The Secret War in El Paso

L. W.

The Secret War in EL PASO

Mexican Revolutionary Intrigue, 1906–1920

Charles H. Harris III
Louis R. Sadler

University of New Mexico Press ■ Albuquerque

Residents of El Paso perch on rail cars in the city railroad yards observing the fighting in Ciudad Juarez in early May 1911. Walter Horne photo courtesy of the El Paso County Historical Society.

Printed in the United States of America

16 15 14 13 12 11 10 09 1 2 3 4 5 6 7 8

Library of Congress Cataloging-in-Publication Data

Harris, Charles H. (Charles Houston)
The secret war in El Paso : Mexican revolutionary intrigue,
1906–1920 / Charles H. Harris III, Louis R. Sadler.
p. cm.
Includes bibliographical references and index.
ISBN 978-0-8263-4652-0 (hardcover : alk. paper)
1. Mexico—History—Revolution, 1910–1920—Diplomatic history.
2. United States—Foreign relations—Mexico.
3. Mexico—Foreign relations—United States.
4. El Paso (Tex.)—History—20th century.
5. Mexican-American Border Region—History—20th century.
6. Mexican-American Border Region—Commerce—History—20th century.
7. Smuggling—Mexican-American Border Region—History—20th century.
I. Sadler, Louis R. II. Title.
F1234.H283 2009
972.08'16—dc22

2009002203

Design and composition by Mina Yamashita.
Text composed in Kepler Std., a contemporary
type designed for Adobe by Robert Slimbach.
Display composed in Frutiger 77 Black Condensed,
designed by Adrian Frutiger in 1976.
Printed by Thomson-Shore, Inc. on 55# Natures Natural.

For Betty and Betty

Contents

Preface / ix

Acknowledgments / xiii

CHAPTER 1: The Díaz-Taft Meeting / 1

CHAPTER 2: The *Magonistas* / 17

CHAPTER 3: Madero's Improbable Triumph / 28

CHAPTER 4: Revolutionary Discord / 51

CHAPTER 5: Orozco's Rebellion / 70

CHAPTER 6: Merchants of Death / 87

CHAPTER 7: Plot and Counterplot / 106

CHAPTER 8: The Constitutionalists / 131

CHAPTER 9: Villa Ascendant / 150

CHAPTER 10: Huerta's Defeat / 161

CHAPTER 11: Villa versus Carranza / 181

CHAPTER 12: Huerta's Comeback Attempt / 192

Illustrations / 210–39

CHAPTER 13: Aftermath / 240

CHAPTER 14: Villa, Columbus, Spies / 247

CHAPTER 15: The War Crisis / 266

CHAPTER 16: Gunrunning / 285

CHAPTER 17: World War, 1917 / 294

CHAPTER 18: World War, 1918 / 318

CHAPTER 19: Exile Futility / 337

CHAPTER 20: Villa's Eclipse / 349

CHAPTER 21: The New Strongman / 365

Conclusion / 377

Abbreviations / 380

Notes / 382

Bibliography / 465

Index / 476

Preface

The Mexican Revolution (1910–20), the first great revolution of the twentieth century, could not have succeeded without the United States. The revolution was primarily a northern movement, the only first-rank figure from southern Mexico being Emiliano Zapata. All the other leading revolutionary personages, including the ultimate winner, General Alvaro Obregón, came from the northern tier of states, and the dominance of the northerners resulted from their access to the American border. Without American territory to serve as a base of operations, a source of munitions, money, and volunteers, a refuge, an arena for propaganda, and a market for revolutionary loot, the Mexican Revolution simply would not have succeeded.

The revolution unfolded under the specter of American military intervention, and in 1914 and 1916 that specter became real. But even when the United States did not overtly intervene, it shaped the course of the revolution by supporting one faction over another, primarily by extending or withholding diplomatic recognition, by imposing or lifting arms embargos, and by selectively applying the neutrality laws. These statutes, which not only prohibited Americans from enlisting under a foreign flag but more importantly prohibited the use of American territory for the purpose of overthrowing a friendly government, were the major tools the United States used to influence revolutionary activity within its borders.

Despite the crucial role of revolutionary intrigues in the United States, this aspect of the revolution hasn't received systematic scholarly study. W. Dirk Raat's investigation of Mexican exiles focuses primarily on the *magonistas*, the followers of the anarchist Ricardo Flores Magón.[1] David N. Johnson's study of Francisco Madero's activities in launching the revolution from San Antonio covers 1910–11.[2] Peter V. N. Henderson has examined exiles for the period 1910–13.[3] Richard Estrada's treatment of revolutionary activity in El Paso ends in 1915.[4] Michael M. Smith has published two important articles about Carranza spymasters.[5] Other scholars such as Victoria Lerner Sigal, Friedrich Katz, and Jacinto Barrera Bassols have also written articles on various aspects of Mexican espionage in the United States.[6] Most recently, David Dorado Romo has touched on intrigue in his cultural history of El Paso and Juárez during the revolution.[7] Each of these works has contributed to our understanding of the revolution, but what they all have in common is that none is based on the one indispensable archive—the records of the Federal Bureau of Investigation.

Contrary to popular belief, the FBI wasn't created in 1935, and it performed distinguished service even before the advent of J. Edgar Hoover. The agency was formed in 1908 and in 1909 was formally named the Bureau of Investigation. Its name was changed in 1935 to the Federal Bureau of Investigation.[8] The agency closely monitored revolutionary activity and amassed a huge archive—some eighty thousand pages—bearing on the Mexican Revolution. This mass of documents contains not only agent reports and administrative correspondence but also thousands of Mexican items—correspondence, codes, and so forth—that won't be found in Mexican repositories because they were seized by American authorities. A number of FBI reports (with the names of the reporting agents deleted) have been available to scholars since 1958, being included in the microfilmed State Department records on Mexico.[9] However, the bulk of the FBI's Mexican files exist only on National Archives microfilm. These twenty-four rolls of microfilm have been available since their declassification in 1977 but have barely been utilized, in part because of the way the documents are arranged.[10] They are roughly chronological, but a page or pages of a report may be in one roll while the rest are scattered through several other rolls.

The FBI records afford the historian almost a day-by-day picture of revolutionary intrigue in places such as New York City, Washington, D.C., New Orleans, San Antonio, El Paso, and Los Angeles, among others. Enhancing the picture are the hundreds of federal court cases and U.S. commissioners' files that include useful testimony and exhibits. And complementing these American sources are the archives of the Mexican Foreign Ministry. We chose El Paso for the present work because it was by far the largest and most important city on the Mexican border and because the revolutionary machinations that occurred there exceeded in degree, though not necessarily in kind, what occurred elsewhere along the border.

We have titled this monograph *The Secret War in El Paso* because for over a decade, El Paso was the base of operations for constant intrigue involving U.S. and Mexican authorities, Mexican revolutionists, and others. The population of El Paso was only sporadically aware of this struggle, usually when some incident got into the newspapers. But in this secret war it was often difficult for the players to keep secrets secret from each other. Heretofore no work has focused on this struggle.[11] It's a complicated tale, for those were complicated times. El Paso may be visualized as a kaleidoscope in which constantly changing combinations and permutations occurred among a cast of characters that included many larger-than-life figures. The city was inundated with refugees and was a magnet attracting revolutionists, adventurers, smugglers, gunrunners, counterfeiters, propagandists, secret agents, double agents, criminals, and confidence men of every stripe, but as one Bureau agent put it, "Valuable information is sometimes obtained from very shady sources."[12] The revolution also became big business, and some of the city's most respectable citizens were quite profitably involved. And it was the Mexican Revolution that produced a huge military buildup in El Paso and transformed it permanently into the "army town" that it is today. What we are concerned with is not the ideology of the revolution, which has been discussed ad infinitum, but rather the mechanics of rebellion. The picture that emerges is one in which treachery was elevated to an art form and factional loyalty was fragile. El Paso as a case study indicates what could be done if an examination of revolutionary intrigue on a nationwide basis for the entire decade were undertaken. Such a study would add an important new dimension to what is known about the Mexican Revolution.

Acknowledgments

As a general rule authors have only a vague recollection as to precisely when they conceived the idea of a topic for a possible book. Such is not the case for *The Secret War in El Paso*. We actually sat down almost thirty-nine years ago and wrote a Memorandum of Understanding laying out the subject of the monograph. To be sure, it was slightly different or, put another way, more focused—on gunrunning in El Paso during the Mexican Revolution. We immediately began doing research—collecting documents on the topic, and so forth, but a variety of events intervened over decades, which prevented us from completing a book-length manuscript.

We did carry out some scholarship on the topic. For example, we wrote an article ("The Underside of the Mexican Revolution: El Paso, 1912," which appeared *in The Americas: A Quarterly Review of Inter-American Cultural History*) in 1982, and in 1993 a history of Fort Bliss (*Bastion on the Border: Fort Bliss, 1854–1943*) for the U.S. Army. We would like to think this historical monograph benefited from the long gestation period.

During our research we benefited directly and indirectly from support from several institutions. These included a generous grant from the Weatherhead Foundation, New York City; the Directorate of Environment, Cultural Resources Management Branch, U.S. Army Air Defense Artillery Center, Fort Bliss, Texas, who asked us to write a history of Fort Bliss; a summer stipend from the National Endowment for the Humanities and several research grants from the Arts and Sciences Research Center, New Mexico State University. We thank them all.

We also received assistance from a number of individuals and institutions. In Washington and College Park, Maryland, (Archives I and II) a number of archivists at the National Archives assisted us. Timothy Nenninger, Mitchell Yokelson, Rick Cox, George Chalou, Rebecca Livingston, and Trudy Peterson were of considerable assistance over a period of years. For historians who have benefited from their advice, Livingston, Cox, Chalou, and Peterson have regrettably retired. In addition, we thank the staff of the Manuscript Division of the Library of Congress for their help. We are most appreciative for the assistance of William Boehm and Derek Nestell (who located and photocopied an important file for us in Archives II).

At the Federal Bureau of Investigation in Washington historians John Fox and Susan Falb provided advice on Bureau documents. At the U.S. Secret Service in Washington, Archivist Mike Sampson was of considerable assistance in providing leads on Secret Service agents who were on the Presidential detail in 1909. At the Federal Records Center, Fort Worth, Texas, the late George Youngkin advised us on pertinent documents and more recently archivists Barbara Rust and Rodney Krajca went out of their way to find Federal Court records for us. At the Federal Records Center, Denver, Marene Sweeney Baker steered us to their holdings on the El Paso region as did archivists at the Federal Records Center, Laguna Nigel, California and the Federal Records Center, East Point, Georgia.

At the Behring Center, National Museum of American History of the Smithsonian Institution, both Alison Oswald and Kay Peterson assisted us in obtaining both documents and a photo from their collections. At the Bancroft Library of the University of California, Berkeley, Cynthia Rollins and Susan Snyder went out of their way to help us obtain a unique photograph.

At the El Paso Public Library, Director of Libraries Carol Brey-Casiano, Deputy Director Jim Przepasniak, Branch Manager Norice Lee, along with Southwest Librarian Marta Estrada and reference librarians Terri Grant, Claudia Ramírez, Priscilla Pineda, Danny González, Danny Escontrías, Ruth Brown, and Public Service Librarian Brian Burns assisted us in our research in the invaluable Otis Aultman Photographic Archive. At the El Paso Historical Society, Patricia Worthington was helpful in providing access to the society's collections. At the University of Texas, El Paso, Claudia Rivers assisted us in examining both their documentary and photographic archives.

We thank the archivists at the British National Archive (formerly the Public Record Office) for their courtesy to a non-British historian.

At the Zuhl and Branson Libraries at New Mexico State University, Dean Elizabeth Titus and Associate Dean Cheryl Wilson (now retired) and Rose Marie Espinosa Ruiz (who helped us both in Special Collections and the Center for Latin American Studies) were of considerable assistance to us; and at Rio Grande Historical Collections Steve Hussman (and before he retired, Austin Hoover); Bill Boehm (now a National Guard archivist in Arlington, Virginia); Tim Blevins and Dennis Daily (both now in Colorado Springs, Colorado) and Martha Andrews also assisted us. At the Center for Latin American Studies at NMSU, Rosa de la Torre Burmeister word processed an early draft for us.

If one does not have daily access to the Library of Congress, "Inter-Library Loan" is an often ignored standby in conducting research. In our case we could not have done without the able assistance of Jivonna Stewart and Deanna Litke (now retired) at the NMSU Zuhl Library. They obtained literally hundreds of obscure documents, articles, and books for our manuscript. We thank them both for their efforts in our behalf.

For several years we compiled lists of thousands of documents from both the Mexican Foreign Relations Archive (Archivo de Relaciones Exteriores de México), and name indexes to the Centro de Estudios de Historia de México, Departamento Cultural de Condumex Archives in Mexico City. Elena Albarrán, a PhD candidate in Mexican history at the University of Arizona, copied thousands of pages of documents from our lists. We are indebted to her.

At the Department of History, department head Jeff Brown with good humor tolerated two emeritus historians whose office was slightly overgrown with tens of thousands of documents. Nancy Shockley, our former graduate student, history instructor, and departmental secretary responded to constant cries for help from the technologically illiterate. We are absolutely certain our colleagues in the history department are delighted they will no longer have to hear interminable stories about the glories of the Mexican Revolution—at least until we start our next manuscript.

Our former graduate student and colleague Mark Milliorn was absolutely indispensable in producing this manuscript. Milliorn, who in our opinion is a technological genius, constantly pulled us out of computer jams. We thank him most kindly.

We thank William Beezley of the University of Arizona who over a substantial period of time strongly encouraged us to pursue this topic. In addition, we benefited from comments by colleagues Colin MacLaughlin, Friedrich Schuler, Lawrence Taylor, Jeff Pilcher, Daniel Newcomer, John Chalkley, Jose García, Jim Hurst, Theo Crevenna, Floyd Geery, and Jack Wilson. We miss the late Michael C. Meyer, Ricardo Aguilar-Melantzon, John Taylor, Bill Timmons, and Jack McGrew, all of whom assisted us over a period of decades. We mourn their absence.

At the University of New Mexico Press, David Holtby got us started on this project before he retired and turned us over to Clark Whitehorn, who replaced David. We suspect Clark did not know what he was getting into when he inherited *The Secret War in El Paso*. We are greatly indebted to both Clark and David for tolerating our various eccentricities. Maya Allen-Gallegos, managing editor, did yeoman duty on this manuscript. In addition Glenda Madden, Amanda Sutton, Stewart Marshall, and press director Luther Wilson all helped. We thank them all.

Finally and not for the first time, we dedicate this monograph to our respective spouses Betty Harris and Betty Sadler. They know why.

CHAPTER 1

The Díaz-Taft Meeting

El Paso came of age on October 16, 1909. For the first time in its history, the city found itself in the international limelight when the presidents of the United States and Mexico met officially at what was the first presidential summit in U.S. history. Press accounts suggested that the meeting in El Paso and Ciudad Juárez between President William Howard Taft and President Porfirio Díaz marked the first time that a U.S. president had violated the unwritten law that American chief executives did not leave the territorial boundaries of the United States during their term of office. These newspaper accounts were wrong. American presidents had met with several presidents of Central American republics, including Panama (although the meeting with Panama's president didn't really count since the United States had created Panama).[1]

Because this meeting was an event of considerable significance, and because historians have tended to gloss over it, it merits discussion in some detail.[2] The border location of El Paso aside, the central question was why would the president of Mexico want to meet with the president of the United States? Politically, no Mexican president should ever have wanted to meet with his American counterpart. After all, only six decades earlier the United States had precipitated a war—the Mexican War (1846–48)—in which Mexico lost by conquest almost half of her national territory. But as the cliché goes, considerable water had passed under the bridge since the end of that war.

What is striking is not that Díaz agreed to meet with Taft but the fact that the Mexican president used clandestine correspondence to arrange the public meeting. Virtually all of the accounts of this first presidential summit are wrong on this critical point.[3] President Díaz cleverly utilized a friend of Taft's, Judge L. R. Wilfley, to send his request for a meeting, allowing him to avoid having to transmit it through the Mexican Foreign Office. Taft's letter in response reads as follows: "I have your courteous note of June 16th, sent me through Judge Wilfle[y]. . . . I sincerely hope that in the course of a trip I hope to take in September and October in the South, I may have the pleasure of meeting you in El Paso or some convenient station on the border."

The Judge Wilfley referred to was Judge Lebbeus R. Wilfley, an attorney who had served as Taft's attorney general in the Philippines when the president was governor of the islands. Wilfley was subsequently named a judge of the U.S. Court in China but was apparently removed by Secretary of State Elihu Root during the Roosevelt administration. As a result, in early 1909 Wilfley was attempting to revive a law practice, and on May 25, 1909, he wrote to his old friend Taft requesting a letter of recommendation to President Díaz so he could help an American client in Mexico who allegedly was being swindled out of a mining property. Taft wrote Díaz the letter, stating that Wilfley was a lawyer of high standing and a gentleman but that he knew nothing about the legal matter Wilfley was pursuing in Mexico. Taft also wrote Wilfley a letter of introduction to the U.S. ambassador in Mexico, David Thompson.

The case in which Wilfley was interested was before the Mexican Supreme Court, and Taft's letter gained him an interview with Díaz, who indeed intervened with the judges on behalf of Wilfley's client. Having won the case, Wilfley was to receive a whopping $250,000 fee, to be paid when the mine in question resumed production. However, Díaz's intervention became known, and stories concerning the case appeared in the Mexico City press. President Taft regretted having gotten involved and wrote Wilfley a rather stiff letter saying that "I want it absolutely understood that you can not quote me as in favor of granting your request. My only function was to present you . . . as a reputable attorney in high standing but I expressly said that I knew nothing of the case."[4] Unfortunately for Wilfley, the outbreak of the Mexican Revolution prevented the mine from reopening, and his substantial fee vanished.

Díaz, who had controlled Mexico since 1876, arranged the summit with Taft because he wanted one more term—an eighth four-year term—as president. The dictator, although vigorous, was an old man (he would be eighty in 1910), and he realized that he needed the cooperation of the U. S. government to remain in power. During the previous administration, President Theodore Roosevelt and his secretary of state, Elihu Root, had enthusiastically supported Díaz and had ordered U.S. attorneys to pursue anti-Díaz Mexican exiles in the United States.

Had Taft chosen to do so, he could have provided a diplomatic answer explaining why he would be unable to meet with Díaz. For example, Taft's wife, Helen, had suffered an incapacitating stroke in May. Furthermore, Taft was in the process of planning a thirteen thousand–mile railroad tour of the midwestern United States that he was to embark on in September. But as the president wrote to his brother after the Díaz meeting, he hoped that American friendship "will strengthen him with his own people and tend to discourage revolutionists' efforts to establish a different government." Perhaps Taft had in mind the several billion dollars of American capital invested in Mexico.[5] And of course there was the matter of geography—the two countries shared a 1,951-mile border.

Following Mexican ambassador Francisco León de la Barra's announcement on June 18 of the forthcoming meeting, the date and location became subjects of discussion between the State Department and the Mexican Foreign Office, although Taft had mentioned only El Paso. On July 9 it was announced in Washington that the presidents would meet in El Paso and Ciudad Juárez on October 16. The date initially caused some consternation in El Paso. Organizers of the annual Southwestern Fair complained that the visit of the two presidents would interfere with their event and suggested changing the date of the summit. The city fathers quickly squashed these protests and notified their congressman, W. R. Smith, that the date was just fine and asked him to so notify the appropriate Washington officials.[6] There was a brief flurry of apprehension in late July that the conference would be moved to San Antonio, but that proposal died a quick death, apparently because of security concerns.[7] San Antonio had a substantial contingent of Mexican exiles who would undoubtedly have led demonstrations protesting Díaz's presence in the city.

Meanwhile, the State Department began to grapple with protocol. At the very least it must have been galling to have the Mexican ambassador making all of the public announcements, not just of the summit but also its date and place. Yet the State Department had never had to arrange a meeting between the president of the United States and the president of Mexico, so the diplomatic protocol was uncharted territory for it. On the other hand, the Díaz regime had come to power three decades earlier, and the Mexican Foreign Office had invested an enormous amount of time and money studying how the major European powers conducted diplomacy; for example, the Mexicans had been collecting menus created for diplomatic dinners. Mexican diplomats examined carefully how officials dressed, what gifts were exchanged between officials, and the general nuts and bolts of diplomatic protocol as practiced by the French, British, Russian, and Italian governments. Therefore, Mexican diplomats were in a position to take the lead in planning the summit.[8]

Ambassador de la Barra in effect "hijacked" the conference. He realized that he was in a position to take the lead rather than let the lackadaisical State Department muddle through. Capitalizing on his relationship with President Taft, he decided to take control. For their part, State Department officials did not plan a major event, because in their view Mexico was not all that important. But from the perspective of the Mexican Foreign Office and Ambassador de la Barra it was imperative to make the most extravagant display possible in order to impress not just Taft and the U.S. government but the American people.[9]

Since he enjoyed an excellent relationship with President Taft, de la Barra arranged to meet with Taft at the president's summer vacation home in Beverley, Massachusetts, to plan the summit. There the two worked out the scope of the summit and formulated detailed arrangements. De la Barra encountered only one obstacle in planning the meeting. He informed Taft that Díaz wanted to be received with "military honors." According to Taft's military aide, Captain Archibald Willingham

Butt, who was present, there was some difference of opinion between "a Latin's idea of military honors and those of the President of the United States." Taft instructed Butt to contact the army chief of staff and have "one or two squadrons of cavalry [sent] to El Paso, but no more."[10]

At the State Department, Taft's appointees, who had been in place for only five months, were confessedly just beginning to settle into their positions. Taft's new secretary of state, Philander C. Knox, was an able lawyer (one of nine in the cabinet) but was unquestionably the laziest secretary of state in history. He did not arrive at his office until between 10 and 10:30 in the morning. He would then go to lunch at either the Metropolitan Club or at the Shoreham Hotel. At the Metropolitan Club he would order terrapin and a bottle of champagne, and at the Shoreham canvasback duck (prepared very rare) with a bottle of Romany burgundy. The secretary would then walk home to his apartment for a nap and if the weather was good drive to the Chevy Chase Country Club for a round of golf. He would not return to the department in the afternoon except on Thursdays, when he received foreign diplomats.[11]

Given the secretary of state's schedule, assistant secretary Huntington Wilson effectively ran the department. Still in his mid-thirties, Wilson had spent nine years at the U.S. legation in Tokyo before returning to Washington as third assistant secretary of state. Secretary Knox had promoted Wilson to assistant secretary (or undersecretary of state as the position subsequently became).

It would be Wilson whom de la Barra would meet in late August with a memorandum detailing what he and President Taft had agreed to. One would suspect that Wilson was nonplussed to receive the document. The summit had to a substantial degree been taken out of the hands of the State Department, which would now have to respond to Mexican Foreign Office initiatives—not the best position for American diplomats to find themselves in.

Ambassador de la Barra delivered the memorandum, which he represented as a report on the meeting between himself and Taft, to the State Department.[12] Wilson's response is found in his memorandum to William Phillips, third assistant secretary of state, and begins with "we had a rather long conversation." Wilson turned the arrangements over to Phillips, noting weighty matters that he and de la Barra had agreed upon, such as "We thought that a glass of champagne and a buffet with sandwiches . . . would be satisfactory when President Diaz met with President Taft." The memo then continued with matters such as "The President will wear a frock coat" for the initial meeting and a "dress suit at the dinner of the Mexican President."[13]

But there were also two serious matters mentioned in the memo. The first was the matter of the Chamizal, a disputed strip of land between El Paso and Ciudad Juárez that had been created when a series of floods on the Rio Grande beginning in 1852 carved a new channel. As a result, a slice of Mexican territory, the Chamizal, had been left on the U.S. side of the river.[14] De la Barra suggested that during the meeting the Chamizal not be decorated with the flags of either country. Wilson countered with the idea that the area be marked with crossed U.S. and Mexican flags. It was finally agreed that no flags would be used in the Chamizal. The second major item Wilson and de la Barra discussed was whether "politics" would be broached by the two presidents. Alvey A. Adee, second assistant secretary of state, apparently mentioned to de la Barra that Taft might wish to discuss serious issues between the two nations. De la Barra rather emphatically dismissed the idea, saying that it would be "detrimental to the intended keynote of the occasion." In his memo Wilson noted rather cynically that "this relieves us of the duty of preparing political memoranda for the President."

The remainder of the memorandum noted that Díaz would probably wear his military uniform, and that President Taft hoped that Ambassador de la Barra might attend the summit.[15] It raised a discussion of the cavalry units that would guard the presidents and whether they would cross the border, as well as the matter of who would be responsible for preparing the toasts (the elderly but able Mr. Adee was detailed to prepare them for the State Department). The final item in the memorandum must have stuck in Wilson's craw. De la Barra mentioned as an aside that he thought President Taft's train would leave early in the evening following President Díaz's banquet. To be informed what his president's train schedule would be must have really irked Wilson. De la Barra was, to put it mildly, not fond of Wilson and considered him a diplomatic lightweight; Wilson heartily reciprocated this opinion.[16]

What is astonishing is that at this first meeting of the presidents of Mexico and the United States, the secretary of state announced that he would not be in attendance. And given the rules of protocol, if the secretary of state were absent, the Mexican foreign secretary must be also. In September, Secretary Knox changed his mind at the behest of the president, and the Mexicans were notified that he would attend. But Knox later changed his mind again.[17] There are no documents in the State Department files that disclose why Knox did not attend. Perhaps he had a pressing engagement to play golf at a course near his home at Valley Forge, Pennsylvania.

Besides dealing with the Mexicans, the State Department had to deal with the city of El Paso, which was raring to take charge of the summit. The committee that had been named to make local arrangements even asked the State Department to send a special representative to assist the city in handling the diplomatic protocol. State dismissed the request out of hand.[18] But the city and its business community were not to be deterred. A huge arrangements committee was assembled, fourteen subcommittee chairs were named and members selected, stationery was printed, and funds were raised. El Paso had every intention of taking charge, and to a substantial degree it succeeded. By the end of August preparations had been under way for three weeks. The historic meeting was even going to be filmed for posterity.[19] And to avoid civic embarrassment, local officials had a fence erected around Chihuahuita, the Hispanic slum in south El Paso.[20]

El Pasoans began pressing the State Department to provide the schedule for the event. Since the State Department apparently couldn't get its act together, the locals decided to put forward their own ideas as to what the two presidents should do. Early on, the El Pasoans suggested that the chief executives meet at the chamber of commerce building. The State Department accepted the offer because the building was convenient and spacious. It would be the location for the first presidential meeting of the summit.[21]

The principal reason the El Paso committee and subcommittees functioned effectively was because the 142 members included virtually everyone locally prominent. Although there were a few ex officio types, such as Joseph Sweeney, the mayor of El Paso, Thomas D. Edwards, the U.S. consul in Juárez, and Antonio Lomelí, the Mexican consul in El Paso, most were local movers and shakers, such as executive committee member and future mayor C. E. Kelly. The largest committee was the press committee, whose twenty members included four women, presumably responsible for hosting parties for reporters. The committee was keenly aware of the favorable publicity El Paso could derive from lavishing hospitality on the visiting press corps. The committee responsible for hosting senators and congressmen included a future collector of customs, Zach Lamar Cobb, and was chaired by a powerful attorney, W. W. Turney. The reception committee for state officials included R. F. Burges, another prominent lawyer, and Joseph Magoffin, a member of the oldest Anglo family in the city. The committee for ambassadors counted among its members Max Weber, the German consul in Juárez, Mexican consul Lomelí, Adolph Krakauer, owner of the largest hardware store in the Southwest and a future chamber of commerce and bank president, and Benjamin Viljoen, who had been a ranking general in the Boer War. Chairing the invitation committee was Félix Martínez, the most prominent Hispanic in El Paso. Finally, the committee on public safety's chairman was leading businessman Zach White; he was assisted by Texas Ranger Captain John R. Hughes and Colonel Joseph F. Huston, commander at Fort Bliss.

With the committee structure in place and working well, Mayor Sweeney decided to take the initiative and present the "Freedom of the City" to President Díaz. The State Department turned Sweeney's request over to Ambassador Thompson, who found that Díaz was delighted with El Paso's gesture and would be pleased to receive Mayor Sweeney in Mexico City for the presentation.[22] It would appear that the Mexican government, realizing that the State Department was a reluctant participant in the summit, decided that the city of El Paso would be an excellent substitute.

Therefore El Paso and the Mexican government would work together to ensure that the meeting was a success.

In the meantime, the U.S. Army prepared for the ceremonial aspects of the meeting. The acting chief of staff suggested that Taft's escort be the commanding general of the Department of Texas, Brigadier General Albert L. Myer, plus three batteries of the 3rd Field Artillery, the 9th Infantry Regiment, two squadrons of the 3rd Cavalry Regiment, and a band. The artillery batteries would fire the 21-gun salute for President Díaz. If additional cavalry units were needed, they could be summoned from other posts in Texas.[23]

It should be noted that the presidential summit was not met with universal acclaim. There were written protests to Taft from several groups, including the Fort Wayne, Indiana, chapter of the Socialist Party and from Carlo de Fornaro, a journalist and virulent enemy of the Díaz government. There was even a letter from the board of managers of the Women's Pennsylvania Society for the Prevention of Cruelty to Animals, requesting that bullfighting be omitted from the program of entertainment.[24] It was.

But there were other problems, and most of them revolved around the Chamizal. President Díaz insisted that nothing at the meeting should be done that would imply that the United States held sovereignty over the Chamizal strip. Unfortunately, the only way to cross between El Paso and Ciudad Juárez was through the Chamizal. It would finally be decided that during the summit the Chamizal would be considered neutral ground and not be marked by the flags of either nation.[25]

The El Paso committee, having been kept in the dark by the State Department as to the agenda, decided to formulate its own. John Wyatt, the chair of the general arrangement committee and the ramrod for the city, wired Taft's secretary that their plan included a parade, the assembling of schoolchildren to sing "America" for the president, a speech by Taft that would be followed by the arrival of President Díaz, the singing of the Mexican national anthem by schoolchildren, a meeting of Taft and the Ohio Society and the Yale alumni, and so forth. One suspects that Alvey Adee, who had assumed responsibility at the State Department for the detailed planning for the summit, was miffed by El Paso's taking over the arranging. He fired off a telegram to Wyatt stating that "it is unlikely that arrangements for meeting . . . as outlined by your telegram . . . can be adopted." Wyatt promptly wired a reply prodding Adee to provide the program as soon as possible.[26] Ironically, much of what the El Paso committee suggested was eventually adopted.

The U.S. consulate in Ciudad Juárez also wished to participate. The vice consul enumerated the vast sums the Mexican government was spending to beautify Juárez and gently suggested that it would be nice if the consulate could be painted before the presidents met. Adee responded by sending three large American flags (which must be returned promptly after the visit), providing a special $50 allocation for decorations, and suggesting that the landlord was responsible for painting the consulate.[27]

The El Paso committee had determined that no one locally was competent to decorate the city. Therefore it was decided that major decorating firms on the East Coast would be asked to bid on a contract. But before the committee could proceed with providing specifications for bidders it was necessary to ascertain where and when the various activities would take place. After twice sending telegrams to the State Department, the El Pasoans gave up and decided to make their own decisions based on what they had learned about the program. However, Adee, after being nudged by William Phillips, did finally provide the outlines of the protocol for the meeting.[28]

Immediately after receiving Adee's telegram Mayor Sweeney wired his response, stating bluntly that "it would inflict great injury on this town and the hundreds of its inhabitants who live on what is known as the Chamizal Tract to even indirectly appear to abandon jurisdiction over that tract during the meeting of the Presidents. Please answer." Understanding Mexican sensibilities over the Chamizal, Adee answered "regret not practicable to consider any modification settled program."[29]

If the Chamizal had been a problem earlier, it rather quickly got stickier. Colonel Huston, the post commander at Fort Bliss, alerted his superior, Brigadier General Myer, that the State Department had ruled that American troops could *not* be used in the Chamizal tract. General Myer then asserted that "under the ruling as understood here from the telegram of the Acting Secretary of State, troops could not enter this zone." Myer wrote to the adjutant general: "It is respectfully represented that if this ruling is to govern, the troops cannot be properly arranged for the safeguarding of . . . the two Presidents. In order to properly safeguard the Presidents, it is necessary that our troops should be posted over the whole line of march and extend to the center of the [international] bridge. To do this these troops must occupy the El Chamizal Zone."[30]

Mayor Sweeney was becoming increasingly angry at what he considered to be incompetence on the part of the State Department vis-à-vis the Chamizal. He wrote a four-page letter to Adee in which he bluntly stated "you evidently do not understand the exact nature and character of that strip of land in the southern portion of this City designated El Chamizal. This strip of land is the most densely populated of any portion of the City. . . . It is a physical impossibility to enter the Republic of Mexico through this city without passing over the El Chamizal district. . . . The El Chamizal district is policed, cared for and lighted . . . by the City of El Paso and . . . we maintain a large number of policemen [to] protect life and property. In no event could we withdraw the police . . . because . . . a large proportion of the people . . . are of the migratory class and frequent disturbers of the peace. This district is about five blocks deep and about two miles long . . . you will see the impossibility of carrying out suggestions of the State Department. . . . Should we withdraw the police from that district, it would leave a population of about 14,000 or 15,000 unprotected, and we could not possibly prevent people from entering that zone during the period that the Presidents would be here, unless we had eight or ten thousand troops to establish a picket line along the northern border of the El Chamizal tract and then, we would also have to dispose and drive from their homes at least 15,000 people so that there would be nobody on the disputed tract."[31] It is curious that the State Department did not have the American consul in Juárez provide a detailed report on the Chamizal. If Adee didn't get the picture before he received Sweeney's letter, he certainly understood now.

Tensions increased on September 24, after the Associated Press filed a dispatch reporting that explosives had been found in Ciudad Juárez "near the place of contemplated meeting of Presidents Taft and Diaz." Consul Edwards, however, deemed the report "unworthy of notice."[32] Yet two days later the State Department changed the protocol—each president would now be guarded by a twenty-man cavalry escort.[33] Ambassador Thompson received instructions to notify the Mexican Foreign Office that the United States proposed using American troops to guard the roadway in the Chamizal.[34] In his discussions with the foreign minister, Thompson suggested that both countries provide troops to guard the road through the Chamizal. The Mexican government's position was now that since the Chamizal was under American control it was the responsibility of the United States to provide the necessary security. Thompson reported that "I am strong in my feeling that a double line of soldiers should hold an open road several hundred feet wide across the Chamizal for the Presidential parties. No one should be permitted within easy throwing distance of the center of the open way."[35]

In view of the increasing security concerns, Wilson proposed that the best solution was for Díaz to have a "diplomatic illness" so the meeting could be canceled. Unfortunately, two of the major decision makers were unavailable: Taft was already on his train trip speaking all over the western United States, and the Mexican ambassador was in Europe and would not return until just a week before the scheduled summit. Secretary of State Knox, who was at his home in Valley Forge playing golf, vetoed the "diplomatic illness" suggestion, declaring that both Mexico and the United States could station troops in the Chamizal if that was required. The summit was still on, but it is noteworthy that the undersecretary of state had seriously proposed canceling it.

By September 30, an increasingly worried Mexican Foreign Office was more than willing for the U.S. Army to guard the Chamizal road and for the cavalry escorts to protect the two presidents; the next day the Foreign Office put its willingness in writing. Ambassador Thompson was able to report that "this is all satisfactory to the Mexican government and thought to be as it should be."[36] The State Department was also worried about security, and Adee held a meeting with Taft's secretary and the secretary of war at which it was decided to take the unusual step of sending the chief of the secret service, John Wilkie, to El Paso to investigate the situation. Based on his report, a decision would be made whether to deploy additional troops to protect the summit meeting.[37]

As if security concerns weren't worrisome enough for Adee, the State Department was stunned to receive a telegram from the governor of Texas, Tom Campbell, informing the secretary of state that he probably wouldn't be able to attend the summit. He did allow as how he'd send a personal representative, though. Adee sent a very diplomatic reply, explaining that Campbell's presence was needed to provide parity, since the governor of Chihuahua would be in attendance, and hoping that Campbell could work the summit into his busy schedule. Not until October 9, only a week before the summit, did Campbell notify Adee that "I expect to be present."[38]

By the first week in October, the State Department and the Mexican Foreign Office had decided that additional security was required. They informed their respective military establishments that in crossing the Chamizal each president would be guarded by twenty cavalrymen from his army and twenty from the other nation's army—the bodyguard had now been doubled. This was in addition to the line of U.S. troops that would be lining the Chamizal road.[39] And the State Department urged the army to assign even more troops to the summit. The chief of staff informed State that on two days' notice an additional one thousand soldiers could be ordered to El Paso from Fort Sam Houston in San Antonio. Secret Service chief Wilkie would assess the situation on the ground and confer with the Fort Bliss commander; they would decide whether additional troops were needed.[40]

Wilkie arrived in El Paso on October 6, and reported the following day on his findings: "Chamizal District thickly populated by Mexicans of lowest class whose sympathies generally anti-Diaz. Conservative El Paso citizens familiar with conditions predict serious complications if Mexican soldiers appear in Chamizal with possible stoning of personal guard while waiting El Paso boundary end of district for President's return. . . . Local idea is that Diaz will be perfectly safe under escort of American cavalry but that presence of armed Mexican force in Chamizal would be like shaking red flag at bull. Please advise me promptly as possible. Delicate situation."[41] Acting Secretary of State Adee replied that the commanding general of the Department of Texas had been directed to order such additional troops to El Paso as he and Wilkie deemed necessary. Adee emphasized that they must do everything in their power "to guarantee absolutely the preservation of peace and quiet and the protection of the Mexican escort from assaults from ill-disposed persons. Since the Government of the United States is responsible, it is expected that you and the Commanding General, Department of Texas, will not hesitate to act in such a manner as will relieve the situation of all possible danger."[42] While U.S. and Mexican officials nervously contemplated the possibility of serious problems, up to and including the assassination of the two presidents, they faced the additional difficulty of keeping the threat secret. There was some discreet leakage of information, but El Paso newsmen downplayed the security threat. The security situation did lap over into the public arena with the announcement that no one would be admitted to the breakfast for President Taft at the St. Regis Hotel without the proper admission card. In addition, press passes were to be issued for journalists.[43]

The public focus was on the preparations for the summit. The citizens of El Paso enthusiastically draped every downtown building from top to bottom in red, white, blue, and green bunting, hung Mexican and American flags, erected reviewing platforms, and scrubbed the city clean for the great day, spending tens of thousands of dollars in the process. The Mexican expenditure was even greater. Early on, the Foreign Office had proposed that President Díaz host the banquet for Taft that would be the concluding event of the meeting. The Juárez Customs House was selected as the site for the banquet and was transformed at enormous expense into a copy of one of the great salons of the Palace of Versailles. A painting of George Washington was hung along with one of Father Miguel Hidalgo y Costilla, the father of Mexican independence. Rich red draperies graced the salon, which was illuminated by hundreds of electric lights and festooned with tens of thousands of fresh flowers (three carloads) brought in from Guadalajara by special train. The gold and silver dinner settings, valued at approximately $1.25 million, had belonged to the Emperor Maximilian, and the crystal and linens had also been brought from Chapultepec Castle in Mexico City. The chef had previously been employed by the king of Spain. The Mexicans were determined to do their president proud.

Over in Juárez for the last month the officials had been engaged in identifying "undesirables" and running them out of town. The mayor ordered all saloons closed and banned the sale of intoxicants. And beginning on October 11, three special troop trains arrived with a regiment of engineers and a regiment of field artillery to bolster security. There was another arrival—Mexican foreign minister Ignacio Mariscal, who had informed the American embassy that even if Secretary of State Knox wouldn't attend the summit, he would. It was Mariscal who would direct the Mexican part of the presidential meeting.[44]

Among the distinguished visitors arriving in El Paso were the neighboring governors: Richard E. Sloan, territorial governor of Arizona, George Curry, territorial governor of New Mexico, Enrique Creel of Chihuahua, and of course a reluctant Governor Tom Campbell of Texas. The Mexican contingent also included Governor Escandón of the state of Morelos.[45]

The summit was going to be an extravaganza. The press corps and the officers from the army units coming from Fort Sam Houston to parade for the presidents were to be entertained with a banquet at the Elks Club. The Ohio Society, most of whose members were from Taft's hometown of Cincinnati, would get to meet informally with the president. The Ohioans had even built their own reviewing stand, and they had commissioned a handsome wool sombrero, which they planned to present to Taft. The planning committee had a local jeweler make two solid-gold loving cups, valued at an impressive $1,500 each, to be presented to the two presidents to commemorate the summit. Anticipating that the crowd that would assemble to watch the parade would be large, two days before the event entrepreneurs began selling reserved seats along the parade route at prices ranging from $1 to $3.

But security remained the paramount concern. Mexican Army units continued to pour into Juárez. These included the 800-man Regiment of Engineers (Zapadores), the 800-man 11th Infantry Regiment, the 11th Artillery Regiment with 600 men and 2 batteries of 75-mm guns, and Díaz's elite 86-man Presidential Guard. Eventually some 2,000 Mexican regulars were deployed. As for the U.S. Army, the local National Guard infantry unit (Company K, 4th Texas Infantry) was mobilized, and the Fort Bliss garrison of four companies of the 19th Infantry Regiment—322 strong—was powerfully reinforced. A constant procession of troop trains rolled into the border city, bringing 115 men (Troops A and D, 3rd Cavalry) from Fort Clark and 1,500 from Fort Sam Houston as well as the remainder of the 3rd Cavalry (Troops B, C, F, G, H, K, and L), Batteries A, B, and C, 3rd Field Artillery, the entire 9th Infantry Regiment, the 3rd Field Artillery Band, and the headquarters contingent of the Department of Texas. The army virtually stripped Fort Sam Houston, the largest post in the western United States. In all, some 2,000 Mexican soldiers and a similar number of American troops were deployed to keep the presidents safe.[46]

El Paso was wild with excitement when shortly after 9:00 a.m. on October 16, President Taft's train pulled into the middle of the business district.[47] Mayor Joseph Sweeney and a formally attired welcoming committee greeted the president and escorted him to the St. Regis Hotel. There the city hosted a sumptuous breakfast in his honor, with the dignitaries and a hundred leading citizens in attendance. (The waiters, incidentally, were brought in from Los Angeles—apparently El Paso waiters were not good enough.) The president's entourage at breakfast included Secretary of War Jacob Dickinson, Postmaster General F. H. Hitchcock, Taft's aide, the inimitable Captain Archibald Willingham Butt, and the president's good friend and golfing partner John Hays Hammond, a wealthy mining engineer. It should be noted that not a single official from the Department of State in Washington was present and that Ambassador David Thompson's invitation to the breakfast never reached him.[48]

Taft enjoyed the breakfast immensely, but perhaps he should have skipped it—he tipped the scales at more than 350 pounds, and he had been gaining weight on the trip as cities vied with each other to provide the most succulent meals possible. Taft also suffered from sleep apnea—he would often fall asleep during meetings, embarrassing both his staff and visitors to the oval office.[49] But whatever else, Taft was a trooper. Immediately after breakfast he was transported to the San Jacinto Plaza to hear four thousand El Paso school children sing "My Country, 'Tis of Thee" before proceeding to the chamber of commerce.

There Taft met Díaz. As per the schedule negotiated between the State Department and the Mexican Foreign Office, President Díaz initiated the proceedings by boarding his elegant presidential coach to meet President Taft for the first time. After a glass of champagne and a sandwich, the two presidents conferred privately for about twenty minutes, Chihuahua governor Enrique Creel as interpreter. The meeting must have been convivial, for the presidents ordered more champagne to be brought in.[50] The most noteworthy aspect of this private meeting was that Taft's chair collapsed under his considerable weight.[51] Although this was most embarrassing, the chief executives took it in stride and presumably had a good laugh.

Following their meeting Díaz returned to Juárez. Taft returned his visit, being transported by coach and posing for photographs before returning without incident to El Paso. There he reviewed a huge army parade through downtown, stretching for three miles and lasting for an hour and a half. Taft then retired to the Sheldon Hotel for a brief rest before being transported back to Juárez by coach at 5:30 p.m. for Díaz's magnificent banquet in the customs house. The splendid decorations, gourmet cuisine, choice wines, and fulsome presidential toasts put everyone in a mellow mood of good fellowship. And as an added bonus, Taft didn't break anything. By any standard, the banquet was a great success, a fitting climax to the first presidential summit in American history.

Taft returned to his train waiting in El Paso and immediately left that night for San Antonio. As the president's train sped away from El Paso, his aide Captain Butt and John Hays Hammond slumped, exhausted from nervous tension. According to Hammond, Taft had commented that "You and Archie seem to have been jumpy all day, Jack. What's the trouble? Perhaps a highball will steady you." Hammond said they gratefully gulped down the offered highballs, and with a sigh of relief he said to Taft, "Thank God we're out of Mexico and the day's over. We've been half crazy for fear somebody'd take a shot at you." Taft replied: "Oh, is that what's been bothering you? Why should you have worried about that? If anyone wanted to get me he couldn't very well have missed such an easy target."[52]

Taft made light of the assassination threat, but it had been real, and those responsible for his safety could congratulate themselves that only his dignity had been injured. Throughout the round of official functions, banquets, and parades there had been a rising undercurrent of concern for the safety of the chief executives. After all, an anarchist had assassinated President McKinley only eight years earlier, and President Díaz certainly had no lack of enemies, incurred during his decades of iron-fisted rule. As early as September 27, the Mexican foreign minister had notified American ambassador Thompson that "the Mexican Government has what it considers good evidence that an attempt will be made, if the situation permits, to take the life of the Mexican President on the Chamizal while he is crossing it." Thompson reported that President Díaz had not been informed of the threat but that the foreign minister was "much exercised over the matter." Thompson stated that "without protection of lines of soldiers that would keep the crowd in the distance I think there is grave danger."[53] When he did not receive an immediate reply from the State Department, the ambassador repeated his warning: "As no mention is made of my recommendation for policing the Chamizal . . . I again urge the importance of this. Thugs understand the protocol leaves this place unpoliced and are planning destruction when the occasion offers. The personal guard agreed to is not sufficient for perfect safety. The Chamizal should not only be well-policed but well-inspected for mines and bombs."[54]

Ambassador Thompson's warnings spurred a series of hurried meetings at the State Department. Assistant secretary of state Wilson met with Secret Service chief John Wilkie. Although Wilkie's agency was under the Treasury Department, he often cooperated with the State Department on matters involving threats against prominent foreign visitors. As we've seen, Secretary of State Knox decided to send Wilkie, the government's expert on presidential protection, to El Paso to evaluate the potential threat, and Wilkie recommended additional security measures.[55]

On October 12, an extraordinary and secret meeting was held in Ciudad Juárez between Díaz and Wilkie. It would certainly have been logical for the head of the Mexican Secret Police and for Foreign Minister Mariscal, both of whom were in Ciudad Juárez, to have been present. However, Wilkie's coded report seems to intimate that there was no one else at the meeting (except an interpreter, since Wilkie did not speak Spanish and Díaz had little English). What Wilkie discussed with Díaz was a change in the security protocol for the summit. He proposed, and Díaz agreed, that for additional security the carriage following Díaz's contain two Mexican secret police operatives and two American Secret Service agents.

For an American intelligence chief to meet secretly with the president of a foreign country without a U.S. diplomat being present was unprecedented. It emphasized that indeed there was in play a serious plot to assassinate one or both presidents. This meeting has never previously been disclosed, and some aspects of it remain obscure. The opening sentence in Wilkie's telegram read: "At a conference between General Diaz and myself this morning." What is mysterious about the meeting is how President Díaz reached Ciudad Juárez. He supposedly had not even reached the city of Chihuahua en route from Mexico City as of October 12. Could Wilkie have taken a train to Chihuahua and met the president secretly there? We simply do not know. While it may be illogical that the meeting was held in Ciudad Juárez, it is unlikely that Wilkie would have been absent from El Paso for more than a brief time prior to the summit. The dating of the telegram is accurate, as is the State Department date stamp, but the location from where the wire was sent is missing. The telegram was sent in a Treasury Department code, deciphered there, and sent over to the State Department.[56]

The upshot of the meeting was that in addition to the four thousand U.S. and Mexican troops providing security, the entire El Paso police department and the El Paso County sheriff's department, a four-man contingent of U.S. Secret Service agents, several federal Bureau of Investigation agents, U.S. Customs inspectors, and deputy U.S. marshals were pressed into service. And the famed Texas Rangers contributed a company of men. The Texas Ranger detail included John Hughes and John H. Rogers, two of the great Ranger captains of that era.[57]

As if all this weren't enough, another level of security was added. A private "off-the-books" security force of an estimated 250 men was added at the last minute, courtesy of John Hays Hammond. When he learned that there was apparently a plot (or more probably several plots) by anarchists to assassinate one or both presidents in El Paso, he arranged for an old friend from his South African mining days, Major Frederick Russell Burnham, to travel to El Paso a few days before the president arrived. Burnham was another of these larger-than-life figures who appeared in El Paso. A native of Minnesota, he was a scout and tracker of international reputation. He had fought with great distinction on the British side in the Boer War (he had turned down a Victoria Cross) and would come to be considered the real father of the Boy Scout movement, having taught Robert Baden-Powell everything he knew.[58]

At Hammond's direction, Burnham proceeded to recruit a group of men who could be described as "shooters"—cowboys, ex-Texas Rangers, former U.S. Customs line riders, and ex-deputy sheriffs—and arranged to have the sheriff swear them in as special peace officers. We do not know precisely how many Burnham recruited. He would later state that there were "a number" of individuals, but one source gives the number as about 250.[59]

These special officers that Hammond paid for earned their money. Major Burnham initiated the plan to protect the presidents along the parade route. A complete census was taken of individuals and businesses along the route. It was divided into sections, and one of Burnham's special deputes was made responsible for each section. The individuals and businesses in each section were ordered to lock their doors one hour before the procession started. Special deputies were also stationed at the rear of the buildings and prevented anyone from entering or leaving the building after it had been locked.[60]

Some deputies cleared the crowds away from in front and beside the presidential carriages, while others scrutinized the crowds lining the route; they had been instructed to look for individuals who scowled or seemed angry. If an officer spotted someone like this he signaled his partner while edging over to the individual. As one deputy talked to the suspect, the other frisked him. According to Burnham, they seized over one hundred weapons. It should be noted that there was one fatality. An Anglo teenager was stabbed to death by "a young Mexican boy," but this was evidently a personal dispute.[61]

There is evidence, in two independently corroborating reports, of at least one planned assassination attempt. At the El Paso Chamber of Commerce building, just before Taft and Díaz met there, Burnham noticed what he described as a "sinister looking man writing in a notebook." He signaled a Texas Ranger, Private C. R. Moore, who was assisting Burnham in guarding the building, and they both moved in on the individual. Moore slipped his arm through the arm of the suspect and Burnham grabbed his wrist. Quickly flipping over his hand, Burnham and Moore discovered that "the pencil sticking out between the first and second fingers was actually the muzzle of a pistol especially designed to be hidden in the palm of the hand." The Texas Ranger report of the incident identified the weapon as a "pencil pistol," an assassin's weapon. Burnham related that the suspect identified himself as a newspaper reporter, but he was obliged to finish his story in jail. However, since the individual had not committed an overt act he was released from the county jail the next day—after the two presidents had left.[62]

Wilkie later claimed that the so-called plot was concocted out of whole cloth and was based on the testimony of an informant for the Department of Justice who was attempting to justify his informant fees.[63] Yet Wilkie's secret meeting with President Díaz and the "pencil pistol" incident belie this assertion. A major tragedy—and international incident—had in all probability been averted. These events underlined the fact that El Paso was a strategic base of operations for Mexican exiles seeking to overthrow the Díaz regime. Ironically, Díaz himself had set the precedent of using Texas soil as a revolutionary sanctuary when he had made Brownsville his headquarters for the 1876 rebellion that had elevated him to power.

CHAPTER 2

The *Magonistas*

Opposition to Díaz's oppressive rule increased significantly during the first decade of the twentieth century, and the opposition revolved around the person of Ricardo Flores Magón. Born in 1874 in the southern Mexican state of Oaxaca, Flores Magón studied law in Mexico City but never received his degree. Instead, he became a student activist and crusading journalist, spending the rest of his life as an uncompromising rebel. In 1900 he was a founder of the opposition newspaper *Regeneración*, which boldly attacked the regime. The authorities soon suppressed the publication, and they imprisoned Flores Magón on several occasions. Mexico finally became too dangerous for him, and on January 3, 1904, Flores Magón and his brother Enrique fled to the United States, entering at Laredo as penniless exiles.

They made San Antonio their headquarters and in November 1904 resumed publication of *Regeneración*. But the long arm of Díaz followed them. They lived in constant fear of Díaz's agents and decided that San Antonio was too close to the border. In 1905, the Flores Magón brothers moved to St. Louis, Missouri, and from there resumed publication of *Regeneración*. But that year they were arrested in St. Louis on defamation charges, and in March 1906, while awaiting trial, they jumped bond and fled to Canada, first to Toronto and then to Montreal. Flores Magón's movement was named the Partido Liberal Mexicano, the PLM or Mexican Liberal Party, so called because the traditional Liberal Party had become indistinguishable from the Conservative Party in its support of the Díaz administration. Members of the PLM came to be called *magonistas* after their charismatic leader. (Mexican factions were usually called by the name of the leader, evidencing the element of *personalismo*, that is, loyalty to a leader rather than to an ideology or political program.) On July 1, 1906, the PLM's junta, headed by Flores Magón, issued a comprehensive indictment of Díaz and proposed a plan for social and economic reform in Mexico. And at the same time the *magonistas* were busy organizing a nationwide uprising against the dictator.[1]

Flores Magón left Montreal in August 1906 to direct the planned revolution, traveling first to St. Louis and then to El Paso, the center of *magonista* activity.[2] The city was strategic for several reasons. First, there were many unemployed Mexican migrant workers in the area who would probably join the movement in hopes of securing food and money. Second, El Paso was a major railroad center. Most importantly, Ciudad Juárez across the river was the largest Mexican border town, and its seizure not only would shatter Díaz's image of invincibility but would provide the *magonistas* with confiscated goods, munitions, cash, and a major port of entry.

Even before Flores Magón's arrival there was considerable rebel activity in El Paso. A *magonista* cell, calling itself the Liberal Club, had been formed in 1905. Several Spanish-language Liberal Party newspapers were published there, of which the most important was *La Reforma Social*.[3] Its editor, Lauro Aguirre, had lived in El Paso for the past ten years. As president of the Liberal Club he functioned as a kind of public spokesman for the *magonistas*, although as a freethinking socialist he privately did not always agree with the *magonista* junta. Nevertheless, he was an effective propagandist who smuggled copies of *Regeneración* across to railroad workers in Juárez, who in turn disseminated them into the interior of Mexico.[4] While Aguirre served as the front man for the *magonistas*, Prisciliano G. Silva operated in El Paso as the contact between the PLM leadership and the movement's rank and file.

Flores Magón was soon joined in his El Paso headquarters by other leading members of the PLM, such as Juan Sarabia, a poet, journalist, and printer, Antonio I. Villarreal, a schoolteacher, and Librado Rivera, an elementary schoolteacher—men who have been described as "intellectuals of low status."[5] A notable exception was Práxedis G. Guerrero, who joined the PLM in 1906. Born in 1882 in Guanajuato into a wealthy landowning family, he became disgusted with the way Díaz was governing Mexico. Guerrero went into voluntary exile, entering the United States at El Paso in September 1904. Repudiating his own background, Guerrero worked as a common laborer and became a libertarian writer and revolutionary militant. He functioned as the PLM's principal organizer in the American Southwest.[6]

Guerrero and his fellow *magonistas* labored under severe handicaps, not the least of which were the neutrality laws of the United States prohibiting the use of American territory for the purpose of overthrowing a friendly government, such as that of Díaz. Flores Magón and some of his associates would undergo periods of imprisonment for neutrality law violations. In addition, the *magonistas* were starved for funds, most of their contributors being Hispanics in the Southwest who were holding down low-paying jobs as, for example, miners who were thus able to contribute little money to the cause. If money is the mother's milk of politics, it is also essential nourishment for revolutions, and the *magonistas* were chronically malnourished. They were also fatally infiltrated by operatives of the Mexican government, by American private detectives hired by the Mexican government, such as the Furlong Detective Agency, and by the federal authorities of the United States.[7] Their plight resembled that of American communists in the 1950s, whose movement was systematically undermined when many of those attending party cell meetings turned out to be FBI informers. Lastly, the *magonistas*, who were the most radical faction in the Mexican Revolution, were indeed fighting for the people, and some fought bravely, but unfortunately they did not fight well. Their military ineptitude eventually caused them to be marginalized by more competent revolutionary factions.

Not that the *magonistas* didn't try. By 1906 the PLM had established a central junta, published a manifesto announcing its reform program, founded a newspaper, and issued a call for members. The PLM had established a binational structure and had formulated tactics. The *magonistas* operated on three levels: clandestine clubs, Liberal Party clubs and front groups operating openly, and revolutionary forces. The PLM divided Mexico into five military zones, the northern zone encompassing Sinaloa, Baja California, Sonora, Chihuahua, Coahuila, Nuevo León, and Tamaulipas. The rebels boasted some forty-four guerrilla bands operating throughout Mexico, groups that historian Dirk Raat refers to exaggeratedly as "armies."[8]

To Flores Magón and his companions in El Paso, overthrowing Díaz seemed quite feasible. By October 1906, the rebel junta, operating from Chihuahuita, the teeming and impoverished Hispanic barrio in south El Paso, was making preparations for an attack on Ciudad Juárez. As historian Richard Estrada has observed, the leaders worked out of "locations close to the international bridge should the plan succeed, and near the railroad station should it fail."[9] Coordinating their efforts with sympathizers in Ciudad Juárez, the *magonistas* formulated an unrealistically grandiose plan of campaign: two hundred armed militants would assemble in El Paso, cross the Rio Grande, blow up the Juárez barracks, police station, and city hall, seize the customs house, the bank, and the house of the richest *juarense*, Inocente Ochoa. A contingent would then take the train and go capture the state capital, the city of Chihuahua. The El Paso junta would continue to supply war materiel, the victorious *magonistas* would name one of their own as governor of Chihuahua, the remainder of that state would rally to their cause, and there would occur a domino effect as state after state repudiated Díaz's rule.[10] It all seemed so simple when being worked out in a smoke-filled room in some cheap rooming house.

Reality was harsher. The Mexican authorities soon learned of the plan. Documents seized in the St. Louis offices of *Regeneración* were delivered to U.S. authorities on the border, who shared this information with their Mexican counterparts. This was a devastating development, for the material included PLM membership lists and a roster of revolutionary agents.[11] On October 4, 1906, President Díaz was informed that a *magonista* revolutionary cell led by Lauro Aguirre was actively operating in El Paso. Díaz promptly ordered General José María de la Vega and one hundred troops to Ciudad Juárez. Upon arriving, the general assigned two of his officers—Captain Adolfo Jiménez Castro and Lieutenant Zeferino Reyes—the mission of infiltrating the rebels and acting as agents provocateur. Since the PLM desperately hoped to enlist the army's support in the planned rebellion against Díaz, the *magonistas* were delighted at this apparent evidence of military defection, especially when Jiménez Castro and Reyes promised to lead a mutiny by the Juárez garrison. The *magonistas* naively took the two officers into their complete confidence. The officers kept General de la Vega and the Mexican consul in El Paso, Francisco Mallén, apprised of the revolutionists' plan and of their difficulties in acquiring munitions.[12]

The attack on Juárez was scheduled for October 21, but it never materialized. On the night of October 19–20, Captain Jiménez Castro led a handful of eager, young revolutionists across the international bridge. The *magonista* militants thought they were going to seize the Juárez jail, but instead Jiménez Castro led them into a trap—the dumbfounded rebels were arrested near the customs house. The captain then crossed back into El Paso to assist the American authorities, who at the request of the Mexican government were preparing to round up the revolutionists. At midnight Mexican consul Mallén led a party of some dozen police, plus a deputy U.S. marshal, plus Captain Jiménez Castro and other Mexican Army officers, in a series of raids on seedy rooming houses on South Oregon and South El Paso streets. Their biggest catch, though, was on Overland Street. They raided the room of one "Pedro González," and hidden "in the jamb of one of the transoms" they found a cache of PLM documents. Having seized them, the lawmen were coming down the stairs when they encountered, and arrested, "Pedro González" himself—who turned out to be Antonio I. Villarreal, one of the leaders of the PLM.[13] Several hours later the raiding party, again led by Mallén with pistol in hand, burst into the home of the journalist Lauro Aguirre and arrested him. Also falling into the net that night was José Cano, the principal arms smuggler for the *magonistas*. In Ciudad Juárez, meanwhile, the authorities arrested a total of seventeen men, including the three PLM ringleaders in that city.

The operation in El Paso was characterized by egregious illegality—a pistol-packing Mexican consul figuring prominently, arrests being made without warrants, Mexican Army officers participating—but it contributed materially to smashing the *magonista* plot. Yet the biggest fish of all had escaped. When notified of the dragnet, Ricardo Flores Magón, who was hiding out in the home of a follower, Modesto Díaz, hurried to one of the international bridges armed with a dynamite bomb in each hand bent on crossing over to Juárez to warn his colleagues there. But he spotted a detective employed by the Mexican government stationed at the bridge and turned back, prudently choosing flight over martyrdom. He and Modesto Díaz unobtrusively made their way to the Union Depot and caught the first train out of town.[14]

As it happened, the captured Antonio I. Villarreal also managed to escape. The Mexican government felt that there would be difficulty in having him extradited, so it adopted a different approach—trying to have Villarreal deported to Mexico for violating U.S. immigration laws. (He'd earlier killed a man in Mexico in a duel and had been imprisoned—thus he had entered the United States illegally because of his criminal record.) The United States cooperated, and Villarreal was indeed turned over to immigration authorities in El Paso for deportation. On the way back to the county jail after his immigration hearing, Villarreal asked permission to send a telegram to his family in St. Louis. Either through the negligence or the connivance of his deputy U.S. marshal escort, Villarreal simply walked out the back door of the Western Union office, and hid in the home of a *magonista* sympathizer. He then made his way to California and rejoined Flores Magón.[15]

The PLM's 1906 attempt to capture Juárez was a disaster, and the *magonistas*' effort to touch off an uprising throughout Mexico also failed. Díaz's image of invincibility was, if anything, enhanced. Yet in one respect the *magonistas* did have an impact. In June, copper miners in Cananea, Sonora, had gone out on strike, influenced by *magonista* organizers and propaganda. Although the authorities quickly crushed the strike, it helped prepare the way for the Mexican Revolution.

On occasion the Mexican government's campaign against the *magonistas* became really outrageous. On June 30, 1907, in Douglas, Arizona, "an intelligent and to a degree, handsome, Mexican," who worked in a newspaper office and was known locally as "Sam Moret," was arrested by an Arizona Ranger and jailed at the instigation of the Mexican consul, Antonio Maza, who charged the man with having committed murder in Mexico. The consul also paid for heavily armed men to guard the prisoner around the clock. But that night the prisoner was turned over to two American minions of the consul who drove up to the jail. The prisoner was forced into their automobile crying "I am being deprived of my liberty" before he was choked into silence. The kidnappers then drove across the border to Agua Prieta and delivered Manuel Sarabia to the Rurales, Díaz's feared mounted constabulary. The jubilant authorities promptly hustled Sarabia off to prison in Hermosillo, the capital of Sonora.

The Mexicans had gotten their man, but what they hadn't counted on was public opinion in Douglas. The citizens were outraged at the blatant violation of the law, which a local newspaper described as "the most startling event yet recorded in the history of Douglas," and they promptly held a mass meeting demanding not only an investigation of American complicity in the kidnapping but also the immediate return of Sarabia to American soil. Arrest warrants were issued for Consul Maza, the Arizona Ranger, a local policeman, and a local constable. It turned out that the constable and Consul Maza's hired guards had delivered Sarabia to his kidnappers (the driver of the automobile confessed). The Department of Justice instructed the U.S. attorney for Arizona to conduct an investigation. Meanwhile, Consul Maza discreetly crossed the border into Mexico, and Sarabia wrote a letter from prison giving his version of the affair. Deciding to cut their losses, the Mexican authorities reluctantly agreed to return Sarabia, thereby ending the affair. A grateful Sarabia expressed his profound thanks to the people of Douglas. Since no charges were pending against him, he walked the streets as a free man.[16]

Despite their failure at Ciudad Juárez and of the collapse of their hoped-for nationwide uprising, the *magonistas* gamely kept on trying. They had to act without their leader, for on August 23, 1907, Flores Magón and several associates were arrested in Los Angeles for neutrality violations and were sentenced to prison. About that same time, Flores Magón became openly more radical; he was no longer a political liberal but now proclaimed himself to be an anarchist. His radicalism of course had the effect of alienating many of his moderate supporters.[17]

As if to symbolize the defeat of the PLM, on January 24, 1907, Enrique Clay Creel passed through El Paso on his way to Washington, D.C., where he was to assume the post of Mexican ambassador to the United States. Consul Mallén arranged an elaborate banquet in honor of Creel and his wife, who occupied the entire first floor of the Sheldon Hotel. The banquet, with music provided by the regimental band from Fort Bliss, was a huge success. Enrique Creel was the son-in-law of the oligarch General Luis Terrazas, who dominated the state of Chihuahua. Creel was extremely well connected and between 1906 and 1911 served as governor of Chihuahua, ambassador to the United States, and minister of foreign relations. In 1909, he was the official interpreter and host for the Díaz-Taft meeting. Significantly, between 1906 and 1911 it was Creel who directed the Díaz regime's campaign against rebels. Creel functioned as the informal head of the government's intelligence service, as liaison with the American authorities, and as employer of American detective agencies combating the *magonistas*.[18] A vital component of Creel's network were the Mexican consuls in the United States, and especially those in cities such as El Paso. We have seen how Consul Mallén played a leading role in the 1906 arrest of *magonistas*. The consuls were authorized to employ their own secret agents, which necessarily meant there would be a certain lack of coordination and effectiveness, and this would be the pattern for years to come.[19]

Although the pursuit of the *magonistas* in the United States is well documented, the full scope of the Roosevelt administration's zeal to stamp out the PLM is in our judgment not yet fully understood. See, for example, a little-noticed September 28, 1907, "confidential" letter from the adjutant general of the U.S. Army to the general commanding the Department of Texas. The adjutant general acknowledged Brigadier General Duncan's letter of September 18, 1907, in which the latter asked what he should do in case a suspicious band, whether armed or unarmed, should try to cross into Mexico with revolution on their mind. The adjutant general instructed him to spread the word along the border that the United States was prepared to use military force "to enforce the neutrality laws and to protect the territory of a foreign state, with which the United States is at peace, from an invasion by an armed party from the territory of the United States."[20]

The *magonistas* did manage to mount several minor raids in 1908 from Del Rio across the Rio Grande against the towns of Jiménez and Las Vacas (today Ciudad Acuña) in Coahuila. But in terms of toppling Díaz these were mere pinpricks. The raids did have a noteworthy effect on the United States, however. The American government established what today would be termed an "interagency task force" headed by Luther T. Ellsworth, the consul in Ciudad Porfirio Díaz, to monitor Mexican exile plotters. Ellsworth, who spoke Spanish fluently, was so proficient at gathering intelligence that by the end of 1909 the Department of Justice appointed him as its special representative for neutrality matters.[21]

While Flores Magón languished in prison, his followers continued the struggle. And his followers included a number of women. In El Paso, for instance, Isidra T. de Cárdenas founded a radical newspaper, *Voz de la Mujer*, in 1907. And a Mrs. Flores de Andrade, a political refugee from Chihuahua, collected clothes, medicine, money, arms, and ammunition for the *magonistas*, who were preparing in 1908 for another attempt to overthrow Díaz.[22] From El Paso, *magonista* organizers spread out through the Southwest, disseminating propaganda and collecting money and weapons; once again the city figured prominently in their plans as the base from which to seize control of Ciudad Juárez. Essentially the plan was a repetition of the failed 1906 strategy—to seize Ciudad Juárez while touching off a nationwide uprising.

A driving force in this endeavor was Práxedis Guerrero. In January 1908, he and a close friend and fellow militant, Francisco Manrique, left Los Angeles for El Paso. Guerrero established his headquarters in the house of Prisciliano Silva, the leading *magonista* in the city. Shortly before the revolt scheduled for June 25, Enrique Flores Magón, Ricardo's younger brother, arrived from Los Angeles to assist in the operation. Unfortunately, most of the letters that Ricardo Flores Magón was smuggling out of the Los Angeles County jail had been intercepted and turned over to the Mexican authorities.[23] One was a letter that he wrote to Enrique in June containing a detailed account of PLM activities and plans for the revolt.[24] This material, supplemented by the reports of informers, meant that the outcome was predictable—another *magonista* catastrophe.

The *magonistas* stockpiled homemade bombs and a growing cache of arms and ammunition in south El Paso. The conspirators' headquarters were "a house on the corner of First and Tays Streets, a stone's throw from the Rio Grande."[25] All this feverish activity was for naught. A woman living next door to the revolutionary headquarters became concerned about the suspicious activity going on there—people carrying munitions into the house in broad daylight, armed men milling around, and so forth. Thinking they must be smugglers or thieves, she informed the authorities. The El Paso police, again working in conjunction with the Mexican consul, raided the place on June 25, arresting four important *magonistas* and seizing arms, ammunition, and a treasure trove of documents, including detailed lists of *magonistas* and the location of revolutionary cells throughout the Southwest.[26] The Mexican consul asked the authorities to arrest León Cárdenas, Lauro Aguirre, Práxedis Guerrero, Enrique Bermúdez, and Manuel Aguilar as accomplices. Only Aguirre was caught. He was released on bail put up by politically active brothers Isaac "Ike" Alderete, clerk of the district court, and Francisco "Frank" Alderete, who worked for the city health department.[27] "The projected assault on Ciudad Juárez came to an end before it even started."[28]

Práxedis Guerrero and Enrique Flores Magón were fortunate enough to escape the dragnet in El Paso. Frustrated and desperate, Guerrero decided they should strike a blow *somewhere.* The target chosen was the godforsaken little village of Palomas, sixty miles west of El Paso and across the border from Columbus, New Mexico. Enrique Flores Magón, although devoted to his brother's cause, was evidently unwilling to die for the cause—he "accidentally" shot himself in the foot and thus couldn't participate in the harebrained attack. Led by Guerrero, ten *magonista* militants assaulted Palomas on the night of June 30. The small garrison repulsed the attack, one man being killed on each side, and Guerrero was left mourning the death of his close friend Francisco Manrique.[29] The attack on Palomas had been a pointless failure, but there was one interesting aspect: among the *magonista* attackers was José Inés Salazar, who in years to come would be a conspicuous player in the Mexican Revolution on the border.

Not only had the *magonistas*' plans in the El Paso area failed miserably, but it also began raining indictments. In the October 1908 term of the El Paso federal district court, indictments were returned against Ricardo and Enrique Flores Magón, Antonio I. Villarreal, Antonio de P. Araujo, Ecarnación Díaz Guerra, and Práxedis G. Guerrero.[30] In addition, the grand jury indicted a number of *magonistas* who had allegedly participated in the raids on Las Vacas and Jiménez.[31]

By 1910, the *magonistas* had become a minor irritant, their activities limited mainly to propaganda and their leaders on the defensive.[32] In El Paso the principal activist was Lázaro Gutiérrez de Lara, a veteran PLM member, who delivered impassioned street-corner harangues advocating anarchism and socialism. He was periodically arrested, but on release he would resume his inflammatory speeches.[33] Most El Pasoans couldn't have cared less about the *magonistas*—they were focused on the city's booming economy.

Although the largest city between San Antonio and Los Angeles, El Paso had historically suffered from its isolated location at the western tip of Texas, six hundred miles from Austin, the state capital. Its reputation had rested principally on the fact that it was the residence of a covey of the West's better-known gunfighters, who enjoyed shooting it out in the local saloons over cards and drinks.[34] All this began to change with the arrival of the first railroad in 1881. "As a city, El Paso's birth and initial growth were due to an entirely external factor. This external factor was the arrival of the railroad in the 1880's. Prior to the railroad's appearance on the scene, El Paso was a sleepy little adobe village completely isolated from the more settled regions of the state."[35] By 1909, when the Taft-Díaz meeting occurred, El Paso had a population of almost forty thousand.[36] And the six railroads serving the city made El Paso the trade and transportation center of the Southwest.[37] In addition, Ciudad Juárez was the largest Mexican border town and the terminus of the Mexico Northwestern Railroad and the Mexican Central Railroad.[38] Although Juárez remained largely a town of one-story adobe buildings and many unpaved streets, the advent of the railroads had propelled El Paso toward modernity. Its adobe structures were being replaced by dwellings of lumber or brick, streets in the downtown area were paved, the city boasted a Carnegie library, and considerable commercial construction was under way.[39]

The American Smelting and Refining Company copper and lead smelter in the suburb of Smeltertown, employing several thousand mainly Hispanic workers, received about 80 percent of its ore from Mexico, brought in by rail. Besides boasting a major smelter, El Paso enjoyed a flourishing traffic in cattle from Mexico. In the spring of 1910, for instance, it was anticipated that sixty thousand head would be imported just between April 1 and mid-May, mainly from the enormous haciendas of General Luis Terrazas in Chihuahua.[40] At this time Terrazas arguably had the largest ranching operation in the world.

The firm of Krakauer, Zork and Moye, established in 1887 and incorporated for $300,000, dominated the regional trade in wholesale and retail hardware, sporting goods, arms, and ammunition. Adolph Krakauer was president, assisted by his sons Robert and Julius. Besides the main office in El Paso, Krakauer had a warehouse and powder magazine in Ysleta and a large hardware store in the city of Chihuahua. The Chihuahua store was an integral part of the firm but was managed independently by Adolph Krakauer's brother-in-law Zork, who was vice president of the corporation. (Moye had been bought out several years earlier.) Krakauer had been branching out in Chihuahua, buying bank and railroad stocks as well as acquiring several mines. By 1912, its investments in the Mexican state amounted to about $1 million. And Adolph Krakauer was one of El Paso's leading businessmen; he served as president of the chamber of commerce and was a director of the First National Bank and of the Rio Grande Valley Bank and Trust Company.[41]

Lumbering was rapidly becoming a pillar of the local economy. Lewis Booker, owner of the Booker Lumber Company of Chihuahua and El Paso, emerged as one of the most active American landowners in Mexico. Booker's timber holdings included a 165,000-acre tract in the Sierra Madre of Chihuahua. His lumber mill on the property had a daily capacity of twenty thousand board feet.[42]

But the big economic news concerned the activities of Frederick Stark Pearson, PhD. A native of Lowell, Massachusetts, he was a prominent consulting engineer who headed the Pearson-Farquhar syndicate, an English organization that conducted large-scale engineering projects in various countries. The syndicate was especially noted for developing electric traction, light, and power projects in Brazil, Spain, and Mexico. Pearson's syndicate formed a Canadian company, the Madera Company, which acquired a 3.5 million-acre timber and colonization concession in western Chihuahua, constituting the third largest landholding in that state. To haul out the timber, Pearson in 1909 organized a Mexican corporation, the Ferrocarril Noroeste de México, the MNW, by merging three existing lines.[43] When completed—there was a 116-mile mountainous gap presenting formidable engineering problems between the towns of Terrazas and Madera—the 400-mile MNW would run in a loop from Juárez to the city of Chihuahua.[44] Besides the considerable sum required to complete the railroad (which was accomplished in 1912), he invested some $600,000 in an enormous sawmill complex at the new company town of Pearson on the MNW. Another company town, Madera, contained many of the railroad's installations as well as a sawmill that by 1910 was producing four hundred thousand feet of rough-cut lumber a day. A branch line ran to a mine, which shipped about 150 carloads of ore a month to the El Paso smelter. And in a subsequent phase of construction, Pearson and his associates planned to extend the MNW across the Sierra Madre to the Pacific.[45] The syndicate's total investment was reputed to be in the neighborhood of $20 million. (By 1912, the Pearson interests had invested an estimated $33 million in Chihuahua.)[46]

Of this breathtaking sum, Ciudad Juárez stood to get at least $500,000 for the terminal of the MNW. As for El Paso, "The estimated expenditures to acquire and complete the company's property in El Paso will aggregate in the neighborhood of $2,000,000. This is assured, provided desirable locations can be secured at reasonable prices and the company receives fair treatment."[47] The prospect of such a massive investment made the leaders of the El Paso business community practically salivate, and it produced an overnight inflation of some real estate values. Landowners who thought the company might want their property were eager to sell, at exorbitant prices, for El Paso would be the hub of Pearson's operations. The company contemplated building a railroad yard in El Paso and using that city's Union Depot, and it was planning on constructing a huge planing mill to finish the rough lumber coming from Mexico, which facility would be capable of handling thirty carloads of lumber daily and would employ four hundred to five hundred men. The El

Paso Milling Company, another Canadian corporation, was established to this end. Moreover, an extensive box factory, and perhaps later a paper mill, was envisioned in connection with the planing mill.[48] To the intense disappointment of the chamber of commerce, which had planned to hold an elaborate banquet in his honor when in May Dr. Pearson and his entourage rolled into El Paso in his private railroad car on his way to inspect the operations in Mexico, he stopped only a short while, promising to enjoy their hospitality on his return trip.[49]

With economic development dominating the news, few El Pasoans had paid much attention to a local newspaper story that had appeared on January 15, reporting the overnight stay of a visitor from Mexico. The headline read: "Predicts Revolution in Mexico if Corral Ever Becomes President," referring to Ramón Corral, Díaz's vice president. A subhead explained: "Mexican Cotton Planter Is Touring His Country Speaking Against Diaz and Corral," on behalf of the Anti-Reelectionist party.[50] The "cotton planter" who was bold enough to criticize Díaz publicly was a certain Francisco I. Madero, who would touch off the Mexican Revolution in November 1910. During the tumultuous decade that followed, El Paso would play a crucial role.

CHAPTER 3

Madero's Improbable Triumph

Madero's rebellion was of a different order of magnitude than that of Ricardo Flores Magón—if the Mexican Revolution were an ocean liner, Flores Magón would be traveling in steerage while Madero would be dining at the captain's table. The anarchist Flores Magón had set out to overthrow the Díaz regime and to abolish capitalism in Mexico, and he was an abject failure on both counts, although some of his ideas were later adopted by more capable factions. Flores Magón remained safely in the United States while urging his followers to risk their lives in Mexico. In short, he was a thinker, not a fighter. Those who have written about Flores Magón have usually described him as the precursor to the revolution, which is a gentler way of describing his failure.

By contrast, Madero was no bomb-throwing anarchist; he not only was eminently respectable but believed in private property, of which he owned an impressive amount. A member of one of the wealthiest families in Mexico, Madero believed in democracy and hoped to bring about change through the ballot and not through bullets. He had the moral courage openly to challenge Díaz, running for president against the dictator in the 1910 election. But Díaz, who initially viewed Madero as a joke, became seriously concerned when in his campaign Madero generated large and enthusiastic crowds. So, Díaz had Madero arrested on a trumped-up charge prior to the election, which effectively neutralized him. When the election was held in the summer of 1910, the government announced that Díaz had won handily. Madero thus faced the dilemma of accepting defeat and returning to a very comfortable life as a private citizen or, as a last resort, denouncing the election as a fraud and issuing a call to arms. Ironically, the Mexican Revolution was initiated by a man who was not really a revolutionary.

On October 5, 1910, Madero eluded the surveillance of the Díaz authorities and fled to the United States, making his way to San Antonio, a center of anti-Díaz agitation. There he organized the Mexican Revolution, issuing the obligatory revolutionary manifesto, the *Plan de San Luis Potosí*, which called for a nationwide rising at 6 p.m. on November 20. Obviously the manifesto couldn't be entitled the *Plan de San Antonio* because of U.S. neutrality laws, so the document was backdated to October 5, the last day Madero had physically been in Mexico, in the city of San Luis Potosí.

Madero's slogan was "Effective Suffrage, No Reelection." In the short space of six weeks it was simply impossible to organize a nationwide revolutionary network, but Madero did the best he could, briefing a steady stream of followers who came to his San Antonio headquarters for instructions. As for himself, to avoid the charge that he, like Flores Magón, was afraid to risk his life, on November 19, Madero traveled secretly to Eagle Pass, Texas, on the Rio Grande, planning to cross the river and lead in person a large contingent of rebels who were supposed to be waiting for him. They weren't, and the crestfallen Madero had to return to San Antonio and await developments.

In a further effort to inflate Flores Magón's stature, Dirk Raat states that "when Madero crossed [*sic*] the border at Eagle Pass the night of 19 November to join his comrades in Mexico, he did not initiate the Mexican Revolution—he joined it."[1] The Mexicans lack Raat's insight—they celebrate the anniversary of the revolution as November 20, 1910, the date Madero initiated it.

Not much happened on November 20, and for a time it seemed that Madero would fail as miserably as Flores Magón had failed, but fortunately for Madero he had some capable subordinates, and the revolution began to gather momentum, especially in the state of Chihuahua. And the reason it did so was due in no small measure to Madero's followers in El Paso, despite an intense rivalry with the *magonistas*, who considered themselves the only true revolutionaries.[2]

The key figure in the *maderista* apparatus in El Paso was Abraham González. The tall, portly González was forty years old when Madero commissioned him as an insurgent, or *insurrecto*, colonel, provisional governor of Chihuahua, and chief of the Second Military Zone encompassing Chihuahua and Durango.[3] A businessman and rancher by background, González was well known in El Paso, where he had lived for some time. A graduate of Notre Dame, he'd worked for many years as a cattle buyer in Chihuahua for the Charles M. Newman Company of El Paso.[4] In his military capacity González tried to capture a border port of entry, the isolated town of Ojinaga, across from Presidio, Texas. But in a series of engagements in December 1910, the Mexican Army thrashed González and his rebels. "He retired to El Paso, disabused of his military abilities, to concentrate on supplying arms to the rebels and reestablishing communications with scattered units in the state."[5]

It was from El Paso that González made an outstanding contribution to the rebel cause. Since early October 1910, there had been a *maderista* junta in that city (led by González's brother Santiago González, Alberto Fuentes, and Cástulo Herrera), but it had been relatively ineffectual. González quickly imbued the junta with his enthusiasm for providing the *insurrectos* with recruits, supplies, and organization. He operated quite openly from rented offices, rooms 507–8 in the downtown Caples Building, 300 East San Antonio Street, frequently giving interviews to the press.[6] At the same time, he made good use of his local contacts while establishing a most effective rebel network that maintained communications with the guerrillas in Chihuahua, gathered intelligence, arranged for volunteers to join insurgent bands, enlisted railroad personnel to drop off arms and ammunition at isolated spots in west Texas, purchased substantial amounts of arms, ammunition, and supplies from El Paso dealers, and smuggled the munitions across the Rio Grande.[7] González was a highly effective recruiter, enlisting among other El Pasoans Doctor Ira J. Bush, who as surgeon general with the rank of colonel would play a key role in establishing a medical service for the insurgent army.[8] Yet Abraham González's major achievement was enlisting Pascual Orozco and Francisco "Pancho" Villa as guerrilla chieftains.[9] These men, who were gifted amateurs, embodied *personalismo*, or allegiance to a leader over allegiance to a political faction or ideology. Orozco and Villa proved adept at defeating small contingents of Díaz's rail-bound army in Chihuahua, and with each victory more and more men became enthusiastic *maderistas*. As insurgent momentum increased, especially in the western Sierra Madre region of Chihuahua, the Díaz government was always behind the curve in sending reinforcements into the state, and the rebels were often able to defeat army units piecemeal. What the regime had initially derided as the activities of "bandits" evolved into full-blown rebellion. And more and more people began to wonder whether Díaz was invulnerable after all.

As revolutionary activity along the border intensified, the United States was hard pressed to enforce the neutrality laws. The federal agencies charged with enforcing these statutes were the Customs Service, the army, and the Department of Justice. The Customs Service could do relatively little except man the international bridges and deploy its few mounted inspectors to patrol the Rio Grande and the land boundary west of El Paso along the New Mexico border to Columbus.[10] As of 1910 the army had been phasing out the chain of border forts built in the nineteenth century. Since Díaz had pacified Mexico, most of these installations were now deemed unnecessary. Some consideration had been given to deactivating Fort Bliss in El Paso, but it was decided to retain it as an active installation. This proved fortunate, because Bliss was the largest post on the border and would prove to be the pivot of border defense. But when the Mexican Revolution erupted, the Fort Bliss garrison consisted of four companies and a machine-gun platoon of the 23rd U.S. Infantry regiment. This force of 310 men could perhaps protect El Paso, but the absence of cavalry severely curtailed the army's ability to patrol the Rio Grande.[11]

As for the Department of Justice, a frustrated Mexican consul reported that the deputy U.S. marshal in El Paso, H. Richard Hillebrand, a former army captain, El Paso police chief, and El Paso County sheriff, was elderly and carried out his duties indifferently, while the assistant U.S. attorney, S. Engelking, seemed much more interested in his private law practice than in prosecuting Mexican revolutionists (being an assistant U.S. attorney was not a full-time job).[12] And the U.S. attorney for the Western District of Texas, Charles Boynton, insisted that Madero had to be caught in the very act of violating the neutrality laws before he could be arrested.[13] The Justice Department's other enforcement arm was the fledgling federal Bureau of Investigation, created in 1909, and it became the cutting edge of neutrality enforcement. Besides being a recent creation, the Bureau lacked money and manpower, and it especially lacked agents fluent in Spanish. It was the Mexican Revolution that enabled the Bureau to hone its counterintelligence skills.

The Bureau eventually assigned several special agents to El Paso, and they used half a dozen Anglo informants. Yet given the level of revolutionary intrigue in the city it was impossible to monitor everything that was going on and keep under surveillance those whom the Bureau would have considered "persons of interest." During the first two years of the Mexican Revolution the Sheldon Hotel was the epicenter of revolutionary activity in El Paso, while in the fall of 1910 revolutionists of lesser status were staying at the Victor Hotel, a rather shabby establishment located at 211½ Overland Street. Just keeping these places under even intermittent surveillance was beyond the manpower resources of the local Bureau office.

In its efforts to enforce the neutrality statutes the Bureau encountered an unusual problem—locating addresses in Chihuahuita, the Hispanic barrio in south El Paso. "It must be stated that this part of the city consists almost entirely of adobe huts, with about two rooms but quite a number have only one. Some of these huts are numbered, and those that are not come between the numbered ones. Neither the blocks nor numbers follow one another with any regularity.... The letter carrier who delivers on the first three blocks states that it is the custom of the poorer class of Mexicans to take with them when they move the small piece of tin containing the number of the house and place it over the entrance of their new house regardless of any of the surrounding numbers.... The majority of the huts are built at random and the inhabitants are very ignorant."[14] Bureau agents assigned to El Paso from the East definitely experienced culture shock.

The Bureau of Investigation agents were also hampered by the fact that smuggling was a time-honored occupation along the border—the only changes being the nature of the goods being smuggled and the direction they were going in. Whereas in earlier decades cattle smuggling had dominated, there had grown up a brisk trade in smuggling Chinese laborers into the United States in violation of the Exclusion Act. "El Paso and Juarez form the smuggling center of opium as well as of Chinamen into the United States."[15] With the outbreak of the Mexican Revolution people quit smuggling Chinese into the United States and began smuggling guns into Mexico.[16]

The view seemed to be that if the Mexicans were determined to kill each other they should be provided with ample weaponry at a price they could afford. Many of the locals did not really consider smuggling a criminal activity, an attitude that became a major source of frustration for the federal authorities. Besides trying to keep track of smugglers, the Bureau was hampered by the fact that Mexican officials were being less than cooperative. Although Bureau agents conferred frequently with the Mexican consul, Antonio Lomelí, he refused to divulge the names of those who came to him with rumors or information regarding neutrality violations, and "every clue furnished by Mexicans has proven on investigation to be without foundation."[17]

Lomelí was running his own secret agents, among them one Manuel Torres, hired for nine days at $2.50 a day and William "Australian Billy" Smith, a local detective who had previously worked for the Mexican intelligence service, at $5 a day plus a limited expense account. Smith, who frequently submitted written reports, stated that revolutionists gathered at several bars, including the Emporium Saloon, run by "a Greek who once lived in Guadalajara." Smith was referring to Teodoro Kyriacopulos, who will appear frequently in connection with revolutionary intrigue.[18]

The level of intrigue was rising. The Bureau was keeping the *magonistas* and *insurrectos* under surveillance and distrusted the Mexican consul. The *insurrectos* conducted countersurveillance on the Bureau and the Mexican consul and his agents. The Mexican consul shared some intelligence with the Bureau and maintained surveillance on the *magonistas* and *insurrectos*.

The consul's men learned, for example, that Abraham González had opened an office in the Victor Hotel, occupying several rooms on the second floor and allowing none but his subordinates to enter. Among those entering was the man who collected González's mail at a post office box and delivered it to the hotel.[19] And it was learned that Cástulo Herrera, a former railroad man operating from his office at the southwest corner of Third and Stanton streets, was busy recruiting men and purchasing weapons for the rebels.[20]

An additional complication for the Bureau was that Madero's network was by no means confined to the border region. Madero's brother Gustavo, who handled the revolutionary finances, enlisted the services of Ed Maurer, a wealthy import-export broker with offices at 30 Wall Street in New York City who specialized in Mexican and South American business. In fact, Maurer had been marketing the guayule rubber being produced at some of the Madero family's haciendas. The Bureau reported that Maurer, "who acted as commission broker for Madero[,] . . . would not hesitate to export anything requested by his trade, although he is represented to be a man of excellent character."[21] Maurer acquired most of the rebels' weaponry from a major international arms dealer, Francis Bannerman and Company of New York City.[22] Francis Bannerman was a fabulous figure. He wasn't just an arms dealer—he was the largest arms dealer in the world. He'd gotten that way by making shrewd purchases of government surplus, mainly U.S. Army surplus but also including virtually all the Spanish weaponry from the Spanish-American War. When the authorities in New York City prohibited him from storing enormous amounts of live ammunition in the city, Bannerman simply purchased an island on the Hudson River fifty-five miles to the north, built himself what was literally a castle, and relocated his massive inventory there.[23]

Maurer arranged to have Madero's munitions shipped from the Bush Terminal Company docks in Brooklyn through Galveston to the border, mainly to the Shelton-Payne Arms Company in El Paso, the principal *maderista* supplier.[24] This firm, of which D. M. Payne was president and W. H. Shelton was general manager, dealt in "fire arms, ammunition, saddlery and sporting goods." But Maurer was under surveillance by one James Silver, an operative working on behalf of the Mexican government.[25] And Edward Laroque Tinker, a former New York assistant district attorney who'd resigned to enter private law practice, was a paid Díaz spy who employed the Burns Detective Agency to "shadow certain members of the Madero party stopping at the Hotel Astor."[26] Tinker neglected to mention this in his memoirs.[27]

In Washington, D.C., Madero's attorney was the urbane Sherburne Gillette Hopkins, who had been born in Washington in 1868, had attended Columbia University, and since 1889 had practiced law with his father as the firm of Hopkins and Hopkins. Operating from his office in room 801 of the Hibbs Building, Hopkins enjoyed a flourishing practice, advising important foreign investors, Latin American revolutionists, and the governments combating those revolutionists.[28] He often held court at his table in the grill room of a leading hotel, consuming copious amounts of whiskey and charming various Central American ministers, American reporters, and Mexican revolutionists, among them the peripatetic revolutionary José Vasconcelos, at the time the secretary of Madero's confidential agency in Washington.[29] Hopkins handled a number of tasks, many of them clandestine, for Madero. For instance, he dispatched an agent, Harvey J. Phillips, first to New Orleans and then to El Paso to arrange for arms shipments to the *maderistas*. The overworked Bureau agents failed to locate the elusive Phillips before he slipped out of El Paso.[30]

Rebel activity increased markedly in 1911. Although San Antonio remained Madero's headquarters, the center of insurgent gravity in the United States rapidly shifted to El Paso. The local junta worked feverishly to supply Orozco's and Villa's guerrilla forces, which were rapidly growing stronger, with munitions. Greatly facilitating the junta's task was the fact that over 90 percent of the city's population warmly supported the *maderista* cause.[31] The federal and state officials in El Paso perhaps did what they could to interdict the flow of weaponry across the Rio Grande, but they were fighting a losing battle. The border was, as indeed it still is, extremely porous, and Díaz took the attitude that it was the responsibility of the United States to stop the arms traffic. The United States kept insisting that the Mexicans furnish convincing proof of *maderista* neutrality violations.[32] A tactic the Díaz government used was the April 24, 1899, extradition treaty, by the terms of which if Mexico accused one of its citizens living in the United States of a crime, the individual could be jailed for forty days while the Mexican authorities provided evidence of the offense. The Bureau of Investigation arrested Madero's secretary, Juan Sánchez Azcona, in Washington, D.C., on an extradition warrant, charging him with embezzlement. Attorney Hopkins secured his release.[33]

On occasion, American officials did work in cooperation with their Mexican counterparts. Information from the Bureau of Investigation and the Immigration Service enabled Mexican officers in Juárez to arrest seven Pullman employees on the night of January 27 and seize several boxes of Mauser rifle cartridges destined for the rebels.[34] And Consul Lomelí was now more cooperative in providing leads, as was Mexican government secret agent Jesús María Arriola. Nevertheless, the Bureau kept the consul under surveillance.[35] Unfortunately for the Díaz regime, it seems Consul Lomelí had been suborned by the *maderistas*, in the person of C. F. Z. Caracristi, one of the most flamboyant figures ever to grace El Paso. With Caracristi it is difficult to determine where bombast ends and reality begins. Caracristi, who had visited El Paso several times before the revolution, described himself as a Virginian of Austrian ancestry, a PhD geologist of international reputation who'd represented major corporations on four continents and who was a close friend of the rich and powerful whose wrath he could call down on anyone who had the temerity to cross him. He was diplomatic agent and legal counsel for the El Paso junta. Caracristi reportedly suborned Consul Lomelí, who provided information on Díaz troop movements and a copy of a Mexican government cipher in exchange for $3,000, paid in weekly installments of $300.[36] This invaluable source of intelligence dried up in March, when the Mexican government, suspicious of Lomelí's loyalty, replaced him as consul with Tomás Torres.

But it was not just Mexican officials who were suborned. The Díaz regime paid R. W. Dowe, collector of customs for the Saluria District, with headquarters in Eagle Pass, for information.[37] And Sheriff J. J. Allen of Terrell County, whose seat was Sanderson, was also on the Mexican government's payroll as a secret agent, as was "Australian Billy" Smith, the El Paso detective.[38] It was further rumored that late in 1910 Díaz personally dispatched a secret agent, James Henry McCloskey, to San Antonio to secure evidence of Madero's violation of the neutrality laws. McCloskey posed as a gunrunner and became acquainted with Madero and his family but never succeeded in catching Madero violating the law.[39] The Díaz administration also funded a San Antonio network operated by William M. Hanson, a former U.S.

marshal; among Hanson's agents were Roy Adams and J. D. Womack.[40] Furthermore, a certain Thomas Foster was a Díaz agent in San Antonio, spying on Madero.[41] These clandestine resources supplemented the regular intelligence reports the Furlong Detective Agency was providing.

In El Paso, Consul Torres ran several secret agents. One was the experienced spy Jesús María Arriola, who'd been working for Torres's predecessor. Arriola, who would become head of the Mexican government's intelligence service in 1916, turned in reports that were rather pedestrian, usually describing the surveillance of unknown Mexicans seen making purchases at local arms dealers, especially at Shelton-Payne.[42] Consul Torres's most effective operatives were the pair signing themselves "Your Informants"—brothers Thomas Branham Cunningham and Ed B. Cunningham, who had been railroad special agents. They operated at a more sophisticated level than did Arriola, for they developed important contacts among the *insurrectos*, including several members of the local junta, and their reports contained intelligence of real value.[43]

But their most intriguing reports concerned the Standard Oil Company. Historians have long debated the alleged involvement of Standard Oil in the Mexican Revolution.[44] The Cunningham brothers informed the Mexican consul in mid-April that C. R. Troxel, a representative of Standard Oil, had approached them with a proposition to be conveyed to the *insurrecto* leadership, who were known to be in dire financial straits: Standard Oil would furnish it $500,000 to $1 million on condition that the insurgent government would issue Standard Oil 6 percent gold bonds and make certain commercial concessions. If the Cunninghams could arrange a meeting between Troxel and the *maderista* leaders the brothers would be well paid. The Cunninghams duly introduced Troxel to J. V. Smith, an executive of the El Paso Brick Company, representing the insurgents, at Smith's room in the Hotel Zeiger. The Cunningham brothers left them to negotiate in private. Smith subsequently stated that he'd seen credentials and a letter from John D. Archbold, Standard Oil's vice president for operations, authorizing Troxel to enter into contracts, and that a tentative agreement had been reached and its provisions transmitted to Madero's headquarters. The next day the Cunninghams saw Luis H. Hernández and other members of the *maderista* junta entering Smith's room at the Zeiger. Hernández told the Cunninghams that Troxel's proposition had been presented to Francisco Madero, who accepted the idea of a loan. Madero told Hernández to put the proposition up to Alfonso Madero, Francisco's brother, who was the local financial agent for the *insurrectos* and was currently staying at the Sheldon Hotel, but said that he would advise Alfonso to accept Standard Oil's offer. Hernández said that Smith and J. J. Bennett, another rebel sympathizer, agreed to meet with Hernández and Alfonso Madero the next morning.

Meanwhile, a side agreement was negotiated by those involved. Bennett asked that a contract be drawn up to divide the 5 percent commission that Standard Oil was to pay Troxel. The commission would be divided equally among Troxel, Luis Hernández, J. V. Smith, J. J. Bennett, F. Sandoval, Thomas Branham Cunningham, and Ed B. Cunningham. The parties agreed not to mention this arrangement to any of the Maderos.

In a further side agreement, Luis Hernández stated that the *insurrectos* had agreed to give the Cunningham brothers all of the hides from the cattle the rebel forces used as compensation for their services in securing the loan. It was then agreed by Hernández and Smith to say nothing about this hide deal to Troxel. A company composed of Hernández, Smith, Bennett, Sandoval, and the Cunninghams would be formed and the profits from the sale of the hides divided equally.

Furthermore, Hernández informed his associates that Francisco Madero had agreed to grant a concession to the above parties to furnish all the ammunition and firearms the *insurrectos* needed. It was agreed by the parties to form yet another company to handle this concession.

The various side contracts were drawn up, and as for the Standard Oil proposition, Alfonso Madero accepted it and told Smith to have Standard's representative come to El Paso at once. However, Troxel was somewhere near the town of Toyah investigating potential oil properties. On April 25, 1911, J. V. Smith sent him a telegram, witnessed by Bennett and the Cunningham brothers, reading "Come to El Paso at once. Parties accept your proposition. Come without fail. [signed] J. V. Smith," but Troxel was fifty miles from the railroad in Toyah and didn't get the telegram as expected. In the meantime, the various contracts were signed by all except Troxel and deposited with attorney H. L. Bennett for safekeeping until Troxel could sign.[45]

All this intrigue and maneuvering came to naught. Not only did the Cunninghams spy for the Díaz consul while maintaining close relations with the *insurrecto* leadership, but they were also informants for the federal Bureau of Investigation.[46] As a Bureau report stated, "Mr. Cunningham imparted to the agent additional information regarding the proposition made to the Madero party by the Standard Oil representative. Immediately upon receipt of Agent Vann's report, such information was embodied in a memorandum and submitted to the Attorney General."[47] The attorney general promptly notified the secretary of state.[48] The American authorities took an exceedingly dim view of Standard Oil's machinations and so informed the company, which of course categorically denied any involvement in the Mexican Revolution.[49]

This affair has been discussed at some length because it illustrates two important themes: it was hard to keep secret intelligence secret and everybody was on the make. Regarding the Standard Oil proposition, it seems reasonable to speculate that Madero agreed to the proposed loan in order to keep his revolutionary movement alive, but in less than a month the *insurrectos* would score a stunning victory that ensured the triumph of the rebellion and made Standard Oil's proposition redundant.

Even while the Standard Oil intrigue was unfolding, Abraham González and the junta could take satisfaction in how things were progressing. González remained quite visible, assuring American officials that he'd consulted eminent attorneys to ensure that he and his colleagues weren't violating the neutrality laws.[50] But it was an open secret that they were. To combat the Mexican consul's clandestine network, González and his associates hired the Thiel Detective Service to spy on Díaz's supporters. Two of Thiel's El Paso operatives, Henry C. Kramp and Louis E. Ross, will soon figure prominently in our story.[51]

The Bureau had its hands full just trying to monitor arms shipments. As an example, *maderista* Captain A. W. Lewis, a Canadian ex-artillery officer and veteran of the Boer War, bought two boxcar loads of ammunition through Ed Maurer in New York City. In January some of the munitions, which were stored at the Bush Terminal docks in Brooklyn, were repacked in seven bales and billed as "upholstery and furniture fixtures" to one Frank Cody in El Paso. The Bureau suspected that the shipment was a trial run and that if it went through without trouble the remainder would be consigned in the same way.[52] While the seven bales were en route to El Paso, the Bureau learned that Harvey Phillips, the agent of Madero's attorney Sherburne Hopkins, had arrived in the city. Assuming that he was connected with the arms shipment, the Bureau placed him under surveillance. A Bureau agent even checked in to the room adjoining that of Phillips in the Sheldon Hotel and listened to the conversations between Phillips and his roommate as they practiced their Spanish.[53] The shipment of "furniture fixtures" duly arrived from New York and was delivered to Shelton-Payne.[54] When the Bureau interviewed manager D. M. Payne he said that half of the shipment had been removed from his store but he "did not know the nature of the shipment and did not know the disposition" of the missing items.[55] The Bureau agents were of course frustrated by this evasive answer. As they continued their investigation they concluded that "Frank Cody" and Harvey Phillips were one and the same person. But they again failed to apprehend Phillips, who was reported to have crossed over to Juárez. The Bureau subsequently located Phillips in Washington, D.C., and in March had a warrant issued for his arrest on a charge of unlawful shipment of munitions in violation of Section 235 of the U.S. Criminal Code. After his arrest Phillips pleaded guilty and was fined $100 and costs—not much of a deterrent, especially since Phillips received a pardon on October 21, 1915.[56]

By then more important matters claimed the authorities' attention. In early February 1911, Pascual Orozco approached Ciudad Juárez intending to attack the town, causing consternation there and in El Paso. Many El Pasoans crowded the roofs of buildings hoping to witness a battle, but after skirmishing with the garrison the insurgents withdrew as Mexican Army reinforcements neared.[57] Then on February 13, 1911, U.S. commissioner George B. Oliver in El Paso, whose hobby was breaking Mexican ciphers, issued federal warrants for the arrest of Francisco Madero and Abraham González, based on letters seized from *maderista* Martín Casillas, whom the army had recently arrested. Oliver gave strict orders to keep the warrants secret so the insurgent leaders could be arrested, but an enterprising reporter learned of this and the Associated Press broke the story.[58] Both men escaped capture, fleeing into Chihuahua. González slipped across the border near Juárez. While Bureau of Investigation agents searched for Madero in El Paso, he made his way from San Antonio to the vicinity of Tornillo, thirty-five miles downriver from El Paso, and on February 14, his partisans smuggled him across the river to the town of Guadalupe. Madero cut a jaunty figure. He had shaved off his short beard and "wore a suit of tan whipcord, Norfolk jacket and riding breeches and smart English boots. He looked like an exhibitor at a fashionable horse show."[59]

One of those involved in this operation was Lawrence Converse, a twenty-two-year-old resident of Glendora, California. According to Converse, he had joined the *maderistas* in El Paso in January and was commissioned as a captain under Orozco. Converse stated that when he conveyed Madero across the Rio Grande he wore his military school uniform (Converse had attended Harvard Military School in Los Angeles for a year) because it was similar to a U.S. Army uniform and would allay suspicion.

Converse soon became the subject of an international incident. He described himself as an officer on Madero's staff who served as a courier between the El Paso junta and various points on the border, averaging three to four trips a week, traveling by rail, horseback, auto, and on foot.[60] He was still wearing his military school uniform and was carrying messages from Madero to the El Paso junta when, on February 21, he was seized, together with Edward M. Blatt, by Rurales while camped on the U.S. side of the international boundary. The Rurales turned the Americans over to Mexican soldiers, who that very evening conducted a drumhead court martial and sentenced them to be shot the next morning. However, Colonel Samuel García Cuéllar intervened, and Converse and Blatt were taken to jail in Juárez.[61] Converse later stated that although his personal papers were confiscated, he'd hidden in the sole of his shoe the Madero messages addressed to the El Paso junta and his captors never found them. Blatt and Converse languished in a filthy prison cell for two months. Influential Los Angeles friends of Converse's family tried through diplomatic channels to secure their release but failed. The two Americans were finally freed through the efforts of General Harrison Gray Otis, publisher of the *Los Angeles Times*, whose help was enlisted by a friend of Converse's family. Otis was a close friend of President Díaz, who personally ordered their release, whereupon Converse returned to Los Angeles.

Converse shed some light on the operations of the *maderistas* in El Paso. He knew Abraham González and Braulio Hernández, the Chihuahua secretary of state in the provisional government, and claimed that Madero himself told him that as soon as the rebels demonstrated real strength, several leading El Paso bankers were prepared to advance Madero $100,000. Moreover, González, Hernández, and Madero told him that Standard Oil had purchased provisional government bonds, and he claimed Madero had told him Standard Oil was behind the insurrection. Converse said that large amounts of cash withdrawn from El Paso banks frequently went across the Rio Grande to Madero, and he suspected it was Standard Oil money. Converse also alleged he had personal knowledge that Krakauer, Zork and Moye and Shelton-Payne sold munitions to Madero's people, knowing full well they were rebels. Converse was miffed because he'd been inadequately compensated. The *insurrectos* were to pay him $300 a month, but he'd only received a total of $50. Madero had promised to compensate him when the revolution triumphed.[62]

Converse exaggerated his own importance, but in fact a number of Americans were involved with Madero. His forces included a foreign legion of sorts, composed principally of Americans.[63] When the revolutionary leader crossed into Chihuahua at Guadalupe in February, awaiting him were some four hundred followers, about seventy of whom were Americans or Europeans. They too had slipped across the border in the El Paso area to join the struggle against Díaz. Contrary to the hackneyed Hollywood plot, there were few hard-bitten Americans who got involved in the revolution for financial gain but met a beautiful señorita, fell in love, developed a social conscience, ended up fighting on behalf of the downtrodden people, and got the girl. (Not to be confused with the hackneyed plot in Mexican movies in which the handsome young peon, outraged at the injustices suffered at the hands of the arrogant landowner, becomes a revolutionist, fights on behalf of the downtrodden people, and gets the girl.)

A reporter for the *El Paso Herald* wrote, "When I asked the American filibusters what they came down for they almost invariably answered 'For the hell of it.'"[64] They were a heterogeneous lot. Some had no military experience, giving their occupation as things such as carpenter, locomotive fireman, plumber, stationary engineer, steelworker, railroad man, boilermaker, hotel and restaurant cook, bridge builder, ironworker, bookkeeper, burglar, chauffeur, jockey, speculator in sheep, big game hunter, and in several cases "no particular occupation."[65] One was a "young man with the derby hat who sported the only stiff collar in the column, a smartly dressed young man, now much bedraggled, but proudly carrying his Remington sporting rifle in precise military position. This lad came from Chicago, not long out of a military boarding school. He turned out to be one of the best sharpshooters in the group."[66] Then there was Richard Brown, stylishly attired in a golf cap and loud plaid overcoat. He had worked as a nurse at Providence Hospital in El Paso and had volunteered "in the name of medicine" to function as medic for the outfit. He later managed to get himself captured.[67] Some had been soldiers, either in the U.S. Army or some other fighting force. Roy Kelly, for example, had been a scout in the Philippines, had been discharged because of bad lungs, and had come to Texas for the climate.[68] The foreign legion included two Swiss professional soldiers as well as a sprinkling of Germans.

Mercenaries flocked to El Paso like vultures to a fresh carcass. They besieged the junta office, pleading to be allowed to join the *insurrectos*. "There was Paul Mason, who bore the scars of half a dozen revolutions and spoke English with a strong German accent. Many thought that Mason was not his real name."[69] There was A. W. Lewis, the Canadian ex-captain of artillery and Boer War veteran. There were "the triplets," Emile L. Charpentier, D. J. Mahoney, and R. H. G. McDonald, who would figure in border intrigue for years to come. There was Edward S. "Tex" O'Reilly, soldier of fortune and writer of magazine articles, who would distinguish himself as "the biggest liar in the legion."[70] The Americans were nothing if not colorful. There was, for instance, John M. Madison, alias "Dynamite Slim," who hailed from the deserts of Arizona.[71]

The foreign contingent participated in the battle of Casas Grandes in March. Madero tried to lead by example and insisted on personally commanding the *insurrecto* forces. Unfortunately, Madero didn't know the first thing about warfare. He led his followers in a straggling column in what proved to be a difficult march from the town of Guadalupe on the Rio Grande across the semiarid Chihuahuan plain, picking up many volunteers on the way. He and his commanders decided to divide the *insurrectos*. Orozco led his original force southward toward the state capital, while Madero, with about 550 men, marched westward toward Casas Grandes, located on the Mexico Northwestern Railroad (MNW), reaching the vicinity of that town on the afternoon of March 5. He ordered a night attack, in which the eighty-odd men of the foreign legion distinguished themselves, although their commander, Captain R. F. Harrington, formerly a sergeant in the U.S. Army and more recently from Bisbee, Arizona, was killed in the early stages of the intense three-hour engagement that resulted in an insurgent victory as dawn broke. But even as the rebels began celebrating the town's surrender, victory turned into disaster. It hadn't occurred to Madero to send out patrols, and thus he was unaware that four troops of Mexican cavalry supported by two field guns were encamped in the vicinity. This federal force, under Colonel Samuel García Cuéllar, swept into Casas Grandes, throwing Madero's men into confusion. The foreign legion again fought bravely, suffering heavy casualties, but the battle soon turned into a rout.[72] Fourteen American and two German legionnaires were captured and marched off to the state penitentiary in the city of Chihuahua. They arrived destitute, but the American colony in Chihuahua collected clothing for them. The legionnaires remained prisoners until June 12.[73] Inexplicably, the victorious federal cavalry commander failed to pursue the fugitives; had he done so he could easily have captured Madero and changed the whole course of Mexican history. As for Madero, who had been slightly wounded in the right arm, the debacle in Casas Grandes convinced him to leave the fighting to those who were good at it, such as Orozco and Villa. For many American *insurrectos*, Casas Grandes took a lot of the fun out of participating in a Mexican revolution. It forcefully brought home to them that one could suffer grievous bodily harm.

One of the American survivors of Casas Grandes, Oscar Creighton, developed a formidable reputation as a warrior. "In appearance he was anything but prepossessing, though he was tall and well proportioned. His face was extraordinarily homely. A thick mop of unkempt red hair crowned his head, and his blue-gray eyes were set too far apart. He had no nose worth the name: merely a small knob above his upper lip. His receding chin was covered by a tangled red beard. Across his broad shoulders he wore a handsome poncho of elaborate design and at his belt were two six-shooters. A Winchester repeater, riding breeches and high laced boots completed his outfit."[74]

Creighton was a man with a past, and that past was rather mysterious. One version was that he had been a safecracker in San Francisco and had robbed a number of banks but then had been persuaded by his fiancée to give up his life of crime. To make a fresh start and redeem himself in her eyes he had gone to Mexico to fight in the just cause of the revolution.[75] Another version came from one who knew him well in El Paso. Creighton had told him that he was a New Yorker born and bred who had worked in a brokerage office there. He also told him he had also served in the New York National Guard and, according to this source, Creighton habitually maintained a stiff military bearing. He was a poor shot but a good rider. Creighton's reputation, however, rested on his impressive prowess at blowing up bridges and stealing whole freight trains in Chihuahua. Another of Creighton's favorite techniques was to capture a locomotive, tie logging chains from it to the track, run the engine down the line a ways, ripping up the ties and twisting the rails. "He was a natural guerrilla fighter, born to it just as all really great artists are born to their work."[76]

This picture of Creighton as the talented amateur is rather romantic, and there was another explanation for his "stiff military bearing." The federal Bureau of Investigation was interested in Creighton, as it was in the other Americans fighting for Madero, and its background check with the War Department revealed that Creighton was really James T. Hazzard, an ex-lieutenant in the 7th U.S. Infantry, who'd been stationed for a time in the Philippines. He'd been retired from the service in 1908 in lieu of trial by court martial for "excessive use of intoxicating liquors and for gross immorality." Furthermore, the Bureau interviewed one Price Hazzard, postmaster in Colorado City, Texas, who said he believed Oscar Creighton was his cousin, who he referred to as Captain Hazzard, who had been dishonorably discharged from the army in San Francisco.[77] Like Creighton, many other American volunteers had murky antecedents.

Commissioned a captain in Madero's forces, Creighton initially worked out of an El Paso boardinghouse, keeping his saddle, rifle, and pistols in his room. He concentrated on smuggling munitions. His sweetheart, the proprietor's daughter, sewed shirts for him with secret pockets for concealing ammunition. But once Madero entered Mexico, Creighton embarked on his spectacular career of devastating the Mexican Central Railroad (MC) between Chihuahua and Ciudad Juárez, driving the federal army to distraction. The measure of Creighton's effectiveness was that, by mid-April 1911, of the seventy-six railroad bridges between Juárez and Chihuahua, all had been destroyed, although temporary tracks had been laid around forty-three of them. It would take at least two weeks of uninterrupted labor to put the railroad back in operating condition.[78]

Another prominent foreigner in Madero's ranks, and like Creighton a survivor of the Casas Grandes disaster, was Colonel Giuseppe Garibaldi, "a tall, blond young Italian" who spoke Oxford English, had exquisite manners, and was the soldier of fortune grandson and namesake of the great Italian liberator. The thirty-one-year-old Garibaldi, a Boer War veteran, had been in Panama and considered going to China on an engineering project but instead went to California, where he found work as an engineer in the oil fields and in railroad construction. But in 1910 the restless Garibaldi decided to go to Mexico and promptly became involved in the Madero revolt. Making his way to El Paso, he offered his services to Abraham González, who was initially reluctant to utilize foreigners in the struggle but then changed his mind and accepted Garibaldi's offer.[79] The new arrival certainly made a fashion statement, for "the Italian filibuster was a jaunty looking fellow in his tan riding suit and his green velour hat with its brim worn down on all sides to protect the face from the sun."[80] Being his famous grandfather's grandson was both Garibaldi's claim to fame and his biggest problem—his grandfather was a hard act to follow, and the younger Garibaldi compensated by developing an inflated notion of his own abilities and by denigrating his associates. For instance, in his memoirs he contemptuously dismissed the contribution of his fellow revolutionary General Benjamin Johannis Viljoen: "Among the new arrivals who attached themselves gratuitously to Madero was a General Viljoen, a Boer from the Transvaal and a veteran of the South African War." He "declared that he was military adviser to [Madero]. In this imaginary capacity he gave out a number of interviews, but we regarded him as a harmless crank."[81]

This description of Viljoen reflected Garibaldi's corrosive jealousy, for he couldn't begin to compare with Viljoen in terms of military reputation. Exactly how Viljoen became associated with Madero remains unclear, but Viljoen was taken on as military adviser to the *insurrecto* leader after the battle of Casas Grandes. One of the first pieces of advice he gave the rebel high command was that "the weak point of the Insurrecto army was its lack of efficient scouting."[82] Viljoen's credentials were certainly impressive, for he had considerable experience in guerrilla warfare. Born in South Africa in 1868, Viljoen became a newspaper editor and a member of the Transvaal legislature, representing Johannesburg.[83] The young Boer was handsome and well built, five feet ten inches tall, with Teutonic features, blue eyes, brown hair, moustache, and short pointed beard.[84] And he was a firebrand, outspokenly anti-British and spoiling for a fight.

When the Boer War broke out in 1899, Viljoen urged his countrymen to put their trust "in God and the Mauser."[85] He transformed himself from politician into warrior: Viljoen led the Johannesburg Commando, with the rank of commandant. During the next three years of savage warfare Viljoen distinguished himself, rising from commandant to assistant commandant-general of the Transvaal forces.[86] But the military might of the British Empire gradually ground down Boer resistance, and the Johannesburg Commando was virtually annihilated. "[I]t was the utter collapse of the Boer rank and file which staggered the great officers. Smuts, Botha, De la Rey, Viljoen—all the stoutest hearts and strongest wills in the Transvaal army—had become convinced of the 'utter hopelessness' of continuing the struggle."[87] Viljoen was ambushed and captured on January 25, 1902. The British interned him on the island of Saint Helena, the scene of Napoleon's final imprisonment, where Viljoen spent much of his time writing his memoirs.[88] After the Boer War officially ended on May 31, 1902, he was freed and allowed to return to South Africa, but he refused to sign the oath of allegiance to Britain and sailed from Capetown, never to see his homeland again.[89]

Viljoen began a new life in the United States, publishing a book entitled *An Exiled General* (1904) and lecturing on his wartime experiences, among other things. But he was primarily interested in establishing a colony for Boers who like himself refused to live under British rule. He visited potential sites both in the United States and in Mexico.[90] Although a number of Boers would eventually settle in Fabens, Texas, Viljoen himself chose to locate in the fertile Mesilla Valley north of El Paso, purchasing land in Chamberino, New Mexico, in 1905. He proved to have a talent for agriculture; he expanded his holdings to seventeen hundred acres and made his Hope Harvest Farm a flourishing enterprise. On the side he raised horses and also got himself appointed as postmaster in Chamberino. Viljoen became a U.S. citizen in January 1909, became an expert in irrigation agriculture, and became involved in politics—in 1908 he was appointed an aide to Governor George Curry of New Mexico, with the rank of colonel. Aiming higher, Viljoen in 1910 applied to become the collector of customs for the El Paso and New Mexico district, an appointment he did not receive.[91] And in twenty-three Sunday installments in the *El Paso Morning Times* between September 27, 1909, and February 27, 1910, he published his Boer War memoirs. Perhaps his involvement in the Madero revolution was an outlet for his frustration. In any case, he joined the *insurrectos* along with his wartime aide, Lieutenant Jack Malan, who had settled in Texas.[92] Ironically, Viljoen had become fast friends with a former Boer War enemy, the Canadian artillery captain A. W. Lewis, whom he had met on shipboard coming to America. Both men were now on Madero's staff.[93]

Events began moving to a climax in late March, and the level of tension in El Paso rose appreciably. There was, for instance, a move afoot, spearheaded by the imprisoned Converse and Blatt's attorney, to assemble a force of about a hundred men in El Paso, cross to Ciudad Juárez, storm the prison, and, by golly, liberate the two young Americans. The authorities were understandably worried by the strong undercurrent of sentiment in favor of such an invasion, and they did everything they could to discourage the idea. To the general relief of everyone, nothing happened.[94]

Also noteworthy was the arrival in El Paso from Los Angeles of Antonio I. Villarreal, one of the leading *magonistas*. He had just been released from the penitentiary in Florence, Arizona, and had broken with Flores Magón over revolutionary policy.[95] Flores Magón had forbidden his followers to have anything to do with Madero, considering him nothing but a rich boy playing at revolution. But some *magonistas*, like Villarreal, decided to put pragmatism ahead of ideological purity and join Madero, who seemed to have a chance of overthrowing Díaz.[96] Villarreal arrived in El Paso on November 30, 1910. Mexican government agents spotted him at the train station but for lack of transportation watched helplessly as Villarreal and his family disappeared in downtown El Paso. The Mexican consul's operative, detective Billy Smith, assigned to shadow Villarreal, located him at the Palace Hotel, a cheap rooming house on South El Paso Street. Villarreal discovered that he was under surveillance and quickly took the train for San Antonio.[97] Another *magonista* who'd joined Madero was José Inés Salazar. This thirty-four-year-old native of Sabinal, Chihuahua, enlisted in the insurgent forces on December 4, 1910, commanding some thirty to forty fighters.[98] As we shall see, changing allegiances would become Salazar's trademark.

Magonista recruits were in the minority, however. Despite the defeat at Casas Grandes, there was no lack of men, both Hispanics and Anglos, eager to join the *insurrectos.* In fact, the junta boldly established recruiting offices in the Planters Hotel on El Paso Street and at 317 Overland Street in addition to at the junta's headquarters in the Caples Building.[99] The principal recruiter was one William P. "Red" Stratton. He had served in the U.S. Army in the Philippines and later had become an immigration inspector but had been fired for allowing ten Chinese to cross the river into the United States, in violation of the Exclusion Act, near the immigration station where he worked. Stratton allegedly got $50 a head for the Chinese.[100] But now Stratton was among the most energetic Madero sympathizers in the city. Besides supervising the enlistment of volunteers, Stratton organized them into groups and smuggled them into Mexico, along with arms and ammunition, in the vicinity of El Paso and downriver at Ysleta and Fabens, where, using the alias of "McKenzie," he'd reached an arrangement with some of the U.S. soldiers patrolling the border to look the other way.[101] According to Stratton, he got a job with the Overland Market that enabled him to meet the soldiers guarding the river under the pretense of selling groceries for their mess. By selling them provisions at a discount (with the Overland Market reimbursing him) Stratton developed rapport with the troops and could more easily pass recruits and supplies through the army's lines.[102] Stratton's relations with the El Paso junta soured as it became evident that besides smuggling into the United States horses stolen in Mexico, he was also smuggling weapons for his own profit.[103] But Stratton was very good at his job, and the junta continued to avail itself of his services. In late April, however, Stratton tendered his resignation to the junta but said that "he would not turn against the men with whom he had been associated even though they had mistreated him."[104] He was now a freelance gunrunner and continued to supply the rebels at their camp across the Rio Grande from the smelter. Stratton, incidentally, also supplied hundreds of crowbars, one shipment of 160 being seized by the army on information from Mexican intelligence.[105] The crowbars were for the rebels to use in their assault on Juárez. Mexican houses were traditionally built up to the sidewalk and contiguous to each other, so by breaking through the walls of houses, rebel fighters could advance down a street without exposing themselves to enemy fire.

Munitions smuggling intensified, not just around El Paso but also through the hamlet of Columbus, New Mexico, sixty miles to the west.[106] In April the El Paso junta reportedly had 37,000 rounds hidden in the city awaiting shipment to Madero. Some of the munitions came directly from New York City. In March, Captain A. W. Lewis had again been at the Bush Terminal docks in Brooklyn arranging with Ed Maurer for a shipment of ammunition, rifles, and two machine guns.[107] And in May, Captain Lewis, posing as an American newspaper reporter, was arrested in Presidio, Texas, by a deputy U.S. marshal, who seized 13,000 rounds shipped from Shelton-Payne to Lewis, "who has acknowledged being an arms supply agent for the insurrectos."[108] Not only did Lewis admit his identity, but "upon his own statement went across the Rio Grande and operated the Napoleon twelve-pounder smoothbore cannon 'McGinty' that was stolen from the plaza in El Paso, Texas."[109] The cannon, though obsolete, evidently got the attention of the Díaz garrison across the river in Ojinaga, for when the rebels attacked on April 30 the garrison and the Díaz officeholders fled.[110]

What was fueling all this frenetic activity was the fact that the rebels, including some forty-five Americans, were massing for a full-scale attack against Ciudad Juárez. Orozco and Villa succeeded in cutting both the MC and MNW, effectively isolating the town.

On the evening of April 22, a force of insurgents under Garibaldi clashed with Mexican troops at Bauche Station on the MNW only twelve miles southwest of Juárez. The engagement developed into a pitched battle lasting into the next day. In the fighting the rebels suffered a grievous loss, for the intrepid Captain Oscar Creighton was killed. According to one account he was shot in the back of the head by a Mauser bullet fired by one of his own men.[111] Creighton's personal effects were delivered to his sweetheart, Miss Frances Hughes, 908 Kansas Street in El Paso.[112]

The Mexican troops fell back into Juárez, while the *insurrectos* took up positions west of El Paso in the hills across the Rio Grande from the American Smelting and Refining Company smelter. There Madero established his headquarters, in an adobe hut. At times there was friction between the Mexican and American insurgents, a manifestation of the growing nationalism that characterized the revolution and was embodied in the slogan "Mexico for the Mexicans." [113] With other rebel contingents closing in from the south, everyone braced for the impending battle of Juárez.

On April 19, Madero had formally demanded that Brigadier General Juan F. Navarro surrender the city. Navarro contemptuously refused. Madero had second thoughts about ordering an attack because inevitably bullets would land in El Paso, and the response of the United States might be military intervention, which was to be avoided at all costs. Therefore Madero was willing to give peace a chance. On April 22 a temporary armistice was declared in Juárez while the rebels and the emissaries of Díaz discussed a permanent end to hostilities.

While the talks were going on there was considerable movement back and forth across the river. Most of this traffic occurred near the smelter, with El Pasoans flocking to visit Madero's camp and *insurrectos* flocking to shop in El Paso for provisions and clothing. And Trinidad Concha's band gave morning and evening concerts at the rebel encampment.[114] A Bureau agent visited Madero's camp, talked with the rebel leader and with General Orozco, as well as with Colonel Garibaldi and Raul Madero, receiving assurances that the *insurrectos* would not fire into El Paso. And the Mexican consul notified American authorities that *insurrecto* officers would be allowed to cross to the U.S. side of the river upon presentation of passes signed by Madero.[115]

Rebel officers repeatedly crossed into El Paso for sightseeing and shopping while the armistice held. An incident on the evening of April 20 gives some idea of the support the *insurrectos* enjoyed in the city. Pascual Orozco, whom Madero had recently promoted to brigadier general, decided to pay a visit to the border city. He walked into the lobby of the Sheldon Hotel followed by a crowd of at least a thousand people cheering and applauding him. He registered and was assigned a room, which he entered as soon as he could escape the crowd. Orozco's presence posed a major problem for the authorities. Two Bureau of Investigation agents promptly interrogated him about his purpose in coming to El Paso. Orozco said that it was to get a good night's rest and to see his family (throughout the Mexican Revolution many personages took care to send their families and their money to the United States for safety) and that he intended to return the next morning to his command in Mexico. Orozco was detained in his room while the Bureau agents conferred with U.S. attorney Boynton, assistant U.S. attorney W. H. H. Llewellyn, Federico González Garza, the *insurrecto* provisional secretary of state, Dan Jackson, of the firm of Jackson and Lessing, attorneys for the El Paso junta, Mayor Charles E. Kelly, and chief of police Jenkins. The conferees concluded it was advisable to convey Orozco to the border and send him back to Mexico without delay. An automobile was secured and Kelly and Jenkins, representing the city, John L. Dibrell, deputy U.S. marshal and Bureau agents J. Herbert Cole and Fred H. Lancaster, representing the U.S. government, and González Garza and attorney Gunther Lessing, representing the *maderista* junta, all crammed in and drove Orozco to the footbridge across the Rio Grande by the smelter and with great relief watched him cross the river and rejoin his troops.[116]

The rebels were furious because General Navarro refused to let them bring their wounded through Juárez for medical treatment in Bush's makeshift hospital at 416 South Campbell Street.[117] One of Madero's sympathizers in El Paso, J. V. Smith, invited the Mexican consul's informants, the Cunningham brothers, to participate in a ridiculous plot to kidnap General Navarro, which would of course facilitate the capture of Juárez. Smith said he'd been offered $5,000 to kidnap the general and deliver him to Madero's camp. The plan was somehow to persuade Navarro to accompany a sexy woman to El Paso, where he would be seized and gagged and delivered. The $5,000 was to be placed in a safety deposit box in El Paso; Smith would receive one key, and when Navarro was delivered he'd get the second key, and the box could be opened. The informants urged Consul Torres to warn General Navarro.[118] Not surprisingly, the plot came to nothing. On a lighter note, there was the case of William Hill, who called on the Bureau of Investigation about his eleven-year-old son. The boy had left home, and Hill suspected that he'd probably gone to the rebel camp opposite the smelter. A Bureau agent accompanied Hill to the camp, where they found the boy proudly wearing a cartridge belt and carrying a rifle. Hill took his son back to El Paso.[119]

Even as the peace talks were under way, Madero adherents continued to arrive, among them Venustiano Carranza on April 25; he checked into room 206 of the Sheldon Hotel. As *insurrecto*, governor of Coahuila, First Chief of the Constitutionalist army, and ultimately president of Mexico, Carranza was to dominate much of the revolutionary decade.[120] The rebels also continued trying to build up their supply of weaponry. On April 29, for instance, the Bureau had the Mexican intelligence agent Jesús María Arriola detail two of his men "dressed as insurrectos" to watch the front and back entrances to the Shelton-Payne store. That afternoon they followed a wagon leaving Shelton-Payne with forty-four Mauser rifles. The wagon went to a feed store where alfalfa was loaded to cover up the sacks of rifles. The wagon then proceeded to the smelter but, in accordance with the Bureau's instructions, the Mexican agents shadowing the vehicle notified the troops patrolling that sector of the river and the wagon was seized.[121] The peace talks eventually broke down over the issue of Díaz's refusal to resign immediately, and the armistice expired without result on May 6.[122]

When the armistice expired, Madero, still apprehensive about the consequences of stray bullets landing in El Paso, canceled the projected attack on Ciudad Juárez, announcing that the insurgent army would retreat southward.[123] By then there was considerable unrest in Madero's camp, for many *insurrectos* had become disillusioned with their leader, feeling that he'd sold out the cause. Some, of course, were just angry at the prospect of being denied an opportunity for rape and pillage.[124] Madero's drastic change in plans did not set at all well in particular with Orozco, who was aching to attack; he was much more concerned with the benefits of capturing Juárez than with the attitude of the United States. Accordingly, Orozco boldly took charge, overruling the indecisive Madero. Orozco ordered the attack to begin at 10 a.m. on May 8. Madero ordered Orozco to desist, but when he refused, Madero could only watch helplessly as his followers eagerly charged the town's defenses.[125]

Orozco shrewdly had his men begin their assault from the west parallel to the river in order to lessen the chances of bullets hitting El Paso.[126] Rebels made their way along an irrigation canal from their camp near the smelter and, protected by the ditch bank and by pilings along the riverbank, opened fire on the Mexican soldiers and customs guards manning the guardhouses at the international bridges. This caused both General Navarro and the Mexican consul mistakenly to protest that firing was coming from El Paso. The consul also complained that rebels were being allowed to cross the footbridge near the smelter, but in reality the army and customs and immigration officers prevented this from happening.[127] The rebels poured reinforcements into their positions along the riverfront, thus entering Juárez from the lightly guarded Rio Grande side while other insurgent units attacked the main defenses to the south and east. For the next three days brutal street-to-street and house-to-house fighting characterized the rebel advance. The *insurrectos* took heavy casualties from the defenders' artillery. The best the rebels could do was to answer back with three homemade cannons, fabricated from locomotive axles at the MNW shops in Madera and commanded by the soldier of fortune Captain Charpentier, a Frenchman who was a bit of a dandy, going into battle wearing kid gloves. General Navarro finally surrendered unconditionally on May 10, and what was left of his battered 450-man garrison wearily laid down their arms. Reportedly the surrender occurred because Navarro's officers realized that their men had had enough and would turn on and kill them if the fight continued another day.[128] As the rebels occupied the town, Garibaldi tried to maintain some degree of calm by ordering that all the liquor in Juárez be destroyed. Some of the *insurrectos* happily destroyed liquor by drinking it. The victorious rebels also liberated from the jail all prisoners, who promptly scampered across the bridges to El Paso.[129]

El Pasoans had finally gotten to witness the real battle they had yearned for. Hoping to minimize casualties, the authorities had closed the international bridges and had ordered that no one without a pass could approach the Rio Grande nearer than Seventh Street.[130] This was a prudent precaution, because bullets from Juárez indeed landed in El Paso. For example, on May 9 the Finnegan-Brown Company's warehouse at Seventh and Kansas, approximately eight hundred yards from the Mexican bank of the Rio Grande, was hit about fifty times in ten minutes by machine-gun fire. The next day the building was hit five or six times in the space of three minutes. Fortunately none of the seventeen workers was hurt.[131] Yet human nature being what it is, crowds of El Pasoans had desperately wanted to get as close a view as possible of the fighting in Juárez, evidently thinking that because they were on American soil bullets couldn't reach them. Despite Colonel E. Z. Steever having deployed all his available troops to keep back the multitudes, the locals swarmed to the bridges, crowded the riverbank, even climbed on top of boxcars in the railroad yards for a better view. Predictably, for some, this maneuvering was the last thing they ever did. On May 9, two men were killed instantly some two hundred feet west of the Santa Fe Street bridge while standing on a railroad track parallel to the river bank. The following day another man was killed in almost the same spot. Some victims of stray rounds weren't even down by the river. Antonio García died from a bullet in the head while standing in the doorway of his home near the Santa Fe stockyards. Another unfortunate died at the corner of Fifth and Santa Fe streets. In all, six El Pasoans were killed by stray bullets. Another fourteen were wounded, among them a child who was hit in the hand while lying in bed in his home on Seventh Street and the owner of a little grocery store on the corner of El Paso and Seventh streets who was shot in the left arm while reading a newspaper. People suffered gunshot wounds as far north from the river as Thirteenth Street.[132]

Barely had the last shots been fired in Juárez before hordes of morbidly curious El Pasoans began rushing across the bridges for a firsthand view of the carnage. Stepping gingerly around corpses and piles of rubble, they avidly sought souvenirs. Sightseers received a shock on the afternoon of May 11 when some 100 shots suddenly broke the calm, but it turned out that it was only jubilant rebel soldiers firing into the air. As the horde of sightseers began returning they created a problem for the U.S. Army, which was busy trying to prevent rebels from entering El Paso and war materiel from crossing into Juárez. The soldiers at the bridges confiscated a number of dynamite bombs and unexploded shells from returning visitors, who were outraged at losing their souvenirs.[133]

In a humanitarian gesture, Colonel Steever permitted the Juárez wounded, mainly *insurrectos*, to be gathered up by American volunteers and brought to Bush's hospital. Hispanic women *insurrecto* sympathizers had held a three-day fundraiser for the hospital in March, raising several hundred dollars by serving meals to the accompaniment of a Mexican orchestra.[134] Now Bush and other local volunteers unselfishly treated the wounded, as did the staffs of the county hospital and Hotel Dieu where some were taken.[135]

The battle of Juárez had provided El Pasoans with all the excitement they could handle.

CHAPTER 4

Revolutionary Discord

The capture of Ciudad Juárez on May 10 was the turning point in the struggle against Díaz. But despite the victory, there was trouble, for the *insurrecto* leaders promptly fell out among themselves. Colonel E. Z. Steever reported on May 13 that "Mayor Kelly has just returned from Juarez [and] informs me that Villa wants to kill Navarro, Orozco wants to kill Villa, Madero is protecting Navarro in the customs house and has turned over his business temporarily to his lieutenants. Mayor says his information is founded upon what was told to him by provisional Governor Gonzalez."[1] Orozco threatened Madero with arrest when they disagreed violently over the disposition of the defeated General Navarro. Orozco and Villa demanded that General Navarro be turned over to them, for they had every intention of executing him in retaliation for his having ordered the killing of *insurrecto* prisoners, some of whom were wounded. There were already charges that the insurgents had summarily shot some of the volunteers who had tried to defend Juárez. Should Navarro fall into Orozco's hands his life expectancy was nil. Madero, in his capacity as insurgent leader and provisional president, was horrified by his bloodthirsty subordinates and brusquely rejected their demands. According to one account Orozco was so angry that he stuck his pistol in Madero's chest.[2] But Madero stared Orozco down, and he saved General Navarro's life by having Gustavo Madero spirit him out of town in an automobile.[3]

The Mexican consul in El Paso informed the Bureau agents that Navarro had swum his horse across the Rio Grande and was now in Washington Park. The consul urgently requested that the Bureau guard the general until arrangements could be made for his protection. Although this request was somewhat irregular, the agent in charge, Fred Lancaster, decided the situation was an emergency. He and two of his men drove to Washington Park but failed to find the general. Upon returning to their office they learned from Oscar Braniff, one of Díaz's peace negotiators, that General Navarro was hiding in the basement of the Popular Dry Goods Company at the corner of Mesa and San Antonio streets. Agent Lancaster detailed his men to guard the general until he could be turned over to Mayor Kelly and the police chief. These officials had Navarro taken to a "safe house," an apartment at 1304 Montana Street, where city detectives guarded him until the excitement subsided, for "there is a great deal of feeling against Navarro among the El Paso Mexicans and the soldiers of Madero in Juarez and there is some danger of his being assassinated if he is not guarded."[4]

Not only was the mercurial Pancho Villa eager to kill General Navarro, but he was making a nuisance of himself in El Paso. Colonel Steever reported that on May 17, "Villa came into the lobby [of the] Sheldon Hotel armed, with [the] avowed purpose to kill some one. Whether it was Garabaldi [*sic*], Obregon, an American former insurgent of the name of Crum or an army officer is uncertain. As Villa was violating a municipal ordinance, I went to the mayor, who had the offender disarmed. I urged Villa arrest [*sic*] but the mayor thought that would cause trouble so Villa was released with a warning."[5] This incident must have been a terrible blow to Villa's self-esteem.

The "Crum" Colonel Steever referred to was ex-*insurrecto* lieutenant Jack R. "Big Dude" Crum, who'd fought at Casas Grandes and at Bauche; he'd been with Oscar Creighton when Creighton was killed.[6] It seems that Crum had been involved in a bit of looting in Juárez. The Bureau learned that several of the American insurgents who'd helped precipitate the battle of Juárez hadn't limited themselves to liberating the town; they'd also liberated a large amount of jewelry and cash from stores they had looted during and after the battle, and they'd smuggled the loot to El Paso.[7] When the Bureau agents began making inquiries about the matter, they learned that the culprits had taken "an immense quantity of silks and jewelry from Juarez stores and had been trying to dispose of it." In fact, the El Paso police had just arrested one of the thieves with twenty watches on him, watches that had been identified as part of the loot. The gang consisted of about five men, who were known to have had some of the stolen goods in their possession. The Bureau was trying to locate the loot.[8] But as the investigation developed, it was learned that fifteen members of Madero's American legion had done considerable looting. They included Captain K. E. Linderfelt, Lieutenant R. H. G. McDonald, and Lieutenant Jack R. Crum. The looters had made off with silks, jewelry, cigars, and fancy drawnwork among other items, and they had smuggled a large amount of stolen merchandise and opium to the American side of the Rio Grande.[9]

The group, who had left the *insurrecto* service, boarded a train in El Paso on the night of May 17 bound for San Antonio. An entrepreneur named C. A. Stewart, a former agent for Buick automobiles, headed the party. Stewart paid for the group's transportation, explaining that he planned to lecture in San Antonio about the battle and exhibit the legionnaires as the real heroes of that engagement. Suspecting that the legionnaires were going to dispose of their loot in San Antonio, the authorities searched them and their baggage several times but found nothing incriminating and reluctantly concluded that the loot had been shipped separately. The show proved to be a fiasco, and some of the stranded legionnaires eventually drifted back to El Paso hoping for new opportunities for enrichment.[10]

One of Madero's peace commissioners inquired of Agent Lancaster whether Madero could travel across U.S. territory en route to Mexico City. The agent replied that although there was a federal warrant out for Madero, the grand jury had ended its term without indicting the Mexican leader. The assistant U.S. attorney in El Paso further assured the commissioner that under the circumstances Madero would not be molested if he wanted to travel to Mexico City to negotiate peace terms with the collapsing Díaz government.[11]

Madero postponed his departure from El Paso, however. He partook in a round of glittering social events sponsored by admiring El Pasoans, among them Mr. and Mrs. Frank Wells Brown, who hosted a luncheon at their home in his honor; the guests included Felix Sommerfeld, Madero's brothers Raul and Gustavo and their father Francisco, and Giuseppe Garibaldi. But the climax of the social whirl came on May 31, at a sumptuous banquet at the exclusive Toltec Club hosted by the El Paso establishment. It was the most splendid banquet in the city's history, even outdoing the fetes El Pasoans had thrown during the Díaz-Taft meeting in 1909. Mayor C. E. Kelly acted as toastmaster, with Francisco Madero seated on his left. On the mayor's right was seated none other than General Navarro, the defeated federal defender of Juárez.[12] No doubt when Pascual Orozco and Pancho Villa learned that Madero was consorting with the enemy whom they badly wanted to kill it did not raise his stature in their eyes.

Whereas the two *insurrecto* chieftains wanted Navarro dead, there were those who wanted Francisco Madero dead. As Colonel Steever telegraphed to his superiors, "For what it may be worth: Confidentially informed two emissaries from Mexico City here [to] bribe Viljoen with 100,000, Orozco with 50,000 dollars. Viljoen apparently will accept bribe induce emissaries into Juarez to be shot."[13] And a member of the *insurrecto* junta received a telegram from a confidential source in Mexico City advising of rumors that an attempt would be made to assassinate Madero upon his arrival in the Mexican capital. Madero publicly dismissed the report, but at his advisors' urging announced on May 20 that he was postponing his trip.[14] On May 29, the El Paso press reported a plot against Madero's life combined with a planned revolt against him. The followers of Porfirio Díaz, generically referred to as *científicos*, had allegedly organized the conspiracy.

What lent substance to the allegation was that on May 28 a Boer, one Daniel De Villiers, was arrested in the Orndorff Hotel in El Paso on a charge of conspiracy to murder Madero. Almost simultaneously, an American, William L. Dunne, was arrested on information from El Paso in Monterrey, Nuevo León, by local police and an American private detective working for Madero. In the days following, details about the conspiracy began to emerge. De Villiers was "thirty-six-years old, tall, well built, with deep-set gray eyes, black hair streaked with gray combed in a pompadour. He speaks with a slight Dutch accent." When interviewed in the county jail, he stoutly maintained his innocence, stating that he lived in San Antonio, was a rancher, and had served under General Benjamin Viljoen in the Boer War. Dunne had lived in Ciudad Porfirio Díaz since 1909 and was a business associate of Andrés Garza Galán, a fervent Díaz supporter and son of a former governor of the state of Coahuila.[15] Dunne had allegedly been a Mexican government agent in 1910 and had intercepted Madero's correspondence. In February 1911, Dunne had forwarded to President Díaz an intelligence report from Garza Galán on insurgent activities.[16]

It was Viljoen who provided most of the details about the conspiracy. The Boer general said that he and General Pascual Orozco had been approached with offers of substantial bribes if they would betray Madero. They immediately informed the Mexican leader of the plot and pretended to go along with the scheme in order to learn more about it. According to Viljoen, De Villiers and Dunne were acting as agents of Andrés Garza Galán. At a meeting in the Sheldon Hotel they not only tried to suborn Viljoen and Orozco but also disclosed that the plan was to kill Madero and have the Mexican congress name Rosendo Pineda, a staunch Díaz partisan and former secretary of the interior (*gobernación*), president. The conspirators had also been busy securing information regarding Madero's travel plans. Convinced that the conspiracy was real, Madero ordered the arrest of De Villiers and Dunne and notified the interim government in Mexico City to put Pineda under surveillance. Dunne went from El Paso to Monterrey to receive the bribe money, accompanied by Madero's operative William "Australian Billy" Smith, who had previously been an El Paso city detective and a Díaz secret agent.[17] Smith pretended to be Viljoen's emissary but was instructed to have Dunne arrested as soon as he received telegraphic instructions from El Paso to do so. Viljoen further stated that he and Orozco had De Villiers pay them a part of the bribe money on May 28. De Villiers was arrested that evening; a search of his hotel room produced a pistol, a notebook, and a cipher telegram to him from Garza Galán.

In discussing the affair, Madero indicated that Rosendo Pineda was the master conspirator, putting up the bribe money and trying to organize the revolt. Madero stated that "I was informed of the plot immediately when General Viljoen received the first telegram from Mexico City, and it was by my orders that he continued to treat with De Villiers and Dunn [*sic*], and I kept Orozco in Juarez for a week after his forces had left for no other reason than to give him an opportunity to vindicate himself before the public for the incident which occurred between us after the battle of Juarez." Madero said there was enough evidence to convict several of Díaz's most prominent supporters, but they'd be given the opportunity to leave Mexico.[18] Rosendo Pineda, realizing he'd been discovered, fled.[19] De Villiers was released on $500 bond at his preliminary hearing, and Dunne didn't fight extradition to the United States. Their trial was scheduled for October 2 in El Paso but was continued to the November term of the court. (Incidentally, on October 4, De Villiers again made news when he attacked Captain Jack Malan, the fellow Boer who had served under Viljoen and more recently had been Madero's adjutant during the revolt against Díaz, in the lobby of the Sheldon Hotel.)[20] The assistant U.S. attorney dismissed the De Villiers–Dunne case in January 1912, because a number of witnesses were in Mexico and because the government would have had to bear very great expense without any appreciable results. The Mexican authorities also dropped the charges against Dunne and De Villiers.[21]

In May 1911, Madero's staff had increased security measures—without a special pass no one was allowed aboard the train that Madero and his entourage, which included Colonel Giuseppe Garibaldi and reporter David Lawrence of the Associated Press, took to Eagle Pass, where they crossed into Mexico en route to Mexico City.[22]

There was another reputed plot against Madero, one that was not too credible. Insurgent Captain Emile Charpentier, who was stationed in Juárez, informed the Bureau that a woman living next door to the *insurrecto* hospital in El Paso and known in European diplomatic circles as the "Red Devil" claimed that on the night of June 1 at a ball in Madero's honor at the Juárez customs house, one Cruz Reyes tried to dynamite the building but was arrested, and she said that, in addition, had the explosion taken place, sixty or seventy of Pancho Villa's men had been deployed to shoot the survivors. Whatever the veracity of her account, Charpentier said the woman knew about the attempted bribery of Orozco and Viljoen and spoke very knowingly about the Dunne case.[23] This episode illustrates the superheated atmosphere in El Paso of intrigue, rumor, and fantasy in which anything seemed not only possible but probable.

What was undeniable was that "El Paso herself" had "lost several million dollars, directly and indirectly, as a result of the insurrection." Between February and April 1911, the quantity of freight to and from Mexico was less than one-third the volume of the preceding year. El Paso had lost her exports of mining machinery and supplies, cement, coal and coke, general merchandise, and food products. Moreover, ore imports for the smelter were drastically down (the smelter normally got 80 percent of its ore from Mexico), which forced the shutting down of nearly all the furnaces and had thrown nearly one thousand men out of work. In addition, cattle imports, normally around two hundred thousand head a year, had dropped precipitously.[24] The real beneficiaries of the upheaval in Mexico were the arms dealers Shelton-Payne and Krakauer, Zork and Moye.

Madero's revolution triumphed, and his brother Gustavo, who handled the finances, submitted a bill to the national government and was reimbursed for:

Arms, ammunition, and equipment	$154,000
Lawyers' fees in New York, Washington, San Antonio, and El Paso	53,000
Confidential agency in New York	6,000
Confidential agency in Washington	5,000
Confidential agency in San Antonio	18,000
Confidential agency in El Paso	15,000
Press campaign	12,500
Expeditions, envoys, trips, and minor expenses	56,000
	$319,500 (or 642,195 pesos)

One of Madero's principal collaborators, Doctor Francisco Vázquez Gómez, questioned these figures, pointing out that the expenses of the confidential agency in Washington, which he had headed, were not $5,000 but merely $650 and expressing surprise at $12,500 for a press campaign, since there hadn't been one.[25] Whatever the actual amount, however, Madero had operated on a financial scale that Flores Magón could only dream about. But although Madero had triumphed, peace was to be a mirage. An armistice was proclaimed on May 21, and on May 25, Porfirio Díaz resigned and left for exile in Paris, where he died in 1915.[26] Yet the revolution had succeeded too easily; Díaz was gone, but most of the Díaz system was still in place. Against all odds, Madero had won, and he had raised expectations sky high. But in the very hour of victory he did something that would have serious adverse consequences—on May 26 he resigned as provisional president, stating that he would run for president in an honest election to be held in a few months.[27] Madero's motive in wishing to avoid the charge that he had shot his way into power was laudable, but his action was incredibly naïve. The interim regime that would conduct the presidential election was headed by a member of the old regime, Francisco León de la Barra, who had been Díaz's ambassador to the United States.[28] De la Barra did what he could to undercut Madero and limit revolutionary reforms.[29] Since he was now just a private citizen, Madero could only suggest and complain. His popularity was diminishing even as he prepared to campaign for the presidency.

The U.S. consul in Juárez, Thomas D. Edwards, left a lot to be desired as a diplomat (one El Paso lawyer would complain that Edwards was "less effective than a notch on a stick").[30] But, despite his inadequacies, he did presciently observe that "the first and apparently the only desire of a majority of the revolutionists is to free themselves from Diaz, and break down the Diaz government. They have no thought of what they will get in its place. Madero serves the purpose for the breaking down, but there will be a need for another Diaz to reconstruct."[31] (Ten long and bloody years of civil war would pass before such a figure emerged, in the person of General Alvaro Obregón.) Madero's military advisor, General Benjamin Viljoen, expressed similar views, saying Madero's mistake was in failing to continue military operations after the fall of Juárez, which would have enabled him to achieve a complete revolution.[32] Viljoen visited Mexico City with his wife as the guest of Madero, who late in 1911 commissioned him to negotiate peace with rebellious Yaqui Indians in the state of Sonora. Viljoen then became involved in 1915 in a plot to foment revolution in Baja California. He subsequently returned to New Mexico and died at his home in La Mesa on January 14, 1917.[33]

But in El Paso in May 1911, there were signs that the Mexican Revolution was over. On May 19, the Treasury Department directed that the port of entry be opened for all traffic into Mexico. This meant that guns and ammunition could now be shipped into Juárez; all that was required was that the goods be properly manifested.[34] Two days later, a thousand *insurrecto* soldiers left Juárez for Casas Grandes, where they would be stationed.[35] Juárez itself was quiet, and the Bureau of Investigation was no longer receiving much information regarding neutrality violations. Therefore the extra Bureau agents brought in to assist the resident agent, Louis Ross, were returned to their stations. And the chief of the Bureau instructed that informants be discharged at the end of the month, or even earlier if practicable.[36]

Disturbingly, both the political Left and Right were plotting to capitalize on the power vacuum in Mexico. The *magonistas* had gotten a new lease on revolutionary life. Operating out of Los Angeles and utilizing a number of foreigners as well as Mexicans, they had managed in early 1911 to seize the northern part of the territory of Baja California, one of the least important regions in Mexico, planning to use it as a base from which to take over the rest of the country. They assembled several hundred men, many of them mercenaries, and that was as close as they ever came to fielding an army. This proved to be the military high point of the whole *magonista* movement. But by June 1911, de la Barra's interim government handily defeated them and regained control of Baja California.[37] As a faction contending for national power, the followers of Flores Magón had shot their bolt and were increasingly marginalized.

Still, they kept trying. Small bands of *magonistas* sprang up downriver from El Paso and raided several American-owned ranches. One target was the 1.25 million-acre T. O. Ranch belonging to Morris Brothers of Chicago and covering sixty miles along the Rio Grande across from Fort Hancock.[38] And *magonistas* clashed with *insurrecto* troops near Del Rio. Other *magonistas* were in the field near Villa Ahumada, between Juárez and the city of Chihuahua.[39] And the Bureau of Investigation had to keep three agents in El Paso after all, because of the upsurge in *magonista* activity and a resurgence of smuggling.[40]

Some things never changed. The Thiel Detective Service, specializing in labor relations, had its headquarters in Chicago and branches in several other American cities, five Canadian cities, and Mexico City. Its El Paso offices were in rooms 414–17 in the American Bank Building.[41] Thiel had worked for the Díaz regime against the *magonistas* and *insurrectos* and was still working for the Mexican government. Agent Ross reported in August that "the Thiel people have received a concession from the Mexican Government which places them practically on the same basis in Mexico as the Bureau of Investigation in the United States. They are therefore watching the situation very closely and have men gathering information in regard to revolutionary activity. For this reason I am keeping in close touch with Mr. Kramp the Manager as he will be in position to give this Bureau information regarding violation of neutrality in case of a counter revolution."[42] Both *magonistas* and diehard Díaz supporters continued to cause concern. *Magonistas* again raided the T. O. Ranch, as well as another American-owned ranch near Ojinaga. The El Paso attorney representing Madero's interests, Dan Jackson, and German-born Henry Kramp, the Thiel manager, wired news of these depredations to Madero in Mexico City and to Abraham González, now governor of Chihuahua. They also notified the commander in Juárez, General José de la Luz Blanco, but he took no action.[43] Kramp had a number of operatives working in Mexico, and one of his men had infiltrated a *magonista* cell in El Paso. Kramp promised to keep the Bureau apprised.[44]

The Bureau was keeping *magonista* sympathizers under surveillance in El Paso as well. A case in point was one José Trujillo, who at one time had worked for the Thiel Detective Service and had been a Díaz adherent until he saw how the revolution was going, at which point he switched sides and secured a commission in Madero's *insurrecto* army. Since Madero's victory, however, Trujillo, like many others, had become disillusioned with Madero because he hadn't kept his promises. Now Trujillo was intriguing with the *magonistas*. "Trujillo has a small fruit stand on the corner of El Paso and Seventh Street. He states that this stand is only a bluff; that he is not making any money out of it and is depending on other means for his living. He has practically no stock of fruit in this stand. Today he had one watermelon and one bunch of bananas. A large number of rough looking Mexicans are always hanging around this place, and Trujillo seems to have a large following among the Mexicans here." Trujillo's attitude mirrored the prevailing unrest, for "the dissatisfaction with the provisional government of Mexico seems to be wide-spread in the northern part of the republic. As far as this immediate locality is concerned the dissatisfaction is general."[45]

Discontent with Madero extended to General Pascual Orozco, who felt that his considerable services hadn't been rewarded. Orozco, whose military prowess had been decisive in the *insurrecto* victory, had hoped to be named secretary of war, or at least to become governor of Chihuahua. Instead, Madero, evidently still rankling from his clashes with Orozco, gave him the insultingly paltry appointment of commander of Rurales in the state of Chihuahua. Discontent extended all the way down to people like Captain Charpentier, who had directed Madero's artillery during the battle of Juárez. Charpentier claimed that he'd spent more than $1,000 of his own money on the *insurrecto* cause, but when he was mustered out, Governor Abraham González had offered him a lousy fifty pesos and a train ticket to El Paso in full settlement of his services. He was "exceedingly angry at the whole Madero crowd."[46]

Another resentful ex-*insurrecto* was John R. Madison, aka "Dynamite Slim." He had been traveling in Mexico and was back in El Paso "to see what the prospects" were "for raising another revolution in Mexico. . . . He is very much dissatisfied with the treatment he has received since the former hostilities ceased[.] . . . [H]e only received fifty pesos for all his services in the insurrecto army. . . . He said that he was 'Johnny on the spot' for anything that was against Madero and Governor Gonzalez."[47] Madison was hardly a trained political analyst, but he made some shrewd observations about the deteriorating situation in Mexico:

> The Cientifico party is financing the Magonistas, both of these parties joining forces against Madero; that the Magonistas, since the end of the revolution have been working actively among the insurrectos of late, and have enlisted the sympathies of a great number of former Maderistas all over the Republic. Madison says that the plan of the Cientificos is to furnish the money while the Magonistas furnish the men, and are determined to get rid of Madero; that the Cientificos believe that with Madero out of the way they can easily do away with any opposition from the Magonistas and regain control over Mexico.[48]

Dynamite Slim further asserted that Madero had promised him $20 a day to operate a machine gun, but when he was discharged he received only fifty pesos, and in addition, he had been cheated out of a valuable mining claim. He reportedly was now cooperating with the *magonistas* in a planned assault on Ciudad Juárez.[49]

Once again El Paso was filled with wild rumors about bands of *magonistas* converging on Juárez, which at the time had only a forty-man garrison and could easily be captured.[50] Adding to the apprehension was unrest in Juárez itself. Interim president se la Barra ordered the *maderista* collector of customs and his staff removed and reinstated the former Díaz officeholders. The ex-*insurrecto* collector refused to step down, and General Orozco strongly backed him. It was feared there would be bloodshed if the regime in Mexico City tried to remove the collector by force. The issue came to a head on August 2. The Díaz officeholders stayed in El Paso, fearing for their lives. The *maderista* collector and his employees showed up for work armed, and they seized the former postmaster and revenue stamp administrator, locking them up in the customs house. These Díaz appointees had promised to resign but had failed to do so. The mayor of Juárez intervened, escorted the two men to the international bridge, and warned them never to return to Juárez. Furthermore, the mayor asked Governor González to remove General José de la Luz Blanco as commander of the Juárez garrison on the grounds that his troops were on the verge of deserting to the *magonistas*. To make matters worse, the Rurales stationed in Juárez were reportedly just awaiting the right moment to defect to the *magonistas*. Evidencing the growing uncertainty was the steady stream of foreigners flocking to El Paso from Mexico.[51]

With renewed revolution in prospect, Mexican officials began maneuvering to protect themselves. For instance, the consul in San Antonio, Miguel E. Diebold, "stated that he was going to Mexico City to investigate the matter and if he is not on the right side that he is going to get on the right side." Diebold also asked Charles Stevens, chief deputy sheriff of Bexar County (and future Texas Ranger captain), if Stevens could furnish two good men to work for him as informants in San Antonio. Stevens agreed to supply one man he knew to be reliable, whom the consul ended up employing. But Stevens had secured a promise from the informant to give him all the information he obtained for the consul, and Stevens turned this information over to the Bureau of Investigation.[52]

The Bureau of Investigation stepped up its surveillance of *magonistas* in El Paso. Ross, the resident agent, not only monitored who was picking up copies of *Regeneración* at the post office but also acted as agent provocateur, making contact with *magonistas* and offering to smuggle arms for them in hopes of thus learning about any filibustering expeditions they were planning.[53] Ross also shadowed Dynamite Slim when the latter went to see José M. Rangel, a *magonista* chieftain who'd been raiding the T. O. Ranch and skirmishing with Rurales sent out from Juárez. Rangel was at the home of a Mr. Stuart on Government Hill east of El Paso. This was where the McGinty "Blue Whistler" cannon had been hidden after being stolen from City Hall Park by Madero sympathizers in 1911. To Ross's disappointment, Rangel, who had been indicted in 1908 for neutrality violations, was no longer wanted, the prosecutor having dismissed the case in 1909.[54]

One of the Bureau's best sources of information was Henry Kramp, manager of the Thiel Detective Service, who frequently passed along reports from his operatives. Among these operatives was none other than the ex-*insurrecto* Emile Charpentier, who was now based in the city of Chihuahua reporting on *magonista* activity: according to Charpentier, Lázaro Alanís was near Casas Grandes heading up a guerrilla band, while Lázaro Gutiérrez de Lara was "making socialistic speeches throughout the state agitating strikes and telling the people to organize and fight for their rights." Gutiérrez de Lara, wanting to avoid problems with the local authorities, was careful to deny any connection with the *magonistas*. Charpentier also reported that "when Dynamite Slim left here he was made an offer by some one, I do not know whom [*sic*], and was offered the rank of colonel and good pay if he would get a few hundred men together. Slim spoke to me about the matter, and offered me charge of the artillery which was to be new artillery shipped from the United States. The offer came from one of the Terrazas family, or from El Paso. There appears to be an effort at organization, and I understand that there are some men in El Paso and San Antonio who are endeavoring to perfect this organization in time to render it of service about [Mexican presidential] election time in October."[55]

In El Paso the *magonistas* maintained a junta, one of whose principal endeavors was to equip the guerrilla bands operating in Chihuahua. Yet bad luck continued to dog the followers of Flores Magón. Their leaders in El Paso, José M. Rangel, Prisciliano Silva, and Rubén Silva, crossed the river below the city and were captured on August 5 by Mexican vaqueros who turned them over to the authorities in Juárez.[56] (It was erroneously charged that authorities in El Paso had seized them and had handed them over to the Mexican officials.)[57] Four nights later their partisans raided the Juárez hospital where the trio were being held, guarded by forty soldiers. The rescue attempt failed, and the luckless prisoners were conveyed to the state penitentiary in the city of Chihuahua.[58] Still, *magonista* militants continued to converge on El Paso. Fifty-four had arrived in just the last few days of August. "They do not seem to have any definite plan of action, but are extremely violent and anarchistic in their talk."[59] Agent Ross was having trouble gathering intelligence on them: "Since these people already know who I am, the only way I can see to get information from them is to make them believe I am crooked."[60] Ross relied on reports from that fastidious soldier of fortune Emile Charpentier, whom the *magonistas* were trying to recruit because of his artillery expertise. The *magonistas* were also offering $5 a day for good fighting men.[61]

Charpentier took a cynical view of the rebels, saying that "these Magonistas are simply crazy and are going to be led into trouble; that they are ready for any kind of idiotic action."[62] Charpentier suggested one idiotic action to them—deploying "war kites." War kites were kites with an attached nitroglycerine charge that could be dropped on the enemy. Charpentier showed Ross "a batch of plans he had given them, showing how to put on the guide lines, how to drop the charge, and how to place the kite in the desired position. He said they intended to make use of these plans."[63] But "the plans for war kites that he gave to the Magonistas were such that if they tried to use them they would blow themselves up."[64] The *magonistas* didn't employ war kites, nor did they enlist Charpentier's services. "He informed these people that if he ever went to fighting again in Mexico it would be for strictly a money consideration, and if he ever took another town he would see to it that he got his; that he was tired of fighting for the fun of the thing."[65]

The Mexican authorities did not of course stand idly by while *magonistas* plotted. In early September, Governor Abraham González of Chihuahua hired Abraham Molina, a resident of El Paso, to function as a secret agent in the city and combat the *magonistas*.[66] Molina had been a freelance purveyor of intelligence to the American authorities during the Madero revolution.[67] In his new capacity Molina persuaded Governor González to send three companies of infantry to the border to conduct patrols in civilian clothes. According to Molina, the governor told him that "the time has now come to put a stop to all disorder in Chihuahua and he is going to adopt Diaz methods to do it."[68] To the great relief of Agent Ross, Molina announced his readiness to cooperate closely with the Bureau. This information Ross received from Molina reinforced the intelligence that he was receiving from the Thiel Detective Service.

The real threat of a counterrevolution came not from the hapless *magonistas* but from the reactionary *científicos*. Despite all their bluster, the *magonistas* turned out to be broke, as usual.[69] The great advantage the *científicos* had was money. This led to a cynical marriage of convenience between the two antagonistic factions—the *magonistas* providing the cannon fodder and the *científicos* paying for it.

The *científico* menace developed during the summer of 1911 when a reactionary cabal began plotting in the elite International Club in San Antonio. Its leader was Andrés Garza Galán, one of the founders of the International Club who had fled into exile in San Antonio in June and was the leader of the Díaz exile community. An engineering graduate of Lehigh University, class of 1895, Garza Galán was no newcomer to intrigue.[70] Back in 1909 he'd acted as an intelligence agent in San Antonio working for Enrique Creel and maintaining surveillance on the *magonistas*.[71] And he had allegedly been the prime mover in the abortive De Villiers–Dunne plot to assassinate Madero.

Significantly, on October 23, 1911, the San Antonio *Express* reported a new plot in Ciudad Porfirio Díaz to assassinate president-elect Madero, who had just won the cleanest election in the history of Mexico.[72] The Bureau of Investigation received word that Garza Galán, Nicanor Valdez, and Dan De Villiers planned to drive from San Antonio to Eagle Pass with the intention of assassinating Madero, timing their trip so as to arrive when Madero was due across the river in Ciudad Porfirio Díaz.[73] But nothing happened. Dan De Villiers continued to be Garza Galán's close associate in the San Antonio junta, whose leaders were Andrés Garza Galan, Dan De Villiers,

Juan Garza Galán, Nicanor Valdez, and "one Negrete, a millionaire from Monterrey."[74] Andrés Garza Galán remained deeply involved in conservative Mexican exile conspiracies for the remainder of the decade.[75]

Another associate, though not a member of the junta, was Garza Galán's close friend Francisco A. Chapa, a prominent San Antonio druggist and the most powerful Hispanic politician in Texas.[76] Chapa was the only Hispanic to receive a signal honor, that of being appointed as a lieutenant colonel in the Texas National Guard on the personal staff of three successive governors (and not because they were "celebrating diversity" but because Chapa could deliver the Hispanic vote in San Antonio). The San Antonio junta received most of its funds from wealthy *científicos* in Mexico and abroad.

Garza Galán's machinations overlapped with the plotting of another prominent Mexican exile politician in San Antonio—Emilio Vázquez Gómez, one of Madero's original associates who then became secretary of the interior in de la Barra's interim government and who resigned on August 2.[77] And there was another right-wing faction emerging—the partisans of General Bernardo Reyes. At one time viewed as a probable successor to Díaz, Reyes was now making his own bid for power. He had campaigned unsuccessfully for the presidency against Madero. Yet when Madero was inaugurated in November he was considerably less popular than he'd been in May as the triumphant leader of the revolution against Díaz, which gave Reyes hope. He'd taken a page from Madero's book and had installed himself in San Antonio in October to organize a rebellion against President Madero, a rebellion that would be set off with an invasion of Mexico from El Paso, Laredo, and Brownsville. Reyes's great advantage was his prestige as a leading member of the old regime, and he soon overshadowed the other plotters. Those factions began coalescing, however reluctantly, behind Reyes.[78] Francisco Chapa, for example, was a great friend of Reyes and became his principal coconspirator. Another fervent *reyista* was Manuel Quiroga, a wealthy exile friend of both the general and of Chapa, with whom he published *El Imparcial de Texas*, the leading Spanish-language newspaper in the state.[79] Then there were the mercenaries. Some forty members of Madero's foreign legion were in San Antonio and, disgruntled because Madero hadn't adequately rewarded them, they were eager to join Reyes's movement. Reflecting the situation in San Antonio, on the sixteenth of September, Mexican Independence Day, there were three celebrations: *magonistas* gathered at San Pedro Park, *reyistas* at Milam Square, and *maderistas* at Bowman's Island, a park on the San Antonio River.[80]

These same factions were of course represented in El Paso. The job of frustrating both *magonista* and *reyista* intrigue fell primarily to Agent Ross and his Mexican counterpart, Abraham Molina. Molina quickly organized a network of agents and informants; most of Ross's intelligence on revolutionary matters came from Molina. For instance, Molina arranged to intercept *magonista* mail. It all arrived addressed to F. M. Franco, who opened and distributed it. Franco sent a man to the post office every day for the mail. Molina cut a deal with the man whereby he would examine and pilfer the mail before delivering it to Franco.

The *magonistas* in El Paso had a very basic problem; they had "no guns and no money."[81] José Inés Salazar, for example, who at this stage in his turbulent career was again a *magonista*, claimed to have twenty-five men ready to cross into Mexico; however, he had only seven rifles for them.[82] There was another group of disgruntled revolutionists or would-be soldiers of fortune in El Paso claiming to be followers of Flores Magón. They "simply follow Magon's standard because there is no one else to follow here at this time."[83] This bedraggled collection included "Colonel" Paul Mason, a "Major" Talbert (E. A. Talbot?), who was currently supporting himself as a floorwalker at the Boston Store, Captain Emile Charpentier, J. Todd McClammy, and one Schodman, who claimed to be an expert bomb thrower.[84] The gunrunner William P. "Red" Stratton remained loyal to Madero, rejecting *reyista* overtures.

The *reyista* contingent in El Paso was much better organized, and certainly much better financed, than that of the *magonistas*. The followers of General Reyes organized a club in El Paso and claimed an initial membership of sixty.[85] A junta was also established; its leader was Doctor Rafael Limón Molina, who resided on East Missouri Street. The doctor had conferred with Reyes while the latter was still in Mexico City, had returned to El Paso, and had initiated an ambitious plan for the El Paso branch of the Reyes network. He intended to recruit at least one hundred good men locally and to equip each with a Winchester rifle, two revolvers, three hundred rounds of ammunition, and one hundred pesos. He also hoped to recruit two hundred men in Juárez on the same basis. All this of course required money, and the doctor was anxiously awaiting the receipt of funds. Abe Molina observed that "if this man can produce the money, he will not have a very hard time getting all the men he wants. The only thing that is causing the magonistas to fizzle is their lack of funds."[86] Abe Molina was in a position to monitor the doctor's progress, for he had managed to get two of his operatives enlisted as *reyista* recruits.

Prominent followers of Reyes, such as Dan De Villiers, periodically appeared in El Paso to help coordinate operations.[87] De Villiers continued to live in San Antonio, where he was engaged in Boer colonization. His wife divorced him in October 1912 on the grounds of cruelty, married a wealthy realtor named Roy L. Glover, and moved to Los Angeles with him. De Villiers followed, demanding to see his children, and got into a heated argument with Glover on the night of December 21, 1913. Glover shot and killed him and pleaded self-defense.[88]

On the morning of November 20, 1912, El Pasoans were rudely awakened by sustained gunfire in Juárez, and their immediate thought was that the Reyes revolution had begun. But it was only the *juarenses* celebrating the first anniversary of Madero's rebellion against Díaz. General Pascual Orozco, who happened to be in Juárez, used the occasion to visit El Paso and renew acquaintances.[89] The day was notable for another reason, however. Limón Molina's efforts as head of the *reyista* junta bore fruit. According to Ross, "The Magonistas in El Paso today consolidated with the Reyistas in a common cause against Madero. They met this afternoon at F. M. Franco's home. He's the Magonista leader. 48 men attended, including Dr. Molina." The doctor agreed to pay to equip *magonista* fighters.[90] Unfortunately for the conspirators, all their actions were being reported by the agents Abe Molina had infiltrated into the movement.[91] Molina then shared as much of the information as he chose with Bureau agent Ross.

Because of his effectiveness as an intelligence chief, Molina's stature grew; Abraham González, now Madero's minister of the interior, followed all of Molina's recommendations for combating insurrection, such as his suggestions that the government deploy additional Rurales to patrol the border and ship additional artillery to Ciudad Juárez.[92] Molina's standing in Mexico City was certainly better than that of the Mexican consul in El Paso, Enrique Camacho, who was relieved of his position in November when it was learned he was a *reyista* and had been attending their meetings. A captain of Rurales in Juárez was likewise discovered to be a *reyista* plotter. He was about to be arrested and executed but managed to escape to El Paso. From there he telephoned his commanding officer in Juárez and roundly cursed him.[93]

Despite all the plotting, the Reyes conspiracy fell apart in November when the U.S. government took action. On November 16, a federal grand jury in Laredo began issuing indictments against Reyes and his principal associates for violating the neutrality laws.[94] On November 18, Reyes was arrested in San Antonio and released on bail, but he jumped bond and fled to Mexico, while the army, the Bureau, and the Texas Rangers dismantled his organization in Laredo. The governor of Texas, Oscar B. Colquitt, had for political reasons turned a blind eye to Reyes's plotting but now was eager to get the credit for smashing the plot. Colquitt sent his adjutant general, Henry Hutchings, and Texas Rangers to Laredo and El Paso to assist the federal authorities.[95]

With his network in San Antonio, Laredo, and Brownsville in shambles, Reyes's new strategy was to revive his movement from El Paso westward along the border.[96] This would be difficult, as the general was now a fugitive in Mexico. Furthermore, the *reyistas* in El Paso had been thoroughly infiltrated. Not only were the Bureau and the Thiel Detective Service uncovering their activities, but Abe Molina had suborned José Elizondo, the treasurer and general purchasing agent of the *reyista* junta. Elizondo disclosed that the Rio Grande Valley Bank and Trust Company was the conduit for their funds, and that they had only 113 recruits on the payroll, each one receiving $1 a day. Elizondo had been purchasing equipment, but to avoid the authorities the *reyistas* intended not to purchase their guns and ammunition until the very day they were to cross into Mexico.[97]

They never got the chance to cross. Texas Ranger Captain John Hughes and seven of his men worked closely with the Bureau and Abe Molina to crush the local *reyistas*, who among other things had been busy making primitive hand grenades. Acting on information from Molina, on November 30 a task force consisting of Hughes and his rangers, a deputy U.S. marshal, Agent Ross, and Molina swooped down on the *reyista* junta, making fourteen arrests.[98]

At one stroke the authorities in El Paso had crushed not only the followers of Reyes but their allies the *magonistas* as well. To the chagrin of the *reyistas*, two of those arrested revealed themselves to be Molina's operatives. As Mexican consul Enrique C. Llorente explained in a letter to the foreign secretary, "They claim to have the most complete oral and documentary evidence of a plot to seize Ciudad Juárez."[99] Most of those arrested were able to post bond. Their trial was held during the April 1912 term of the federal court, at which Limón Molina was sentenced to a year and a day in the federal prison in Leavenworth.[100]

Whatever hopes the *reyistas* might have entertained for the future of the movement were dashed by General Reyes himself. He failed to generate much support in Mexico and, having no stomach for the life of a fugitive, he surrendered to the Madero government on December 25, 1911. Although this was probably the best Christmas present President Madero received, other plotters would rush to fill the anti-Madero conspiratorial vacuum. Intrigue remained a constant; all that changed was the cast of characters.

El Paso's attention was of course not entirely focused on the Mexican Revolution. In September 1911, the business community was agog over news that the Pearson syndicate was actively negotiating the purchase of a large tract of land on which to build a box factory, planing mill, and paper mill.[101] Additionally, the Pearson people were hoping to construct a large factory to manufacture paper for the Mexican trade in Pearson, Chihuahua. The initial phase of the El Paso complex, which when complete would be the largest wood-finishing plant in the world, would pump an estimated $666,000 into the local economy.[102] As if to underline the city's growing importance, El Paso was chosen as the site on October 19, 1911, for a meeting of the governors of Texas, New Mexico, Arizona, Chihuahua, and Sonora. The occasion was to celebrate the admission to statehood of New Mexico and Arizona. The city went all out, beginning with a grand military and civic parade followed by welcoming speeches in Cleveland Square. Governor Abraham González of Chihuahua and

Braulio Hernández, the Chihuahua secretary of state, were greeted with enthusiastic cheers.[103] And on November 30 the annual winter horse-racing season opened in Ciudad Juárez on an unprecedented scale. This was the only winter race meeting in 1911 in all of North America, and El Pasoans flocked to enjoy the races, which would be run for a hundred days. Streetcars ran directly to the track every five minutes, and ladies were admitted free. Adding to the general enjoyment, the Juárez bullring announced a special program on December 24 that would combine a bullfight and a pantomime. All this was in addition to a fiesta in Juárez with illuminations, a concert orchestra, and dancing girls. Streetcars ran all night on this occasion.[104]

But the Mexican Revolution would not go away. With General Bernardo Reyes out of the picture, Emilio Vázquez Gómez quickly emerged as the new anti-Madero standard-bearer.[105] On October 31, 1911, he issued the obligatory revolutionary manifesto, the *Plan de Tacubaya,* which amended Madero's *Plan de San Luis Potosí,* and like Madero and Reyes had done, he established his headquarters in San Antonio. He was, however, very careful not to violate the neutrality laws while he plotted against Madero.[106] For lack of an alternative, conservative and disaffected elements in the Southwest and in northern Mexico coalesced around him. In January 1912, the *vazquista* junta moved from San Antonio to El Paso.[107] Bands of nominally *vazquista* guerrillas appeared, mainly in western Chihuahua.

Disaffection in that state against the Madero regime assumed critical proportions on January 31, 1912. In what the government described as an economy measure, it had ordered that one hundred men—roughly 40 percent—be discharged from the Juárez garrison, which was composed of Rurales (not the old Díaz mounted constabulary but irregular *maderista* cavalry). But the designated troops had no intention of joining the ranks of the unemployed. Not only did they refuse to be disarmed and demobilized, but they mutinied and were joined by the rest of the garrison. The uprising occurred around 7 p.m., and Juárez was quickly plunged into anarchy. The mutineers imprisoned their commanding officer and the chief of police, released all the prisoners from jail, ransacked the customs house and took all the money they found there as their back pay, broke into the district court and took the records into the street and burned them, guzzled anything alcoholic they could get their hands on, staggered drunkenly through downtown firing their weapons, prevented the Mexican Central train from leaving the station, stopped all streetcars, engaged in an orgy of looting and arson, among other things burning down the large warehouse of Ketelsen and Degetau, the German hardware firm, and generally terrorizing the civilian population. In short, Juárez was wrecked.[108]

Nor was disaffection confined to Juárez. In mid-January the former *maderista* Antonio Rojas rebelled against the government, proclaiming himself a *vazquista.* He was captured and taken off to prison in the city of Chihuahua.[109] Mutinous Rurales decided to liberate Rojas. Accordingly, they stormed the prison. After some skirmishing the warden freed Rojas who, with his followers, triumphantly rode out of the city of Chihuahua under circumstances that indicated General Pascual Orozco had permitted him to do so.[110] On February 1 the town of Casas Grandes repudiated President Madero's authority. On February 8, Colonel Roque Gómez, who had been an *insurrecto* captain, seized the border town of Palomas with 165 men. Gómez was second in command under Salazar; both he and Salazar had been *magonistas* and then *maderistas* but had recently decided to become *vazquistas*.[111] The American consul in Chihuahua telegraphed: "Am astounded at extent disaffection against Government. . . . Loyalty troops here very uncertain."[112] Madero was rapidly losing control of the largest state in Mexico.

A further indication of the growing apprehension was that the Pearson Company shipped to its Madera mills 1,000 new Mauser rifles, 100,000 rounds of ammunition, and 2 Gatling guns and installed a powerful searchlight mounted on a 140-foot tower to sweep the area around the mills.[113] Ironically, the company had finally completed the monumental engineering job of building the Mexico Northwestern Railroad on January 31 and announced that as of March 1, trains would run directly from Juárez to the city of Chihuahua.[114] Refugees, both Mexicans and Americans, flooded into El Paso.

In this crisis the man of the hour was General Pascual Orozco, for only he had sufficient prestige to pacify the mutinous troops in Juárez. Many doubted Orozco's loyalty to the regime.[115] Nevertheless, Orozco obeyed the government's command to go to Juárez and restore order. Meanwhile the mutineers had elected a new municipal government and had proclaimed their loyalty to Pascual Orozco and Emilio Vázquez Gómez.[116] Orozco arrived on February 4; he conferred not just with the leaders of the mutiny but also with the Mexican consul, Colonel Steever, and Mayor Charles E. Kelly, in El Paso. He announced that he was taking the rebellious garrison to Chihuahua and replacing them with other troops, who in fact arrived on February 5.[117]

Ciudad Juárez returned to something approaching normality, much to the relief of El Pasoans, who had been both terrified and fascinated at the prospect of a repetition of the 1911 battle. The chamber of commerce on February 1 had fired off rather hysterical telegrams both to the governor of Texas and to the president exaggerating the seriousness of the unrest in Juárez and requesting that all necessary steps be taken to protect life and property and especially to prevent firing into El Paso. Troops were rushed from Fort Bliss to guard the American ends of the international bridges, but what many El Pasoans wanted was for American troops to occupy Juárez and pacify the town.[118]

Although Juárez remained quiet, nerves were very much on edge, as illustrated by an incident on the morning of February 15. Lieutenant Benjamin W. Fields and nineteen men of the 18th U.S. Infantry were ordered to the Santa Fe Street international bridge to relieve the detachment on duty there. They secured their rifles and boarded a streetcar. The line ran south on Stanton, across the Stanton Street bridge, looped through downtown Juárez, then swung north over the Santa Fe Street bridge back to the U.S. side of the Rio Grande. The lieutenant asked the motorman where the international boundary was and was informed it was the middle of the bridge. But inexplicably the officer kept his men aboard the streetcar as it crossed over into Juárez, planning to disembark once the Santa Fe Street bridge was reached. Mexican customs guards quickly massed to repel this invasion by streetcar. The befuddled Lieutenant Fields and his men were soon surrounded by hundreds of outraged *juarenses*, most of them armed, and it looked as though an ugly international incident were imminent. Large crowds gathered to vent their anti-American anger, and these demonstrations continued throughout the day. All the Americans in Juárez scurried back to El Paso as quickly as possible. The Juárez municipal authorities stopped any further travel between the two cities. This volatile situation was defused, however, when Colonel Steever apologized to the Mexican consul for the lieutenant's blunder, whereupon the consul used his good offices to secure the release of that officer and his men. Steever placed the wretched Lieutenant Fields under arrest pending further investigation and court martial. By the next day conditions had returned to normal, and streetcar traffic across the bridges had resumed.[119]

Yet American authorities remained concerned. On February 22 Colonel Steever telegraphed the War Department that "Madero's trusted agent in El Paso tells me Orozco no longer loyal. Much unrest and scheming among Mexican population [in] El Paso against United States government—20,000 residing here augmented largely recently from Juarez." The colonel added that the exodus of foreigners from Mexico was increasing and that considerable Mexican property had been moved to the safety of El Paso. Steever commented that "many Mexicans ugly towards Americans. Last year El Paso was unanimously pro-Madero. Now large portion Mexican population anti-Madero and anti-American, because apprehensive of intervention."[120]

CHAPTER 5

Orozco's Rebellion

The threat of American intervention loomed over Juárez because once again serious rebellion had erupted in Chihuahua. General Pascual Orozco resigned his position and broke openly with the Madero administration, probably in response to a public appeal on February 18 by the leaders of the guerrilla bands already fighting against Madero in Chihuahua: self-proclaimed generals Emilio P. Campa and José Inés Salazar, Colonel Demetrio Ponce, Colonel Lino Ponce, and Major Enrique Portillo. In the most flattering terms they urged Orozco to become their caudillo and the supreme commander of the "Liberating Army." That force swelled to some seventeen hundred men by February 24, as rebel contingents massed at Bauche, only twelve miles from Juárez, and at Madero's old camp opposite the El Paso smelter. As a precaution the U.S. Army had the 22nd Infantry Regiment and a battalion of field artillery ready to move by rail at a moment's notice to reinforce Fort Bliss.[1] Rumors filled the air in El Paso; the mayor and the sheriff feared a race riot should the United States intervene in Juárez. The Madero government did what it could to defend the city—the Mexican consul in El Paso rushed 600 rifles, 2 Colt machine guns, some 300,000 rounds of ammunition, cartridge belts, pistols, and so forth to Juárez to arm five hundred civilian volunteers.[2] All to no avail—on February 27, rebel general Emilio Campa with eight hundred men occupied Juárez after only token resistance. El Pasoans, who had swarmed the border to witness a battle, were bitterly disappointed.[3] In short order the troops of generals José Inés Salazar and Antonio Rojas entered the city, and within days the number of rebels swelled to some four thousand. On March 1, Emilio Vázquez Gómez's emissaries David de la Fuente, Paulino Martínez, and Ricardo Gómez Robelo arrived in Juárez from San Antonio and addressed a large and enthusiastic crowd in front of the city hall.[4]

The rebel cause got a huge boost on March 1 when General Pascual Orozco, whose loyalty to Madero had been suspect for months, disavowed the president, issuing a statement explaining his reasons for doing so. There is, by the way, convincing evidence that Orozco had supported Reyes's conspiracy: Reyes's chief of staff, Samuel Espinoza de los Monteros, kept a roster of *reyistas*, and Orozco's name is on the roster. Moreover, a cipher used by the principal followers of Reyes includes Orozco, code-named "Bueno"; F. A. Chapa is "Clarke," General Reyes is "Antonio" or "Miguel," and

Manuel Quiroga is "Pedro Ríos." The cipher was among the documents that American authorities seized in El Paso from the luggage of Manuel Quiroga.[5]

On March 3, Orozco formally joined the rebel cause. He quickly marginalized the ineffectual Emilio Vázquez Gómez, whose presidential ambitions he was unwilling to support. On March 4, Orozco took control of the rebellion.[6] He was the nominal leader of the rebels, but in reality he was more like the chairman of a very obstreperous board, composed of ambitious generals, each of whom had his own agenda and his own band of followers. Ciudad Juárez was firmly in rebel hands, and despite President Madero's public statements that the loss of the city was of little importance, the reality was that the *orozquistas* now controlled the largest Mexican port of entry on the border. Orozco soon dominated the rest of the state of Chihuahua. Because of the color of their banner, the American press referred to Orozco's followers as "Red Flaggers."

El Paso businessmen were eager to capitalize on this latest turn of events, but there was initial uncertainty regarding what kinds of merchandise could be exported to Juárez, given the fact that the American government staunchly supported Madero and refused to accord Orozco diplomatic recognition as a belligerent. It turned out, however, that as long as goods went through the customs house in legitimate fashion, anything could be sent over.[7] An avalanche of exports resulted. Much of this traffic was in munitions, the rebels' first priority. They had to amass a huge amount of war materiel quickly if they entertained any hope of overthrowing Madero. Complicating things for them was the almost total lack of fire discipline in their ranks, which meant that ammunition was expended at an astounding rate. Even the U.S. military attaché in Mexico commented on "the capacity of the Mexican soldier for expending ammunition."[8] The Madero government protested vigorously against "the enormous importation of arms and ammunition through the port of Ciudad Juarez" and urged the United States to stop the traffic.[9] This was ironic, since it was the same complaint Porfirio Díaz's regime had registered during the Madero revolution.

The booming munitions traffic through the El Paso customs house relied heavily on the use of manifests signed by men using fictitious names.[10] As long as the paperwork was properly executed, the goods went across the river. Making a killing was the venerable firm of Krakauer, Zork and Moye. They exported, for example, a substantial shipment of arms and ammunition consigned to the Madera Company. When the munitions arrived in Juárez the shipment was diverted to the rebel General Antonio Rojas.[11] A frustrated Colonel Steever observed that there was "little likelihood of attempted smuggling when arms can be carried across [the] bridges by [the] wagon load."[12]

As with arms, so with money, the lifeblood of revolutions. The El Paso Bank and Trust Company, conveniently located in the Sheldon Hotel, facilitated the funding of the insurrection. According to a federal Bureau of Investigation agent, the bank's vice president, Alfred H. Kerr, stated confidentially that he was doing a good business changing pesos at a discount for dollars to be used by the rebels to purchase munitions. Dollars—one transaction involving $80,000—were also being deposited for the same purpose. Kerr said that those putting up the money included General Luis Terrazas, who was currently staying at the Sheldon, where he had rented a whole floor, ex-president Díaz, and Enrique Creel, Díaz's sometime foreign secretary and Terrazas's son-in-law. Kerr also said that Krakauer, Zork and Moye were the principal purveyors of armament to the Orozco rebels.[13] The *orozquistas* thus planned to import through El Paso whatever war materiel—even including aircraft—they needed in order to topple Madero. But they blithely ignored the fact that when in 1911 General Reyes had plotted to overthrow Madero, whom Washington recognized as the constitutionally elected president of Mexico, the United States had supported Madero and had dismantled Reyes's revolutionary network. Now the *orozquistas* naively believed that the United States would at least remain neutral while they fought Madero.[14] It would prove to be a miscalculation of monumental proportions.

Orozco's rebellion got off to an impressive start. He was widely popular in Chihuahua and in short order controlled the state. Orozco then began advancing southward down the line of the Mexican Central Railroad. On March 24–25, at the first battle of Rellano, near the Durango border, he inflicted a catastrophic defeat on Madero's federal army, causing General José González Salas, the secretary of war who had received a leave of absence to command the field force, to blow his brains out rather than return to Mexico City in disgrace. It seemed as though the city of Torreón, the next important target on the central rail line, would be Orozco's for the taking, as more and more people decided they were really *orozquistas*. But the days of bitter combat culminating in the battle of Rellano had used up 5 million cartridges, most of Orozco's supply. So instead of maintaining his momentum toward Mexico City, a frustrated Orozco spent the next two months in place trying to rebuild his stock of ammunition. By then he had lost the initiative and was forced into a fighting retreat.[15]

He failed because of the United States. The good times for the Red Flaggers had ended abruptly on March 14, when a joint resolution of Congress enabled President Taft to impose an arms embargo on shipments to Mexico, an embargo that would be lifted on March 25 for the Madero government.[16] Overnight the rebels, who had confidently anticipated being able to import all the munitions they could afford—and they were well financed—found themselves in mortal peril. Without a steady flow of supplies coming to the rebels through El Paso, the insurrection was doomed. The only recourse was to smuggle, and this produced an intense struggle in El Paso involving *maderistas*, *orozquistas*, and American authorities. The atmosphere reeked of intrigue, bringing to mind West Berlin at the height of the Cold War.

The initial epicenter of intrigue was the five-story Sheldon Hotel. Spies, revolutionists, smugglers, mercenaries, and sharp operators hoping to make a quick score habitually thronged its lobby. By November 1912, however, the Sheldon had been relegated to second place by the opening of the luxurious Paso del Norte Hotel, which boasted a magnificent Tiffany cut-glass dome. Thereafter, the important personages involved in revolutionary plotting usually stayed at the Paso del Norte. Another structure that figured prominently in revolutionary activities was the Mills Building, overlooking San Jacinto Plaza, where many of those involved in the revolution had their offices.[17]

The struggle between *maderistas* and *orozquistas* in El Paso was also fought out in the local newspapers, both sides being keenly aware of the importance of public opinion. The *El Paso Morning Times* championed the Madero regime, while the rival *El Paso Herald* was equally vehement in its support of the rebels. (It is instructive to compare the two newspapers' accounts of the same event.) The *Morning Times* was unabashedly contemptuous of the Red Flaggers, referring to Orozco as "Pascualito" and to his subordinates as thieves, rapists, and murderers. The *Morning Times* was also contemptuous of its rival newspaper, referring to the *Herald* as "the Red Headed official rebel organ." For its part the *Herald* was particularly bitter about the unneutral way the neutrality laws were being enforced, and it alleged that Madero officials were handing out checks to *El Paso Morning Times* reporters.[18] But there were also allegations that the *Herald* was receiving a subvention from the rebels.

The Red Flaggers deployed secret agents in El Paso to watch the *maderistas*, the rebel operatives meeting in a private wine bar under the Hotel Zeiger. But their activities were routinely reported on by agents of the Thiel Detective Service, who had infiltrated the group.[19] Orozco's followers also appointed a consular agent, Jesús Morales Guevara, whom the United States refused to recognize. The consul focused his activities on recruiting—the *orozquistas* were offering $2 a day—and on organizing a network of ammunition smugglers, the network being directed from Juárez by Colonel Cástulo Herrera, who was Orozco's quartermaster general.[20] He had been an *insurrecto* in Ojinaga in December 1910, then an *insurrecto* recruiter in El Paso. After the capture of Juárez, he had served as police chief there for a time, resigning because of disillusionment with Madero. What the rebels had going for them was that there was no lack of people, Anglos as well as Hispanics, eager to make a fast buck by smuggling. And their efforts had the enthusiastic cooperation of Krakauer, Zork and Moye as well as that of some less prominent El Paso businessmen. There developed a booming "cash and carry" munitions traffic.

The federal Bureau of Investigation was the cutting edge of neutrality enforcement, but when the Orozco rebellion erupted there was only one agent stationed in

El Paso, working out of a cramped office in the federal building. Louis Ross proved to be a most effective agent.[21] For one thing, he was fluent in Spanish; for another, he got along with Mexicans. Prior to becoming an agent, Ross had worked in Cananea, Sonora, in the office of the Sonora Packing Company, and then as an operative of the Thiel Detective Service in 1911.[22] Now he was overwhelmed with work. Several other agents arrived to assist him, but they neither spoke Spanish nor had much border experience. The problem the Bureau faced in 1912 was not unlike the problem it faces today: then, few of its agents were fluent in Spanish; now, few are fluent in Arabic, which has a crippling effect on the agency's counterintelligence capabilities. However, in 1912 the Bureau received decisive assistance from the Madero government's intelligence agencies. It was this unique arrangement that made neutrality enforcement effective.

Realizing the crucial importance of El Paso, the Madero regime pulled out all the stops to choke off Orozco's lifeline, spending lavishly. One prominent El Paso banker testified in September 1912 that he understood that the Mexican consul, Enrique Llorente, had "handled upward of $2,000,000 since the success of the Madero revolution, and that he has cleared it or expended it in this vicinity. . . . I know he has expended large sums here. He has accounts with at least four or five banks in town."[23] Another local banker estimated that $1 million had passed through Llorente's hands.[24] But a Mexican intelligence chief, who should have known, declared that the consul had handled only $600,000 to $700,000.[25] A considerable part of this expenditure was for arms and ammunition. To take only two examples, in February Consul Llorente purchased in El Paso 2 machine guns, 100,000 cartridges for the guns, a consignment of .30-.30 rifles, and ammunition for them.[26] In August he sent 1,500 rifles and 450,000 cartridges to Sonora.[27] And according to the Mexican government's official figures, the Interior Ministry (Gobernación) furnished $283,943.39 for the El Paso consulate's secret work.

March 1912	$28,265.22
April to June 1912	107,993.39
July 1912	36,121.37
August 1912	24,455.31
September 1912	26,907.55
October 1912	no figure
November 1912	45,045.31
December 1912	2,379.11
January 1913	7,770.49
TOTAL	$283,943.39[28]

Ironically, the minister of the interior, and thus the head of the Mexican intelligence service, was Jesús Flores Magón, brother of the anarchist leader Ricardo Flores Magón. The Mexican government flooded El Paso with secret agents and informers, some of whom circulated among the crowds of men who daily congregated downtown in places such as in front of the Sheldon Hotel or on San Jacinto Plaza. The Mexico City newspaper *El Imparcial* even sent a special correspondent, Leopoldo Zea, to El Paso to write a story on Mexican government spies. Zea was less than complimentary, commenting that the city was overrun with agents recruited by the Mexican consul. These people were amateurs; they were indiscreet, most of them were shabbily dressed, and they were lazy to boot. Zea was especially derogatory in discussing "hybrids," "who the legitimate Yankee disowns and the real Mexican gazes on with suspicion. They are Mexican-Texans."[29] The *El Paso Herald* reported on June 7 that "Rebel sources declare that there are in El Paso 217 of these Maderista spies." On June 20 the newspaper claimed that over one hundred Mexican spies were active; some estimated there were even as many as four hundred.[30] The Bureau of Investigation had a much more conservative estimate: "As many as 50 have been employed at one time covering a period of several months."[31] Whatever the precise number, and the number fluctuated, Mexican operatives were everywhere—at the international bridges, on the street corners, watching the Shelton-Payne Arms Company at 301–3 South El Paso Street and Krakauer, Zork and Moye at 115–17 San Francisco Street, keeping *orozquistas* under surveillance, and maintaining a vigil along the Rio Grande.[32] The Mexican intelligence apparatus in El Paso not only comprised numerous individuals but also was rather complex.

A key figure was Felix Sommerfeld, who was a most unlikely spymaster. Sommerfeld was a thirty-four-year-old native of Posen, Germany. He was described as being "5' 6", heavy build, apoplectic complexion, short neck, heavy eyebrows, broad shoulders, prominent nose, heavy dark brown wavy hair worn pompadour, protruding forehead, German type, clean shaven, several gold teeth, arrogant in appearance and wears a large signet ring on left hand."[33] He had served in the German Army, in a unit sent to China during the Boxer Rebellion. Sommerfeld had a gold medal from his Boxer service of which he was very proud. He wore it on special occasions, such as the kaiser's birthday. He emigrated to the United States during the 1890s and worked for a time in Albany, New York, as manager of the local Associated Press agency. Sommerfeld returned to Germany, obtained a degree in metallurgy at the University of Berlin, then came back to the United States, working as a mining engineer in Idaho, Arizona, and Colorado as well as in Chihuahua. From September 1909 to August 1, 1911, he lived in the house of Leonard Worcester Jr., in the city of Chihuahua. Worcester employed him sporadically to sample ores that Worcester was buying for his customers in the United States. During this time, Sommerfeld, a German reservist, reported regularly to the German consul in Chihuahua and also acted as a confidential agent for that official.[34]

When the Madero revolution began, Sommerfeld went to Francisco Madero's headquarters, the hacienda of Bustillos west of Chihuahua. Thereafter, in the capacity of stringer for the Associated Press, he alternately visited the federal troops and the *insurrectos*. But he then attached himself to Madero. The Mexican leader took a great liking to him, and when the revolution triumphed Sommerfeld formed part of Madero's entourage. Madero as president gave Sommerfeld a roving commission as his confidential agent on the border. One of Sommerfeld's duties was distributing watches, as Christmas presents from Madero, to those American officers who had been instrumental in smashing the Reyes conspiracy.[35] Initially, the German's headquarters were in San Antonio, where he supervised the *maderista* intelligence network whose head was Teódulo R. Beltrán, owner of the Alamo Safe and Lock Company on the corner of Market and Presa streets.[36]

On February 4, 1912, Sommerfeld shifted his base of operations to El Paso, armed with a presidential letter ordering Mexican civil and military officials to render him every assistance. He installed himself in that center of intrigue, the Sheldon Hotel, occupying room 103.[37] Sommerfeld reported directly to President Madero. He ran only two or three agents personally, relying by and large on the horde that the Mexican consul financed. For the next few years Sommerfeld would move through the Mexican Revolution like a wraith.

On Madero's orders he sought to hire an aviator to use against the rebels. Initially Sommerfeld hoped to contract the services of one Brownrigg.[38] He did hire an English aviator named Lee Hedgson to bring his airplane to El Paso in order to smite the Red Flaggers from the air. Hedgson later recalled that Sommerfeld offered him a great deal of money to bomb the rebel forces. Hedgson secretly brought his disassembled airplane to El Paso and hid it under the grandstand at the baseball park. Hedgson was having second thoughts, imagining what his fate would be if the rebels shot him down, when somebody in the secret agent community managed to locate the airplane. This impelled Hedgson to act, and he notified Sommerfeld that he was willing to go if the German could have the aircraft reassembled and provide a pretext for Hedgson to take off. The resourceful Sommerfeld complied, arranging for an aerial meet at the baseball park—with only Hedgson's plane participating. Just as the Englishman was poised to take off and fly across the Rio Grande, U.S. army intelligence operatives learned of the plan and informed Colonel Steever, the ranking officer in El Paso. Steever promptly informed Hedgson that if he tried to cross the river, American soldiers would shoot his plane down. To Sommerfeld's undoubted disgust, Hedgson gave up the plan.[39]

Another major figure in the clandestine war in El Paso was Mexican consul Enrique C. Llorente, a suave individual whose previous posting had been Genoa, Italy, and who arrived in El Paso in December 1911.[40] He quickly ingratiated himself with the El Paso establishment, counting Mayor Kelly among his close friends.[41] Following the pattern established by the Díaz administration, the consul supervised a network of agents and, most importantly, handled the money that financed their activities. The Mexican consulate at 816 North Oregon Street, where Llorente and Sommerfeld conferred morning and afternoon on a daily basis, was the scene of intense activity: "Enter the sightseer through lanes and aisles of high hatted, cape coated Mexican soldiers, citizens and officials who block the North Oregon street traffic and clutter up the perfectly good scenery in the immediate vicinity of Oregon and Montana."[42] Not only did Llorente direct and pay secret agents, but he also paid the salaries of more than one hundred refugee *maderista* soldiers who'd been part of the Juárez garrison and those of several hundred *maderista* public employees who'd likewise fled to El Paso. These men, combined with those Llorente was busy recruiting, potentially constituted a striking force that greatly concerned the rebels in Juárez. The rebels literally had to keep looking over their shoulders to guard against a surprise *maderista* attack from El Paso. Accordingly, they closely watched the international bridges.[43]

Llorente demonstrated a real flair for intrigue. When the rebels occupied Juárez, he managed to steal the firing pins from several machine guns that were about to be shipped to them.[44] And on the night of March 14, 1912, Llorente and Sommerfeld dispatched into Chihuahua a three-man team led by an American, "a tall, lank fellow," Peter S. Aiken, who claimed to be a veteran of the Boer War and to have been a Japanese spy in Washington, D.C., during the Russo-Japanese War. It appears that Aiken padded his résumé; he had been a locomotive engineer in Chihuahua who had enlisted with the Red Flaggers for a promised $5 a day but had received only 11.60 pesos for fifteen days' hard work and had deserted. He then tried his hand at smuggling but was caught on the streetcar with a pistol and 125 cartridges; he was released on $1,000 bond. This then was the leader of the team sent to dynamite the railroad bridges between Juárez and the city of Chihuahua.[45] The mercenaries were to be paid $100 each. Sommerfeld gave them each $50 in advance, while Consul Llorente contributed twenty-five pesos to each man for expenses and provided two .38 revolvers and fifty rounds of ammunition. The consul also arranged with Aiken to have the necessary dynamite crossed for the team downriver at Ysleta.

The expedition proved to be a fiasco. The saboteurs got cold feet. They returned to El Paso and by March 19 reported their failure to a furious Consul Llorente.[46] Aiken was convicted on an attempted smuggling charge and was sentenced to six months in the county jail, subsequently earning one month off for good behavior.[47] Interestingly, the Bureau later reported that "Aiken is doing time in order to keep the Mexican Consul, Enrique C. Llorente and Abraham Molina, out of jail themselves. Pressure was brought to bear upon him to plead guilty in order to keep the consul and Molina out of it. However, these persons have not kept their promises to Aiken and have turned him down completely. Therefore he talked." Aiken gave the Bureau a detailed statement.[48]

The *maderista* intelligence chiefs in El Paso continued their efforts to interdict the strategic Mexican Central line to the city of Chihuahua, and they continued to rely on mercenaries to do it. In June, Llorente had hired four soldiers of fortune from among the many hanging around El Paso ready for anything that paid reasonably well. One was Captain Emile Charpentier, who had recently been fighting on the *maderista* side. Charpentier had been operating a fieldpiece for Pancho Villa, who had remained loyal to Madero and had raised a force of irregulars to combat the *orozquistas*. But the rebels defeated Villa in Parral in a battle fought April 2–4, and Charpentier had narrowly escaped death. Not so lucky was his comrade in arms Thomas Fountain, a soldier of fortune from Mesilla, New Mexico, who had enlisted in Villa's command as a machine gunner. He was captured by the *orozquistas* in Parral and executed. His killing became an international incident and further increased the U.S. government's distaste for Orozco's rebellion. The *El Paso Morning Times* blamed his death on the rebel general José Inés Salazar, calling him "the cowardly scum of Mexican creation." The newspaper speculated that the battle cry "Remember Tom Fountain" might inflame the American public the way the battle cry "Remember the Maine" had done in 1898.[49] It didn't.

Charpentier had managed to escape the Red Flaggers in Parral, and he continued to fight under Villa. But then his horse fell on him, and so he'd come to El Paso for medical treatment.[50] To assist Charpentier in sabotaging the railroad, Consul Llorente had hired R. H. G. McDonald, D. J. Mahoney, and J. H. "Jack" Noonan, alias "A. Monahan." McDonald, the ex–*insurrecto* legionnaire lieutenant, had gone to San Antonio, then to New Orleans. In the Crescent City, he went looking for new revolutionary employment somewhere in Latin America, but finding none, he hired himself out instead for a time as an operative for the local Burns Detective Agency office. In April 1912, however, he'd returned to El Paso, where he ended up finding employment with the *maderistas*.[51]

Llorente promised the mercenaries a handsome salary and furnished them money with which to outfit themselves at Shelton-Payne. On June 11 the expedition was ready to depart.[52] They traveled on horseback a few miles west of El Paso to Pelea, New Mexico, and picked up their equipment, which had been tossed off a passing freight train by a bribed railroad employee. The group encountered a U.S. Army patrol, whose commander warned them against crossing into Mexico, which they did anyway. After a week they returned to El Paso with a tale of woe and derring-do. According to Charpentier, they fought off *orozquista* patrols and endured thirst and other hardships, but they failed to accomplish their mission and were exceedingly fortunate to have escaped with their lives. Incidentally, they claimed that one reason they failed to dynamite any railroad bridges was because their dynamite had washed away in a rainstorm.[53]

Agent Ross discussed this expedition with Felix Sommerfeld, and they both viewed it with considerable scorn. Ross related that:

> I remarked sarcastically to Felix Somerfelt [*sic*] to the effect that it was a wonder he would not send someone with a little brains on an expedition of this character, stating that none of the four men sent out had the nerve to blow up any railroad. He told me that this was just the trouble with all of them; that they had spent between $8000 and $9000 sending out parties to blow up these railroads and not one of them had done anything yet. He said he agreed with me in the belief that these men would go out into the mountains and stay a week or so and return with some cock-and-bull story about their difficulties. His whole conversation was an open-and-shut admission that he had sent these men out, or rather that he and the Consul were together on the deal.[54]

Powell Roberts, another *maderista* intelligence chief, took the same unflattering view of the expedition as Sommerfeld and Ross, for Ross wrote that: "Roberts' talk indicated plainly that he knew all about the proposition, and agreed with me that the Consul didn't have any sense . . . and also agreed with me that they [Charpentier et al.] didn't have the nerve to accomplish anything."[55] The expedition had been a fiasco, like that of Peter Aiken back in March.

Besides employing mercenaries, Consul Llorente employed the 1899 extradition treaty to great effect. Llorente repeatedly had rebels arrested and jailed awaiting extradition. The Mexican government would fail to produce evidence and they'd be freed, but they'd been taken out of circulation for forty days.[56] In addition to working to frustrate *orozquista* schemes, Llorente handled the export of munitions for the Madero government, something that was sanctioned by Washington, and he also directed the recruiting of men for the Madero forces, in direct violation of U.S. neutrality laws.

In order to begin collecting evidence of this breach, Agent Ross hired two ex-*insurrectos*, Gilford Jones and Abraham A. "Kid" Lea, a former professional boxer who'd been an *insurrecto* captain, at $3 a day each to get themselves recruited.

They did so, although the *maderistas* were becoming leery of recruiting Americans, fearing diplomatic complications. There was growing evidence that Llorente was directing recruiting in El Paso and Giuseppe Garibaldi was doing likewise in Arizona.[57] Agent Ross reported that Abraham Molina had lied to him by denying that any *maderista* recruiting was going on. Ross also used an *insurrecto* veteran, Ray M. Jones, as an informant monitoring the arms traffic in El Paso and Silver City, New Mexico. Felix Sommerfeld had recruited Jones, at $3 a day, and turned him over to Ross.[58]

Abraham Molina was the third *maderista* intelligence chief. A U.S. citizen, he listed himself as a contractor residing at 213 North Florence. The listing was accurate in the sense that he did contract out a lot of intelligence assignments. As we've seen, he had been combating *magonistas* and *reyistas*. He now focused his efforts on the *orozquistas*. He operated rather openly, being described by one local newspaper as "chief of the Madero secret service in this city." And in December 1911, Consul Llorente had referred to him as the "secret Agent of the Interior Ministry."[59] Molina took on the Red Flaggers with gusto. On March 1, he tried to arrange for dynamite to be placed in the boilers of the Mexico Northwestern locomotives that the rebels had seized in Juárez, and he soon thereafter bribed a watchman to steal the breechblock from a howitzer that the rebels had sent over for repair.[60] And he may have been responsible for two unsuccessful attempts to dynamite the Mexico Northwestern bridge between El Paso and Juárez.[61] He also offered a standing reward of $25 for information about *orozquista* activities.[62]

Basically Molina relied on an extensive network of operatives and informants to accomplish his mission. When, for instance, one Edgar Held, a merchandise broker with offices in the Mills Building, was suspected of shipping ammunition to Juárez in cans of oatmeal, Molina informed the Bureau "that he knew a young woman who could get information from Held, and that he would put her to work on this job."[63] Molina's informant was Miss X. Reynolds, who had worked for him before and who just happened to be Held's secretary. She readily accepted Molina's offer of a reward for information.[64] But Molina concentrated his efforts against the largest arms dealers in town, Shelton-Payne and Krakauer, Zork and Moye. He bribed some of the clerks in these firms, and he detailed his operatives to watch the Krakauer store continually. He also rented room 1 at the Planters Hotel across from Shelton-Payne; two men in this room watched the front of the store, while two more covered the alley in back.[65] Molina's people tried to follow every customer and every shipment of munitions leaving these establishments. They also maintained a close watch along the Rio Grande, on one night in May deploying twenty-five men along the river.[66] This may have been Molina's entire roster, for Felix Sommerfeld estimated that Molina had about twenty-six agents working for him.[67] Whenever they detected smuggling they notified the American authorities, usually the local police, the army, or the Texas Rangers, who made the arrests.

But monitoring the activities of smugglers was not without risk. Take the case of James Enos, a forty-nine-year-old runner for the Hotel Carlyle on San Francisco Street. He told the proprietor he'd landed a soft job that paid $3 a night for two hours' work, a job that had something to do with watching smugglers. But while Enos was watching smugglers they were watching him. Although he had armed himself with a pistol, smugglers jumped him, disarmed him, and two held him by the arms while a third stabbed him twenty-three times. His body was found in the brush near the smelter. A Madero intelligence agent confirmed that Enos had indeed been employed to watch smugglers.[68]

Like Llorente, Abe Molina readily employed mercenaries. Three Americans, E. A. Talbert (Talbot?), G. C. Steele, and G. Z. Stevens, applied to the local Bureau of Investigation office for employment as special agents. Their credentials left much to be desired, and they were rejected. Abraham Molina, however, readily hired the unsavory trio, explaining that he was now using American operatives because he hadn't gotten good results from many of his Mexican agents. Molina quickly wrote out notes in English stating that the men were Mexican secret agents working in accord with the United States government and requesting that they be given every assistance. He signed himself "Chief of Mexican Secret Service, El Paso" with offices at 310 Texas Street.[69]

Some of the mercenaries with whom Molina dealt were unstable personalities. One was James C. Bulger. Born in Brooklyn, New York, he left home at age seventeen to join the army. Though small in stature—five feet four inches and 120 pounds—he had an enormous lust for adventure. He served in 3rd U.S. Cavalry for a year and was discharged in the Philippines on July 24, 1901, as a private. Bulger was a soldier of fortune in Central America for a time. He then became a rancher in Colorado, where he founded the town of Bulger City and raised a regiment of volunteers, becoming a colonel. Bulger participated in the Madero revolution, fighting at the battle of Ojinaga. He remained a Madero sympathizer, coming to El Paso in 1912 to combat the Red Flaggers. He promptly got into an altercation with some soldiers in the Sheldon Hotel lobby and shot one of them in the hand. He pleaded self-defense.[70] In September, Abe Molina assigned him to Douglas, Arizona, where he passed himself off as a rebel sympathizer and also got involved in a proposed filibustering expedition into Sonora with the flamboyant former *insurrecto* E. S. "Tex" O'Reilly, who was now a war correspondent. Bulger eventually returned to El Paso, but in a fit of depression, on the night of October 5, 1912, he tried to commit suicide by shooting himself in Abe Molina's hotel room.[71] Failing in this endeavor, he participated briefly in the Mexican Revolution in 1913, in Laredo.[72] Bulger then drifted to Nicaragua where he was said to have taken part in a revolution.

Bulger's life took a dramatic turn on the afternoon of May 6, 1914, at the Savoy Hotel in Denver. He'd been drinking heavily and got into an argument with a cattleman from Cheyenne, who knocked him down and took away his pistol. Mortified and humiliated, Bulger raced to a nearby hardware store, purchased two .38 revolvers and ammunition, and returned to the hotel bent on revenge. Storming through the lobby brandishing his revolvers, Bulger went looking for his antagonist. He failed to find him, but in his drunken condition he managed to shoot the hotel proprietor, who died three days later. Bulger was found guilty of murder and was sentenced to hang. The sentence was later commuted to life imprisonment. According to a feature story on Bulger in the inmate magazine of the Colorado State Prison in 1960, by that time he had been an inmate for forty-four years and would soon be eighty years old.[73]

The Thiel Detective Service's operatives reinforced the *maderista* intelligence effort. One of Thiel's most effective agents was Thomas B. Cunningham, the former Díaz spy who with his brother had reported as "Your Informants."[74] Cunningham later became a special officer for the Chino Copper Company and then for the El Paso and Southwestern Railroad.[75] Thiel's manager, Henry Kramp, duly sent his operatives' reports, entitled "Revolutionary Information," to the Madero government, but he also sent copies to Alberto Madero, the president's uncle who participated in anti-Orozco operations in El Paso, to the management of the Mexico Northwestern Railroad, and to the federal Bureau of Investigation.[76] However, he insisted on sending his copies directly to the Bureau's regional office in San Antonio, for he feared leaks in the Bureau's offices in El Paso and elsewhere along the border.[77] Kramp exemplified a widespread phenomenon, namely that many of those involved in revolutionary intrigue served more than one master.[78]

For example, Abraham Molina was very good at his job, but his loyalties were in question. On May 10, Bureau agent Louis Ross had a long discussion about Molina with Consul Llorente. Ross's information, as well as that reaching Llorente and Sommerfeld, "proves to a moral certainty that Abraham Molina and a number of his men have given us all the double-cross and has [*sic*] been working both ends at the same time. Molina is to be separated from the Mexican secret service, and all of his men are to be removed next Saturday and an entirely new bunch put in to operate under my direction. We are to have all the men we want and the Mexican Consul will pay their salaries. We expect to have about 10 or 12 good Americans and about 20 good Mexicans from San Antonio and locally, and with this bunch of men, and with the privilege to get as many more as we require, we should be able to get some results," Ross reported.[79]

The new chief of the Mexican secret service in El Paso was to be W. Powell Roberts, formerly a local sergeant of police for many years. Roberts was well respected and spoke fluent Spanish, always an asset. On April 1 he'd been arrested in Juárez by the rebels on the charge of being a *maderista* spy and was transferred to the state penitentiary in Chihuahua before being released in response to American demands.[80] Another American, Lee L. Hall, was to be Roberts's deputy. Roberts was instructed to cooperate fully with the Bureau and with Charles H. Webster, the Texas Ranger most involved in enforcing the neutrality laws. Roberts established his espionage Bureau in the Roberts-Banner Building and began assembling his operatives and informants, who would allegedly number between twenty and eighty, paying them between $2 and $4 a day.[81] But Roberts proved to be a rather ineffectual spymaster. In June, Agent Ross would complain that "when this arrangement was first put into effect, I arranged for close co-operation with the various forces at work. I have been unable to secure this from Roberts. Neither Roberts nor any of the men under him have done anything worth while since they have been working."[82] Roberts was eventually transferred to Douglas, Arizona, a less important post.

As matters developed, Molina simply refused to be fired, and he knew so much about *maderista* organization and machinations that if he decided to go public it would be devastating. Agent Ross discussed the matter with Molina: "I remarked to him that they did not dare to fire him, because he knew too much about them, and he agreed that this was true."[83] However reluctantly, Llorente and Sommerfeld acquiesced to Molina's demands, and he remained in charge of his network. Powell Roberts and his subordinates played a supporting role (and were also used to keep Molina under surveillance). As for Molina, when in May the Bureau arranged to work with a detective named José Martínez sent directly from Mexico City, Molina out of jealousy had his men arrange the arrest of Martínez's undercover operative Pedro Cruz, who was taking 1,000 rounds into Juárez in order to infiltrate a smuggling ring. Interestingly, the policeman who arrested Cruz took him first to Molina's house, then to jail. When Cruz identified himself he was released on his own recognizance.[84]

In a very real sense the Mexican secret agents were the eyes and ears of the federal Bureau of Investigation, and on occasion also of the U.S. Secret Service (Molina, for example, helped on counterfeit cases). Molina, Roberts, and Ross worked very closely together. In one case, Ross, Molina, Texas Ranger captain John Hughes, and two of Hughes's men raided a printing shop and seized a scurrilous anti-American manifesto signed by Gonzalo Enrile, a noted *orozquista* who functioned as the liaison between Orozco and his *científico* backers.[85] Ross later reported that "I have got a list of all the men working for Roberts. As a sort of identification in case of necessity, these men have all been furnished with a small three-cornered card with the word 'Chicago' written on it."[86] Ross's superior, H. A. Thompson, the special agent in charge in San Antonio, would write to the chief of the Bureau of Investigation that "*the Mexican secret service agents, both at El Paso and at San Antonio, have aided us materially in the investigation of neutrality matters, and it is only just here to state that if it had not been for them, and their co-work, it would have been next to impossible for us to have accomplished the results thus far obtained.*"[87] The Mexican agents proved to be a double-edged sword, though; they enabled the Bureau to accomplish its mission, but they also made the Bureau see things largely through a *maderista* filter.

The figurative joining at the hip of the Bureau of Investigation and the Mexican secret service quickly became controversial. In April, public outrage erupted over an egregious violation of American civil liberties—armed Mexican operatives searching the passengers on streetcars for ammunition *at the American ends of the two international bridges.*[88] Abe Molina declared that his agents at the bridges reported to him but if they searched anyone they were acting on instructions from the U.S. Department of Justice. Ross publicly approved of this outrageous practice of armed agents of a foreign government searching Americans on American soil; he stated to the press that he was directing the activities of these Mexicans, who were employed by the Mexican government and were paid by that government, but he claimed that they'd never molested Americans—they just pointed out suspects to the soldiers, who did the actual searching.[89] Ross's statements were at variance with the facts, but they illustrate his concern for curtailing ammunition smuggling by whatever means necessary.

This view certainly wasn't shared by the local officials. Mayor Kelly announced that he'd ordered the chief of police to station men at the bridges and arrest anyone not an officer of the United States who tried to search people. Sheriff Peyton Edwards announced a similar policy. And indeed local law enforcement began to arrest Mexican agents on the charge of impersonating an officer and hauled them off to police court. On one occasion an Anglo El Pasoan who objected to being searched administered a severe beating to a Mexican attempting to search him. The battered agent was then arrested. Moreover, Mexican agents keeping a house under surveillance were arrested when the homeowner complained. They were charged with loitering.[90] Nevertheless, searches of travelers on the U.S. side of the international bridges, and the footbridge near the smelter, resumed, albeit in modified form. American soldiers now did most of the searching, although with Mexican government funds, several American inspectresses were employed in an effort to cope with the numerous women, primarily Mexicans, who took the streetcars and smuggled small amounts of ammunition on their persons.[91] Mexican agents stationed at the crossings now simply pointed out suspects to the soldiers and the inspectresses.[92] Since, however, the inspectresses were on duty only four hours a day, it wasn't too difficult to evade their attentions. On August 23, the searches of women ended. Soldiers continued to search the men.[93]

Mexican agents operating in El Paso still went around armed. As a Bureau agent admitted, "Strictly speaking, Madero men have no specific authority to carry arms except as comity is extended by local officers. They are assisting this Department and have not been elsewhere molested for carrying arms."[94]

Tom Lea, of the firm of Lea and Nagle, 512–14 American Bank Building, attorney for the *orozquistas* and future mayor of El Paso, complained bitterly to Washington about the searches.[95] The El Paso Bureau office tried to justify the practice by reporting that ammunition smuggling had declined sharply and that "no one [is] being searched unnecessarily and no undue harshness [is] used. No woman at any time [is] made to take off any clothing whatever." Not unnaturally, Mexican women objected to being searched, and they frequently scratched and slapped the inspectresses.[96] What the controversy illustrated was the differing priorities of federal and local authorities regarding the Orozco rebellion. In an interview published in the *El Paso Herald* on April 11, Agent Ross readily admitted that his informants were paid by the Mexican government and had been working with the Department of Justice for the past six months.

On occasion Sommerfeld passed along information directly to Ross: "Felix Somerfelt [*sic*] informed me that a Jew with a broken jaw who works for Abe Molina is giving information to the rebels about our operations on this side."[97] And Agent Ross gratefully availed himself of the *maderistas*' largesse, for his informants were on Consul Llorente's payroll.[98] As might be expected, the informants were of uneven quality. On May 11, for instance, Ross wrote: "I today discontinued the services of A. W. Hicks as Informant, because he would not stay under cover but began to advertise himself as a government employee."[99]

But that same day Ross hired two men who proved to be the gold standard among informants—Maurice L. Gresh and Virgil L. Snyder. They ran the Western Detective Agency's branch office in El Paso, located in rooms 224–25 of the Mills Building, and had considerable experience as railroad special agents. Ironically, that same day the *orozquistas* hired them to gather intelligence in El Paso. Ross employed them to work under cover against the *orozquistas*, primarily by gathering intelligence on gunrunners. Ross prudently arranged to keep an eye on them until he was satisfied with their performance. His precaution was mirrored by the Red Flaggers, who were also suspicious about the pair's loyalty. Gresh and Snyder were subjected to the third degree in Juárez. They were thrown into jail and accused successively of being "U.S. Customs officers, U.S. secret service men, and Maderista spies." The double agents were able to bluff their way out of trouble, and Cástulo Herrera explained to them that he was suspicious of Americans as he had been double-crossed by every one with whom he had dealt. Herrera directed them to smuggle some ammunition to him as evidence of their good faith. Agent Ross arranged for them to smuggle three hundred rounds, the soldiers guarding the footbridge near the smelter being ordered not to interfere with the pair as they crossed into Juárez on the night of May 15 with the contraband. Herrera was reassured of their bona fides. The double agents reported that the Red Flaggers were currently paying eighteen pesos ($9) per 1,000 rounds delivered.[100] About this same time Ross got another informant on Consul Llorente's payroll by persuading Abraham Molina to employ a certain Ed W. Mebus to cover munitions shipments by rail in and out of El Paso.[101] As we'll see, these shipments were substantial.

CHAPTER 6

Merchants of Death

What frustrated both the American and Mexican authorities was the attitude of the two large El Paso hardware dealers, much of whose trade was in death-dealing hardware. The Shelton-Payne Arms Company had been the principal supplier for Madero's *insurrectos*. As of September 1912, the firm had during the preceding two years purchased 4,000 rifles (mainly Remingtons) for $60,000, 2 million cartridges for $70,000, 4 machine guns for $2,500, 100 pistols (Colts) for $1,500, 1,000 rifle scabbards for $1,500, 100 pistol holsters for $125, 2,000 cartridge belts for $3,000, 500 saddles for $7,500, 1,000 cartridge bags for $1,000, 25 Mannlicher rifles for $375, and about 20,000 8-mm cartridges for $800, making a total of $148,300.[1] These are the amounts that can be documented. Undoubtedly there were others.

Most of the *orozquista* business went to Shelton-Payne's competitor, Krakauer, Zork and Moye. This was the largest hardware firm in the Southwest, whose financial statement on January 1, 1912, listed assets of $1,180,000 ($115,000 in cash).[2] Adolph Krakauer, who ran the firm with his sons Robert and Julius, was not just an arms dealer. He was one of the city's leading businessmen, a director of the First National Bank and the Rio Grande Valley Bank and Trust Company, president and director of the Two Republics Insurance Company, and president of the chamber of commerce.[3] And he was not at all apologetic about his munitions business, testifying that "for all I know, some of these cartridges that were bought may have been for the Madero government. I do not know. I was not supposed to know; but our business is supplying arms and ammunition, it has been for the last 25 years, and I do not propose on account of this revolution to stop it."[4] Krakauer asserted that "the Mexican consul and the so-called personal representative of Mr. Madero, Mr. Sommerfeld, have made it a business to surround our store and warehouse with 25 to 30 spies, who were there night and day." He also complained that they'd bribed some of his store employees; in one case Krakauer had discovered the spy.[5] Since it was not illegal to purchase munitions, only to attempt to cross them into Mexico in violation of the president's proclamation, there raged a battle of wits between the smugglers and their adversaries. The hardware companies were understandably reluctant to disclose information about their clients. In the case of Krakauer, an innovative system was used. The *orozquistas* reportedly deposited $300,000 with the firm, then drew against this sum for ammunition purchases. Individuals in Juárez would be given a note by Cástulo Herrera, for, say, "one pound of nails." The person would present this note to Krakauer and receive 1,000 rounds of ammunition.[6] The price would be deducted from the *orozquista* funds on deposit. The customer would try to get the goods across and if successful would receive payment when the ammunition was delivered to Herrera at the customs house. But evidently Robert Krakauer, who handled the *orozquista* account, not infrequently engaged in sharp practice, for some smugglers complained that when they presented a note to him he would keep the note and tell them to return later for the ammunition. When they returned he would profess to know nothing about the note and tell them to go back to Juárez and get another note.[7] He was thus presumably double-billing the *orozquistas* by deducting the amount represented by both notes from the rebel funds on deposit.

The Krakauers did everything they could to frustrate the federal authorities and facilitate the export of munitions by their *orozquista* customers. The firm protested to the Texas and Pacific Railroad that it was permitting "individuals unknown to us" to inspect arms shipments, and Krakauer threatened legal action unless the railroad stopped this practice immediately.[8] The Krakauers employed the same tactics with the El Paso and Southwestern Railroad. The Bureau countered by threatening the railroads with legal action for conspiracy, and both lines reluctantly agreed to permit inspection of their freight manifests and freight houses.[9] The Krakauers tried everything they could think of, though. For example, Adolph Krakauer attempted, unsuccessfully, to persuade the owner of the Alberta Hotel to evict Abraham Molina, who had rented a room overlooking Krakauer's yard and warehouse, which had a railroad siding from where many a clandestine arms shipment departed. Krakauer even filed a police complaint about men leaning against his building in a transparent attempt to clear the premises of Molina's spies. Once the Bureau got access to the railroads' freight records, Krakauer, Zork and Moye largely discontinued making large shipments by rail.[10]

The railroads might be cooperating with the federal authorities to curtail smuggling, but individual railroad employees were making good money by working with the smugglers. As the rebellion spread from Chihuahua into the neighboring states of Coahuila and Sonora, one of the quickest ways to supply ammunition to the rebels there was by rail from El Paso. Accordingly, train crews were routinely bribed. Cars with ammunition under false manifests were set out on lonely blind sidings, where revolutionists could unload them at their leisure. Or, conductors would put gravel in the journals of a boxcar's trucks, creating a "hot box," and the car would have to be uncoupled from the train and left behind on a siding. Or, members of the crew would toss packages off at agreed-on locations.[11]

In short, it appeared as though only a handful of people in El Paso were doing honest work and everybody else was mixed up in the Mexican Revolution. Some of the soldiers guarding the river spent as much as $100 a night in the red-light district after coming off duty[12] (this on a salary of $15 a month). Ammunition smuggling was carried on by virtually every means that human ingenuity could devise. Not only did people smuggle by rail (shipping by train even large iron pipes filled with ammunition), by automobile, and by wagon, but they concealed ammunition on their persons, sometimes in specially made vests. Some conductors and motormen cashed in by concealing contraband in their streetcars. Small-time smugglers bought ammunition at Krakauer, Zork and Moye and turned 100 rounds over to a conductor each trip, knowing that passengers were searched at the bridges but not the streetcars. The crews secreted the ammunition under the seats and once in Juárez returned the goods to the smugglers, who paid them a few dollars for their services. Once the practice was discovered, streetcars were also searched, and Abe Molina had one of his men get a job in the streetcar barns in order to keep an eye on the crews.[13] Smugglers employed young boys pulling toy wagons with ammunition concealed under firewood. They emptied the contents of large tin cans of food, filled the cans with ammunition, and resealed them. Still, the Red Flaggers were losing the struggle. Agent Louis Ross claimed that by May 1912, Orozco's partisans in Juárez were receiving on average only 1,000 rounds of smuggled ammunition a day, transported mainly by women riding the streetcars over the Stanton Street bridge when the inspectresses weren't on duty. Moreover, Ross estimated that between March 14 and May 1, about 800 rifles had been crossed one at a time by gunrunners.

By May, the army had substantially increased its presence in the El Paso area. The 22nd Infantry Regiment plus one battalion of infantry, one battery of field artillery, and four troops of the 4th Cavalry, a total of 1,350 soldiers, were commanded by Colonel E. Z. Steever. "The section in El Paso and contiguous to it is pretty well patrolled, but at the present low stage of water in the Rio Grande, the officers there state that the river can be waded at almost any point and that nothing short of a continuous line of sentinels can prevent individuals from slipping across, carrying small amounts of ammunition."[14] Even after summer rains increased the water level in the river, the army still had its hands full trying to cope with smugglers.[15]

Despite the enhanced military presence, Agent Ross complained about a lack of cooperation from other federal agencies: "I have repeatedly taken up with the military and customs authorities the matter of proper inspection of exportations of merchandise and railroad cars going across the river, but I have been unable to get any results along these lines. It is impossible to get the soldiers to do anything, and the inspection of shipments by them and by the customs people is a very casual matter. Ammunition is being taken over in all sorts of ways. I understand the last shipment going as Medicine."[16] In June there was an upsurge in smuggling by women because there was only one inspectress to cover three bridges. The local Bureau office requested authorization to hire a few more.[17] The necessary funds were not forthcoming but Ross went ahead anyway. He was especially concerned about the situation at the footbridge opposite the smelter, for his informants Maurice Gresh and Virgil Snyder, in the course of their smuggling duties in Juárez, reported that thirty to forty Mexican women crossed that bridge every day, taking the *orozquistas* between 2,000 and 3,000 rounds daily. Ross, Powell Roberts, and Texas Ranger Charles Webster called on Colonel Steever, the Fort Bliss commander: "We told Steever that the women [the inspectresses] would work 'on their nerve' and that we had no authority to put them there, but that if he would furnish us a tent for their work, we would arrange the rest. He agreed to furnish us a tent." The Mexican government's man Powell Roberts paid the salaries—$3 a day each—for two inspectresses, who now worked from 6 a.m. to midnight in two shifts of nine hours each.[18]

The Red Flaggers had developed new smuggling techniques and routes. On May 29, Colonel Castúlo Herrera, the rebels' chief ammunition smuggler, using the alias of "George Valencia," traveled to Albuquerque, New Mexico, with two associates. They went to the office of John McGinnis, manager of the Spanish-language weekly *La Opinion Pública*. The owner of the newspaper, which had a decidedly pro-*orozquista* slant, was McGinnis's father-in-law Elfego Baca, a prominent New Mexican lawyer and politician. When Herrera and company visited McGinnis they presented him with a letter from Baca instructing McGinnis to do everything in his power to assist the Mexicans. McGinnis, who subsequently stated "that he is employed by Elfego Baca, and would do anything he told him to," arranged for the repackaging into three barrels marked "lime" and twelve kegs marked "nails" of 49,000 cartridges Herrera had purchased from the McIntosh and Whitney hardware stores. On May 30 Herrera shipped the ammunition by Wells Fargo Express to Deming, New Mexico, where Eduardo Ochoa, using the alias of "A. Gonzalez," waited to receive it. Ochoa and his accomplices moved the ammunition by wagon thirty miles south to the border town of Columbus, where they successfully crossed the shipment on June 1. Herrera and his associates Jesús de la Torre, Ignacio Núñez, and Eduardo Ochoa had scored a major coup. Ochoa made his way back to Juárez, but the military arrested the other three in Deming. Their bond was set at $3,000 each.

The Bureau was determined to keep Herrera in jail even if he could post bond, for he was already under indictment in El Paso for conspiracy to export munitions (Herrera had posted a $1,000 bond but had failed to appear for trial). However, the Bureau hadn't counted on the *orozquistas*' lawyer, Thomas C. Lea Jr., who quickly took the morning train to Deming, convinced the deputy U.S. marshal there to get approval from his superior in Albuquerque—who hadn't yet received the Bureau's request to hold Herrera—to allow Herrera to post his $3,000 bond. Lea and his client took the first train back to El Paso and, to evade any Bureau agents who might be waiting at the Union Depot to rearrest Herrera, they alighted in Pelea, New Mexico, a whistle stop just west of El Paso and took a leisurely stroll into Juárez. A furious and frustrated Agent Ross admitted that Lea had "slipped one over on me."[19] It was good to have competent legal representation.

It perhaps needs to be reiterated that in addition to large firms such as Shelton-Payne and Krakauer there were literally scores of independent operators involved in arms smuggling. In June the Bureau received word that Henry Mohr, who operated a new and secondhand hardware store three doors south of Shelton-Payne on South El Paso Street, had just begun smuggling arms and ammunition. Agent Ross conferred with Abe Molina about the matter, and Molina promptly took care of the problem—he put Mohr's head clerk on his payroll as an informer.[20]

Those engaged in smuggling at times included the very people supposed to be combating the practice. For instance, Abraham Molina came up with the bright idea of fleecing the *orozquistas* (while doing himself some good) by selling them a 14,000-round shipment of bogus ammunition. He loaded boxes with bricks to the exact weight of 14,000 rounds, but before he could conclude the sale, federal agents and Texas Rangers raided the house where the goods were stored, thinking they were really contraband.[21] Then there was the case of El Pasoan Floyd S. Sitler, whom Molina employed to gather evidence against Krakauer, Zork and Moye. Sitler went to Juárez, secured an order for 2,000 rounds, picked up the ammunition from Krakauer, and started to smuggle it back to Juárez on the streetcar. Molina, however, had discovered that Sitler was trying to double-cross him, so he pointed Sitler out as a smuggler to the soldiers guarding the Stanton Street bridge. They seized Sitler, who had 200 rounds of .44 ammunition concealed in his socks (which must have made walking a bit awkward), and off he went to jail. Unable to post a $500 bond, he stayed there.[22] Then there was a certain James McKay, who was indicted for neutrality violations. It turned out that he was really W. B. Scott, who'd been working for the Madero government since March 1 and had been sent to Juárez to secure information.[23]

Prominent among local ammunition smugglers were the brothers Sabino and Abelino Guaderrama, whose activities shed light on the complexities of the traffic. In one instance, rebel colonel Demetrio Ponce arranged to purchase from Shelton-Payne 67,000 rounds and 390 rifles for the *orozquistas*. But repeated efforts to move the munitions to Juárez failed. Ponce then arranged for the Guaderramas to try their luck at smuggling the consignment. An order signed by General Pascual Orozco, Demetrio Ponce, and Cástulo Herrera was sent to Shelton-Payne stating that the Guaderramas had bought the munitions and instructing the firm to deliver the goods to the brothers. The Guaderramas took 15,000 rounds, hid them under a shipment of flour, and tried to smuggle the goods over to Juárez, but Texas Rangers seized the shipment and turned it over to the army. The Guaderramas then stored the balance—52,000 rounds and 390 rifles—at the American Grocery Store instead of at the Guaderramas' stores, one of which was on the corner of Sixth and Stanton and the other of which was in Smeltertown. Warrants were issued for Sabino and Abelino Guaderrama and Cástulo Herrera for gunrunning. The brothers were arrested and released on bond; since Herrera was in Juárez he was beyond the reach of American law. To prevent the authorities from seizing their arms and ammunition, the Guaderramas had cleverly given their attorney, P. E. Gardner, a lien on the munitions, and thus they could claim that they didn't own the merchandise. The Guaderramas were able to smuggle small amounts of this cache but became frustrated at their lack of success. The resourceful brothers then approached Consul Enrique Llorente and offered to sell him the munitions surreptitiously for half price, thereby double-crossing the *orozquistas*.[24]

On June 22, Abraham Molina informed Bureau agents Ross and H. A. Thompson that the Guaderrama brothers, Isabel Larrazolo, and Longino González had bought 10,000 Mauser and Winchester cartridges from Krakauer and had concealed them in the hills north of El Paso, planning to smuggle the munitions at night. The Bureau agents searched but failed to locate the cache. On June 24, however, one of Molina's men discovered the ammunition hidden in a gulch, covered with leaves and brush. There was also a pile of gunnysacks for transporting the ammunition on burros. The Bureau agents, Molina, and several peace officers staked out the scene and waited for the smugglers. But one of Molina's operatives watching the cache from afar thought that the group was the smugglers and raced back to town to inform Consul Llorente, who immediately notified the police, who rushed ten heavily armed officers to the location. In the darkness each group thought the others were the smugglers and prepared to open fire. Tragedy was only averted when someone in the Bureau group recognized the voice of the chief deputy sheriff in the other party. The police left, and after waiting another two hours the Bureau group decided that the smugglers had been scared off. They loaded the ammunition into an automobile and took it to the federal building. The Guaderramas and their accomplices were arrested. The accomplices' bail was fixed at $750 each, but the Guaderramas had to post a bond of $3,000 each because it was their second arrest for ammunition smuggling.[25]

In the spring a new player appeared on the scene, one of the most remarkable figures in this whole outlandish cast of characters. Victor Leaton Ochoa's revolutionary career had begun decades earlier, when he had earned the distinction of having been among the first to rebel against the regime of Porfirio Díaz. Ochoa was born in 1850 in Ojinaga, Chihuahua, of Spanish and Scotch ancestry.[26] His parents moved to Presidio, Texas, when he was three years old. In 1885, he ran unsuccessfully for the office of alderman in El Paso. In May 1889, he became a naturalized U.S. citizen.

Turning to journalism, by 1892 he was the founding editor of two Spanish-language newspapers and was president of the Spanish-American Press Association. Ochoa worked in Las Vegas, New Mexico, as a crusading newspaper editor, defying Hispanic vigilantes who tried to run him out of town.[27] Motivated by radical liberal ideals, he decided in 1893 to join a rebel movement in the state of Chihuahua.[28] In December 1893, he was arrested in El Paso and charged with being a revolutionary agent. The charge wasn't proven, and in January 1894, Ochoa slipped into Chihuahua and raised a guerrilla band.[29] But as the Las Vegas, New Mexico, newspaper observed, "The opinion of Ochoa here is that he has more courage than discretion, and that he is hardly destined to die in his bed."[30] Indeed his military career was brief—within weeks Díaz troops virtually annihilated Ochoa's force, hanging on trees the corpses of forty-two of his followers as a warning to other rebels. Ochoa was one of four survivors, and he only managed to escape by donning the uniform of a dead soldier.[31]

His whereabouts became a matter of intense speculation. Mexican government agents prowled around his house in El Paso day and night, according to his wife.[32] The American authorities were also looking for Ochoa, for violation of the neutrality laws, and on October 15, 1894, a federal grand jury in El Paso indicted him on a charge of leading a military expedition against Mexico, a friendly nation.[33] About that time Ochoa was arrested, not in El Paso but in Fort Stockton, Texas, where he'd been posing as a cattleman. Texas Rangers recognized him and took him in charge. But the slippery Ochoa conned the sheriff into letting him go, and he fled toward El Paso. He got as far as the hamlet of Toyah before the Texas Rangers recaptured him a few days later.[34] He was tried in El Paso on April 10, 1895, and being found guilty, he was sentenced to two years and six months in Kings County Penitentiary, Brooklyn, New York, plus a $1 fine. On August 15, Ochoa was committed to prison. He was released on May 10, 1897. As a convicted federal felon he lost his citizenship, but since his conduct following his release from prison was good, both the trial judge and the district attorney recommended the restoration of his rights of citizenship. The U.S. attorney general concurred, and a presidential pardon on February 15, 1906, restored his civil rights.[35]

Ochoa resided in Poughkeepsie, New York, and Paterson, New Jersey. He was a versatile inventor who tried to patent two flying machines and did patent a fountain pen, a revolving signboard, a streetcar brake, an improved windmill, an adjustable clincher wrench, and a pen clip. He also founded the Ochoa Tool and Machine Company and the International Airship Company of Paterson, New Jersey.[36] In 1911, he sued—unsuccessfully—*Everybody's Magazine* in New York City for libel because it had published an article on the Texas Rangers entitled "Guarding the Rio Grande" that stated Ochoa had been arrested in Fort Stockton in 1894 and was subsequently convicted of neutrality violation and sentenced to prison.[37]

Ochoa supported the Madero revolution. In October 1911, he sent to Gustavo Madero, the new president's brother, clippings of sensational articles about Mexican conditions that had appeared in American newspapers. Gustavo thanked him for sending these examples of yellow journalism. When the Orozco rebellion broke out, it became evident that Ochoa had lost none of his fiery rhetoric; in a letter written in April 1912, he fulminated against the plight of Mexicans in the United States and threatened that if the United States meddled in the affairs of Mexico, El Paso, San Antonio, and other southwestern cities would immediately be burned and all the territory from San Antonio to San Diego and from San Francisco to Denver would be laid waste by Mexicans.[38] Perhaps to be in a position to participate in all this he traveled to El Paso to join the *orozquistas*. After a quick trip in May to Orozco's headquarters in the city of Chihuahua, Ochoa informed the press in El Paso that Madero's ingratitude was the real cause of Orozco's rebellion, which he asserted was on the verge of triumphing.[39]

To aid in that triumph, Ochoa, "the reputed head of the rebel secret service," established his residence at 406 Texas Street (a block away from Abe Molina's office), adopted the aliases of "Wallace" and later "Perkins," and began directing local smuggling operations.[40] He had brought a group of women with him from Chihuahua and put them to work smuggling ammunition, of which the rebels were desperately short.[41] But his movements were closely watched by Powell Roberts's *maderista* network, by Abraham Molina's men, and by the Bureau of Investigation.

Victor Ochoa lived in a world of intrigue. He claimed to have fourteen men working for him who were ostensibly working for Consul Llorente, and he declared that these double agents were providing a steady stream of useful intelligence.[42] Ochoa always went around heavily armed, even in his own house. And he thought big; his schemes were usually grandiose. For example, he instructed an American associate—the private detective Maurice L. Gresh—to escort his brother, Eduardo Ochoa, who had crossed the 49,000 cartridges at Columbus, New Mexico, to the El Paso railroad depot, for he was on a special mission for General Orozco. He ordered Gresh to kill anyone who interfered with Eduardo Ochoa. The only trouble was that Gresh was a Bureau of Investigation undercover operative paid by Molina, and Gresh promptly informed Agent Ross of the plan. Agents Ross and Robert L. Barnes placed Eduardo Ochoa under surveillance. Ross also boarded the train and arrested Eduardo Ochoa in Ysleta.[43] Ochoa was considered a prize catch, as is indicated by his bond, which was set at $5,000. He couldn't post it and was remanded to the county jail.[44]

Suspecting nothing, Victor Ochoa increasingly relied on the energetic Gresh, who in the parlance of the time was a real "live wire." Gresh ended up being his right-hand man. (Gresh didn't lack nerve. On one occasion while in Cástulo Herrera's office in Juárez he sneaked a look at the book in which the rebel colonel recorded payments for smuggled ammunition.)[45] The Bureau thus learned that Ochoa had received some shipments billed as "disassembled machinery" from Paterson, New Jersey, his former home, the items presumably to be used for smuggling.[46] Some inkling of what they might be came from informant Gresh. He accompanied Ochoa to the Juárez customs house, the headquarters for *orozquista* smuggling. There Ochoa showed the informant "what looks like a toy balloon made of heavy duck containing ribs. Ochoa said that they put 5,000 rounds in one of these things, which are six feet in diameter and about five feet high when inflated; that they then sealed up the open end and tied a string to it; a man would take this thing and swim the river, and whenever he could get a footing he would pull the balloon after him, which, on account of being full of air, would not drag on the bottom." Ochoa boasted to Gresh "that during the last sixty days he had crossed about 300,000 rounds of ammunition in these things, and that they are now worn out and of no further use. He stated further that they had others which are in use at the present time. Gresh asked Ochoa where they got the stuff across and he told Gresh that they operated just below Washington Park, not very far from the place where the soldiers are camped." Ochoa subsequently informed Gresh that he'd successfully smuggled ammunition in automobiles and, most intriguingly, said that "he had a much better arrangement now for getting the ammunition across the river, that he had a bag about three feet in diameter and fifteen feet long and it would hold 10,000 rounds. He told Gresh that he was awaiting the arrival of this bag and until it came he would not do anything."[47]

Gresh kept the Bureau and Abe Molina abreast of Victor Ochoa's schemes. Ochoa was furious because his brother Eduardo had been arrested, and he plotted to break him out of the county jail, along with some other *orozquista* prisoners. He was under the impression that Eduardo had been betrayed by the latter's mistress and told Gresh that "arrangements had been made to put her out of the way so that she would not tell any more stories." Regarding the proposed jailbreak, none other than Gresh was to head the nighttime raid, impersonating a constable. Ochoa even purchased a constable's badge for Gresh to wear. Ochoa's plan was for Gresh to approach the jail leading a Mexican supposedly under arrest. As soon as the jail door was opened, Gresh and his men would rush the jailer and liberate the prisoners while twelve picked men from Juárez would be deployed outside to prevent any interference and to cut the telephone line. Ochoa planned to confer in Juárez with Cástulo Herrera and other prominent Red Flaggers to work out the final details of the operation.[48]

As it happened, the proposed jail delivery was postponed because of trouble between Ochoa and Herrera. An article appeared in *El Paso del Norte*, a local Spanish-language newspaper, charging Herrera with misappropriation of *orozquista* funds and with incompetence in directing smuggling operations, stating that in Columbus it had been Eduardo Ochoa who'd done all the work of getting the ammunition across while Herrera had just spent money. Felix Sommerfeld, always anxious to sow dissension in the ranks of the Red Flaggers, had obtained the article prior to its publication and had added Victor Ochoa's initials to the manuscript. When the article appeared, Herrera was livid, and he had a warrant issued for Ochoa's arrest. The latter happened to be in Juárez at the time but was warned by friends and fled back to El Paso. So, Herrera refused to provide the twelve picked men for the jailbreak. The irony in all this was that Ochoa had in fact written the article but expected it to be published anonymously. However, Herrera made overtures of reconciliation toward Ochoa, and the dispute was smoothed over. Still determined to liberate his brother, Ochoa showed Gresh some saws he planned to slip into his brother's cell so Eduardo could saw his way out if all else failed. But the scheme to rescue Eduardo came to naught. It wouldn't have succeeded anyway because the sheriff, anticipating a jailbreak, had several extra deputies sleeping in the jail.[49]

Another Ochoa plan was for Gresh to secure employment with Abe Molina in order to act as a double agent. Gresh conferred with the Bureau and with Molina, who arranged to employ him under the name of "R. McGrath."[50] When Gresh so informed Ochoa, Ochoa announced that he'd abandoned that plan, telling Gresh that the man he really wanted to get was Felix Sommerfeld. He offered Gresh $5,000 to shoot Sommerfeld or, better still, to blow up the Mexican consulate with Sommerfeld and Llorente in the building, thus eliminating them and destroying the records of the consulate.[51] Gresh came up with plausible reasons as to why this wasn't feasible.

Next, Ochoa, who considered himself a criminal mastermind, a veritable Professor Moriarty, but was really a loose cannon, told Gresh to get a job in a garage so he could steal a car to use in smuggling. The Bureau arranged for Gresh to work nights temporarily at the Two Republics Garage, so he could "steal" a car when Ochoa needed one.[52] Yet it turned out that what Ochoa really wanted was an automobile engine of about forty horsepower—to use in an airplane he claimed to have received disassembled that he'd hidden in several places in El Paso. He planned to have Gresh help him smuggle the components across the river.[53] Ochoa never managed to get his airplane to Juárez, but he was certainly imaginative, being among the first in the smuggling community to envision using an aircraft.

Ochoa was also of a practical bent of mind. To raise working capital he proposed running a kidnapping ring, in which Gresh would play a leading part.[54] Ochoa told Gresh to come to his house at night and to bring his revolver, for they were going "to do a little business." Gresh of course informed the Bureau, whose agents, along with Abe Molina, staked out Ochoa's house. Gresh later reported that Ochoa had organized not just a kidnapping ring but a very businesslike criminal enterprise that was to operate under the name of the Mexico Mine and Investment Company. Its members would commit all kinds of crimes from murder on down. Ochoa of course was the president of the organization, and Gresh was named the vice president. In addition, Flavio Sandoval, who had lived in El Paso for several years and who bought cattle in Mexico, was the secretary. José Trujillo, an old-time partner of Ochoa's who had accompanied him on the ill-fated Chihuahua filibustering expedition in 1894, was the treasurer.[55] (We've already encountered Trujillo, the sometime Thiel operative, *insurrecto* officer, and *magonista* sham fruit-stand proprietor.) Two of Ochoa's associates who'd failed to attend the meeting would be inducted into the organization the following day. At Ochoa's suggestion each man made out his will and delivered it to Sandoval. It was further agreed that if any member betrayed the organization one of his colleagues would kill him and place his will on his person to give the impression he'd committed suicide. Having gotten the ground rules out of the way, Ochoa announced that their first caper would be to locate the *orozquista* colonel Cástulo Herrera's wife and rob her of $18,000 supposed to be in her possession.[56] Ochoa subsequently informed his colleagues that he'd located Mrs. Herrera's residence, at 520 South Florence, but the plan to rob her was put on hold.

Ochoa was increasingly nervous about his house being under surveillance; when Gresh offered to have the gang meet at Gresh's house Ochoa gratefully accepted. Gresh also arranged for Agent Ross to eavesdrop on the gang's deliberations.[57] Ross crawled into the attic to try to overhear, but "all I got, however, was an imitation Turkish bath as the conversation was held in such low tones that I was unable [*sic*] to hear but very little." Therefore, Ross decided to plant a dictograph in hopes of having better luck.[58] Ross went to an optical store and purchased an "electrophone," which he installed in Gresh's house. Ross again took up station in the attic. The machine's microphone was concealed in the meeting room, and although the device worked, apparently no information of importance was conveyed.[59]

Meanwhile, the fertile mind of Victor Ochoa had been concocting yet another scheme. He traveled to Chihuahua in late June for an audience with General Orozco.[60] Ochoa hoped to be named chief rebel ammunition smuggler in El Paso, which under the circumstances was something akin to intriguing to become the captain of the *Titanic*, for by July the Orozco rebellion was disintegrating. Under the Red Flaggers Juárez became a dreary place: "Ciudad Juarez has changed from the lively little town of former times to a city of vacant streets, vacant houses and stagnant business. Americans have scratched the Mexican town from their visiting list lately and very few sightseers make the trip across the line." Even the gambling dens and saloons had few patrons and closed at 10:30 p.m.[61]

The most important battle Orozco lost was the battle of El Paso, and it made his defeat inevitable. A powerful column of Madero's federal army under General Victoriano Huerta was driving north up the central rail line. Huerta inflicted a series of major defeats on the *orozquistas*, who were desperately short of ammunition.

What little was being smuggled to them through El Paso was almost exclusively small arms ammunition, smugglers finding it difficult to conceal artillery shells on their persons. Orozco's artillery simply couldn't respond to Huerta's many fieldpieces and their seemingly inexhaustible supply of shells.[62] For example, at the second battle of Rellano, May 22–23, federal artillery was decisive.[63] Facilitating Huerta's advance was the intelligence he received from *maderista* spies in the state of Chihuahua operating out of El Paso.[64]

With the rebellion in decline, Emilio Vázquez Gómez had tried to rally the rebels. On May 2 he left San Antonio. He arrived in El Paso on May 4 and crossed over to Juárez, where he proclaimed himself provisional president of Mexico and established his headquarters in the customs house. But he and Orozco couldn't agree on the terms that would install him as provisional president. The frustrated politician was virtually a prisoner in the customs house, and on May 11, he gave up and returned to San Antonio to sulk.[65]

Orozquistas began pouring across the international bridges seeking asylum. On June 10, for instance, Gonzalo C. Enrile, who had been the architect of the revolution, serving not just as Orozco's secretary but as the liaison between Orozco and the conservatives financing the revolt, set foot in El Paso, as did Colonel Agustín Estrada, at one time commander of the Juárez garrison. Consul Llorente promptly had them arrested pending extradition proceedings.[66] Moreover, the Bureau reported on June 17 that the rebels had virtually ceased smuggling, speculating that they were saving their money for their getaway. "Several of the rebel officials in Juarez came to the American side tonight with the statement that they had quit the revolution for good and all." But most significantly, the families of General Pascual Orozco and his father, Colonel Pascual Orozco Sr., came to El Paso with all their baggage and effects, "and it appears that they are not going back to Mexico in the near future."[67]

The Orozco families settled in Los Angeles, where two operatives of the local Mexican consul kept them under surveillance. They were already watching prominent conservative exiles suspected of helping to fund the Orozco rebellion, such as General Luis Terrazas, his two sons and their families, who were living in Long Beach. The Terrazas clan first stayed at the Hotel Virginia in Long Beach but then moved to the Bixby Apartments in that city. Reportedly they moved because Terrazas didn't like the cuisine at the hotel. He rented the whole apartment building at $800 a month to house the family, who numbered about twenty, and the servants.[68] The man had style. The exiles had formed a revolutionary junta in Los Angeles, one whose meetings an informant of the Bureau attended.[69] Gloom prevailed among the exiles in Los Angeles and panic among their comrades in Juárez.

General Terrazas, who had dominated the state of Chihuahua for decades, was not just the largest rancher in Mexico; he was arguably the largest rancher in the world. One of the ways in which he supported Orozco's rebellion was through the export of cattle, a device that various revolutionary factions employed. In May, Terrazas signed an agreement with the *orozquistas* by which he'd be allowed to ship forty thousand head of cattle to El Paso over the rebel-controlled railroads in Chihuahua. The American consul in Juárez stated that "I am told that a liberal export duty besides the freight goes to the army of liberation."[70] The first shipment, one thousand head, arrived in El Paso on May 9. That same date another Chihuahua ranching operation, the Corralitos Cattle Company, crossed one thousand head, presumably under the same kind of arrangement.[71] But whatever export duties were collected were too little and too late. And Terrazas stoutly denied that he had ever willingly supported the Orozco rebellion.[72] A variation on using cattle to finance revolution occurred in the fall of 1912, when several Americans gathering cattle in Chihuahua for export claimed to have been held for ransom by rebels. The ransom was paid, but this proved to be merely an innovative method of funneling money to Madero's enemies.[73]

The Orozco rebellion was rapidly running out of ammunition, money, and morale. To accelerate its collapse, Consul Llorente and Felix Sommerfeld were still determined to sabotage the vital railroad line between Juárez and Chihuahua. This time they recruited the most famous soldier of fortune on the border—Sam Dreben, "the Fighting Jew." Dreben hardly fit the romantic image of the mercenary—he was short and squat and spoke in a guttural voice. But he had a sunny disposition despite being a perennially unlucky gambler, and he had a prodigious capacity for alcohol and women. His principal talent was as an expert machine gunner, a skill much in demand during the Mexican Revolution.

Dreben was born in Poltava, Russia, on June 1, 1878. To escape both oppression and grinding poverty he did what thousands of other Europeans did and emigrated to the United States, arriving in New York in 1898. His ambition had always been to become a soldier, and he promptly enlisted in the U.S. Army, serving in the Philippines and in China. After completing several enlistments, he was discharged in 1907 and drifted to Panama, where he became a saloon keeper for a time. Yet soldiering was in his blood. He became a mercenary, fighting in Nicaragua, where he met and became fast friends with another professional machine gunner, Tracy Richardson. The pair made their way to New Orleans and eventually enlisted in an expedition that the celebrated filibuster General Lee Christmas was organizing to overthrow the government of Honduras. The revolution triumphed, and after Honduras, Dreben and Richardson returned to New Orleans. In 1911, *maderista* emissaries recruited Dreben to fight in southern Mexico, in the state of Campeche. With Madero in power, Dreben again returned to New Orleans, and there in 1912, *orozquistas* hired him and Richardson as machine gunners at a salary of $500 a month.

By February 29, the two had traveled to El Paso, then into Chihuahua, serving in the forces of rebel generals Emilio Campa and José Inés Salazar.[74] They performed quite professionally, although by his own admission Dreben ordered his men to shoot a badly wounded federal officer agonizing in bed; when the officer pleaded for his life because he had a family, Dreben spared him. But General Salazar entered the room and personally blew the officer's brains out.[75] One account states that Dreben and Richardson narrowly avoided execution—their commander, General Emilio Campa, in a fit of pique ordered them shot but at the last moment relented. Campa was, of all things, an anarchist physician; he'd practiced medicine in Saint Louis, Missouri, before joining the rebels, and his wife still lived there. This incident, coupled with the fact that Orozco was losing and that Richardson had been badly wounded, figured in the mercenaries' decision to return to El Paso. While Richardson convalesced, Dreben secured a job as a recruiter for the rebels.[76]

Dreben and Richardson, "late of Orozco's army," arrived in El Paso on June 23 and took rooms at the Hotel Angelus. Agent Ross suspected they were there to arrange the smuggling of some fieldpieces, and he detailed an informant to cover their movements.[77] They may also have been under surveillance by John Barbrick, who operated in Chihuahua as an agent of Consul Llorente's.[78]

The Bureau gained further information about Dreben from Joseph Rothman, an ex-Bureau agent who'd carried out assignments in China, the Philippines, and Panama. He informed the El Paso office that the Mexican government had employed him "to keep track of Sam Dreben" who was at present in El Paso and Juárez on some special mission. Rothman said he'd known Dreben and Tracy Richardson in the Panama Canal Zone: Dreben worked for the Quartermaster Department in Cristóbal, later opened a saloon on Cass Street in Colón, and subsequently was a pimp for Nancy Hanks's brothel in Colón. He lost track of the mercenary pair until February when he saw them in New Orleans. Rothman reported that they were now staying in room 136 at the Angelus Hotel in El Paso. He promised to keep Agent Ross apprised of Dreben's movements. (Rothman later followed Dreben to Douglas, Arizona.)

Rothman was not the only man who ended up keeping Dreben under surveillance. Bureau informant Snyder, of the team of Gresh and Snyder, made Dreben's acquaintance in a Juárez cantina. Dreben told Snyder he was trying to recruit fifty good Americans to fight against the federal army when it attacked Juárez. Dreben also mentioned that Orozco had sent him to Juárez to have three machine guns repaired there. He'd done so, and the *orozquistas* in Juárez now boasted four machine guns, two cannons, and a mountain howitzer (hardly enough, however, to offset General Huerta's superiority in artillery). Dreben acknowledged that the rebels' chief problem was securing ammunition. Snyder then offered to help smuggle munitions, but Dreben said he was unwilling to risk involvement in the smuggling trade. Snyder invited Dreben for supper at his house the following night, and the Bureau planned to have Gresh attend also, so there'd be two credible witnesses in case Dreben tried to recruit them.[79]

Disappointingly, Gresh and Snyder reported that they'd had little success with Dreben, who hadn't talked business over dinner. They invited him back the next night to try again. Agent Ross was nervous about entrapment, however: "I have instructed those informants that they should not lead this man on; that they should let him do the talking and not try to induce him to violate the law in order to make a case against him."[80] Soon afterward, Snyder reported that Dreben had discontinued trying to recruit the fifty Americans and that he "appears to have gone into some scheme to smuggle ammunition and appears to be figuring on where to buy his stuff."[81] Informant Gresh, who went to Juárez on an errand for Victor Ochoa, met Dreben there and returned to El Paso with him, in the course of which Dreben told Gresh he'd be able to use him in a "money-making proposition in about 10 days." Shedding light on what this proposition might be was the fact that Dreben was now working for Felix Sommerfeld, gathering intelligence on the *orozquistas* in Juárez—Dreben had no intention of going down with a sinking ship.

Reportedly Sommerfeld had hired Dreben to complete the work of destroying the railroad bridges south of Juárez.[82] Dreben must have declined to carry out the bridge sabotage mission, for he soon surfaced in New Orleans, working for the Mexican government investigating an arms cache in New Orleans.[83] He registered at the St. Charles Hotel under the alias of "Lakowski" and appeared to have ample funds. From there, Sommerfeld sent him to Douglas, Arizona, to make contact with General Salazar and ingratiate himself with the *vazquista* rebels in order to report on their activities.[84] Still working for Sommerfeld, Dreben also operated in San Antonio, where he infiltrated a group of rebels who planned to transport a load of munitions from New Orleans to the vicinity of Tampico. "Dreben states that he will miss the boat when this party leaves New Orleans and that the Mexican officials will be apprised of the destination of the party where they will be captured when the boat lands on Mexican territory."[85]

Dreben's partner, Tracy Richardson, was the second most famous mercenary to set foot in El Paso during the Orozco rebellion. Unlike Dreben, Richardson *looked* the part: he was "a lean, sunbaked six-footer with a perpetual squint in his eyes from staring into tropical suns, a well-trimmed dark moustache, prominent nose, close-cropped sandy hair; if not exactly handsome, at least looking every inch the professional soldier-adventurer."[86] Richardson was born on a farm in Broken Bow, Nebraska, on November 21, 1892, but his family moved to Lamar, Missouri, when he was an infant. He never attended high school, working instead as a timekeeper, purchasing agent, and commissary clerk for an oil company. By 1909 he had decided to become a soldier of fortune and went off to Nicaragua, joining a revolutionary army and remaining in that country until 1910. There he reportedly performed the feat of bluffing the garrison into surrendering the capital, Managua. After a brief stint as a mercenary in Venezuela, in 1911 he enlisted with Lee Christmas and fought in Honduras.

In 1912, along with Dreben, he signed on with the *orozquistas*. He suffered a severe chest wound and, as we have seen, he and Dreben returned to El Paso.[87] In October 1912, he hired out in El Paso once again as a machine gunner for the Orozco faction.[88] The Bureau learned of this from one R. M. Jones, having "arranged with him to enlist, if possible, and accompany Richardson as these two boys are rather friendly."[89] Richardson returned to the ranks of the *orozquistas*, participating in the battle of Ojinaga in January 1914. Thereafter he continued his career as a professional soldier.[90] In 1914, when the United States seized the Mexican port of Veracruz, Richardson served briefly in an intelligence capacity with the American occupation forces. In September 1914, he went to Canada and enlisted in the elite Princess Patricia's Canadian Light Infantry Regiment as a machine gunner. By January 1915, the regiment was in Belgium fighting the Germans. During the second battle of Ypres, Richardson, on May 4, 1915, suffered severe shrapnel wounds. After a lengthy convalescence he returned to service, this time as a captain in the 97th Battalion of the Canadian Expeditionary Force. He subsequently transferred to the Royal Naval Air Service, during which time he flew patrols over the North Sea and served as a flight instructor in England. But in 1918 he again transferred, this time to the U.S. Army Signal Corps as a pilot. By the end of World War I he commanded an aerial gunnery school in France. He was discharged in 1919.

Richardson's postwar career included a dizzying variety of jobs. He was a prospector in Canada, explored for minerals in Honduras, oil in Guatemala, and mahogany in southern Mexico. He was also an operative for the Burns Detective Agency in New Orleans, where in 1922 he was acquitted of murder after shooting a man in self-defense. Richardson then became a realtor in Florida and Washington, D.C., did a stint as a police reporter for the *Chicago Herald-Examiner*, was a prohibition agent in New York City, managed a gold mine in Mexico in 1930, was a roustabout in Tyler, Texas, and worked in mines in Washington and Colorado. As the Depression intensified, Richardson's fortunes declined further. He spent 1933 working in Albuquerque in low-paying jobs. He then moved back to New Orleans and scratched out a living at various endeavors, including writing articles for pulp magazines.

But with World War II, Richardson's situation improved markedly. In 1941 he returned to military service as intelligence officer in the Eastern Procurement

District, then became an air inspector and a base commander in Colorado. He also served briefly in the Aleutian Islands. On January 13, 1946, he was discharged from the army with the rank of lieutenant colonel.

Again, the postwar years were anticlimactic. Richardson spent the last three years of his life around Lamar, Missouri, as a door-to-door salesman of household appliances. He died in Springfield, Missouri, on April 22, 1949, virtually forgotten—a sad end for a remarkable larger-than-life figure.[91]

Unlike Dreben, who abandoned the doomed Orozco rebellion, Victor Ochoa intensified his efforts to replace Colonel Cástulo Herrera as chief ammunition smuggler. Among other things, he planned to get Herrera court-martialed by Orozco and, hopefully, shot. To this end, Ochoa intended to use Gresh, his trusted right-hand man, as a witness against Herrera.[92] Ochoa claimed he'd uncovered a plot by Herrera to defect to the *maderistas*, post bond in El Paso to placate the American authorities, recruit men locally, and then use them to attack the rebels in Juárez. Ochoa instructed Gresh to go to Juárez and get a job as Herrera's chauffeur and then when Herrera started for El Paso to have him arrested and jailed.[93] Ochoa also gave Gresh a letter to deliver to Orozco denouncing Herrera as a traitor to the rebel cause. Gresh promptly took it to the Bureau office, where it was opened and translated, then took the letter to Juárez and delivered it to Orozco as instructed.[94]

Ochoa's machinations succeeded—at least in part. He wasn't able to get Cástulo Herrera court martialed and executed, but he did undermine Herrera to the point that General Orozco ordered Herrera and his operatives to the battle front. On July 18, an ecstatic Victor Ochoa replaced Herrera as chief ammunition smuggler for the rebels—with Gresh as his assistant.[95]

Agent Ross commented that "Ochoa stated to Gresh that he himself could not afford to appear in any smuggling operations. This is exactly in line with Ochoa's schemes to play safe himself and let the other fellow do the dirty work." Ochoa enthusiastically outlined his plan of operations to Gresh. Three of Abe Molina's former operatives now worked for Ochoa. They had agreed to lure Molina's current watcher away from Krakauer, Zork and Moye during the noon hour when the warehouse was closed. Ochoa had arranged with Krakauer to deliver a substantial amount of ammunition to Gresh, who would haul it to a downtown furniture store, whose proprietor agreed to conceal it in his storehouse. From there, Gresh and his associates, each accompanied by an attractive female, would drive buggies carrying 5,000 rounds past the military camp to the island, where they would unload. Ochoa also had an alternative plan: to have the ammunition transported to the home of a personally recruited associate, Roberto Limón, who would see to smuggling it into Mexico. Unbeknownst to Ochoa, Limón was also a Bureau informant. The agency had Ochoa covered whichever scheme he chose.[96]

Victor Ochoa's elation was short lived, for Orozco was now unwilling or unable to continue funding Ochoa's network, even though Ochoa and Gresh went to Juárez and pleaded with him to do so. And Krakauer, Zork and Moye had no intention of extending credit to the *orozquistas*; until and unless they replenished the funds deposited with the firm, no more ammunition would be forthcoming.[97] But even if Krakauer had agreed to provide the ammunition the plan wouldn't have worked—not only was Gresh a Bureau informant but so was Limón. As if this weren't enough, Limón was also a secret agent of the Mexican government.[98]

Orozco informed Ochoa that if, for example, General José Inés Salazar wanted ammunition smuggled, Salazar could put up the money himself. Orozco wouldn't contribute a single cent. Orozco's attitude resulted in part from an attempt to dump him as leader of the failing rebellion and replace him with Emilio Vázquez Gómez. Under this new leadership, General Salazar would become commander of the rebel forces, in which capacity he hoped to get a new lease on life by opening a major campaign in the neighboring state of Sonora.[99] Victor Ochoa was deeply involved in this conspiracy. All he could do now was to pin his hopes on Salazar, who was currently in Casas Grandes.

Ochoa's problems were not limited to matters of ammunition. He was furious to learn that he'd been duped. He had been paying one T. C. Cabney (alias J. Harris) $30 a week—recently reduced to $15 because of the *orozquistas*' troubles—for information, Cabney being a Bureau of Investigation agent. Agent Ross decided to ruin Ochoa's day by having informant Gresh take Ochoa to the federal building, leave him in the lobby, go up to the Bureau office, and on returning inform Ochoa that he'd talked with the three agents assigned to El Paso, and Cabney wasn't one of them. Once Ochoa recovered from the shock of realizing that Cabney had been playing him for a sucker, it dawned on him that Cabney was probably an operative of the Thiel Detective Service. Ochoa had seen Cabney going into that office but had thought nothing of it at the time.[100] Predictably, Ochoa informed Gresh that Cabney knew too much about him and "that the only thing to do was to have Cabney put out of the way permanently."[101] As with Ochoa's other death threats, which Gresh would presumably be assigned to carry out, nothing came of this call to have Cabney removed. And Ochoa was unaware that Cabney was really a double agent working for Abe Molina and was at the same time an informant for the Bureau.[102]

While waiting for General Salazar to return to Juárez and hopefully provide funds for arms smuggling, Ochoa decided to raise some quick cash by means of a kidnapping. He rented a house in Juárez, and he, Gresh, and Flavio Sandoval, the gang's secretary, would lure a wealthy *juarense* from a gambling den to it and hold him for ransom. The details were still to be worked out. Worried that things were getting out of hand, Agent Ross arranged with the El Paso police to have Sandoval arrested on a vagrancy charge "in case this action is necessary to prevent carrying out the scheme, as it is impossible to allow Gresh to take any active part in a scheme of this kind."[103]

For good measure the Bureau decided to have Victor Ochoa arrested, along with Flavio Sandoval, José Trujillo, the gang's treasurer, and T. C. Cabney, charging them with conspiring to export munitions of war (to General Salazar): "They are an organized band of bandits, and are organized for no other purpose than to rob and steal and do any other illegal act they are able to accomplish, for money."[104]

Ochoa's arrest occurred, fittingly enough, at that hotbed of conspiracy, the Sheldon Hotel, on July 20, while he was chatting with Sam Dreben and other colorful characters. Ochoa informed the authorities that "I am a nice man. Ask anybody, they will all tell you that I am a nice man. I came to El Paso to die. To die, remember." And he announced to the U.S. attorney: "[Y]ou are not going to send me to the penitentiary either." He was jailed in default of a $3,000 bond. On the way to the county jail Ochoa claimed that Orozco had been executing a federal for every rebel arrested in El Paso. "I guess he will kill about a dozen for me," he blustered.[105] Ochoa's bond was later reduced to $1,000 on July 30, however, because at the preliminary hearing the government presented only one witness, the Mexican government agent Roberto Limón, as it had decided it was content merely to establish the element of conspiracy by having Limón claim he'd gathered the evidence against Ochoa and the others. The Bureau did not want to reveal Gresh's role by having him testify at this time. Ochoa was thus spared a major shock.[106] Predictably, Ochoa wanted Gresh to kill Limón for him.[107]

Besides arresting Ochoa and his associates, the authorities seized a wealth of documents. Bureau of Investigation agents went to Sandoval's house and secured a tin box in which he kept his valuable papers, including "the wills written out by members of the gang at the time they organized recently at Ochoa's home."[108] Moreover, informant Gresh said he knew where Mrs. Ochoa had hidden her husband's papers at the time of his arrest; she had told Gresh they were very incriminating. Agent Ross, together with informants Gresh and Snyder went to the Ochoa residence at 2 a.m. to carry out a "black bag" job. Gresh entered and secured the papers, which were hidden at the bottom of a bucket of sugar in the pantry.[109]

Remarkably, Gresh's cover remained intact. In August, he called on Mrs. Ochoa, who received him cordially. Her husband planned to use Gresh as a courier to carry letters to General Orozco. If Gresh was satisfied that he was still under cover, the Bureau wanted him to go to Juárez and try to learn how much ammunition was getting over and who was smuggling it.[110]

Ochoa's arrest had stemmed in part from his involvement in the Vázquez Gómez movement, which was still struggling to get organized.

CHAPTER 7

Plot and Counterplot

A *vazquista* junta that included Victor Ochoa was organized in El Paso in late June. The junta was, however, thoroughly penetrated, for Abe Molina had arranged for one of its members, Doctor José S. Saenz, to be an informant. He'd be known as "Mr. Sterling" in his written reports, which he sent to Molina and to the Bureau. Saenz was a local physician but was also well known in Douglas, Arizona, where several months earlier he'd been financial agent for Vázquez Gómez.[1] The doctor did provide useful intelligence: Emilio Vázquez Gómez received his mail at P.O. Box 1068 and at 113 City Street, San Antonio, under the name "W. Castor." Paulino Martínez, head of the El Paso junta, resided under cover at 816 East Missouri Street and got his mail at P.O. Box 918 under the names of "J. E. Hernández" and "Mr. Letcher." In addition, Martínez sometimes received mail addressed to "Luis González" and "Mrs. C. G. Martinez." Lauro Aguirre, the old *magonista* militant, received mail from Vázquez Gómez at P.O. Box 711, El Paso. According to Saenz, Vázquez Gómez enclosed communications in this mail for other *vazquistas*, which Aguirre then distributed.

Regarding the proposed rebel military campaign in Sonora, Saenz said that General Orozco had agreed to provide Manuel Mascarenas Jr., a wealthy and well-connected native of Sonora, eight hundred to one thousand men for the enterprise. The point of attack would be the town of Sahuaripa, whose government officials sympathized with the *vazquista* cause. Saenz also claimed that Colonel Reyna, in command at Nogales, Sonora, had agreed to deliver the town to Mascarenas for fifty thousand pesos. Mascarenas was to command *vazquista* forces in that state and to serve as provisional governor as well. He was receiving his mail in Nogales, Arizona, under the name "José Camberes." Juan B. Larrazolo, who at present got his mail at 814 South Hill Street, El Paso, under the name of "Antonio Sánchez" was to be secretary of state in Sonora.[2]

In preparation for the campaign, Mascarenas and Larrazolo came to El Paso and stayed in room 37 of the Alberta Hotel annex. In light of his status as the rebel military commander and provisional governor, Mascarenas wanted to look good. He made the acquaintance in the Sheldon Hotel bar of a lieutenant in the 22nd U.S. Infantry Regiment, part of the El Paso garrison, and mentioned that he wanted a riding suit made. Mascarenas asked to be introduced to the regimental tailor. The lieutenant was happy to oblige. Not only did Mascarenas have the tailor make him two uniforms, but he casually informed the tailor that he was in the market for an additional fifteen hundred uniforms. The tailor immediately informed the authorities, and Mascarenas was arrested on July 11 at the Stanton Street bridge and charged with conspiring to export munitions—two coats and four pairs of trousers—uniforms being considered munitions of war, as was everything used by an army except food and ordinary clothing. A search of his person and hotel room produced a *vazquista* cipher, Mascarenas's commission as a lieutenant colonel in the national liberating army, and his appointment as provisional governor of Sonora by authority of Emilio Vázquez Gómez and the revolutionary junta, signed by Paulino Martínez. The Bureau also moved to secure from the local Western Union office copies of all telegrams Mascarenas had sent and received in El Paso prior to his arrest. Mascarenas had no difficulty in posting a $750 bond, which he then forfeited by fleeing to Juárez.[3]

A few days later Saenz reported to the Bureau that a provisional *vazquista* government had been organized in El Paso, and that Braulio Hernández, sometime Chihuahua secretary of state, had just arrived with substantial funds supplied by "certain Boston capitalists," who unfortunately he didn't name. As for the rebel government being organized, Emilio Vázquez Gómez was provisional president and the members of his cabinet named so far were:

Paulino Martínez	Minister of War and Marine
Dr. José S. Saenz	Sub-Secretary of War and Marine [and informant for Abe Molina and the Bureau]
Braulio Hernández	Minister of Justice
Delio Moreno Cantón	Minister of Foreign Relations
Dr. Policarpo Rueda	Minister of Finance
David de la Fuente	Commander of Chief of the Army

Juntas were to be organized in El Paso and Douglas. Saenz would head the one in Douglas. The good doctor asserted that the movement had the support of rebel generals José Inés Salazar, Antonio Rojas, Francisco del Toro, and Luis Fernández. But General Emilio Campa had declared that he was an anarchist and wouldn't support either side yet. (He finally joined the rebel movement.) According to Saenz, the plan was to execute General Orozco shortly after the rebel force left Casas Grandes for Sonora. Manuel Mascarenas was to be executed as well, presumably because he was a bungler, and a new provisional governor of Sonora appointed. (In the event, neither execution occurred.)

Saenz further informed Agent Louis Ross that Paulino Martínez had moved to 1508 Wyoming Street and that he'd prepared a cover story for his revolutionary activities: he had various letters and documents dated at different points in Mexico in the hope that if arrested he could prove that he wasn't in the United States at the time. Saenz stated that Martínez had been in El Paso the whole time except for a few trips to San Antonio to confer with Vázquez Gómez. The doctor said he could give the Bureau the dates of these trips.[4]

When it came to the matter of security, the *vazquista* movement leaked like a sieve. Saenz was providing the Bureau with a steady stream of intelligence. Abe Molina declared that he'd arranged to get all correspondence received by Jesús Navarro, alias "Andrés Avila," who was also connected with the *vazquistas*, and he promised to inform Agent Ross of their content.[5] Francisco Pérez, a representative of the Douglas junta, was really a *maderista* sympathizer. He not only furnished the Bureau office in El Paso with information, but when dispatched with letters for Vázquez Gómez and Paulino Martínez he brought them to the Bureau office, where they were translated. Pérez then delivered the letters as instructed.[6] One of Abe Molina's operatives, Alberto Estrada, had ingratiated himself with the El Paso *vazquista* junta. Also, the Mexican government agent Lee Hall was working his way into the rebels' confidence—Ochoa's associate T. C. Cabney claimed to be the intelligence chief for the junta, and he had offered Hall a job.[7]

And Harvey Phillips reappeared. It will be recalled that in 1911 during the Madero revolution he was an agent for Madero's attorney, Sherburne Hopkins, who sent Phillips to El Paso to arrange for the smuggling of munitions. The Bureau of Investigation eventually tracked down Phillips, who pleaded guilty, was fined $100 and costs. Now in 1912, still working for Hopkins on behalf of the Madero regime, Phillips gathered intelligence on rebel arms procurers in New York. But at the same time he was also a "special informant" for the Bureau of Investigation.[8] Phillips later went from Washington, D.C., to San Antonio to infiltrate the *vazquista* movement. He was armed with credentials from Juan Pedro Didapp, a prominent *vazquista*, who had been Mexican consul general in Istanbul, Turkey, Santander, Spain, and Norfolk, Virginia, during the preceding fifteen years, and was now the Washington, D.C., representative of the Mexican revolutionists. Didapp wrote a glowing recommendation for Phillips and urged Vázquez Gómez and his associates, among them Doctor Policarpo Rueda, to admit Phillips to their councils. Phillips provided the Bureau with the letters and ciphered telegrams that he received from Didapp.[9] But the Bureau didn't trust Phillips. On September 12, 1912, the chief of the Bureau telegraphed the agent in charge in San Antonio: "Suggest you have as little to do with Phillips as possible." (The chief later changed his mind—in 1915, Phillips was a special employee of the Bureau.)[10]

Just as the expedition to Sonora was about to depart, a wave of arrests threw the *vazquista* movement into disarray. Emilio Vázquez Gómez and several of his companions were arrested in San Antonio on July 20, the authorities seizing among other documents Vázquez Gómez's personal cipher. Testimony at his preliminary hearing revealed a plan to overthrow Orozco as leader of the rebels and replace him with Antonio Rojas.[11] On July 21, arrests were made in El Paso. Among those apprehended was Paulino Martínez, head of the local junta and currently using the alias "Luis González." A cipher and a number of documents were seized from his person and home and later translated by the Bureau.[12] José Saenz, secretary of the local junta, was also taken into custody. A search of his house turned up a trove of documents, letters, and telegrams. In default of $3,000 bonds each, both men were jailed on federal charges of conspiracy to instigate a military expedition. Saenz could easily have posted bond but chose to stay in jail for five days, to avoid suspicion. Both Saenz and Martínez were bound over to the grand jury, which "no billed" them.[13] Saenz was not only a useful informant; he would also be a very valuable government witness when the *vazquista* cases came to trial.[14]

J. Evaristo Hernández also came under suspicion, the Bureau maintaining surveillance on his mail received at P.O. Box 918. In the hunt for revolutionary documents, Texas Ranger Charles Webster and Abe Molina raided Hernández's place of business, where *El Eco del Comercio*, a *vazquista* newspaper, was printed. What Webster and Molina seized was a mass of torn-up papers, which Ranger Webster delivered to Agent Ross, who undertook the unenviable task of trying to paste the papers back together. After considerable labor, Ross discovered to his disgust that the material consisted only of copy for the newspaper. The one item of interest was an anti-Orozco piece written and signed by Rueda.[15]

A ray of hope for the rebels appeared in August in the person of Senator Albert B. Fall of New Mexico.[16] Although from New Mexico, Fall was sometimes referred to as the "senator from El Paso" because of his strong ties to that city. In 1907, for instance, he built a most imposing mansion at 1725 Arizona Street.[17] Fall had had close ties to the Díaz administration. He now urged that the United States recognize Orozco's belligerency and mediate between rebel factions and the Madero administration.[18] With Senator Fall due to arrive in El Paso shortly, on August 20 Numa Buchoz and Bernard Schuster, real estate agents who were strong rebel sympathizers and were suspected of smuggling arms to the rebels in the vicinity of Ysleta, wired the senator: "If necessary we can get both Orozco and Vazquez Gomez for a conference with you."[19] The senator was certainly interested, and allegedly Orozco even delayed the evacuation of Juárez for a few days in hopes of conferring with him.[20] Fall didn't arrive until early September, but he was anxious to meet with prominent *vazquistas*, although he told Paulino Martínez that he didn't want to be seen speaking with them and wanted them to come to him. Fall wanted to interview Ricardo Gómez Robelo, but he was in the county jail on charges of neutrality violations. So, elaborate arrangements were made by the Bureau and the U.S. marshal to take Gómez Robelo out of jail whenever Fall requested.[21] Buchoz and Schuster made the arrangements for the secret meetings, at which the informant José Saenz was present. According to the doctor, Fall was working on a scheme to bring about peace in Mexico and profit for himself—Fall wanted to unite Vázquez Gómez and Orozco against Madero, believing that that would convince Madero of the necessity of negotiating. By acting as peacemaker, Fall hoped to secure some valuable concessions for himself. Thus Fall was working for U.S. recognition of the rebels merely as part of his larger plan.[22] Fall's scheme as reported didn't come to fruition, but the senator continued to interest himself in the affairs of Mexico.[23]

Fall was a prominent member of a six-man subcommittee of the Senate Committee on Foreign Relations, chaired by Senator William Alden Smith of Michigan. The subcommittee's brief was to investigate "whether any interests in the United States have been or are now engaged in inciting rebellion in Cuba and Mexico." Smith and Fall conducted hearings in El Paso, Los Angeles, Washington, D.C., and New Orleans. When they were in El Paso at the Sheldon Hotel taking testimony that was initially secret, they were continually under surveillance by Mexican intelligence to learn who was testifying and if possible of what their testimony consisted.[24] John Barbrick, former secret agent for Consul Enrique Llorente, worked as an investigator in New Orleans for the Senate subcommittee.[25]

Meanwhile, the *vazquistas*' problems had continued to mount. General David de la Fuente, who'd defected from Orozco to become commander of Vázquez Gómez's forces, arrived in El Paso from San Antonio together with Ricardo Gómez Robelo, another prominent *vazquista*, in mid-August. De la Fuente was promptly arrested on a federal warrant out of San Antonio charging him with involvement in the Vázquez Gómez conspiracy. He was apprehended at the home of Paulino Martínez, 1508 Montana Street, and the authorities seized a cipher that de la Fuente was carrying.[26] Gómez Robelo, for whom there was also a warrant, abandoned his luggage in his room at the Linden Hotel and crossed over into Juárez. The Bureau maintained surveillance over the luggage in hopes of arresting him should he return.[27] Gómez Robelo was imprudent enough to return to El Paso, and the Bureau had him arrested at the international bridge. He was confined in the county jail pending arraignment. However, at his hearing before the U.S. commissioner on September 3, Gómez Robelo was released for lack of evidence.[28] As for de la Fuente, he posted a $2,500 bond for appearance before a grand jury at its October term. He was released on the neutrality charge but was immediately rearrested on an extradition warrant from the Mexican government charging him with bank robbery in Chihuahua—the old forty-day ploy. Off he went to jail.[29]

The authorities might have been neutralizing the leadership of the Vázquez Gómez movement, but rebel representatives continued their efforts to secure ammunition. For example, Shelton-Payne was approached by a man wanting to purchase 30,000 rounds of .30-.30 ammunition. He asked that the goods be repacked and delivered somewhere in El Paso. The firm had only 8,000 rounds on hand, so the man said he'd return when they could fill the entire order. The Bureau learned of this from the assistant manager of Shelton-Payne as part of its routine monitoring of ammunition sales. The manager's cooperation went beyond providing information; he even offered to let a Bureau agent drive the delivery wagon if the deal materialized.[30] A few days later Shelton-Payne sold 15,000 Mauser cartridges to a customer who wanted them repacked and delivered but gave no destination. He paid for the ammunition and said he'd provide delivery instructions later. The firm immediately informed the Bureau of this transaction.[31] The firm of Krakauer, Zork and Moye was less forthcoming. The Bureau received word that Julius Krakauer had traveled to Albuquerque, New Mexico, around July 3 and was thought to have made a deal with the rebels to sell 338 cases of arms and 60 cases of cartridges consigned to Krakauer that were scheduled to come by rail from Galveston. The Bureau agent who investigated went to the store and learned that Krakauer had returned to El Paso. Later that day a fully loaded railroad car with the 338 cases of arms and 60 cases of cartridges was switched to the Krakauer warehouse and unloaded. The Bureau was convinced these munitions were for the *vazquistas*.[32]

But the federal authorities moved cautiously against the Krakauers. The assistant U.S. attorney was adamantly opposed to seeking an indictment prematurely because it would require a public hearing and force the government to present its evidence, or at least its witnesses. In his opinion the Krakauers "are shrewd and unscrupulous and will not hesitate to go to any extremes to get these witnesses out of the way." He preferred to wait until the grand jury was in session.[33] The federal grand jury did indict Robert, Julius, and Adolph Krakauer for conspiracy to export and ship munitions to Mexico. They were arrested on October 8 and arraigned shortly thereafter. They posted a $5,000 bond each, and were quickly released.[34] The Krakauers then hired the Western Detective Agency, run by Maurice Gresh and Virgil Snyder, the Bureau's crack informants, to learn the names of potential witnesses so that allegedly they could try to bribe them. Western supplied the Bureau with the names of these seven persons, commenting that they'd likely be desirable witnesses for the prosecution.[35]

On August 1, Shelton-Payne received 100,000 cartridges by freight and express for which the rebels had already paid. The *vazquistas* instructed the firm to ship 50,000 rounds the next day by freight to one "Frank Jenkins" in Columbus, New Mexico, and to send the bill of lading to Juárez. They also wanted Shelton-Payne to repack the ammunition in plain boxes, billing it as hardware. Shelton-Payne refused to do so and assisted the Bureau in surveilling the shipment.[36] The Bureau immediately notified Major Sedgwick Rice, the commander in Columbus, who made arrangements to guard the shipment upon its arrival. A party of rebels was waiting across the border in Palomas to receive it, and on August 12, they crossed into the United States to pick up the ammunition. A brisk firefight ensued. One rebel and one cavalryman were wounded, and the army seized the ammunition.[37]

Among the most proficient smugglers in El Paso were the brothers Abelino and Sabino Guaderrama, whom we have already encountered. Their bond for attempting to smuggle 10,000 rounds in June 1912 had been set at $3,000 each, since that had been their second arrest. They readily furnished the bond.[38] Not only that, but they boldly offered to become informants for the Bureau against smuggling operations provided they were paid $5 a day for their services and provided further that Agent Ross would use his influence to secure the release of 67,000 rounds of ammunition and 390 rifles now stored at Fort Bliss, which had been seized from the brothers at the time of their previous arrest. Ross told them he could do nothing to help recover their munitions and he suggested that they contact Abe Molina with regard to hiring out as informants. Ross "later advised Molina not to employ these crooks under any circumstances as it is inadvisable to employ Ammunition Smugglers to turn up these cases for us, especially under the circumstances surrounding this Guaderrama gang. It is evident that they wish to use their employment as a cover for further smuggling operations."[39]

The Guaderramas and their fellow defendants, Isabel Larrazolo and Longino González, waived their preliminary hearing and were bound over to the grand jury, each of the Guaderramas posting a $2,000 bond and their associates $750 each. When the case came to trial in October, Abelino Guaderrama and Longino González were found not guilty; a hung jury resulted for Sabino Guaderrama and Isabel Larrazolo. The case was continued.[40]

While the *vazquistas* were trying to move munitions to the west of El Paso for their Sonora campaign, the Guaderramas continued to supply the Red Flaggers in Juárez. On August 6 they crossed about 4,000 rounds near the smelter, apparently using the ruse of having shots fired from the Mexican bank of the Rio Grande to distract the American troops patrolling the river. They didn't get the whole shipment across, however, and in an effort to prevent their crossing the remainder the next night, the Bureau deployed four of Molina's men along the river. A complication was that a Bureau informant reported that at least one of the soldiers guarding that sector was in cahoots with the smugglers.[41] However, Agent Ross conferred with Abe Molina and decided there was enough evidence to charge Sabino Guaderrama, José Cerros, and Israel Rangel, who were then arrested. Since this was his third offense, Guaderrama's bond was set at $5,000, which he posted. The others' bonds were $500 each.

The government's case was that Guaderrama had hired Cerros, Rangel, and a certain Juana Carmona to help him smuggle, and that Guaderrama had suborned two U.S. soldiers. Juana Carmona had agreed to testify for the prosecution and thus wasn't charged. She alleged that on the night of August 6, she, Cerros, and Rangel, helped by two soldiers, crossed the 4,000 cartridges between Old Fort Bliss and the smelter pump house. The woman became dissatisfied with her treatment and after crossing her share of the ammunition brought it back across the river and hid it in a woodpile near her home at the smelter. The authorities went with her to the woodpile but found nothing; they speculated that one of the defendants had spirited the ammunition away. Carmona claimed that ammunition had been crossed many times with the connivance of the two soldiers, but she was unable to identify them—it seems she was an alcoholic and Guaderrama had been keeping her drunk. A Texas Ranger was detailed to put her in jail until she sobered up in hopes that she could then point out the alleged soldier confederates of Guarderrama's.[42] The government felt it had a strong case—not just Carmona's testimony but also that of two eyewitnesses, Molina's men—to the crossing of the ammunition. But a furious Agent Ross reported that on August 14 when Guaderrama and his colleagues had their preliminary hearing before the U.S. commissioner, the witness denied knowledge of the smuggling: "Our witnesses appeared to have been bought off by the defense and threw us down with the exception of Juana Carmona; her testimony, however, was uncorroborated, and the defendants were released."[43] The Guaderramas not only enjoyed this legal triumph but were evidently planning to expand their business by dealing with rebel representatives in Arizona. On August 20, Abelino arrived in Douglas and registered at the Roy Hotel.[44]

What may have accounted for this development was that the Guaderrama brothers' Juárez customers were disappearing. The federal army occupied the city of Chihuahua on July 7, and everyone knew that it would be Juárez's turn next. Orozco, in retreat, reached Juárez on July 10. During his short stay there he, among other things, tried to make some quick cash for the journey. An American movie company, the Gaumont Company of Flushing, New York, had dispatched a cameraman to El Paso to try to film Orozco and to take scenes of Juárez. However, the cameraman telegraphed the company that Orozco had demanded $1,000 to pose with his troops. The Gaumont Company not only refused to pay but indignantly informed the State Department: "It has occurred to us that this telegram gives a fairly clear insight into the character of the Mexican Revolutionists and the telegram might be of interest to the Department."[45]

On August 16 the *orozquistas* carried out their long-anticipated evacuation of Juárez. Orozco and his forces left on two trains heading south on the Mexican Central Railroad. He'd sent a message to General E. Z. Steever advising that at 1 a.m. on August 16 he'd evacuate and asking Steever to keep anyone from crossing to Juárez to prevent looting and disorder. Steever then ordered that the international bridges be closed as of 1 a.m. on the sixteenth.[46]

Madero's army moved cautiously into Juárez on the afternoon of August 20 to the acclaim of the local citizenry and of some twelve hundred Mexicans from El Paso who, with a band at their head, marched over to Juárez to welcome the federals. Some twelve hundred soldiers occupied the town while patrols were sent out to locate *orozquista* bands along the border.[47] Yet the federal army seemed in no hurry to finish off the rebels. The American consul in Chihuahua commented: "I regret to say the campaign seems a perfect exhibition of inefficiency and incompetence."[48] Even so, there was one benefit for the American authorities. They entered into an agreement with the federal army occupying Juárez under which the army would apprehend those for whom there were outstanding warrants in the United States and deliver them at the international bridges as undesirables. The army would notify the Americans so that a U.S. marshal could be waiting.[49] And the commanders of the Mexican federal army in Juárez, General Victoriano Huerta and his successors Joaquín Téllez and Fernando Trucy Aubert, frequently crossed over to El Paso in uniform in their staff cars, complete with flags flying, to confer with Sommerfeld and Llorente in the Sheldon Hotel. Sommerfeld disingenuously maintained that they came only to dine because there wasn't a decent restaurant in Juárez.[50]

The departure of the *orozquistas* had major repercussions not just for the smuggling community but also for the Bureau of Investigation. H. A. Thompson, the agent in charge of the San Antonio office, reported that now the Bureau would have to shift its attention along the border to the east and west of Juárez and unfortunately would have to rely on its own meager resources because the Madero government was virtually dismantling its intelligence apparatus in the El Paso–Juárez area. "This will make it extremely difficult for the reason that heretofore we have been able to call upon them at any time for a Mexican whom we could place at a designated point to furnish information for us and this has helped us materially in preventing the exportation at El Paso."[51]

The cash-strapped Bureau of Investigation cut expenses as quickly as possible. Thompson, who'd been directing operations in El Paso, declared on August 21 that there was no further need for the Bureau to have a stenographer in El Paso, and Thompson himself returned to his home station in San Antonio.[52] At the outbreak of the Orozco rebellion, the Bureau's presence in El Paso had been limited to the resident agent, Louis Ross, and so it was now again.

With Orozco's rebellion on its last legs, the U.S. government could finally address a rather delicate matter—the flagrant violation of the neutrality laws by Consul Llorente. For months he had been sending teams of saboteurs into Chihuahua and had been recruiting men in and around El Paso for military service in Mexico. The American authorities hadn't exactly turned a blind eye to these activities; they'd been slowly and deliberately gathering evidence against Llorente. The U.S. attorney wanted to make absolutely sure of an ironclad case before seeking an indictment.[53] This attitude had infuriated the *orozquistas* and their sympathizers in El Paso, who complained bitterly about the "unneutral" way the neutrality laws were being enforced—zealously against those opposing Madero and gingerly against his regime, which the United States recognized as the legitimate government of Mexico. In July the State Department asked the Mexican government to stop Llorente's recruiting activities immediately. The Madero administration replied that Mexico had been scrupulously observing the neutrality laws and quoted Llorente's denial that he or any of his agents had been involved in recruiting, inviting the United States to conduct an investigation and declaring that "if any person has violated the neutrality laws I have ever been the first to become active in punishing him." Llorente dismissed the allegations as propaganda by Madero's enemies but later amended his blanket denial by alluding to the sabotage operations: "The only thing it [the consulate] has done is to accept the service of several persons, never more than four at a time, for the performance of certain secret commissions on Mexican territory, but they have not been armed or equipped here." He blasted Tom Lea and yellow journalism for the scurrilous accusations.[54] And of course Sommerfeld also stoutly denied any recruiting: "[W]e did not ever hire any men for the purpose of going and carrying arms to defend the constituted Government against the rebels—never."[55]

Consul Llorente was understandably concerned by the knowledge that the Bureau of Investigation was developing a case against him. Reportedly he planned to avenge himself against Agent Ross, who'd been gathering the incriminating information. Llorente hired the soldier of fortune Captain Emile Charpentier to bribe Ross and arrange for Ross to be caught with the money on his person.[56] Although Llorente's plan was never implemented because Charpentier told Ross about it, the relations between the *maderistas* and the Bureau of Investigation were becoming less cordial as the Bureau moved to apply the neutrality laws to Madero's followers. When Agent Ross asked the help of the rebels' attorney, Tom Lea, in gathering evidence against the consul, Lea responded enthusiastically: "He said that he would do so; that he would go to Juarez and find out for me just what they had, and thought that he could be of material assistance to me in this matter; that it was really a pleasure for him to do this, as he knows that the Consul is nothing but a crook."[57] In fact, Lea said "he did positively know the Mexican Consul to be a dirty double-crossing scoundrel and that he could bribe him in one minute."[58] Perhaps, but if so one wonders why Lea hadn't already bribed the consul. Ross also tried to persuade Jesús Morales Guevara, who had been the Orozco consul in El Paso, to give evidence of recruiting by Llorente.[59] Morales Guevara said he had three former employees of Llorente's ready in Juárez to be witnesses but they feared prosecution if they came to El Paso to testify, for they had smuggled ammunition for Abe Molina. The Bureau assured him the witnesses wouldn't be arrested.[60]

Consul Llorente didn't help his cause any by the way he treated Emile Charpentier. As in the case of Peter Aiken, Llorente reneged on his end of the arrangement with mercenaries. This time, however, Llorente's chicanery produced a sensation, because an infuriated Charpentier went public in the press. Texas Rangers, acting on Bureau instructions, arrested Charpentier in El Paso on July 8 on a charge of violating the neutrality laws. Charpentier steadfastly refused to give the Bureau a statement. Unable to post a $1,500 bond (and Llorente refused to post it for him), he was remanded to the county jail. From there, a very bitter Charpentier decided to tell all, informing the press that if he were guilty then so was Consul Llorente. According to Charpentier, he and the others had entered into a written contract with Llorente, witnessed by Sommerfeld and Alberto Madero, the president's uncle, in the Mexican consulate, by which Llorente agreed to pay the mercenaries $500 a month each plus expenses. The contract included a clause whereby the adventurers waived their rights as American citizens should they be captured either in Mexico or by American authorities. (Charpentier had no problem with this stipulation—he was French.) The mercenaries solemnly promised not to involve Llorente and to shield him in every way. But since Llorente hadn't kept his end of the agreement by paying the men, Charpentier felt amply justified in revealing the plot.[61] When Charpentier and his confederates were tried in October for conspiracy to export munitions the judge held that the government hadn't proved a conspiracy, and he instructed a verdict of not guilty.[62]

As the authorities continued to build their case against Consul Llorente, Felix Sommerfeld became worried because one Joaquín Alvarez, who had been vice consul under Llorente, was reportedly prepared to testify against Llorente regarding the recruitment of men for the Madero army. As part of his duties, Alvarez had handled the records and the cash of the consulate, and his testimony would be devastating.[63] In the event, Alvarez refused to testify. Many potential witnesses in Juárez were afraid to come to El Paso, fearing that Llorente would have them arrested on extradition warrants.

The Bureau had mixed results in dealing with potential witnesses on the American side of the Rio Grande. Someone who was most eager to help build the case against Llorente was Victor Ochoa. He called on the Bureau on August 21, immediately after his release on bond from the county jail, to offer the names of persons who could provide evidence both of Llorente's hiring of mercenaries and of his recruiting activities.[64] At the same time, Agent Ross, accompanied by Mexican agent Lee Hall, went to the hamlet of Tornillo downriver from El Paso to interview witnesses, using a certain Mr. Walbridge as an intermediary: "We went to the ranch of Mr. Walbridge for the purpose of getting him to accompany us to talk to these witnesses, as it is useless for a stranger to try to do anything with the Mexicans in that section by reason of the fact that they are all thieves and crooks themselves and are exceedingly suspicious of strangers."[65] On a subsequent occasion Ross took Abe Molina with him to interview witnesses in Tornillo and Fabens.[66]

The pressure on Llorente increased when on September 27, the El Paso law firm of Goldstein and Miller, with offices in the American National Bank building, wrote to Secretary of State Philander C. Knox denouncing the consul's enlisting men for the Mexican Army, sending the Charpentier sabotage team into Chihuahua, attempting to coerce a jailed rebel, Felipe López, to perjure himself, and engaging in "malicious prosecution" by repeatedly employing the forty-day extradition technique.[67] Secretary of State Knox ordered a special investigation of these allegations. The Bureau took affidavits from men who'd been enlisted by Llorente's agents as well as from Felipe López. Charpentier's statement was already public record. As for "malicious prosecution," the Bureau reported that eight individuals had been charged with extraditable offenses by Llorente, who had made no effort to prove these charges while the accused languished in jail for forty days.[68] The Bureau concluded that Goldstein and Miller's allegations were pretty well substantiated.[69] Evidence was closing in on Consul Llorente.

Neutrality enforcement in El Paso received a stunning blow from federal judge T. S. Maxey on October 7. He was presiding over the case of *U.S. v. Arnulfo Chávez*, Chávez having been charged with exporting munitions, specifically with transporting rifle ammunition between two points in El Paso with the intent to export.[70] Chávez's attorney moved to quash the indictment on the grounds that since there had been no actual exportation, the indictment didn't charge an offense. To the consternation of the U.S. attorney and the Bureau, Judge Maxey held that indeed there must be an actual exportation in order to constitute an offense. He therefore quashed the indictment, stating that it was his opinion that in order to constitute an offense a person must actually transport to Mexico munitions of war. This devastating ruling affected not just the Chávez case but another fifteen to twenty-five federal cases pending in El Paso, the defendants in which had been apprehended just before crossing munitions into Mexico. During the day of October 7, all prisoners jailed in El Paso charged with neutrality offenses were arraigned and released on their own recognizance, except those charged with conspiracy to violate these laws, their cases being set for trial.

Attorneys for these defendants filed the same motion to quash the indictments as were filed in the case of Arnulfo Chávez. The government immediately notified Judge Maxey that it would appeal his ruling.[71]

A despondent agent in charge Thompson soon thereafter informed his superiors from San Antonio that rebels were becoming active in Chihuahua and Coahuila, and they were receiving quantities of ammunition from Texas, but Judge Maxey's ruling tied the Bureau's hands. The agency would of course attempt to apprehend smugglers in the very act of crossing munitions, but it currently had no agents assigned to the areas of greatest activity.[72]

Adding to Thompson's frustration, Sabino Guaderrama et al., charged with trying to smuggle in July 10,000 rounds of .30-.40 Winchester and 7-mm Mauser cartridges purchased from Krakauer to the *orozquistas* (when the firefight between two groups of peace officers was narrowly avoided), would be acquitted. The trial was set for October 16, and Judge Maxey held that the government hadn't clearly established the element of conspiracy and that therefore a verdict of acquittal would be approved. The Bureau agent complained that "it seems [the] Judge is against us in all these conspiracy cases."[73] Compounding the Bureau's chagrin, the Guaderrama brothers' attorney, P. E. Gardner, secured a court order for General Steever and the Bureau to release to the Guaderramas all of their munitions held at Fort Bliss because the grand jury had failed to return an indictment.[74]

On October 14, agent in charge H. A. Thompson wrote: "Every effort possible is being made here by persons under indictment and others in sympathy with the rebel cause to discredit all government officers connected [with] neutrality investigations. They are having these persons taken before the Senate Committee and examined evidently for this purpose, also for the purpose of showing [the] use [of] Mexican informants [in] connection therewith." Thompson stressed to his superiors that he needed more agents.[75] The Bureau reluctantly authorized Thompson to hire two or three informants on a temporary basis. Thompson quickly hired Ross's chief informant, the private detective Maurice Gresh, and former Bureau agent John W. Vann at a salary of $4 a day and necessary expenses when away from El Paso.[76] As an economy measure, however, their services were discontinued on October 31.[77]

Regarding Mexican government activity in El Paso, one prominent citizen complained in October to Senator Fall:

> I note your remarks this morning with reference to the actions of the Secret Service men and other employes [*sic*] of the Mexican Government as is being carried on now in El Paso. I believe I voice the sentiments of this city in most heartily approving of what you said. It seems to me that the battles of the Mexican revolution have been transferred from Mexican to American

> territory and any man that the Mexican Government wishes punished can be sentenced to forty days imprisonment at the will of Mr. Llorente from his castle on North Oregon Street. He seems to have more power in this community than Genl. Steever, Gov. Colquitt and Mayor Kelly combined. . . . I wonder what influence is being exercised over some of our Federal officials that allows this. . . . My sole object in writing this is to make a protest to you against the abuse of power by the Mexican officials in our city. I suppose you know that it is almost impossible for two gentlemen to stand in conversation in this town on the public streets without some spy quietly getting as close to them as possible to overhear and then misquote and garble such conversation. You are right, El Paso is being seriously damaged by the Mexican revolution in Mexico, but a great deal worse by the Mexican revolution in El Paso. I believe I represent the feelings of 90% of the American citizens in El Paso.[78]

Furthermore, there were disquieting allegations about Agent Ross. His superior thought very highly of him, writing in August that if the rebels attacked along the Arizona border he planned to send Ross to Douglas to assist the Bureau agent on the scene. "My purpose in sending Ross there is the fact that he is familiar with the Spanish language and is known to most of the Mexican informants along the border and [is] in their confidence and can secure more information for us than nearly any other Agent now available for this work."[79] However, evidence was mounting that Ross and his counterpart Abe Molina had been doing a brisk business on the side by selling and smuggling some of the munitions being seized.[80] There were, for example, accusations that arms had disappeared from the Bureau office, which was frequently overflowing with confiscated munitions. For example, seven canvas-wrapped trunks, each weighing 250 pounds and containing 4,000 cartridges, that *orozquista* agents had shipped by railway express from New Orleans to El Paso were stored in the office. One of the operatives had become disillusioned and had informed Lee Hall of Mexican government intelligence about the impending delivery to El Paso. When the trunks arrived on May 21, Bureau agents seized them.[81]

A disgruntled Bureau agent, C. D. Hebert, later testified that some of the rifles mysteriously disappeared, Agent Ross claiming that some scoundrel had broken in and stolen them, although there was no evidence of forced entry. One of the trunks of ammunition also vanished, and Ross allegedly said that Thompson had taken it to San Antonio with him. A skeptical Agent Hebert decided to investigate. He went to Shelton-Payne and learned not only that Ross had sold the firm 2,000 cartridges but that on July 24 he'd sold them 5 rifles, for $50. Hebert was shown the canceled check, endorsed by Ross, and Shelton-Payne allowed him to make a photograph of it.[82] Ross sold a total of 10 rifles, for $100, to Shelton-Payne, claiming that he'd found them abandoned.[83]

There was additional hard evidence of Ross's shady activities. He and Texas Ranger Charles Webster, who specialized in neutrality enforcement, had gone into business together. On April 17, 1912, they offered Julius Krakauer some ammunition, no questions asked. Krakauer bought 2,780 .30-.30 and 920 7-mm cartridges for $102.35. Webster being out of town, Ross went to get the payment. Krakauer wanted to pay by check, but Ross demanded cash. Krakauer paid cash but insisted that Ross sign a receipt, dated on April 18 and listing the ammunition sold and the price paid. Krakauer later produced the receipt and testified that he subsequently refused to purchase additional munitions that Ross and Webster offered him—on one occasion 30,000 cartridges.[84] Ross's ventures in private enterprise came to the attention of his superiors, who were not amused. The chief of the Bureau telegraphed the agent in charge on September 8: "Letter second received, advise Ross suspended until further notice will present matter to Attorney General Wednesday, utterly unable understand his action have him write me how he came to make sale in question."[85]

Interestingly enough, Ross continued performing his usual duties for several weeks thereafter. On September 22, for example, accompanied by two Madero intelligence operatives, one of them being Felix Sommerfeld, Ross personally arrested Juan Pedro Didapp, the prominent *vazquista*, on a warrant from San Antonio, in a downtown drugstore while Didapp was sipping lemonade and being interviewed by a local reporter, took him to the Bureau office for interrogation, then turned him over to the U.S. marshal for incarceration.[86] Then Ross "went to his room at the Angelus Hotel and secured his grips, which we went through, taking out a large number of documents which I read over and segregated. I did not have an opportunity to translate these documents today."[87]

But there was really nothing Ross could say to explain his munitions sales. On October 14 the acting chief of the Bureau wired to the agent in charge: "Attorney General directs cannot reinstate Ross. Have him forward resignation, letter following."[88] Ross publicly and emphatically denied the rumor that he intended to resign.[89] Ross's replacement as resident agent arrived on November 2 in the person of Charles E. Breniman, who had previously been stationed in Cheyenne and in Douglas. Regarding the neutrality enforcement snake pit that was El Paso, Breniman wrote: "I deem it necessary to handle the situation here with extreme caution."[90]

Ross promptly went to work for Consul Llorente, who publicly and emphatically denied that Ross worked for him.[91] Llorente might not have liked Ross, but he certainly could have used the former Bureau agent's expertise.[92] And Ross was involved in some nefarious activities. On October 19, he was in the lobby of the El Paso Bank and Trust Company and was introduced to a notary public, whom he tried to induce to notarize a document without reading it. The notary refused but tantalizingly caught a glimpse of the figure $12,000 on the document.[93] In his new job Ross worked closely with the Mexican government agent Lee Hall instead of Abe Molina, and they readily shared information with Ross's former Bureau colleagues, who didn't hold Ross's peccadilloes against him.[94] Evidently Hall had displaced Molina as the dominant Mexican government spymaster in El Paso.[95] Ross's connection with Mexican government intelligence seems to have ended by December 1912.

Ross then became an operative for the Western Detective Agency in El Paso, managed by his former informant Virgil Snyder.[96] The Western Detective Agency didn't confine itself to investigations; Ross, Snyder, C. P. Pitman, and R. F. Atkinson planned a daring robbery. On the night of January 13, 1913, Ross and Atkinson put on masks and held up a poker game in the McCoy Hotel. They relieved the eleven high rollers of some $3,000 in diamonds and jewelry and $1,300 in cash. However, Atkinson had lost his nerve, had informed the police about the forthcoming heist, and had been instructed to go through with the caper. Thus the police were waiting for Ross as he fled the hotel and arrested him in the lobby. Ross was indicted on nineteen counts of armed robbery, and his bond was set at an astronomical $20,000. A special venire of 150 men was ordered for his trial, scheduled for February 17 in the Thirty-fourth District Court.[97] Snyder and Pitman, his associates were each indicted on seven counts for complicity although they weren't present during the robbery. Pitman's bond was set at $10,000 and Snyder's at $2,500. None of the defendants furnished bail, and they stayed in the county jail.[98] "R. F. Atkinson who, it is said, informed the police that the robbery was going to take place and then participated in it to apprehend the others," noted the *El Paso Morning Times*, "was the star witness during the examining trial and will probably be the main witness during the trial."[99] Ross's attorney moved for a change of venue on the ground that the numerous rebels and gamblers in El Paso had it in for Ross. He also moved to sever Ross's case from that of his associates. The judge denied both motions, as well as one for a continuance.[100]

Ross was tried on one count, the trial starting on February 22; the state's star witness was indeed R. F. Atkinson. The defense argued, by introducing a note found in Ross's pocket after the robbery, "that Ross was engaged in ferreting out gambling games with a view of prosecuting when he was arrested for alleged connection with the robbery."[101] As for the money and jewelry found in Ross's pockets when he was arrested, the best the defense could do was to maintain that they'd been placed in his pockets while he was asleep. At least some of the jurors were convinced—after forty hours of deliberation, the jury remained deadlocked—seven for conviction, five for acquittal. The hung jury was discharged.[102] Ross moved for a reduction in bail, which was refused. Snyder's bail was reduced from $2,500 to $1,500, which he posted. He was then released.[103] Pitman also made bail. Not until his bond was reduced to $5,000 did Ross finally make bail and secure his release, on May 31. He and his wife soon left for Santa Ana, California to visit relatives.[104] Ross seems to be a case of a good man corrupted by the tools of the trade.

Ross wasn't the only one having troubles. The opposition to the Madero regime was also having a hard time. We've seen that Orozco's rebellion was not just failing but fragmenting. Many of his partisans in desperation attached themselves to Vázquez Gómez, who'd already proved his inability to succeed.[105] Orozco's disaffected generals such as José Inés Salazar and Emilio Campa failed miserably in their campaign in Sonora. Among those repelling the *vazquistas* was the future president and strongman of Mexico, Alvaro Obregón, who commanded a unit of *maderista* volunteers. Another factor was that on August 26, Madero had announced that the law of "suspension of guarantees" would go into effect in northern Mexico—under this law, captured rebels could be summarily executed on an order from a colonel or higher-grade officer in command.[106] The Madero government now offered amnesty to all rebels there except the leaders, most of whom slipped across the border and laid low.[107] Campa, for instance, sought refuge in the United States but surrendered to American authorities thirty miles south of Tucson. Although he wasn't wanted by the Americans he was arrested on an extradition warrant from Mexico. He managed to escape back to Mexico and once again become a revolutionary player.[108] Salazar also made it back to Chihuahua and continued the struggle, capturing the border village of Palomas on November 21. His 350 rebels defeated the 85-man federal garrison, seized 15,000 cartridges, and promptly evacuated the town.[109] As for Orozco himself, on September 11, he occupied the town of Ojinaga across from Presidio in the Big Bend.[110] As conservative Mexican exiles were floundering around trying to find a viable leader or at least some funds, both of which were often much more important than ideology, juntas accordingly kept springing up like dandelions in places such as El Paso.

Complicating the situation, the loyalty to Madero of some of the federal army officers in the state of Chihuahua was questionable. General Huerta had been moving unaccountably slowly against the rebels; there was always a span of two to five days between rebel evacuations and the arrival of federal troops. The federals, who now had three thousand troops in Juárez, weren't trying very hard to capture Orozco. It seemed that Huerta had no intention of finishing off the rebels. Interestingly, informants Snyder and Gresh called Agent Ross to their office and told him that Snyder had become acquainted with a young Mexican woman who was of good family and was well connected both with rebels and federals. She told him that a new rebellion was brewing against Madero—General Huerta would be president and Emilio Vázquez Gómez would probably be vice president. Snyder thought there was an element of truth in the story. Agent Ross instructed the two informants to pursue the matter. Snyder turned her over to Gresh to cultivate because Gresh was a college man. The woman was well educated, and she and Gresh would have more in common.[111]

The woman's story might just have been idle gossip, but lending it credibility was none other than Abe Molina. He stated that General Huerta was in league with the rebels to overthrow Madero and eliminate Abraham González as governor of Chihuahua. The spymaster added that informant Saenz had attended a meeting on September 13 between rebel representatives and officers of the federal army representing General Huerta at the hotel room of Ricardo Gómez Robelo. The conspirators agreed that Madero would be overthrown, Huerta would be installed as president, and the rebel partisans would name the cabinet. According to Molina, messengers had been sent to inform Orozco, Salazar, Emiliano Zapata, and others of the agreement.

Reportedly there was widespread disaffection among the federal officers in Juárez. There were between two hundred and four hundred rebels within forty miles of the town, but the federal garrison had made no effort to engage them. And those Juárez policemen who had been Bureau informants were notified that if they testified in El Paso federal court against any of the rebel arms smugglers they wouldn't be tolerated on the Mexican side of the river. Molina had persuaded all who were U.S. government witnesses to resign and come to El Paso. The situation was so threatening that "Abe Molina, who has reported the true condition of affairs to Governor Gonzalez at Chihuahua and to President Madero, is afraid to cross the river to Juarez."[112] In light of the coup that would topple Madero in February 1913, these allegations are intriguing.

At the same time, the *orozquistas* were trying to get back in the game. But Madero's forces captured Ojinaga on September 15, and every *orozquista* who could run fled across the Rio Grande into Texas. Orozco himself was sheltered by sympathizers in the Big Bend and avoided capture.[113] His father, Colonel Pascual Orozco Sr., wasn't as fortunate. He and several companions were arrested in Presidio by the U.S. Army and delivered to the deputy U.S. marshal in Marfa.[114] As it happened, back in April Pascual Orozco Sr. had been among those indicted in El Paso charged with conspiracy to export munitions.[115] The arrest warrant for the elder Orozco was forwarded to Marfa together with an extradition warrant sworn out by the Mexican government.[116] The elder Orozco and his companions were transported to El Paso, where there was a public outcry at the way Orozco was humiliated. A crowd of Madero partisans gathered at the railroad station to hoot and jeer as Orozco was escorted off the train, and they followed him all the way to the county jail. And, refusing offers of an automobile or a carriage, the deputy U.S. marshal escorting Orozco marched him coatless and hatless, shackled to another prisoner, through downtown El Paso to the jail.[117] At the railroad station José Córdova, who'd been General Pascual Orozco's secretary, was arrested by a deputy U.S. marshal on an extradition warrant from Mexico, and he joined Orozco and the others in jail.[118]

The elder Orozco and two of his associates—Cástulo Herrera and Braulio Hernández—were tried in federal court on October 18.[119] They were found not guilty and were immediately released, to Agent Thompson's intense displeasure:

> In this case the Government made up a strong case, the jury had no doubt been reached, at least this is the opinion of the United States Attorney, Judge and ourselves. It was found that the jury had been in communication with noted revolutionists, in spite of every effort made by ourselves to prevent this thing being done. The sentiment here has been very much against us on account of the Senate investigation committee who have been using their efforts to discredit our witnesses no doubt for the purpose of bringing about intervention.[120]

Orozco was immediately rearrested on the Mexican extradition warrant and returned to the county jail. The Bureau was most interested in what he had to say because "we believe that Orozco is in conference daily with revolutionary leaders and that they are planning violations of neutrality."[121] So, steps were taken to bug his cell. After consulting with jail personnel, a Bureau agent concealed a dictograph wire in the cell to which Orozco, Didapp, and Córdova were transferred, a cell previously occupied by several insane women. The dictograph wire ran to the jailor's quarters. The machine worked well enough, but since the cell had no lights Orozco and his companions went to bed early, and the Bureau obtained no information of value. "Orozco said he would see his lawyer the next morning and try to get transferred back to his comfortable cell. This will make no difference in our arrangements as the Sheriff's office is working in harmony with us in this matter."[122] But evidently the dictograph never picked up anything incriminating.

While Orozco and Córdova were serving out their forty-day incarceration, Consul Llorente allegedly tried to bribe a fellow prisoner to testify against them.[123] One Felipe S. López, who had run the military hospital in Juárez, was also serving a forty-day sentence on an extradition warrant, the Mexican government having charged him with stealing furniture from the hospital. According to López, two Mexican secret agents approached him in the jail and showed him a commission authorizing them to represent the consul. They handed him the consul's card on the back of which were written the names of the two agents over Llorente's signature. They offered López $25 in cash and dismissal of the case against him if he would perjure himself by testifying that in his presence Córdova had ordered the execution of two *maderista* spies, who were shot on August 8 with the approval of Colonel Pascual Orozco Sr., who at the time was commanding in Juárez. For good measure, they wanted López to testify that Orozco and Córdova daily received large sums of money stolen from the Juárez treasury. López refused, and when the U.S. commissioner freed him on October 5 after forty days for lack of extradition evidence, López got himself a lawyer and considered suing Llorente for damages but eventually dropped the idea.[124]

Córdova and the elder Orozco were also freed after forty days when the Mexican government failed to substantiate the charges against them. But when Orozco was released on October 30, Texas Rangers immediately rearrested him. A letter from Texas governor Oscar B. Colquitt stated that Governor Abraham González of Chihuahua had requested that Orozco be held until charges of robbery and theft could be filed against him by the state of Chihuahua. This transparent ploy failed because at a habeas corpus hearing the judge ruled that no warrant had been issued against Orozco, and Colquitt's letter didn't justify his arrest and incarceration.[125] Orozco was finally a free man. He of course immediately resumed plotting.

A pro-Pascual Orozco Jr. junta had appeared, headed by Ricardo Gómez Robelo (who used to be a *vazquista* and before that an *orozquista*) who had been released after his preliminary hearing.[126] He called at the Bureau office requesting the return of the papers seized at the time of his arrest, announcing that he represented officially the whole revolutionary movement in northern Mexico and that a Madero peace commission had called on him to arrange for a peace conference and that he'd sent word to Madero detailing what the revolutionists wanted. Abe Molina provided the Bureau with documents confirming what Gómez Robelo had said. Molina also supplied a copy of the statement Gómez Robelo had presented to Senator Fall. But the Bureau's informant, José Saenz, declared that Gómez Robelo was a man without integrity, always on the side where the most money was, a man without patriotism or scruples. The doctor claimed that Gómez Robelo had fallen out with Vázquez Gómez because the latter couldn't trust him. In short, Gómez Robelo was "an intelligent writer but a man of shallow character."[127]

As had been the case with previous juntas, this one, meeting at 609 Third Street and later at the Oklahoma rooming house on South El Paso Street, was thoroughly penetrated. Lee Hall had an informant who provided him with a full account of the junta's activities.[128] There was no lack of people willing to do just about anything for money. For example, Colonel Lázaro Alanís, a prominent *orozquista* officer living with his wife in a rooming house on First Street, was jailed on October 8 by a Texas Ranger on a fugitive warrant from Mexico charging him with murder.[129] The justice of the peace soon released him because the Mexican government hadn't substantiated the charge. But on October 16 Alanís was again arrested, this time on a federal warrant, for he'd been indicted in Santa Fe for conspiracy to export munitions.[130] Alanís was released on bond on November 14 and immediately contacted Hall, not only offering to work for the Mexican government but also asking for a liberal consideration to bring General Pascual Orozco Jr. to a place where he could be arrested by American authorities. Lee Hall put Alanís on his payroll but declined the offer about luring Orozco, doubting that Alanís could deliver. In return for informing on his colleagues in El Paso, Alanís also asked that four of his close friends—Roque Gómez, Enrique Portillo, Rodrigo Quevedo, and Manuel Meléndez—receive protection from the American authorities; he guaranteed they would lay down their arms and live peacefully. What made Alanís's treachery especially disgusting was that his fellow *orozquista* Aristarco Carascosa had mortgaged his home to contribute to the bond for his friend Alanís to get him out of jail so they could take the field.[131]

And there was of course Saenz, who reported to Abe Molina and the Bureau. According to the doctor, Vázquez Gómez had absolutely nothing to do with this junta, which consisted entirely of Orozco partisans. The junta's avowed purpose was to support General Pascual Orozco as chief of the revolution against Madero. Vázquez Gómez and his junta were denounced as being "no more than a gang of ambitious persons without civil or moral worth, and persons who only desire to avail themselves of the opportunities offered in the provisions of the famous and ill-considered Plan of San Luis Reformed in Tacubaya."

Ricardo Gómez Robelo, who was Orozco's official representative, "and in which character he has presented himself to the country," was president of the junta. The group's second secretary was none other than the informant José Saenz.[132] José Córdova, who had been General Orozco's secretary and who'd been captured in Presidio, became the junta's secretary as soon as he regained his freedom. Colonel Pascual Orozco Sr. was the military chief of the junta and also acted in an advisory capacity. Saenz described the junta's organization and enumerated its objectives, which were certainly ambitious. He also declared that the junta had the financial support of the Terrazas clan and of reactionary Mexican exiles in New York City led by Rosendo Pineda, who'd organized the plot to assassinate Madero in 1911. The doctor attended all the junta's meetings, and he ended his report by mentioning that in order to carry out his important mission of informing he needed expense money.[133] But the Bureau became disenchanted with Saenz as an informant: "We've been able to get an informant on friendly terms with the junta, other than Jose Saenz, whose services have not proved overly satisfactory. This informant reports to Mr. L. L. Hall in written daily reports."[134]

General David de la Fuente, who'd been a strong *orozquista* but who'd abandoned Orozco to ally himself with Vázquez Gómez, had decided that the latter was an even bigger loser than Orozco, and had accordingly resumed his *orozquista* allegiance. After serving the forty-day incarceration from the Mexican extradition warrant, he became a prominent member of the junta. Agent Ross's evaluation of the situation was that the junta apparently was "not very well organized yet and as yet have not entered into any unlawful conspiracy."[135] De la Fuente established his residence at 908 Rio Grande Street. He and Gómez Robelo were soon under investigation because they, among others, were involved in recruiting men in El Paso for the rebel movement. The recruits were usually given a few dollars and told to stand by and wait until they were notified they were needed.[136] A technique repeatedly used by several factions was to have recruits ostensibly be hired as laborers by a local employment agency, to ship them by train westward from El Paso but have them disembark at the nearest station, cross into Mexico, and there receive their arms and ammunition.[137]

The junta suffered a series of major blows in November. The U.S. Army arrested Colonel Pascual Orozco Sr., confined him briefly at Fort Bliss, then transferred him to Fort Sam Houston in San Antonio.[138] The same thing happened to General David de la Fuente. They were confined in the guardhouse, but Judge Maxey freed them, ruling during habeas corpus proceedings that their arrest and imprisonment by the army had been illegal.[139] De la Fuente was released, but on December 21 a U.S. marshal arrested him for neutrality violations. He waived a hearing, and his bond was fixed at $2,500, which he posted. When Orozco was released on December 26, he was immediately rearrested on an extradition warrant sworn to by the local Mexican consul, Manuel Esteva.[140]

In October 1912, there appeared in El Paso a soldier of fortune who would figure on the border for decades—Emil Lewis Holmdahl. He was at the time working for the Mexican government gathering evidence against rebel recruiters. Holmdahl worked under Hall of Mexican intelligence, as for that matter did Jack Noonan, of the failed bridge blowing expedition, and Juan Parra, whom the resident Bureau agent described as being "of the better class of Mexicans; does not speak English . . . but is a Mexican of some intelligence."[141]

Holmdahl was born on August 26, 1883, in Fort Dodge, Iowa, into a farming family of Swedish immigrants. In 1898 during the Spanish-American War he enlisted in the 51st Volunteer Iowa Infantry and fought against Filipino insurgents. When his regiment returned to the United States in September 1898, Holmdahl elected to stay behind. He'd developed a taste for fighting, and he enlisted as a soldier of fortune in China. Returning to the Philippines in 1900, he reenlisted in the U.S. Army, this time in the 20th U.S. Infantry. He fought against Filipinos and rose to the rank of sergeant. He returned to the United States in 1906, landing in San Francisco just before the great earthquake. Holmdahl was discharged from the army in January 1907. He then drifted down to Central America and fought as a mercenary under General Lee Christmas. By 1909, Holmdahl was in Mexico, somehow connected with the *magonistas*. When the Mexican Revolution erupted he reportedly obtained a commission as a captain of Rurales in Sonora, then became a *maderista* and a naturalized Mexican citizen. Following the capture of Ciudad Juárez in 1911, Holmdahl was a captain of Rurales in that city and subsequently served in Sonora, Sinaloa, and Morelos.[142]

During the Orozco rebellion Holmdahl had fought on the side of the federal army. He'd recently been commissioned as a first captain of Rurales attached to the command of General Fernando Trucy Aubert. Holmdahl had several conversations in the Sheldon Hotel lobby with one Colonel Felipe Cáceres, a recruiter for the reconstituted Orozco junta, who told the adventurer that if he joined the rebels they'd make him a major in their army. But, Cáceres said, he wanted Holmdahl to remain at his post in the Juárez garrison and attempt to suborn other federal officers, so that when the rebels attacked, the garrison would mutiny.[143] Holmdahl played along, suggesting that two of his colleagues might be amenable to rebel blandishments. A delighted Cáceres urged him to bring the pair to room 29 at the Hotel Zeiger, where Cáceres was staying, saying he could guarantee them a better position than their current federal rank. For several weeks Holmdahl concocted excuses for not bringing the officers to see Cáceres, who admitted that rebel morale was declining because of a lack of money.[144]

The Mexican government agent Juan Parra likewise was stringing Cáceres along; in fact, Parra got himself invited to meetings in Cáceres's hotel room, meetings that included General David de la Fuente, the military chief of the *orozquistas*. The meetings must have been rather depressing, for the *orozquistas* were broke.[145] The Bureau was intensely interested in what went on in room 29 at the Hotel Zeiger. Special Agent E. M. Blanford was dispatched to El Paso to check into the Zeiger and work under cover to monitor Cáceres and his associates.[146] Blanford's undercover assignment soon ended, for David de la Fuente, like Pascual Orozco Sr., was soon arrested by the U.S. Army and transported to Fort Sam Houston in San Antonio.[147]

The *orozquistas* were now not only broke but largely leaderless; revolutionary activity was at a virtual standstill in El Paso and in San Antonio as well. This at least was the opinion of Lee Hall, General Steever at Fort Bliss, Consul Thomas Edwards in Juárez, and the government officers in El Paso. The Bureau agent in charge in San Antonio even began assigning some of his agents to other work.[148]

Nevertheless, the enemies of Madero kept trying. A particularly intriguing rumor was that General Orozco had slipped into El Paso during the first few days of December. Hall of the Mexican intelligence service was convinced that the report was true. And when "some party or parties known to the County Sheriff alone, stated that for a $1,000 reward they would locate Pascual Orozco Jr. in El Paso" on the night of December 4, Consul Llorente immediately advanced that sum to Hall with instructions to pay the reward if Orozco were arrested and jailed. But despite an intensive search the elusive rebel leader was not located.[149]

On December 5, 1912, General José Inés Salazar, modestly styling himself "Major General in Chief of the Revolutionary Army of the North," issued a manifesto from the mountains of Chihuahua in favor of Doctor Francisco Vázquez Gómez, Emilio's brother.[150] And Captain Emil Holmdahl continued to be courted by Ricardo Gómez Robelo, Irineo Ponce, and Lázaro Alanís, on behalf of the moribund Orozco–Vázquez Gómez movements, in the hope that he would agree to induce federal officers in Juárez to revolt at the opportune time.[151] Gómez Robelo professed to be a particular admirer of Holmdahl, telling him that he'd checked his record, found him to be a great fighter, and "that he had confidence in his purpose to join them at the proper time, and made his flattering promises as to the reward he should receive."[152] Holmdahl kept the Bureau and the U.S. attorney apprised of the conspiracy. He acted as agent provocateur with the knowledge and consent of General Trucy Aubert, the federal commander in Juárez, and reported to Consul Llorente as well as to Hall.[153]

In a convoluted development, Lázaro Alanís came to suspect Holmdahl of being a *maderista* spy rather than a rebel recruit. Alanís boldly went to see Consul Llorente and denounced the mercenary as an agent of Llorente's. The consul expressed surprise, denied any connection with Holmdahl, and informed the latter of Alanís's suspicions. Holmdahl immediately contacted Gómez Robelo and expressed his outrage at Alanís's having blown his cover. Gómez Robelo "swore at Alanís and declared that he always had suspected him and would not trust him with any more of his plans." A relieved Agent Blanford reported that Holmdahl still had "a standing with the revolutionary leaders."[154] The American continued to attend meetings of the revolutionary junta at Felipe Cáceres's room in the Hotel Zeiger, where the participants discussed how to smuggle munitions across the border and how to send small groups of recruits out from El Paso as railroad laborers, utilizing an employment agency. "The junta also organized a secret service corps to watch the Mexican Consul's office and trail the Consul's Agents. The men in charge of this service are Major Angel Lopez and Florentino Caballero with as many men as they think the occasion may warrant." This information was contained in the regular written reports that Holmdahl submitted to Lee Hall, who shared them with the Bureau.[155] Holmdahl also reported that to raise funds the rebels planned to steal cattle in Mexico and sell them in the United States. Alanís had made arrangements with an unnamed American cattleman to buy them at an agreed-on price.[156] In a subsequent report to Hall, Holmdahl identified the employment agency the rebels were using to ship out recruits as the R. J. González agency. The recruits went out on the El Paso and Southwestern Railroad to or near Douglas and then slipped across the border.[157]

Rebel activity in the El Paso area seemed to be at a low ebb. Hall informed the Bureau that he thought the Mexican situation would be quiet for a long time to come, or at least while the cold weather continued, but that in the meantime, the revolutionists would be formulating plans for an aggressive campaign in the spring. In his opinion, no munitions were being crossed at present.[158]

As one piece of evidence that things were returning to normal, on November 25 there arrived in Juárez the first regularly scheduled through train on the Mexican Central Railroad since February 27.[159] And the American consul in Juárez was decidedly optimistic: "Political conditions continue to improve in this district and the entire border territory. About eight hundred additional Federal soldiers have been added to the force of the district during the past few days part of which were cavalrymen and which were greatly needed. Railway traffic has attained its normal condition."[160] General Steever was less sanguine, telegraphing the War Department that he needed an ample force for border patrol: "Conditions along border no better now than last July. Salazar, Rojas, Caraveo, Gomez, Cano and others still in field. The only side that attacks is the rebel. . . . Under existing conditions not justified recommending depletion border patrol just now."[161] The Bureau of Investigation shared his caution. Agent in charge Thompson reported that if Orozco and Salazar united and reignited the rebellion in Chihuahua "it will be necessary for us to cover the shipments of arms and ammunition and the enlistment of men closely at El Paso. Agents Breniman and Blanford are being kept at El Paso and instructed to keep a close lookout for this movement and keep us fully advised of the further developments, and use every effort to prevent violations of neutrality."[162]

The situation in El Paso had even gotten the attention of President Taft. After conferring with senators Fall and Smith the president directed the attorney general to launch an investigation of Senator Fall's complaint that the Bureau and the army had been overzealous in their efforts to enforce neutrality, specifically citing the cases of Pascual Orozco Sr. and David de la Fuente, as well as an incident in which an American sentry had fired at the automobile of an El Pasoan who had refused to stop. The president inferred from the senators' remarks that "there was a sort of reign of terror there instituted by the representatives of the Department of Justice, instigated by Llorente, the Consul-General of the Madero Government at El Paso, who had a great deal of money for the purpose, and more or less sustained by Colonel Steever, who, however, was acquitted by the Senators of any wish to violate the rights of other people."[163]

The situation in El Paso was soon overshadowed by momentous events in Mexico.

CHAPTER 8

The Constitutionalists

Prospects for peace seemed to improve in January 1913. The American government continued to harass the *vazquistas*—Emilio Vázquez Gómez and thirty-eight others were indicted in San Antonio on January 9 for conspiring to instigate a military expedition and for enlistment.[1] Among those arrested were Ricardo Gómez Robelo and Juan Pedro Didapp, as well as the memorably named Dr. Luis J. Snowball. The *vazquistas* were released on bond, and the term of the federal court ended without their being tried. Rebel bands in Chihuahua entered into peace negotiations with the Mexican government, negotiations that ended in stalemate because a confident government demanded unconditional surrender.[2] It seemed only a matter of a month or so before the demoralized rebels would surrender. The American consul in Juárez could report that "the general feeling among Americans having interests in the state of Chihuahua is that the worst is over, and that they are justified in returning to their labors."[3]

With the rebels in disarray, the level of intrigue declined sharply. Accordingly, the Mexican government drastically curtailed its intelligence presence in El Paso. The spymaster Lee Hall now had only six agents working for him; one, a newcomer, fabricated a report about an arms cache, admitting that he felt he had to report *something*. John Neville, a former newspaperman, and Jack Noonan were also operatives of Hall's, and Emil Holmdahl was still reporting to Hall and Llorente. Ironically, another of Hall's agents was W. Powell Roberts, who had originally been Hall's boss. Roberts was assigned to make the rounds of the freight stations to monitor arms shipments in and out of El Paso. Although on a much smaller scale, the Bureau was still largely dependent on Mexican intelligence, for its budget usually didn't permit the luxury of hiring informants. The Bureau did dispatch an additional agent to El Paso and continued to receive some intelligence from Henry Kramp of the Thiel Detective Service.[4] From the Bureau's point of view the situation was about to worsen; Consul Llorente notified Hall that as of February 1, Hall and his operatives would be discharged and Mexican intelligence activities would be discontinued. Hall, in fact, had already arranged to become chief of security at the American Smelting and Refining Company smelter. (By 1915, Hall had become a captain in the El Paso police force.)[5]

As for Llorente, the government still hesitated to charge him with conspiracy in view of the fact that the trial of the saboteurs Charpentier, McDonald, and Mahoney had resulted in their acquittal because the prosecution hadn't been able to prove conspiracy. Matters came to a head when on February 5, 1913, McDonald filed a complaint with U.S. commissioner George B. Oliver against Llorente and Alberto Madero. McDonald hated Llorente's guts and was determined to get even with him before Llorente left El Paso. Commissioner Oliver obligingly issued an arrest warrant for Llorente that same day. Interestingly, the U.S. attorney in San Antonio instructed the U.S. marshal not to serve the warrant pending additional investigation.[6] Incensed at being overruled, Commissioner Oliver assumed entire responsibility for the arrest warrant and appointed a special officer to serve it. The consul couldn't be located in El Paso, however. He'd learned of the warrant and had gone to Juárez. From there Llorente stated to an Associated Press correspondent that he wouldn't return to El Paso but would leave that day, February 6, for Mexico City and would return in two weeks to face the charges. He admitted to hiring the four saboteurs but stressed that he had warned them not to buy their munitions in the United States.[7] The Bureau agent in charge interpreted these events as follows: "[I]t appears to be that this complaint is being filed for the purpose of harassing and discrediting Mexican Government officials in order that their testimony might be disregarded in future prosecutions to come up at El Paso, particularly in the case of the United States v Krakauer, the main case now pending for violation of neutrality."[8]

This proved to be a rather shrewd observation. When the case of the *United States v. Robert, Julius, and Adolph Krakauer, Cástulo Herrera, and Victor Ochoa* for neutrality violations came to trial before Judge T. S. Maxey in April, at the close of the government's case the defense entered a motion to direct a verdict of acquittal for Adolph and Julius Krakauer and Cástulo Herrera. Judge Maxey granted the motion. The cases of Robert Krakauer and Victor Ochoa went to the jury. In these cases the government was confident that the evidence was sufficient for conviction, "but owing to an apparent prejudice against the presentation of such cases, and against certain parties who worked up this and other cases, particularly former Mexican Consul Llorente, former Special Agent Ross, Jose Martinez, Abe Molina and others contemptuously referred to by attorneys for the defense as Mexican spies, the jury returned a verdict of 'not guilty' as to all defendants at 6:00 p.m. having been out less than 15 minutes."[9] This crushing defeat for the federal government was a dramatic expression of local resentment against what were perceived as the arrogant feds and their Mexican cohorts. From the Bureau of Investigation's point of view it certainly didn't help that Judge Maxey also dismissed cases against nineteen more defendants accused of neutrality violations on the ground that it was almost impossible to secure convictions.[10]

The outcome of the Krakauer case powerfully reinforced the arms traffic, which had continued unabated. Because of Judge Maxey's 1912 decision in the Chávez case it was very difficult for the Bureau to arrest and detain people for violating the president's proclamation and the joint resolution of Congress. Since it would be some time before the Supreme Court ruled on the government's appeal of Maxey's ruling, all Bureau agents and other government officials along the border had received instructions merely to seize munitions but not to arrest those attempting to smuggle them. "The U.S. commissioners along the border hesitate to issue warrants for the apprehension of these persons," noted agent in charge H. A. Thompson.[11]

What had lent urgency to the seizure of munitions were persistent rumors in January that rebels were planning to attack Ciudad Juárez, which was easy pickings—a garrison of less than three hundred men plus the piles of cash from the racetrack, the gambling concessions, the bullfights, and the annual fiesta then in full swing that thousands of Americans attended daily.[12] But then there were always rumors that Juárez was about to be attacked.

Reportedly, José Inés Salazar and Antonio Rojas were encamped with between 250 and 400 men at the village of Guadalupe, across from Fabens, while David de la Fuente was approaching Juárez from the west, from Palomas, with a similar force, and other rebel bands were operating along the Mexican Central Railroad to the south of Juárez. At Guadalupe, Salazar released the American cattle broker Todd McClammy, whom de la Fuente had captured near Palomas when McClammy was traveling to the ranch he owned in Mexico.[13] An intriguing development was that General José de la Luz Blanco, of the federal army, who'd reportedly been captured by rebels, appeared in El Paso from Salazar's encampment in Guadalupe bearing peace proposals, which he delivered to Consul Llorente. Evidently an informal armistice ensued, in which the federals didn't attack Salazar at Guadalupe and Salazar didn't attack Juárez, being content to improve the lot of his troops by spending five thousand pesos to buy them underwear, shoes, and so forth. Reinforcements in the form of one thousand cavalry made the Juárez garrison capable of repelling any attack by Salazar.[14] El Pasoans breathed easier.

A disquieting development was that Emilio Vázquez Gómez slipped out of San Antonio with several companions on the night of January 27 and headed west. To the delight of his partisans in El Paso, he secretly passed through that city on February 14 and made his way to the dingy hamlet of Palomas, where he once again proclaimed himself provisional president of Mexico and began trying to organize a government.[15] This was Vázquez Gómez's big chance, for which he'd yearned for so long—to supplant Orozco, secure United States diplomatic recognition as a belligerent, and take on Madero. Vázquez Gómez proclaimed himself provisional president on February 15, naming Salazar general in chief of the army of the North and David de la Fuente chief of the general staff. The proclamation was signed by a number of lesser officers.[16] On February 25, Vázquez Gómez informed the American secretary of state that he'd formed a provisional government. He also began issuing decrees.[17] In addition to carrying out his military duties, David de la Fuente also served as subsecretary of foreign relations in the provisional government.[18] However, José Inés Salazar subsequently had charge of that department as well as communications and public works.[19] Talent was in extremely short supply in Palomas.

The fates continued to be against Emilio Vázquez Gómez. While he'd been trying to get organized in Palomas, momentous events had transpired in Mexico City, events that once again marginalized the would-be provisional president.

In January 1913, President Francisco Madero could take some satisfaction. He had survived rebellions by General Reyes, General Orozco, and General Félix Díaz, Porfirio's nephew. True, Emiliano Zapata was still leading a rebellion in the state of Morelos against Madero, one centering on immediate and drastic land reform, something Madero refused to implement. Yet Zapata was a regional threat, as was Salazar in northern Chihuahua. What the well-meaning Madero failed to grasp was that the real threat to his regime lay in Mexico City itself. Followers of the exiled Porfirio Díaz and disaffected army officers were busy plotting. On February 9, 1913, mutinous troops freed Reyes and Félix Díaz from the prisons where they were awaiting trials for treason, and the rebel column marched on the national palace, planning to seize Madero. However, the palace guards opened fire, and in the resulting firefight Reyes had the distinction of being the first one killed.[20] His coconspirator Félix Díaz and the remainder of the rebels barricaded themselves in a downtown arsenal. The coup had failed.

Madero selected General Victoriano Huerta to command the loyalist troops and finish off the rebels. This was Huerta's opportunity.[21] He promptly became Félix Díaz's coconspirator, and for the next ten days Mexico City endured a bloody and cynical charade in which rebels and loyalists devastated the downtown area, seeking to create chaos and give the appearance that Madero had lost control of the situation. On February 18, Huerta made his move, arresting Madero and the vice president and forcing them to resign.[22] Huerta and Félix Díaz met under the auspices of the American ambassador to divide the spoils—Huerta would become provisional president and Díaz would select the cabinet. On the night of February 22, Madero and the vice president were shot down by their military guards as they were being driven to the penitentiary, and the next day the Huerta regime announced that unfortunately the president and vice president had been killed in a clash when their partisans tried to rescue them.[23] Huerta had made himself the new strongman of Mexico. But he'd also made Madero a martyr, and a wave of revulsion against Huerta the "Usurper" began to spread.

Huerta's seizure of power created a dramatic new phase in the Mexican Revolution. Heretofore the revolution had been fought along a north-south axis with the principal battleground being the state of Chihuahua and the Juárez–El Paso area being decisive in determining who won and who lost. Now, however, opposition to Huerta appeared in the entire northern tier of Mexican states. Venustiano Carranza, the governor in Coahuila, initially accepted the new regime in Mexico City but then changed his mind and seized the opportunity to become the standard-bearer in the struggle against Huerta.[24] He issued the inevitable revolutionary manifesto, the *Plan de Guadalupe*, and announced the formation of the Constitutionalist army. He shrewdly did not proclaim himself provisional president. Instead, Carranza proclaimed himself First Chief of the Constitutionalist army, a position whose powers were whatever Carranza wanted them to be.

One of the great strengths of the Constitutionalists was their organization. They not only raised guerrilla bands but soon established a junta, or an office, in almost every city and town in the border region. In the cities, Constitutionalist "consuls" headed the offices, which became magnets for neutrality violators. These juntas were accepted and approved by the public as an additional enterprise for the community, and no questions were asked as to their real purpose.[25]

From Coahuila Carranza provided the political leadership but initially the state of Sonora supplied much of the Constitutionalists' military muscle. The governor, José María Maytorena, secured a six-month leave of absence and fled to Arizona.[26] His absence proved no great loss, for the state government raised units of volunteers to fight Huerta, who began losing control of Sonora. It was this campaign that would make Alvaro Obregón an outstanding revolutionary commander.

In Chihuahua, Governor Abraham González, who had been a staunch supporter of Madero and who could have provided invaluable leadership, informed the American consul in confidence on February 10 that the overthrow of the state government by the army was imminent and that he was preparing to flee.[27] He didn't make it. On February 22 the army arrested the state officials for their alleged connection with a plot to restore Madero to power. There was widespread fear for González's life.[28] The Panhandle and Southwestern Stockmen's Association, ironically a member of whose executive committee was General Luis Terrazas, adopted a resolution praising González and requesting a fair trial for him.[29] On the other hand, the U.S. ambassador to Mexico reported unsympathetically to the State Department that González "had committed many crimes against Americans and many more against Mexicans and I would suggest to the Department the desirability of avoiding any active steps in his behalf. His reputation is so limited and his character so doubtful that I doubt the wisdom of any vigorous intervention in his behalf."[30]

Concerned for González, the American consul in Chihuahua called on General Antonio Rábago, the new military governor of the state, on February 28.[31] Rábago vehemently denied that González was in any danger and gave his personal guarantee of González's safety. The Huerta regime claimed that González had been sent to the American border under an escort of his own choosing.[32] But on the night of March 6, González was hustled aboard a military train headed south. Besides González, the train carried a colonel, a major, and twelve soldiers. Some forty miles south of Chihuahua near Bachimba Pass the train halted, the party got off, and the train proceeded on to Ortiz station, some fifteen miles down the track. After two hours the train returned, picked up the officers and soldiers, and returned to Chihuahua without González. The military party had shot the unfortunate governor and had buried him in a shallow grave beside the track.[33] Constitutionalist propagandists would seize on González's murder and embroider it, alleging that the federals hadn't just killed the governor but had done so with fiendish glee—tying him hand and foot and throwing him under a moving train.[34] The revolution had gained another martyr. But to put González's murder in perspective, the Constitutionalists employed exactly the same technique—in March, prominent *vazquista* attorney Joaquín Cantú Cárdenas and four other prisoners were forced aboard a special military train in the middle of the night, transported a few miles, and shot dead by the side of the track.[35]

There was frantic realignment as triumphant conservatives coalesced around Huerta, while Madero's followers suddenly found themselves in the political wilderness. Juárez was firmly in the hands of *huertistas*.[36] The absence of Abraham González meant that initially Chihuahua lagged behind the neighboring states in organizing against Huerta. This delay significantly affected the position of El Paso. The city functioned as the major entrepôt on the border, and, as in the past, the contending Mexican factions struggled either to increase or to impede the arms traffic. It was observed that "the hardware firms are very influential among the business men of El Paso, most of whom are favorable to the constitutionalists."[37]

Krakauer and Shelton-Payne were the largest wholesalers of munitions in the entire Southwest, and they had no hesitation in selling both to the federals and the Constitutionalists. Increasing quantities of arms and ammunition flowed from El Paso eastward to the Big Bend and especially to Eagle Pass, for Carranza had established his provisional capital in Piedras Negras across the river.[38] Likewise, a torrent of munitions flowed westward from El Paso to the Arizona border, especially to Douglas, for the Constitutionalists under Alvaro Obregón were rapidly taking control of Sonora.[39] Dealers such as Francis Bannerman in New York City also supplied arms and ammunition to the Constitutionalists. In June, for example, he sold them two three-inch fieldpieces. Edward Maurer was approached to sell a quantity of Springfield rifles, two machine guns, and several fieldpieces that Madero had originally ordered but had been left over in New York City when his revolution triumphed. And an enterprising broker tried to interest Carranza in buying a torpedo boat, for a mere $35,000 to $40,000. Carranza wasn't interested.[40]

Besides acquiring weaponry, Carranza began organizing a coalition of Constitutionalist chieftains under his leadership. East-west communications on the Mexican side of the border were lacking, and so in April he requested U.S. permission to cross the border and proceed by rail to Sonora to confer with rebel leaders there. Permission was refused.[41] Carranza had to make the difficult journey on horseback.

Huerta too was desperately negotiating to attract support. General Pascual Orozco, the man whom Huerta had defeated in 1912, announced his adherence and was given a military command. David de la Fuente traded the delights of Palomas for a position in Huerta's cabinet as secretary of communications. The United States granted him safe passage through American territory via El Paso on his journey to Mexico City.[42] José Inés Salazar reiterated his allegiance to Vázquez Gómez as a bargaining chip, for reportedly "Salazar, Rojas and Campa are holding off for a large sum of money or a lucrative position under the new Government."[43] The Huerta administration was unimpressed and planned to have Salazar arrested and held for extradition if he appeared in El Paso. Salazar succeeded in cutting a deal with Huerta—to abandon Vázquez Gómez and accept a commission as a brigadier general in Huerta's army, undertaking to pacify the Casas Grandes region with his two hundred men. Campa also got himself commissioned as a brigadier general in Huerta's army.[44] Pathetic Emilio Vázquez Gómez finally gave up the illusion of becoming powerful; he left his provisional capital of Palomas, arriving in El Paso on March 31. He refused to grant reporters an interview.[45] The press viewed him as a huge joke, pointing out that no one took him seriously except himself and the U.S. officials who kept arresting him for neutrality violations. In short, he was harmless.[46] One conservative Mexican writer described him as the "perpetual candidate" for the presidency.[47]

Vázquez Gómez's capitulation seemed to mark another step in Huerta's consolidation of his control of Mexico. Pascual Orozco Sr. had been doing his bit—he, Andrés Garza Galán, and Sheriff Amador Sánchez had organized in Laredo the bloodless seizure of Nuevo Laredo from the Madero authorities. Huerta now entrusted the elder Orozco with the delicate mission of persuading Emiliano Zapata to submit to Huerta. When Orozco led a delegation to negotiate with Zapata, Zapata reacted by having Orozco shot.[48] Huerta interpreted this as a definite "no."

Someone else who was adamantly opposed to Huerta was Pancho Villa. He had served under Huerta as commander of irregular cavalry in the 1912 campaign against Orozco. Huerta, the professional, despised Villa, the amateur, and seized on a flimsy pretext to have him condemned to death by a drumhead court martial. One of Madero's brothers informed Madero, who countermanded Huerta's order in the nick of time. (There is a photograph of Villa standing in front of a wall with the firing squad drawn up, minutes away from death.) Huerta never forgave Madero for this interference. Villa was consigned to prison in Mexico City to await a proper trial, but he managed to escape with the help of a prison employee, Carlos Jáuregui, and made his way to the United States, joining the throng of Mexican refugees in El Paso. Villa arrived on January 3, 1913. He first stayed at the Roma Hotel, 419 South El Paso Street, then moved to a house at 510 Prospect Avenue in Sunset Heights.

The chief of the Bureau advised the El Paso office that "Francisco 'Pancho' Villa, a former Federal officer," had escaped from the federal penitentiary in Mexico City and was now residing in El Paso and asked that "a close watch be kept on him, as it is believed he will attempt to start some kind of proceedings in violation of the neutrality laws. Kindly cover the movements of this party, and advise us of all the facts obtainable."[49] Teodoro Kyriacopulos, an intimate friend of Villa's in El Paso, gave an interview in 1930 describing how Villa lived as an exile. Kyriacopulos evidently had a lot of fun with the reporter, for he declared that Villa coped with boredom by purchasing an Oliver typewriter and spent days, and sometimes nights, hunting and pecking. And, according to Kyriacopulos, Villa frequently gave away $100 or more daily to destitute *orozquistas* because, even though they'd been his deadly enemies, they were now fellow exiles in need.[50] Somehow this picture of a kinder, gentler Villa seems just a bit out of character.

Villa, who idolized Madero and hated Huerta, initially told the local press that he intended to remain a neutral refugee in El Paso, but the next day he announced that he intended to take the field against Huerta. Yet Villa seemed to be totally inactive, and the Bureau relaxed its surveillance.[51] The agency belatedly learned that Villa had purchased 3 rifles and 500 cartridges from Shelton-Payne. When Agent Charles Breniman subsequently interviewed the personnel at Shelton-Payne, he learned that Villa, Juan Dozal, and other Madero supporters had made substantial arms purchases in El Paso.[52]

Sometimes the Bureau's intelligence really went awry. Hearing a rumor that Manuel Mascarenas Jr., the onetime *vazquista* would-be provisional governor of Sonora who had jumped bail, was in town, Agent E. M. Blanford went looking for him, taking along Earl Heath, a former Mexican government intelligence operative, who said he could positively identify Mascarenas. They met the train from Los Angeles that Mascarenas was supposed to be on, but he wasn't on it. Then Heath announced that a party had registered at the splendid new Paso del Norte Hotel under the name of C. R. Thomas, and he thought it was Mascarenas. Embarrassingly, C. R. Thomas turned out to be the chief of detectives for the city of Los Angeles.[53] But then Henry N. Gray, who had worked for Mexican intelligence in southern California, told Blanford he had actually seen Mascarenas in El Paso. The Bureau agent got a deputy U.S. marshal to accompany him and went looking for Mascarenas, finally locating him in the Parlor Saloon on the corner of El Paso and San Antonio streets in the company of Manuel L. Luján, a prominent *orozquista*, and Arturo M. Elías, a former Mexican consul in Los Angeles. The marshal arrested Mascarenas, who was unable to post a $2,500 bond and went to jail.[54]

The Bureau had less luck watching Pancho Villa, who on March 6 quietly crossed the border with eight followers, the nucleus of what would become the formidable Division of the North.[55] Agent Blanford commented: "There has been a lot of general talk in El Paso of a counter-revolution in Mexico, and I won't be surprised to see it materialize. There is much and bitter resentment at the way the Huerta Government gained control."[56] As El Pasoans had been overwhelmingly pro-Madero in 1911, they were now overwhelmingly anti-Huerta. Smuggling increased dramatically, and the Bureau "found it hard to interest those who have heretofore helped U.S. officers in apprehending those guilty of violating neutrality."[57]

The Constitutionalists began organizing at 602 Upson Avenue, the residence of Juan Medina, former Juárez mayor, and at the Hotel México on South El Paso Street.[58] Despite a desperate shortage of cash, the junta tried to accommodate those offering their services. Every day volunteer officers appeared, many of them having endured great hardships just to reach El Paso. The junta arranged to lodge them in a third-rate hotel on credit. As for food, a lady agreed to feed them for forty cents a day per man.[59] The Huerta regime requested that those attending revolutionary meetings in El Paso be arrested and helpfully sent a list of these miscreants.[60] Huerta agents, among them Victor Ochoa, informed the Bureau that a Constitutionalist recruiting center had opened at the Emporium Saloon, owned and operated by Teodoro Kyriacopulos, on South El Paso street. It was said he recruited four American machine gunners and two telegraph operators for the Constitutionalists in Sonora, offering them $125 a month, the money coming from the junta in Douglas. There were even rumors that some Texas law enforcement officers had declared that they weren't going to arrest Constitutionalists.[61]

The players continued to choose sides. In general, those who had supported Orozco and Vázquez Gómez now supported Huerta, whereas Madero partisans now supported Carranza and the Constitutionalists. Felix Sommerfeld belonged to the latter camp, and he'd had a rather exciting time of it. When the coup against President Madero broke out, Sommerfeld was at home in Mexico City. He raced to Chapultepec castle, the presidential residence, to look after Mrs. Madero. The German remained in Chapultepec throughout the fighting, then escorted Mrs. Madero to the Japanese legation, after which he fled to the German legation. Sommerfeld had learned that, because he was a staunch Madero partisan, General Huerta had put a $1,000 price on his head. At the German legation he demanded protection as a German subject, which was granted. He remained hidden in the legation from February 18 to March 14, when the German minister, Admiral Paul von Hintze, secured a safe conduct for Sommerfeld and personally escorted him to Veracruz. From there Sommerfeld made his way to Havana, Key West, New Orleans, and San Antonio, where he spent a few days in the Hutchins Hotel before leaving for New York City.[62] Like Sommerfeld, Sam Dreben, whom one source described as "assistant to Captain Burnside, United States military attaché at the embassy in Mexico City," had had to flee the city during the fighting because of Huerta's animosity. He and Sommerfeld teamed up to travel to Piedras Negras, Carranza's headquarters, to offer him their services.[63] They subsequently advanced the Constitutionalist cause by operating from New York City, New Orleans, San Antonio, and El Paso procuring armament.

Abraham Molina also became a Constitutionalist secret agent, communicating with Governor José María Maytorena of Sonora. But he was a double agent. The Huerta consul, Miguel Diebold, reported that he was employing Molina, "who has the confidence of almost all the leaders of the parties that have their juntas here." But Diebold labored under no illusions about Molina's loyalty, calling him "a man of little education, very shrewd, and in my opinion having little conscience. He has no political allegiance nor does he care about politics, having no other aim than that of serving whoever pays him best, whether as a smuggler, a recruiter, or a secret agent." Diebold added that Molina's reports had been most valuable but that his services perhaps would have to be dispensed with because his salary, that of his two subagents, and their expenses came to $20 a day: a stiff $600 a month. But he felt that the money was well spent, as long as Molina served loyally. Diebold included letters between Constitutionalists that Molina had intercepted as well as several exchanged between Molina and Maytorena, letters that Molina had loaned him to prove that he was indeed in contact with the Sonora rebels.[64] By contrast, Enrique Llorente genuinely lent his talents to the Carranza cause. After a spell in prison in Mexico City for allegedly misappropriating government funds, he made his way back to the United States and eventually became inspector of Constitutionalist consulates.[65]

The Washington attorney Sherburne Hopkins represented Venustiano Carranza as he had represented Francisco Madero. In his correspondence with Carranza, Hopkins initially used the pseudonym "F. González Gante," but in May he informed the Washington press corps that "that mysterious gentleman" had left for Europe on a special mission. Henceforth Carranza could write to him as "S. G. Hopkins, 723 15th Street, Washington, D.C.," or, in case discretion were necessary, he could address his letters to "Royal Gold Mining Co." at the same address. Hopkins lobbied to get the arms embargo lifted and to secure United States diplomatic recognition of the Constitutionalists as belligerents. He was particularly effective in persuading his contacts in the press to publicize Constitutionalist victories. Hopkins reported that he and Carranza's Washington representative, Ignacio Pesqueira, were working closely together in perfect harmony, and that many ranking United States officials sympathized with the Constitutionalists.[66]

The *huertistas* were of course intensely interested in Hopkins's activities, and on occasion they managed to intercept his mail.[67] In June 1914, Hopkins's office was burgled and his files stolen. Selections of his correspondence were soon published in the *New York Herald*, containing embarrassing and sensational information on Hopkins's relations with prominent politicians, businessmen, and Mexican revolutionaries.[68]

Emil Holmdahl deserted from the federal army and traveled to Sonora to join the Constitutionalists there.[69] Jack Noonan, the sometime saboteur for Llorente, also joined the Constitutionalists in Sonora, smuggling munitions for them in Nogales, Arizona.[70] (In 1916–17, Noonan was a customs inspector in Arizona.)[71] R. H. G. McDonald, who'd been Noonan's colleague, traveled to Nogales to enlist in the Constitutionalist forces but Colonel Alvaro Obregón rejected him when he learned that McDonald was the man who'd preferred charges against Consul Llorente and who had participated in looting Juarez in 1911. After returning to El Paso, "McDonald states that if he had succeeded in joining their forces, he intended to make a 'clean up' at the first opportunity, and then desert."[72]

Others decided to support the Huerta regime. Colonel Paul Mason, the *insurrecto* in 1911, offered his services to the Constitutionalists, who decided to have no dealings with him, suspecting that he was a Huerta spy. Mason then worked as a secret agent for the Huerta consul in Laredo.[73] Lawrence Converse, "an American of doubtful reputation and known unreliability," the *maderista* whose kidnapping in 1911 near El Paso had caused a furor, was employed by the Huerta War Department and the Foreign Office as a secret agent in New Orleans but "had acted in such a way in Mobile and other places that the War Dept and Foreign Office became suspicious, and they no longer trust him."[74]

Victor Ochoa became a secret agent in El Paso for the Huerta regime. He called at the Bureau office to inquire about the government's attitude regarding neutrality violations. The Bureau wasn't inclined to take Ochoa too seriously. Agent Blanford reported: "I asked a news reporter if he had talked to Ochoa recently and without any questioning on my part he described Ochoa as one affected with hallucinations and the faculty of seeing things, and further stated that he could not rely on anything that Ochoa had to say. I talked to another party about Ochoa and this person stated that he took no stock in anything that Ochoa had to say."[75]

Initially the overthrow of Madero produced little excitement in Juárez, the population adopting a wait-and-see attitude. But as it became obvious that the garrison was going to support Huerta, Madero supporters began seeking safety in El Paso. On February 24, the police chief and the city treasurer fled across the international bridge, bringing the municipal treasury with them for deposit in an El Paso bank. And on February 25, the Juárez garrison surrounded four hundred pro-Madero volunteers and disarmed them without a shot being fired. Military rule now prevailed.[76] For El Pasoans the positive side of military rule was that Juárez was orderly. Tourism picked up, Americans flocking over the border to enjoy not only the usual diversions such as the races, bullfights, and keno games but also more exotic spectacles such as bullbaiting—four bull terriers fighting a bull to the death.[77]

The latest turn of events in Mexico underlined the importance of Fort Bliss as a bastion protecting El Paso from attack. The post was in transition—what had been an infantry installation was becoming the premier cavalry post in the country. And Fort Bliss was growing. The government appropriated $200,000 in March for improvements to the post, whose payroll was already pumping some $70,000 a month into the El Paso economy.[78]

The secret war in El Paso continued unabated, with much of the action revolving around the new Mexican consul. The local press reported on March 8 that the Huerta regime had formally relieved Enrique Llorente as consul and had appointed Miguel Diebold as his replacement. Diebold, who'd just arrived in El Paso from Arizona, was experienced, having been in the consular service for some fourteen years both at border locations and most recently in San Francisco. At one time he'd been Mexican consul general in the United States.[79] His formal title was inspector general of Mexican consulates. As such he supervised the administrative and financial affairs of the consulates, but the inspector's primary responsibility was to supervise the Mexican secret service in the United States. Diebold immediately plunged into his clandestine responsibilities—he referred, unfortunately without naming names, to a bribe made to American officials to secure the release of ammunition seized in El Paso.[80] And shortly after his arrival Diebold began shipping Huerta soldiers disguised as laborers by rail to Arizona to reinforce the garrison in Naco, Sonora.[81] Another of Diebold's top priorities was to establish a network of secret agents. He offered Lee Hall the position as head of his intelligence operatives.[82] Hall, employed at the smelter, turned down the offer, although from time to time he did moonlight to conduct "some special investigations" for Diebold.[83] Huerta's Foreign Office notified Consul Diebold in May that Agent Blanford was investigating the Constitutionalist junta in El Paso and would welcome whatever information Diebold could provide.[84] By July, Diebold was able to inform the Bureau that he had a number of men engaged in secret work and would notify the Bureau whenever he received definite information about neutrality violations.[85]

The Bureau needed all the help it could get. The level of revolutionary activity had increased along the Texas border, and Agent H. A. Thompson informed his chief that because of overwhelming sympathy for the Constitutionalists, people were most reluctant to cooperate with the Bureau. And because of its limited manpower, the Bureau had a number of important points uncovered and had to rely largely on Mexican government informants. The army, customs, and deputy U.S. marshals were willing to assist the Bureau but had their own duties to perform. Thompson reiterated that he needed more agents.[86]

The Bureau, and other agencies involved in neutrality enforcement, got welcome news in May 1913. The U.S. Supreme Court ruled on the government's appeal against Judge Maxey's decision in October 1912 that munitions must be crossed into Mexico before an offense could be deemed to have occurred. The high court on May 8 reversed Maxey's ruling in the Chávez case.[87] The Bureau could finally resume arresting violators instead of merely seizing contraband munitions. Unfortunately, by the time the Supreme Court handed down its ruling many government witnesses, especially Mexicans, had scattered, and the government had to dismiss a number of neutrality cases.

The matter of storage had become critical; in the Bureau's office in the federal building there were some 30,000 confiscated cartridges being held as evidence. The Treasury Department, which had jurisdiction over the building, demanded that the ammunition be removed forthwith.[88] But the Bureau had bigger problems than just determining where to store ammunition. The shortage of agents had reached the point where the agency's manpower resources were laughable—there was no agent for San Antonio and only *three men* to cover the entire border from Yuma to Brownsville.[89] One of them was Agent Blanford in El Paso who had all he could do just trying to keep up with the large amounts of ammunition that Shelton-Payne and Krakauer were receiving. Agent Thompson pointed out that "it would be advisable, if appropriations will permit, to have someone cover the local freight stations in El Paso, in the capacity of an informant."[90]

During the spring and into the summer of 1913, the Constitutionalist cause flourished. On July 21, the United States halted shipments to the Huerta government. This return to a policy of impartiality and nonassistance to all sides leveled the playing field.[91] Felix Sommerfeld traveled from San Antonio to New York City in May to arrange substantial arms purchases through Ed Maurer, who'd performed similar services during the Madero revolution.[92] Sherburne Hopkins, the Constitutionalists' legal representative in Washington, was busily lobbying on their behalf.[93] In Chihuahua, not only were chieftains such as Villa winning victories south and west of the state capital but the morale of the Huerta forces was crumbling. For example, in April about three hundred of José Inés Salazar's troops deserted, taking with them a large quantity of ammunition they'd recently received from the Huerta government. And there was a steady trickle of desertions from the Juárez garrison.[94]

Yet General José Inés Salazar, at least, kept up a brave front. On June 16, he appeared in El Paso for the first time since the outbreak of the Orozco rebellion, nattily attired in a black business suit, new cowboy boots, and an expensive panama hat. Salazar strolled through the lobby of the Sheldon Hotel and along a main street, attracting a crowd of the curious. He was preparing to have lunch with officials of the Mexico Northwestern Railroad and two of his staff at the St. Regis Hotel, but he hadn't been in town more than half an hour before a deputy U.S. marshal served him with a federal warrant charging him with conspiracy to violate the neutrality laws (a federal grand jury in Santa Fe had indicted him for conspiring to export 50,000 rifle cartridges from New Mexico on August 6, 1912) and took him into custody. Unperturbed, Salazar instructed his aide Felipe Cáceres, who was well known to the Bureau, to go to the bank and have $1,000 withdrawn from his account so he could post a cash bond. Cáceres soon returned with Alfred F. Kerr, vice president of the El Paso Bank and Trust Company, who posted the bond. Salazar was promptly released and departed for Juárez to enjoy his delayed lunch. He subsequently failed to appear before the U.S. commissioner, to the disappointment of a large crowd hoping to glimpse him, and the bond was forfeited.[95]

By late June, the city of Chihuahua and Ciudad Juárez were practically the only places of importance still in *huertista* hands. The federal army had virtually abandoned the western and southern sections of the state. And the Constitutionalists engaged in disinformation, announcing that Juárez was about to be attacked.[96] Emil Holmdahl, who had joined the Constitutionalists in Sonora but had transferred to Villa's command as an artillery captain, appeared in El Paso on July 30 telling the press that Villa was approaching Juárez with five to six thousand men.[97] Instead, Villa isolated the state capital. On July 29, the American consul in Chihuahua telegraphed: "A heavily-guarded train arrived here from El Paso on 27th with food supplies and made the first since June 3. Orozco arrived here on July 22 with 1500 troops—raw, undisciplined, poorly armed. Noticeable friction between them and the regulars."[98]

While the federal garrison in Juárez braced for the inevitable Constitutionalist attack, some El Pasoans cheerfully worked both sides of the street. For example, in the Western Union office two Hispanic brothers were employed as telegraphers, one of whom passed information to the federals and the other to the Constitutionalists.[99]

If there is one incident that encapsulates the sheer cynicism of the El Paso business community during the revolution it is the following. As part of its defensive measures the Huerta garrison had practically surrounded Juárez with barbed wire entanglements. Krakauer, Zork and Moye sold the federals one thousand rolls of barbed wire for this purpose. Then the firm sold to the Constitutionalists every pair of wire cutters in stock.[100]

In the event of a rebel attack the federals planned to electrify the barbed wire entanglements by hooking them up to the overhead electric line feeding the international trolleys. But this line was powered from the El Paso Gas and Electric Company's plant, and there was apprehension that rebels might blow up the installation to foil the federals. Accordingly, a detachment of soldiers was assigned to guard the power plant. They weren't too observant, for adjoining the power plant was the Badger Fuel Company, 212 West Second Street, where on the night of July 15, four Mexicans were frantically shoveling coal into a railroad gondola car to cover boxes containing 448,000 7-mm and .30-.30 cartridges destined via Douglas for the Constitutionalists in Sonora. Since the ammunition boxes had been loaded into the car during the afternoon, "it seems almost impossible for a man to patrol the back of the Gas & Electric plant for two hours and not see what was going on at the back of the Badger Fuel Co., so near are the two places together, unless, of course, the man was being paid to look the other way."[101]

The ammunition had come from Shelton-Payne, but on the advice of his attorney, W. H. Shelton wasn't telling who had ordered and paid for the shipment. However, faced with the threat of criminal prosecution, Shelton's lawyer advised him to be forthcoming. Speaking through his attorney, Shelton said that an individual giving his name as G. Padres had ordered the ammunition by phone from Douglas on June 20. A few days later, Padres appeared at Shelton-Payne and made a down payment, whereupon Shelton ordered the goods from Winchester. On July 12, Padres again came to Shelton-Payne, made another payment, and directed that the boxcar coming from Galveston with the ammunition be turned over to Powell Roberts. This was done, and Shelton stoutly maintained that this ended his involvement in the affair.

Roberts purchased ten tons of coal from J. B. Badger to cover the cartridges, and he supervised the transfer of the ammunition from the boxcar to an adjacent gondola. He was directing the laborers covering the cartridges with coal when a raiding party suddenly appeared. Alerted by one of his agents, Consul Diebold notified deputy U.S. marshal Charles R. Moore and accompanied Moore and ex-Texas Ranger Charles Webster, who now apparently worked for Diebold, in seizing the shipment and arresting the shovelers. Roberts escaped by rolling under a boxcar and running away.[102] The cartridges were hauled off to Fort Bliss for safekeeping, and arrest warrants were issued for Roberts and Padres. The latter, it developed, was Gustavo Padres, a paymaster for the Sonora rebels. Padres, who was the chief defendant in this case, was arrested in Douglas and posted a $2,500 bond. Powell was arrested at his home in El Paso. Since he couldn't post his $1,500 bond, Powell went to the county jail.[103]

As more details about the affair surfaced, it began to resemble a sordid little soap opera. One Cecil Durrell, an ex-prostitute who lived in a small house behind three prostitutes' cribs she owned and who was J. B. Badger's common-law wife and Powell Roberts's former mistress, had contacted a local police captain offering to divulge information about the arms shipment if there was a reward. There wasn't, and she soon had a visit from the Bureau of Investigation and two deputy U.S. marshals, on July 18. At first she was defiant, alleging that the officers were trying to frame her, but then she calmed down and began talking. On July 13, Badger had taken her to his fuel company and had pointed out the gondola in which the ammunition was to be shipped, covered in coal. And on the night of the seizure, a soldier had come to her door and informed her about it. Moreover, the deputy marshal who'd seized the shipment had seen Badger at the coal yard shortly before the seizure and had asked him if the Mexicans shoveling coal worked for him. Badger said no, whereupon the marshal asked sarcastically if Badger was in the habit of letting people come into his yard at night and shovel coal without his consent. Badger grudgingly admitted selling the coal to Roberts but tried to disclaim any knowledge of the use to which it was to be put. He was arrested for complicity and posted a $1,500 bond. Cecil Durrell was served with a subpoena to testify as a key government witness.[104]

From a legal standpoint the government's case was weak: there was no evidence that the defendants intended to smuggle the ammunition in the coal car, and Cecil Durrell repudiated her statement, alleging that she was an alcoholic, that she had been drunk for a week at the time she had talked with the officers and didn't know what she was saying, that everything she had said was a lie, and that she had been intimidated by the lawmen. This was now her story, and she would so testify in court. Nevertheless, the grand jury indicted Roberts, Padres, and Badger, whose trial was scheduled in the October term of the federal court. The defendants claimed that witnesses material to their defense were absent and thus secured a continuance until the next term of court.[105] But at least the 448,000 cartridges—the largest seizure so far in El Paso—were being held as evidence. And the seizure caused a decided slump in the local arms traffic. Shelton, for one, was now warning all purchasers of ammunition that he had to give the government any information requested regarding sales.[106]

The slump in gunrunning was only temporary. Although the U.S. government refused to recognize Huerta as the legitimate president of Mexico, Washington had been issuing permits for the export of munitions to the Huerta regime, extending the privilege accorded to Madero during the Orozco rebellion. During July, Shelton-Payne was authorized to ship 40,000 cartridges to the Huerta commander in Juárez, and that same month Consul Diebold shipped 83,000 rounds to Juárez and 1,000 carbines and 500,000 rounds to the Huerta commander in the city of Chihuahua.[107]

But the United States suspended this practice on July 21, decreeing that no Mexican faction would be permitted to buy arms in this country.[108] This was in effect a significant victory for the Constitutionalists, for now the Huerta government was on the same footing as they were, having to rely on smuggling.

Entrepreneurs such as the Guaderrama clan were ready to help. Sabino Guaderrama was at one level a legitimate and successful businessman—at the corner of Stanton and Seventh streets he owned the Tres Piedras Saloon and an adjoining billiard parlor and motion picture theater—but he also smuggled munitions to the federals in Juárez. Responding to informant reports that a number of cases of arms had been taken from the saloon, the police raided these premises on the night of September 15, confiscating 5,500 .30-.30 Winchester cartridges and arresting Guaderrama as a suspicious person. The authorities tried to connect him with the smuggling of some rifles near the smelter, but he was subsequently released for lack of evidence. Sabino Guaderrama had business dealings with an unsavory pawnbroker named Joe Ravel, who "will sell anything he has and ask no questions as to what use is intended to make of it, if he thinks he is not being watched."[109] At Smeltertown, Manuel Guaderrama, who owned a saloon there, together with his father José, crossed a shipment of ammunition for the federal garrison in Juárez, according to Lee Hall.[110]

Besides investigating actual cases of smuggling the Bureau spent a considerable part of its time checking out leads that proved worthless, most of them provided by volunteer Constitutionalist agents lurking around the hardware stores. "Reports of this character are of almost daily occurrence. Volunteer detectives see something and surmise much more, and then report to this and the marshal's office that they have actually seen ammunition being purchased or in course of transportation."[111]

Everyone waited for the Constitutionalists to move against Juárez. Anxiety was running so high that any incident could trigger an emergency. On the afternoon of September 6 a Mexican from Juárez came to the American end of the Stanton Street bridge and opened fire on immigration officers with a rifle. They fired back and killed him. But it was reported that troops were forming on the Mexican side of the bridge. Troops from Fort Bliss were rushed to the American side. The situation was extremely tense for a while, until it was learned that no Mexican troops were massing. The excitement died down, and it was thought the dead Mexican had probably been drunk. Nevertheless, guards were doubled at the American ends of the international bridges. While all this was occurring, a train arrived in Juárez from the state capital with an escort of about twelve hundred Huerta troops. The mere fact that it had taken an escort of this size to get a train through served to increase the anxiety level in Juárez. This anxiety manifested itself in growing lawlessness and in resentment against Americans for the killing of the drunken Mexican at the bridge.[112]

In fact, conditions in Juárez became so menacing for Americans that the American consul recommended closing the port of El Paso to all imports and exports "until such time as the Mexican government can or will maintain a safe and honest port on her side of the line." He believed it would take only a few days to bring the Juárez authorities to their knees.[113]

October was a memorable month for several of our characters. Sabino Guaderrama went to Juárez to dispose of 54,000 cartridges originally bought for Orozco's troops and that the Bureau of Investigation had seized and later released. He was, however, arrested on October 2, jailed for six days, and hauled off to the penitentiary in Chihuahua, where he remained for twenty-one days under grim conditions until he could bribe his way out for four hundred pesos. After his return to El Paso he filed suit against the mayor of Juárez and the Mexican Foreign Office for $50,000 for great mental and physical anguish and humiliation.[114] To the surprise of many El Pasoans, former Consul Enrique Llorente appeared and surrendered to federal authorities, being under indictment for neutrality violations. He had come from Mexico City, where he had spent several months in prison accused of misappropriating government funds before being exonerated by the Mexican Supreme Court and released. In El Paso he posted a $2,000 bond to appear for the April 1914 term of federal court. He then departed for Los Angeles. Shortly thereafter he offered his services to Venustiano Carranza, who accepted them.[115] Felix Sommerfeld blew into town from San Antonio, announcing that he planned to remain in El Paso indefinitely. Four days later he surfaced in Nogales, Sonora, where he had gone to confer with Carranza.[116] Still another player appeared on the streets of El Paso. Tracy Richardson, machine gunner extraordinaire, returned to town from a six-week hunting trip near Silver City, New Mexico.[117] You just never knew who you might run into.

During the October 1913 term of the El Paso federal court the grand jury refused to indict eleven defendants accused of neutrality violations, which greatly raised the morale of the merchants-of-death community.[118] An impressive amount of ammunition poured into El Paso. On August 2, for instance, Shelton-Payne received 450,000 cartridges straight from the factory in New Haven, Connecticut.[119] The overstretched Bureau received some assistance from an unexpected source. In what was an extralegal operation, soldiers in plain clothes helped to keep the freight depots, pawn shops, and major hardware stores under surveillance.[120] Most of the arms traffic out of El Paso was directed toward Arizona, as was the case with the 448,000 seized cartridges. During the summer and into the fall of 1913 a flood of weaponry inundated the Arizona border, which together with the New Mexico border was initially devoid of any Bureau agents.[121] The Constitutionalist junta in Douglas, headed by Francisco Elías, was most effective in securing enormous amounts of weaponry for their colleagues in Sonora, who were well on the way to gaining military control of the state.

As of September 30, Douglas merchants had received 1.2 million cartridges since June, at least 95 percent of this total consisting of 7-mm and .30-.30 ammunition. The Douglas Hardware Company alone had retailed not less than 700,000 rounds.[122] In all, the Douglas junta smuggled some 3 million cartridges, spending money lavishly to bribe American soldiers guarding the border and to purchase a fleet of automobiles for transporting the contraband into Sonora. Krakauer shipped not only ammunition but also three sets of reloading tools to Douglas.[123] The Bureau urged extreme measures to suppress the arms traffic and hoped that the commanding officer in Douglas would be ordered to adopt the "most drastic methods possible."[124] The members of the Douglas business community didn't dispute the fact that most of the ammunition they sold went into Mexico in violation of the law but insisted that they were not involved in the unlawful traffic.[125]

The government thought otherwise. Agent Thompson telegraphed from Douglas on October 2: "Wave of arrest of dealers believe have [*sic*] destroyed smuggling operations to a large extent this locality; several dealers have returned ammunition to consignor, others have stated will discontinue traffic."[126] The grand jury in Phoenix returned indictments against ammunition dealers in Douglas, Bisbee, Tucson, and Patagonia, Arizona, as well as against Krakauer and Shelton-Payne in El Paso.[127] The arms traffic had been dealt a body blow. Whether convictions would result remained to be seen.

CHAPTER 9

Villa Ascendant

The focus of attention shifted suddenly and dramatically away from the Arizona border and the arms traffic. On November 5–10, Villa attacked the city of Chihuahua, among whose federal defenders were units of irregulars commanded by brigadiers Pascual Orozco, Marcelo Caraveo, José Inés Salazar, and Antonio Rojas.[1] With attention focused on Chihuahua, Villa carried out his most spectacular feat of arms, one that won him international fame—by a brilliant ruse he captured Ciudad Juárez.

While operating against the city of Chihuahua Villa learned from an intercepted telegram that General José Inés Salazar and his command were expected to arrive in Juárez at dawn on November 15 to reinforce the garrison. Quickly seizing the opportunity, Villa loaded fifteen hundred troops aboard a captured Huerta railroad train and had the train return to Juárez. At 1:30 a.m. on November 15 this Trojan horse on rails disgorged the *villistas* in the railroad station. Before the befuddled Huerta garrison grasped what was happening, Villa had captured Ciudad Juárez with ridiculous ease, the scattered resistance ending by 8 a.m. Besides capturing the town, Villa captured 95,000 cartridges, 2 machine guns, 2 fieldpieces, and a mountain of small arms. Order was quickly restored. Villa forbade looting and began executing federals, starting with Colonel Enrique Portillo, the old Red Flagger.[2] Great numbers of morbidly curious El Pasoans, including some well-dressed women, flocked to Juárez to gawk at the dead bodies, and if lucky they got to witness an execution or two. Unlike the last time Juárez was captured, in May 1911, there was no exodus to the safety of El Paso; Villa prohibited the citizens from leaving.[3]

Villa had already sent his wife to the safety of El Paso on September 15. She traveled via Columbus, arriving there in a covered carriage drawn by five mules. Mrs. Villa "had on a gold wrist watch and chain and another gold watch and chain on her person among many jeweled rings on her fingers."[4] No doubt she was holding these items in trust for the people.

Because Villa's surprise attack had succeeded so quickly and decisively, El Pasoans hadn't even had the opportunity to worry about an attack on Juárez. True, some bullets had landed in El Paso, but the only casualty was a boy who was shot through the hand. With Villa firmly in control, entertainment in Juárez resumed—the fiesta and the racing season got under way, bullfights started being held again, and the gambling houses reopened. But Villa operated the fiesta, and the proceeds from the games went to outfit his troops. In short order he bought ten thousand uniforms and pairs of shoes in El Paso. His officers likewise replenished their wardrobes there. Villa took the lucrative keno concession away from *huertistas* Salvador Rojas Vértiz and Ike Alderete and conferred it on his loyal followers Carlos Jáuregui, who had helped him escape from prison in Mexico City in 1912, and Teodoro Kyriacopulos, who besides being a prominent Constitutionalist in El Paso was a personal friend and confidant.[5]

The population of El Paso awoke on November 16 to a significantly changed strategic situation, one in which the city's importance was similar to what it had been during the Madero and Orozco phases of the revolution. The El Paso–Ciudad Juárez region would be Villa's logistical lifeline, and his campaign, as had Orozco's, would develop largely along the line of the Mexican Central Railroad. And as in the earlier phases, adventurers rushed to El Paso to join the revolution, but Carranza had decreed that no foreigners should be enlisted. Captain Emil Holmdahl, who arrived in Juárez in charge of a *villista* artillery unit, was an exception, for he was a naturalized Mexican citizen. In December, he accompanied Colonel Juan N. Medina to Hermosillo to confer with Carranza and returned with Medina to El Paso.[6]

One of the more exotic specimens trying to join Villa was Ivor Thord-Gray, a self-proclaimed artillery expert. A Swede, born in 1878 as Ivor Thord Hallstrom, he had emigrated to South Africa, where he became a naturalized British subject and changed his surname to Thord-Gray, which sounded more English and rather aristocratic. He saw extensive military service in South Africa, fighting in several colonial campaigns as well as in the Boer War. By 1906 Thord-Gray was a captain in the British colonial forces, but he decided to broaden his horizons by becoming a mercenary. He fought in French Indochina in 1909, in Tripoli in 1911, and in China in 1912.

In his memoirs he relates that he was in Shanghai in October 1913, when he decided to seek further adventure by going to Mexico. He prevailed on the local Mexican consul to issue him a "special permit to travel throughout Mexico for six months on archaeological and anthropological work."[7] The Swede said he landed in San Francisco in early November and left immediately for El Paso, where he registered at the Hotel Paso del Norte. Armed with his permit, he crossed over to Juárez and offered his services to Pancho Villa, who had just captured that town on November 15. Villa wasn't impressed, thinking that Thord-Gray might be a Huerta spy. Thord-Gray then walked out of Villa's presence "without saluting" and started back to El Paso. But while walking through Villa's camp he chanced on a forlorn American deserter, an army sergeant who was Villa's artillery officer and who had no idea of how to repair a damaged fieldpiece. Thord-Gray, who had some experience with artillery, was able to repair the gun, and a grateful Villa made him his new "chief of artillery," with the rank of captain. His command consisted of two 75-mm guns, no officers, no noncommissioned officers, and ten "Apache-speaking" gunners.[8] Besides giving Villa valuable advice on how to train and employ his cavalry, for example by establishing a school for officers, Thord-Gray whipped his pitiful artillery command into first-class shape in a suspiciously short time—less than ten days. Thus when the pivotal battle of Tierra Blanca occurred south of Juárez November 23–25, Villa won a smashing victory against a powerful Huerta column advancing to recapture Juárez (with El Pasoans swarming rooftops and along the Rio Grande trying to get a glimpse of the fighting and flocking to the battlefield after the engagement to collect souvenirs and stare at the dead).[9] Villa not only routed the *huertistas* but captured 15 75- and 80-mm cannon, along with 29 boxes of projectiles for these fieldpieces, each box containing 12 shells.[10]

In achieving this victory, Villa's artillery, which Thord-Gray claimed to have commanded, played no small part. An appreciative Villa then dispatched Thord-Gray on a confidential mission, to convey a large shipment of munitions across the Arizona border. Thord-Gray successfully carried out the assignment.[11] His association with Villa ended on November 29, when the Swede left Juárez for Arizona. Thereafter he joined Obregón's army. He fought in a cavalry regiment under General Lucio Blanco and participated in the campaign that ultimately resulted in the capture of Mexico City.[12] On September 3, 1914, Thord-Gray, by then a colonel in the Constitutionalist army, was honorably discharged.

He left Mexico to join the British Army. In October 1914, he was promoted to major and raised and trained the 15th Battalion of the Northumberland Fusiliers. The following year he was promoted to lieutenant colonel and saw action in France from June 1915 to May 1916, when he was wounded and was treated for shell shock. His command, at that time the 26th Battalion of the London Regiment, was disbanded. Thord-Gray secured his discharge from the British Army, and he claimed he then turned down appointment as chief of staff of the Mexican Army, going instead to New York City, where in March 1917, he tried to raise a British-American brigade for service with the U.S. Army. In July 1918, Thord-Gray was attached to the U.S. Shipping Board, making patriotic speeches to shipyard workers.[13] This being rather humdrum employment, in 1918 he went to Siberia with the Canadian contingent, as part of the Allies' ill-fated intervention against the Bolsheviks in Russia. When Thord-Gray arrived in Vladivostok he left the Canadians to join the White Russian Cossacks under General Demionoff, who promoted him to the rank of major general.[14] After his stirring adventures, Thord-Gray devoted himself to more peaceful pursuits, such as compiling a Tarahumara-English/English-Tarahumara dictionary, which the University of Miami Press published in 1955, and in writing his Mexican memoirs, published in 1960 and entitled *Gringo Rebel*. As of September 1960, he was living quietly in Coral Gables, Florida.

As we have seen, Thord-Gray's memoirs contain an extensive section recounting his association with Pancho Villa. This account has been accepted at face value by Villa's biographer.[15] There is a problem, however. The battle of Tierra Blanca, of which Thord-Gray gives a detailed account as a participant, occurred on November 23–25, 1913. Yet on November 27, the "hotel arrivals" column of the *El Paso Morning Times* stated that "among the arrivals in El Paso yesterday was Captain I. Thord Gray, of Stockholm, who registered at the Paso del Norte[.] . . . Captain Gray expects to remain in El Paso some time and today will visit General Villa at Juarez. It is not improbable that the soldier of fortune will enlist in Villa's army."[16] Since he didn't even get to El Paso until *after* the battle of Tierra Blanca, and since Colonel Martiniano Servín commanded Villa's artillery in that engagement, Thord-Gray's account of his dealings with Villa was a figment of his imagination.[17] Even in the unlikely event that there is some explanation for the hotel arrivals notice, what conclusively proves that Thord-Gray tried his hand at writing fiction is his file in the Office of Naval Intelligence (ONI). During World War I there were allegations that Thord-Gray was really a German and a spy, and ONI investigated his background. The American naval attaché in London received from the British War Office in 1920 a confidential report on Thord-Gray, concerning whom the British had a considerable dossier. The British report said that "Lieut. Colonel Grey [*sic*] states that he has served in the following campaigns before the outbreak of the late war, and there does not appear to be any reason to doubt his statements regarding his service." He listed his Mexican service as: "1913–1914—Mexican Revolution—Chief of Staff to General Lucio Blanco (Carranza's Army) raised and trained eight infantry and cavalry brigades."[18]

What Thord-Gray *didn't* list was anything connected with Villa, surely something that didn't just slip his mind. One can thus conclude that the Pancho Villa story was a fantasy Thord-Gray indulged in to spice up his memoirs. This naturally makes one wonder how much of the rest of his book is also fantasy.

Villa having repulsed the federals at Tierra Blanca, his base of operations in Juárez was safe, and he could concentrate on planning his advance to the south. This would necessitate a considerable supply of munitions, so smuggling through El Paso surged.[19] To try to deal with this upsurge, Agent Thompson recruited an able informant in the person of John Wren, formerly employed by the Madera Company in Madera, Chihuahua.[20] Wren would eventually become a Bureau agent.

When the cases involving the Arizona arms dealers and Krakauer and Shelton-Payne came to trial in Phoenix in December, the government suffered another devastating defeat. The court sustained demurrers in all arms case where conspiracy wasn't specifically charged, which meant that eleven indictments involving the direct shipment of arms and munitions to Mexico were thrown out.[21] The court then sustained a defense motion to instruct the jury to render a verdict of not guilty in five cases alleging conspiracy, on the grounds that the facts the prosecution presented weren't sufficient for the jury to return a guilty verdict. The Bureau agent on the scene wrote: "We were very much astonished at the action of the court in this case in directing a verdict of 'Not Guilty' as we had been advised that an exceptionally good case had been made out."[22] The U.S. attorney threw in the towel and asked that the conspiracy cases against Douglas Hardware Company, Shelton-Payne, and Krakauer be dismissed.[23] The government planned to appeal the not guilty verdicts, but the morale of those trying to enforce the neutrality laws must have been sagging; if it wasn't a resentful jury freeing defendants it was a judge doing so. And part of the fallout of these decisions was that W. H. Shelton, of Shelton-Payne, was now disinclined to cooperate with the government. A Bureau informant reported that "Mr. Shelton was very cool and stated that he had no more information for the Government."[24] Nevertheless, the Bureau gamely soldiered on, trying to interdict the arms traffic. The agency received some help from the Treasury Department, which in late November assigned a special agent to El Paso.[25]

Despite their dismal track record, Emilio Vázquez Gómez's supporters in El Paso doggedly tried to instill new life into that failed movement. They sent an emissary, then a three-man delegation, to Ojinaga, where the federal forces who had evacuated the city of Chihuahua were entrenched, to sound out Orozco and Salazar as to whether they'd support a new revolution in favor of Vázquez Gómez. Orozco rejected the overture. The *vazquistas* also formed yet another in what seemed an interminable succession of juntas in El Paso. As usual, a member of the junta was an informant, this time for a deputy U.S. marshal. According to the informant, the junta stated that Luis Terrazas had contributed money to the new movement and would contribute further, and that at present the junta had all of $900 in the treasury. Further, the seven-man junta had appointed Braulio Hernández as their secret agent.[26] Some of the junta's revenues came from the collection of a heavy export duty on cattle being crossed through Palomas. Doing the collecting was Maximo Castillo, "thief and bandit," whose band of fifty men was the nucleus of what the junta optimistically if unrealistically hoped would become a new *vazquista* army of twelve hundred men.[27] Castillo captured Palomas without a fight. Planning to control it indefinitely, he appointed municipal officials, imported armament, and collected customs duties.[28]

By engaging in this activity the *vazquistas* were stepping on some powerful and dangerous toes—they were depriving Pancho Villa of export revenues on cattle. Villa had authorized an American from El Paso who dealt in Mexican cattle, Todd McClammy, to collect these monies for him. McClammy, born in 1869 in Alabama, was an "old Mexico hand" who had known Villa since 1907.[29] Not only was McClammy an experienced border character, but he was also feisty. In 1912, he had managed a horse ranch southwest of Casas Grandes that the rebels had stripped of the best livestock, and McClammy was not at all reticent in expressing his distaste for the *orozquistas*. During an argument with some of them in the lobby of the Sheldon Hotel, one made the mistake of insulting McClammy, who tweaked the nose and pulled the mustache of the offender, touching off a small riot.[30]

To make it perfectly clear who was in charge of collecting export duties, Villa detailed a hundred of his soldiers to chase Castillo from the Palomas area and ordered them to shoot Castillo on the spot if they captured him. The *villistas* routed Castillo, driving him far from the border, and occupied Palomas.[31] Now McClammy demanded ten pesos ($5) a head on 2,165 head being exported by the Bigham and Love Cattle Company, threatening to prevent the firm from exporting any more cattle unless they paid.[32] Export duties would now go to Villa, who was on his way to becoming the most powerful general in Mexico.

Huerta's control of the border was nearly gone by early 1914. The federals held only the towns of Ojinaga, Las Vacas (today Ciudad Acuña), and Nuevo Laredo. Constitutionalist forces threatened Las Vacas, and General Pablo González was preparing to attack Nuevo Laredo.[33] Villa's forces were attacking Ojinaga. The demoralized *huertistas* had evacuated the city of Chihuahua in December 1913, accompanied by hundreds of civilians fearing Villa's wrath. Isolated from the rest of Mexico, the fugitives were putting up a desperate resistance against the troops Villa had assigned to capture Ojinaga.

With Villa firmly based in Ciudad Juárez, the arms traffic through El Paso flourished, and the army resumed searching suspicious persons at the bridges on streetcars going to Juárez.[34] There was one mysterious development. Bureau agent Blanford had been focusing on a suspicious lot of 300,000 rounds, 78,000 of which belonged to the Constitutionalists. Soldiers of the 13th U.S. Cavalry in civilian clothes were still keeping Shelton-Payne under surveillance, and they had observed 300 cases of ammunition being transported from that establishment and loaded into a boxcar. The ammunition was destined for New Orleans and was consigned to the Guatemalan government in Puerto Barrios. Blanford notified the Bureau's New Orleans office, suspecting that an effort would be made to divert the shipment "because it is almost unbelievable that a car of ammunition would be shipped to the Government of Guatemala from El Paso."[35] The car might be unloaded at some lonely siding near the border, and Blanford intended to prevent this. The railroad agreed to place the car next to the caboose, in which rode Blanford, informant John Wren, a deputy U.S. marshal, and two cavalrymen, armed with Winchesters and sandwiches. They rode without incident as far as Sierra Blanca, "which was believed to be the limit of the danger zone" and returned to El Paso on a passenger train (one that had a wreck at Fort Hancock, but luckily none of the party was injured).[36]

In New Orleans the Bureau also located 25 cases of .44-caliber Winchester ammunition (2,000 rounds per case) and 200 rifles, all consigned to the Guatemalan government. The munitions were loaded aboard a United Fruit Company steamer bound for Guatemala. Significantly, Sam Dreben and his friend T. M. Solomon, who was "indirectly connected with revolutionary parties in New Orleans" were watching at the wharf while the ammunition was being loaded on the ship.[37] According to Emil Holmdahl, who reappeared in El Paso after serving as a captain in Villa's forces, the shipment was landed at Matamoros and conveyed to the Constitutionalist army.[38] But Holmdahl was disseminating disinformation. The United Fruit Company adamantly denied that any of its vessels stopped at any Mexican ports under any circumstances and stated that the ship in question's first port of call after New Orleans was Belize, British Honduras.[39] In all probability the munitions were destined for an anti-Huerta faction headed by the *maderista* former governor of Campeche, Manuel Castillo Brito. Carranza had urged Castillo Brito to open a southern front against the dictator in order to relieve the military pressure on the northern Constitutionalists. While making his preparations in New Orleans, Castillo Brito was frequently accompanied by Sam Dreben. The principal routes for Castillo Brito's munitions were across the borders of Guatemala and British Honduras.[40]

Felix Sommerfeld, "special representative of General [*sic*] Venustiano Carranza," reappeared in El Paso in January. He called at the Bureau office to urge the interdiction of alleged ammunition shipments that were sent by rail from El Paso through Marfa and then conveyed overland to Presidio and smuggled to the beleaguered federal garrison in Ojinaga.[41] The matter was urgent enough for Sommerfeld to go to Marfa, where he joined another Constitutionalist agent, both of whom then proceeded to Presidio to investigate smuggling personally. The other Constitutionalist agent was none other than H. A. Thompson, former Bureau of Investigation agent in charge in San Antonio. Thompson had resigned to accept more lucrative employment with the Constitutionalists, who of course were delighted to acquire the services of one so well versed in neutrality enforcement matters. As had been the case with former agent Louis Ross, Thompson maintained cordial professional relations with active Bureau agents. Thompson now worked mainly out of El Paso.[42]

Villa had assigned the capture of Ojinaga to subordinate generals. Becoming impatient with their lack of success, Villa went to Ojinaga and took personal command of the assault. The town fell in one day, January 10, 1914. In a remarkable grasp of the obvious, the Bureau agent in Marfa reported on January 12 that "it is not likely that the smuggling contemplated by the Federals will now materialize, they having been defeated by the Constitutionalists at Ojinaga."[43]

The defenders of Ojinaga and their civilian camp followers stampeded across the Rio Grande to the sanctuary of Presidio. There were several familiar figures in the mob of refugees. "Bob Dorman and Tracy Richardson of the Aultman & Dorman Photographic company returned yesterday from the Ojinaga battle field where they have been for the last two weeks, snapping pictures for the Hearst papers." Dorman had been with the *villistas*, Richardson with the federals. The federals had, however, become angry with the versatile soldier of fortune because he took photos of the federal entrenchments prior to Villa's final assault. On the night the federals abandoned Ojinaga, Richardson was arrested and jailed. His guards fled across the Rio Grande, and so did Richardson, who broke down the door to his cell and sprinted for the river. He barely escaped the victorious *villistas*.[44]

Defeated generals Orozco and Salazar also fled across the Rio Grande. Orozco was believed to be hiding at the mine in Shafter, protected by American sympathizers, as had happened in 1912. Although the mine owner and the local officials stoutly denied it, there was strong suspicion that the mine superintendent, Bill Russell, again hid Orozco.[45] Orozco subsequently made his way to New Orleans, from where he sailed in February for Mexico in the Huerta gunboat *Zaragoza* (Orozco had already sent his wife and family to San Antonio).[46] José Inés Salazar was arrested on the train at Sanderson as he tried to make his way to San Antonio. The U.S. Army detained all *huertista* military personnel seeking safety in Presidio. Brigadier General Tasker Bliss, the commander of the Southern Department, ordered that if the civil authorities released Salazar, who was under indictment, the army would detain him.[47]

The army marched its prisoners—3,300 Huerta troops, 1,067 women, and 312 children—from Presidio to the railroad in Marfa, from where they were transported to a prisoner of war stockade established at Fort Bliss. The camp was built on the mesa beyond the fort and was surrounded by barbed wire. The prisoners lived in tents. By March, the number of interned Huerta soldiers numbered 3,658 and included General Salvador Mercado, the commander, and eight brigadier generals, among them José Inés Salazar. While Salazar was confined at Fort Bliss the army confiscated a number of interesting letters and telegrams from him.[48]

The U.S. attorney in Albuquerque wrote to the Bureau agent in charge in San Antonio in March regarding the forthcoming neutrality trial of José Inés Salazar. The Mexican consul in El Paso had hired a defense attorney, one Sweeny, for Salazar, "and an attorney of Albuquerque not of the highest standing here [Elfego Baca]," who "after the employment of Mr. Sweeny gained an audience with Salazar through representations to General Scott of his intimacy with the two New Mexico Senators." After the interview with Baca, Salazar fired Sweeny and telegraphed to Huerta, who remitted $3,000 to attorney Baca with the promise of an additional $5,000. The U.S. attorney continued: "It is said the Albuquerque attorney went to Washington to get the Salazar prosecution dropped through his influence with the New Mexico senators. I understand his visit was futile." Baca had availed himself of his friendship with Senator Albert Fall, who wrote him letters of introduction to President Woodrow Wilson, Secretary of War Lindley M. Garrison, and Secretary of State William Jennings Bryan. Although Baca's attempt to use political influence proved futile, he still received his additional $5,000 fee.[49]

Although "not of the highest standing here," as the U.S. attorney discreetly put it, Elfego Baca was a folk hero in New Mexico. In October 1884, at the age of nineteen he had held off a reputed eighty Texas cowboys in a thirty-three-hour gun battle in what is today the village of Reserve, then called Upper San Francisco Plaza, in southwestern New Mexico. This exploit made Baca a legend. In 1958 Disney even aired a TV miniseries entitled *The Nine Lives of Elfego Baca*. According to the *Albuquerque Journal*,

> during his tumultuous career—during an equally tumultuous time in New Mexico—Baca was a deputy, gunfighter, lawyer, private detective, sheriff, Juarez barroom bouncer, county clerk, school superintendent, Socorro mayor, Socorro and Sierra counties district attorney and Indian agent. In all capacities, Baca's methods have been described as brash, impulsive, unorthodox, sometimes dangerous. He was three times charged with murder and acquitted on all counts. He is said to have engineered at least one jailbreak. He often defended in court the downtrodden and oppressed. He was first-name friendly with many leading and politically prominent New Mexicans of the era. He ran unsuccessfully for governor.[50]

This then was the flamboyant figure who was now Salazar's attorney. It will be remembered that back in 1912 Baca had been an *orozquista* sympathizer and had instructed his son-in-law to provide every assistance to Orozco's emissaries who went to Albuquerque to purchase ammunition and smuggle it across the border. Now he was defending Salazar, and not just because everyone deserves competent legal representation but because he sympathized with the *huertistas*.[51] And of course the money was a not inconsequential consideration. Salazar was charged with having ordered 100,000 rounds from Shelton-Payne through third parties in 1913. Some 50,000 of these cartridges had been seized by the U.S. Army near Columbus, and Salazar had instructed his representatives to sell the other 50,000 back to Shelton-Payne, which they did.[52]

Salazar, who had been transferred to confinement in Fort Wingate, New Mexico, was brought to Santa Fe for trial in May. The U.S. attorney wrote: "If statements made to me are true, I feel confident that an effort will be made to influence the trial jury," and he strongly suggested that as a precaution the government detail some special agents in Santa Fe during the term of court to obtain evidence of any attempted jury tampering.[53] Agent Blanford got the assignment. When he got to Santa Fe he conferred with the U.S. attorney, alerting him to the fact that the confiscated ammunition being held at Fort Bliss could be introduced as evidence. The attorney immediately telegraphed the Fort Bliss commander requesting that the ammunition be dispatched to Santa Fe by express. Agent Blanford hovered as closely as possible around the jury in order to spot any attempt at tampering.[54] But what Blanford witnessed in Santa Fe turned out to be educational.

Salazar was incarcerated in the county jail, and the deputy U.S. marshal who delivered him there left strict instructions with the jailer that only Salazar's lawyer, Elfego Baca, was to see him. A bemused Blanford reported: "It was learned, however, that the jailer disregarded this instruction and permitted everyone who called at the jail to see Salazar, to see him, and that among the crowd were a number of the jurors. It appears that no conversations were had with the defendant, the visitors merely passing through and speaking to Salazar."[55] The trial began on May 11, and the government felt it had an open and shut case. But one of the prosecution's key witnesses recanted his earlier statement, and the U.S. attorney discharged him, whereupon Elfego Baca put him on the stand as a defense witness. However, a parade of other government witnesses seemingly discredited his testimony. At the end of the day the jury was sequestered, supervised by two bailiffs. Blanford concentrated on the witnesses, fearing an attempt to suborn one or more of them. At the noon recess on the second day, Blanford followed three government witnesses who left the federal building in the company of attorney Baca. They went to the bar of the De Vargas Hotel, where they had a few drinks. Then they went up to Baca's room. Blanford managed to enter an adjoining room and overheard them deep in conversation trying to agree on certain dates. On May 14, the jury returned a verdict of not guilty.[56]

Salazar had beaten the rap; he wasn't, however, out of the legal woods yet. His attorney secured a habeas corpus hearing for the Mexican general, but he was still held in confinement because he was charged with having committed perjury when he had sworn he had resigned from the federal army in Ojinaga five days before the federals fled to the United States and that he had left Mexico at that time with the intention of residing permanently in the United States. The government argued that he'd crossed over from Ojinaga on January 10 along with the rest of the federal fugitives. The U.S. attorney in Santa Fe, still smarting from Salazar's acquittal, was "convinced Salazar should be prosecuted to the full extent of the law for his repeated perjury in connection with this matter."[57] The government began locating witnesses who'd seen Salazar in Ojinaga after the date he'd sworn he'd left.[58] A federal grand jury in Santa

Fe returned an indictment for perjury charging Salazar with having lied at his habeas corpus hearing. His trial was to begin on November 30 in Albuquerque.[59]

But on the night of November 20, Salazar escaped from jail in Albuquerque under very questionable circumstances indicating that the jailbreak was an inside job that Elfego Baca had organized for a hefty fee. The Bureau agent in Albuquerque characterized Baca as "unscrupulous, would stoop to anything and stop at nothing."[60] To gather incriminating evidence, the Bureau agent in Albuquerque even wanted to install a dictograph in the Graham Brothers' Saloon, which Baca and his cronies frequented.[61] On April 10, 1915, Baca and his associates were indicted for conspiracy in the Salazar escape, but on December 18, 1915, an all-Hispanic jury acquitted everybody.

Meanwhile, on January 31, 1915, Baca had shot and killed Celestino Otero, one of his fellow conspirators, on an El Paso street. Indicted for murder, Baca pleaded self-defense. At his trial, Otero's widow testified that her late husband had gone to see Baca to collect a promised $1,000, presumably payment for his role in the Salazar escape. The jury, however, acquitted Baca on January 25, 1916, after deliberating for twelve minutes. Interestingly, a New Mexico lawman acquaintance of Baca's who investigated the Otero killing later claimed that Baca had rushed to a pawn shop, purchased a pistol, and placed it on Otero's body.[62]

While Elfego Baca's machinations were unfolding, Sabino Guaderrama, who'd been smuggling ammunition to the Huerta garrison in Juárez until Villa captured the town, was negotiating with the Constitutionalist garrison commander, General Eugenio Aguirre Benavides, to supply him with ammunition.[63] Guaderrama provided samples and a price list, using as his agent one Luis R. Goldbaum, a Constitutionalist operative. And there were reports that Sabino's father, José, had 75,000 cartridges concealed in the attic of his store in Smeltertown. The district attorney secured a search warrant on the very dubious ground that "the ammunition is being assembled for the purpose of insurrection and riot." A party composed of Bureau informant John Wren, a Texas Ranger, and two El Paso county deputy sheriffs searched the premises but found nothing.[64] The Guaderramas were not garden-variety smugglers. They were businessmen of substance in Smeltertown: "The Guaderrama property is composed of store, restaurant, residence, rooming house, motion picture theater and corral. Another piece of property which was covered by the warrant and which was searched is composed of grocery store, saloon, residence, and corral."[65] What the Guaderramas illustrate was the propensity of El Pasoans, regardless of ethnicity and socioeconomic status, to profit from the Mexican Revolution.

CHAPTER 10

Huerta's Defeat

By 1914 the Mexican Revolution had become big business. Ammunition smuggling increased as Villa sought to stockpile supplies for his forthcoming campaign southward along the Mexican Central Railroad. The local Constitutionalists had become more sophisticated in their operations. They put the word out on the street assuring anyone wishing to engage in arms smuggling that if they were arrested, bond would be furnished, attorneys would be provided, and any fines would be paid. So, smugglers had only to fear a prison sentence if convicted. The firm of Brown and Terry, the attorneys for the Constitutionalists in El Paso, was prepared to represent anyone smuggling for their clients.

According to the Bureau, Brown and Terry weren't considered the best lawyers in town, and it was suspected they'd been hired for ulterior motives. It seems that Volney Brown, the firm's senior partner, was the brother-in-law of U.S. commissioner George Oliver. Their hiring Brown and Terry, E. M. Blanford thought, "rather shows the tendency of the Mexicans to endeavor to take advantage of such circumstances in the hope of securing lighter bonds or of probably getting a man turned loose when, otherwise, he might be held." However, the Bureau considered Commissioner Oliver to be a man of integrity, and so Bureau agents did not feel compelled to give any preferential treatment to the Constitutionalists. Saloon keeper Teodoro Kyriacopulos coordinated smuggling activities and functioned as bondsman for Constitutionalist smugglers. In fact he incurred such a great liability in signing bonds that Commissioner Oliver finally refused to let him sign any more. Kyriacopulos's father-in-law succeeded him as bondsman.[1]

Constitutionalist activity in El Paso was at a fever pitch. For example, a single shipment for Villa consisted of eight thousand uniforms, and at least $50,000 was spent with local merchants for foodstuffs and for fifty carloads of coal for Villa's locomotives. In addition, there was a sharp increase in the sale of army surplus. Most importantly, arms smuggling reached unprecedented levels.[2]

A development that profoundly altered the dynamics of the secret war in El Paso occurred on February 3, 1914, when President Wilson lifted the arms embargo.[3] The military guards at the El Paso bridges were removed, ammunition smugglers were suddenly thrown out of work, and a veritable flood of munitions poured into Mexico.

It was estimated that within the next few days some 3 million small-arms cartridges were exported to Ciudad Juárez in addition to thousands of rifles Villa had ordered for immediate delivery. Another 1 million rounds, several hundred rifles, and two machine guns were held at Fort Bliss, but on February 6 the Justice Department ordered the immediate release of all munitions seized in Texas, New Mexico, and Arizona except those used as evidence in pending cases. The munitions were delivered to the Constitutionalists.

The chief of the Bureau telegraphed to his agents: "Suspend investigations arms matters which have not yet resulted court proceedings."[4] All neutrality investigations were put on hold while the agency adjusted to this dramatically different state of affairs. The result in El Paso was that "all ammunition and gun smuggling cases were presented to the Grand Jury and on instructions from the District Attorney that the law under which these cases were sought to be presented had been repealed, returned 'no bill.'"[5] Jubilation reigned in many households.

Besides what crossed the border at El Paso, there were 2 million rounds sent across from Brownsville, while in New Orleans some 15 million cartridges, 13,700 rifles, 4 machine guns, and 600 revolvers started for Mexico by sea. Most of the backlogged munitions went to the Constitutionalists, but the Huerta government tried to get its share, sending a gunboat to New Orleans to stock up.[6]

And in preparation for his forthcoming campaign against Torreón, Villa ordered from American manufacturers 5,000 shrapnel shells for his 30 70- and 80-mm fieldpieces, an order worth $50,000. He also purchased a machine for making shrapnel shells, and it too was exported through El Paso. (Villa had tried to manufacture his own shrapnel shells but they proved worthless.)[7] The Mexican general even purchased three airplanes, which were delivered in El Paso. As of March 21, Villa had imported through El Paso since February 4 some 3.5 million rifle cartridges, 20 small mountain howitzers, and thousands of rifles. He was anxiously awaiting the arrival of five siege guns he had purchased in the East. He had also equipped his forces with forty-five automobiles.[8]

With the lifting of the arms embargo the nature of the arms traffic changed significantly. No longer could border firms such as Shelton-Payne and Krakauer meet the demand. Not that they didn't try; W. H. Shelton, of Shelton-Payne, gave a talk in 1916 entitled "Villa as a Customer." He recalled that when the embargo was lifted he promptly went to Juárez, met with Villa, and "contracted to sell him enough ammunition to kill all the revolutionists in Mexico if it had been judiciously used."[9]

The arms traffic into Mexico had assumed monumental proportions.[10] Yet this traffic has received little scholarly attention.[11] The Constitutionalists increasingly dealt directly with the munitions manufacturers in the East, ordering enormous quantities. On May 18, 1914, for example, Remington Arms Company received a wire from Lázaro de la Garza, Pancho Villa's confidential commercial representative in El Paso, regarding an order for 5 million cartridges, 3 million to be shipped to El Paso and 2 million to some seaport on the Gulf Coast. Charles Flint and Company, 25 Broad Street, New York City, a firm that had been doing business with Mexican revolutionists for some time, handled this transaction. This was in addition to a 3-million-round order other Constitutionalists placed with Flint.[12]

Charles R. Flint was a businessman and financier with an international reputation and an intimate knowledge of Latin America. He'd been a partner in W. R. Grace and Company, had consolidated rubber interests in South America, had bought warships and munitions for the Brazilian government, had negotiated the sale of warships for Argentina, Chile, and Japan, was prominent in establishing the Bureau of American Republics in Washington, D.C., and had founded the forerunner of IBM. He was known as "the Father of Trusts."[13] And he was a partisan of Carranza and Villa, whose photographs graced his office.[14] What Flint arranged was a steady series of shipments by sea from New York usually to Galveston but occasionally to Tampico or through Havana. Munitions would be shipped on the Southern Pacific Railroad from Galveston to El Paso. Juan T. Burns, the Constitutionalist consul in Galveston, was a key figure in this traffic. Remington kept the Bureau informed of the amount and date of each shipment and the vessel it was sent on.[15]

The arms traffic reached ludicrous heights when some American businessmen tried to sell Pancho Villa a submarine. In February 1915, Enrique Llorente, Villa's representative in Washington, D.C., informed the general that they had been offered a submarine, the property of an unnamed but leading shipyard in the United States. He included a photograph and specifications of the sub, whose owners were asking $340,000, which included the batteries, valued at $26,000. The craft had a crew of ten, three torpedo tubes, a range of 850 miles at six knots per hour, and ran on gasoline. It had been built for the Russian government but in the wake of the outbreak of World War I, the United States had prohibited its export on the grounds that it would violate the neutrality laws. This of course raised the issue of how it could be sold to Villa. The owners assured Llorente that they had dispatched the submarine to Key West, Florida, where the U.S. Navy was about to test several submarines. In a moment of naval inattention, the sub would simply put out to sea and head for the coast of Tabasco or Campeche. Llorente informed the owners that Villa probably could not buy the vessel but that he would send the particulars to the general, who would make the final decision.[16] Not surprisingly, Villa did not buy the submarine, but the affair conjures up delightful images of a *villista* navy.

Lázaro de la Garza handled the logistics for Villa. He was a U.S. citizen born in Laredo who had established himself in Torreón, where he had become wealthy by selling mining properties and managing a mining enterprise. He built himself a mansion costing some $50,000. When Villa captured Torreón on October 1, 1913, he assessed a war tax of three million pesos against the city and named a three-man commission, one of whom was de la Garza, to collect the forced loan.[17] Villa was so pleased with de la Garza's performance that he placed him in charge of the Division of the North's finances. De la Garza was one of the comparatively few civilians of outstanding ability to attach himself to Villa, who was a dangerous man to work for given his penchant for flying into a rage and having people shot.

The press reported on February 24, 1914, that de la Garza had been appointed Villa's commercial and financial agent, with headquarters in Juárez.[18] De la Garza was crucial to Villa's continued success. Not only did he negotiate the purchase of millions of cartridges and other munitions but he also orchestrated the purchase of enormous quantities of supplies. As with munitions, at the height of Villa's power El Paso merchants could not meet the demand by themselves, and de la Garza's representatives in New York signed large contracts: in June 1914, for example, they contracted for 55,000 pairs of shoes, 25,000 khaki uniforms, 2,000 suits of knitted underwear, 10,000 pairs of leggings, and 10,000 campaign hats, to be delivered through El Paso to Juárez.[19]

De la Garza also supervised the sale of loot to pay for the munitions and supplies. When Villa recaptured Torreón in the spring of 1914 he confiscated the entire cotton crop of the surrounding Laguna region, loaded thousands of bales of cotton into boxcars, and rushed them to El Paso for sale to American buyers. One hundred carloads of cotton arrived in Juárez on April 8 alone. Despite the legal obstacles that the cotton's owners, many of them Spaniards and thus particular targets of Villa's wrath, put in the way, enough cotton was marketed in the United States to enable Villa to reequip the Division of the North into the most formidable army in Mexico.[20]

Helping to market this crop in the United States was T. M. Solomon, who, having considerable experience in shipping munitions to Mexico, knew his way around the murky world of arms trafficking.[21] Felix Sommerfeld telegraphed to Solomon in June to come to El Paso to handle cotton deals. Solomon did so, moving into Sommerfeld's room at the Sheldon Hotel, Sommerfeld being out of town at the time. Sam Dreben, Solomon's associate, soon made his appearance. (We last saw the pair at the wharf in New Orleans supervising the loading of the 300,000 cartridges consigned to the Guatemalan government.) Agent Blanford's former informant and interpreter John Wren was now working for Solomon, helping him import and market the vast quantities of Laguna cotton. Solomon bought the cotton through an arrangement with the cotton's rightful owners and Villa whereby the owners dropped their legal challenges to the sales in return for a small percentage of the sales price.

Blanford asked Wren about Solomon's operations, and Wren replied "that Solomon is known to be willing to turn almost any sort of a deal for the money."

Wren had heard that Todd McClammy, "who is a Villa sympathizer and assistant," had introduced Solomon to a prominent Constitutionalist, saying "He has helped us many times with ammunition." Solomon was also representing someone in New York or New Orleans anxious to sell khaki uniforms to the Constitutionalists. He had samples in his room at the Sheldon and was showing them to Constitutionalist agents.

The frenzy in munitions was accompanied by a sharp increase in the sale of all kinds of army surplus in El Paso.[22] Besides those engaged in the profitable arms traffic, various other businessmen were getting in on the action. Haymon Krupp, a local wholesale dry goods dealer, had already sold $7,726 worth of hats, shorts, khaki suits (2,200), shoes, socks, handkerchiefs, and underwear to the Constitutionalists in Douglas.[23] In January 1914, Krupp reportedly sold to the Sonoran Constitutionalists some ten thousand uniforms "of the jumper and full trouser, and while not like the ordinary military khaki uniforms," these "are, of course, to be used for clothing the rebel soldiers."[24] He became one of the major suppliers for Villa's Division of the North. Villa sent Venustiano Carranza a letter of introduction for Victor Carusso, Krupp's partner and brother-in-law, stating that the firm had been "one of our best friends" in El Paso and had helped the cause significantly. Villa had arranged to buy from Krupp a considerable amount of clothing and equipment for his troops and had agreed to a down payment of 175,000 pesos in Constitutionalist currency, which he asked Carranza to have paid. Carranza did so. On one occasion Krupp sold Villa fifty thousand pairs of shoes, the shipment filling twelve boxcars. Krupp also sold clothing to the *huertista* troops interned in Fort Bliss.[25]

Outsiders who sold supplies on a smaller scale soon appeared in El Paso. One W. S. Kirk, for instance, opened an army surplus store at 310 San Antonio Street, initially stating that although he had a large stock of weaponry and ammunition in New Orleans, he wasn't trying to sell these items on the border because he didn't want to break the law. So he confined himself to dealing in cartridge belts, scabbards, canteens, and so forth. Kirk did a flourishing business, especially after Wilson lifted the arms embargo.[26] A major outfit that moved into El Paso to get its share of revolutionary business was the Cal Hirsch Army and Navy Goods Store of St. Louis, Missouri. Hirsch already had a branch store in Los Angeles and now established another in El Paso, at 120 East Overland Street, dealing in ammunition, equipment, and clothing.[27]

Not only was Villa's logistical network flourishing but so was his intelligence network in El Paso. The key figure was Héctor Ramos, an experienced operative whose office, complete with secretary, was room 418 in the First National Bank Building. He had been the head of the Thiel Detective Service's branch office in Mexico City and later had served as chief of the city detectives in that capital. He had joined the

Constitutionalists in Matamoros in 1913. Ramos represented a new approach to the Mexican intelligence service in the United States. He felt that experience had shown that authorizing consuls to recruit their own secret agents had resulted in wasteful expenditures, spotty results, and lack of oversight of agents. Therefore, he favored a consolidated intelligence network. He had proposed such a structure to Carranza in November 1913, but at that time the First Chief didn't think it necessary.[28] However, Ramos now secured Villa's blessing to implement his scheme. Ramos stated that El Paso was the headquarters for the entire border from Tijuana to Matamoros for the following reasons:

1. El Paso had the best communications network, facilitating the dispatch of agents.
2. The archives of the intelligence network could be safeguarded in El Paso in case of calamity.
3. Because of El Paso's size, it was easier to keep agents under cover there than in any other border town.
4. Because of El Paso's commercial importance, intelligence headquarters could be established under commercial cover.
5. Finally, El Paso was strategically located on the border.

Ramos wanted agents in Nogales, Eagle Pass, Laredo, Brownsville, and perhaps in Los Angeles and New Orleans, but, interestingly enough, he did not mention San Antonio. These agents posed as small independent businessmen and passed themselves off as enemies of the Constitutionalist cause. Under Ramos's system, one copy of reports filed by the agents went to headquarters and one copy to the civil or military authorities. The services of consular personnel were enlisted as needed, and El Paso was the headquarters of the Constitutionalist consular service.[29]

Ramos claimed to have a dozen men working for him in and around town. His agents included former Bureau agent in charge H. A. Thompson, Powell Roberts (he of the coal-covered ammunition fame), Henry Kramp (formerly of the Thiel Detective Service), and Henry Gray, who had previously operated in California. In addition, Todd McClammy operated semi-independently of Ramos, on occasion traveling to Deming and Las Cruces, New Mexico. These assignments could get dangerous; while investigating an alleged federal filibustering expedition being organized in Las Cruces, McClammy pursued suspicious characters by auto one night, encountering on the road pieces of tin with nails poking through them and a potentially lethal wire strung across the road. Fortunately for McClammy he had the windshield up.[30] Our old friend Abe Molina handled a subagent, Luis Regalado Guillén, but played only a minor role, a far cry from his heyday in 1912. Presumably the Constitutionalists had doubts about his loyalty, and Molina soon faded from the scene. (But as of April 1918, Molina was working for the Mexican consul in Tucson as a secret agent, reporting on anti-Carranza activities.)[31] Then there was Emil Holmdahl, who operated on the fringes of the Villa network, quietly advertising himself as a freelancer and willing to become an informant for whoever paid best.[32] Holmdahl was acting as an agent provocateur against the federals.[33] Sometimes Charles Stevens, a Constitutionalist agent who operated mainly in San Antonio, would appear in El Paso.[34] Stevens had been the chief deputy sheriff of Bexar County and would in time become a Texas Ranger captain. And of course Felix Sommerfeld was periodically in El Paso combating *huertista* machinations.

The Bureau of Investigation relied heavily on the *villista* operatives for information. Perennially short of money, the Bureau could afford only one Anglo informant in El Paso. The agency did get some help from the army, specifically from several men of Troop D of the 13th Cavalry, who were still stationed within El Paso at Eighth and Florence streets and who still maintained surveillance in plain clothes over Krakauer, Shelton-Payne, and the pawn shops. Yet on occasion the soldiers also apprehended those believed to be carrying ammunition and turned them over to the police.[35] This whole operation was extralegal, and everyone seemed uncomfortable with it, but until some flap occurred it would continue.

The Bureau got an enormous break in September. R. L. Hall, a Los Angeles arms and ammunition dealer, with offices at 602 Garland Building, was also a Constitutionalist agent. He gave the Bureau the cipher used by Carranza agents throughout the United States.[36]

Trying to fend off this formidable combination of Bureau and Constitutionalist operatives was Miguel E. Diebold, Huerta's inspector of consulates in the United States. (Consul Enrique de la Sierra handled the routine business of the El Paso consulate.) Diebold's principal assignment was to direct Huerta's intelligence apparatus on the border. To that end, all reports went to Diebold in El Paso.[37] Consul Diebold spent some time in San Antonio, and Felix Sommerfeld urged the Bureau to watch him, as he was probably up to no good. Agent Blanford was already suspicious, for the last time he'd been in the El Paso Mexican consulate he casually inquired about Diebold's whereabouts, and the consulate staff said they didn't know. "This looked very suspicious to me as I had previously suspected, and had some reason to believe, that Mr. Diebold was doing work aside from the usual and ordinary duties of his office."[38]

What Diebold was doing was arranging to reduce the number of *huertistas* in El Paso. The city swarmed with them between the refugees on the streets and those confined in the Fort Bliss internment camp. In collusion with a railroad ticket agent,

Diebold was sending out almost nightly by rail to Eagle Pass and other border points parties of from ten to twenty Huerta soldiers under the command of an officer.[39] Some of these were men who'd escaped from the Fort Bliss detention camp. A notable escapee was the commander of irregulars General Blas Orpinel, who as a Red Flagger in 1912 had gone by the name of "Luis Fernández." He got all the way to Amarillo before immigration inspectors captured him. He was returned under military escort to the Fort Bliss prison camp.[40]

The object of Diebold's exercise to get soldiers back into the fight against the Constitutionalists. When asked about these activities, Diebold replied that he was helping to repatriate refugees, strictly as a humanitarian gesture, and that those he was assisting included men, women, and children. He pointed out that he was actually performing a service for the El Paso authorities, for otherwise these indigent refugees would have to be supported from public funds.[41] Diebold did express concern to his government about indigent Mexicans and the obstructive attitude of the local authorities, but no one ever saw women and children being shipped out, only able-bodied men. But the chief of the Bureau was of the opinion that a federal indictment against Diebold couldn't be successfully prosecuted.[42]

Diebold further irritated the Bureau by complaining that the Constitutionalists were operating an organized spy system to watch the Mexican consulate. He was shadowed everywhere he went. "This spying is entirely arbitrary and uncalled for and cannot be justified by any acts of mine or of the Mexican Consular office at this city." In particular Diebold complained that Constitutionalist agents were circulating false reports that the Mexican consulate was recruiting or organizing a military expedition.[43]

The reason Constitutionalist agents were circulating reports of the Mexican consulate being involved in a filibustering expedition was because the Mexican consulate was involved in a filibustering expedition. On February 12 and 13, the El Paso newspapers carried stories of an armed expedition having crossed the Rio Grande into Mexico at Ysleta and alleging that the expedition had been recruited and equipped in El Paso.[44] *Villista* agents Todd McClammy and Héctor Ramos informed the Bureau that the expedition was organized in El Paso under Consul Diebold's supervision and that the men were sent by automobile and by the interurban to Benigno Alderete's ranch near Ysleta.[45]

The Alderete family—Benigno and his sons Francisco (known as "Frank") and Isaac (known as "Ike")—were staunch partisans of conservative Mexican factions. They'd supported Orozco and now supported Huerta. Ike had even informed the U.S. commissioner that he wanted to sign the bond for José Inés Salazar.[46] Although ideology doubtless played a role, the Alderetes' support of Huerta also stemmed from self-interest: while the *huertistas* occupied Juárez, Ike Alderete had enjoyed the extremely lucrative keno concession, which he lost when Villa captured the town and awarded that juicy prize to his good friends Teodoro Kyriacopulos and Carlos Jáuregui.[47]

A certain Juan Natividad was the recruiting officer for the filibustering expedition, operating under Consul Diebold's direction. Victor Ochoa, now a Huerta secret agent, also worked for Consul Diebold and helped to organize the enterprise. Assisting Natividad were the Alderete brothers, especially Frank.[48] Those being recruited were taken to the Mexican consulate, where Diebold or one of his staff gave each one $5 and informed them they were going to the Alderete ranch, where they'd be issued horses, saddles, and armament. Most of the 257 recruits were men with no military experience but who were anxious to eat. Taking them to the Mexican consulate in the Caples Building was not really a good idea, for two reasons. First, Emil Holmdahl was stationed across the street observing who entered and left the building. Second, there was such a crush of recruits that other tenants in the building complained bitterly, and the consulate had to move to Magoffin Avenue, where men then congregated outside the building by the dozen, prompting the neighbors to complain.[49]

On February 11, the recruits were transported to the Alderete ranch. Most of them departed from the house Frank Alderete owned in the city. The neighbors probably noticed the several hundred men milling around outside and the twelve automobiles assembled to transport them. In the midst of this crowd was recruit Alejandro D. Chávez, who happened to be a *villista* secret agent working for Todd McClammy. Using the pretext that he was trying to locate two men whom he was hoping to recruit, Chávez periodically slipped away to telephone McClammy and keep him abreast of developments. Chávez managed to avoid going to Ysleta by claiming that he was still trying to locate the potential recruits. Most of the multitude went to Ysleta by automobile. Each vehicle made several round trips, transporting men even as night began to fall. A few of the recruits took the interurban to Ysleta. There they were met, exchanged password and countersign, and were directed to the ranch, where more than two hundred horses were waiting in the corral.[50] The horses, some of them ex-federal mounts seized in Presidio after the battle of Ojinaga, had been obtained at a U.S. government auction sale.[51] Most of the rifles for the expedition were either purchased from smugglers or, after the arms embargo was lifted on February 3, on the open market. The ammunition and some rifles, ironically enough, may well have come from Fort Bliss.

On February 17, Captain A. P. Watts, the post quartermaster, who had charge of ammunition, reported to the assistant U.S. attorney that he believed there was a shortage. The distraught captain was right. Ammunition seized for neutrality violations was kept in a root cellar at the post, and when Watts made a casual estimate he discovered to his horror a serious shortage. When the U.S. attorney sent

Agent Blanford to help conduct a detailed inventory, it was found that the shortage amounted to:

	Cartridges Seized	Short
Powell Roberts, G. Padres, J. B. Badger case	448,000	10,000
Fermín Ríos case	7,000	1,000
Marcos B. Castillo case	20,000	16,000
Hilario Limón case	8,000	1,000
Lázaro Alanís case (seized by Major Rice in Columbus, N.Mex.)	50,000	42,000
	533,000	70,000

There were also some rifles and other small quantities of ammunition missing.

It turned out that Watts's superior officer had received confidential information from the jealous wife of a sergeant that the ammunition had been stolen by the quartermaster sergeant with the assistance of a city water works employee and a Signal Corps soldier. The stolen cartridges were initially hidden at Logan's ranch, just north of the Fort Bliss reservation.[52] An informant later told the Bureau that Ike Alderete had received the stolen ammunition. The army found fourteen carbines whose serial numbers "were proximate" to seized carbines still stored at Fort Bliss. When called before the grand jury the informant denied everything he'd said about the arms from Fort Bliss having been delivered to Alderete. The witness was arrested and charged with perjury.[53]

Wherever the ammunition came from, very little of it was used by the filibustering expedition. The commander of this force was the former *orozquista* and more recently *huertista* Rodrigo Quevedo, assisted by his brother Silvestre and by José Orozco, a cousin of General Pascual Orozco. Quevedo's mission was to destroy sections of the Mexican Central Railroad between Juárez and the city of Chihuahua. At the request of Frank Alderete, Consul Diebold provided $722 to support the expedition.[54] Quevedo's subordinate officers, like himself, were federals who had been defeated at Ojinaga and had been released from the Fort Bliss internment camp. The rank and file were a pretty motley crew whose combat effectiveness was problematical. For example, Quevedo had personally recruited one Gabino Guillén, promising him the rank of sergeant. When Guillén was later asked about his military experience he replied that he had none but he was a good friend of Quevedo's.[55]

On the night of February 11 the first few members of the expedition began entering Mexico at the Socorro ford, three miles south of Ysleta. Their comrades back at the ranch scattered like quail, because they'd received an urgent warning that the U.S. Army was on the way to arrest them.[56] And in fact two troops of cavalry from Washington Park in east El Paso and one troop stationed in the hamlet of Clint were bearing down on the Alderete ranch in response to a report that an armed expedition would try to cross the Rio Grande that night. When the soldiers arrived around midnight they seized 225 horses and mules from Alderete's corral and a corresponding number of saddles and bridles. They also arrested six men who were caring for the stock. Inexplicably, the army didn't conduct a search for arms and ammunition until the following night, February 12. Some twenty soldiers spent three hours searching Benigno Alderete's premises but came up empty.[57] Somebody had spirited the munitions away. Imagine that.

The newspapers reported that some twenty-seven to thirty filibusters had been captured on the Mexican side of the Rio Grande on the night of February 11 and that some of them were being held as prisoners in Juárez. Blanford and Ed Bryant, a deputy U.S. marshal, decided to go to Juárez and try to interview the prisoners in hopes that they might shed further light on the expedition. The two American lawmen were ushered into the presence of General Francisco Villa himself. When they explained their mission Pancho Villa informed them that only seven men had crossed and that they had all been killed in a skirmish with his troops. He had no prisoners in Juárez. The Americans explained that they were anxious to get to the bottom of the affair and apprehend whoever was responsible for the expedition. As Blanford later reported, "Villa was not altogether reasonable in his talk, asserting that Don Luis Terrazas, a man named Cuilty, and certain others, for example Juan Creel, were responsible for this attempted invasion and that the fact that horses and men were accumulated at Ysleta ought to be sufficient evidence, apparently not realizing to what degree of proof the Government is put in proving a criminal case. Villa was, however, very courteous in his treatment of us."[58] This was good, because Villa obviously wasn't concerned about the rules of evidence. He'd recently ordered a certain Domingo Flores executed in Juárez because Flores had allegedly embezzled $3,500 Villa had given him to purchase ammunition ($3,500, by the way, would buy a lot of ammunition—the 70,000 cartridges stolen from Fort Bliss were worth $2,600).[59]

Since there was suspicion that the Terrazas clan were behind the filibustering expedition, Lieutenant W. N. Hensley, the acting Fort Bliss provost marshal (and intelligence officer), decided to take action. He and Powell Roberts, now working as an agent for Héctor Ramos, went to the Bureau office and inquired as to where a Spanish stenographer might be found. They'd installed a Dictaphone in Terrazas's office in the Mills Building, and the initial conversation Lieutenant Hensley had overhead concerned the purchase of a quantity of shoes. Since the Terrazas clan weren't noted for their interest in footwear, their references to "shoes" was no doubt code for arms or ammunition. Hensley and Powell thought that important information could be obtained if a stenographer systematically transcribed what was being said in that room.[60] There were also reports that the Terrazas were involved in another filibustering expedition, one being prepared in Las Cruces, New Mexico. Both Todd McClammy and Agent Blanford investigated these rumors and found them baseless, although some members of the Terrazas clan were indeed living as refugees in Las Cruces.[61]

Whether anything important resulted from this exercise in bugging an office is unknown, but the affair does illustrate the close connection between the army and Bureau of Investigation on the one hand and the Constitutionalists on the other, even though Constitutionalists had been violating the neutrality laws as had been the *huertistas*. As the above incident illustrates, the connection went beyond the mere sharing of information. On the night of March 7 a party consisting of Agent Blanford, police detective Fred Delgado and *villista* agents Héctor Ramos and H. A. Thompson went to the Union Depot and arrested eight Mexicans whom they suspected were being shipped out of El Paso by Consul Diebold.[62] *Villista* agent Thompson was left in charge of those arrested while Blanford and Delgado boarded the train and rode it for a short distance searching for other *huertistas*.[63] It's hard to imagine this kind of cooperation between the American authorities and, say, Consul Diebold.

In fact, the next day, March 8, after conferring with assistant U.S. attorney Robert T. Neill and U.S. commissioner Oliver, the Bureau filed a federal complaint against Miguel Diebold, consul general of Mexico at large, E. de la Sierra, consul, Alfredo Margáin, vice consul, and F. de J. Saldaña, paymaster, charging them with "conspiring to hire and retain men to go beyond the limits or jurisdiction of the U.S. to enlist in the service of a foreign people, to wit: the Federal or Huertista Army."[64] Arrest warrants were issued, and when the defendants were arraigned before Commissioner Oliver, he fixed their bonds at $2,000 for Diebold and de la Sierra and $1,000 for Margáin and Saldaña. Diebold wrote a check for $6,000 on the First National Bank, officials of that bank signed the bonds, and the defendants were released.[65]

Consul Diebold retained the firm of Walthall and Gamble, attorneys for the Mexican consulate, to defend the men arrested in the Union Depot on the night of March 7 and charged with enlisting in a foreign army. On March 8, federal complaints were filed against the three who had confessed as well as against the five who had not. The Bureau thought it desirable to get the three out of jail because they had given signed statements. They were released on their own recognizance to appear as government witnesses against their five companions at a preliminary hearing. So they'd have no excuse for leaving the United States, it was arranged for two of the three to get work at a ranch in Anthony, New Mexico, across the state line. The third lived in El Paso, and he was an informant for Héctor Ramos.[66] The Bureau learned that Diebold was trying to bribe the three witnesses, the go-between being a Hispanic El Paso attorney, Felipe Seijas, whose office was room 202 in the Mills Building. Seijas would reportedly give them each $200 to leave town. One of the witnesses was observed entering the Mexican consulate with his father and another man, and they were then followed to Seijas's office. But the consul and Seijas had second thoughts about suborning witnesses. Seijas informed them he couldn't offer them money to leave town as that might involve them in even greater legal difficulties.[67] At the preliminary hearing Diebold, de la Sierra, and Saldaña were bound over to the action of the grand jury, while Margáin was discharged.

Despite the Bureau's having taken action against Consul Diebold and his staff, the flow of *huertista* soldiers by rail to the Eagle Pass area continued. One Ben Coltman, a South El Paso Street secondhand dealer who also peddled articles at the Fort Bliss prison camp, pointed out to Captain Harry N. Cootes, the Fort Bliss provost marshal, certain Mexicans at the Union Depot who had escaped from Fort Bliss and who were about to leave for Eagle Pass. The captain arrested seven of them on the spot. Coltman knew them because he had sold the Mexicans some of the clothing they were wearing in their attempt to escape from El Paso.[68]

In an unusual development, Victor Ochoa informed Agent Blanford that Carlos H. Echegaray (whom Blanford had employed as an informant in Douglas in 1913) was one of those who had crossed at Ysleta. Ochoa's motives for informing on Echegaray, a fellow *huertista*, are unclear; perhaps he was suspicious of Echegaray on account of his connection with the Bureau. Blanford arranged for Echegaray to call at the Bureau office, where the Mexican made a clean breast of the Ysleta expedition and his involvement with the federals in recent months. He claimed the Huerta government owed him $900 for his services as a rebel major in the Orozco rebellion. In early January he had gone to the Mexican consulate, had spoken with de la Sierra, and had asked for his money. De la Sierra told him the best way to get his money was for him to go to Piedras Negras and report to the federal commander there. He would be given a military command at his former rank. On February 9, he received a railroad pass to Eagle Pass for this purpose. Echegaray showed the document to Agent Blanford—it was identical to those Diebold had issued to the eight "refugees" arrested at the Union Depot on March 7. Echegaray had also asked Diebold for some money and had received $5 for travel expenses.

On February 11 he had been approached by José Orozco with a proposition—to join the Ysleta expedition. Echegaray was offered the rank of major, and he readily accepted. Frank and Ike Alderete supervised the dispatch of men to their father's ranch, where recruits were herded into a corral behind Benigno Alderete's house.

According to Echegaray the plan had been to cross 150 men that night, but only forty-two got across mounted, armed, and otherwise equipped before American troops raided the ranch. Echegaray said he was one of those who crossed. They burned several bridges on the Mexico Northwest Railroad and had one skirmish with Villa's forces. "Echegaray stated that he left the men because Quevedo was using him and the other men to get money for himself and did not give the men anything." Echegaray also stated that Victor Ochoa helped to organize the expedition and that there were seven other men in El Paso who had abandoned Quevedo. He claimed he could locate them and that they would probably testify. He offered to become an informant and help assemble the witnesses and secure their statements. Blanford received permission to employ Echegaray to gather evidence in the Diebold case. Echegaray was willing to provide information but wanted Blanford's assurance that he would not be called as a witness.[69]

Blanford's tradecraft left something to be desired. Instead of meeting with his informant Echegaray either at some inconspicuous location or else in some crowded place, Blanford had Echegaray phone him every time he wanted to come to the Bureau office to report, "as it might happen that someone from the Mexican Consulate or others familiar with his role in the Ysleta expedition would be present who I would not care to see Echegaray call at my office." The U.S. Commissioner's office was across the hall from Blanford's office, and there was a constant procession of people being arraigned, which would make Echegaray's presence in the Bureau office rather dicey.[70]

Echegaray was playing a dangerous game. He followed the seven potential witnesses all the way to the camp of the Quevedo brothers and José Orozco, located about twenty-five miles south of Columbus. Despite his efforts to persuade the seven to return to El Paso so they could be subpoenaed, they refused, and Echegaray returned alone and unscathed to El Paso. There, Agent Blanford persuaded Echegaray to pretend to be arrested and be confined in the Fort Bliss detention camp so he could pump inmate Juan Natividad, the Ysleta expedition's recruiting officer, for further details about the affair. If it were discovered that he was a snitch his life expectancy would be brief. Blanford stated that "I arranged with Major Michie, District Adjutant, to place Echegaray in the camp with the privilege of taking him out at my pleasure." To substantiate Echegaray's cover story, Blanford had him arrested at the Gem Saloon, taken to the camp, and placed in the same enclosure with Natividad.[71]

Echegaray reported that Ike Alderete, whom the Bureau planned to have indicted in connection with the Ysleta expedition, had visited Natividad at the internment camp and had cautioned him not to talk about the expedition, promising to secure Natividad's freedom in a few days. Blanford commented that Alderete was merely trying to keep Natividad in line, for "Alderete, of course, has no means of getting any one out of the camp as the men are held without bond," but "if Natividad were released the Alderetes would get him out of the way before Court, or if he were put in county jail under an appearance bond, Alderete would give the bond and again get him out of the way. It was decided for the present to leave Natividad in camp."

Blanford had Echegaray released from the camp and instructed him to produce witnesses of the Ysleta expedition and the Eagle Pass recruiting organization.[72] Echegaray now reported verbally to Blanford on a daily basis. He stated that Frank and Ike Alderete not only had managed to bribe the three original witnesses and get them out of town but had tried to induce Echegaray himself to leave so he couldn't testify.[73]

Blanford assisted U.S. attorney C. C. Cresson to present the Diebold case to the grand jury, which returned indictments against Diebold, de la Sierra, Saldaña, and one F. Mármol. "It was thought better not to include Frank and Ike Alderete in the indictment but to make a separate case against them, probably taking the matter before [the] Commissioner at a later date rather than let [the] Grand Jury pass on the matter at this time."[74] Echegaray, "a valuable witness," testified before the grand jury. The government had such a strong case that Walthall and Gamble, the attorneys for Diebold and the other defendants, proposed a plea bargain: two defendants would plead guilty if the charges were dropped against the other two. The U.S. attorney replied that if Diebold and de la Sierra would plead guilty he would dismiss the charges against Saldaña and Mármol. The defense attorneys went off to consult with their clients. Meanwhile, the cases were set for trial the next day, April 15.[75] The government announced it was ready for trial, but the defense requested a continuance, which the judge granted. The witnesses were discharged on their own recognizance to appear at the October term of the court. "No further use being had at this time for the services of informant C. R. Echegaray, the same were dispensed with."[76]

A few days later one of Frank Alderete's henchmen summoned Echegaray to the Alderetes' real estate office at 103 Mesa Avenue, where "Alderete took him to task in no uncertain manner about his, Echegaray's, having testified before the Grand Jury against the Mexican Consul. . . . Alderete became very abusive and presently attacked him with his fists, beating him up generally and giving him a black eye. Ike Alderete, Frank's brother, heard the noise, came into the room and upbraided Frank for his conduct, saying the Alderetes were not in the clear regarding the matter about which Echegaray had testified. Ike then put Frank out of the room and dressed Echegaray's face, which had been cut up considerably by a heavy ring on Frank's hand."[77]

Echegaray's troubles were soon vastly overshadowed by an event that plunged El Paso into crisis mode. On April 21, 1914, the U.S. Navy bombarded and seized Veracruz, the principal port in Mexico and Huerta's lifeline to Europe. Ostensibly this exercise in gunboat diplomacy occurred because Huerta hadn't fully complied with American demands stemming from a perceived insult to the American flag, but the occupation of Veracruz was also designed to deny Huerta a huge shipment of munitions arriving on a German vessel. There was of course a surge of patriotism in Mexico against this American invasion, and in El Paso, a city with a large Hispanic population, there was considerable anxiety among Anglos as to what Hispanics would do. Would their loyalty lie with Mexico or with the United States?

There was a lot of fiery rhetoric among some Hispanics about taking extreme measures against Anglos in the event of war between the United States and Mexico. Former informant Echegaray reported "that there was talk of blowing up the smelter, the gas tanks and plant, the electric power plant, the banks and appropriating the money, the ammunition houses and appropriating the arms and ammunition and other buildings in the city. Echegaray also stated that a storage warehouse where a lot of ammunition was stored for the Constitutionalists would be raided and the ammunition obtained." Agent Blanford promptly informed the military where the Constitutionalists' ammunition was stored, the warehouse having been pointed out to him by Emil Holmdahl "who had been with the Constitutionalists, but who is with the U.S. in case of trouble between the two countries." The 275,000 cartridges were in the warehouse of Gutiérrez-Velarde and Company, 338 South Leon Street. Velarde was a member of the local Constitutionalist junta.[78]

The army took steps to ensure that this ammunition didn't fall into the wrong hands. A guard was placed around the warehouse, as well as a boxcar with 675,000 rounds that arrived for the Constitutionalists on April 23. And on April 23 the United States reimposed the arms embargo on the export of munitions to Mexico. This time the embargo would last until September 8, 1914.[79] Moreover, the El Paso Spanish-language newspaper, *Mexico Libre*, which published an inflammatory article on April 23, was suppressed by the local authorities and its editor jailed on a charge of inciting a riot. And the Mexican consulate was placed under surveillance. Agent Blanford advocated strong measures to curtail Consul Diebold's activities; Blanford especially wanted to see Diebold's request that railroads furnish him with prepaid orders for tickets from California, Arizona, New Mexico, and Texas localities to points on the border turned down. This smacked of rushing men to Mexico for military service should full-scale hostilities ensue.[80] The U.S. attorney wanted to demonstrate that Diebold and de la Sierra were merely posing as officials of a foreign government. The State Department checked and reported that it had not recognized Diebold as consul general of Mexico at large but that an exequatur had been issued to de la Sierra in Naco, Arizona, on August 13, 1912.[81] Agent Blanford reported that during the tense period, April 21–23, "scarcely a Mexican could be seen on the streets, while usually one can hardly get through them on the sidewalks and parks are congested with them. Somebody circulated a report that in case of further trouble with Mexico, all the Mexicans in El Paso were going to be shot. It had the effect of clearing the streets for a few days. . . . There is probably more or less of an understanding among Mexicans that in case of war they will go to the other side, if they can get there, and join the army, but as for organized enlisting and recruiting . . . I do not think there is any going on."[82]

Another result of the war crisis was serious unrest at the Fort Bliss prison camp. This stemmed in part from the hardships the *huertistas* experienced; the best the Mexican consulate could do was to provide some clothing and a little cash from time to time.[83] But with war between the United States and Mexico seemingly imminent, the army took no chances, mounting machine guns, assigning two battalions of the 20th Infantry to guard the Huerta soldiers and their families, and issuing shoot-to-kill orders for those attempting to escape. El Pasoans were worried about an uprising among the five thousand interned Mexicans and wanted the 20th Infantry free to defend the city in the event of war. The solution was to transfer the prisoners away from the border. Accordingly, they were all transported by rail to Fort Wingate, west of Albuquerque. The first trainload arrived there on May 6, 1914, soon followed by four more.[84] El Pasoans breathed easier.

In the event, war did not break out, and passions cooled, although it would be November before U.S. forces evacuated Veracruz. Action against Diebold was deferred. By June, Diebold was recalled to Mexico City and his replacement as inspector of consulates was Arturo Elías, formerly consul in San Antonio. Elías reported that intelligence activities in El Paso were at a virtual standstill because Diebold left only $36 in the secret service fund.[85] Consul Enrique de la Sierra was transferred to Los Angeles, and his replacement in El Paso was Juan Hernández.[86]

At the April 1914, term of the federal court the government, which had doggedly been building a case against former Consul Enrique Llorente for neutrality violations, was able to present as key witnesses J. H. Noonan, J. D. Mahoney, and R. H. G. McDonald (who had just been discharged as a lieutenant in the Colorado National Guard).[87] Only Charpentier was absent. He'd worked for Thomas B. Cunningham, security chief of the Chino Copper Company, for a time and had last been heard from in February, writing from Canutillo, Durango, that he was a first captain in Constitutionalist general Tomás Urbina's command and had charge of his artillery. Thereafter Charpentier drifted to Central America, then back to the United States. In 1919, he testified before a Senate subcommittee. Cunningham, the old Díaz spy, didn't work as a security chief permanently. In March 1918, when working as a special agent in El Paso, the thirty-six-year-old investigator obtained a special Texas Ranger commission. By the time of his death on March 29, 1931, he'd become a prominent El Paso financier and president of the Nevada Consolidated Mining Company.[88] As it happened, the presiding judge over the Llorente trial was Waller T. Burns, who'd presided at the 1912 trial of the *reyistas* in Brownsville. He intimated to the U.S. attorney that in his opinion Llorente had been indicted under the wrong section of the U.S. Penal Code, for enlisting men for foreign service rather than for organizing an armed expedition, and that the case "had better be passed, which was done. Had this intimation come sooner a new indictment could have been returned."[89] (On April 14, 1916, the case was dismissed.)

The government suffered another setback when former Bureau informant and witness Carlos Echegaray came to a bad end in June. He'd been enticed across the border to Juárez, having been assured of safe conduct. But his record as an *orozquista* major in 1912 and his more recent participation in a federal filibustering expedition in Ysleta had sealed his fate. The *villistas* executed him.[90]

Blanford asked Héctor Ramos, Villa's intelligence chief in El Paso, about Echegaray, and Ramos gave a preposterous version of events. According to Ramos, Echegaray had gone to Juárez several times and had been warned to stay away because of his past *orozquista* and *huertista* affiliations. The *villista* authorities in Juárez were anxious to lay hands on him. One day when Ramos was in Juárez he happened to see Echegaray on the street and pointed him out to an official. Echegaray was arrested, and on his person was a letter in his own handwriting stating that he and his men were ready to serve Huerta at any time and all they needed were arms, ammunition, and equipment. Ramos added that Echegaray had been sent to Chihuahua along with a dossier containing his record. When Blanford first asked Ramos about Echegaray, Ramos maintained that he was in the penitentiary in Chihuahua, but when the Bureau agent pressed the issue Ramos finally said he "suspected" that Echegaray had been executed.

In a striking display of callousness, Agent Blanford had asked the *villista* operative Henry Gray to use his influence, in case Echegaray hadn't yet been shot, to have the execution postponed until after the October term of federal court in El Paso, so that Echegaray could testify against Consul Diebold. Gray replied, reasonably enough, that *villista* officials wouldn't allow Echegaray to cross to back to El Paso under any circumstances. Besides, he had already been executed.[91]

The loss of Echegaray, Blanford later noted, was a great blow to the government's case against Diebold.[92] At the October term of the federal court Diebold, de la Sierra, and Saldaña were tried. Their defense was that they had merely been repatriating Mexican refugees.[93] After deliberating about four hours, the jury returned a verdict of not guilty. Blanford commented that "the loss of this case may be attributed to the absence by death and otherwise, of four of the most important witnesses. So far as the quality of the testimony presented is concerned, a perfect case was made out. The prosecution lacked quantity. It is believed that had all the witnesses present at the last term of court testified at the trial this term, the case could have been easily won."[94] The agent touched on a favorite tactic of defense lawyers in neutrality cases—obtain continuances of a case, thereby gaining time to eliminate one way or another the witnesses, so that by the time it actually came to trial few of the government's witnesses could be produced. "It has been the experience," Blanford observed, "of the U.S. Attorney's office here that after the lapse of one year, and possibly longer, the witnesses in cases of this character have disappeared—especially the most important cases."[95]

Of course sometimes the loss of witnesses was not the result of defense attorneys' machinations. On November 23, 1914, the police received an anonymous call telling them where to find the bodies of two Mexicans: José Morales had been shot and his friend Pedro Méndez had his throat cut. Both men were prospective witnesses in neutrality cases pending in federal court. They had claimed they'd been offered money to testify that the defendants had enlisted them for military service in Mexico, and they had threatened to testify about the bribery attempt.[96] On occasion a witness was lost for personal rather than political reasons: on December 23, 1914, Harry Mahoney, a probable government witness in an important case, was shot and killed, "it being alleged that he was caught violating the sanctity of another man's home."[97]

But perhaps the most improbable impediment to a smoothly functioning justice system in El Paso was that—whether by accident or design—a British subject, Homan C. Myles, had been serving on both the petit and grand juries. His nationality was only revealed when he was appointed British consul in March 1914. The consequence of the discovery that a foreigner had been serving on a federal grand jury was that all of that jury's indictments had to be thrown out and the whole procedure gone through again, necessitating the kind of delays that delighted defense attorneys.[98]

In the summer of 1914, El Paso seethed with intrigue. Agent Blanford commented that "aside from the police and other authorities, this city is full of spies and informants of the various contending factions in Mexico."[99] To complicate matters further, the *felicistas*, the followers of Huerta's onetime coconspirator General Félix Díaz, began organizing in San Antonio and El Paso. Huerta had shunted Díaz aside, and the *felicistas* were trying to get back into contention. Villa's intelligence agents alerted the Bureau in July to the fact that José Bonales Sandoval, the Mexico City attorney who had been a staunch *reyista* in 1911, was now a leading *felicista* and was in El Paso organizing. Since General Huerta was losing his war against the Constitutionalists, *huertistas* would ally themselves with the *felicistas* in hopes of salvaging something.

There were already reports that men were being recruited in El Paso to join the Huerta contingent commanded by Rodrigo and Silvestre Quevedo and José Orozco lurking near the border south of Columbus.[100] Agent Blanford, city detectives, and "several other men," presumably *villista* secret agents, went to the Union Depot to prevent recruits from boarding the train for Columbus to join the proposed filibustering expedition.[101]

As frequently happened, much of the Bureau's information about the expedition came from Héctor Ramos, who claimed to have a dozen men working for him. He was certainly better supported than his Bureau counterpart, who usually had to work alone. Bureau agent Blanford and Lieutenant W. N. Hensley, of the Fort Bliss provost marshal's office, were frequent visitors to Ramos's office. Ramos asserted that Victor Ochoa, who had an office in the Trust Building and was a close friend and adviser to Juan Hernández, the Huerta consul in El Paso, was one of the prime movers in recruiting men for the expedition and getting them across the border near Columbus. The man in charge of the actual recruiting was Vicente Carreón, a former Huerta officer. Ramos stated that two of his operatives had already been approached by Carreón, and he produced two typed notes allegedly signed by Carreón acknowledging receipt from the Mexican consul of $4 "for the administration of a secret mission to Deming, in the interests of war." Of course Ramos may have forged the receipts to encourage the Bureau to take action against the consul.

That official had his own problems, one of which was that Carreón kept drinking up the money the consul gave him to pay the railroad fares of recruits and for other expenses.[102] Furthermore, the consul was trying to impose unity of command on the squabbling officers in the *huertista* camp south of Columbus. By threatening to withhold funds he got their grudging agreement to have General Roque Gómez command all the filibusters. On the night July 14, Gómez received seven trunks of ammunition that had been smuggled across the border from Columbus, but they were filled with dirt and wood; ammunition smugglers often had ethical issues. The next day Gómez led an attack on Palomas but was repulsed by the *villista* garrison. By August, Gómez's total force numbered only 110 men, hardly a threat to Villa's control of Chihuahua.[103]

Things continued to go downhill for the *huertistas*. Colonel Rodrigo Quevedo fled across the border near Columbus, and on October 29, civilian lawmen captured him and turned him over to the U.S. Army. He was taken to El Paso and confined in Fort Bliss.[104] Roque Gómez proved incapable of holding the increasingly demoralized force together, and "the band of filibusters, desperados, and bandits" scattered, many of them slipping across to the United States. Silvestre Quevedo and Roque Gómez were reportedly in Metcalfe, Arizona, trying to recruit new followers.[105] Héctor Ramos maintained that Gómez was hiding in Deming. But even as the military and civil authorities prepared to arrest him for a gunrunning indictment pending against him in New Mexico, the case was dismissed.[106] Gómez had been indicted along with José Inés Salazar, but with Salazar's acquittal the government saw no chance to convict Gómez.[107] There was no point in going through another farcical trial in Santa Fe.

CHAPTER 11

Villa versus Carranza

Pancho Villa, whose Division of the North numbering some forty thousand men was the most powerful Constitutionalist formation, increasingly resented Carranza's demand that Villa and his counterparts, generals Alvaro Obregón and Pablo González, obey his orders without question. Carranza resented Villa's growing power and insubordination and manifested his displeasure by designating Obregón's and González's forces as army corps while Villa's more formidable army remained a mere division. A break between Villa and Carranza was inevitable, and it occurred in June. Although the quarrel was papered over, Carranza and Villa were on a collision course. By August, Huerta gave up the fight and fled into European exile. The victorious revolutionists soon began fighting each other in a savage power struggle.

On September 22, 1914, Villa formally disavowed Carranza's authority.[1] Mexicans began choosing sides for what would become the decisive phase of the revolution. Supporting Carranza were generals such as Alvaro Obregón, Pablo González, and Benjamín Hill. Among Villa's allies were the Maderos and generals such as Felipe Angeles and Emiliano Zapata, who had his own grievances against Carranza, and ex-governor José María Maytorena of Sonora, who resented the rise of Obregón and of Colonel Plutarco Elías Calles (both future presidents of Mexico).[2] Carranza cleverly referred to all of his enemies as "reactionaries."

This new and bloodiest phase of the Mexican Revolution produced a strong reaction from U.S. attorney judge J. L. Camp, who discussed with Agent E. M. Blanford ways and means of driving away from the border towns the swarm of agitators who seemed bent on causing strife between Carranza and Villa. Camp declared that he would like to see them deported and would vigorously prosecute them for white slavery, for smuggling diamonds ("a great many of these prominent Mexicans wear diamonds which were probably not declared"), for violations of the neutrality laws, or for any other charges that could be brought against them.[3]

It was in this heated atmosphere that Victor L. Ochoa had an epiphany. He suddenly realized he had been a *carrancista* partisan all along, abandoned his *huertista* associates, who were going down the drain, and enthusiastically began working for the Carranza cause. He still lived in a world of intrigue, being armed with two pistols whenever he left his home, and often sleeping in his real estate office in the Trust

Building, rooms 507–9. Ochoa had come into money, evidenced by his having a secretary and being driven around the city in an automobile. The source of his newfound affluence was his new position as chief recruiter in El Paso for the Carranza faction.[4] Ochoa claimed he had recruiting officers in Douglas, El Paso, and San Antonio, and that he had three or four hundred men in El Paso ready to go provided he could equip them. As usual, his approach was grandiose. An unemployed former Immigration Service inspector asserted that Ochoa wanted him to take a few men, travel to New Mexico and Arizona, steal as many horses as he could, and cross them into Mexico. Ochoa offered to pay $5 a head delivered in Mexico. The local Bureau agent wasn't impressed with Ochoa's choice: the man was "55–60 yr. old, very stout, and would seem a bad pick for a horse thief." Ochoa was also in the market for machine gunners. Héctor Ramos, who was still Villa's intelligence chief in El Paso, promptly began trying to get several of his men hired by Ochoa so they could testify against him.[5]

Agent Blanford was concerned because there were several unsavory Americans hanging around in Columbus. One of them was R. H. G. "Mac" McDonald, whose presence always meant trouble. Another was William "Red" Stratton who, like McDonald, had been involved in border intrigue since 1911.[6] The third was a little-known individual, Fred Mendenhall, who said he'd once been a lieutenant of a machine-gun platoon in Villa's forces but "got in bad" and had to leave.[7] The Bureau agent suspected them of involvement in a rumored filibustering expedition that Ochoa and José Orozco, the former Red Flagger and *huertista* who was now a *carrancista* (not to be confused with Jorge Orozco, the *carrancista* consul in El Paso) were organizing. Blanford and Ramos repeatedly went to the Union Depot to arrest suspected recruits taking the train for Columbus or for Douglas to join the forces of the *carrancista* general Benjamín Hill.

Planning for the *carrancista* filibustering expedition in Columbus was disrupted when on October 24 the El Paso police arrested Victor Ochoa on a state charge of swindling based on a recently enacted Texas statute covering the making and passing of counterfeit Constitutionalist money. They searched Ochoa's office and home but found no evidence of counterfeiting. Ochoa blamed his *villista* counterpart Héctor Ramos for his arrest, and he was quite right. Ramos maintained cordial relations with the El Paso police department. He persuaded the police to arrest Ochoa on a state warrant for counterfeiting and to use a search warrant to ransack his office and house, confident that they would find enough evidence to convict Ochoa of neutrality violations and remove him from the revolutionary scene. At his preliminary hearing before a justice of the peace, Ochoa launched into a tirade and threatened the life not just of Ramos but also of Gunther Lessing, the Villa faction's attorney. The magistrate put Ochoa under a peace bond. "However, Lessing and Ramos did not feel secure behind this peace bond as they felt that Ochoa could shoot through it at any time he might get a fair chance." They were so afraid that they appealed to the federal Bureau of Investigation for protection.[8] They need not have worried. As we saw with Ochoa in 1912, he was all just big talk and bluster. Interestingly, Ochoa's arrest "was made without the knowledge, advice or consent of the federal officers who were working on this neutrality case." It seems that two months earlier Ochoa had purchased a hundred fifty-peso counterfeit bills for $50. Henry Kramp, former manager of the Thiel Detective Service's local office, was now a secret agent working on this counterfeit Constitutionalist currency case.[9]

Ochoa had been arrested in his office, and among those also arrested with him was José Orozco, the reported commander of the Columbus expedition. In Columbus itself the expedition was hardly a secret anymore because the few hotels were overflowing with men who had been sent to Ochoa's office to receive a few dollars before taking the train to Columbus to join the enterprise. The Bureau was gathering testimony from several of the recruits about Ochoa's role, but the assistant U.S. attorney insisted that since Ochoa was a notorious character who had been indicted several times with little success, no action be taken against him until an ironclad case existed.[10]

Besides filibusters, there was in Columbus an entire boxcar load of munitions—111 cases of ammunition and 19 boxes of small arms, plus saddles, stirrups, bridles, girths, canteens, rope, leather goods, belts, and blankets—that Ochoa had purchased from F. J. Feldman and Company of El Paso for the expedition. The army had seized the boxcar, and the authorities were deciding what to do with it. The El Paso law firm of Lessing and Bowes, with offices in the Caples Building, was eager to help. The firm's senior partner, Gunther R. Lessing, who had been the attorney for Madero in 1911, was now the attorney for the Division of the North, that is, for Pancho Villa. Lessing was trying to get a complaint filed against Ochoa, asserting that he was implicated in the boxcar of ammunition as well as in funding seventeen men just arrested in El Paso bound for Columbus. Lessing complained bitterly that the government required an overwhelming amount of evidence before permitting one to file a criminal complaint.[11]

Agent Blanford arranged with the justice of the peace in Columbus to have all the Mexicans in town whom Blanford designated arrested on a charge of vagrancy so that Blanford could interrogate them about their connection with the proposed filibustering expedition. After he had interviewed them, he reported, "Agent desires to state that this bunch of Mexicans were without doubt the greatest aggregation of liars ever gathered under one roof. I expect to profit by the experience." After deliberation, the army decided to release the boxcar, which reached Douglas on November 1 consigned to General Benjamín Hill.[12]

The delicious irony in all this was that Victor Ochoa later confided to Bureau agent Charles Breniman that "they intended to smuggle" the boxcar load of ammunition and supplies the Carranza consul had paid for "across the border near Columbus, sell the equipment to a faction operating against Carranza and divide the profits."[13]

The government finally filed a complaint charging Ochoa and his associates with conspiracy to instigate a military expedition and to enlist men for foreign service.[14] The authorities tried to keep the defendants' names secret so they could be arrested. Ochoa was the first to be arrested, could not post a $2,000 bond, and went to the county jail.[15] Emil Holmdahl, who had been commissioned as a major in the Carranza forces, was also under suspicion of recruiting. Héctor Ramos helpfully gave the Bureau three enciphered telegrams that purportedly were copies of telegrams Holmdahl had sent. (Western Union later confirmed that indeed Holmdahl had sent these and others as well.)[16] When Ochoa was arrested on November 11 on the counterfeiting charge, he carried a memorandum book containing names and addresses of interest to the authorities, people such as Emil Holmdahl, R. H. G. McDonald, and Roque Gómez.[17] A search of Ochoa's office had turned up a list of officers and soldiers and a number of telegrams from McDonald and others sent from Columbus between October 19 and 23, when the filibustering expedition was being organized. Holmdahl and José Orozco were also arrested, charged with conspiracy to recruit, and released on a $2,000 bond each.[18] At the hearing before the U.S. commissioner the clerk at Feldman and Company testified that the *carrancista* consul, Jorge Orozco, had ordered and paid for the carload of munitions.[19] At the conclusion of the hearing Ochoa was held to the grand jury under a $1,500 bond, while José Orozco's and Emil Holmdahl's bonds were $500 each. Holmdahl was subsequently held to the grand jury as well, posting a $1,000 bond. Shortly thereafter he left for Veracruz.[20]

The two Mexican leaders who would have the greatest impact on El Paso were Venustiano Carranza and Pancho Villa. Since racism is of such great concern these days, it should be mentioned that Venustiano Carranza was a racist, a subject on which Carranza apologist Douglas Richmond is silent.[21] On January 24, 1914, from his headquarters in Sonora, Carranza issued an official decree declaring that Chinese constituted a national menace and barring them from entering Mexico. The Constitutionalist state government of Sonora, for its part, issued a decree forbidding Chinese from changing their residence within Sonora and prohibiting Chinese from elsewhere in Mexico from entering Sonora. And a subsequent decree forbade more than four Chinese from living in one house, forbade their visiting one another for more than two days, and increased the occupational tax of merchants sixfold.[22] As for Pancho Villa, he was not just a racist, he was a vicious racist. His biographer Friedrich Katz states that "he may have hoped that the killings of Chinese that he perpetrated might appeal to the xenophobia of some of the Chihuahuans." And that "he had given orders to all of his men not to molest Americans, or any other foreigners except Chinamen, whom he claimed were a pest in the country, and would be run out of Mexico." And that "while the few Americans in Ciudad [*sic*] Chihuahua managed to hide, the Chinese the Villistas found were mercilessly massacred."[23] One of the uglier features of the Mexican Revolution was the pogroms of inoffensive Chinese, to say nothing of how Mexican regimes crushed indigenous peoples such as the Yaqui in Sonora. Racists also came in colors besides white.

As if to symbolize the atmosphere of intrigue that permeated El Paso, the Adventurers' Club was organized in April 1915, at a meeting in the Aultman and Dorman photographic studio on San Antonio Street. It was the Burro chapter of the organization, whose parent chapter in New York City had been established on December 7, 1912, by thirty-four charter members at Mouquins Restaurant on Sixth Avenue.[24] The *El Paso Morning Times* proudly commented that "El Paso has more adventurers than any other similar-size city in the world." Membership in the club was open to those who had seen combat in Mexico during the last four years as war correspondents, American army officers, or soldiers of fortune. Timothy G. Turner, the newspaperman and correspondent, founded the club and prepared the bylaws. The only officer (secretary and treasurer) of this purely social organization was R. P. Dorman, who had been a news photographer in several campaigns in Mexico. The charter members were Turner, Dorman, J. H. Noonan, Otis A. Aultman, Edward "Tex" O'Reilly, Bert B. Caddle, Sam Dreben, Philip A. McLaughlin, and Laurence M. Shadboldt. Membership requirements were relaxed, and the club soon boasted some thirty members, including General Benjamin Viljoen, Tracy Richardson, Felix Sommerfeld, R. H. G. McDonald, Gabriel Conrad, D. J. Mahoney, and Captain Ben Marias. Marias was a Boer who had served with distinction in the Boer War but who died the day after his election to membership when the English liner he was traveling on en route to South Africa was torpedoed.[25] The members presumably toasted his memory at one of their monthly banquets, at which several of them gave brief talks, everybody had a few drinks, and they swapped war stories and lies.

Victor Ochoa probably resented not being included, for he continued to have adventures. He was now counterfeiting *villista* currency in Anthony, New Mexico, just across the state line, in order to evade the recent Texas statute against printing foreign currency.[26] In this connection, Ochoa was in all probability counterfeiting for profit, but there is evidence that the Carranza faction counterfeited Villa currency as a form of economic warfare, a topic that merits further research. In fact, the whole subject of the financial aspects of the Mexican Revolution is one that has been inadequately studied.[27]

Ochoa was also enlisting men for the *carrancistas* in conjunction with Rafael E. Múzquiz, the new Carranza consul in El Paso (who happened to be Carranza's nephew) and C. S. T. Folsom, a local attorney representing that faction.[28] Ochoa did not have a telephone at his home; he used that of a neighbor, one Denman. The

Bureau and the sheriff's office seriously "discussed [the] possibility of getting a room at [the] Denman house, tapping the phone line, and picking up what we could in that way." Ochoa reportedly enlisted men at the rate of about fifty a day, at his office in the Trust Building. The recruits were dispatched westward by rail to cross into Mexico at various points along the line and eastward to Presidio, crossing the Rio Grande around Ojinaga.[29] What particularly infuriated Héctor Ramos was that Ochoa openly boasted of his influence with the authorities.[30] Enrique Llorente, now Villa's representative in Washington, complained bitterly to the State Department about Ochoa's activities.[31] One potential recruit was none other than General José Inés Salazar, who was still on the run after escaping from the Albuquerque jail. Salazar was currently trying to find a faction that would have him and was negotiating with the *carrancistas*. He wrote to Ochoa, who was suspected of helping Salazar evade the lawmen searching for him, that he planned to go to Sonora and join General Benjamín Hill's forces. Salazar eventually decided that the deal Villa was offering him was better, and he became a fervent *villista*.[32]

Of course it wasn't just the *carrancistas* who were enlisting men; a *villista* agent was doing the same in Smeltertown.[33] Carranza's representative in Washington indignantly protested against this shocking *villista* violation of the neutrality laws.[34] It was even reported that Huerta's sometime collaborator General Félix Díaz had an agent in El Paso recruiting men for a new enterprise he was currently planning in New Orleans to launch a rebellion in southern Mexico in yet another bid for power.[35] Recruiting for factions in Mexico remained a constant, as it had been even before 1910, and El Paso was a seemingly inexhaustible source of cannon fodder. In fact, the El Paso and Southwestern Railroad's nightly 7:45 p.m. train westward to Douglas was commonly known as the "filibusters' special."

Another constant was the arms traffic, and here too Victor Ochoa was an active participant. On February 13, two men were arrested near old Fort Bliss on the Rio Grande with nine boxes of ammunition and thirty rifles. They told the police officer who arrested them that the munitions had been purchased "on an order from Victor L. Ochoa."[36] The *villistas*' attorney, Gunther Lessing, was eager to have this case prosecuted because, according to Lessing, "Ochoa had boasted that no U.S. government official could catch him, nor could Villa's men nor anyone else."[37] Ochoa's lawyer, Juan Larrazolo, argued that Ochoa had sold the munitions to a small-time grocer. When the Bureau agent investigating the case asked what a small grocer wanted with them, Larrazolo pointed out that "no matter what business a man was engaged in he could be assured of a small profit at least by dealing in arms and ammunition."[38]

Sam Dreben also remained involved in the arms traffic. He sued Leonardo Camou, purchasing agent for the Sonora state government headed by Governor José María Maytorena, Camou's brother-in-law, claiming that $1,140 was due him as his broker's commission on a consignment of 557 rifles bought from the Fred J. Feldman Company of El Paso. Dreben got a judgment for $346.20. What is interesting, though, is that Dreben and Camou bought the rifles for $12 each but billed the Sonora treasury for $15.50 each, the difference being what the two were grafting.[39]

Another experienced arms dealer was Sabino Guaderrama. This time he was attempting to peddle 3,240 cartridges that were the property of the United States.[40] Through an intermediary Guaderrama offered them to Héctor Ramos, who promptly informed both Brigadier General John J. Pershing, commanding the El Paso Patrol District, and the provost marshal at Fort Bliss. Ramos had the intermediary instruct Guaderrama to have the ammunition sent to Shelton-Payne merely so as to give the transaction the appearance of legitimacy. A Bureau agent was watching outside of the store and noticed Guaderrama loitering, obviously waiting to receive the money from the sale. But Guaderrama realized he'd been spotted and strolled away. The authorities confiscated the ammunition and issued a complaint against Guaderrama, who was already under a $1,000 bond. At his hearing before the U.S. commissioner Guaderrama presented no defense and was bound over to the grand jury under a $750 bond.[41]

Significant amounts of arms and ammunition flowed through El Paso, most destined for Villa. Just from April 12 to June 4, for instance, 7,717,485 cartridges and 4,381 rifles were exported, and in the third week of June Villa received another 1,030,600 cartridges.[42] But as has been mentioned, the arms demand had expanded far beyond what El Paso could supply (this despite a tightening market resulting from the demand for munitions by those nations fighting World War I). In February 1915, Felix Sommerfeld, now a *villista* agent operating mainly out of the Astor Hotel in New York City, signed a contract with the Western Cartridge Company for 12 million rounds, the price to be $35 per thousand FOB at the company's factory in East Alton, Illinois, payment to be made on presentation of invoices to Boatman's Bank, Saint Louis, Missouri. Sommerfeld delivered a down payment of $50,000, and a delivery schedule was specified. If Western Cartridge failed to make deliveries as scheduled, the $50,000 would at once be returned to Sommerfeld.[43] Between April 6 and May 24, Western Cartridge shipped to El Paso by express for Pancho Villa 5,079,284 7-mm and .30-.30 cartridges consigned either to Villa's brother, Colonel Hipólito Villa, who headed the *villista* commercial agency in Juárez, or to the Rio Grande Valley Bank and Trust Company, where the *villistas* did much of their banking.[44] Pancho Villa needed all the ammunition he could lay his hands on, for he was engaged in a decisive campaign in the Bajío region north of Mexico City against the Carranza forces commanded by General Alvaro Obregón and was expending ammunition at a prodigious rate.

With his reserves perilously low, Villa dispatched his financial agent Lázaro de la Garza to New York to arrange for a substantial shipment of ammunition by express to El Paso. De la Garza was not only Villa's financial agent; he was also collector of customs Zachary Cobb's most valuable informant. De la Garza kept Cobb apprised of Villa's military difficulties. And Cobb was most interested in gathering intelligence about Mexico; he was both collector of customs, working for the Treasury Department, as well as an undercover agent for the State Department's elite Bureau of Secret Intelligence, which reported to the counselor of the department.[45] Carranza had seen to it that Villa was prevented from importing any munitions by sea through Tampico, and he had cut off Villa's supply of coal from Coahuila for his locomotives. More than ever El Paso represented Villa's military lifeline. He was largely dependent the single-track Mexican Central from Juárez for his supplies.

As the April term of federal court approached, the government began preparing its case against McDonald, Holmdahl (who had returned from Veracruz where he had reportedly been acting as bodyguard for *carrancista* general Benjamín Hill), Ochoa, José Orozco, and former Carranza consul Jorge Orozco stemming from the abortive 1914 *carrancista* Columbus filibustering expedition. An important witness was Fred Mendenhall, who had considerable experience operating a machine gun for both the *villistas* and the *carrancistas*. Mendenhall, who was currently employed as a waiter in a local café, made no bones about fearing for his life. He carried a pistol at all times and was careful to stay away from the border, fearing kidnapping by *villistas* for his role in the Columbus expedition. The Bureau tried to reassure him, and he agreed to testify before the grand jury. Among other things, he declared that José Orozco had skimmed enough money from the Columbus expedition to set himself up as the proprietor of a local wood yard.[46] But as far as the Bureau was concerned, the key witness against Ochoa and the others would be McDonald.

That veteran soldier of fortune had been having a lively time of it. In the fall of 1914, he had reportedly eluded the federal authorities in a most imaginative way—he shaved off his mustache and was hidden by his soldier friends in Battery C, 6th Field Artillery, at Fort Bliss for nearly a month and accompanied that unit when it was transferred to Naco, Arizona, in December 1914.[47] In early 1915, he was prospecting in the vicinity of Nogales, Arizona.[48] By March 1915, he was engaged in mining in northern Chihuahua and had the bad luck to be captured near Palomas by a detachment of *villistas*. They were taking him under guard to Palomas, probably to execute him since he had aided the *carrancistas*, when he managed to escape, flee across the border to New Mexico, and hide in a mine near Deming, where he was arrested on March 27, 1915. The government decided to grant him immunity in return for his testimony. After a Bureau agent interviewed him, McDonald gave a detailed account of the Columbus filibustering expedition and in effect turned state's evidence.[49] McDonald then unsuccessfully worked a mine on the border near Hachita, New Mexico, but gave it up to travel to Canada in February 1916 to enlist in the Canadian

Expeditionary Force. Because of his previous military experience he was made a sergeant. In April 1916, while drilling recruits in Windsor, Ontario, he died of a heart attack, an end more honorable than that of many of his mercenary colleagues.[50]

By early April 1915, the government had lined up its witnesses and was confident of their testimony in the forthcoming trial. But Héctor Ramos informed the Bureau that Ochoa and Holmdahl were trying to persuade certain Mexican witnesses to leave town and hide out during the trial.[51] Through Ramos the Bureau instructed the witnesses to pretend to accept, and they had several meeting in Ochoa's office with Ochoa and Holmdahl. Ochoa even treated them to supper and cigars. He also asked them to write statements to the effect that Ramos had paid them to testify against him and Holmdahl. One of the witnesses craftily said he was illiterate, whereupon Ochoa helpfully wrote the statement himself. The witnesses agreed to go to Presidio. Holmdahl gave one of them $60 for traveling expenses, and Ochoa and Holmdahl drove them to Ysleta to catch the train. Instead, the witnesses took the interurban back to town and reported to Ramos. The Bureau secured an additional indictment against Ochoa and Holmdahl, and Agent Breniman jubilantly stated that "in this matter the evidence against Ochoa and Holmdahl appears to be conclusive."[52] Ochoa and his associates were indicted for conspiracy to begin a military expedition.[53] In addition, Ochoa and Holmdahl were indicted separately for enlisting men and jointly for bribing witnesses.[54] The government was most anxious to avoid any continuances because of the difficulty of keeping its witnesses together and away from influence by the defendants.[55] Holmdahl's attorney, by the way, was Tom Lea, who had represented the *orozquistas* in 1912.[56] Lea was elected mayor of El Paso in the fall of 1915.

As if the government didn't have enough problems, a number of cases, including those of Ochoa, had to be re-presented to the grand jury because of the British subject who had served on the federal grand jury.[57] Ochoa had three cases pending against him in federal court: one for enlisting men, one for organizing a military expedition, and one jointly with Holmdahl for bribing witnesses.

The government decided to try the Ochoa and Holmdahl bribery case first because it seemed open and shut. Trial was set for April 28.[58] The defense immediately requested a continuance because Ochoa was ill. The prosecution was understandably skeptical. A physician was sent to Ochoa's house to examine him. The good doctor reported to the court that Ochoa was indeed experiencing discomfort, "suffering from inflammation of the testicles from being kicked." In a subsequent report to the court the doctor changed his story, stating that Ochoa was confined to bed suffering from gonorrhea and thus couldn't appear. Interestingly, one of Ochoa's neighbors later stated that Ochoa said he'd been warned of the forthcoming examination and barely had time to jump into bed and feign illness and "was laughing and telling what a job he had put up on the Court," which of course made the Bureau most skeptical about the doctor's integrity; it was also suspected that Ochoa's lawyer knew of the fraud. One report stated that it was Holmdahl who had warned Ochoa.[59]

The outcome of the trial was another bitter disappointment for the Bureau. Although the prosecution laid out a clear-cut and well-corroborated case, the jury returned a verdict of not guilty. The defense had vigorously attacked the credibility of the government's Mexican witnesses and argued that the case was really a frame-up by the Villa faction in El Paso. When Bureau agents interviewed members of the jury after the trial, they readily admitted that the evidence had been clear enough but stated that they did not care to send defendant Holmdahl, a white man, to prison on the testimony of any Mexicans, and although they would have liked to convict Ochoa, they couldn't acquit Holmdahl and convict Ochoa on the same evidence. Furthermore, although the evidence was fully corroborated, they considered the witnesses as disreputable as the defendants, a case of "dog eat dog." The jury had split five to seven, and rather than have a mistrial they had decided to acquit both defendants with the hope that the government might be able to convict them in some future case.[60]

A jubilant Ochoa walked out of court a free man, but Texas authorities immediately arrested him, this time in connection with the burglary of the local Kress store several nights earlier, when about $1,200 was stolen.[61] Ochoa's attorneys filed a petition for a writ of habeas corpus to reduce his bond, which the justice of the peace had fixed at $7,500. The bond was reduced to $2,000, which Ochoa posted. Local officers feared he'd flee the country, and had papers ready to serve him in another case should he make bond in the burglary case. However, he was later released on his own recognizance, which must have given him a good laugh.[62]

Fred Mendenhall stated that he wanted to testify for the government in the enlisting case but that he feared Ochoa who was "doing everything he could to have the case go over [i.e., be continued], and had made the boast that it wouldn't be tried this term and that next October there would be no witnesses." Mendenhall claimed that Ochoa had approached him and urged him to get two of the Mexican witnesses out of the way, "suggesting that they go on a hunting trip up in the mountains in an automobile, and after they got up there to disable the car so they couldn't get back, and had made other similar propositions."[63] Ochoa's tactics were partially successful: all hope of trying the conspiracy and enlisting cases during the April term was abandoned, and the cases were continued until the October term of federal court.[64]

In the meantime recruiting continued apace, with representatives of the contending factions denouncing each other to the Bureau of Investigation and demanding prosecution. For example, Gunther Lessing, counsel for the *villistas*, and their agent Henry Kramp called at the Bureau office to report another contemplated *carrancista* expedition of about twenty-five men scheduled to leave Union Depot for Douglas. The men were allegedly to gather at a nearby alley, where railroad tickets would be distributed about an hour before departure. Lessing urged that they be arrested, mentioning that two or three of them were *villista* informants whose testimony would be sufficient to secure a conviction. Commissioner George Oliver agreed that Lessing's assumptions were justified but declared that the admissions of coconspirators just didn't set well with juries. He wanted stronger evidence. It was finally agreed that the best course would be to watch them leaving for Douglas and if necessary have a Bureau agent follow them on the train and connect their activities in Douglas with those in El Paso. A Bureau agent was designated to go to Douglas with the *villista* agent Powell Roberts acting as interpreter. It was learned, though, that instead of twenty to twenty-five Carranza recruits, only five were going to Douglas, and Roberts could handle them alone.[65] In the event, the army apprehended them in Columbus, and Héctor Ramos furnished the money to have them returned to El Paso. They were then taken to Ramos's office, where Lessing took their statements. Lessing delivered copies the Bureau, which then filed complaints against the men for enlisting.[66]

The Bureau could be most accommodating to the Villa faction on occasion. In January, *villista* secret agent (and former Bureau agent in charge in San Antonio) H. A. Thompson claimed to have uncovered a plot to assassinate Pancho Villa, the plot originating in New York and the assassination to occur in Monterrey. Thompson lacked a secure cipher in which to transmit the warning to Villa's brother Hipólito in Juárez, and he asked the Bureau to transmit it for him at his expense in the Villa agency's cipher. As a courtesy the Bureau did so, without commenting on the reliability of Thompson's information. A Bureau agent accompanied Héctor Ramos to Juárez and personally delivered the message to Hipólito at the Turf Exchange.[67]

In the spring of 1915, the Bureau's El Paso office could no longer focus on *villistas* and *carrancistas*—another faction made its appearance.

CHAPTER 12

Huerta's Comeback Attempt

A new conspiracy was brewing, one that would have significant implications in El Paso. Bureau of Investigation agent Steve Pinckney commented on the general situation, informing his chief that the border was in more turmoil at present than at any time since the revolution began. Every faction that existed or had existed was well represented, each faction having scores of informants and agents keeping tabs on the others, "and there is more *double-crossing* and crooked dealings going on than any other place on the globe." The juntas were busily holding their meetings and directing their partisans in Mexico, the city was crawling with soldiers of fortune, many El Paso merchants and bankers were doing business with the various factions, and there were swarms of refugees. Worst of all, it was virtually impossible to get a jury that would decide any case wholly on its merits.[1]

With regard to the new conspiracy, initially there was uncertainty about just who was involved.[2] Suspicion centered on the usual suspects, people like Emil Holmdahl and Victor Ochoa. It was reported that Ochoa was the mastermind, which must have delighted the old plotter. He was credited with a new approach to organizing an assault against Ciudad Juárez, the presumed object of the exercise being for the *carrancistas* to wrest the vital border town from the *villistas*. Men were enlisted on an "on call" basis. Their names and addresses were taken down and they agreed to assemble whenever and wherever they were summoned. To ensure security a cellular structure was employed—they were divided into groups, a lieutenant heading each group, and each group was ignorant of all the other groups. Moreover, houses were being rented close to the Rio Grande and munitions hidden within them. At a given signal a particular group would assemble at a certain house, arm themselves, and participate in a simultaneous attack across the river. The *villista* defenders would necessarily have to fire into El Paso, and this would embroil them in difficulties with the United States. This possibility was taken seriously; General John Pershing made a personal reconnaissance along the river, having received a report that the Juárez garrison had trained artillery on the riverside houses the conspirators were using.[3]

According to Héctor Ramos's agents, this new movement represented an alliance between the conservative *científico* faction, which currently consisted largely of the remnants of the Red Flaggers, and the *carrancistas*.[4] Carranza was willing to cooperate with his sworn enemies—at least temporarily—in order to deprive Villa of his vital supply base in Juárez. Ramos claimed to have thoroughly penetrated the movement, which was well organized, equipped, and financed. Reportedly the movement had even hired a public relations man to accompany the invading force and issue press releases.[5] The principal conspirators in El Paso were José Orozco, Marcelo Caraveo, and Francisco Escandón (who used the alias of Francisco Mendivil). Ramos complained bitterly to the Bureau that the American government was aware of what was going on but refused to take action. Bureau agent Pinckney proceeded to lecture him on the necessity for evidence, emphasizing that this wasn't Mexico, where people were shot on mere suspicion.[6]

What caused increasing concern was that this revolutionary movement had noteworthy leadership—General Victoriano Huerta, no less. Ever since his defeat and exile in the summer of 1914, Huerta had dreamed of regaining power. During his sojourn in Europe he had succeeded in persuading Germany to finance his comeback bid.[7] He had arrived in New York in April and immediately began conferring with German embassy personnel and secret service agents.[8] He also began directing the preparations in El Paso. From Carranza's point of view Huerta, a proven loser, posed no real threat to Carranza's power, but Huerta could be strategically employed to deny Villa the use of Ciudad Juárez. Carranza could deal with Huerta later.

Throughout the spring of 1915, El Paso figured prominently in a flurry of communications among Huerta's adherents. For example, exiled Huerta general Luis Medina Barrón, who was living in El Paso, wired Querido Moheno in New Orleans urgently requesting his presence.[9] And a certain L. López, "formerly employed by the Mexican secret service" and living in El Paso, corresponded by registered mail with José B. Ratner in New York City.[10] This was significant, for Ratner and his brother Abraham were among Huerta's closest advisers. The Ratners were wealthy Germans who had lived in Mexico for years. They had owned the Tampico News Company, a mercantile corporation with stores in Tampico and Mexico City, and under this innocuous name, they had engaged in arms smuggling. In 1912, however, President Madero had unceremoniously deported the Ratners. When Huerta seized power in 1913 they returned to Mexico, became *huertistas*, and made fabulous profits as Huerta's official munitions purchasers in the United States. Abraham Ratner, for instance, bought twenty-five Colt machine guns in New York for Huerta in April 1914 and had the weapons shipped to the Tampico News Company.[11] In 1915, José Ratner was living in New York City, operating an import-export business at 130 Fulton Street and acting as the conduit for the money Germany was providing Huerta. When Huerta arrived in New York in April, José's brother Abraham was a member of the general's entourage.[12]

Huerta installed himself in a suite at the Hotel Ansonia and was immediately a "person of interest" to the Bureau, which made arrangements with the hotel management to keep the Mexican dictator under surveillance. Several pro-Allied Czechs and Slovaks, who were nominally Austrian subjects but were cooperating with American authorities, intercepted letters and eavesdropped on conversations.[13] At the same time the Bureau was examining Abraham Ratner's account at the Irving National Bank, tracing a series of nine drafts between banks in Mexico City, Paris, and the Irving, drafts totaling $400,000.[14] The Bureau subsequently examined the accounts of other members of the Ratner family as well.[15]

The Bureau's interest in Huerta's activities increased sharply when it learned that General Pascual Orozco had been calling on Huerta at the Hotel Ansonia.[16] No federal charges were pending against Orozco, and a Mexican extradition complaint filed against him some time earlier had been shelved because of the unsettled conditions in Mexico.[17] He allegedly went to Washington, D.C., together with Ricardo Gómez Robelo, who had been attorney general in Huerta's cabinet, to sound out some high government officials regarding the attitude of the U.S. government and public toward the developing revolutionary movement. They also tried to have the American Bank Note Company of New York City print 5 million pesos of currency, hoping to finance the movement in this manner. The company quoted them an exorbitant price and refused to print without the consent of someone in authority in Mexico.[18]

Seeking greater privacy, Huerta moved in May from the Ansonia to a large summer residence he had leased in Forest Hills, Long Island, a house large enough for the twenty-odd family, advisers, and servants constituting his entourage. Huerta's neighbors were less than thrilled to have him in Forest Hills. When a member of the Fourth of July committee suggested inviting the Mexican dictator as a guest at the forthcoming festivities the committee rebelled, "stating that they would not have a murderer amongst them on such a day."[19] Huerta's new place of residence represented a problem for the Bureau: "It will," an agent noted, "be very hard to keep track of visitors without spending lots of time and money."[20] The Bureau lacked both the manpower and funds to maintain adequate surveillance.

Funding was not a problem for the conspirators in El Paso. They bought arms, ammunition, equipment, and supplies on a wholesale basis. One purchaser wanted twelve to fifteen machine guns.[21] Among the principal suppliers was the local branch of the Saint Louis, Missouri, army surplus firm of Cal Hirsch and Sons, who were doing a land office business.[22] In fact the store had trouble keeping some of its customers from finding out that it was dealing with their enemies: Haymon Krupp, the local wholesale dry goods merchant, had evolved into a merchant of death, a little-known aspect of his career.[23] In April he purchased 500,000 7-mm cartridges (at $49 per 1,000), 700 cartridge belts, and 70 yards of olive drab cloth, for $10,000. Presumably these goods were for delivery to the new revolutionary movement, for the store manager wired the home office: "Sold them to Krupp don't say anything to Sommerfeld."[24] In May 1916,

Krupp sold 1 million Mauser cartridges and 5,000 Mauser carbines.[25] Felix Sommerfeld was of course procuring munitions in the United States for Pancho Villa. Interestingly, Sommerfeld was reportedly intriguing with German agents to foment civil war in Mexico in order to provoke American intervention.[26] Hirsch and Sons had for some time been selling munitions to anyone who could pay. During the arms embargo, for instance, the company had shipped a thousand rifles to Hamburg, Germany, then had them reshipped through the United States by rail billed as machinery to El Paso and on into Mexico.[27]

Some of the new movement's funds were locally supplied. José Zozaya was a wealthy Mexican who dealt in wholesale groceries and merchandise and operated a bonded warehouse.[28] Zozaya was a shrewd businessman and enjoyed an excellent reputation. He had recently sold his considerable interest in the Popular Dry Goods Company and was a prominent stockholder in the Union Bank and Trust Company. He was one of the financial agents of the new movement. His warehouse at Fifth and Santa Fe streets was a major depository for the munitions being amassed. For example, ten thousand cartridges were shipped on May 28 to José C. Zozaya, Frontier Commercial Company, 106 San Francisco Street. That same day the Hensinger Hardware Company in San Antonio shipped eleven boxes of ammunition to Zozaya. And on June 11, Huerta's supporters in El Paso received four machine guns shipped by one C. A. Eron, 50 John Street, New York City. Eron ostensibly operated a stationery store that was really a front for the conspirators.[29] On the second floor of Zozaya's warehouse there was a rooming house, where suspicious individuals were gathering. Frank and Ike Alderete, who owned a good deal of real estate, likewise figured prominently in the funding of the movement, although the extent of their financial contribution remains murky.[30]

Felix Sommerfeld, comfortably ensconced in an apartment in the Astor Hotel, had agents keeping the conspirators under surveillance in New York City, while his representative Sam Dreben was doing likewise in El Paso.[31] Operating independently, Héctor Ramos kept the Bureau informed on a daily basis of the conspirators' activities, hoping that the United States would smash the movement as it had those of Reyes, Vázquez Gómez, and Orozco. But "feeling that the information I was getting through the Villa agency, while helpful, was too vague, indefinite, and generally without corroboration," the Bureau agent in charge, Clifford G. Beckham, requested authorization to hire a capable Spanish-speaking informant at $3 a day for general neutrality work. The Bureau's chief approved hiring such an informant for at most thirty days, subject to renewal if necessary.[32]

Beckham hired Spanish-born Louis Azopardi, recently honorably discharged from the U.S. Infantry. Azopardi had been a guard and the interpreter for the five thousand Mexicans interned at Fort Bliss. In addition, he had been the army's chief secret agent in El Paso. And he had escorted José Inés Salazar to jail in Albuquerque and had acted as his interpreter. Azopardi came highly recommended by the army and was familiar with most of the Mexicans active in local revolutionary intrigue.[33]

In an ironic development, Enrique Llorente, who was now the Villa faction's confidential agent in Washington, D.C., wrote to the secretary of state complaining about *huertista* officers who were gathering in El Paso and planning to attack Juárez—a clear violation of the neutrality laws—and whose fire could pose a danger to the city.[34] Although Llorente's concern for the neutrality laws was laughable, he was right about *huertista* officers gathering in El Paso. It was looking like an ex–federal generals' convention, the upscale Hotel Paso del Norte serving as the venue.[35]

But persuading the generals to subordinate their own egos and ambitions for a common cause was like trying to herd cats. Generals Pascual Orozco and Guillermo Rubio Navarrete were holding meetings trying to patch up differences between Orozco, Marcelo Caraveo, and Emilio Campa. What proved to be only a temporary reconciliation was effected between Orozco and Caraveo, and it was a topic of conversation at a meeting in the Saint Charles Hotel on El Paso street between generals Trías, Rubio Navarrete, Castro, Manuel Landa, Aduna, and Nicolás Bravo. General Roque Gómez also arrived on the scene and demanded his piece of the action. They and lesser-ranking Huerta officers were being assisted by civilian sympathizers such as the Alderete brothers and Jesús Guaderrama, who transported arms for the conspirators.[36]

While supporting the new movement, Frank Alderete had also been dealing with Héctor Ramos and supplying munitions to the *villistas*. Preparing his next shipment, he amassed 500 hand grenades, 156 rifles, and 60,000 cartridges. He even hired a watchman to guard the cache, which was stored in a house near the river. But on the night of May 20, everything was stolen. The watchman later confided to Fred Delgado, a former city detective now working for Héctor Ramos, that for some time he had contemplated stealing the munitions, and on the night of May 20 he'd done so. He took everything to Juárez and sold it to Villa's people, who paid him $2,000.[37] It was hard to get good help.

Frank Alderete's luck didn't improve. In October 1916, a disconsolate Frank reported to the police that somebody had stolen 38,000 rounds of .30-.30 ammunition from his place of business a few days earlier.[38]

The atmosphere of secrecy, rumor, anticipation, and apprehension reached a frenzy in June. There were unconfirmed reports of huge sums of money arriving in local banks to fund the rebellion and of major arms shipments being received, but it became harder and harder to ascertain what in fact was happening because everybody claimed to have the real story. Adding to the air of uncertainty were allegations that Mayor Tom Lea and his political ally District Judge Dan Jackson were the legal advisors for the new movement and that conferences were sometimes held in city hall.[39]

Moreover, General Pascual Orozco arrived in town on May 11, rented a room in the house of a Mrs. Susan Finch at 604 Myrtle Avenue, and used it as an office for a month, transacting business in connection with the Huerta movement. Assisting Orozco were his secretary Crisóforo Caballero, who always carried a pistol, and a son of General Jose de la Luz Blanco. Orozco spent much of his time pounding out letters on his Oliver typewriter and conferring with a steady stream of callers, including the Alderete brothers, José Zozaya, and Elfego Baca, whom he asked to send his regards to Senator Fall. Mrs. Finch on several occasions saw Orozco and his associates poring over maps. Héctor Ramos was able to intercept some of Orozco's correspondence, and had at least one Orozco letter photographed by the Aultman and Dorman studio.[40]

Orozco's activities were disquieting to the authorities, but even more disquieting was when Orozco dropped out of sight in late June, producing intense speculation as to his whereabouts and intentions. Orozco, it turned out, had made a quick trip to New York; he returned to El Paso on June 24.[41] What caused the most excitement, though, was the report that General Victoriano Huerta himself was on his way to El Paso, ostensibly to visit old friends—a lot of whom had been congregating in the city of late.[42]

The Bureau had been having considerable trouble keeping Huerta under surveillance. The agency had arranged with the Forest Hills postmaster to receive tracings of all envelopes addressed to Huerta at his home at 129 Seminole Avenue. But because of a scarcity of agents and the pressure of work in the New York office, it was not until May 26 that an agent was dispatched to check on the Huerta residence.[43] And in response to reports that Huerta and his adherents were becoming quite active, and that Orozco was planning an attack on Ojinaga, the Bureau belatedly assigned a couple of agents to observe visitors at Huerta's home and to monitor those with whom he met in New York City, usually at Abraham Ratner's office at 61 Broadway.[44] On June 26, the chief of the Bureau, having received reports that Huerta and his staff, as well as personal friends in San Antonio, were heading to El Paso, sent an urgent cipher telegram to have agents fully cover their movements both in San Antonio and El Paso.[45] Bureau agents checked Huerta's residence on June 26 and were told by the mailman that he hadn't seen the general for the last two or three days (Huerta had left on the twenty-fourth). The Bureau learned interesting but useless things such as that Huerta had two Chalmers automobiles, one a touring car and the other a limousine, both registered in the name of his son-in-law, Alberto Quiroz. The Bureau also obtained Huerta's home telephone number; when an agent phoned, someone answered in Spanish that Huerta was gone and would be away for some time and suggested trying Ratner's office. When that number was called the agent got the cleaning lady.

Meanwhile, in San Antonio, a Bureau agent called on the local Villa representative, who was happy to provide a list of Huerta's associates who had left for El Paso during the last twenty-four hours.[46] On June 26 the Bureau agent in charge in San Antonio wired his counterpart in El Paso: "Reported here about ten former Huerta generals left San Antonio four a. m. en route to join Orozco. Cover closely. Wire development. . . . Detain Huerta generals 'by finding some suitable charge if necessary.' . . . by all means prevent crossing of parties mentioned. They may leave train before El Paso in view of contemplated attack on Ojinaga. Get Immigration to help." The Bureau also rushed its agent in Naco, Arizona, to El Paso to help.[47] And the Bureau's New Orleans office reported that three prominent *huertistas* had left by rail for El Paso.[48] Huerta had become a top priority.

The Bureau received invaluable assistance from Zach Cobb, the collector of customs in El Paso, who was primarily responsible for enforcing the arms embargo. His principal informant continued to be Lázaro de la Garza, Villa's financial representative.[49] Cobb went to the Bureau office on June 26 and showed Agent Beckham a telegram, the gist of which was that Cobb had wired the State Department that he had been informed that Huerta had left Kansas City and would arrive in El Paso on Sunday morning, June 27.[50] Cobb also showed Beckham the answering telegram he had received from State: "Immediately advise and cooperate with El Paso representative Department of Justice." Beckham, Cobb, a deputy U.S. marshal, and two of Cobb's men rushed to the Union Depot to meet the train arriving from San Antonio and detained two suspicious Mexicans. They were Pablo Cortines and Balbino Dávalos. The latter's business card read: "Envoy Extraordinary and Minister Plenipotentiary from Mexico." Dávalos claimed diplomatic immunity because Porfirio Díaz had appointed him ambassador to Russia years earlier, and he threatened to complain to the State Department. Cobb and company were not impressed. And it turned out that Dávalos was on his way to join Huerta. Huerta, however, was not on the train.

Before leaving the station, Cobb informed the Bureau agent that it had been some newsmen who had notified him that Huerta would arrive in El Paso on Sunday morning. Cobb, a deputy U.S. marshal, and Beckham agreed to meet that train, by which time Beckham hoped to have received instructions from his superior "as I felt a delicacy in detaining Gen. Huerta, in view of [the] fact that he had, for such a length of time, been sojourning in East U.S., and that I had received no instructions to apprehend him."[51]

Cobb telephoned Beckham at 2:30 a.m. on June 27 and stated that he had received a wire from the conductor of the Rock Island train due to arrive in El Paso at 6:30 a.m. to the effect that Huerta was on board but was to leave the train in Newman, a way station just across the Texas–New Mexico line about twenty miles northeast of El Paso. Furthermore, there were said to be five autos, presumably full of Huerta partisans, in Newman awaiting the general. Beckham immediately wired his superior in San Antonio: "Five automobiles awaiting Huerta at first station. Shall I detain? Please rush answer."[52] An hour's frantic telephoning resulted in the assistant U.S. attorney authorizing Beckham to file a complaint against both Huerta and Pascual Orozco for conspiring to violate the neutrality statutes.

Believing that there were five automobile loads of supporters waiting for Huerta in Newman, Agent Beckham decided that he needed some muscle. Accordingly, he turned to the army. The provost marshal at Fort Bliss declined to participate in any way in confronting Huerta. However, the colonel commanding the 16th U.S. Cavalry agreed to accompany Cobb and Beckham, taking with him fifteen troopers in automobiles Cobb provided and dispatching another ten troopers on horseback. The soldiers were not to participate in arresting Huerta and Orozco or any of their entourage or those meeting Huerta but were merely to be on hand in the event of trouble. Beckham awakened the U.S. commissioner and hurriedly filed complaints against Huerta, Orozco, and José Zozaya charging them with conspiracy to organize a military expedition, citing the accumulation of rifles, ammunition, and machine guns in Zozaya's El Paso warehouse as justification. (When federal agents raided Zozaya's warehouse on June 27 they found 14 machine guns, 500 rifles, and 100,000 cartridges).[53]

The commissioner issued arrest warrants. Then, at 4:30 a.m., Beckham and Cobb drove to Fort Bliss, picked up the colonel, his men, and two waiting deputy U.S. marshals and started for Newman. Since he had not received an answer to his telegram to the agent in charge in San Antonio, a worried Beckham stopped on the road and telephoned his office; to his great relief a telegram had been received: "Yes. Detain party." When they reached Newman, Agent Beckham was dumbfounded when the deputy U.S. marshals informed him that they had no authority in New Mexico. Beckham then had Cobb wire his personal friend the superintendent of the El Paso and Southwestern Railroad and have him get the train stopped across the line in Texas.

When the train arrived, Beckham sought out Huerta in his Pullman drawing room, introduced himself and the deputy marshals, and informed Huerta that he was not under arrest but that he would have to accompany them to the El Paso federal building for investigation. Huerta admitted that his destination was El Paso and that he had planned to proceed there from Newman by automobile. Beckham also took charge of General Pascual Orozco, who was waiting to meet Huerta. The photographer Dorman recalled that he had asked Orozco what Huerta was coming for, and Orozco had replied "To fight, of course. What do you suppose?" Dorman also saw Orozco over in the bushes behind the station outhouse doing something that looked like removing his belt.[54] Orozco was frantically tossing a checkbook, pistol, and cartridge belt into the brush. (Unknown Mexicans later searched for these items on several occasions, but they were found by persons who delivered them to the Bureau, which had translations made of everything in the checkbook. There were forty-two check stubs, all for June and all written by J. C. Zozaya and J. C. Zozaya Company to Orozco and others in the new movement).[55] Orozco and Huerta were understandably glum on the drive back to the federal building. Even a brief stop at the country club for refreshments failed to raise their spirits.

At the federal building Mayor Tom Lea called and declared that he feared violence might result when it was learned that Huerta was detained in the city; he strongly recommended that the Mexican general be removed to Fort Bliss. As Beckham later reported, "At the time I did not know that Mayor Lea, as a member of a law firm, had been retained to represent Huerta and Orozco, and supposed that he was acting strictly in his capacity as mayor. Soon learned [the] law firm of which Lea is senior member had been retained for such services." The military reluctantly agreed for the two Mexican generals to be kept in one of the administrative offices on post, guarded by federal agents, until the civil authorities decided what should be done with the prisoners. Huerta and Orozco were transferred to Fort Bliss. Later that day, deputy U.S. marshals took them before the U.S. commissioner, who set Huerta's bond at $15,000 and Orozco's at $7,500 (Beckham's superior had telegraphed, "Insist on large bond"). They immediately posted the bonds and were released. The Alderete brothers, Max Moye, Rodolfo Cruz, and R. E. Thomason, a future Congressman, posted Orozco's bond.[56]

On June 28, the chief of the Bureau instructed the San Antonio office to "Wire full report immediately all details Huerta matter."[57] The chief also telegraphed Agent Beckham: "Understand from press reports parties released on bond. Cover carefully and employ all assistance necessary to prevent crossing Mexico. Apply court for increase in amount bond. Keep in touch military authorities." Beckham checked on Huerta and Orozco's whereabouts. Huerta was at the fashionable Georgette Apartments on Stanton Street, where his daughter and her husband Alberto Quiroz had resided for the last three weeks, and he had held a press conference insisting that he had made the trip to El Paso merely to visit his daughter before proceeding on to the San Francisco exposition. But Huerta also conferred with twelve of his former generals, who insisted they had merely gone to pay their respects. Beckham was unable to locate Orozco but had Zozaya arrested on June 29.[58]

Huerta and Orozco's cases were postponed until July 12. Not surprisingly, Villa's military governor in Chihuahua wrote to Governor James Ferguson of Texas requesting Huerta's extradition under the 1899 treaty, charging him with Abraham González's murder.[59] This of course was a matter for the federal authorities to decide, and when Venustiano Carranza formally requested Huerta's extradition, Washington refused to send Huerta to certain death.[60] Huerta's public appearances were noteworthy. A mob of Mexicans demonstrated when the defendants, their entourage, and their attorneys left the federal building, and a near riot ensued, causing Mayor Lea to ban street demonstrations.[61] And on July 1, as Huerta was leaving the First National Bank building after consulting with his attorneys, someone tried to kill him by dropping a large chunk of lead out of a window. The missile landed a few feet from the startled Mexican general.[62]

On June 29, General José Delgado arrived from New Orleans, and Bureau Agent Pinckney met his train and interrogated him. Delgado had been with Huerta in Europe and in New York City, until two weeks earlier when he'd gone to San Antonio. He said Pascual Orozco had recently gone to New York to see Huerta. Delgado had a memorandum book on his person, with the names and addresses of some of Huerta's closest associates. Pinckney reported that "I told Delgado he could find Huerta at the Georgette Apartments and some of his entourage at the Paso del Norte, and that they would all be under surveillance while in El Paso. He went to the Paso del Norte and joined J. B. Ratner."[63]

The federal Bureau of Investigation was determined to spare no effort or expense in order to prevent Huerta and Orozco from crossing into Mexico. To that end, Agent Pinckney arranged for soldiers of the provost guard to provide the necessary security. He went to Huerta's lodgings at the Georgette Apartments and informed the general that "he would be guarded night and day; his every move would be accounted for, and our men would accompany him wherever he went; that he should make no suspicious moves that would cause us to take further steps. He was given to understand by me that it was not the purpose of the Department to inconvenience him in his regular and ordinary affairs." Huerta said this arrangement was satisfactory, and he mentioned that he had been invited to dinner at Fort Bliss. Provost guards escorted him there and back.

The Bureau hadn't a clue as to where Orozco was. Agent Pinckney had to ask Huerta for Orozco's home address. Pinckney, a deputy U.S. marshal, and two guards drove there to give Orozco the same message. His wife said he wasn't home and suggested they try his headquarters, at 624 Myrtle Avenue. They went there but didn't find him, "and none of his force would tell us where he was, stating that he had not been there during the day. It was apparent that they did not desire to give the information." Finally one of them suggested the officers try a residence at 1024 Myrtle. The officers went there, and after some discussion, the occupants produced Orozco. Pinckney "told him substantially what I had told Huerta, but even more emphatically." But while Pinckney was conferring with the guards in front of the house as to their shifts, Orozco disappeared. Pinckney and the others "searched the premises, which we found to be an unending confusion of several houses joined together, with all manner of avenues of escape, closets, etc. After some twenty or more minutes one of the provost guards found Orozco in company with one of the Mexicans a short distance from the premises, headed towards town. The Guard accompanied them both. Orozco apparently was worried as to the procedure, and his assent was merely a silent one."

There was also reason for the Bureau to worry. As Agent Pinckney put it, "Because of the keen activity of the 'new movement' in and about El Paso, there has been an almost-continual stream of people in and out of the office all day, offering information of various sorts, much of it unreliable, but much of it affording leads that we will try to follow as soon as time permits. Agent Beckham and I have not been able carefully to investigate each matter, but are giving each matter such attention as it would seem to merit for the time being. . . . The city and border country is simply alive with the followers of Huerta or the 'new movement,' and the most that can be accomplished at this time is to give check to their movements."[64]

So widespread was espionage by Mexican factions against each other that Mayor Lea on July 3 notified the chief of police that a stop must be put to it. He ordered the police to cooperate in ridding the city of Mexicans who were continually shadowing each other. If a person believed he were being followed he could telephone the police station. A policeman would personally answer the call, and when the suspected spy was pointed out he would arrest him for prosecution in police court as a vagrant.[65] However well intentioned, the policy made little difference, for now instead of shadowing a member of an opposing faction one could simply have him arrested for vagrancy. Intrigue remained a way of life.

On July 3, an apprehensive Agent Beckham reluctantly wired the chief of the Bureau: "Deputy Marshal reports Orozco escaped last night; every effort being made to prevent crossing border; military immigration and customs services assisting Department of Justice to arrest."[66] There had been indications that something was going on in the Orozco residence. On July 1, one of the soldiers guarding the house had informed Agent Beckham that bedclothes had been placed over the windows. Beckham went to the house and insisted that Orozco remove them, but U.S. commissioner George Oliver declared that Beckham had no right to make such a demand.[67] The bedclothes had been rehung.

The authorities were now in panic mode. Stopping only to pick up a lieutenant of the provost guard, Agent Pinckney raced to the residence and learned that the escape had occurred during the night. The guards coming on duty at 6 a.m. had become suspicious when they hadn't seen Orozco stirring about as usual. They entered the house, searched it, and found him gone. A next-door neighbor recalled that about midnight she had heard someone going through her back yard and had asked her husband to check. He did but found nothing. Her mother, who lived two doors down the street from Orozco, stated that about that time she saw a man go through her yard and jump over her back fence. Pinckney had the guards conduct a meticulous search of the Orozco residence, even making one of them check under the house with a flashlight. The Bureau agent also examined the premises and concluded from the evidence that Orozco had jumped out of a window on the east side of the house and had gone over the fence. He had had to cross only about fifteen feet of open ground before he reached heavy shrubbery. More to the point, a disgusted Agent Pinckney reported: "I believe that the guards simply were asleep on the job, as there was an ample number of men, six in number, to guard the place."

As part of the frantic damage-control operation, Pinckney had the provost marshal deploy guards to all of Orozco's usual haunts in the city, but they had no success. Pinckney himself helped to search Zozaya's warehouse at Fifth and Santa Fe, finding in a padlocked room upstairs lots of empty ammunition boxes, some bearing the stamp of Shelton-Payne. He participated in another raid, at the Alderete brothers' Alcazar Theater, during which the officers seized 3 brand-new Colt 1914 model machine guns, complete with tripods and three extra barrels, from the basement. Every trace of the consignees, addresses, and so forth, had been completely chiseled off the boxes. Frank Alderete protested mightily, arguing that there was no law against selling munitions to the leaders of the new movement.[68]

To prevent further embarrassing escapes of prominent Mexican revolutionaries, the Bureau's San Antonio office instructed the El Paso agents to file complaints against Victoriano Huerta and eleven others (including the fugitive Orozco).[69] Moving quickly, the authorities managed, to their great relief, to arrest Huerta, along with five of his associates.[70] Their bonds were set at $15,000 each, in default of which they were remanded to the county jail. The anti-Huerta *El Paso Morning Times* gleefully reported that Huerta, a heavy drinker, had now endured the first day in forty years without a drink, and perhaps for that reason, a disconsolate Huerta had wept.[71]

All the defendants except Huerta eventually posted bond and were released. But Huerta was a problem. For one thing, there was the matter of physically protecting him. The sheriff's department notified the Bureau that it had received information that an attempt to assassinate Huerta would be made by hurling a bomb into the jail. Taking no chances, Pinckney and the U.S. marshal arranged to assign two extra deputies and to double the number of soldiers guarding the jail.[72] Subsequent investigation by the El Paso police indicated that, predictably, it was the *villistas* who wanted Huerta dead.[73] Perhaps because of the additional security, nothing happened. It was decided to transfer Huerta to Fort Bliss, both for safekeeping and to prevent his escaping as Orozco had done. He went before the U.S. commissioner and waived both an examining trial and bond, as per an agreement between his lawyer Tom Lea and the U.S. attorney.[74]

The *El Paso Morning Times* published an article on July 9 citing Department of Justice agents who claimed that Mayor Tom Lea and certain local policemen were unduly friendly toward Huerta.[75] It turned out that there were indeed grounds for thinking that Mayor Lea was unduly friendly toward Huerta. In November, the Bureau gained new insights into the Huerta conspiracy by securing statements from a number of those involved. It was learned that Huerta had continued plotting even after his arrival in El Paso. While still at the Georgette Apartments he had been busy conferring with his officers and handing out money to them as well as making arrangements for *huertista* filibusters to assemble secretly at Tom Lea's ranch, located between El Paso and Ysleta. By July 3, some 250 men had assembled there. They had been transported from El Paso over several days in automobiles, one of them driven by Jesús Guaderrama.

(On February 24, Guaderrama had been kidnapped in south El Paso, knocked unconscious, and had awakened in the Juárez jail. He was then put under guard on a train bound for Guadalajara, apparently to answer with his life for counterfeiting *villista* currency. He said he managed with the help of two friends to make his way back to El Paso. In the meantime his father had offered a $1,000 reward for his safe return. Hipólito Villa and Héctor Ramos were charged with conspiracy in connection with the case but were acquitted. Jesús Guaderrama later sued Hipólito Villa for $50,000 in damages. The two friends sued the elder Guaderrama for the $1,000 reward. The whole affair was quite mysterious, although Victor Ochoa claimed that the motive for Guaderrama's abduction was to learn from him where Ochoa had stored a quantity of arms and ammunition.)[76]

One of the filibusters stated that Tom Lea had driven to the ranch on July 2. He didn't think Lea knew what the men were there for. "He heard or someone told him that Lea asked one of his employees What are these men doing here, and was told they were just some men passing through, and Lea said Oh well, if that is the case, it is all right, and drove off." Perhaps, but this story sounds pretty lame. Some of the arms for the proposed operation came from a cache at José Delgado's house in El Paso, while Victor Ochoa provided other weapons left over from the 1914 Columbus expedition. The men were given twenty-five cents a day to live on in El Paso and were issued a "Benito Juárez Club" card as identification. They were promised $2 a day as soon as they crossed into Mexico. The recruits were told they were going to fight against Villa and were assured that the United States government had given its blessing to the enterprise. When they learned that this was not the case, many refused to participate further. The expedition collapsed on July 4 when a U.S. Army patrol entered the ranch. The filibusters scattered.[77]

Knowing nothing of this at the time, the authorities treated Huerta with consideration. His family arrived from Forest Hills, traveling with upward of sixty pieces of luggage, and took up residence at 415 West Boulevard Street.[78] Huerta was permitted to visit them, being escorted under guard from Fort Bliss and back by a deputy marshal and four provost guards. Agents Beckham and Edward B. Stone went to the house prior to the general's arrival to familiarize themselves with the lay of the land and with the thirty to thirty-five family and servants. Huerta was of course in a good mood, and when the Bureau agents were about to leave so that he could enjoy his family, Huerta insisted that they stay for refreshments and cigars. A large tray filled with glasses of beer was produced, but Huerta accompanied the servant back to the kitchen before anyone partook, and after he returned the servant brought in a tray filled with small glasses of liquor. Fearing that the booze was doped, the Bureau agents and the guards were reluctant to drink anything, although out of curiosity Agent Stone did take a small sip of the fiery liquor. In all probability, however, Huerta was simply being the gracious host. After visiting with his family for an hour and a half, he was escorted back to Fort Bliss.[79]

The Huerta affair was of such importance that the chief of the Bureau of Investigation, A. Bruce Bielaski, arrived in El Paso on July 11 to direct operations in person.[80] Besides the chief, there were now three Bureau agents in El Paso. One of them, Stone, had been operating under cover and had the considerable advantage of speaking Spanish. The Bureau's agent in charge in San Antonio recommended to Chief Bielaski that a $25 reward be offered for information leading to Orozco's arrest.[81] It was all the Bureau could afford given its meager budget, but it was hardly enough to get anybody excited about informing on Orozco.

Continuing their investigation of the Huerta conspiracy, agents Stone and Pinckney called on José Zozaya at his Frontier Commercial Company and tried to interview him about his dealings with Orozco and Huerta. Zozaya, on the advice of his attorney, Mayor Tom Lea, refused to talk. In another development, the U.S. marshal informed the Bureau about a rumor concerning an automobile owned by the Guaderramas and inquiries about how to approach Fort Bliss by car. Agent Beckham reported that "we concluded to go to Fort Bliss and asked Colonel Morgan for a detail of men to be ready in case of an attempt to release Huerta or to molest him. He agreed to furnish a detail at night."[82] Further fallout from the Huerta affair involved Victor Ochoa, who was apparently up to his old tricks. Guns and ammunition were said to be stored at the house of an ex-Huerta general. The man who hid them there had told Ochoa about the cache, and Victor immediately planned to steal the munitions. He enlisted the assistance of one H. H. Boyd and showed him where the arms were concealed but not the weapons themselves. Unluckily for Ochoa, Boyd turned out to be an informant for the Bureau. But when Agent Beckham secured a search warrant and raided the house he found nothing.[83] Another of Ochoa's schemes had fizzled.

Orozco's escape caused the El Paso rumor mill to shift into overdrive. Confusing the situation even more were the imaginative stories appearing in the local press. John W. Roberts, a staff writer for the Hearst News Service, informed agents Stone and Beckham on July 28 that he had interviewed Pascual Orozco in El Paso the previous day, in a house in the 800 block of Magoffin Avenue. Orozco had told him that he planned to remain in El Paso, that he'd moved about town disguised by a heavy black beard, and that he would forfeit his $7,500 bond rather than remain in custody and be persecuted the way Huerta had been. Furthermore, it would do the authorities no good for Roberts to tell them where the interview had taken place because Orozco kept moving from place to place. The story appeared in that day's *El Paso Herald*, the afternoon newspaper. Not to be outdone, the next day the *El Paso Morning Times* published an article stating the letters had been received in El Paso from Orozco saying that he was in Mexico with a band of two hundred men and that he had crossed the border four days after he escaped from his guards. Agent Beckham observed that "the consensus is that both stories are 'fakes.' It is customary for each of the El Paso papers to deny practically any and everything published by the other."[84]

Another, and much more important, complicating factor was the suspicion regarding the loyalty of Mexicans in El Paso. Any intimation of an uprising by the local Hispanic community was taken with the utmost seriousness. On August 25, a confidential informant of the Bureau, Antonio Garibay, a graduate of the Mexican military academy in Chapultepec who was currently working for the local Carranza consul, came to Agent Stone's room in the McCoy Hotel and told him about a planned *huertista* plot in which he was involved: a simultaneous uprising in El Paso combined with an attack on the city by the Villa garrison in Juárez, which would mutiny, and that all this would occur at midnight. Mounted men had been designated to ride through the barrio in south El Paso throwing hand grenades and giving the signal for insurrection. Since General Tomás Ornelas, the *villista* commander in Juárez, wouldn't participate in the attack on El Paso he was to be assassinated. Stone, who was still operating under cover, not only summoned his superior, Agent Beckham, to his room but also telephoned General Pershing requesting that he come at once to the room for a conference. Pershing arrived at 9:45 with his aide, Lieutenant James L. Collins. Beckham, meanwhile, had called Edwin M. Dubose, deputy U.S. marshal, and Peyton Edwards, the sheriff, to the room. Pershing suggested that Mayor Lea be called to attend the meeting; this was done. As soon as Lea arrived, Stone gave a detailed account of the purported rising and his source for that information.

About 10 p.m. Garibay returned with additional details, and the military and civilian authorities interrogated him at length, with Stone interpreting. "He stood the test well. He was instructed to go ahead with the plan; he would be arrested along with the others in the event of trouble, to maintain his cover. He then left the room." General Pershing announced that he was going immediately to order out a sufficient force of troops to protect the city and prevent any uprising. Two battalions of infantry were deployed along the riverfront and at strategic locations in the city. The rest of the brigade that Pershing commanded remained under arms at Fort Bliss throughout the night. The mayor and the sheriff, meanwhile, left to give their orders to the police and sheriff's departments. Stone's companions suggested that he remain in his room to keep in touch with Garibay should he return unexpectedly with new information.

"The night passed off very quietly," Stone recounted, "and no trouble of any kind was reported in El Paso or Juarez. Very likely the placing of the armed troops about the city before midnight, and the presence in the vicinity of where we had been informed some of these Mexicans were going to gather, of the provost guard and many police and deputy sheriffs all armed with riot guns, had a deterrent effect on the leaders about carrying out their schedule as originally planned."[85]

The entire alleged plot, attributed to Orozco, seems highly improbable, but the mere fact that experienced civilian and military officials who were not given to hysterics took it seriously demonstrates the apprehension felt regarding the large Hispanic population in the city. Further evidence of the nervousness of the Anglo citizenry is the fact when the 13th and 15th U.S. Cavalry Regiments conducted maneuvers on the mesa on August 27, the blanks they fired caused a panic in El Paso, many of whose residents thought a Mexican uprising had begun.[86] And on September 16, Mexican Independence Day, the military patrolled the streets of south El Paso, the bridges, and the bank along the Rio Grande, but nothing untoward occurred.[87]

The Bureau received good news on July 20, when Zach Cobb telephoned that two of his mounted customs inspectors had apprehended the fugitive José Inés Salazar and had him in custody in Columbus. Agents hurried there to interrogate him. Salazar said that after his escape from the Albuquerque jail, he had crossed into Mexico with one follower, who had since been killed in action. Salazar's subsequent career had been an exercise in downward mobility. He had joined the Villa faction, had seen action in the Ojinaga vicinity but in a subordinate capacity, and had been humiliated by the notorious bandit Chico Cano, who had temporarily been a *villista* captain himself before becoming a *carrancista*. Cano had run Salazar out of town with only four followers. Thereafter, Salazar had become a garden-variety bandit operating south of Columbus at the head of a band of twenty-three men. His force had been shattered by *villistas* on June 30, and the survivors had fled into New Mexico and surrendered to the U.S. cavalry. Hungry and without supplies, Salazar himself had crossed into New Mexico at Gibson's ranch, located on the international boundary, the night before his capture. He was caught when the customs inspectors had sneaked up on him as he sat near a water tank looking back into Mexico with field glasses. They got the drop on him, and he surrendered without resistance. The U.S. marshal for New Mexico arrived to take charge of Salazar.[88]

Another fugitive Mexican revolutionist was also taken out of action. Pascual Orozco had been on the run ever since his escape, and the authorities launched a desperate search for him, fearing that he might cross the Rio Grande and start the revolution even without Huerta. The search was fruitless.[89] Allegedly Sabino Guaderrama drove Orozco in his automobile from El Paso to a friend's house near Fabens. This seems plausible, since Sabino's brother, Jesús, was among those indicted along with Huerta and Orozco.[90]

According to Mrs. Orozco, her husband had hidden out at his Montana Street residence and had slipped out of El Paso on the night of August 24 on horseback. Whether this was true or not, Orozco surfaced on August 29, having joined up with four of his closest associates: Crisóforo Caballero, General José F. Delgado, Andrés Sandoval, and Miguel Terrazas. The group's objective seems to have been to reach Bosque Bonito, across the Rio Grande. They made their way to Dick Love's ranch near Sierra Blanca, where they made the ranch hands prepare breakfast for the party and shoe a horse.[91] When Love and two friends rode up the Mexicans rode away; Love and his companions followed, and the Mexicans opened fire on them. A posse was quickly organized and took up their trail. Although Culberson County sheriff John A. Morine nominally led the posse, the real leader was William Davis "Dave" Allison, the constable in Sierra Blanca, "a very quiet looking old man with a sweet face and white hair" whose grandfatherly appearance gave no indication that he was a gunslinger of fearsome reputation. He had been a sheriff, a city marshal, a Texas Ranger, and an Arizona Ranger. And he had absolutely no use for Mexicans.[92] The posse caught up with Orozco and company the next day, August 30, encamped in Green River Canyon, some thirty miles from Sierra Blanca. The posse unceremoniously mowed them down; the Mexicans never knew what hit them. According to several sources, it was Dave Allison who killed most, if not all, of the Orozco party.[93] It has been said that Texas Rangers and U.S. cavalrymen were involved, but there is no credible evidence to support that claim.

When he received word of the killings, Agent Beckham took the first train to Van Horn to identify the bodies. Also on that train were two young men from the Orozco household. One was named Russell and was the son of William Russell, formerly manager of the mines in Shafter, in whose mine and under whose protection Orozco hid after the fall of Ojinaga. Young Russell told the agent that Orozco was like a brother to him. At Van Horn on September 1, Beckham was met by Sheriff Morine and various citizens who took him to the courthouse, where the five naked bodies were laid out on an improvised table in the courtroom. The Bureau agent identified Orozco by flashlight. The sheriff gave Beckham all the documents found on the deceased. He had also secured their personal effects in his office vault. These consisted of five Marlin rifles, a Smith and Wesson .44 revolver that supposedly was Orozco's, ten canvas cartridge bags, a large quantity of .30-.30 rifle ammunition, knives, scissors, medicine for venereal diseases, a small amount of cash, and Orozco's gold signet ring and Elgin watch. Also, one man, probably Orozco, had what was locally known as a "war bag," a canvas double sack that could be thrown over a saddle or over a man's shoulder.[94] Interestingly, José Zozaya later maintained that each of the five men had $500 on his person when he was killed.[95] So there would be no legal loose ends, Sheriff Morine insisted that he and the rest of the posse be indicted for murder. Their defense was that the Mexicans were rustlers and had fired first. The trial ended quickly; an all-Anglo jury acquitted everybody.[96]

The embalmed bodies were brought by train to El Paso the night of September 1. Informant Garibay raised the possibility that Orozco sympathizers might riot at the Union Depot when the corpses arrived.[97] However, "an anticipated demonstration was prevented by the action of the military and police by having the bodies removed from the train at an unexpected point and by keeping the crowds from gathering in such a manner as might lead to a demonstration."[98] On September 2, the bodies lay in state for two hours in the Nagley and Kaster mortuary, while several thousand people filed by to pay their respects. The funerals of Orozco and his companions took place at Concordia Cemetery on September 3, with some three thousand mourners, mainly Mexican, in attendance. A Protestant minister conducted the services for Orozco, Roman Catholic priests those for his four companions. Orozco's casket was placed in a vault, with Orozco wearing the uniform of a general in the Mexican Army, the rank he had held under Huerta. A Mexican flag covered his coffin. Orozco's onetime comrade in arms and subsequent implacable enemy Pancho Villa sent a telegram of condolence to his widow. Huerta sent a wreath.

On November 2, All Souls Day, hundreds of Orozco's friends gathered at his tomb to pay tribute to his memory. There were speeches, a band, and a profusion of flowers.[99]

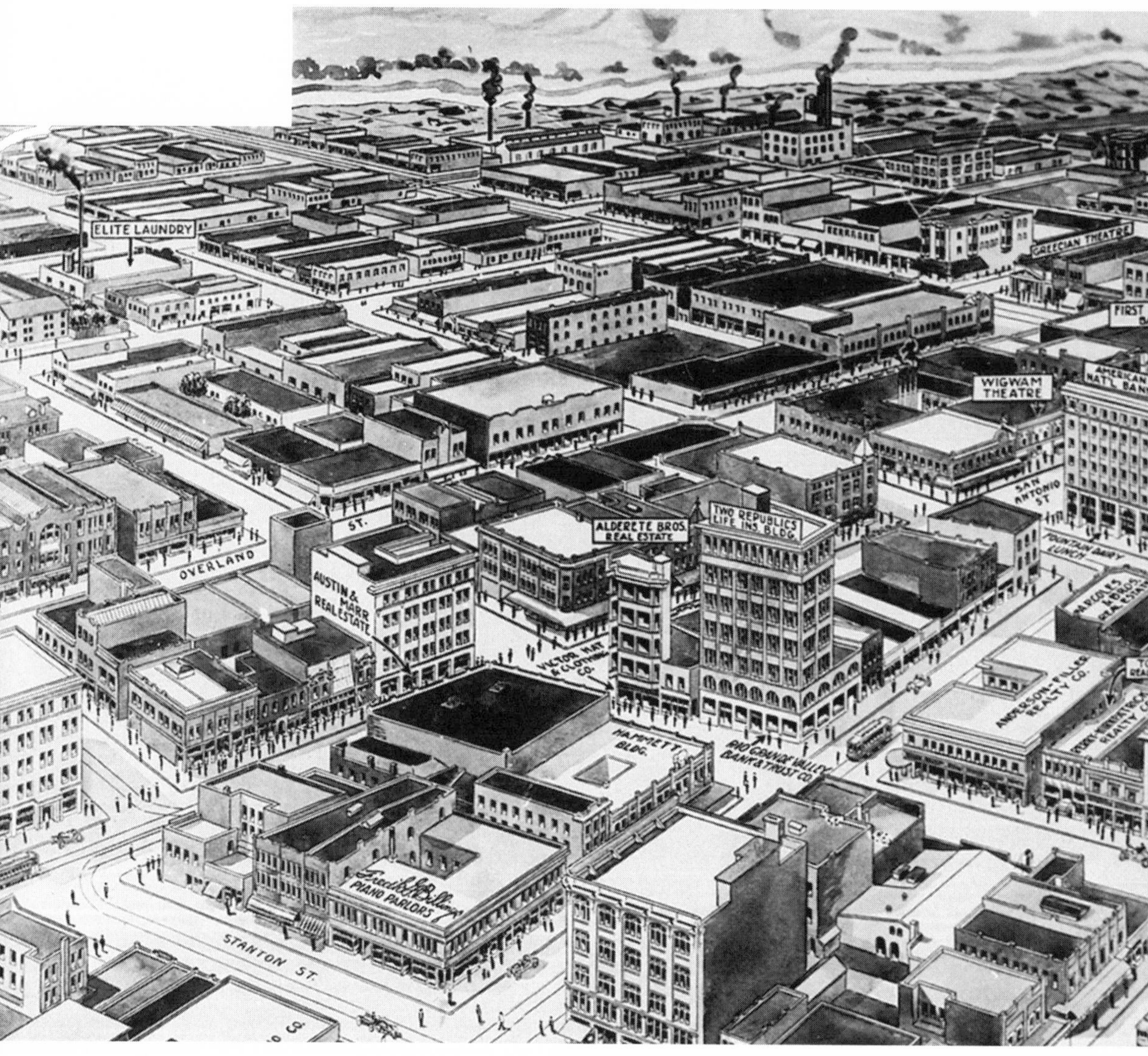
ELITE LAUNDRY
GRECIAN THEATRE
WIGWAM THEATRE
SAN ANTONIO ST
TWO REPUBLICS LIFE INS. BLDG.
ALDERETE BROS. REAL ESTATE
ST.
OVERLAND
AUSTIN & MARR REAL ESTATE
VICTOR HAT & CLOTHING CO.
HAMMETT BLDG.
RIO GRANDE VALLEY BANK & TRUST CO.
ANDERSON-FILLER REALTY CO.
PIANO PARLORS
STANTON ST.

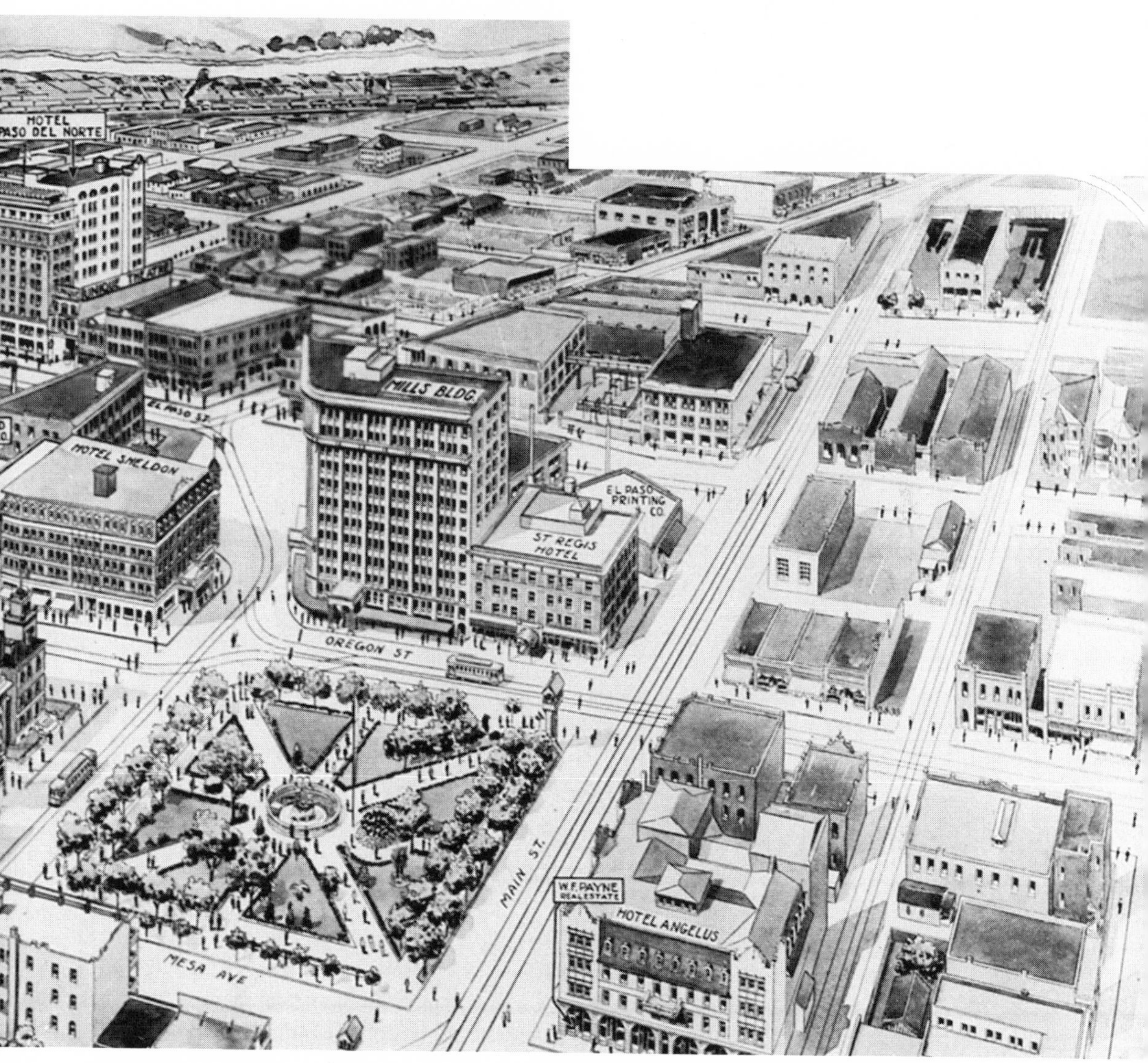

Map/drawing of downtown El Paso. This drawing of downtown El Paso shows the growth of the city from a tiny town of eight hundred in 1880 to an already imposing skyline by 1912. A number of street and building names appear in the drawing. Drawing courtesy of El Paso Public Library.

Figure 1. President William Howard Taft and Mexican president Porfirio Díaz pose in El Paso on October 16, 1909, during their historic presidential summit—the first meeting of an American president and a Mexican president. Standing directly behind the two presidents and between them is James McGavock Dickinson, secretary of war. Fortunately, a plot to assassinate both presidents was thwarted because of an elaborate security screen. The meeting of the two presidents was marked with much pomp and circumstance—two thousand U.S. Army troops paraded in El Paso and more than two thousand Mexican Army regulars marched through the streets of Ciudad Juárez during the ceremonies. Photo courtesy of El Paso Public Library, Otis Aultman Collection (A5989).

Figure 2. Major Frederick Russell Burnham, DSO, was a decorated American veteran of the Second Boer War, serving as chief scout for the British commander Lord Roberts. Burnham was in part responsible for preventing the assassination on October 16, 1909, of President William Howard Taft in El Paso. President Taft's close friend, the millionaire John Hays Hammond, learning of the plot to kill the president, arranged for Burnham to recruit an estimated two-hundred-man security force to protect Taft. Burnham and Private Charles Moore, a Texas Ranger, disarmed the assassin only a few feet from the president. Photo in Frederick Russell Burnham, *Scouting on Two Continents* (Garden City, N.Y., Garden City Publishing, 1926).

Figure 3. Texas Ranger Charles Moore, a member of Captain John Hughes Company A, was an outstanding ranger. He and Major Frederick Russell Burnham probably prevented the assassination of President William Howard Taft in El Paso on October 16, 1909, by grabbing the potential assassin who was within a few feet of Taft armed with a concealed pencil pistol (also known as a palm gun). Photo courtesy of Texas Ranger Hall of Fame and Museum, Waco, Captain "Lone Wolf" Gonzaullas Papers.

Figure 4. This is probably the type of "pencil pistol" that the potential assassin was carrying concealed in his hand on October 16, 1909, when Major Frederick Russell Burnham, who headed an unofficial security force to protect President William Howard Taft, and Texas Ranger Charles Moore grabbed him within a few feet of the president. Bullets from the pistol supposedly could penetrate a two-inch plank. The gun was sold by the Pencil Pistol Sales Company of New York. This photo was used in an advertisement for the pistol in an unidentified magazine dated September 1909. The assassin did not have the opportunity to take a shot at the president, so, although he was arrested, he was only held briefly before being released after the Taft/Díaz summit. We are indebted to our colleague Mark Milliorn, who found the advertisement on the Internet and brought it to our attention.

Figure 5. El Paso's impressive Union Depot was one of the principal reasons for the city's growth both in population and industrial capacity. Six railroads arriving from north, south, east, and west subdivided the city. Because of El Paso's geographical position on the north bank of the Rio Grande, which divided Mexico and the United States, by 1910 the city boasted the largest population of any city between Dallas/Fort Worth and Los Angeles. Furthermore, the city was a key railroad terminal tying the southwestern United States to Mexico through which cattle to American markets, ores to smelters, and rail passengers were funneled. Photo courtesy of El Paso Public Library, Otis Aultman Collection (A5448).

Figure 6. The principal industry in El Paso was smelting. Smelters processed the ores from the mines of Chihuahua and southwestern New Mexico. This photograph was taken from the south bank of the Rio Grande on the outskirts of Ciudad Juárez. In the foreground is Smeltertown, the community that housed the workers at the adjacent smelter. The four smokestacks of the smelter are visible in the background. Photo courtesy of El Paso Public Library, Otis Aultman Collection (B199).

Figure 6A. Felix Sommerfeld (at the time an Associated Press correspondent), Francisco Madero, H. Allie Martin, managing editor of the *El Paso Herald*, and Chris Hagerty at Madero's headquarters opposite the American Smelting and Refining Company smelter. This photograph was taken sometime during the period April–May 1911. Photo courtesy of El Paso Public Library, Otis Aultman Collection (B763).

Figure 7. The Sheldon Hotel (to the right of the streetcar) in downtown El Paso was probably the best-known hostelry in the city. Virtually every revolutionary figure of consequence drank there, stayed there, and sometimes even engaged in fistfights there. General John Pershing liked to drink coffee (and sometimes something stronger) under the portico visible at the front of the hotel. Gunrunners, spies from every faction, and U.S. government secret agents all hung out at the Sheldon. Photo courtesy of El Paso Public Library, Otis Aultman Collection (A5610).

SHELDON
HOTEL SHELDON
DEPOT
23
23

Figure 8. Adolph Krakauer was the senior member of the firm of Krakauer, Zork and Moye. Based in El Paso, the firm was the largest hardware company in the southwestern United States. During the Mexican Revolution the company competed with Shelton-Payne for the title of largest arms dealer along the Mexican border. Photo courtesy of El Paso Public Library (Portraits K).

Figure 9. Madero family dinner party at Mr. and Mrs. Frank Wells Brown home in El Paso following the capture of Ciudad Juárez in May 1911. Left to right seated: unidentified, Francisco Madero Jr., Mrs. Frank Wells Brown, Francisco Madero Sr., Bryan Brown, Felix Sommerfeld, Ethel Brown, Giuseppe Garibaldi, Mrs. Sara Pérez de Madero, Frank Wells Brown, Gustavo Madero, Roque González Garza. Standing left: Emilio (?) Madero. Standing right: unidentified. Photo courtesy of El Paso Public Library, Otis Aultman Collection (B816).

Figure 10. One of the more famous photographs of the Mexican Revolution is the May 1911 snapshot of Pancho Villa and Pascual Orozco Jr. at El Paso's Elite Confectionary. Villa (front left) and Orozco (center) are shown relaxing over a dish of ice cream after having captured Ciudad Juárez. Seated far right is Todd McClammy, one of the toughest and most dangerous characters on the border, who hung out in El Paso throughout the revolution. McClammy is often cut out of this photo and is never identified. Photo courtesy of El Paso Public Library, Otis Aultman Collection (A5257).

Figure 11. Soldiers of fortune rest, cradling their rifles after a hard day's work. Left to right are Tracy Richardson, Sam Dreben, and possibly Edward "Tex" O'Reilly. The date and place of the photograph are not known, but presumably the photo was taken in the state of Chihuahua because it was an Aultman picture. Photo courtesy of El Paso Public Library, Otis Aultman Collection (A2449).

Figure 12. Emil Holmdahl is shown posing for a photographer. Holding a rifle and outfitted with a sword, pistol, and five bandoliers (count them) containing large caliber rifle ammunition, Holmdahl was ready to go to war. Although less well known than other El Paso–based soldiers of fortune, he would acquire a formidable and well-deserved reputation for his exploits during the Mexican Revolution. In 1917 he would receive a presidential pardon so that he could go to France as a U.S. Army officer. Photo courtesy of Bancroft Library, University of California at Berkeley.

Figure 13. El Paso Mayor Tom Lea (1915–17) was also a renowned criminal lawyer. He represented Pascual Orozco Jr. in 1912 and represented Orozco and former Mexican president Victoriano Huerta, who were arrested outside El Paso as they prepared to invade Mexico, in 1915. Lea seldom lost a case. His son Thomas Calloway Lea III would garner a well-deserved reputation as a great landscape artist of the American West. His art would hang in the White House during the George W. Bush administration. Photo courtesy of El Paso Historical Society.

Figure 14. Victor Ochoa is shown nattily attired with coat, tie, and sporty fedora in a photograph probably taken in the 1930s. Ochoa twice went to federal prison, received a presidential pardon, and kept the U.S. Patent Office busy with applications (some successful) for several decades, but he was principally the irrepressible (and always unsuccessful) conspirator and gunrunner of the 1912 Orozco rebellion. At the very least Ochoa kept Bureau of Investigation agents and informers in El Paso busy throughout the decade of the revolution. Photo courtesy of Victor Ochoa Papers, National Museum of American History, Kenneth E. Behring Center, Smithsonian Institution, Washington, D.C.

Figure 15. Mercenaries enjoyed posing for photographers. This photograph taken after the May 1911 capture of Ciudad Juárez unfortunately does not have any accompanying identifications. Recognizable on the back row are, left to right, unidentified; Giuseppe Garibaldi; Abraham González, who became governor of Chihuahua; unidentified; Benjamin Viljoen, a Boer War general; unidentified. None of the three men kneeling can be identified. Photo courtesy of El Paso Public Library, Otis Aultman Collection (2599).

Figure 16. Attired in a three-piece suit with appropriate tie, Pancho Villa more closely resembles a Mexican businessman in this photo than the best-known general in the Mexican Revolution. Villa probably spent more time in El Paso than any of his contemporaries. Photo courtesy of El Paso Public Library, Otis Aultman Collection (A2680).

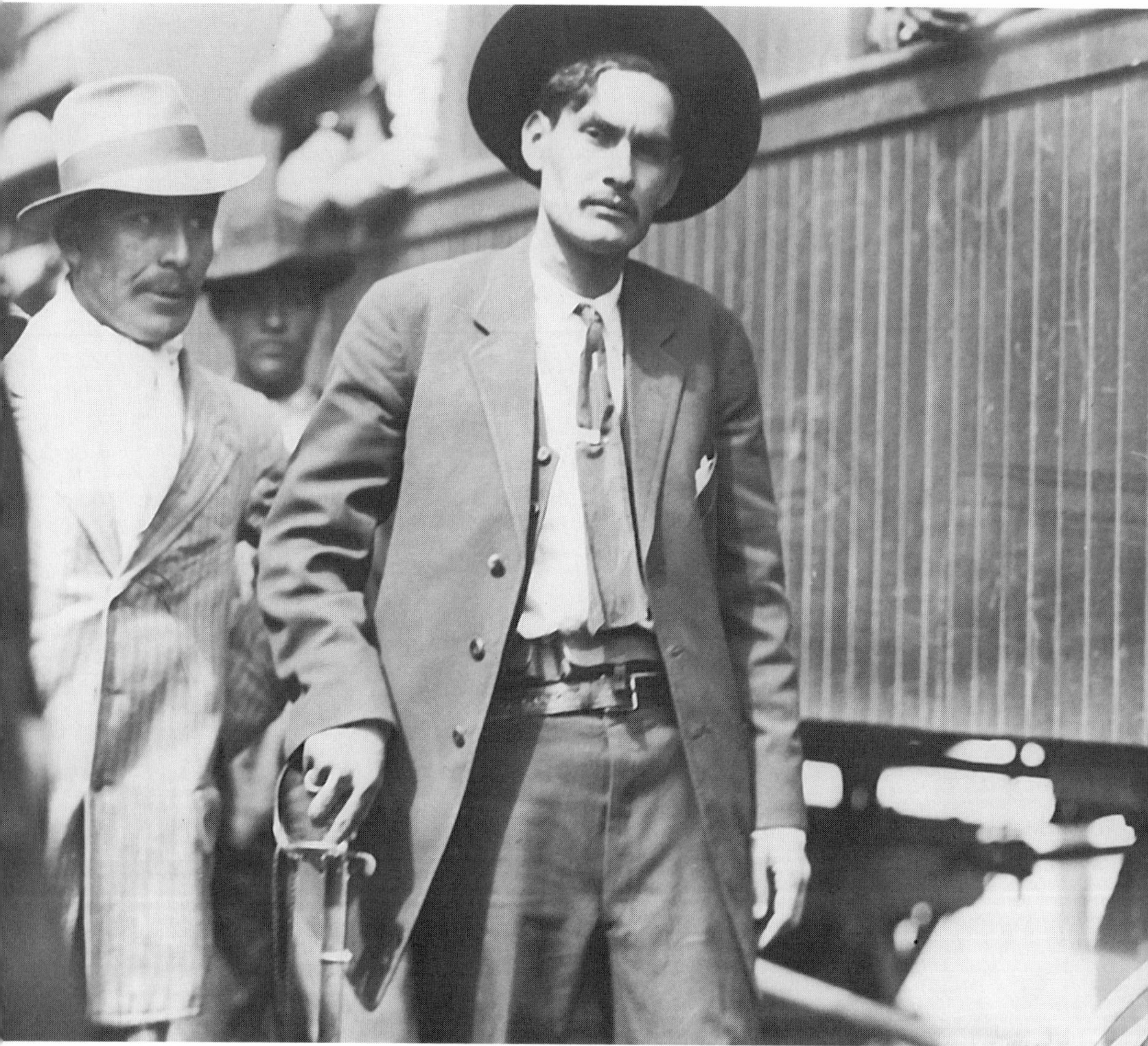

Figure 17. Antonio Rojas, shown posing with his hand on a sword, was a Chihuahua revolutionary commander who acquired his reputation as a cold-blooded killer during the 1912 Orozco Rebellion. Photo courtesy of El Paso Public Library, Otis Aultman Collection (3842).

Figure 18. This large three-story office/warehouse with a railroad siding conveniently located alongside the building was the El Paso home of Krakauer, Zork and Moye. The company was probably the largest arms and ammunition dealer along the U.S.-Mexican border. Photo courtesy of El Paso Public Library, Otis Aultman Collection (A5769).

Figure 19. Shelton-Payne was one of the two largest arms dealers in El Paso. Located on the first floor of the Merrick Building, it sometimes sold more guns and ammunition than its principal competitor Krakauer, Zork and Moye. Despite arms embargos by the U.S. government and one arrest (but no conviction), the firm made large profits on the sale of munitions throughout the revolution. Photo courtesy of El Paso Public Library, Otis Aultman Collection (A5095).

Figure 20. This impressive four-story building housed the Haymon Krupp and Company in El Paso. The owner of the company, Haymon Krupp, built a substantial fortune selling uniforms, shoes, and underwear to Pancho Villa and other revolutionaries. Utilizing the capital he had acquired during the course of the Mexican Revolution, he invested his fortune in oil drilling and was a co-owner of the famed discovery well Santa Rita No. 1, which in the early 1920s opened up the great oil fields of the Permian Basin. Photo courtesy of El Paso Public Library, Otis Aultman Collection (A5057).

Figure 21. The man who would be president: Emilio Vázquez Gómez. Vázquez Gómez spent a lot of time in El Paso plotting in vain to become president of Mexico. He is shown here seated. Behind him left to right are Colonel Pascual Orozco Sr., Francisco Pradillo, and Delio Moreno Cantón. Photo courtesy of El Paso Public Library, Otis Aultman Collection (A1589).

Figure 21A. General and former Mexican president Victoriano Huerta is surrounded by a group of newsman following his arrest by the U.S. district director of customs Zach Cobb outside El Paso as he prepared to invade Mexico with Pascual Orozco in the summer of 1915. Huerta had the covert financial backing of the German government. This photograph was taken in El Paso during the period in which he was held at Fort Bliss. Photo courtesy of El Paso Public Library, Otis Aultman Collection (B759).

Figure 22. Left to right are Santiago González, collector of customs at Ciudad Juárez; Andrés García, consul general of Mexico in El Paso; a Professor Vicarte; Rafael Rembao, director of the Chihuahua State Penitentiary in Chihuahua city; Mrs. Rembao; unidentified. García ran an effective intelligence operation in El Paso keeping track of opposition factions and their plans. Photo courtesy of El Paso Public Library, Otis Aultman Collection (A2289).

Figure 23. General José Inés Salazar (fifth from left with sword) never encountered a Mexican revolutionary faction he did not want to join. From left to right are Colonel Silvestre Quevedo, General Emilio Campa, Ricardo Gómez Robelo, Paulino Martínez, Inés Salazar, Jenaro Ceniceros, and Colonel Jesús San Martin. Photo courtesy of El Paso Public Library, Otis Aultman Collection (A1943).

Figure 24. Although El Paso was not the only city in America with residents who were soldiers of fortune during the decade 1910–20, it probably had the largest number. They even had a club—the Adventurers' Club. This photo was taken after WWI. Sitting left to right are Timothy Turner, a journalist who wrote a well-received autobiography of the early years of the Mexican Revolution; Jack Carlisle; Edward "Tex" O'Reilly of San Antonio, whose reputation exceeded his exploits; and B. Zimmerman. Back row: Bob Dorman; Otis Aultman, an El Paso photographer who was probably the best American photographer of the Mexican Revolution; the famed Sam Dreben, probably the second most famous soldier of fortune of his era—second only to Lee Christmas of New Orleans; Bert Caddle; and an individual identified only as McDonald. Photo courtesy of El Paso Public Library, Otis Aultman Collection (B291D).

Figure 25. Gus (Buster) Jones was a former Texas Ranger who in 1916 became a special agent of the Bureau of Investigation (the name of the Federal Bureau of Investigation prior to 1935) based in El Paso. After special agent Edward Stone was arrested (by Jones ironically) for shaking down an El Paso madam, Jones replaced him as head of the Bureau's El Paso office. A crack agent, Jones would become a special agent in charge in El Paso, a division superintendent of the Bureau, the Bureau's first legal attaché overseas (in Mexico), and Bureau liaison to British intelligence in the Caribbean during WWII before retiring. Photo courtesy of Federal Bureau of Investigation.

Figure 26. Of all of the tragic heroes of the Mexican Revolution, General Felipe Angeles is perhaps the most important. Angeles, who late in the revolution owned a ranch downriver from El Paso, was a professional soldier who had served as Villa's artillery commander in the heyday of the great División del Norte. In 1919 Angeles went to Chihuahua again to support Villa but was captured and executed. Photo courtesy of El Paso Public Library, Otis Aultman Collection (A5322).

Figure 27. On June 14, 1919, Pancho Villa and his troops attacked Ciudad Juárez and had virtually captured the Mexican border city when thousands of American cavalry, infantry, and field artillery opened up on Villa's troops. This photo shows a 24th Infantry unit on June 16 wading across the Rio Grande back into El Paso after having driven the *villistas* from the border city. Photo courtesy of El Paso Public Library, Otis Aultman Collection (B716).

CHAPTER 13

Aftermath

In the aftermath of the failed Huerta-Orozco conspiracy, Ike Alderete visited the county jail and told all those connected with the movement to keep their mouths shut and the Alderete brothers would post their bonds and provide them with a lawyer.[1] Meanwhile, for those conspirators not under arrest, there had occurred a rapid exodus of the *huertistas* and *orozquistas* who had recently flocked to El Paso.[2] There was also a temporary glut in the local arms market, a scramble to sell off the munitions that had been amassed for the ill-fated new movement. Zach Cobb, collector of customs, declared that he could use fifty men to watch the caches of ammunition secreted around El Paso.[3]

It seemed that everybody got into the act, even some widows. Mrs. Pascual Orozco and the widows of his companions Crisóforo Caballero, José Delgado, and Miguel Terrazas had been left in straitened financial circumstances when their husbands had been killed. So they got together to dispose of 375 rifles, 2 machine guns, and 70,000 cartridges that had belonged to their late husbands. Mrs. Orozco received half the proceeds, Mrs. Caballero one fourth, and the other two women split the other fourth. In a separate transaction, Mrs. Caballero sold 290 rifles and 7,000 cartridges.[4] Andrés García, the Carranza consul, was busily purchasing all the armament he could find in order to prevent its falling into *villista* hands.[5] Carranza secret agents, attorneys, and private detectives (the Ben Williams Agency in El Paso) were also monitoring the widespread smuggling of weaponry to the Villa garrison in Juárez.[6] The Alderete brothers were the prime movers in selling to the *villistas*.[7] Their attorney was Mayor Tom Lea, and there were allegations that he was actively involved in the arms traffic. The Alderetes, by the way, cheerfully sold ammunition to the Carranza faction as well, including one lot salvaged from a vessel sunk in the Galveston hurricane of 1900. The *carrancistas* indignantly returned the corroded cartridges because they were defective.[8] "The business instinct of the Alderetes," it was observed by one agent, "in all probability prevails over partisan feeling."[9]

Others who figured prominently in supplying munitions to the *villistas* in Juárez were Villa's old friend Teodoro Kyriacopulos and Victor Carusso, the brother-in-law and partner of the wholesale clothing merchant Haymon Krupp. Carusso had been a traveling salesman for the Friedman Shelby Shoe Company of Saint Louis, Missouri.

For the last several years he had worked in El Paso for his brother-in-law, who was president of the Haymon Krupp and Company. Shortly after Villa captured Juárez in 1913, Carusso secured large contracts with the *villistas*, earning commissions estimated at $40,000 or $50,000. He became an intimate friend of Colonel Hipólito Villa and through him secured other lucrative contracts.[10] Carusso then organized, next door to Krupp's establishment, the Everwear Shoe Company, which he owned together with Krupp, and they sold thousands of dollars' worth of goods to Villa. It was estimated that Carusso had made $300,000 to $500,000 in the last few years. In October or November 1915, customs inspectors found arms stored in the basement of the Everwear Shoe Company.[11] While people like Krupp and Carusso might be making thousands of dollars by supplying the Juárez garrison, ordinary soldiers of that garrison were also participating in a modest way. *Villista* officials were dismayed to learn that their own ammunition was being stolen by the troops, who gave it to their womenfolk, who took it to El Paso and then smuggled it back to Juárez and sold it to the Villa commercial agency for four cents per cartridge. This scam was only discovered when guards at the Mexican end of the international bridge took several Mexican women off the streetcar and found a quantity of cartridges on each.[12]

The fortunes of Pancho Villa, who had earlier seemed a sure bet to defeat Carranza, were declining. Carranza's general Alvaro Obregón inflicted a series of devastating defeats on the hitherto invincible Division of the North, driving Villa northward along the Mexican Central Railroad. And Villa's financial problems increased. The value of Villa's fiat currency dropped precipitously, reflecting the military situation.[13] At times Villa was unable to pay for munitions he had ordered, such as a 3-million-round consignment of 7-mm cartridges from New York, rushed to El Paso by railway express. The broker promptly sold them to Arturo González, Carranza's purchasing agent in El Paso, who arranged for the goods to be shipped through Laredo.[14] Villa was able to get some ammunition via El Paso; 920,000 rounds were exported to Juárez on August 4.[15] According to Cobb, "The chief element of Villa cohesion is his commercial organization at El Paso and Juarez. The profits come from property stolen in Mexico and marketed through El Paso. Villa can continue to operate after losing any number of officers so long as he is permitted in conjunction with American and Mexican grafters to market his loot here."[16] Cobb complained that all he could do was to hold up imports for forty-eight hours. The state courts, he noted, "have no jurisdiction over bonded shipments. Otherwise reputable lawyers, bankers and business men sharing in this loot are devising means to get around that half way remedy. Villa's profit from stolen sheep alone in the last few days has been over twelve thousand dollars. There is no way for the owners to protect themselves in court because the sheep cannot be identified. They continue to bring out cattle and to keep owners from protecting themselves through threats of what would be done to remaining herds in Mexico. They are stealing large quantities of ore, bullion and *matte*." Owners of livestock, mainly the Terrazas family, had to sign under duress contracts for export by which Villa received most of the profits. Cobb urged vehemently that the port of El Paso be closed, not only to prevent the marketing of Villa's loot but also to prevent coal, on which Villa's locomotives ran, from reaching him. Cobb's efforts to close the port were unsuccessful, but he did manage to delay coal shipments.[17]

At the October term of federal court the government's case against Victor Ochoa, Emil Holmdahl, José Orozco, and the former Carranza consul, Jorge Orozco, stemming from the abortive 1914 Columbus filibustering expedition, finally came to trial. Fred Mendenhall turned state's evidence, which was a major victory for the prosecution.[18] The trial began on October 14, and the government presented a very strong case. After deliberating for one hour, the jury acquitted Jorge Orozco but found Ochoa, Holmdahl, and José Orozco guilty as charged. Agent Charles E. Breniman reported: "There was much elation locally over the conviction of Ochoa and Jose Orozco, and especially Ochoa who for many years has caused the State and government officers in this locality much trouble and expense."[19] Ochoa's and Holmdahl's attorneys moved for a new trial, but the motion was denied, and the defendants were sentenced to eighteen months in the federal penitentiary at Leavenworth. They promptly served notice of appeal and their bond was set at $7,500 each.[20]

These convictions represented a real triumph for the government, and especially for the Bureau of Investigation—they were the first major victories obtained on charges of violation of the neutrality laws since the fall of 1911.

The State Department's policy toward Mexico sheds considerable light on the lucrative cross-border commerce about which Cobb complained. Officially the United States was merely watching to see which faction would emerge victorious in this latest round of civil war, but off the record Washington had quietly enabled Villa to remain a contender. In regard to cattle exports from northern Mexico, a puzzled President Wilson inquired of Secretary of State Lansing on August 7 "why you think it wise to put Villa in the way of getting money just at the moment when he is apparently weakest and on the verge of collapse?" Lansing's reply was revealing: "The reason for furnishing Villa with an opportunity to obtain funds is this: We do not wish the Carranza faction to be the only one to deal with in Mexico. Carranza seems so impossible that an appearance, at least, of opposition to him will give us an opportunity to invite a compromise of factions. I think, therefore, it is politic, for the time, to allow Villa to obtain sufficient financial resources to allow his faction to remain in arms until a compromise can be effected."[21]

Such a compromise was not to be. The Carranza forces continued to win on the battlefield, and on October 19, the United States extended diplomatic recognition to Venustiano Carranza as the de facto president of Mexico, thus sealing Pancho Villa's fate. The Villa consulate in El Paso closed its doors, as did the headquarters of Villa's foreign minister, Miguel Díaz Lombardo, located in the Paso del Norte Hotel. And a jubilant Victor Ochoa expressed his confidence that the Carranza ambassador in Washington would secure pardons for himself, Holmdahl, and José Orozco.[22]

The immediate benefit that Carranza received was permission from Washington on October 23 to rush about five thousand of his troops and 6 artillery pieces through Eagle Pass and Laredo by rail via El Paso to the border town of Agua Prieta, Sonora, across from Douglas, Arizona.[23] These reinforcements utterly disrupted Pancho Villa's attempt to retrieve his fortunes by launching a new offensive in Sonora, and he had to withdraw what was left of his forces back across the Sierra Madre into western Chihuahua. In December, another twenty-three hundred Carranza troops were moved through Eagle Pass and Douglas to Agua Prieta. Hipólito Villa was indicted on a state charge of being implicated in an attempt to wreck one of these troop trains by removing spikes from the rails on a sharp curve sixty miles east of El Paso, near Fort Hancock. Fortunately, a trackwalker discovered the sabotage; the train, luckily, was running about five hours late, so a tragedy was averted.[24]

The United States also permitted the export of munitions to the Carranza government but not to its foes, a policy that sharply accelerated Villa's decline.[25] There was an exception, however. For the time being, arms shipments into Chihuahua, Sonora, and the territory of Baja California were prohibited because the de facto government was not in complete control of these entities. The Bureau of Investigation was ordered to take vigorous action to enforce the above policy.[26] The policy of course stimulated smuggling to the Villa garrison in Juárez.[27]

As Villa's military fortunes declined so did the number of his followers. Lázaro de la Garza, whose financial acumen had kept the Division of the North supplied and equipped during a critical year, left the Villa commercial agency in July, forced out by the jealousy of Villa's brother Hipólito, who succeeded in supplanting de la Garza. The latter became an independent dealer in munitions, establishing Lázaro de la Garza and Company, an import-export and commission business, at 115 Broadway in New York City. He repeatedly found excuses not to accede to Pancho Villa's invitations to visit him. One reason he didn't want to see Villa was because he allegedly made a profit of $220,000 by selling to J. P. Morgan, who represented the French government during World War I, an ammunition contract he had obtained when he was Villa's representative. Felix Sommerfeld had originally signed the contract but had later signed it over to de la Garza.

De la Garza hung onto the money like grim death. When Manuel E. González, Hipólito Villa's secretary, sought out de la Garza and demanded that he return the money, claiming that it belonged to the revolution, de la Garza not only refused but said rude things about Pancho Villa.[28] And when in December 1918, Alberto Madero sued him in Los Angeles superior court under an assignment from Pancho Villa, de la Garza successfully defended himself in court.[29] He prudently declined Villa's invitation in 1919 to rejoin him, even though Villa assured him that all was forgiven, for "he was in great fear of assassination at Villa's hands, as he had been told that Villa had made the statement that he was the only man against whom he held sufficient enmity to have killed in the United States."[30] De la Garza settled in Los Angeles, in a walled mansion at 305 South Manhattan Place, which he purchased for $100,000 cash. There he entertained important Mexicans.[31] In 1933, Hipólito Villa sued de la Garza in Juárez federal court to recover $120,000 allegedly stolen when de la Garza was the Division of the North's commercial agent. The Mexican Supreme Court ruled in de la Garza's favor in 1935.[32]

De la Garza was not the only important *villista* to abandon the cause in late 1915. In September, Carranza consul Andrés García entered into secret negotiations with General Tomás Ornelas, the *villista* commander in Juárez. Using the mayor of Juárez as intermediary, García was trying to induce Ornelas to defect and surrender the city and to convince Villa to submit to the First Chief. Villa evidently discovered the intrigue, and in October, Ornelas defected and fled to El Paso. Ornelas stated that, at the risk of his life, he had recently proposed to Villa that the latter retire as commander of the Division of the North and allow his principal subordinates to enter into peace negotiations with Carranza. Ornelas claimed that his attempt failed because Villa's entourage convinced Villa that Ornelas was a traitor. On the night of October 13, Villa telegraphed to General Manuel Medinaveitia to take Ornelas under escort to Casas Grandes, ostensibly to discuss matters of great importance. He sent a second message reiterating the order. And Villa sent a third message, but Ornelas managed to intercept this communication, which stated, "Dispose of General Ornelas before reaching Casas Grandes, his presence is not necessary." Rightly interpreting this as a death sentence, Ornelas fled to El Paso with his family. Twelve other ranking Juárez officials did likewise on learning that Villa had ordered them to be shot.[33] By November, the able chief of *villista* intelligence, Héctor Ramos, had also abandoned the sinking ship, moving to Los Angeles to engage in private business. Ramos decided to study auto mechanics, for he contemplated opening a car dealership in Mexico when conditions permitted. Ramos later established an automobile repair shop in Los Angeles. His assistant Henry Kramp also ended his association with Villa, becoming the house detective for the Popular Dry Goods store. (In 1918, Kramp was a special peace officer in El Paso County and in 1926 was appointed acting postmaster in El Paso.)[34]

General Felipe Angeles, the professional artillery commander, graduate of both the Mexican military academy in Chapultepec and the French military academy in St. Cyr, whose expertise had contributed significantly to Pancho Villa's impressive string of military triumphs in 1913 and 1914, announced that he was ending his participation in Mexican political and military affairs and took refuge in El Paso. Unlike some other Mexican generals, Angeles had not amassed a fortune. He arrived destitute with his family but was rescued by José María Maytorena, ex-governor of Sonora and a Villa ally, who sent him enough money to purchase a small dairy farm near Ysleta and live in a modestly dignified manner. Angeles's chief of staff, General Federico Cervantes, arrived in El Paso as a refugee in December but was less fortunate. The best job he could find was as driver of a jitney car, or taxi.[35]

Colonel Hipólito Villa, who had been running the Juárez commercial agency, had troubles of his own. "Some of [the] El Paso parties heretofore associated with Villa commercial organization," Cobb wrote, "have quit, and seem [to be] seeking to curry favor with [the] Carranza agency."[36] Bowing to the inevitable, Hipólito didn't desert his brother's cause, but he did try to ensure that he and his family wouldn't starve while in exile; the authorities located over $130,000 in jewelry and cash in his El Paso residence.[37] Hipólito and family subsequently settled in Havana, keeping in close touch with Pancho Villa. The United States attempted unsuccessfully to have Hipólito extradited on the charge of trying to sabotage the Carranza troop train. (The charge was eventually dismissed.)

Pancho Villa's hold on Juárez loosened. Hipólito Villa had had to disarm most of the garrison because he feared mutiny. Moreover, Carranza operatives had been busy suborning Villa officers, distributing about $1,500 each to some thirty officers in Juárez and the city of Chihuahua in exchange for their allegiance.[38] It cost the Carranza regime $92,120 and 236,440 pesos to secure the surrender of Juárez.[39] It was an excellent investment.

On December 20, 1915, a group of *villista* officers went to the Mexican consulate in El Paso to receive amnesty. As of 12:10 p.m. they recognized the Carranza regime and gave it their allegiance. More importantly, they delivered Ciudad Juárez and its four-thousand-man garrison and offered to secure the allegiance for Carranza of Villa garrisons in Guadalupe, San Ignacio, Villa Ahumada, Casas Grandes, and other towns in Chihuahua. Carranza consul Andrés García received them with pleasure, guaranteeing amnesty for all but Francisco and Hipólito Villa, and offering financial assistance to pay the Juárez troops. The Carranza government retained the option as to whether to use the services of those receiving amnesty.[40] Lázaro de la Garza was one of those congratulating Consul García and President Venustiano Carranza on the unconditional surrender of Ciudad Juárez.[41]

General Alvaro Obregón arrived in El Paso with a hundred thousand Carranza pesos in currency to pay off the troops in the Juárez garrison who were being discharged. Obregón established his temporary headquarters in the Paso del Norte Hotel and announced on December 28 that a Carranza recruiting office would be opened in Juárez. Moreover, nearly three thousand Carranza troops began entraining with their camp followers in Naco, Arizona, that same day for El Paso. They were to be sent directly to Juárez to reinforce the garrison. Shortly thereafter Obregón departed for the city of Chihuahua to plan military operations against Villa.[42]

The Carranza regime's occupation of Juárez underlined the extent to which Pancho Villa had been reduced from the most powerful general in Mexico to a regional figure, but, still, one whose activities would continue to preoccupy El Pasoans for years to come.

CHAPTER 14

Villa, Columbus, Spies

Advertising the Carranza government's control of Chihuahua, Mexican consul Andrés García hosted a banquet on January 7 in the private dining room of the Paso del Norte Hotel for General Jacinto Treviño, Carranza's commander in Chihuahua. Besides Treviño's staff and the staff of the consulate, among the many attendees were General Gabriel Gavira, commander of the Juárez garrison, and C. S. T. Folsom, El Paso attorney for the Carranza regime.[1] On January 10, General Eulalio Contreras, Villa's commander in Palomas, surrendered with his four hundred troops to the Carranza government.[2]

The U.S. authorities continued to investigate the failed new movement and at the same time prepared to try General Huerta and his associates for neutrality violations. The Bureau intensified its efforts to locate key witnesses. Emil Holmdahl obligingly assisted in this endeavor, using his association with his codefendant José Orozco, who was currently in the county jail, to do so.[3] With the appeal of his neutrality conviction pending, Holmdahl was eager to earn merit with the authorities. His other codefendant, Victor Ochoa, was also eager to help, although the Bureau took a rather jaundiced view of him, Agent Frederick Guy commenting that "Ochoa is occasionally correct in his statements."[4]

The government's case was presented to the federal grand jury on January 6, but it was an open question whether Huerta would be in attendance at his forthcoming trial.[5] His physical condition was rapidly deteriorating. On November 5 he had been transferred for humanitarian reasons from detention in Fort Bliss back to his home in El Paso. An operation on January 1, 1916, to drain fluid from his abdomen brought little relief.[6] The procedure was repeated on January 3 but produced no improvement, nor did a repetition on January 7. Huerta seemed to improve slightly three days later, but he took a turn for the worse and died at his home at 8:35 p.m. on January 13, 1916. He was buried next to Pascual Orozco in an unpretentious grave in Concordia Cemetery. Huerta's secretary, General José Alessio Robles, issued a statement condemning the U.S. government for its treatment of Huerta and charging it with responsibility for his death.[7]

Unlike the outpouring of sympathy that accompanied Orozco's funeral, there was no great public manifestation when Huerta died, for his death was overshadowed by the aftermath of the Santa Isabel massacre. On January 8, 1916, eighteen American mining personnel, several of them well known in El Paso, were traveling by train to reopen a mine in Cusihuiriachic, west of the city of Chihuahua. The Carranza government had assured them that it controlled the area and that it was safe for them to travel. Shortly after the train passed through the way station of Santa Isabel, some forty miles west of Chihuahua, a band of *villistas* stopped it, forced the Americans to get off, and gleefully shot them down. Only one lived to tell the tale.[8] The massacre caused a sensation in El Paso, and it significantly increased the tension between Anglos and Hispanics that had grown during the revolution.

The tension exploded on January 13, the day Huerta died, when the first two Santa Isabel victims were buried in Evergreen Cemetery. During the morning an "indignation meeting" was held in the office of Charles Hunt, the wealthy cattle dealer, and fifty thousand "vengeance" cards were printed by friends of the victims for distribution in El Paso. The cards bore the ominous inscription "Remember the Alamo—Did we watch and wait? Remember Cusi—Shall we watch and wait?" That night sporadic street fighting broke out between Anglo civilians and soldiers and Hispanics. It started in the red-light district after the saloons closed, but at the height of the disorder hundreds of men were brawling along Broadway and Overland streets. Soon a race riot was in full swing, with many Hispanics getting beaten up. Overland Street not only was only a principal shopping street for south El Paso and for customers from Juárez, but was also an unofficial border line between the Anglo and Hispanic districts of the city. The sixty-five-man police force was unable to cope, and the local National Guard company was also unable to quell the disturbance. With the situation getting out of hand, General John Pershing offered to use his regulars to restore order, an offer the city fathers gratefully accepted. Pershing deployed a battalion of the 16th U.S. Infantry. Companies A and B patrolled the streets and established a cordon along Broadway, preventing Anglos from making a concerted attack on Hispanic south El Paso. Companies C and D were kept in reserve at the police station. These measures, and the arrest of about 150 men, turned the tide. An uneasy calm settled over El Paso.[9]

As part of the campaign to reduce the level of tension and intrigue in the city, the police began deporting many former *villistas*, charging them with being vagrants, among them Miguel Díaz Lombardo and General Manuel Banda. Díaz Lombardo, Villa's former foreign minister, had to post a $1,000 bond for his release, after which he was quietly told to get out of town.[10] The Immigration Service also did its bit—General Manuel Medinaveitia, Villa's former chief of staff, was deported to Juárez as an undesirable alien. Fearing arrest by the Carranza authorities, he made his way back to El Paso after two days, only to be deported once again.[11] But both Banda and Medinaveitia slipped back into El Paso, only to be arrested. And it was not only *villistas* who were being rousted for vagrancy—José Orozco, out on bond after his conviction in the abortive 1914 *carrancista* filibustering expedition, was also arrested.[12]

Someone who certainly should have had wit enough not to reenter Mexico was General Tomás Ornelas, the former Juárez commander who had defected from Villa in October 1915. He had been living quietly in El Paso, and against the repeated advice of his friends he decided to visit the city of Chihuahua. Ornelas took the train in Juárez and got as far as Sauz station, where Pancho Villa at the head of some sixty men captured the train and personally shot Ornelas dead on the station platform.[13] The incident not only illustrates Ornelas's incredible stupidity, but also the caliber of Villa's intelligence network, which alerted him to the fact that Ornelas would be aboard that particular train.

An unrelated incident further contributed to lessening the level of intrigue. Sabino Guaderrama, at the age of twenty-eight the most dynamic member of the prominent clan, met an untimely end on January 22, 1916. He was in the front passenger seat of an automobile driven by his brother David, with two friends in the back seat. They were en route to Nogales, Arizona, and shortly after crossing into New Mexico, Sabino was shot in the back and died soon afterward. Although the coroner ruled the incident an accident, the stories of the back seat passengers don't quite ring true. Joe Madrid, the man who actually shot Sabino, said a pistol went off accidentally as he was removing it from a pocket in the car door. His companion Emiliano Valverde, however, stated that the pistol was on the back seat and that Madrid was reaching for it when the car hit a bump and the weapon discharged.[14] Whatever the facts of the case, Sabino's death removed one of the boldest and most colorful characters in revolutionary El Paso. Furthermore, he had been the moving spirit in most of the Guaderramas' enterprises; with his death the clan ceased to play a significant role in revolutionary intrigue.

The demise of Orozco and Huerta marked yet another turn of the revolutionary wheel. Their followers were left scrambling to find other factions to which to attach themselves. To keep them under surveillance the Carranza consul employed four secret agents, among them Captain W. A. George, the former chief of El Paso city detectives. Another of the consul's operatives was Henry Gray, who declared that some of the original Red Flaggers—generals Emilio Campa and Marcelo Caraveo—were in town buying arms for the reactionary movement that General Félix Díaz was trying to get off the ground in southern Mexico.[15] Gray also told the Bureau about a rumored deal between one Al Roca, staying at the Hotel Zeiger, and one Walter Randall, staying at the Sheldon, for Roca to buy 5,000 rifles and 1.5 million rounds from Randall. Agent Guy was skeptical, for "Mr. Gray's information has rarely been found to be reliable and it was thought proper to hold up the matter pending confirmation." But several newspaper reporters had received information along the same lines, and Lieutenant Shallenberger, the provost marshal, stated that the deal had actually been closed two days before at Ike Alderete's office for 5,000 rifles, although he said he hadn't heard about any ammunition. The shipment was on its way from either Pittsburgh or Philadelphia bound for one of the Gulf Coast ports. From there the shipment would proceed via Cuba to Yucatán. The arms were intended for the Félix Díaz movement.[16] And Gonzalo Enrile, once Pascual Orozco's principal adviser, had for some time been living comfortably in the Waldorf Hotel in New York City but had recently made several trips to Toronto to confer with General Aureliano Blanquet, the former *huertista*, who was now supporting Félix Díaz. On February 29, 1916, Díaz issued the obligatory revolutionary manifesto, entitled *To the Nation*, formally launching a new rebellion against Carranza.[17]

Félix Díaz merited some of the Bureau's attention, but its top priority was monitoring Pancho Villa, who still commanded widespread support in Chihuahua and in El Paso as well. State Department special agent George Carothers wrote on March 3: "I anticipate renewed Villa activity in [the] very near future."[18] General Manuel Medinaveitia, Villa's former chief of staff, stated that in December 1915, Villa had planned to attack El Paso, but that Villa's generals balked, whereupon he called them cowards and abandoned the plan.[19]

General Gabriel Gavira, the commander in Juárez, announced to reporters on March 6 that Villa was proceeding to the border and that Gavira had asked American military authorities to be on the lookout for him. That same day Zach Cobb reported, "My tip is that he is due tonight or tomorrow. I have instructed [the] deputy [collector] at Columbus to rush any information."[20] On March 7, Cobb informed the secretary of state that "deputy [at] Columbus phones report that Villa with estimated four hundred men is on river southwest of Columbus, fifteen miles west and fifty odd miles south, where they stopped round up of cattle by employees of Palomas Land and Cattle Co., all of which [*sic*] employees except one are reported to have hastened to American side."[21] Colonel Herbert Slocum, commanding the 13th U.S. Cavalry in Columbus, also received reports of Villa moving toward the border but discounted them amid a spate of rumors. He should have paid attention.

In the predawn hours of March 9, Villa attacked the hamlet of Columbus, New Mexico, with about 480 men, taking the garrison by surprise and burning down part of the town. The 13th Cavalry quickly rallied, though, and repelled the attack, inflicting an estimated 110 casualties and pursuing the marauders into Mexico for some fifteen miles. The cavalry suffered ten dead. In addition, eight civilians died in the raid.[22]

The fleeing *villistas* left behind a number of documents, including a letter from Villa to General Emiliano Zapata inviting the latter to bring his army to the border and make a joint attack on the United States.[23] (Villa's invitation of course begged the question of just how Zapata was supposed to march his army through more than a thousand miles of Carranza-controlled territory in order to link up with Villa.) In April 1916, Agent Edward Stone in El Paso obtained a mass of correspondence and telegrams that had been sent among members of the Villa faction between May and August 1915. Stone sent this material to his superiors, and Agent L. S. Perkins of the New York office translated it, producing 104 typed pages of documents.[24]

The response of the United States to the Columbus raid was to dispatch Brigadier General Pershing and the Punitive Expedition into Chihuahua after Villa. This must have pleased Senator Fall, who arrived in El Paso on March 21 to see the situation for himself. Fall even hired the Ben Williams Detective Agency of El Paso to investigate the army's response to the Columbus raid.[25] Columbus, rather than El Paso, became the expedition's base of operations because Carranza forbade the U.S. Army to use Mexican railroads (although he later granted partial permission). Accordingly, the army embarked on a crash program of mechanization, to keep Pershing supplied by truck convoys. There has been some controversy concerning Pershing's mission—was it merely to disperse Villa's guerrillas or was it to capture or kill Villa himself? Pershing, at least initially, thought it was the latter, for on March 12 he issued a public statement that the expedition's object was the "pursuit and capture of Villa."[26]

In El Paso the immediate response to the Columbus raid was panic, fear that Villa was about to attack the city with the help of its Hispanic population. The Anglo citizenry stampeded to gun stores to arm themselves. Krakauer, Zork and Moye, for example, quickly sold its entire inventory, which was substantial, of arms and ammunition to a frenzied mob that clamored for more.[27] The military did not share in this hysteria but nevertheless took precautions. Brigadier General George Bell, who had replaced Pershing as commander of the El Paso Patrol District, placed the troops at Fort Bliss on alert and deployed five companies of the 16th U.S. Infantry and a doubled provost guard. In addition, a doubled police presence helped the army patrol the river and south El Paso. The international bridges, the smelter, and the city's power and light plant were guarded, and trolley service to Juárez was halted. A detachment of Texas Rangers arrived and also began patrolling. Mayor Lea requested that stores not sell arms to Mexicans, because of the many Villa supporters in the city, and the local authorities suppressed six Spanish-language newspapers.[28] One was *El Paso del Norte*, a Carranza mouthpiece newspaper, whose editor, Fernando Gamiochipi, was arrested. Mayor Lea subsequently allowed Spanish-language newspapers to publish, provided they avoided political pronouncements. However, Emilio Valenzuela, editor of *La Constitución*, was arrested, presumably for not obeying Lea's decree.[29]

Although no disturbances occurred, and 150 additional policemen were sworn in to ensure that they didn't, Agent Robert Barnes noted that "considerable apprehension is felt among officials and citizens in this vicinity concerning the friction which they fear will arise as a result of the punitive expedition in pursuit of General Villa. This action of the United States is distasteful to most of the Mexican population." Worried consultations occurred between local officials, Cobb, and agents of the Bureau of Investigation and the Immigration Service.[30]

Not surprisingly, the Columbus raid led to a new roundup of Villa partisans in El Paso. They had a horror of being deported to Juárez to face the tender mercies of the *carrancistas*. As mentioned, General Manuel Banda, a former commander of the Juárez garrison, was arrested, as was General Manuel Medinaveitia, who had been Villa's chief of staff. Also arrested was Cecilio Luna, who held a commission from Villa as a lieutenant colonel. The Bureau obtained a number of letters that Luna had on his person when arrested. They were translated and copies were forwarded to the San Antonio office. Representatives of the police, the Bureau, and the Immigration Service interrogated the numerous suspects, who were eventually released.[31] Roundups of *villistas* continued into April, when more than seventy were deported to Juárez, ostensibly because, as with the eighteen arrested in the plaza near the Sheldon Hotel, they were plotting to capture Juárez. Seven, including General Marcelo Caraveo, were held for investigation by federal agents. Prominent but unnamed local businessmen were prepared to furnish their bail.[32]

Generals Banda and Medinaveitia provoke a certain amount of pity, for they were harshly treated by the police and greedily exploited by their attorney, Juan Larrazolo. They related that the El Paso police had detained them in jail for fifteen days without permitting them to see anyone but their attorney. The day captain of police, Lee Hall, the former *maderista* intelligence chief, ordered that if any other prisoners talked to them the prisoner would receive fifty lashes. In addition, Hall refused to let them be fed.[33] The night captain did, however, permit the feeding of the imprisoned *villista* generals. Their attorney, Larrazolo, told them he would guarantee their immediate release for $1,000 in cash each, assuring them that his influential contacts in Washington had arranged the matter. Larrazolo claimed that the United States was positively going to intervene militarily in Mexico, presumably declaring war, which would result in the two men rotting in jail for at least five years. The frightened *villistas* met Larrazolo's terms: Banda signed over his house in El Paso, worth $1,500, and Medinaveitia sold his home in Torreón for $1,000. They were released on March 26. Having received the cash, Larrazolo told them they would have to leave the United States within fifteen days. He asked them to pay his expenses to accompany them to New Orleans and see them safely off to Havana. Or, for another $250, he could arrange for them to remain in the United States indefinitely. The police put them on a train for New Orleans, where they related their tale of woe to the Bureau. As a final touch, Larrazolo went to court to prevent Banda's wife from selling her furniture and possessions to get cash she could send her husband in New Orleans. Banda's wife and child were left destitute.[34] This was most certainly not the only instance of Mexican refugees being abused and exploited.

There were of course also American partisans of Villa, among them George Milton Holmes, a cattle dealer born in 1867 who figured prominently in the intrigue that characterized El Paso. Holmes's early life paralleled that of Villa: "Born in Uvalde, Texas, Holmes, like Villa, came from a poor family; and, like Villa, he soon became a cattle rustler."[35] Now, Holmes marketed the cattle that Villa confiscated in Chihuahua, mainly from the Terrazas clan. Holmes even had Villa's picture on his stationery. A close friend of both Pancho Villa and his brother Hipólito, Holmes was a major *villista* agent, a go-between who carried confidential messages from Pancho to Hipólito, at that time living in exile in Havana. Holmes had escorted Mrs. Villa no. 1 (Luz Corral, Pancho Villa's legitimate wife) to Havana three weeks earlier. There he had conferred with Hipólito Villa, returning a few days before the Columbus raid. Perhaps significantly, Holmes and his wife immediately checked out of the elegant Paso del Norte Hotel, where they had lived for two years, announcing that they were going to Tennessee but instead leaving for the West. Holmes had since returned to El Paso but not to the Paso del Norte. The Bureau was trying to locate him, and it was suggested that Alfred H. Kerr, vice president of the El Paso Bank and Trust Company, a close friend of Holmes, could tell them the latter's whereabouts. Kerr either couldn't or wouldn't.[36] Kerr was known to have handled financial transactions for Villa, and Holmes was suspected of being Villa's principal financial agent in El Paso, allegedly enjoying a power of attorney for both Francisco and Hipólito Villa. Reportedly there were Villa funds on deposit in the Rio Grande Valley Bank and Trust in Holmes's name.[37]

Holmes's "associates in his enterprises scale from that of high officials of banking institutions in this city down to the lowest criminals and crooks," observed Military Intelligence, which also had its eye on Holmes. The Fort Bliss intelligence officer was especially frustrated by the close ties between Holmes and Captain Monroe Fox, whose Texas Ranger company covered the El Paso area. Holmes and his associates frequented Fox's headquarters in Fabens, and Holmes allegedly boasted of having furnished horses and weapons to his Texas Ranger friends. Thus Holmes could carry on with impunity his flouting of the neutrality laws from his ranch near San Elizario.[38]

Haymon Krupp and Victor Carusso were also zealous in protecting Villa's interests. In May, a woman won a judgment against Villa for $2,275, which she paid him in a vain effort to save her brother from the firing squad. In February 1914, Villa had commissioned her brother, Domingo Flores, nicknamed "El Coyote," to purchase $3,500 worth of ammunition in El Paso, and Flores had kept the money. Villa ordered that Flores be shot, but he informed his sister that if she paid $3,500 his life would be spared. She scraped together the money in installments. The day after she paid the last installment Villa had Flores executed. To collect the judgment, the sister attached a luxurious seven-passenger automobile of Villa's. Carusso and Krupp signed the replevin bond, and the auto was returned to the Villa family. However, shortly thereafter Villa's longtime friend Teodoro Kyriacopulos attached the same automobile, alleging that Villa owed him money.[39]

One of Pancho Villa's staunchest supporters in El Paso had been the *El Paso Morning Times*, which had consistently backed the revolutionaries ever since 1910. The *Times* was in fact banned in Chihuahua by the Carranza authorities because of its pro-Villa slant. In March 1915, Consul Andrés García had reported that to justify the subvention that Villa was paying the paper, it had started a Spanish-language edition with Ramon Prida, "a known *cientifico* who has sold his pen to the reactionaries," as editor. García then arranged for *carrancista* sympathizers to finance *El Paso del Norte*, a daily newspaper whose editor was Fernando Gamiochipi, in order to counter the propaganda of the *El Paso Morning Times*, "our most powerful enemy."[40] *El Paso del Norte* received $400 a month from Consul García.[41]

Although the *Times* ceased being pro-Villa in the wake of the Columbus raid and subsequently referred to "the bandit Villa," at a political rally in July 1916 Mayor Tom Lea accused the newspaper of having secretly received a subsidy from Villa and boldly declared that he knew where there was irrefutable proof. The newspaper categorically denied the charge and invited inspection of its books and accounts.[42] Nevertheless, it became known that several people had seen a receipt, and the *Times*'s rival, the *El Paso Herald*, triumphantly published "the picture of two pieces of paper. One was a photograph of a draft directing Pedro Maese, Villa's collector of customs in Juárez, to pay $10,000 to 'Wyche Greer, manager of the El Paso Morning Times.' The second was a receipt from Wyche Greer, accepting the $10,000. The draft was dated August 31, 1915, and the receipt was dated September 1, 1915." All the *Times* could do was lamely to repeat that the company had never received the money and invite an inspection of its books, where presumably any such subsidy would be neatly listed under "bribes."[43] The point is, of course, that the *Times* never received the money from Villa—its editor Wyche Green did. He was fired, went to Fort Worth where he got a job on the *Record*, then moved on to become the editor of the *Wichita Falls (Tx.) Tribune*. He filed an unsuccessful $50,000 libel suit against the *El Paso Herald* over the bribe allegation.[44]

In the highly charged atmosphere produced by the Columbus raid, El Pasoans were jumpier than usual. A near panic ensued when residents on both sides of the river were jolted by "heavy cannonading" at 9 p.m. on May 30. They thought the war had started. What had occurred was that a furnace had burst at the El Paso smelter and leaked ten tons of molten metal on wet ground and standing water. The resulting explosions, which could be heard two miles away, lasted for two hours, shattering the nerves of many residents.[45] Then on June 13, the army practiced for an exhibition in Washington Park, firing artillery, machine guns, rifles, and pistols; the din could be heard throughout El Paso, and "newspaper offices, the police station, detective headquarters, the sheriff's office, and Fort Bliss" were besieged with frantic telephone calls asking whether El Paso was under attack.[46]

The Columbus raid also produced a swarm of war correspondents in El Paso. By March 12, eighteen had arrived, notable among them Damon Runyon of the *New York American* and Floyd P. Gibbons of the *Chicago Tribune*.[47] Some of the stories this press corps filed, however, were so utterly false and sensational that Mayor Lea quickly had an ordinance passed making the sending of false and alarming reports a misdemeanor.[48]

The tense days following the Columbus raid also impelled Robert Barnes, the Bureau agent in charge in San Antonio, to come to El Paso to direct operations for a time. He informed his superior that "if conditions do not continue to improve and the situation takes a turn for the worse, I anticipate that there will be in the United States along the border a large number of Mexicans who will be dangerous to the community and against whom there will be neither evidence on which to base a prosecution nor to cause their deportation. It has occurred to me that probably the only way they could be handled would be for the military authorities to hold them as a war measure. I have discussed this matter briefly with General Bell commanding the forces here and he expresses a dislike to be bothered with prisoners."[49]

The Bureau was desperately trying to improve its intelligence-gathering capabilities, and Bruce Bielaski, the chief, authorized Barnes to employ up to three informants. Barnes personally recruited Colonel Darío Silva, who had been Villa's secretary, as an informant. Silva was quite amenable to working for the Bureau, and he was confident that by using his *villista* connections he could obtain valuable information. Barnes notified his chief on March 24 that "Silva is the only informant who has been employed in El Paso to date," explaining that "I have interviewed a number of people in this vicinity and find it very difficult to secure a Mexican informant who could be trusted at this particular time" and adding that "I might also say that the people generally in this vicinity are very much excited and a large number of rumors have been followed up without any results."[50] Barnes considered Silva a real prize: "In reporting on information furnished by Informant Dario Silva, he will be referred to in the reports as 'Informant Avlis.' ["Avlis" was "Silva" spelled backward.] This is done in order to more carefully guard his identity."[51]

Silva not only reported on *villista* activities in El Paso, but on occasion he was dispatched to places such as Clifton, Arizona, to ferret out conspiracies there.[52] He did provide the Bureau with insights into Villa's character. Agent Charles Breniman noted that "Avlis believes that Villa will fight our forces. He said that since the United States recognized Carranza, Villa has many times in his presence expressed the most virulent hatred for the 'gringoes' [*sic*]. I asked about Villa's personal characteristics. He said Villa is subject to fits of intense anger and he would on such occasions order the execution of any one among his own forces to whom he happened to take a dislike. On one occasion he ordered his brother Hipolito executed" (he then changed his mind). "Avlis believes Villa is being backed by German money and influence."[53] Silva continued to supply a steady stream of information, and sometimes acted as agent provocateur to sound out persons known to have ties with Villa.[54] He discussed with Todd McClammy, the *villista* cattle dealer and secret agent, the idea of an expedition of cowboys and border characters going into Chihuahua to capture Villa. McClammy proposed that he himself lead such an expedition, hoping thereby to collect a substantial reward. Reportedly, $50,000 had been deposited in a New York bank by Mrs. Russell Sage, the wealthy mother-in-law of Colonel Herbert Slocum, commander of the 13th Cavalry in Columbus, whose reputation had been severely damaged by the Villa raid. McClammy stipulated, however, that he would lead an expedition only if the U.S. government approved. The government didn't, and the idea died.[55] Informant Silva diligently made the rounds of the saloons, cafés, rooming houses, and tenements in south El Paso where revolutionary plotting was a cottage industry.[56]

Silva advised that George Holmes was indeed back in El Paso, living at 719 West Missouri Avenue, and was buying horses and equipment for the Villa faction. George Carothers, who was staying at the Paso del Norte, obtained letters addressed to Holmes from Havana that were being held for him at the hotel and had Bureau agents read them.[57] The Bureau employed detective "Australian" Billy Smith to shadow Holmes when he called at the Paso del Norte for his mail and had meetings at the hotel and elsewhere.[58] Holmes subsequently moved into the house of Raymond Bell, a Villa sympathizer who had become wealthy selling hides and cattle for Villa, who had conferred the lucrative Juárez packing plant concession on him. An admiring Gus Jones, a Bureau agent, remarked that "Mr. Bell is probably the most consummate and cheerful liar we have ever dealt with."[59]

Holmes traveled to Columbus, New Mexico, on June 1 with two young Mexican women, one of them Mrs. Pancho Villa's secretary. The trio wanted to cross into Mexico, and Holmes applied to General Pershing for permission to bring out some cattle. Pershing ordered that Holmes be watched and under no circumstances be permitted to enter Mexico. General Bell informed the Bureau that Holmes had retrieved secret papers from the shoes of two *villista* couriers recently killed by the U.S. Army as they headed for El Paso. The general was most anxious to learn Holmes's whereabouts. The elusive Holmes, however, went from Columbus to Las Cruces and from there back to El Paso. The Bureau tried to ascertain his intentions by checking his usual haunts: the El Paso Bank and Trust Company, the Coney Island Club over the Coney Island Bar, and the room of his friend Roy G. Martin, residing at the Linden Hotel.[60] A Bureau agent finally located Holmes and talked with him, learning that Holmes was desperate to enter Mexico, where he had important business, and that he hoped to secure letters of recommendation to Pershing from Mayor Lea and Sheriff Edwards. He did secure a letter of recommendation from Monroe Fox. According to one informant, Holmes's "important business" consisted of trying to deliver sensitive papers and maps to Pancho Villa.[61] The effort failed.

Informant Silva reported that José G. Hernández, who resided at 506 East Rio Grande Street, was Pancho Villa's financial agent in El Paso and through a stream of couriers was in constant touch with Villa.[62] Sometimes Silva met his Bureau handlers in out-of-the-way places, such as Evergreen Cemetery on the city's outskirts.[63] This was a considerable improvement over the practice of earlier years, when informants came to the Bureau office to report. Although Silva provided a quantity of information, Agent Steve Pinckney was concerned about its quality: "Avlis is not a worthy informant. He has been instructed time and again to be able to state explicitly the sources of his information, to secure names etc. when asked from time to time; he is seldom able to state things exactly, saying 'Some man whose name I don't know told me so.'"[64] Pinckney's superior, Agent Barnes, who had recruited Silva, instructed Pinckney to check Silva's reports.[65]

Pinckney's reply was not what Barnes wanted to hear, for it was essentially "I told you so." He reminded Barnes that he had never had faith in Avlis but that Barnes had overruled him and ordered him to be Silva's case officer. Captain Robert E. Grinstead of Military Intelligence, unaware that Silva was working for the Bureau, had been reporting to Pinckney from time to time that one of Grinstead's informants kept seeing Silva in the company of various Mexicans and believed that Silva was active in revolutionary matters. To test Silva, Pinckney arranged with Grinstead to have his movements covered. Pinckney gave Silva specific assignments, and Grinstead's people kept him under surveillance. When Silva reported back to Pinckney the next day, Pinckney realized that Silva had lied to him outrageously. Pinckney repeated the test the following day, with the same results. He informed Barnes that "Avlis lied totally. I feel that most of the information he has reported during the past two or three weeks was worthless. On Monday I will discontinue his services unless you instruct otherwise. If you want a detailed report of the two days' cheating of him I will be happy to send it."

Barnes replied: "Dismiss Informant Avlis."[66] Barnes, who was a very good agent, must have been mortified over the Avlis fiasco, for he had been well and truly suckered. However, the affair was a learning experience for the Bureau, driving home the point that it was essential to corroborate the reports of any informant. From time to time Silva continued to provide information, on an informal basis, and State Department special agent George Carothers also used him as an informant.[67] However, Zach Cobb's opinion was that "Silva was for [a] long time and I believe has been continuously and still is Villa's principal confidential man. I believe he is Villa's alter ego here."[68]

The Bureau still had to rely heavily on informants—either Carranza secret service agents, local officials, or its own small number of operatives. One of these, referred to as "Informant Samot" (whose name was presumably "Tomás") was hired in April at $2.50 a day, provided he could "deliver the goods." He evidently did, with his handler meeting him in places such as the sunken gardens in Houston Park. There was also Jack Flynn, who lived in Juárez and who reported on the Mexican military.[69] And in some unspecified manner Agent Stone secured on April 11 a list of people who had been Villa confidential and consular agents.[70] The Bureau also enjoyed the invaluable cooperation of post office officials, who provided tracings of the writing on envelopes addressed to persons of interest.

The Bureau not only used human intelligence but also periodically utilized technology. A potential source of intelligence appeared in the person of "Mrs. Villa the second," Juana Torres de Villa (Pancho Villa was not monogamous) who arrived in March from Los Angeles along with her brother, Colonel Zenaido Torres, two sisters, two children, and a German maid. The party took rooms in the Detroit Hotel, a hostelry once favored by Pascual Orozco and Hipólito Villa. Anxious for any crumb of information, Barnes had Agent Stone rent an adjoining room, and Stone installed a Holliday Detecto ("similar to a dictograph") in his room, connecting the transmitter to the room of Mrs. Villa's brother. The device couldn't be installed in Mrs. Villa's room because she never left it. Unfortunately the dictograph produced nothing useful, and after three days of frustration Barnes ordered the surveillance ended. It was from the landlady that Stone learned the party's plans—Mrs. Villa had left Los Angeles to avoid newspaper publicity and planned to travel on to New Orleans, then to Cuba. The landlady promised to notify the Bureau of any developments.[71]

Undaunted by the failure to learn anything of value by bugging the Villa party, the Bureau was prepared to try again. The potential target was Luis Terrazas, the patriarch of the clan who had controlled Chihuahua prior to the revolution.[72] Terrazas was living in a suite on the third floor of the Paso del Norte and was protected by bodyguards. Agent Stone learned that there was to be in the suite an important meeting of prominent *felicistas, científicos,* and Red Flaggers. This opportunity was too good to pass up, and agents Pinckney and Stone went to the hotel. There they encountered a Major Laubach of Military Intelligence who was also interested in the meeting and had rented a room on the same floor.[73] Laubach informed the agents that he had seen a high-powered automobile drive up with three Mexican passengers who immediately went to Terrazas's suite. He thought one of them was General Marcelo Caraveo. The major had taken the elevator to the third floor and found two men guarding the entrance to the suite and thirteen Mexicans standing in the corridor waiting for admittance. Agent Pinckney sent Agent Stone to the third floor to investigate. Stone saw one of Terrazas's nephews, whose last name was Horcasitas, sitting on guard by the elevator while the meeting was in progress. Stone knew him and his brother by sight and knew they handled Terrazas's correspondence and confidential matters. He reported back to Pinckney, who instructed him to continue surveillance. Stone hung around in the lobby and saw one Brant Elliot, a cattleman from Alpine, conversing with the agent who handled Terrazas's livestock and with the other Horcasitas brother, who was Terrazas's secretary. He also saw Senator Albert Fall of New Mexico enter the lobby about 11 a.m., go to the bar, and have drinks with two Americans and an unknown Mexican. Then a few minutes later Terrazas, his two sons, his private secretary, and several others emerged from the elevator and left the hotel.

Stone and Pinckney later went to the third floor to inspect the two rooms adjoining the Terrazas suite with a view to determining whether a Dictaphone could be successfully installed. They were encouraged by what they saw, especially Stone, who had had "experience with Dictaphones and that sort of work."[74] Unfortunately the available documents do not reveal whether the Bureau in fact bugged Terrazas's suite, but it was a technique that was being used with greater frequency.

Agent Pinckney did continue to investigate the meeting in Terrazas's quarters and learned that General Marcelo Caraveo and General Fidel Avila, a prominent *villista* now living quietly on his large farm in Vado, near Las Cruces, New Mexico, had indeed attended. Avila had some forty to ninety ex-*villista* soldiers, mainly deserters, working for him on the farm for $1.00 a day clearing brush and grubbing out mesquite roots. Recently there had been reports of considerable activity by Avila and his laborers. That many *villistas* together in one place on American soil made the authorities nervous.[75]

The object of the meeting was apparently to forge an alliance between *científicos, huertistas*, Red Flaggers, and other reactionary elements. Francisco León de la Barra, José Yves Limantour, and Enrique Creel were working in Washington, D.C., and New York City on behalf of this movement, and those handling the military end of it were generals Aureliano Blanquet, Manuel Mondragón, and Félix Díaz. Stone hoped eventually to learn exactly who had attended the meeting and more precisely what its purposes were.[76]

One of the attendees, General Caraveo, must have had a sense of humor. He had confidentially proposed to George Carothers, the State Department special agent, that the United States arm and equip the two thousand men he claimed to have in the vicinity of El Paso and then he would lead them into Mexico to capture Pancho Villa, thereby avoiding the necessity of American troops having to enter the country.[77] Now, since Caraveo was involved with other reactionaries, the Bureau called him in for a talk. Agent Barnes, with Stone as interpreter, was especially interested in Caraveo's relations with General José Inés Salazar. Caraveo denied any connection and gave his word of honor that he would live quietly in El Paso and have nothing to do with Salazar. He was then permitted to go home.[78]

Salazar, who had been apprehended in New Mexico and taken to Santa Fe to be tried for perjury, had been acquitted on December 9, 1915, in yet another farce of a trial. He then made his way back to El Paso. Bureau agents had questioned him, and he stated that between his two trials he had stayed in Las Cruces but was now residing at 1402 East Missouri Avenue with his family. He was, he admitted, unemployed, but he was apolitical, although he did plan to return to Mexico when it was safe to do so. Salazar had come down in the world; he was now destitute. He asked Ike Alderete for monetary help, and Alderete and his friends took up a collection.

On the night of April 9, 1916, Salazar slipped out of town with a handful of followers, and on April 11, issued a revolutionary proclamation urging Mexicans to rally around him. It was speculated that Salazar's attorney, Elfego Baca, actually wrote the proclamation and that Salazar still owed Baca money for having arranged his escape from the Albuquerque jail. Few heeded Salazar's call; his followers dropped from thirty to four by May, and he wrote to General Gabriel Gavira, the commander in Juárez, requesting amnesty and permission to become a *carrancista* general. Gavira was agreeable, and he issued a written guarantee of amnesty. Salazar surrendered in May. Described as a "professional Mexican revolutionist," Salazar was pretty grubby when he arrived in Juárez with his followers—a one-eyed man, a one-armed man, and a deaf mute. But he was soon nattily attired in a new suit, and it seemed his fortunes had taken a dramatic upward turn.[79]

Back in April, Salazar had had a compelling reason to leave El Paso—he feared being killed, as there were several Americans whom he had wronged and who were just waiting for a chance to get even.[80] One of them was Todd McClammy. Some of Salazar's men had captured McClammy and had "strung him up"—tying him up by his wrists to a tree limb and leaving him to die an agonizing death. McClammy hung there for forty-eight hours before a compassionate passerby cut him down. His wrists bore the scars of his ordeal.[81] It's surprising that McClammy had not retaliated, for he was a violent individual. He had a dispute over a business deal with Alberto Madero, the late president's uncle, in Madero's office in the First National Bank Building. In the midst of a heated exchange, Madero drew a small automatic pistol; McClammy drew his six-shooter, disarmed and pistol-whipped Madero, and kicked him down a flight of stairs. (In an attempt to save face, Madero initially claimed that two unknown Anglos had jumped him as he walked down the corridor.)[82]

Mayor Lea was determined to purge El Paso of Mexicans who might cause trouble. When Mrs. Villa no. 2 (Juana Torres de Villa) returned to El Paso from exile, the mayor had the police deport her and her party to Juárez. This action miffed Agent Stone: "The police acted very arbitrarily in [the] matter, not waiting for any explanation from [the] government as regarding our position in matter."[83] Mayor Lea also had the police arrest General Juan Medina on a vagrancy charge. The police informed Medina that he would be jailed overnight and would have to leave town the next day. Medina had a lawyer and made bail to appear in police court. Medina had been a prominent follower of Villa and was arrested at the home of a longtime friend, Mrs. Lucero, where he had been hiding for several weeks. She was interviewed by Agent Stone, Captain Grinstead, the Military Intelligence officer, and Lieutenant H. B. Lewis of the provost guard. Mrs. Lucero said Medina told her he had been commissioned by Villa to go to Japan to obtain arms and ammunition. Medina claimed he had wanted to desert Villa and, through Lucero, had approached Zach Cobb about the matter. Medina had persuaded Villa to send him to Japan to purchase munitions as a ploy to get beyond Villa's reach. Since Villa had given him money for the trip he decided to take both the money and the trip. He said he had lived in Lucero's home for many years. She operated a curio business in Juárez and accompanied him in order to purchase stock for her shop. To save money they traveled as man and wife but absolutely no sex was involved (although she was his longtime mistress). She didn't know if in fact Medina tried to obtain munitions; he denied making any inquiries about munitions.

When they arrived in El Paso in late February 1916, Mrs. Lucero claimed that she informed Cobb of Medina's presence, and on the advice of Medina's counsel he had remained in seclusion in her home ever since. Medina's lawyer, U. S. Goen, stated that he'd informed the district attorney and other local officials of Medina's presence but had not gotten around to informing the mayor and the police chief. Medina and Lucero refused to permit Agent Stone to examine Medina's papers, and on the advice of his attorney, who was present, Medina refused to discuss his mission to Japan. Determined to be rid of Medina, the local authorities and General Bell himself insisted that Agent Pinckney file a white slave charge. Pinckney declined, for lack of evidence. The agent then called on Medina's attorney, who said he would contest any attempt to run Medina out of town on a vagrancy charge, but if Medina's presence was obnoxious to the authorities he'd advise his client voluntarily to leave town until conditions improved. Pinckney thought this was a splendid idea. Vagrancy charges against Medina were suspended and he was released on a $400 bond.[84]

Medina left town, but about that time Sam Dreben, the redoubtable soldier of fortune, reappeared. He had continued to work with Felix Sommerfeld, and they were suspected not just of acquiring munitions for Villa but also of being the conduit between Villa and German intriguers. Shortly after the Columbus raid, Dreben, in a patriotic gesture, had volunteered to join the Punitive Expedition as a scout for General Pershing. The general accepted the offer, and Dreben spent about a month with Pershing. But the general expelled Dreben from the Punitive Expedition because Dreben was gambling with—and cheating—the troops. Dreben returned to El Paso, and in September he opened a brokerage business with offices in the Sheldon Hotel. That month he also got married, to Helen Spence.[85]

Another soldier of fortune who joined the Punitive Expedition as a scout was Emil Holmdahl, out on bail pending his appeal on the neutrality conviction. On May 17, 1916, Holmdahl was one of two civilian guides for a detachment of ten soldiers commanded by Lieutenant George Patton. They were searching a ranch headquarters in Chihuahua for *villistas* when a firefight erupted. The Americans killed three Mexicans, including Colonel Julio Cárdenas, one of Villa's top aides. Patton wounded Cárdenas, but it was Holmdahl who killed him, as Patton himself stated in his official report of the incident.[86] The point is worth mentioning because the press made Patton the hero of the engagement, and Patton made no effort to set the record straight. The incident became part of the Patton legend. The flamboyant Patton had the three Mexican corpses tied to the hoods of the cars the Americans were using and transported them back to camp like a deer hunter returning from a successful outing.

The presence of the Punitive Expedition (the number of troops assigned to it eventually reaching some fourteen thousand) in Chihuahua severely strained relations between the United States and Carranza, who steadfastly demanded the withdrawal of the Americans, considering the Punitive Expedition an invasion of Mexico. Washington's position was that unless Carranza could guarantee the protection of the American border the expedition would remain in Mexico. Carranza could give no such guarantee, for his control of Chihuahua was questionable. Pancho Villa might be down, but he was certainly not out. He enjoyed considerable popular support and dominated areas of southern and western Chihuahua. The Carranza army vastly outnumbered Villa's forces but showed no great offensive spirit. And Carranza's commanding general in Chihuahua, Jacinto Treviño, was suspected of disloyalty, or at least of culpable stupidity—he had dispatched an important shipment (500,000 cartridges, hundreds of rifles, and several machine guns) south from Chihuahua by rail without an escort. Villa had captured the lot.[87]

On April 12 in the city of Parral in southern Chihuahua a clash occurred between elements of the Punitive Expedition and Carranza troops. On April 15 the United States reimposed an embargo on all war materiel for Mexico. (With two exceptions, the embargo lasted until July 20, 1917.)[88] These developments prompted an important conference in El Paso and Juárez beginning on April 29 between General Alvaro

Obregón, who was the secretary of war in Carranza's cabinet, and American major generals Hugh L. Scott and Frederick Funston.[89] Amid all the pomp and ceremony the presence of the Punitive Expedition dominated the discussions, which also included talks concerning Mexican raids into south Texas. It was later charged that Obregón had stalled for time in order to make important troop movements involving a buildup along the lower Rio Grande, a proposed attack by Mexican regulars against Laredo, and an uprising by Hispanics in the Brownsville area in support of the notorious *Plan de San Diego*.[90] May 10 was the target date, but because the United States had learned of these plans the operation was called off. Nevertheless, precautions were taken in El Paso, as elsewhere along the border. Two companies (E and F) of the 20th U.S. Infantry, plus the machine-gun platoon, camped on the courthouse lawn ready for trouble.[91]

As U.S.-Mexican relations deteriorated in the spring of 1916, the Bureau's El Paso office took on an importance second only to the agency's Washington headquarters. Chief Bielaski directed that "whatever force is necessary to adequately handle the situation be kept at El Paso and that all necessary arrangements be made to keep in closest possible touch with General Bell or whoever may be commanding the military forces in that vicinity."[92] The El Paso office was sent a stenographer from the San Antonio office and was even authorized to employ an additional stenographer (for thirty days at $65 a month) to handle the vastly increased workload.

The office's duties had expanded from investigating revolutionary activity to gathering military intelligence. On June 30, the San Antonio office instructed that "in the future please furnish this office with an extra copy of any report which you may submit containing military information, such as movements of troops, etc. Your compliance with this request will enable me to submit a copy of your report to the Chief of Staff here without the delay necessary in having the same copied."[93]

Former informants Ed Mebus and John Wren were back on the payroll, the latter this time as an agent. Wren was a deputy sheriff whose connection with the Bureau was kept secret.[94] But finding reliable informants was difficult. One Anastacio Gamboa, who had been an informant for the local police, the Immigration Service, and the military at Fort Bliss, was hired on May 25. Although he came highly recommended, his services were so unsatisfactory that by June 2, Agent Stone recommended he be fired.[95] The El Paso office had better luck with informant José E. Solanos, who at irregular intervals reported in code on military information from the interior of the state of Chihuahua.[96] Occasionally Solanos was able to travel to El Paso and report in person.[97] Considerable information was obtained by Bureau agents and informants interviewing persons arriving from Mexico, although misinformation, exaggeration, and fabrications had to be sifted from what they related.

Agent Stone recruited two unusual but promising informants in the persons of Gemichi "Gustavo" Tatematsu and Lucas G. Hayakawa, two Japanese residing in El Paso who had been personal servants of Pancho and Hipólito Villa. On May 31, Hipólito's wife had written to Tatematsu from Havana telling him that her husband was leaving Havana for Los Angeles and instructing Tatematsu to meet him there.[98] As for Hayakawa, until recently he had been working as an informant for Military Intelligence at Fort Bliss. Stone realized that employing the pair was a gamble in that their principal allegiance was probably to Japan, but he felt it was a gamble worth taking. He received authorization to hire them and to advance them expense money. Tatematsu was given the code designation "Jat" and Hayakawa "Jah." On the enthusiastic recommendation of the local immigration authorities, Stone recruited a third Japanese informant, Hidekichi Tuschiya, codenamed "Frank" and subsequently "Jaf." Tuschiya, however, was handled out of San Antonio by Stone's superior, Agent Robert Barnes, who assigned him the mission of traveling from Ciudad Juárez through Chihuahua to Eagle Pass observing and reporting on the Mexican Army's dispositions. It should be noted, however, that Tuschiya, on reentering the United States, informed the Immigration Service that he worked for the Department of Justice and was "also on [a] special mission for [the] Japanese embassy at Washington."[99]

As for Hayakawa and Tatematsu, Stone initially used them to report on the Juárez garrison, but in early July he dispatched them into southern Chihuahua with the cover story that they were couriers carrying important messages from Hipólito Villa to his brother Pancho. They were unable to make contact with Pancho Villa but reported (and "Frank" corroborated independently) that there were several Japanese in Villa's entourage. Unknown to the Bureau's Japanese, the intelligence section of the Punitive Expedition had recruited several Japanese of its own, not just to report on Pancho Villa but to attempt to poison him. Agent Stone also considered the idea of assassinating Villa: "Agent took up with Informant Jah the matter of capturing Villa alive and delivering him on the border to agent; the matter was also taken up of whether or not Villa could be delivered dead, on the border, if same was requested." Stone sent copies of his report to his Bureau superiors, but Chief Bielaski did not approve Stone's request.[100] The incident does illustrate, however, that some Bureau agents were not averse to using extreme measures. Hayakawa and Tatematsu continued to report in detail on *carrancista* activities in the Juárez area and later in code from the interior of Chihuahua to an El Paso letter drop in the name of "S. Yoriugi."[101] The U.S. Army also gained some of its intelligence on the Juárez garrison from an observation post on the roof of the Paso del Norte Hotel, the tallest building in El Paso.[102]

The Carranza government had its own agents busily collecting intelligence about the U.S. Army. It would appear that being a Mexican government spy was one of the softest jobs around—all one really had to do was to read the local newspapers, which carried a wealth of military information. The *El Paso Morning Times*, for instance, ran a daily column entitled "Fort Bliss Notes." When a preparedness parade was held in El Paso on June 7, some three thousand soldiers marched in a column two miles long. Two Mexicans, believed to be agents of the Carranza garrison in Juárez, were arrested by city detectives on Pioneer Plaza in front of the Sheldon Hotel while they were busily taking notes on the military units passing by. At their arraignment they claimed they were just drawing pictures of the wonderful parade. They received a ten-day jail sentence.[103]

CHAPTER 15

The War Crisis

Relations between the United States and Mexico reached a crisis in June 1916. Because of raids across the Rio Grande into south Texas by Hispanic militants and *carrancista* troops, units of the U.S. Army crossed the river on June 17 near Brownsville, withdrawing the next day after the raiders had been dispersed. But to support the regular army, President Wilson reluctantly mobilized the entire National Guard of the United States on June 18—some 158,000 men—and rushed as many units as possible to the border as quickly as possible. Ultimately about 112,000 guardsmen were deployed; the remainder stayed at their mobilization camps ready to reinforce the border, freeing the regulars for action in Mexico if necessary. Then on June 21, a clash occurred on the outskirts of the hamlet of Carrizal, Chihuahua, between two troops of the 10th U.S. Cavalry, part of the Punitive Expedition, and a much larger contingent of *carrancista* regulars. The American cavalrymen were defeated, suffering eight dead and eleven wounded; twenty-three, plus their civilian guide, were taken prisoner.[1] There were numerous reports that Mexicans were planning to attack El Paso, and Zach Cobb, for one, believed that the reports were true.[2]

The Wilson administration sent Carranza an ultimatum demanding the immediate return of the Carrizal prisoners, the corpses, and the captured equipment. There would be dire consequences otherwise. Carranza, who had been engaged in a policy of brinksmanship, realized that a war would be catastrophic for Mexico. Not only did the United States have more men of military age available (20 million) than the entire population of Mexico (14–15 million), but Mexico was dependent on the United States for war materiel, and any supply from overseas would be quickly interdicted by the U.S. Navy. Carranza reluctantly complied with Washington's ultimatum, and war between the two countries, which had been imminent, was avoided. Diplomats met to discuss the issues outstanding.

In El Paso, distrust of the Hispanic population increased markedly when on June 18, bugle calls in Juárez summoning those residents to the colors produced a stampede in south El Paso—"virtually every Mexican in south El Paso ran for street cars and jitney busses, climbing on much like firemen to a fire truck, and hurried to answer the call."[3] There was considerable doubt regarding the loyalty of Hispanics in case of a war with Mexico, especially since many exiles offered to fight on behalf of their native country. General Felipe Angeles, former chief of Villa's artillery, who had been living quietly on his dairy farm, was quoted in the press as stating that "if the United States intervenes to fight the people of Mexico as a nation, which will be considered conquest, then will all the refugees in the United States unite and return to the land of their birth to fight the invaders." Mayor Tom Lea took umbrage, sent for Angeles, and told him in no uncertain terms to desist from anti-American talk or go live across the river. Enrique Llorente, among other prominent exiles, offered his services to the Carranza government in case of U.S. intervention. The offer was accepted. General Marcelo Caraveo made his way from El Paso to the city of Chihuahua, secured amnesty from the Carranza officials, and offered his services. He left behind his correspondence and codes that the Bureau had seized from his residence.[4]

The war crisis caused Robert Barnes, the agent in charge in San Antonio, to suggest on June 22 to his counterpart in El Paso, Edward Stone, some drastic measures:

> As you know, room 907, Paso del Norte Hotel, El Paso, has been the center of interest for a long time and we have apparently not yet obtained any very definite information with reference to what activities are being handled from this room.
>
> Under all the circumstances and especially because of the tense situation along the border, I think it might be well for four or five agents to go to this room openly, thoroughly question every body in it and examine all documents and papers which may be found therein, seeking the assistance of the local and military authorities, if necessary.
>
> While I know there is no specific authority for such action, I doubt very much whether the occupants of the room will make any serious objection and even if they should, I believe the border situation warrants such action.[5]

Apparently, however, this was not done.

At the height of the crisis the military in Columbus detained the Carranza consular agent in Palomas. An examination of his personal baggage revealed letters from the Mexican consul in El Paso, Andrés García, instructing him to forward to that consulate information about American troop movements, as well as a telegram partly in cipher. Consul García was busily expanding his intelligence network during the war crisis, requesting his government to send him additional agents who were not known in El Paso because he was having difficulty enlisting operatives who were both loyal and trustworthy. The military wanted the consular agent prosecuted, but the U.S. attorney for New Mexico decided that there was insufficient evidence, and he was freed. His documents were of course copied.[6]

Seeking to capitalize on Carranza's troubles, reactionary Mexican exiles formed a new coalition—the *legalista* party, headed by Manuel Bonilla, ostensibly committed to establishing a government of laws, not of men. As in the past, the only thing the opposition groups had in common was their hatred of the incumbent president, in this case Carranza.[7] They made strenuous efforts to attract the support of Villa, who had his own quarrel with Carranza. The *legalistas* also approached Felix Sommerfeld, who had been devoting himself to investing in the New York Stock Exchange, because of his connections with the major arms manufacturers and his connections with prominent Mexicans. Sommerfeld refused to associate himself with the *legalistas*.[8]

Predictably, a *legalista* junta appeared in El Paso, led by Enrique Bordes Mangel and Rodolfo Farías, who held their meetings in the Union Hotel, oddly located on the second and third floors of the Union Bank and Trust Company's building. Bordes Mangel had started out as a fervent *maderista*. He had, in fact, helped Madero draft the *Plan de San Luis Potosí* in San Antonio back in 1910.[9] Now, hoping to make himself relevant again, he had become a *legalista*. Two Bureau informants were detailed to watch the conspirators, and the Mexican consul's secret agents were of course also monitoring the *legalistas*, composed largely of followers of Huerta and some of Villa's partisans.[10] According to Consul García, both Victor Carusso and Abraham Luján were active members of the local organization.[11]

The Carranza intelligence service was quite active in the United States. Its chief was a twenty-nine-year-old native of Durango, Jesús María Arriola.[12] Despite his relative youth, Arriola was an experienced operative. He had worked for printing firms in El Paso from 1904 to 1911, when he became a spy in that city for the Díaz regime's consul, submitting daily reports on *insurrecto* activities. He was then attached to the Mexican consulate in Los Angeles as an agent throughout the Madero regime. When Huerta seized power in 1913, Arriola was dismissed but was reinstated by the Carranza consul in late 1914. Early in 1915 the consul in San Francisco recruited him to head the Mexican Bureau of Investigation, a detective agency the consul secretly financed. Arriola's mission was to track down criminals who were printing counterfeit Constitutionalist currency. He succeeded so well that the consul recommended that Arriola be named head of Mexican intelligence in the United States. In May 1916, he was summoned to Mexico City and was formally appointed as chief. His title was that of special commissioner appointed by the secretary of foreign relations to head the Mexican Secret Service in the United States. He faced a formidable challenge for, as he reported, all the consulates, except for the ones in El Paso and San Francisco, lacked a permanent secret service component, having only a small amount of money with which to pay occasional agents and informants.[13]

Arriola traveled to the United States under his own name to reorganize the service and recruit additional agents, distribute a new code book to the consuls and instruct them in its use, and to have the consuls collect and forward to Mexico City information of military value about the United States. He was also supposed to recruit men to fight for Mexico in case of war with the United States.[14]

From the time Arriola entered the United States on June 10 at Eagle Pass, the Bureau covered him like a blanket, tracking him from California to New Orleans and reporting his activities down to and including his getting drunk in San Antonio and shacking up in room 11 at the Victoria Hotel with a pimp and two prostitutes.[15]

When Arriola arrived in El Paso on June 22, the Bureau was waiting for him. Agents met the train at the Union Depot and followed Arriola to the Sheldon Hotel, where he checked into room 105.[16] Shortly thereafter he met in the lobby with Charles E. Minck, with whom he was already acquainted, Minck having lived in the city of Chihuahua. Unknown to Arriola, Minck was an undercover Bureau informant who had been instructed to make contact with Arriola. Interestingly enough, Arriola showed Minck a letter of recommendation from Tom Ross, an ex–Texas Ranger captain who was a Bureau agent in Laredo and one from Fred Lancaster, a former Bureau agent who was the police chief in San Antonio. Besides explaining that he was engaged in reorganizing the Mexican service in the border towns, Arriola made Minck a proposition: to become chief of Mexican intelligence in either San Antonio or Los Angeles. If Minck accepted, Arriola was prepared to appoint him immediately. Minck said he needed a week to settle some affairs but would write to Arriola informing him of his decision. Minck informed his superiors of Arriola's proposition as well as of Arriola's departure for Douglas that same night.[17]

When Arriola arrived in Nogales from Douglas, Bureau agent William Neunhoffer and a deputy sheriff went to his hotel room and rifled his luggage, finding his credential as chief of the Mexican secret service and his notes containing information from his American informants. Neunhoffer and an army officer then interrogated Arriola at the customs house. Arriola presented his commission and the letters of recommendation from Ross and Lancaster, stating that his activities were confined to gathering information on those unfriendly to both Carranza and the United States. The Mexican was then allowed to continue on his way to Tucson and San Francisco.[18] It has been said that

> hostility and suspicion limited the willingness of North American officials to cooperate with the Constitutionalists intelligence operatives. For example, in October 1916, federal agents detained Arriola in Phoenix, Arizona, treated

> him with open disrespect, searched his personal belongings, ransacked his room, and seized copies of the new regulations[.] . . . The written reports of North American agents clearly reveal the suspicion and low regard in which they held both their Mexican counterparts and the government they represented.[19]

Arriola didn't operate in a vacuum, however. The United States's recent difficulties with Carranza, which had nearly produced a full-scale war in June, hardly endeared either Carranza or his minions to American federal agents. Moreover, Arriola himself reported to the Mexican foreign secretary on October 29 that "it is not my intention to accuse or criticize the American government, because I can attest that on many occasions the agents have been very well disposed to assist our Government, whenever I have approached them."[20]

Minck's case officer authorized him to accept Arriola's proposition. Accordingly, Minck wrote to Arriola in San Francisco that he would be ready to begin by the end of July. Arriola wrote back on July 20 from the "general office of the Mexican secret service" at 250 Hyde Street, San Francisco, located in "the office of the *Pan American Review*, a sham printing operation that afforded a cover for his real activities," that he was proposing Minck's appointment to the Mexican government.[21] Arriola was back in El Paso in September and offered Minck the position of chief in San Antonio.[22] But as it happened, Minck apparently never became a Mexican intelligence chief.

The Bureau did score a coup by obtaining both Arriola's code and the instructions for its use. It seems that Arriola and an associate, one Eneas Levi, were on a double date in San Antonio with some fast women, and during the course of the evening Levi picked Arriola's pocket, secured the code, and delivered it to the Bureau.[23] It has been stated that "As the result of uncharacteristic carelessness and lapse of judgment on Arriola's part, one of Barnes's men in San Antonio acquired a copy of the new Mexican code."[24] The Bureau also obtained the general regulations for Mexican secret agents. As in the past, these secret agents were "entirely subordinate to the consul."[25] Bureau agent J. J. Lawrence in Del Rio obtained cipher messages from the Mexican Foreign Office to the consul in Del Rio informing him that Arriola had been appointed chief of the Mexican secret service. Lawrence deciphered the messages and sent the translations to the Bureau office in San Antonio.[26] And in December the Carranza representative in Washington sent the Bureau a memorandum Arriola had prepared attributing much of the anti-Carranza activity and violations of the neutrality laws to the lack of Bureau agents and urging that more agents be assigned exclusively to investigating such nefarious goings on. Arriola characterized El Paso Mayor Tom Lea as a "terrible enemy" of the Carranza regime. He also described the ammunition smuggling of Henry Mohr as a case in point, stating that Mohr had sold substantial amounts of ammunition to *villistas*. Mohr evaded surveillance by sending ammunition in small lots from his store to his house, a technique that one of his employees who was a *carrancista* sympathizer revealed. Further, Arriola stated that Sabino and David Guaderrama "are constantly purchasing ammunition without any notice of this having been given to the Department of Justice." Sabino most certainly wasn't purchasing ammunition. He had been dead for nine months, and Arriola should have known it.[27]

At about the same time that Arriola was in El Paso, Agent Minck was also keeping under surveillance Enrique Goldbaum y Padilla, reputed to be the intelligence chief for General Plutarco Elías Calles, the Carranza commander in Sonora. Goldbaum, who had arrived from Nogales, was suspected of coming to spy on American troop movements. Minck located him at a saloon patronized mainly by Mexicans and charmingly named el Ultimo Cartucho (the Last Cartridge) on South El Paso Street. (In 1917, the manager was Pascual Cesaretti, an active *villista* who had previously handled artillery for the Mexican chieftain.)[28] Goldbaum had little to say beyond stating that he was staying at the Grand Hotel and would be in town for several days. He arranged to meet with Minck the following noon. Minck left the saloon and hurried to the police station to have the cops arrest Goldbaum and hold him for interrogation. But by the time the police acted, Goldbaum was nowhere to be found. Bureau agents then went to his hotel hoping to arrest him, but he was gone. It was later determined that he had suddenly left El Paso that night by train with a ticket for San Diego.[29] Goldbaum turned up in San Antonio, though, and was promptly arrested, on July 4, 1916. He claimed American citizenship and asserted that he had been separated from the Carranza government since January. Yet in April and May he had distributed business cards reading "Major Constitutionalist Army and Chief, State Police, headquarters Hermosillo, Sonora, Mex." Bureau agents went through Goldbaum's trunk, found numerous telegrams, and had them copied and translated. In February 1917, Goldbaum was arrested in Nogales, Arizona, charged with inducing U.S. soldiers to desert and with helping a German agent to escape to Mexico.[30]

Although it combated *carrancista* espionage, the Bureau at the same time cooperated with the *carrancistas* in some other respects, since El Paso was a focal point for the intrigues of Carranza's enemies.[31] For example, Agent Stone instructed his subordinate Agent Minck to accompany Carranza consul Andrés García's secret agent, Captain Henry Gray, to check out a house on South El Paso Street where *legalista* recruiting was reported.[32] Gray, a longtime operative, had earlier been discharged because of office politics but had since been rehired.[33]

The Bureau's El Paso office had to concern itself with the strong *villista* sentiment in the city; many Hispanics were quite prepared to support Villa if he succeeded in capturing Ciudad Juárez. With the approval of General Bell, a corporal in the 23rd

U.S. Infantry band who had been working under cover for Captain Robert Grinstead of Military Intelligence was detailed to assist the Bureau in neutrality matters, still working under cover and using his own informant. The corporal managed to purloin one of the letters George Holmes received.[34]

The El Paso office received reinforcement on July 2 in the person of Agent Gus T. "Buster" Jones, a former Texas Ranger and customs and immigration inspector who had joined the Bureau in 1916. Jones would prove to be one of the agency's most capable agents, remaining with the FBI until he retired in 1944. Initially he was detailed to uncover ammunition smuggling. Although handicapped by his lack of Spanish, Jones soon discovered that substantial amounts of ammunition were being smuggled in beer kegs; as long as the kegs had proper manifests customs allowed them to cross into Mexico.[35] Jones also received the assignment of investigating one T. F. Jonah, a former customs inspector in El Paso who had resigned on August 6, 1915, and had been an active Villa partisan even before his resignation, arranging the export of cattle from Chihuahua. Agent Jones arrested Jonah, who was interrogated and released for insufficient evidence of violating any specific statute. This, even though when he was searched at the Bureau office and his house was searched with a warrant, the mass of documents that Jonah voluntarily provided showed conclusively that he was a Villa agent. The Bureau kept the documents it deemed useful.[36]

Jonah had been corresponding with George Holmes and acting together with one Frank S. Thomas of Topeka, Kansas, who dealt in investments and real estate loans and was a Villa propagandist. Jonah and Thomas had been corresponding by Wells Fargo Express rather than by the ordinary mail, to evade government monitoring, with Thomas using the alias of "T. N. Dyer." Thomas wrote to Jonah, instructing him to cover the movements of American troops. Furthermore, Jonah was a known associate of George Holmes, the *villista* agent. (The Bureau and Military Intelligence were so anxious to make a case against Holmes that they arrested and interrogated his chauffeur.) Thomas arrived in El Paso in September, allegedly to help provide Pancho Villa with an alibi for the Columbus raid; Thomas argued unconvincingly that it had been *carrancistas* who had raided the border hamlet. Thomas and Jonah's efforts to absolve Villa met with some success—General Hugh Lennox Scott, the army chief of staff, recalled that Villa had sent an emissary to him in Washington, but "I refused to have anything to do with him until I had proof from two Americans that he had cleared himself of his attack on Columbus." Not that Scott needed a lot of convincing, for "I have always believed he was too wise to make such an attack willingly."[37] And while defending Villa, Thomas and Jonah had been meeting with *legalistas*.[38]

Legalista intrigues produced uprisings in several parts of Mexico, but in the Juárez area the results were more modest. On August 4, Colonel Mariano Támez, second in command of the Carranza garrison, defected and took to the hills with some of his troops. A Bureau informant reported that Támez met secretly with other Carranza officers to discuss defecting to the *legalistas*. When the meeting ended he, thirty other officers, and three hundred soldiers deserted, taking with them six Colt machine guns and a large quantity of ammunition. Támez also helped himself to some $70,000 from the Juárez customs house, which he needed to pay his followers and retain their loyalty, an important consideration since the garrison was being paid two pesos a day in virtually worthless Carranza currency.[39] He also issued the obligatory revolutionary proclamation, exhorting the Mexican people to rise in support of the *legalista* party. Like many of his contemporaries, Támez was experienced at turning his coat—he was a former federal who then became a *villista* and who seven months previously had surrendered to the Carranza authorities, receiving amnesty and a military command. Támez illustrates a frustration that Mexican regimes were presented with throughout the decade—when rebels were bought they frequently didn't stay bought.

Not surprisingly, given the atmosphere of nervous anticipation that characterized El Paso, Támez's defection caused great excitement. There was widespread speculation as to whether the remainder of the Juárez garrison would desert and turn the town over to the *legalistas*, whose junta, headed by Enrique Bordes Mangel, had recently been holding its meetings in room 411 of the First National Bank Building. It was said that General Eugenio Rascón and General Ignacio Bravo would direct *legalista* activities on the border. These activities would of course include efforts to suborn *carrancista* officers. The Carranza military rushed four hundred presumably loyal troops from the city of Chihuahua to reinforce what was left of the Juárez garrison.[40]

General Jacinto Treviño, the *carrancista* commander in the state of Chihuahua, had been in contact with the *legalistas* and had indicated that he was prepared to join them with his troops when conditions were right. Instead, he suddenly imprisoned in the Chihuahua penitentiary General José Inés Salazar and some thirty other ex-federal officers who had received amnesty from the Carranza government, considering them *legalista* sympathizers. The *legalistas* of course considered Treviño a traitor to their cause. The Bureau monitored these developments through the reports of their Mexican informants, who had thoroughly penetrated the El Paso *legalista* leadership.[41] That leadership gamely tried to win over public opinion by starting a weekly newspaper, *El Legalista*, whose first number appeared on August 26 with Bordes Mangel as editor.[42] The effort was not very successful. By 1917, the *legalista* party dissolved because it was ineffectual, and Bordes Mangel applied to the Carranza government for amnesty.[43] The nimble Colonel Mariano Támez once again became a *villista*.[44] But by August 1918, he had deserted Villa and had allied himself with the *felicistas*.[45]

Increasingly the Bureau focused on *villistas*. One cause for concern was Hipólito Villa, who was back in town. Overshadowed by his famous brother Pancho, Hipólito was described as being "about thirty eight, height five feet four, weight one thirty, black hair and mustache, ends turned down, dark complected and [dark] eyes, nervous movement, usually wears large black felt hat, dark clothes, neatly attired."[46] Pancho Villa had dispatched George Holmes to Cuba to rescue Hipólito. Holmes had arranged to smuggle Hipólito, traveling as "Jesús M. Salazar," from Havana through Key West to his ranch near Ysleta. Hipólito hid there until he was arrested. Immigration authorities in El Paso were deciding whether to deport him. In the meantime he was held at Fort Bliss and in the county jail. During his questioning he expressed support for the *legalista* movement. Immigration finally decided to release Hipólito from custody. He was promptly jailed on a state warrant: the former customs inspector and *villista* agent T. F. Jonah claimed that Hipólito owed him $500 from a transaction in November 1915. Agent Minck went to the jail and asked Hipólito about the matter. Hipólito acknowledged the debt but thought it was more like $200, and he disclaimed any knowledge of the transaction in question, it having been between his agent George Holmes and Jonah.[47] Hipólito was released on bond and promptly resumed his close association with George Holmes.

Holmes, who played a major role in *villista* intrigue, was indicted in October 1916, for having fitted out at his ranch a small military expedition commanded by ex-*villista* general Manuel Ochoa.[48] The general was now reportedly a *legalista*, that faction having merged with Villa's. Consul Andrés García's agents thoroughly penetrated the *legalistas*, who had frequent meetings at 612 Campbell Street, the home of ex-*villista* general Macrino Martínez.[49]

The filibusters had crossed into Mexico on August 22 near Fabens but most were captured two days later by Carranza forces. Holmes was released on a $2,500 bond, and his case was continued until the next term of federal court.[50] Most of the Bureau's evidence in this affair came from C. S. T. Folsom, Consul Andrés García's attorney, who delivered the information that García's secret agents had uncovered. The Bureau offered one of those arrested, Rodolfo Farías, a local *legalista* leader, immunity if he would testify against the others. Farías immediately became a Bureau informant, reporting on a daily basis to Agent Stone at the Bureau's office. However, Carranza secret agent "X" was well aware that Farías was a Bureau snitch.[51] Holmes had lots of cattle, horses, and equipment on his ranch, and it was suspected that the fugitive general, Manuel Ochoa, was hiding there. Agent Stone sent an informant under cover to that vicinity to learn what he could, which wasn't much.[52]

Presumably Holmes continued his involvement with ammunition smuggling, for Pancho Villa continued to receive a supply. Some came through El Paso, because the soldiers at the international bridges were rather lackadaisical about searching those crossing into Juárez.[53] But since Carranza forces occupied Juárez, most of Villa's munitions supply was smuggled across at places such as Fabens and Palomas.

The Bureau's focus on Pancho Villa became more pronounced as a result of a spectacular feat by the Mexican revolutionist. At 2 a.m. on September 16, Mexican Independence Day, Villa launched a surprise attack against the city of Chihuahua. The much larger Carranza garrison, commanded by General Treviño himself, offered only disorganized and feeble resistance. Villa forces shot up the garrison, wounded Treviño in the shoulder, stormed the state capitol, the federal building, the penitentiary and freed the prisoners (including General José Inéz Salazar, who immediately became a fervent *villista*), made off with enormous amounts of supplies, ammunition, equipment (including some of Treviño's artillery), loot, and hundreds of recruits—*carrancista* troops who defected. By 9 a.m. the *villistas* withdrew in triumph.[54] Although José Inés Salazar had been liberated by Villa and professed his undying loyalty to the chieftain, by November, Salazar was reported on good authority to be only an ostensible *villista*, busily building up his forces so that he could switch sides and join Félix Díaz should the latter decide to negotiate with him.[55]

The Carranza regime tried to put the best face possible on the catastrophe in Chihuahua, but it was clear that the First Chief's control over the state remained shaky and that General Treviño was something less than a capable commander. On orders from Mexico City, martial law was proclaimed throughout Chihuahua on September 17. Bureau informant Tatematsu, who with his colleague Hayakawa was in the city of Chihuahua when Villa's attack occurred, was arrested by the Carranza authorities on suspicion of being a *villista* spy, but he was able to talk his way out of trouble. The Japanese continued to send in their reports, as did the Bureau's Mexican informants.[56] Troop reinforcements were rushed from Chihuahua to Juárez, where the population was in a panic because of rumors that Pancho Villa was approaching.[57]

Villa's raid on Chihuahua thrilled his partisans in Ciudad Juárez and El Paso. Among those who celebrated the victory were his brother, Hipólito, his El Paso attorney, Gunther Lessing, and his agent, George Holmes. On September 19, Hipólito was released from the county jail. His lawyer had negotiated a deal whereby instead of being deported, Villa would reside no closer to the Mexican border than San Antonio.[58] Hipólito was immediately taken to the Bureau office for a chat. Agent John Wren then escorted Hipólito and Lessing to the Saint Francis Hotel where they found Holmes, who was waiting to talk with Hipólito. Wren reported: "I was instructed by Mr. Stone to watch closely and note anything of importance that transpired as the Government was interested in the movements of both Holmes and Villa. Lessing, myself and Villa stayed in the room. Holmes had been drinking and talked freely" about his friendship with the Villa brothers. Hipólito, Wren, and Holmes then adjourned to a café for supper.[59] The next day Wren and Holmes accompanied Hipólito to San Antonio, where by arrangement Hipólito would report daily to the Bureau. Hipólito and Holmes checked into the Saint Anthony Hotel.[60]

Of great importance to the Bureau was any inkling that Ciudad Juárez was about to change hands. As General Funston, commander of the Southern Department, informed the War Department, if Villa succeeded in capturing Juárez it would be impossible to continue supplying the Punitive Expedition using the Mexico Northwestern Railroad.[61] This possibility of course also concerned Military Intelligence at Fort Bliss, which had its own stable of informants and worked closely with the Bureau. The *legalista* leader Bordes Mangel had been working feverishly to suborn the Juárez garrison, holding meetings with General González, the *carrancista* commander. Agent Stone, with the approval of the U.S. attorney, freely exchanged intelligence with Carranza consul García to prevent either the *legalistas* or the *villistas* from seizing this vital border town. García explained that General González had been authorized to meet with *legalista* leaders, in the hope of learning more about their plans. Stone was of the opinion that General González was getting so much easy graft that it would take a great deal to make him give it up by turning the place over to some other faction.[62] Nevertheless, General González took the precaution of sending his family to the safety of El Paso, where they lived at 1410 Myrtle Avenue together with the family of General Jacinto Treviño, who had taken the same precaution.[63]

The Mexican generals' decision to send their families out of harm's way seemed amply justified, for Pancho Villa continued his rampage. On November 23, he again attacked the city of Chihuahua, and heavy fighting continued for more than a day. Villa captured the city, extorted considerable sums from the business community, massacred some more Chinese, and withdrew. Some of the *carrancista* defenders withdrew not merely to Juárez but fled all the way to El Paso.[64]

The Carranza authorities as well as the Bureau were understandably nervous about *villista* intrigues. The connections between the *legalistas* and the *villistas* remained a source of concern. On November 10, Agent H. B. Mock reported: "I was on this date reliably informed that Rodolfo Farias Flores, one of the *legalista* leaders in this city, was associating freely with Todd McClamy [*sic*], a notorious Villa agent."[65] And General Fidel Avila, who had been Pancho Villa's governor of Chihuahua, was constantly visited by Villa partisans at his ranch near Las Cruces.[66]

In November, about 180 Carranza customs guards in Juárez, more than half of whom had been Villa soldiers, were disarmed and dismissed, charged with being secretly in league with Villa and planning to defect to him.[67] And the Carranza authorities sometimes took action against Americans whom they suspected of *villista* ties. A scout with the Pershing expedition, one Benjamin Brahn, who was a lifelong El Paso resident, was in town on leave from the Punitive Expedition. On the night of November 10, he was lured to a saloon in south El Paso, where Carranza operatives drugged him, drove him to Juárez, and tossed him in jail, charging him with being a *villista* spy. Brahn had been a trainmaster on the Mexican Central Railroad when Villa dominated Chihuahua and had thus aided in the movement of Villa's troop trains. More to the point, he had been in charge of Villa's personal train.[68] Strenuous efforts by American authorities and the good offices of Mexican consul García secured Brahn's release a week later. It turned out that Brahn had been working for Captain Grinstead of Military Intelligence and had recently gone to San Antonio to talk with Hipólito Villa in an attempt to renew his *villista* ties. The *carrancistas* suspected Brahn of being a *villista*, but at the same time the *villista* George Holmes had written to Hipólito denouncing Brahn because he'd been a scout with the Punitive Expedition.[69]

In early December, General Jacinto Treviño was relieved as *carrancista* commander in northern Mexico. His replacement was General Francisco Murguía, who promised to wage a more aggressive campaign against Villa.[70] Murguía caused the Bureau some concern, for he made little effort to conceal his pro-German sympathies. One of the Bureau's manifold duties was to keep track of Germans and their sympathizers, as the United States moved closer to entering World War I on the Allied side. For example, Henry Gray, the veteran secret agent for the Mexican consulate in El Paso, informed Agent Stone that in the lobby of the Orndorff Hotel he had conversed with one William Ibs, who had just arrived from New Orleans and who denounced President Wilson in profane language and expressed himself as being strongly pro-German. Gray subsequently gave the Bureau a written memo to that effect. What Gray presumably didn't know was that Ibs was a longtime Bureau informant employed by the New Orleans office.

Gray's information of course galvanized the El Paso office into action. Agent Stone detailed Agent Wren to watch Ibs, merely telling Wren that Ibs was a suspicious character but not revealing Ibs's connection with the Bureau. Stone took into his confidence the local assistant U.S. attorney. The latter asked Stone to bring Ibs to his office, which was done. There, Ibs stated his connection with the Bureau and asserted that Chief Bielaski could vouch for him. According to Stone, Ibs was very nervous and showed the effects of drinking. The next day, Stone encountered Carranza agent Gray on the street, who asked, "Say, Mr. Stone, what is the matter with that fellow Ibs; is he crazy or is he really employed by your Bureau?" Gray had met Ibs earlier that morning and Ibs had boasted about working for Chief Bielaski and being in El Paso on a special assignment and greatly outranking Agent Stone. Whether he believed it or not, Gray said he thought that Ibs was only a damn fool who was flat broke, that he looked like a bum, and that he tried to borrow money from everyone he met. Agent Stone merely replied that he considered Ibs a suspicious character "who would bear watching for pro-German activities or for legalista or Villista activities in this vicinity." Stone impressed on Gray that to his knowledge Ibs had no connection whatsoever with the American government and that if he so claimed he must have been either drunk or crazy.

Several days later, Gray telephoned Stone to advise him that Ibs had skipped out on his bill at the Orndorff Hotel and had left some baggage behind in his room. Gray speculated that Ibs had gone to Juárez and had gotten himself arrested. He subsequently asked Stone again whether Ibs had any connection with the United States government, offering if so to use his good offices in case Ibs were languishing in the Juárez jail. Stone reiterated that Ibs had no connection whatsoever. However, Stone's superior instructed him that if indeed Ibs were in trouble in Juárez, then Stone was to take Gray into his confidence, reveal Ibs's connection, and state that any mistreatment of him by Mexican authorities would be viewed with extreme disfavor by the United States. Ibs's whereabouts remained unknown.[71]

Gray informed Stone that Ibs had been in the Juárez jail for the last five days, suspected of being a *legalista* agent. Mexican consul General Andrés García was summoned to the office of the assistant U.S. attorney, who disclosed Ibs's connection with the Bureau and asked the consul's assistance in securing Ibs's freedom. García obligingly went to Juárez to investigate the matter but reported that there was no Ibs in the jail. However, the two El Paso newspapers ran stories asserting that Ibs was a prisoner in Juárez.[72] But it turned out that Ibs had really gone back to New Orleans. He said he could not pay his hotel bill and had skipped out on the charges, but he denied drinking heavily or making pro-German statements while in El Paso. And he denounced Henry Gray as being a notorious liar, explaining that he had "played" Gray in order to get information from him. Moreover, he had met with a prominent *legalista*, Demetrio Bustamante, whom he had known for some time, to the same end. His explanation was met with skepticism.[73]

The upshot of this affair was that Ibs's usefulness to the Bureau had been badly compromised. Nevertheless, the New Orleans office continued to use his services. Among other things, the Bureau had him shadow the Mexican secret agent Jesús María Arriola, who had been touring the border in December and was expected in New Orleans.[74] Military Intelligence in Arizona had been keeping an eye on Arriola and had obtained a copy of one of his reports.[75]

But the immediate concern for the El Paso Bureau office was what was going on in Juárez. Not only was there worry that Villa might attack the town, but there was serious dissension among the Carranza officers there. General Alvaro Obregón, the secretary of war, assigned Colonel Luis Comadurán to relieve General González as commander in Juárez. When Comadurán arrived with a small escort and demanded that González turn over his command, González refused, and a factional fight ensued that resulted in Comadurán fleeing to El Paso for protection.[76] The mortified Comadurán went to the Bureau office in El Paso to ask Agent Stone, whom he knew personally, whether he should make his complaint public by giving the story to the El Paso newspapers and thereby embarrassing González. Agent Stone advised against doing so but was most interested in Comadurán's account of Villa's latest capture of Chihuahua. At a subsequent meeting Comadurán provided valuable military intelligence to Captain Grinstead.[77] Comadurán decided to join the numerous members of the Mexican exile community in El Paso.

General José Murguía, whose brother Francisco had replaced General Jacinto Treviño as commander in Chihuahua, arrived in Juárez to relieve General González, and this time González relinquished his command without resistance. There were, however, shooting affrays in Juárez involving subordinates of the two generals. In one of these a drunken major of Murguía's command waved his pistol around in the Tivoli Saloon and cursed all the officers of González's command. When the nineteen-year-old police chief of Juárez, Raul Loya, a follower of the deposed General González and until recently a resident of El Paso, attempted to disarm him, the major shot and killed Loya.[78]

At the same time the Bureau had to closely monitor the turbulence in Juárez, it also had to concern itself with Villa's followers on this U.S. side of the border. When George Holmes returned to El Paso in early October, the Bureau kept him under surveillance while the government prepared its witnesses against the slippery *villista*, whose trial for neutrality violation was imminent.[79] In San Antonio, Hipólito Villa was served with a subpoena in this case but dropped out of sight, producing considerable anxiety in the Bureau. The agency's chief tartly commented to the San Antonio agent in charge: "From recent reports it seems that Hippolito [*sic*] Villa was able to leave the Saint Anthony Hotel without this fact coming to the knowledge of the agents in San Antonio for several days. Will you please make arrangements to see that nothing of this character is possible hereafter. A specific definite time should be set for Villa to report to an agent of this Department each day, and unless he does so report, inquiries should be made to locate him."[80] Villa surfaced and began reporting daily to the Bureau while seemingly avoiding any political involvement. He did, however, continue to meet surreptitiously with persons who sympathized with his brother. Some of them had come down in the world: Cesar Moya had been a *villista* general, but now he operated a jitney car in San Antonio.[81] Other *villista* associates of Hipólito's continued to do quite well, among them George Holmes. When informed that the government would not put up with this behavior, Hipólito rather lamely asserted that Holmes had been to see him in connection with the purchase of a ranch. The Bureau required Villa to supply every other day a list of the names of persons who had called at his house.[82]

The government's problems in keeping track of persons of interest is illustrated by the conflicting information it received about Felix Sommerfeld. The State Department was informed that Sommerfeld had arrived in El Paso and was actively working for Pancho Villa, but a Bureau agent in New York City notified his superiors that he had just spoken on the telephone with Sommerfeld, who was still there at the Hotel Astor on Times Square. The agent had lunch with Sommerfeld a few days later.[83]

The Mexican secret service varied in its effectiveness. Jesús María Arriola, Carranza's crack secret agent, was based in San Francisco, where he called at the Bureau office to impart information of mutual interest, mainly concerning the *felicistas*.[84] But in Laredo the Mexican consul complained that he lacked an agent because his government would pay only $2.11 per day for an operative. The consul asked the local Bureau agent, Tom Ross, to recommend somebody. Ross did so, instructing the operative to report everything he did to Ross, who held out the possibility of future employment with the Bureau.[85] In El Paso, by contrast, Consul García enjoyed the services of Captain Henry Gray, the longtime secret agent, who had a friendly relationship with the Bureau.[86] And as a check on Gray's information, Bureau agent Victor Weiskopf in Presidio wrote that "I am meeting the Mexican consular agent almost daily, as it appears the Mexicans have an excellent secret service in El Paso judging by information this party is receiving here in coded messages which I have deciphered and also communications he receives from the Mexican Consul at El Paso, Texas, which he frequently shows to me."[87]

In November, Jesús María Arriola, coordinating the activities of some thirty agents in the United States, transferred his headquarters to El Paso, owing to the obvious advantages of the city as a base of operations. From his office in room 315 of the First National Bank Building he supervised, among others, agent Roberto P. Ticcioni. Arriola readily cooperated with the Bureau in trying to locate a former Bureau informant, Juan N. Echegaray, who was thought to be a *felicista* and who was going around town showing his reports and claiming to be a Department of Justice agent. But Arriola also traveled widely, leaving in December for Los Angeles. Operating under cover as "José Molinar" he secured a letter of introduction from *felicistas* there to General Manuel Velázquez, a prominent *felicista* in New Orleans. Arriola proudly showed the letter to Agent Stone on his way through El Paso before he and Consul García left to combat *felicista* intrigues in New Orleans. When Arriola arrived in that city he stayed in the fashionable Monteleone Hotel.[88]

There was a notable change in the priorities of the Bureau's El Paso office. Whereas in earlier years monitoring the munitions traffic had been paramount, now the army had primary responsibility for that task. The Fort Bliss intelligence office ran its own network of informers and, to prevent duplication of effort, requested that the Bureau stay out of these investigations until it was time to prepare a case for indictment. Captain Grinstead and Agent Stone seemed to work quite well together in this regard.[89]

In the shadowy world of intrigue in El Paso, an emerging player was Frank Thayer, operating from rooms 402–3 of the Mills Building. He was a sometime newspaperman and ammunition smuggler, full-time adventurer and member of the Adventurers' Club, and definitely on the make. He had attempted in 1914 to bribe a customs inspector to let him smuggle a carload of ammunition across the river to Juárez and had been slapped silly for his trouble. Undaunted, Thayer now announced that he planned to make his way into Chihuahua and secure an interview with Pancho Villa, to whom he had smuggled ammunition in 1914 and 1915. Thayer believed that the publication of such an exclusive interview in the American press would command a lucrative fee. But this was a hazardous undertaking, given Villa's habitual suspicion and his well-known volcanic temper and propensity for having people shot. Nevertheless, as Thayer later recounted, he took with him as a peace offering a pair of expensive riding boots for Villa and some medical supplies for the Mexican leader's troops. Despite warnings that he would surely get himself killed, Thayer entered Chihuahua through Columbus on October 22, accompanied by Milt Brennan, with whom he roomed at the exclusive Aragon Apartments in El Paso. Brennan, like Thayer, had been deeply involved in revolutionary intrigue; in 1914 he had worked for the Carranza consul in El Paso, conducting surveillance on arms shipments. The Bureau had been interested in both men for some time. The two American adventurers joined Regino Corral, Pancho Villa's brother-in-law, in Columbus. Thayer later claimed that through the influence of a colonel he knew in the Punitive Expedition, the group was able to travel down the army's line of communications and that on October 29, the Thayer party struck off toward the town of San Andrés in search of Villa.

They made contact with a unit of Villa's followers, who treated them well, but on the night of October 30 the *villistas* were attacked and routed by *carrancista* troops. Thayer and his companions had to run for their lives, abandoning everything except a few blankets, and they hid in a hole all day within earshot of the Carranza soldiers searching for them. But they survived and reached Pancho Villa's camp, about twelve miles south of San Andrés, on November 1. Thayer got his interview, in which Villa refused either to admit or deny a role in the Columbus raid, but "he said when the proper time came, he would prove where he was on that day by three American citizens." Villa maintained that he had no hard feeling against Americans and that "he had given orders to all of his men not to molest Americans nor any other foreigners excepting the Chinamen whom he claimed were a pest in the country and would be run out of Mexico; that they came to Mexico with nothing and sent all their earnings out of it; that they did not make good citizens." After the interview Thayer and

Brennan were escorted to the outskirts of the city of Chihuahua, from where they took a train back to El Paso.

This account of daring adventure made for a good story, but it also produced considerable skepticism. Thayer and Brennan did reach Villa's camp and talk with the Mexican leader, but to Thayer's dismay newspapers were quite dubious about publishing his purported exclusive interview.[90] Thayer offered to sell his interview for $1,000. Some newspapermen offered him $400 provided he could prove the interview was genuine and that Villa's signature on documents he produced was authentic. He implored various people to attest to this but they all refused, for they knew him too well.[91]

Thayer's claim that he was Villa's representative in the United States and the credentials he produced to substantiate that claim were a complete scam. After his return to El Paso he approached Alberto Madero for a $300 loan, saying he needed the money to go to New Orleans in order to purchase ammunition for Pancho Villa. He showed Madero some credentials purportedly signed by Villa authorizing Thayer to act as his agent in the United States. Madero refused Thayer's request because he suspected that the letters Thayer produced were forgeries and because he feared Thayer was setting him up for some kind of trap.

Carranza agent Henry Gray promptly informed the Bureau of these developments. Agent Stone was most interested in building a case against Thayer for violation of the neutrality laws, and he interviewed Alberto Madero about the matter. Subsequent investigation revealed that Thayer and an unidentified companion, presumably Brennan, had approached Todd McClammy, the *villista* partisan, and asked to see whatever Villa documents McClammy had in his possession. For whatever reason McClammy obliged, and Thayer spent considerable time practicing Villa's signature.[92] Thayer subsequently traveled to Washington and Los Angeles trying to secure loans or quantities of ammunition on credit. He apparently had some success because he spent money lavishly.[93]

Alberto Madero not only had to fend off Thayer but also a certain E. A. Talbot and two of his companions. Talbot was a soldier of fortune, well known to the Bureau. He had been a secret agent for Abe Molina in 1912 and had been a machine gunner for Villa during the struggle against Huerta. Talbot and two friends had appeared in Madero's office on November 16, saying they had been with the Punitive Expedition and had several automobiles and machine guns available. If Madero would kindly put them in touch with Pancho Villa these items would be at Villa's disposal. Madero said he couldn't help them, and they left. Afterward Madero thought the matter over and decided to inform Agent Stone. The latter investigated and learned that Talbot and the others had been civilian truck drivers for the Punitive Expedition. They had been involved in a plot to smuggle a group of Chinese out of Chihuahua through

Columbus and had arrived in El Paso several weeks earlier.[94] Emil Holmdahl, who knew something about being a soldier of fortune, told Military Intelligence that he knew Talbot and his associates, "that Talbot has induced some of his associates to believe in his, Talbot's, wild schemes about filibustering, gun running and revolutionary expeditions and that his associates have advanced money to him to help him carry out some of his visionary schemes." Holmdahl said that Talbot "is irresponsible and so visionary that he might be called crazy, . . . whether it is because of want of mental balance or from the use of a drug. Talbot talks of all sorts of schemes, from developing mines in the United States, smuggling ammunition and joining revolutions in Mexico down to starting revolutions in Central America, but never carries his schemes of yesterday into today."[95] El Paso continued to be a magnet for outrageous characters.

As a result of the National Guard mobilization, the city in the summer and fall of 1916 had the largest concentration of troops in the country—forty-thousand-plus regulars and guardsmen. For the first time in a long time, El Pasoans had reason to feel secure.[96] The Bureau, in the meantime, had more to do than just follow the adventures of *carrancistas*, *villistas*, *legalistas*, and garden-variety criminals such as fugitives and smugglers; it also had to spend its energies on more mundane matters: "Instructions were also received to watch very close [*sic*] the Dry Goods Stores belonging to the Jews and find out if the Soldiers were disposing of Goods, like shoes, cloth etc."[97] The army not only pumped gratifying amounts of cash into the local economy, but the massive troop concentration put the Mexican Army on notice: there were in El Paso and its immediate vicinity three regular provisional brigades and three National Guard divisions. To advertise how well the National Guard had been trained, on September 21 the largest military review in the city's history was held. Some twenty-seven thousand regulars and guardsmen, the equivalent of a war-strength division, paraded through downtown with their equipment in a column twenty miles long and were reviewed at Fort Bliss. This was the largest review in the United States since the Union army's victory parade down Pennsylvania Avenue in Washington at the end of the Civil War.[98] Presumably the Mexicans were suitably impressed.

The tumultuous year closed on an appropriately warlike note—the battle of Hart's Mill. On Christmas Eve a detachment of Company L, 3rd Kentucky Infantry, on outpost duty at Hart's Mill on the bank of the Rio Grande (where the Hacienda Restaurant was later located) took a fusillade of some twenty rounds from Mexican snipers in Juárez. The Kentuckians were fed up with being continually sniped at, and they cut loose with everything they had, firing more than two hundred rounds and silencing their attackers. The captain commanding the Kentucky company reported that he had plainly seen the flashes of the Mexicans' rifles as they withdrew up the river. During the engagement some three hundred shots were fired, awakening the city and producing hundreds of frantic phone calls to the authorities.

Army officers on both sides of the Rio Grande promptly investigated the firefight. Regulars from Fort Bliss declared that all the firing came from the American side of the river. Mexican officers, however, declared that a Mexican outpost had believed that Americans were firing on Juárez and by prearrangement fired five shots from their rifles to signal the next outpost that they were under attack. That outpost fired a prescribed volley. Kentucky officers openly scoffed at the regulars' assertion that no shots had come from the Mexican side, pointing to impacts of bullets around their position. Further investigation revealed that the cause of all the trouble was piles of slag at the nearby smelter exploding as they cooled in the freezing night. This caused the Mexican outpost to believe they were under attack, and everything flowed from that.[99] The "battle of Hart's Mill" turned out to be just another of those occurrences that jangled the nerves of El Pasoans during the Mexican Revolution.

CHAPTER 16

Gunrunning

As the new year opened, that perennial adventurer Emil L. Holmdahl was on his best behavior. He was out on bond pending his appeal for his neutrality conviction. On January 10, 1917, the Fifth Circuit Court of Appeals affirmed the sentence of eighteen months in the federal penitentiary at Leavenworth. Holmdahl was given a sixty-day respite to get his affairs in order before surrendering to begin serving his sentence. He used the time wisely, formally applying for executive clemency on January 29 and traveling to Washington to make his case in person. He also generated a stream of letters of recommendation from influential persons such as Mayor Tom Lea of El Paso and the prominent Washington attorney Sherburne Hopkins as well as from army officers who had known him during the Punitive Expedition, among them Brigadier General George Bell Jr. and Major General John Pershing.[1]

More importantly, Holmdahl had a vigorous champion in the person of Texas state senator Claude B. Hudspeth of El Paso, who declared that Holmdahl "was convicted upon perjured testimony bought by Villa gold."[2] Declaring that he was acting strictly in the interests of justice, Hudspeth mounted an impressive campaign where it counted—among politicians. He asked U.S. Senator Morris Sheppard of Texas to approach President Wilson about Holmdahl's pardon and to inform the president that if necessary Hudspeth could secure letters requesting clemency from every one of the thirty-one Texas state senators.[3] Hudspeth's greatest feat, however, was organizing a petition on Holmdahl's behalf that was signed by most of the Texas congressional delegation, plus attorney Sherburne Hopkins. Senator Sheppard sent the petition to the pardon attorney in the Justice Department. The indefatigable Hudspeth also enlisted the support of U.S. Senator Oscar W. Underwood.[4]

This letter-writing campaign resulted in several more postponements of Holmdahl's incarceration.[5] Given his track record, his application for a presidential pardon merited extensive investigation, and the Bureau got the job.[6] Not surprisingly, some of those who knew Holmdahl had nothing good to say about him. They included the U.S. attorney for the Western District of Texas, J. L. Camp, who stated that "I emphatically decline to recommend his pardon," and Charles Breniman, Bureau agent in charge in San Antonio, who said Holmdahl had shown utter disregard for the neutrality laws and if pardoned would continue to violate them.[7]

Samuel Belden, the San Antonio attorney who represented the Carranza regime in that city, was even terrified of Holmdahl—Belden didn't want his name used because he feared Holmdahl would kill him when he was released from prison.[8] The Bureau compiled considerable correspondence, pro and con, concerning Holmdahl, and the chief prepared a memorandum for the pardon attorney in the Justice Department.[9] On July 13, the very day when he was finally scheduled to surrender and begin serving his sentence, Holmdahl received his coveted pardon, based largely on his service in the Punitive Expedition and on his assisting the government in securing the names of important witnesses in the case of *U.S. v. Huerta*.

What then transpired was most unusual. Back on May 31, 1917, Holmdahl's friend Sam Robertson, a prominent engineer in south Texas serving at the time as a major in the Detroit headquarters of the 6th U.S. Reserve Engineer Regiment, had written to Texas congressman Jeff McLemore saying that if Holmdahl received his presidential pardon and would contact Robertson, he could "place him with this regiment as Sergeant." On June 6, Robertson telegraphed McLemore asking him to see the attorney general and try to get Holmdahl pardoned at once: "The Regiment needs his services badly and he will be more valuable to his country in France than in prison."[10] On July 12, Attorney General Gregory wired Robertson: "If Holmdahl is pardoned can you still place him with your regiment. Please wire immediately." Robertson replied: "Your wire. Can use Holmdahl as sergeant first class if he can come at once. Col. [Harry] Burgess [regimental commander] requests that you have him sent to Washington Barracks enlisted and assigned to this regiment."[11]

To ensure that Holmdahl indeed enlisted, the warrant for his pardon was sent to Colonel Burgess. Holmdahl immediately enlisted but failed the physical examination because of the wounds he had suffered in his turbulent career. In a most unusual development, the adjutant general and the secretary of war intervened and ordered his enlistment despite his disabilities. This may be the only instance of such personages interesting themselves in the troubles of any recruit. Holmdahl was quickly promoted to sergeant, went to France with his regiment, distinguished himself in combat, and ended World War I as a captain.[12] This must have pleased Texas senator Morris Sheppard, for on July 13, the day of Holmdahl's pardon, he had approached the secretary of war trying to secure an army commission for the adventurer.[13] Rarely have so many influential people exerted themselves on behalf of a soldier of fortune.

Holmdahl's coconspirator José Orozco likewise appealed his conviction to the Fifth Circuit Court of Appeals, but on January 8, 1917, that body affirmed his sentence of eighteen months in Leavenworth. Orozco spent nearly a year in the El Paso

County jail before beginning to serve his prison sentence. However, like Holmdahl, he furnished information about cases involving Huerta, and this helped to gain him his freedom. On May 23, 1917, he received a pardon, the attorney general stating that Orozco had been punished enough. In October 1919, however, José Orozco, by then a livestock dealer in El Paso, was found guilty of selling morphine. At his trial he had introduced his 1917 pardon as evidence that he was law abiding.[14]

Their codefendant Victor Ochoa was taken in charge by the authorities on February 14, 1917, and did hard time in the federal penitentiary in Atlanta, scheduled for release in May, 1919. To add to Ochoa's troubles, his wife divorced him while he was in prison. But Victor persevered—from Atlanta he wrote to the Naval Consulting Board offering plans for an aircraft with metal wings that folded back and to the War Department's Board of Ordnance and Fortifications offering plans for a tank with a huge plow for trench digging. He received politely noncommittal replies. By the time he got out, the Mexican Revolution was winding down, and Ochoa was a has-been in terms of revolutionary intrigue.

He returned to El Paso, establishing a real estate office in room 609 of the Caples Building. But Ochoa was also involved with the city's underworld. In 1920 he was an informant for the U.S. Treasury Department. On September 19, 1921, Ochoa was arrested and charged with three counts of violating the Harrison Narcotics Act by selling five ounces of morphine. He of course pleaded not guilty. At the trial it was revealed that on July 25, 1921, one C. L. Brite, who unbeknownst to Ochoa was an Internal Revenue officer acting on instructions, asked Ochoa to smuggle twenty-five ounces of morphine into El Paso for him. Brite hoped to arrest a certain woman who was to deliver the drugs. Just before the delivery, however, Brite, acting on his superiors' instructions, called off the transaction because he learned that Ochoa was acting with the knowledge and consent of J. D. Reeder, supervisor of mounted customs inspectors in El Paso, and E. D. Elfers, assistant U.S. attorney. It was thus an embarrassing case of federal agencies working at cross-purposes. The jury quickly found Ochoa not guilty.[15]

Thereafter Ochoa devoted himself to securing patents for his inventions and to promoting mining schemes, becoming president of the Caballo Development and Mining Company. As of 1933, at the age of seventy-three, Ochoa was engaged in prospecting near Caballo Lake, New Mexico, claiming to have discovered two abandoned mines dating back to Spanish colonial times. After getting into a shooting scrape in El Paso in 1936, he relocated to Mexico, where he spent the rest of his life. In 1942, he was prospecting for gold in Sinaloa, but by 1945 was sick and destitute. He reportedly died, alone and forgotten, in El Tambor, Sinaloa, in the fall of 1945.[16] This was a pathetic end for the man who had once been the senior revolutionist in residence in El Paso.

Holmdahl, as evidence that he was a reformed individual, assisted the Bureau in El Paso in identifying ammunition smugglers. Ammunition continued to be an important component of the city's economy, since both the Carranza government and Pancho Villa were dependent on an American supply. As with the present-day narcotics trade, the authorities were able to seize some shipments, but most got through. The El Paso district of the Customs Service, for example, had only nineteen mounted inspectors to patrol more than three hundred miles of the border.[17] As General Frederick Funston commented in January 1917, "Any one with money can buy almost any amount in El Paso."[18] And the Bureau's San Antonio office advised that "reported from a reliable source that Villa has more than enough ammunition, that his partisans in El Paso have sent him large quantities, which were smuggled over between New Mexico and Arizona in automobiles, wagons, and even on railway trains."[19]

Krakauer, Zork and Moye's manager, Robert Krakauer, was quite candid regarding the sale of military ammunition that was to be smuggled into Mexico; he stated that "business is business." The Bureau was not amused and put Krakauer on notice that "any shipments of .30-.30 or 7 m/m cartridges to border points will be looked upon with extreme disfavor by the military and this department, and they [Krakauer, Zork and Moye] have promised that they will be very careful that no consignments of this nature go to border points in the future."[20] Presumably Shelton-Payne received the same warning. That firm handled large amounts—one shipment in July alone totaling 792 cases of small-arms ammunition. Yet, unlike Krakauer, Shelton-Payne cooperated with the Bureau. Agent Gus Jones wrote that: "Mr. Shelton has been very accommodating to the Government and has consulted with this office and the Intelligence office relative to any sale or shipment of ammunition in his territory. The Shelton Arms [*sic*] Company is a reputable concern in this section and Mr. Shelton the head of this firm is a very loyal, law abiding American Citizen."[21]

But proprietors of hardware stores, pawn shops and secondhand stores on South El Paso Street were more than happy to take up the slack. Of these, an increasingly prominent dealer was the Henry Mohr Hardware Company, located at 309 South El Paso Street. Mohr had come up in the world; when we last saw him in 1912, he had been a minor member of the ammunition smuggling fraternity. Although customs and the military had primary responsibility for monitoring the munitions traffic, the Bureau was called on to build a case against Mohr. It compiled a substantial dossier on him but had difficulty securing enough evidence to warrant filing a complaint. It adopted measures such stationing provost guards in front of Mohr's store and a customs inspector in the back, and it even assigned several informants exclusively to watch Mohr, after carefully checking out their backgrounds.[22] Mohr's firm dealt largely in .30-.30 and 7-mm Mauser ammunition and sold it to any faction, knowing that it would be smuggled into Mexico. Surprisingly, though, Agent Jones reported that "Mrs. Mohr is the leading factor in the business. From what I know of Henry Mohr personally, I do not believe that he has the nerve to engage in any business that is liable to get him into trouble, but on the other hand Mrs. Mohr will take any kind of chances to make a dollar." Mrs. Mohr, a "Mexican of German descent," didn't hesitate to march into the Bureau office and assert what she termed her legal right to receive ammunition and to denounce what she considered persecution by the authorities. But the Bureau's pressure had an effect—Mrs. Mohr actually returned a great deal of ammunition to her suppliers.[23] This turned out to be only an interlude, however; Mohr soon began receiving shipments again, although on a much reduced scale, and the battle of wits resumed, but with less intensity.

Still, the Bureau could not develop enough evidence to convince the U.S. attorney to file charges.[24] A frustrated chief of the Bureau advised that "in the present situation along the border, Government officers should be willing to take some chances in examining the contents of vehicles going into Mexico for articles which may be carried there in violation of the President's proclamation." (Chief Bielaski was referring to President Wilson's embargo on munitions shipments to Mexico.)[25] And the chief had "no objection to the placing of a military guard in the vicinity of stores that persistently sell ammunition to Mexicans, under the circumstances which reasonably indicate that it is intended to be smuggled into Mexico, providing it can be arranged with the military authorities."[26]

The district office of Military Intelligence, operating from room 822 in the Mills Building, cooperated closely with the Bureau, on occasion setting up a sting operation. For example, Captain Robert Grinstead, the Fort Bliss Intelligence officer, notified Agent Jones that an informant of his, one Alfredo Argüelles, had advised him that a certain Luis Herrera had approached Argüelles with the proposition that Argüelles find him a buyer for some 15,000 rounds of ammunition. Grinstead had arranged for a Lieutenant Estévez of the 23rd U.S. Infantry, who was a Filipino and thus looked like a Mexican, to be the alleged purchaser. The lieutenant was to meet Argüelles and Herrera at the Lone Star Saloon on Alameda Avenue and have two autos parked nearby to haul away the ammunition. The plan was for the three men to leave the saloon in Herrera's car and drive to where the ammunition was stored; the lieutenant's two autos would follow. Once the ammunition was received and paid for the entire party would be arrested.

Agent Jones advised Captain Grinstead that the plan was too obvious and that ammunition smugglers did not usually work that way, but that the Bureau would cooperate. Jones would drive one of Lieutenant Estévez's autos and a Lieutenant Catron of the Military Intelligence office would drive the other. Captain Grinstead was to hide in the rear of Catron's car and a customs inspector would hide in the rear of Jones's car. At the appointed hour of 9 p.m., Lieutenant Estévez entered the saloon. Jones and Catron were parked across the street, from where they could see the interior of the saloon. Jones was determined not to let the lieutenant out of his sight, for he suspected that the affair would end in a holdup. He didn't mention this suspicion to Captain Grinstead because he "did not desire to throw a damper on any of the schemes of the Intelligence office." When after an hour the other parties failed to appear, Grinstead called the operation off.

The next day Captain Grinstead notified Jones that Grinstead's informant said the deal would definitely take place that night. This time the meeting place was a vacant lot three blocks from the saloon. Again the officers secreted their cars where they could observe the proceedings. A car containing Argüelles and Herrera appeared, and they spoke with Lieutenant Estévez, telling him that the ammunition couldn't be delivered until midnight. Agent Jones advised Grinstead that he had better take charge of the $1,000 Estévez was carrying as bait money because in Jones's opinion it was to be a holdup pure and simple, and Argüelles and Herrera might snatch the money and run before the officers could intervene. Grinstead reluctantly agreed. About twenty minutes later Argüelles returned alone and told Estévez they would meet at midnight and that Herrera was waiting on Alameda Avenue in their car. The officers decided that the matter had gone far enough. They descended on Herrera and Argüelles as well as on Estévez, to preserve his cover. They took the trio to the customs house, where after an hour of intensive interrogation Herrera admitted that his intention had been to hold Estévez up. Herrera confessed that he had no intention of selling ammunition, and that Argüelles had approached him several days earlier and said he had a sucker who wanted to buy ammunition and that if Herrera went in with him they could either fill some ammunition boxes with sand or simply hold the man up. Agent Jones "advised the Captain that I was going to release Herrera with a talk that he would not forget for some time and that he could handle his former informant in any manner he desired."[27]

Besides munitions, another prized commodity was information, whether accurate or fabricated or merely hearsay. The press frequently ascribed its information to "federal agents" without specifying who they were or even what agency they represented. The local Bureau agents were adamant that there were no leaks emanating from them. Agent Gus Jones pointed out that a correspondent of the *Chicago Tribune* had remarked to him "that he had often heard the Bureau of Investigation called the 'Secret Service' and he was beginning to think that it was properly named because it was the hardest place he ever saw to get any news from." By contrast, General George Bell held regular press conferences, as did the collector of customs, Zach Cobb. Moreover, the customs inspectors at the international bridges spoke quite freely, and sometimes indiscreetly, to the press.[28] Much of what they had to say concerned the activities of Pancho Villa.

When the Punitive Expedition withdrew from Mexico on February 5, 1917, there was the real prospect that Villa would fill the resulting vacuum and end up dominating northwestern Chihuahua. Relations between the United States and Carranza improved somewhat as they faced the common enemy. One result was that the Mexican agent Jesús María Arriola cooperated more with the Bureau. Arriola was involved in trying to assert his authority over an extensive spy network based in El Paso, although the secret agents reported to Andrés García, inspector general of Mexican consulates, the official who traditionally directed Mexican intelligence in the United States. To combat the leaks that characterized intelligence operations on the border Mexican agents used code names such as "Equis" ["X"], "Don," and "Dormilonas" and sometimes submitted unsigned reports. However, Arriola considered it illegal to accuse anyone based on reports from those using code names, because this system lent itself to intrigues and abuses. Consul García, to whose agents Arriola referred, categorically rejected Arriola's views.[29] The two were locked in a power struggle, a struggle in which García would ultimately triumph.

Arriola passed some of his information on to the Bureau. He advised that Victor Carusso and the Alderete brothers had had a falling out because of a debt Carusso owed the Alderetes. The brothers had come to Arriola's office and had supplied a code that Carusso and his business associate Abraham Luján were using. Carusso was in New York; he ostensibly making purchases for his Everwear Shoe Company, but the Bureau suspected he was there to purchase ammunition for Villa.[30] Arriola furnished the information and the code to the Bureau, which kept Carusso and Luján under surveillance in New York and on their return to El Paso. In addition, Arriola provided a pamphlet, published in El Paso, of regulations for the Mexican intelligence service in the United States.[31] Furthermore, the inspector general of consulates, Andrés García, provided copies of documents captured from Villa by the Carranza forces.[32] And a former Bureau employee, Adolfo Osterveen Jr., who was now working for the Mexican consul in Laredo against the *felicistas*, advised that he had applied to work for Arriola. Osterveen had informed Agent Brennan in Laredo, who had been his handler, before going to work for the consul and before applying to Arriola. Brennan was confident that if hired Osterveen would not reveal any information he had learned while a Bureau employee.[33] At a more mundane level, Carranza agents were helping the Bureau locate a fugitive, Prudencio Miranda, and Agent Edward Stone requested authorization to pay a $25 reward. He received authorization. The reward went to Mrs. Luisa Escobar, who betrayed Miranda.[34]

But sometimes Arriola was too helpful. He told Agent Jones that "an informant" had advised him that on January 19, he was in Henry Mohr's store and overheard a conversation between Mrs. Mohr and Teodoro Kyriacopulos, proprietor of the Emporium Saloon, located in the same block as Mohr's establishment. The Greek wanted to purchase two cases of ammunition and two cases of rifles, on credit. Mrs. Mohr refused. But the next day cases of rifles and ammunition were in fact carried down the alley into Kyriacopulos's saloon. Kyriacopulos was a well-known *villista*, which accounted for Arriola's enthusiasm in sharing this information with the Bureau. Arriola then revealed in confidence to Agent Jones that his informant was Frank Alderete, whose informant in turn was a clerk in Mohr's store. But in his eagerness to get the Bureau to act against Mohr, Arriola said too much—to keep Agent Jones from getting confused, Arriola emphasized that the two boxes that went down the alley were the ones going to the Emporium Saloon and the two boxes that went up the alley were "for us and all right. He then realized who he was talking to and immediately tried to change the subject." When Jones questioned him about the boxes going up the alley, Arriola lamely said he had been only joking. Jones was certain that Arriola's statement slipped out "before he realized that he was not talking to one of his own operatives" and that Alderete had gone to Mohr's to purchase the two boxes that had gone up the alley, for "it is a known fact that Alderete is the present purchasing agent of the Carrancistas insofar as ammunition is concerned."[35] Several days later, Agent Jones interviewed Mrs. Henry Mohr and came away convinced that despite her denial Frank Alderete had recently purchased 33,000 rounds of 7-mm ammunition for the Carranza government.[36] Frank Alderete was also involved in trying to unload 200,000 7-mm Mauser cartridges salvaged from a vessel sunk in the Galveston hurricane of 1900. The ammunition had been shipped from El Paso in 1916 to General Plutarco Elías Calles in Sonora, but, we recall, he had indignantly returned the merchandise because it was corroded and defective. The cartridges were then taken to Smeltertown, polished, and put back on the market.[37]

A German named Franz Gottwald was also a munitions purchasing agent for the Carranza government. According to Krakauer, Zork and Moye, he tried to buy their entire stock, which they claimed they indignantly refused to sell because they knew he planned to smuggle it into Mexico.[38] The fact that Gottwald was a German citizen immediately aroused the Bureau's interest. Collector Cobb considered him a dangerous enemy alien, pointing out that Gottwald was involved in ammunition deals with the Alderete brothers, who were "renegade American Mexicans," and urging that he be held without bond. Acting on instructions from the Justice Department, Agent Stone arranged with General Bell for Gottwald to be confined in "the German detention camp at Ft. Bliss" even though no charges had been filed against him. However, after two weeks a judge at a habeas corpus hearing ordered Gottwald's immediate release. The U.S. marshal immediately rearrested him for conspiring with Mrs. Henry Mohr to violate the president's embargo and smuggle ammunition into Mexico.[39] Gottwald freely admitted being commissioned by the Carranza government to purchase ammunition and supplies in the United States, and he admitted smuggling ammunition across to Juárez. He was released on a $7,500 bond, despite efforts to have him interned as an enemy alien. Gottwald quickly posted bond and disappeared across the border.[40]

Increasingly the Bureau focused on the activities of Germans, especially on anything even hinting at cooperation between Germany and Mexico. In large measure this alarm resulted from the publication of the notorious Zimmermann telegram on February 27, 1917. The telegram, from German foreign minister Arthur Zimmermann to the German minister to Mexico instructed the latter to negotiate an alliance between Germany and Mexico whereby with German support Mexico would declare war on the United States. The inducement for Mexico was German help in recovering the territory she had lost to the United States in the nineteenth century.[41]

CHAPTER 17

World War, 1917

With the entry of the United States into World War I on April 6, 1917, at least one arms dealer voluntarily curtailed his activities. *Villistas* continued their efforts to acquire ammunition, on one occasion trying to buy 500,000 rounds of 7-mm cartridges from the Curtis Manning Company of El Paso. J. S. Curtis admitted that in the past he and Sam Dreben had sold a lot of ammunition together but stoutly maintained that he was no longer in that line of work.[1] Manning had in years past bought more than 8 million 7-mm cartridges from Remington Arms, but he now informed the company that although his Mexican customers were clamoring for 1 million rounds, which he could sell at a very nice profit for $40,000, as a loyal American he refused to engage in this business.[2] No doubt the Bureau appreciated his patriotism.

The federal authorities gained several invaluable wartime tools for monitoring revolutionary activities. Passports became mandatory. Postal censorship offices were established in New York, Seattle, San Francisco, New Orleans, San Antonio, San Diego—and El Paso. By the end of the war the El Paso office had a staff of fourteen, who read all mail coming from and going to Mexico, as well as all mail to and from countries friendly to the Central Powers. A military censor supervised the thirty-six employees reading all Western Union telegrams. In May 1918, telephone lines between El Paso and Juárez were severed.[3] And in September 1918, wartime passport regulations were put into effect requiring men of military age to secure permission from their draft board in order to enter Mexico. Lastly, Military Intelligence expanded, as civilian employees, such as clerks and translators, were added to the payroll.[4]

The Bureau was zealous in combating disloyalty and German espionage. It filed charges against Henry Beach and the Toenniges family for conspiring to induce unnamed Mexican military commanders to "invade and make hostile incursions from Mexico into the United States." But on April 26, the U.S. attorney stated in court that the evidence was insufficient to support the indictment; the court ordered the case dismissed.[5] The authorities did a little better with regard to August Winter, charged with making obscene statements about the U.S. flag, cursing and abusing the United States, and urging American soldiers to fight for Germany instead of the

United States. He pleaded not guilty but was found guilty and sentenced to sixty days in the county jail.[6]

As mentioned, the Bureau was particularly interested in any connections between Mexicans and Germans. Agent Hyman Harris was loitering in front of the Arlington Bar when two Teutonic-appearing men passed, speaking English. One said to the other that he wanted him to accompany him to Mexico. This immediately got the attention of Harris, who followed them into an ice cream parlor on South El Paso Street. The Bureau agent introduced himself as "Heinrich Levy from Siebenbergen, Austria." The men in turn introduced themselves as Robert Ullman, of El Paso, and one Brill, recently discharged from the Georgia National Guard. The conversation turned to current affairs, whereupon Harris asserted that "I don't care how many more countries will declare war against Germany the Germans will be the victors." This delighted Ullman, who described German military prowess and declared that Pancho Villa was the best friend the Germans had in Mexico. Harris then innocently asked where Villa got his ammunition, and Ullman boasted that Villa had it smuggled to him every day, and that Regino (he was referring to Regino Corral), Villa's brother-in-law, had recently been in El Paso recruiting men, buying ammunition, and smuggling both across the Rio Grande near Fabens. Furthermore, Regino Corral was expected back in El Paso for more men and arms. Harris then confided that he had in Del Rio 500 .30-.30 rifles and 50 cases of ammunition for sale and that he would appreciate Ullman talking with Corral about the matter. Ullman rose to the bait and inquired about price and condition of the merchandise. Ullman and Harris agreed to meet the following day to conclude the deal. After several delays Ullman introduced Harris to a *villista* purchasing agent named "Inez," and they got down to business. Harris stated that he wanted $25 per rifle and $45 per case of ammunition. Inez agreed to those terms provided Harris could deliver the goods in Marfa, explaining that the munitions had to be delivered in the Big Bend, close to where Villa's forces were operating across the Rio Grande. Harris said he could do that, and he and Inez made an appointment to meet the next day at room 102 in the Trust Building. This turned out to be the office of J. L. Tyler and Joe Dunn, "old time smugglers." After Inez introduced Harris to Tyler and Dunn, Tyler asked about price and quality of the munitions, and they agreed to close the deal the next day.[7] This was the end of the affair, but as a result of Agent Harris's initiative the Bureau had gained additional insights into the arms traffic.

German activities were a constant source of concern. The Bureau reported that "On September 23rd one John Seibel, a German, went from Juarez to Chihuahua, where he received from the German consul there a sum sufficient to cover his traveling expenses from San Antonio, Texas, to the city of Chihuahua. The third day after his arrival in the latter place, Seibel went to work for General Murguia in the Mexican government harness shop. In El Paso this man applied for employment at the Depot Quartermaster Machine Shops, but was refused. It is evident that he was trying to obtain a government position in order to have some status in the city, while acting as a German spy."[8]

A German spy may have been involved in an incident on December 21 on Córdova Island. A man approached the cavalrymen manning an outpost on the international border and repeatedly tried to cross into Mexico, saying he wanted to take some pictures for his personal use. The soldiers refused him permission because he didn't have a passport. The man later asked two Texas Rangers to help him cross the boundary, and they also refused. At dusk the man made a dash for the boundary. The cavalrymen repeatedly ordered him to halt. When he kept running they fired at him three times with their pistols, missing him; one of the soldiers then shot him in the back with a rifle at a distance of a hundred yards, when he was already in Mexico. A passing Mexican obligingly loaded the body into his wagon and delivered the corpse to the army outpost.

Papers on the body and subsequent investigation revealed that the name of the deceased was Charles H. Feige, a thirty-two-year-old electrical engineering graduate of the University of Wisconsin, class of 1906. He wore tailored clothing, carried a bank book showing large deposits in the Savings Bank of New York, a camera, a number of documents with the addresses of many Germans in New York and Chicago, a letter showing that his application for a passport had been denied, a large sum of money, and sketches and pictures of munitions factories, radio towers, and the international boundary at El Paso. As far as the authorities were concerned, he was a German spy who had been desperately trying to enter Mexico to deliver the information he had gathered.[9] And the army reported that the discovery of the papers Feige was carrying caused certain Germans in Juárez to leave suddenly for Chihuahua, presumably because they feared the papers would incriminate them.[10]

On occasion there were genuine German agents operating in El Paso. One was William Gleaves, a black Canadian, born in Montreal in 1870. He had been living in Mexico City since 1893. There in 1917 he became an agent of Kurt Jahnke, head of German Naval Intelligence in Mexico. On Jahnke's orders, Gleaves joined the radical Industrial Workers of the World (IWW), for the Germans were interested in sabotaging the huge oil fields in Tampico, which supplied the British Royal Navy with much of its fuel. Gleaves performed so well in the IWW that Jahnke gave him a more important assignment—to foment mutiny among the U.S. troops stationed on the border. Supplied with $1,500 for expenses, Gleaves traveled from Mexico City to Ciudad Juárez, then crossed over to El Paso, where he remained for several weeks assessing the situation. On his return to Mexico City he reported that he had established useful contacts among the soldiers but needed to make another trip to the border. This time, however, the Germans sent him to the Arizona border to suborn members of the black 9th and 10th U.S. Cavalry regiments. The operation failed because what the Germans didn't know was that their crack agent William Gleaves was a double agent—an operative of British Naval Intelligence in Mexico City.[11]

Sometimes the Bureau's efforts to deal with suspicious Germans didn't turn out well at all. In April a German named Von Linder, "alias Leinenbert, alias Leinen, a unit of the German espionage system, operating in the southwest," was arrested in the town of Toyah and brought to El Paso. He confessed to the Bureau that he had been engaged in espionage in the United States since August 1914. He revealed that his instructions were to go to a street corner one block from the American end of the Santa Fe Street international bridge on the last day of each month and there meet a captain in the German Army, one William Brinck. Von Linder would deliver the information he had collected during the month and receive instructions for the next month. Hoping to improve his situation, Von Linder assured Agent Edward Stone that if he were allowed to keep his usual rendezvous he would point Captain Brinck out so he could be apprehended. Stone leaped at this chance to neutralize an important German agent. Stone conferred with the supervising immigration inspector and the sheriff of El Paso County, and a team of eight picked men from the Bureau, Immigration Service, and the sheriff's office was assembled to seize Brinck. Von Linder gave the agreed-on signal as an automobile with five men in it passed. The officers pursued in another car, and Agent Gus Jones and an immigration inspector detained the occupants as they were about the enter the Paso del Norte Hotel.

The four men and their driver were taken to the Bureau's office for interrogation.[12] "One of the party, Carlos B. Austin, to all appearances a German of the decided [*sic*] blonde type, claiming Mexican citizenship, was the one pointed out by Von Linder as being Captain Brinck." After several hours of interrogation and investigation, Agent Stone reluctantly concluded that Von Linder was either mistaken or had duped him, and he ordered all four men released. Still, Stone was anxious to learn where the party's chauffeur had intended to take them in El Paso. Therefore, Stone asked the supervising inspector of immigration to send two of his inspectors with the driver and have him point out his intended destination. He did so, and it turned out to be the residence of Andrés García, inspector of Mexican consulates. The two immigration inspectors had been instructed merely to identify the destination, but they exceeded their instructions by entering the house and briefly looking around. The local Mexican consul, Eduardo Soriano Bravo, immediately lodged a protest, and Agent Stone offered a verbal apology. But the matter didn't end there. The Mexican ambassador formally protested to the State Department, which required a full explanation from Bruce Bielaski, the chief of the Bureau, who of course required a full explanation from Agent Stone. The latter's explanation cleared the Bureau, which had not only not caught a German spy but had been involved in an international incident.[13]

The Bureau not only investigated German spies but also took an interest in the transfer of money to banks in El Paso, such as $200,000 through the Hanover National Bank in New York City to the First National Bank in El Paso for the account of the local Mexican consul, Soriano Bravo. And the Deutscher Sud-Americanische Bank in Mexico City transferred $160,000 to the First National Bank for the account of A. Rodríguez, cashier of the Juárez customs house. Some local banks, such as City National Bank, were involved in ammunition matters. The Rio Grande Bank and Trust Company, for another, was very pro-Villa and transacted a lot of business with George Holmes. Furthermore, representatives of the Carranza regime arrived in Corpus Christi with $495,000 (half of which was in dollars, the rest of which was in Carranza currency), which was transferred by the Corpus Christi National Bank to the First National Bank of El Paso. These funds were to be used to pay General Francisco Murguía's troops in Chihuahua, whose salaries were badly in arrears.[14] Illustrating the importance of El Paso to the Carranza regime was the fact that its financial agency, headed by Roberto V. Pesqueira, which handled financial affairs for the entire border, was located in the city.[15]

While monitoring Pesqueira's activities, the Bureau also kept tabs on Carranza secret agent Jesús María Arriola. Agent Jones wrote that "I am of the frank opinion that Mr. Arriola will bear special attention from this office, as there is no doubt that his purpose in El Paso, Texas is to supervise generally the purchase and smuggling of ammunition for his Government, and the information he gives this office is for the purpose of distracting our officers from his own operations. . . . The operations of Mr. Arriola will be covered on as closely as circumstances will permit."[16] The problem of course was that ammunition could easily be smuggled downriver from El Paso and in the vicinity of Columbus.[17]

Ammunition was much on the mind of Hipólito Villa. He met on January 11 at his home in San Antonio with several persons of interest, among them Teodoro Kyriacopulos and Haymon Krupp, as well as attorney Ignacio Borrego Esparza, who had been a congressman during the Madero administration and who had arrived from El Paso. Hipólito, in his daily report to the Bureau of his visitors, listed Borrego but not the others and of course neglected to mention the meeting.[18] It didn't matter. The Bureau had an informant at the meeting, and Mexican agent Jesús María Arriola presumably also covered the meeting, since he was in San Antonio at the time. The Bureau learned that Hipólito and Borrego had discussed the prospects for Pancho Villa's success and that they had established offices in New York City, putting John J. Hawes of San Antonio in charge.

Hawes was one of the many slick operators hoping to cash in on the Mexican Revolution. The Military Intelligence Division reported that Hawes, an Englishman, was formerly on the staff of the *Mexican Herald*. "Hawes is described as about forty five years old, very distinguished looking, a free spender, heavy drinker of Scotch whiskey, [and] . . . claims at one time to have been an officer in the United States Army and has a captain's uniform in his possession. While he was in Houston, he was well supplied with money and built a couple of apartment houses in this city."[19] Hawes claimed he had the support of important American officials and of powerful American companies with business interests in Mexico, apparently large mining and cattle companies operating in Chihuahua. Agent Barnes was skeptical about Hawes's commitment to the cause: "From what I can find out, I believe that Hawes is the financial agent of such large corporations as are contributing to the Villista cause and that Hawes receives the collections, deducts his commission and remits the balance to some agent of Villa. I also believe that Hawes is more interested in his commissions than he is in the Villista cause and in order to continue a prosperous business he leads the Villistas to believe that he is enlisting the sympathy of high United States officials and financiers, and, on the other hand, induce certain corporations interested in Mexico to believe that through him protection to their interests can be secured from Villa."

Hawes, it might be mentioned, stayed at the Waldorf Astoria when in New York.[20] He also dropped names; when interviewed by the Bureau in New York he mentioned that he was acquainted with Charles Warren, assistant attorney general of the United States, with whom he had recently conferred in Washington. However, Warren had only a slight acquaintance with Hawes, thought little of his activities, and took great exception to his name having been used. Hawes also declared that he was well known to Agent Barnes in San Antonio. Barnes, as we have just seen, was hardly an admirer of Hawes. And Agent Willard Utley, who also knew Hawes personally, stated that he was busily putting out pro-Villa propaganda. State Department agent George Carothers, who had been attached to Pancho Villa, also had a low opinion of Hawes.[21]

At the meeting Hipólito and Borrego stated that they had also received letters from Frank L. Thomas of Topeka and claimed that Senator Curtis was interested in their cause. Borrego said that Hipólito had received letters from Hawes and Thomas regarding advancing money for Villa's cause and that soon they would have plenty of money. The interests backing Villa monetarily included the Madero family and coal companies in the state of Coahuila. Villa allegedly informed Hipólito from Torreón that he was receiving money from the Alvarado Mining Company in Parral and from William Randolph Hearst, who owned the huge hacienda of Babícora in Chihuahua, and that indirectly Standard Oil had offered financial assistance.[22]

Hawes, and especially Borrego, became frequent visitors to Hipólito's house. Borrego was arrested and jailed in San Antonio in April for neutrality violations, and the Bureau seized a number of codes, letters, and other documents from his effects.[23]

The ultimate object of all this activity was to persuade Washington to extend belligerent status to Pancho Villa, the same goal every opposition Mexican faction had sought since 1910. A resurgent Villa was defeating Carranza's commander in Chihuahua, General Francisco Murguía, as he had defeated Murguía's predecessor General Jacinto B. Treviño. More and more of Villa's old comrades were rejoining him, among them General Medinaveitia and General Banda, who had made their way from New Orleans into Chihuahua.[24] But expecting the United States to grant belligerency status to Villa after he had carried out the Columbus raid was just a bit unrealistic.

Nevertheless, Pancho Villa's partisans were optimistic, not only in San Antonio but also in El Paso, where Todd McClammy, George Holmes, Darío Silva, Frank Thayer, T. F. Jonah, Manuel Icaza, M. E. González, and Demetrio Bustamante, among others, had been spotted on the streets. Holmes boasted that Villa would capture Juárez no later than January 25. Teodoro Kyriacopulos and Haymon Krupp, although claiming they were not connected with any faction, spoke enthusiastically about Pancho Villa's campaign.[25]

Furthermore, Colonel Charles Hunt, the prominent cattle dealer who was president of the "El Paso Live Stock Commission Company" with offices in the First National Bank Building, was trying to contact Pancho Villa.[26] It seems that Hunt and his wife, Alice, his assistant, R. E. Saddler, and Todd McClammy made overtures to Villa. Hunt wrote to the Mexican chieftain offering to use his influence with Senator Albert Fall to secure immunity for Villa and also to furnish him with arms and ammunition if he agreed to protect foreigners' properties. Hunt certainly had influence with Senator Fall, for he was "a former business associate and a political backer of the senator."[27] However, one of Consul García's operatives, Agent X, acquired Hunt's letter, which was published in the *New York Times* on March 26, 1917. Hunt's overture proved abortive because Villa doubted Hunt's ability to secure immunity for him, and the affair caused Senator Fall considerable embarrassment.[28] As Agent Barnes observed, "There are scores of Americans along the border of more or less consequence, who are in sympathy with Villa to the extent that should his regime be restored in Mexico south of here their opportunities to exploit in Mexico would be similarly restored."[29]

Villa's partisans were so bold that several Mexicans even approached Jesús María Arriola soliciting money to finance a filibustering expedition under Roque Gómez and José Quevedo that would join forces with Manuel Ochoa and Mariano Támez, who were operating south of Juárez. And in Brownsville, Sam Dreben was reportedly acting on Villa's behalf under instructions from Felix Sommerfeld.[30]

Several important figures were said to be meeting in New Orleans in the interest of Pancho Villa. The reason they didn't meet in El Paso was that Miguel Díaz Lombardo, Villa's sometime foreign minister, had had some unpleasant experiences in that city, having been arrested for vagrancy, and he was afraid of Mayor Tom Lea.[31] He had reason to—Lea was still determined to rid the city of *villista* activists. He informed the Bureau that a great many *villistas*, including José Rochín and Carlos Jáuregui, were frequenting Teodoro Kyriacopulos's Emporium Saloon and that munitions might be stored in the basement. Agent Wren investigated but found nothing incriminating.[32] Mayor Lea wasn't the only one trying to purge the city of *villista* activists—Agent Stone gave General Manuel Chao forty-eight hours to get out of El Paso and called other prominent Villa followers into his office, sternly warning them that if they continued intriguing they too would soon be gone.[33]

Despite his promise to the authorities not to engage in Mexican politics, former *villista* colonel Juan B. Medina was once again a player: "Juan Medina formerly active with the Villistas at Juarez is in San Antonio and recently asked one of the Maderos to furnish him with $10,000 with which to finance a Villa junta in New York City. Mr. Madero told [Carranza] Consul [Teódulo R.] Beltran of this request on the part of Medina. According to Consul Beltran and Mr. Belden, attorney for the consulate, [David] de la Fuente and Juan Medina are engaged here in an effort to unite the Felicista and Villista factions. Medina and Fuente are representing Villa in this matter. According to Beltran, the two factions have no faith in each other, but each needs the assistance of the other for the common purpose of eliminating Carranza, after which it will be a case of the 'survival of the fittest' between them."[34] Medina later moved back to El Paso, receiving a regular stipend from Pancho Villa, but to avoid deportation he accepted the government's demand that he not reside near the border and in May relocated to Albuquerque. In August, some friends in that city gave Medina $70 with which to go to New York City and seek gainful employment.[35]

Another player was Darío Silva, "who for several months has been Villa's organizer and representative in El Paso, receiving shelter by pretending to be an informant [Avlis] of our government."[36] In February 1917, he wrote to Pancho Villa from El Paso suggesting a way for the Mexican chieftain to acquire a substantial amount of ammunition. He stated that the U.S. government held about 750,000 Mauser cartridges destined for Mexico but which weren't actually confiscated. Therefore it could be requested that "they be returned to us," but to do so General José Inés Salazar needed to grant a power of attorney to his lawyer. Silva included the document and asked Villa to secure Salazar's signature and return the power of attorney. Then Silva could proceed to secure the munitions. "The ammunition here at Fort Bliss I have been able to see availing myself of specious excuse for the purpose. They amount to about 350,000 and are in magnificent shape." With regard to expense, the only cost would be the storage charges. Silva closed with a very smarmy passage reiterating his undying devotion to Villa. This was one of the intercepted letters the Bureau received from Consul Andrés García.[37]

Agent Stone maintained friendly relations with Silva, from whom he obtained information from time to time, for Silva met almost daily with fellow *villistas* who were plotting nonstop at General Macrino Martínez's house. The general was head of the junta, being unaware that his private secretary, Canuto Reyes Vázquez, was Consul García's crack agent X ("Equis").[38] Predictably, Carranza's ambassador in Washington had a cynical view of Martínez: "Macrino J. Martinez is the organizer or purveyor of armed expeditions to Mexico, due to the profits he derives thereof."[39] Darío Silva was also closely associated with George Carothers, the State Department agent in El Paso, who used him as his principal informant on *villista* activities.[40] By July 1917, though, Silva had reportedly given up his political involvement and had a job as a sales representative with a Dallas company. However, he continued to participate in *villista* intrigues.[41]

George Holmes continued to be a major Villa agent, smuggling thousands of rounds of ammunition from his ranch on the Rio Grande near El Paso to waiting *villistas*. State Department agent Carothers reported that "Holmes is a rancher who lives near here, down the valley, and he is the only man who is actually in communication with Villa. He has a criminal record as a cattle thief, and is now under indictment for violation of the neutrality laws."[42] Interestingly, it was said Holmes had transferred all his property over to a trusted friend for fear of being convicted when his trial in federal court came up.[43] Whether or not this was true, the Bureau paid particular attention to Holmes, as for that matter, did the Mexican secret service, which reported that he continued to outfit small *villista* filibustering expeditions from his ranch.[44]

Holmes was quite cocky, telling Agent Stone that "a few days ago I bought some guns and saddles on El Paso Street and any time you fellows want to know what I am doing, I will tell you; I am helping Villa all I can and I have been trying to buy some guns but I am not doing smuggling." Stone added: "Holmes is turning these guns and ammunition over to some one else, but he declines to state who." As with the Mohrs, the Bureau was engaged in a battle of wits, and as with the Mohrs, the assistant U.S. attorney kept telling a frustrated Bureau that more evidence was needed to file a complaint. In an effort to secure such evidence, Agent Stone assigned an informant (Joe Solanos, aka Informant "Mes") exclusively to cover Holmes. Because the informant needed an automobile to keep up with Holmes, the parsimonious Bureau authorized the rental of one for a "few days" at $5 a day.[45] The Bureau seemingly scored a victory in April when it filed a complaint against Holmes, José de Luna, General Manuel Ochoa, José Castillo, and Pablo Carbajal for having mounted an expedition into Mexico near the village of Guadalupe against the Carranza government on August 19, 1916, and a federal grand jury bound them over for trial. Holmes and De Luna were freed on bond, while Manuel Ochoa fled into Chihuahua, where he was subsequently killed in battle.[46]

The *carrancista* spymaster Jesús María Arriola continued to focus on George Holmes while complaining that the Bureau's few agents were primarily interested in German surveillance. (One would have thought there was a war on.) Arriola learned that Holmes was preparing yet another filibustering expedition. Because Consul García hated Arriola, Arriola couldn't use any of the consul's operatives. He therefore relied on Agent Antonio Haro, who'd been sent directly from Mexico City and was his only associate in El Paso. Although it wasn't in the budget, Arriola rented an automobile so Haro could cover potential crossing points on the Rio Grande. After three days of surveillance, Haro notified Arriola that the expedition was preparing to cross on May 18, 1917, at Clint. Arriola had Haro alert the nearest army unit, and that night a detachment of the 8th U.S. Cavalry and a mounted customs inspector captured all eighteen filibusters, including "renegade American George Holmes," Holmes's chauffeur C. F. Tinnin, Manuel González, who was Hipólito Villa's private secretary, and General Juan Andreu Almazán, who had come to El Paso to promote, allegedly with Senator Fall's assistance, an alliance between Villa, Félix Díaz, and Emiliano Zapata.[47] The army seized 18,000 rounds of ammunition and 15 rifles, besides horses, saddles, and other equipment. Those arrested were confined in Fort Bliss while the Bureau prepared charges against them. The Bureau and Military Intelligence also seized at Holmes's ranch a trunk containing various articles, later returning it to Holmes.[48]

The Bureau, Military Intelligence, and the Customs Service launched an investigation and determined that the object of the expedition was to retrieve some $300,000 worth of silver bullion and gold that Pancho Villa had buried. Holmes had enlisted the aid of Hipólito Villa to recover the treasure. Twenty-two men were arrested in connection with this case, of whom eighteen were arraigned. Holmes posted a $3,000 bond, the others $1,000. At the preliminary hearing, however, all the government's witnesses had developed amnesia, and the case had to be continued.[49]

The U.S. Circuit Court of Appeals ruled that the indictment of Holmes had been defective, and so the principals in this case had to be reindicted.[50] A federal grand jury did this in April 1917.[51] But as Zach Cobb observed:

> Holmes is under indictment for violation of the neutrality law. He has been under indictment many times. After getting a continuance six months ago, he was to have been tried at the present term, but, presumably by his connivance, the Government's necessary witness is gone. Holmes is so confirmed a criminal, and so slick an individual, that indictments haven't affected

> him any more than water on a duck's back. This man is more dangerous on the border than are the German alien enemies, because he could and would do things, particularly with Villa, for the Germans, that they could not do for themselves.
>
> If our Government, to meet the conditions existing on the border, could find it consistent to summarily detain, along with the dangerous alien enemies, such characters as Hipolito Villa, Dario Silva, Francisco Villa's old private secretary, who now plots and schemes in El Paso, and George Holmes, the most criminal and dangerous renegade American of the border, the good that would be accomplished cannot be estimated in words. It would not be necessary to act summarily with many. It would be sufficient to make examples of the few notoriously vicious ones.[52]

Because the government couldn't locate its principal witness, José de Luna, its only recourse was to ask for a continuance rather than risk going to trial without the witness. The continuance was granted for the next term of federal court, in October.[53] The irrepressible George Holmes must have had a good chuckle before resuming his nefarious activities. In June, there were rumors that he was organizing yet another filibustering expedition.[54] Moreover, according to the Mexican consul in Presidio, the *villistas* planned to raid Ojinaga again in July in order to cross a herd of Terrazas cattle; Terrazas representatives would be ready to receive them, and among these representatives was George Holmes.[55]

Another problem for the Bureau was Frank Thayer, who alternated between his office in the Mills Building and the lobbies of the Paso del Norte and Sheldon hotels. He was described as "an active Villa sympathizer and pro-German" by a Bureau informant who cultivated him. Thayer was still passing himself off as Villa's agent in El Paso, told the informant that he had gone to Mexico to see Villa after the Columbus raid, and showed him the forged Villa letter accrediting Thayer as his agent. Thayer also claimed that Villa had not been in Columbus during the raid.[56] Cobb referred to Thayer as "the notorious ammunition smuggler." From time to time, Agent Stone chatted with Thayer, sometimes eliciting interesting information about arms deals from him.[57] Fortunately, Thayer left for Los Angeles to participate in what he described as a "big deal" and thus became some other Bureau agent's problem, at least temporarily.

Hipólito Villa requested permission to make a trip to El Paso because the Customs Service was suing him to retain confiscated diamonds that Pancho Villa's wife had allegedly brought into the country illegally. According to Clifford C. Perkins, an immigration inspector who knew Pancho and Luz Corral de Villa personally, "she loved the diamonds Villa gave her and wore lots of them." Perkins recalled that while

Pancho Villa still controlled Juárez, for reasons of safety he sent his wife in a new chauffeur-driven Hudson automobile to El Paso every evening to sleep in a house he rented for her at 610 North Oregon Street. Perkins learned that an El Paso city detective intended to detain Luz and "relieve her of the diamond rings and earrings she usually wore, plus the large sum of money it was her habit to carry," figuring that Villa would be unable to do anything about it. Perkins telephoned Villa's headquarters and warned of the plot. That evening when Luz crossed into El Paso two city detectives indeed stopped her auto and took her to the police station. To Perkins's great satisfaction, they were furious to discover that Luz was wearing no diamonds and was carrying only small change in her purse.[58] When Villa lost control of Juárez, Luz had made her way safely to El Paso, diamonds and all.

The Bureau was not enthusiastic about Hipólito being that close to the border but at the same time did not want to interfere in his legitimate affairs. Agent Stone speculated that George Holmes would have Hipólito subpoenaed as a defense witness in the neutrality case pending against him.[59] State Department agent George Carothers stated that "there are three men whom I would suggest be locked up, [John J.] Hawes, Hipolito Villa and George Holmes. This would clear the atmosphere on the border considerably, and be an object lesson for others."[60] Nevertheless, the Bureau agent in charge in San Antonio recommended that Hipólito be allowed to make the trip to protect his property rights since he had agreed to report to the El Paso Bureau office as often as required, return immediately when his business was concluded, and refrain from any revolutionary activities. Although Hipólito's own attorney said that his client's presence wasn't necessary, the Bureau decided to allow Hipólito to make the trip. But a female operative borrowed from Military Intelligence, a Mrs. Gray, shadowed him on the train. Hipólito was given permission to stay in El Paso for eight days; he had to report to the Bureau upon arrival and daily thereafter and was closely watched while in El Paso.[61]

Predictably, as soon as Hipólito reached El Paso he "was soon conspiring with his old criminal associates of the Villa regime, particularly George Holmes."[62] Informant "Mes" assigned to cover Hipólito reported that Hipólito with four others, including Carlos Jáuregui and Teodoro Kyriacopulos and probably Roy Martin, departed unexpectedly and very suddenly from the Hotel Linden where Hipólito was staying, in a big Packard limousine without a license plate. The following morning George Holmes suddenly drove up to the hotel and drove off with Hipólito and two other men. The informant, lacking an automobile, was unable to follow. The Bureau later learned that the party had driven to Holmes's ranch before returning to the hotel. In a belated effort to level the playing field, the Bureau prohibited Hipólito from using an automobile, or even from riding in a streetcar.[63] An exasperated Agent Stone had Hipólito brought to his office and read him the riot act, warning that any more shenanigans would result in Hipólito's arrest. Hipólito promised to be good, confining himself to seeing his lawyer and walking to the movies at night.[64] But what Hipólito really had to fear was not the Bureau but the *carrancistas.*

One Bruno Seibel, who worked for the local military intelligence office as a translator and investigator on pro-German matters, was loaned to the Bureau to assist Informant "Mes" in covering the movements and activities of Hipólito Villa. Siebel reported that he had been approached by Carranza agent Henry Gray with a proposition to divide $3,000 with him if Seibel would arrange for Gray and some other Carranza agents to kidnap Hipólito and smuggle him into Juárez. The U.S. attorney advised that there was no federal statute under which the kidnappers could be prosecuted, but he suggested that Siebel accept Gray's offer so that the military could arrest the Carranza agents in the act of crossing the Rio Grande with their captive. Agent Stone came up with a plan whereby as soon as Gray handed Siebel his share of the money, soldiers would seize Gray and rescue Hipólito.[65] Informant Seibel had several more meetings with Gray, who raised the price on Hipólito's head to $7,500. Stone's superior approved of Stone's idea, but the chief of the Bureau, while commending Stone's initiative, squelched the plan "as there is too much danger of a flare back."[66] In the event, it didn't matter because Gray failed to appear for scheduled meetings with Seibel and the matter came to an end. Informant "Mes" was of the opinion that the whole affair had been a ploy of Gray's.[67]

Stone's superior suggested he tell Hipólito that unless he had further legitimate business in El Paso he should return to San Antonio forthwith.[68] Since Hipólito's business was finished, the judge having ruled in his favor in the jewel case, Agent Stone had Hipólito's hotel room searched, called him into his office, told him he must leave, had a Bureau agent accompany him to purchase his train ticket and see him off for San Antonio. Mrs. Gray shadowed him on the return trip.[69]

Immigration authorities in San Antonio informed Hipólito that he would have to leave the U.S. immediately and remain away until World War I ended or else he would be deported to Mexico. He received permission to go to Cuba and to stay in San Antonio for a few days to wind up his affairs.[70] As matters developed, in the end Hipólito was permitted to remain in San Antonio provided he reported daily to the Bureau and listed the persons who visited him.

Hipólito had difficulties with the El Paso attorney who had successfully defended him in the jewel case; he had agreed to pay $1,500, but now the lawyer was demanding $4,000 as his fee.[71] Hipólito didn't have that kind of money, so he borrowed $4,000 from the El Paso businessman Haymon Krupp. Krupp explained that Hipólito owed him $60,000 for merchandise delivered to the Villa commercial agency in Juárez when Hipólito was running that operation, and in the forlorn hope of someday receiving some of this money he had loaned Hipólito the $4,000 to keep on his good side.[72] Hipólito received permission to return to El Paso for "a reasonable amount of time" to resolve the matter, and he received strict instructions not to engage in revolutionary activity. But as we have seen, Hipólito's real reason for returning to El Paso was to assist George Holmes in retrieving thousands of dollars worth of silver bullion and gold.

Hipólito left San Antonio on May 22 by train. Traveling on the next train was John J. Hawes, "confidential advisor" to Hipólito. Since Hipólito had neglected to inform the Bureau about Hawes, when they reached El Paso Hipólito was interrogated, and Hawes's person, baggage, and steamer trunk were examined, over the strenuous protests of Hawes and his attorney, Volney Howard.[73] Hipólito gained possession of some of the disputed jewelry, which he valued at $25,000, but his lawyers kept $4,000 worth as their fee. And Mrs. Luz Corral de Villa arrived to assist Hipólito in an unsuccessful attempt to recover her automobile, which Pancho Villa's erstwhile friend Teodoro Kyriacopulos had seized in default of a debt and refused to relinquish to Hipólito.[74] Mrs. Villa and Hipólito left for San Antonio on June 7, and the Bureau placed them under surveillance upon their arrival.[75] (Before leaving El Paso Hipólito had demonstrated his patriotism by purchasing a Liberty Bond.)[76] It was rumored that Pancho Villa had severed connections with Hipólito and Hawes, presumably on the grounds that they were incompetent, and that Miguel Díaz Lombardo, who had served as Villa's foreign minister, was now his authorized agent in the United States.[77]

Back in San Antonio, "Matias Garcia, ex-Villista and at present posing as a preacher, is staying at Hipolito Villa's and taking care of the family during Villa's absence."[78] Also awaiting Hipólito's return at his residence was Gustavo Tatematsu, the former Villa servant and Bureau informant, who was once again Hipólito's employee. When the San Antonio office learned of this, Tatematsu was called in for questioning about *villista* activities and also to explain his presence in Hipólito's house. "He refused to make any statement regarding the actions of the Villa faction, claiming that there was nothing of importance taking place in their circles. He also claimed that his object in being in San Antonio was to secure money from Villa in order to start a produce business." These answers sounding quite fishy, the Bureau turned Tatematsu over to the Immigration Service for deportation proceedings. Tatematsu had been permitted to leave El Paso on a "trip which he stated would be solely for business purposes . . . [but] our information shows Tatematsu misinformed us regarding purpose [of] his departure from El Paso."[79]

While the Bureau in El Paso had been focusing on Hipólito Villa, other persons of interest had been busy. Frank Thayer, "who has the reputation on the border of being a smuggler, is in San Antonio, living on Camden Street. Claims to [be] selling curios to the soldiers. Employee suspects that he may be selling something else besides curios."[80] Todd McClammy, by contrast, was still operating in west Texas. He was sighted, along with George Holmes, in the small town of Valentine making cattle deals with the notorious bandit Chico Cano, who was now, temporarily as it turned out, a *villista*. The middleman between them and Cano was Dawson D. Kilpatrick of Valentine. McClammy, with the help of Kilpatrick, smuggled across a herd of cattle that Cano had assembled near the riverside hamlet of Candelaria. McClammy's pattern was to trade ammunition for Mexican cattle.[81]

Cano was operating in the vicinity of Ojinaga, along with José Inés Salazar, a fellow *villista*. Salazar allowed his men to rape some young girls near Candelaria. Cano wanted to punish the miscreants, but Salazar refused, whereupon Cano ran Salazar out of camp with only a handful of followers, most of his men having opted to join Cano.[82] This was quite a comedown from Salazar's glory days as a prominent Red Flag general back in 1912. What must have infuriated Salazar even more was the fact that Chico Cano captured the town of Ojinaga on the morning of May 30, 1917, giving Pancho Villa a desperately needed port of entry. The Bureau recommended closing commercial traffic through Presidio in order to deprive Villa of this advantage. The port of entry was indeed closed, and the disgruntled *villistas* withdrew the following night.[83]

A major figure in border revolutionary intrigue passed from the scene in July. General José Inés Salazar, whose fortunes had declined to the point that he was nothing more than a common bandit, had been raiding the Nogales ranch, headquarters of the Palomas Land and Cattle Company's extensive holdings across the border from Columbus. Tom Kingsbery, general foreman of the company, received word that Salazar and his followers—reduced to a grand total of three men—planned to capture him for ransom or perhaps even kill him. Kingsbery took precautions. When Salazar's three men rode up singly at intervals on July 26, Kingsbery's vaqueros, stationed strategically around the ranch house, shot them down without warning and dragged the bodies off. When Salazar himself arrived at 4 p.m. he expected his men to be in control and confidently approached the building. He dismounted, entered, and chatted for nearly an hour with Kingsbery, who assured a puzzled Salazar that none of his men had been there. They strolled out of the house, Kingsbery keeping a prudent distance from Salazar. One of Kingsbery's men, stationed in the house, took a shot at Salazar but missed. Another vaquero, posted by a water tank, didn't; Salazar "grabbed himself and bellowed like a calf." Kingsbery sprinted into the house. The badly wounded Salazar pulled his pistol and fired three wild shots toward the house, whereupon the man at the tank fired again. Salazar fell. The sniper shot him again, then approached and shot him in the head just to make absolutely sure he was dead. Salazar and his men, incidentally, were armed with U.S. government rifles and pistols presumably obtained from American deserters.

Kingsbery hurried to El Paso to report Salazar's demise confidentially, because he feared being killed by Salazar's friends.[84] Thus ended the checkered career of General José Inés Salazar, who had been a *magonista*, a *maderista*, a *magonista* again, a *vazquista*, an *orozquista*, a *vazquista* again, a *huertista*, a *carrancista*, a *legalista*, and a *villista* as well as self-employed. He differed in degree but not in kind from a lot of other professional revolutionists.

An unrelated but remarkable incident occurred in August. Assistant U.S. attorney R. E. Crawford informed Agent Jones that a client of the prominent local attorney Dan M. Jackson was the victim of an extortion attempt. The client, Mrs. Leona Alderson, was a well-known madam who had operated several elegant brothels over the years. She claimed that a man purporting to be a Department of Justice official had called at her house, announced that he had the evidence to convict her of a white slave offense, showed her certain telegrams as proof, and demanded $200, for which he would not only keep quiet but would permit her to ignore the law banning prostitution within five miles of a military camp or post. The shaken madam agreed to pay him the following day. In her professional career she'd encountered more than one lawman on the take, but never a crooked federal officer. She informed her attorney, who informed U.S. attorney R. H. Crawford, who called the local Bureau office and requested an investigation.

Agent Gus Jones handled the case. He interviewed Alderson at length and carefully wrote down the serial numbers of the $200 to be used in the payoff. The next day Jones and a deputy U.S. marshal hid themselves in Alderson's home to observe the transaction. To Jones's horror, when the extortioner entered the room, he proved to be none other than his own superior, agent in charge Edward Stone, who had very capably headed the El Paso office for the past eighteen months. Jones and the deputy marshal sprang from their cover and seized Stone, taking from him the marked money. Stone could only shriek "I am ruined" before he collapsed in hysterics. When he was able to speak, Stone confessed, explaining that grave financial difficulties stemming from illness in his family had caused him to succumb to temptation.

Not surprisingly, Stone's arrest on August 6 caused considerable consternation. Agent Jones was devastated: "I will state that in all my experiences as an officer I have never conducted an examination or performed a duty that was more painful to me." Crawford interviewed Stone and even wept when Stone again broke down. It was decided to arraign Stone before the U.S. commissioner but to do it behind locked doors. Stone was released on a $2,500 bond, which attorney Tom Lea posted. The Stone affair was so serious that the division agent in charge, Robert Barnes, rushed from San Antonio to take personal charge, and he suggested that Chief Bruce Bielaski also go there immediately. Although Agent Jones had sworn Mrs. Alderson to secrecy, the press got wind of the Stone scandal and promptly published an account of it, with Alderson's name changed.[85]

The sympathy that Stone's colleagues had for their disgraced comrade quickly evaporated. Once Stone recovered from the initial shock of his predicament he desperately lashed out. Stone got himself a lawyer, one W. W. Bridges, claimed he had been framed, and blamed Jones and Crawford for his troubles. The Bureau not only fired Stone but urged that he be prosecuted.[86] Stone had his case continued several times but on April 10, 1918, he pleaded guilty to accepting a bribe and was sentenced to a year and a day in the federal penitentiary at Leavenworth, plus a $100 fine. He began serving his time on April 20, 1918, but was paroled on October 17, 1918, and thereafter conducted himself in a law-abiding manner. The U.S. attorney general recommended that he be granted a pardon to restore his civil rights. On February 22, 1919, the pardon was issued to Stone, the second Bureau agent to meet his downfall in El Paso.[87]

The upshot of the Stone affair was that Gus Jones became the agent in charge of the El Paso office.[88] This was a positive development, for Jones was an excellent operative and quite capable of contending with Jesús María Arriola, Carranza's intelligence chief.[89] Arriola operated quite openly, signing himself "El Jefe del S. S. Mexicano" or "El J. del S. S. M. en los E. U. de A." He used letterhead reading:

> Servicio Secreto Mexicano
> Oficina Central
> Commercial National Bank Bldg.
> Room 315—El Paso, Texas[90]

Arriola complained about the lack of Bureau agents on the border and advocated the creation of a special task force to cooperate with the Mexican Intelligence Service in combating anti-Carranza elements. It has been stated that "After entering World War I, the United States government did in fact significantly increase the number of agents along the border, but suspicion toward carrancistas persisted and cooperation did not appreciably improve."[91] The fact that President Carranza's policy during the world war was one of pro-German neutrality may explain the Bureau's absence of warm comradely feeling toward their *carrancista* counterparts.

The chief of the Mexican Secret Service also faced "suspicion, hostility, and resistance to his authority from within the Constitutionalist ranks."[92] Arriola's problems lay not so much with the Bureau as with inspector of consulates Andrés García, who bitterly resented Arriola's position as head of Mexican intelligence. García headed the consuls' opposition to Arriola, for they naturally resisted loss of control over their own secret agents. For instance, Consul Eduardo Soriano Bravo in El Paso ran four secret agents (one special agent, at $100 a month, two first-class agents, at $75 a month each, and one second-class agent, at $60 a month).[93] In February, the consul had informed the foreign secretary that for the last eight months, thanks to García, there was established in El Paso a system of strict surveillance of revolutionists and resident *villistas* and listed the most important successes.[94] On June 9, 1917, Arriola ordered the consul to dismiss one first-class agent and one second-class agent, because he had learned that they frequently performed routine administrative duties, or turned in false reports, or performed no work at all, but their salaries were charged to the secret service appropriation, which amounted to $455 a month (or $5,460 annually) for El Paso alone.[95] Soriano Bravo protested to the Foreign Office, which allowed him to continue employing all four operatives.[96]

García had a particular grudge against Arriola, suspecting him of having blown the cover of García's best agent, General Canuto Reyes Vázquez, who used the code name "Equis" ("X"). The general had been a *villista* but had helped to deliver Ciudad Juárez to the Carranza faction in December 1915. He nevertheless maintained his *villista* credentials and penetrated the *villista* junta of General Macrino Martínez in El Paso, reporting on, among others, George Holmes, whose ranch was always a hotbed of *villista* activity.[97] In January 1917, "Equis" had acquired, for $50 from Darío Silva, a prominent member of the junta, the letter in which Charles Hunt had offered Villa assistance in his struggle against Carranza if Villa agreed to protect American property in Chihuahua.[98] García engaged in a vicious campaign to remove Arriola, questioning his loyalty to the regime, emphasizing that he had been a spy for Porfirio Díaz and Victoriano Huerta, and accusing him of appointing unworthy agents.[99] The turning point in his campaign came when Carranza named García inspector general of consulates, a position he held until he resigned on January 9, 1920.

García ultimately succeeded in having President Carranza order Arriola's dismissal as chief.[100] The Bureau acquired two telegrams referring to Arriola. The first, on August 27, was from the Mexican foreign secretary to Arriola: "Do not give any more orders at the Consulate and leave at once for Mexico City." The second, on August 29, was from García, in Los Angeles, to Guillermo Seguín, consul general in El Paso: "President Carranza advises me 'The Sub-Secretary of the Exterior has given orders for the retirement of Arriola.' Do not pay him salary September." Arriola was officially notified of his dismissal on September 7, 1917.[101] Agent Jones, for one, was delighted to see Arriola go: "It has for some time past been suspecting [*sic*] that he is engaged in matters that were not exactly for the good of this government. It is with sincere satisfaction that we note his severance of relations with the Mexican Government."[102]

These telegrams referring to Arriola were but a small part of the steady stream of decrypted and translated Mexican government coded telegrams that the Bureau was acquiring. Some of this material came from the military censor and from Zach Cobb, but most was produced by the Bureau's superb cryptanalyst Victor Weiskopf, who had owned a store in Monterrey and had lived in Mexico City. He broke and translated Mexican ciphers on a routine basis, and he had recently been transferred from Presidio to El Paso. After his assignment in El Paso he went to Washington as a cryptanalyst for Military Intelligence, although he remained on the Justice Department payroll.[103] And the army in the Big Bend obtained another *villista* cipher, delivering a copy to the Bureau.[104]

Players in the arena of revolutionary intrigue came and went, and one who yearned to get back in the game was Hipólito Villa. He applied at the Bureau's San Antonio office for permission to make yet another trip to El Paso, ostensibly in order to take a young relative to school there. The agent in charge did not see any necessity for such a trip, and further, Hipólito made his request just when his close associate John J. Hawes again appeared on the scene. This was viewed as more than coincidental.[105] Hipólito's request was denied, and Hawes proceeded on to El Paso without him. According to Military Intelligence, Hawes "has maintained his reputation as a 'four-flusher,'" his object being to make contact with Pancho Villa with an eye to obtaining some of the bullion Villa had cached.[106] The San Antonio office of the Bureau kept Hawes under surveillance.[107] The Bureau also employed a female special informant, Hazel Cordill, to keep an eye on George Carothers, the State Department agent who was close to Pancho Villa.[108] Interagency rivalry was alive and well.

Hipólito was determined to escape his exile in San Antonio. His brother Pancho sent him instructions on how to make his way to Presidio, where *villistas* would escort him across the Rio Grande and conduct him to Pancho Villa's headquarters.[109] The Bureau picked up rumors that Hipólito planned to make a move but could learn nothing definite.[110] As of October 29, Hipólito was still dutifully reporting daily on his visitors. But by November 4 he had disappeared, and it was several days before an embarrassed Bureau realized that he was missing.[111] Hipólito surfaced by November 9, near Ojinaga, having made contact with his brother Pancho, whose forces were maneuvering to seize that port of entry again.[112] The Bureau at the time had no agent in the Big Bend and hurriedly rushed one there.

In an effort to determine how Hipólito had managed to disappear and cross into Mexico, Agent Jones and Colonel H. O. Williard, of the District Intelligence Office, dispatched a confidential Mexican informant who was a close friend of George Holmes to the latter's ranch to spend the night with Holmes. During a convivial evening Holmes revealed that Hipólito had slipped out of San Antonio by rail on November 1 dressed as a peon. He left the train in Sierra Blanca, where an automobile was waiting to transport him to Holmes's ranch. Hipólito was then driven at night in Holmes's auto to a spot near Fort Hancock, frequently used by Villa's partisans, where he crossed the Rio Grande on November 3 or 4 and was met by *villista* colonel Porfirio Ornelas and a ten-man bodyguard. The party made its way to the vicinity of Ojinaga and Pancho Villa's headquarters. The confidential informant later spoke with Manuel González Sr., "a well-known and influential Villista sympathizer of El Paso" (whose son Manuel was Hipólito Villa's private secretary). González told the informant that a messenger from Villa's camp had just told him he had personally talked with Hipólito.[113]

Pancho Villa launched his expected assault against Ojinaga on November 14. The next day the demoralized *carrancista* garrison stampeded across the river to Presidio and were interned by the U.S. Army and later repatriated through El Paso at the Mexican government's expense.[114] Agent Jones commented sarcastically in a November 23 report: "A special train arrived in El Paso this morning, via the G. H. & S. A. Ry, conveying the heroes of Ojinaga. All seemed to be intact, which bears out their claim of having executed a very successful retreat to United States territory (according to established precedent). This train was immediately switched to the Santa Fe tracks, and taken across the River to Juarez, where the battle scarred (?) veterans, including women, children, new-born babes and dogs, were detrained."[115]

Villa's capture of Ojinaga, while demonstrating once again that the Carranza military was mediocre at best, did the Mexican chieftain little good. His objective was to seize a desperately needed port of entry, but the United States once again closed the port of Presidio. After holding Ojinaga for three days, Villa withdrew. The *carrancistas* reoccupied the town on December 12, claiming a major triumph.[116] Villa had hoped to cross a quantity of buried bullion into the United States to finance his operations, but this project went awry. A *villista* sympathizer, Doctor O. L. Orr, who had practiced in Presidio for years, went to El Paso to make arrangements for smuggling at least $100,000 worth of bullion in several shipments and marketing it in El Paso in small lots. However, the Bureau shadowed him all the way to El Paso and kept him under close surveillance there. Orr lost his nerve, returned to Presidio, and divulged the whole project, as well as the code the local *villistas* used, to the army.[117] Thereafter the good doctor, whom the *villistas* used to carry messages between Presidio and Ojinaga, took everything to the local Bureau agent, who opened and read the messages. Orr also functioned as a Bureau informant.[118]

One who never lost his nerve was George Holmes. He left El Paso for Presidio with the avowed intention of crossing into Mexico to see his good friend Pancho Villa. Agent Jones was convinced that Holmes was going in order to arrange for handling smuggled bullion: "Holmes is closer to Villa than any other American. Keep him under constant surveillance; is a bad one." Jones urged that Holmes be prevented at all costs from crossing and suggested that recently enacted passport regulations could be used to accomplish this; he could be denied entry into Mexico unless he had an American passport. "He is an unscrupulous American renegade, and can be handled as such." When Holmes and Manuel González, Hipólito's private secretary, arrived in Presidio on November 17, they were promptly detained by the authorities. Furthermore, Todd McClammy and John J. Hawes were en route. The presence of Holmes, McClammy, and Hawes together in the same town could only mean trouble. Agent Jones telegraphed: "Referring Tod [*sic*] McClammy, he is of [the] same type as Holmes, and should be kept [under] close surveillance. J. J. Hawes was formerly publicity agent for [the Villa] bandits and lives in New York. Should be watched, altho' will not get ten feet from coattails of Holmes or McClammy." But Jones later advised: "Reference my last message regarding Holmes: after conference with Intelligence Officer here, it is decided not to interfere with his crossing into Mexico, but keep close watch on him, as it is desired [to] catch him red-handed with stolen bullion he is arranging [to] take care of for Villa." Ultimately, however, it was decided not to risk letting Holmes enter Mexico.

In hopes of gathering intelligence, Agent Jones dispatched a spy. One Elías Ochoa, a former captain in Villa's army, had been a member of the filibustering party that Holmes had organized the previous spring and had been arrested along with Holmes and the other *villistas*. But Holmes had failed to post bond for Ochoa, who had understandably grown resentful as he wasted away in the El Paso county jail. The Bureau finally secured his release, and Ochoa gave a complete statement regarding his participation in the expedition. Since his release Ochoa had also been furnishing information to a customs inspector in Fabens. The inspector arranged a meeting between himself, Ochoa, and Agent Jones, a meeting at which Ochoa agreed to cross the Rio Grande near Fort Hancock and rejoin Villa's forces. He was confident of resuming his rank of captain, for he was still in good standing with Villa. Ochoa would learn all he could about Villa's movements and intentions and then bring the information back. He would either get himself assigned as one of the many couriers Villa used to communicate with his partisans on the American side of the Rio Grande, or failing that he would simply desert. Ochoa was willing to undertake this hazardous mission without pay, in gratitude for the American authorities having treated him more decently than his own people. Jones advanced him $5, "as he had practically no money at all, and leaves a wife and children here . . . and if anything should happen to Ochoa in the way of battle, murder or sudden death, I would still consider the five dollars well invested, in view of the prospect we have of valuable information."[119]

J. D. Reeder, the superintendent of customs inspectors, escorted Ochoa downriver to Lajitas, Texas, on November 26, 1917, and saw him safely across the Rio Grande.[120] Ochoa passed himself off as a cattle dealer. When he reached the town of Valentine he entered the Villalva and Támez store and was surprised to see that the Villalva of Villalva and Támez was Ramón Villalva, "an old time Villista colonel."

When Ochoa expressed his own undying *villista* allegiance, Villalva introduced him to his partner, who turned out to be none other than Mariano Támez, the former Carranza colonel who had rebelled in Juárez in 1916 and had joined Pancho Villa, remaining with him until recently. According to Ochoa, the store was merely a blind, being nothing more than a meeting place for *villistas*. He was introduced there to several who claimed to be officers in Villa's forces. Ochoa was even invited to spend the night at Villalva and Támez's house, for they had "the utmost confidence in him, knowing his former connections with the Villistas." Ochoa was passed along a line of Villa sympathizers, including Dawson D. Kilpatrick of Candelaria, who told Ochoa "that he was more Villista than Villa himself" and offered to sell him arms and ammunition. Ochoa returned to El Paso and gave the Bureau information, sometimes on a daily basis, identifying various *villistas* operating in the city under cover. By 1918, Jones did not need Ochoa's services regularly but paid for any information provided, Jones deciding the value of such information. At their last transaction Jones paid him $3, stating that this amount, plus the money already paid to Ochoa, "squares matters with him as far as this office is concerned."[121]

Thwarted in Presidio, the imperturbable George Holmes returned to El Paso and calmly strolled into the Bureau office to complain about being prevented from visiting his friend Pancho Villa. Holmes declared that if he were accorded the privilege of crossing the Rio Grande he would guarantee to return with a signed statement from Villa setting forth his plans, intentions, desires, ambitions, and so on. Agent Jones suavely assured Holmes that the government had no intention of interfering with his pursuit of legitimate business, but "in view of the past career of his friend Pancho Villa, it was more than likely that any negotiations opened with him might become of interest to this Government, and any one having 'business' transactions with Villa was almost certain to be regarded with embarrassing suspicion by the authorities on this side; therefore, in a purely friendly spirit, and having Mr. Holmes' best interests at heart, this office felt compelled to discourage any friendly overture on his part toward his 'compadre' Pancho, at this juncture."[122] Jones's sarcasm had little effect, for Holmes was soon engaged once again in his ammunition-smuggling endeavors, this time in conjunction with Dawson Kilpatrick. The Mexican consul's agents reported that Holmes was moving munitions to the vicinity of Ojinaga, undeterred by the fact that Carranza forces had reoccupied that town on December 12.[123] An informant for Military Intelligence reported that while in the vicinity of Ojinaga Villa had received about 60,000 rounds of ammunition.[124]

Another El Pasoan who continued to profit from the revolution was Haymon Krupp. His firm, Haymon Krupp and Company, had a net worth on December 31, 1916, of about $600,000.[125] He had profited handsomely by supplying Villa during the zenith of that leader's career. Now in the fall of 1917, Krupp sold to the U.S.

government twelve thousand quilts manufactured in El Paso. He paid $15 a dozen and charged the government $36. Although this particular transaction was perfectly legal, Military Intelligence took a dim view of Krupp: "This firm of Haymon Krupp & Co. have been doing all kinds of stunts in El Paso for the past four years. Mixed up in many ammunition deals, selling guns, shoes, clothing, etc. to the various factions in Mexico. Have been 'sailing close to the wind' (meaning the law) in all these transactions, but because of trickery have been able to evade any actual entanglements. It is known, however, that they have cleaned up a million or more dollars out of the Mexican troubles. Are they going to continue such work in mulcting the U.S.?"[126]

Speaking of mulcting a government, there was a lot of that going on among the Mexican military. General Francisco Murguía, the commander in Chihuahua, bitterly blamed his predecessor, General Treviño, for the mess that the state's military and civil affairs were in.[127] Yet Murguía seemed as incapable of crushing Pancho Villa as had Treviño. An informant of Military Intelligence provided one explanation:

> During conversation with one of the army officials this afternoon in Juarez I asked why it was the forces did not get Villa and his bunches of bandits out of their way, having so many men, money to pay them, and ammunition as well. The reply was that if the taking of Villa was left with the minor officials and the files, Villa would not last a month, but the pursuit of Villa was in the hands of the Jefes, who had the authority to continue the chase or not, just as they pleased. He said, however, that these Jefes were not anxious to get Villa for the reason that while in the field Villa was a gold mine to them. Whenever funds ran low, they called for more money to continue the work of extermination, and with Villa out of the way there would be no reasons for special appropriations for the purpose of cleaning up the country.[128]

Graft was by no means confined to the Carranza military. "Wholesale grafting," Military Intelligence reported, "has been discovered in connection with Mexican consular invoices at the Mexican Consulate [in El Paso] and Guillermo Seguin is expected to be removed. He will be replaced by Andres Garcia, now acting as Consul General of Mexico."[129]

There were even allegations of collusion between General Murguía and Pancho Villa. In September, a Military Intelligence report stated that: "About two weeks ago [General Francisco] Murguia wrote to Villa, calling the latter a patriot, and saying he did not want to pursue Villa, as the country might need his services at any time now. At the same time he told the bandit leader that he would be glad to furnish him with provisions if his supply ran low, although Murguia could not, of course, do this openly."[130]

It's not known whether this was true or not, but General Francisco Murguía's brother, General José Murguía, who commanded in Juárez, made preparations against a *villista* attack. His forces were so few, however, that there was little he could do. On the night of November 14, he stationed two outposts three miles east and southeast of Juárez, each consisting of twenty-five men and a machine gun. Only about 150 soldiers remained in Juárez itself. General Murguía spent that night, and the succeeding one, in the saddle, riding from place to place to see that all was well. The advance guard of the *villistas* was reported on the sixteenth as being very near Juárez.[131] All saloons in the town were closed until further notice, to keep the garrison sober.[132] On November 30, General Murguía ordered all horses confiscated as of December 1. Horse owners desperately tried to hide them.[133] Further evidence of the precarious conditions was that although passenger trains traveled to and from Juárez, Murguía experienced great difficulty in getting the guards to board them. Trains often sat in the station for hours until the Juárez military authorities finally compelled the fearful soldiers to take their stations on the trains.[134]

The security of Ciudad Juárez was obviously of great concern to the *carrancistas*, and on occasion their efforts extended into El Paso. In December, a Cuban midwife living in El Paso was kidnapped by Juárez policemen and spirited across the river. It developed that she had been friendly with some prominent *villistas* in El Paso and was charged with being a Villa spy. From the Juárez jail she managed to get word of her predicament to her husband in El Paso, with the result that American authorities exerted intense diplomatic pressure on her behalf and finally secured her release. She and her husband immediately left for New Orleans.[135]

The security of Ciudad Juárez concerned not only the Carranza authorities but by extension the officials and residents of El Paso. Villa's shadow still loomed large over the border.

CHAPTER 18

World War, 1918

During 1918, a major source of concern for the American authorities continued to be German espionage. On March 14, a Swiss governess, Catherine Schmid, was arrested and charged with attempting to obtain military information from American soldiers. Specifically, she was charged with having entered Fort Bliss to chat up soldiers and learn the order of battle, types of equipment and weaponry used, and if possible obtain photographs of fortifications, the information being sought for use by the imperial German government. These were serious charges, but an indication that the government's case was shaky came when the U.S. attorney had her bond reduced from $10,000 to $1,500, which the Swiss legation guaranteed. What ensued was anticlimax—on December 10, 1918, on the U.S. attorney's motion, the court dismissed the case.[1]

Schmid fared considerably better than did one Claus Freese, a German subject who tried to sell to the German consul in Juárez the plans for a gun that would allegedly shoot for 105 miles. The hapless Freese was tried and sentenced to five years in a federal penitentiary.[2] Even so, Freese fared better than did a certain Ed Peterson, or Petersen. On the night of August 17, he tried to cross the border and was apprehended by three customs inspectors. They suspected he was a German, although he claimed to be Norwegian. As they were taking him to the customs house for interrogation he broke away and dashed into the Rio Grande, trying to escape to Mexico. This proved to be a serious error in judgment on his part, for the customs inspectors shot him dead when he was halfway across.[3] The vast majority of the wartime investigations that Gus Jones and his men conducted dealt with matters such as draft dodgers, propaganda, and disloyal utterances.[4]

Whereas German espionage wasn't a major problem, the attitude of the *carrancistas* was. Fortunately, there did not occur a pitched battle between the U.S. Army and the Carranza troops in El Paso such as happened in Nogales, Arizona, on August 27, 1918.[5] Nevertheless, in El Paso and vicinity a repeated cause of tension had to do with that time-honored occupation, smuggling. Not only was ammunition being smuggled; because of the wartime embargo on the export of foodstuffs to Mexico, commodities such as lard and sugar were being smuggled too, and for a handsome price.

What really irked American authorities, though, was that elements of the Carranza military were in league with the smugglers. A serious incident occurred on the night of January 25, when an American patrol near the Santa Fe Street bridge discovered a Mexican crossing the river with a sack of sugar. They ordered him to halt, and when he failed to do so they opened fire. Immediately there was a fusillade from the Juárez bank of the Rio Grande. The Americans fired back, and for the next thirty minutes there was a brisk firefight, with some three hundred shots being exchanged.[6] Investigation revealed that regular Carranza troops had provided covering fire for the smugglers. One American soldier was wounded, while the *carrancistas* had two killed and three wounded including a lieutenant, who later died. Agent Jones reported that "the soldiers receive a part of the commissions paid the smugglers, and are really finding this more remunerative than their pay as soldiers; I am informed that this is done not only with the sanction of their superior officers, but with their actual assistance." Corroborating this view was the commander of customs guards in Juárez, who resigned and moved to Nogales, Sonora, because "the Mexican guards and Mexican soldiers at Juarez were smuggling every night, whiskey and other things, and that hardly a night passed that some of his men did not snipe at American soldiers. He said further, that there is going to be some awful trouble there very soon, for which reason he resigned and came home."[7] On April 13, Major Robert Barnes, who had been the Bureau's agent in charge in San Antonio and was now the intelligence officer for the Southern Department of the army, reported to his superiors in Washington that "shootings across the border have been more frequent recently, in the vicinity of El Paso particularly. Mexicans in that vicinity are in [a] very ugly mood due to German propaganda carried on in Juarez."[8]

The night of February 25, two customs inspectors on a stakeout on the river by the smelter spotted five smugglers. The result was another firefight in which some two hundred rounds were exchanged between the inspectors and an estimated twenty-five to thirty Mexicans across the river. And on January 29, there was a skirmish near Ysleta between American soldiers and Mexicans covering smugglers crossing the river. A similar incident occurred on the night of February 5.[9] Then on March 24, an American patrol was fired on near Fabens by *carrancista* customs inspectors. The troopers, reinforced by another patrol, fired back, and in the ensuing clash five of the Mexicans were killed. They received a heroes' funeral in Juárez.[10] The ultimate irony was that an appreciable amount of the ammunition smuggled across the Rio Grande for the *carrancistas* ended up in the hands of the *villistas*. In desperation, Carranza troops, who hadn't received their miserable pay in months, sold cartridges to *villista* agents, often for just a few pesos, sometimes as cheaply as one peso for a hundred rounds.[11] They may later have questioned the wisdom of this practice when the ammunition was fired back at them.

Not only were smugglers profiting; the Mexican Revolution was a bonanza for the legal profession in El Paso. We've seen, for example, that Tom Lea did quite well for himself representing—and associating himself with—conservative Mexican factions. More colorful, if less reputable, attorneys deeply involved in revolutionary matters were partners Harry C. Miller and Volney Howard, with offices in suite 612 in the Mills Building. They were a full-service law firm, not only representing *villistas* in legal matters, but also conspiring with their clients in smuggling schemes.[12]

Howard submitted a claim to the Bureau in January 1918 for articles confiscated from his client José Sedaño, a former *orozquista* but now a *villista* colonel who represented himself as a cattleman. The articles, consisting of field equipment, had been seized and Sedaño arrested in connection with George Holmes's filibustering expedition in May 1917. But since no indictment had been returned against Sedaño, he wanted his property back. At the Bureau's insistence, George Holmes, who was also Howard's client, submitted an affidavit disclaiming ownership of the property, which was duly returned to Sedaño.[13]

Howard's solicitude for Sedaño was such that he tried to use political influence to get Sedaño hired as a Bureau of Investigation confidential informant, which would have been a real joke. The attorney wrote to U.S. senator A. A. Jones of New Mexico making the suggestion. The senator forwarded the letter to the chief of the Bureau, Bruce Bielaski, who dryly replied that "Mr. Howard is well known to our representatives along the border and they will not hesitate to call on him for any assistance that they might consider him in a position to render."[14] Bielaski also sent a copy of Howard's letter to Leland Harrison, counselor at the State Department, with the comment that "I presume that Howard's reputation is well known to you."[15] When he received a copy of Howard's letter, Agent Jones exploded: "I want to say that I have carefully read the copy of Mr. Howard's letter, and desire to say that I consider same as unparalleled a piece of effrontery and as beautiful an exhibition of pure nerve, as it has ever been my privilege to peruse." Besides emphatically recommending that Sedaño not be hired under any circumstances, Jones stated that "I have reason to believe that the true motive behind his sudden anxiety to be of service to this Government is the fact that he knows where Villa has cached some of the bullion 'confiscated' (or in plain English—*stolen*) from various American companies in Mexico, and he is exceedingly eager to get over into Mexico and dig this up, then if possible, get it across into the U.S. No doubt Miller and Howard, his attorneys, are accessory in this plan, because Miller stated here, in El Paso, before two responsible men, one of them a Government employee, that Sedaño knew here this bullion was buried, and they meant to get it, 'sooner or later.'"[16]

Attorney Howard continued to advocate for himself as well as for Sedaño. He again wrote to Senator Jones asking his help in securing a passport to enter Mexico, which he urgently needed for business reasons. As for Sedaño, "I rather feel from past experiences and conferences that the attitude of the local Department of Justice will not be favorable to the matter I suggested. The only objection that I anticipate they will make is that he is a Villista which of course he freely admits. . . . I feel confident that he is guiltless of any wrong doing, and in view of the fact that in most of the federal prosecutions those criminals who turn state's or rather Government's evidence go free in consideration of their testimony and as we know that the Carranza Government is unfriendly to us and the revolutionists appear anxious to conciliate us, I personally think the local office is taking the wrong position."[17]

Agent Jones just had no use for Howard. Commenting on a report that a band of *villistas*, including three Americans, "and no doubt one of these men the shyster lawyer, Volney Howard," had been defeated by Carranza troops and several prisoners summarily hanged, he observed that "it is to be regretted that Mr. Howard was not a star performer in the . . . necktie party."[18]

Agent Jones didn't think much either of Volney Howard's equally slick law partner Harry Miller, formerly of Albuquerque, whom he also categorized as a shyster lawyer. Agents Jones and Albert S. Burleson interrogated a Mexican and an American whom the Texas Rangers had arrested at a hut on Córdova Island where four horses, four saddles, two boxes of rifle cartridges, a pair of field glasses, an automatic pistol, and suspicious letters were found. Significantly, the arrests occurred at the house of Abel Arroyo, the very same house where in May 1917, José Sedaño had been taken into custody by the army. The American, a certain J. Dean Gauldin, disclaimed any knowledge of the items found in his room and claimed that the papers "were given him by an unknown Mexican boy, who asked him to keep them until he 'came back.'" The Mexican who was arrested, one Anastacio Espinosa, said he lived in El Paso and worked for attorney Harry Miller and had come to the island to get some horses for Miller. In fact, the four horses seized belonged to Miller.

Despite prolonged questioning by Bureau agents, Gauldin stuck to his story: he was a twenty-two-year-old Dallasite, the son of a prominent physician, who had recently arrived in El Paso. He was an attorney by profession and "in looking up various law firms in El Paso, met Harry C. Miller; and after some conversation, was told by Miller that he believed they might make a mutually advantageous arrangement, as Miller had available office space." He had driven to Fabens with Miller and Miller's wife to look for a Mexican servant girl, and they had dropped him off at the hut where he was later arrested. He had no explanation as to why an unknown Mexican would hand him a mysterious package of papers.

The Bureau agents failed to get him to change his exceedingly improbable story. In fact, Agent Burleson was so frustrated that he wrote that "had it been permissible to resort to the methods of the Inquisition, the water cure or something of that sort, more information might have been obtained, but as it was, we were forced to accept the above with the comforting conviction that he was lying but the Bureau could not prove it."

What was particularly galling was that after questioning Gauldin exhaustively and learning exactly nothing, Agent Jones had Harry Miller come to the office for an interview, and although the attorney was questioned separately from Gauldin, his story was exactly the same as Gauldin's:

> In fact, it may be said that the stories of the three; Miller, Gauldin and Espinosa, dovetailed so neatly as to smell of pre-agreement in case of eventualities. Mr. Miller was very amiable and uncommunicative. He stoutly denied that Gauldin was attempting to cross into Mexico at all, much less on any mission for him, or that Gauldin had any particular connection with Anastacio Espinosa. Neither could he explain the letters and so on being in the possession of Gauldin. After considerable backing and filling he acknowledged the authorship of the letters, but stated most emphatically they were NOT written to his partner Volney Howard. Blandly insisted that Howard was not in Mexico at all; far from it—he was in fact at that time in Seattle, Washington. . . . When questioned as to who then was the addressee of the letters from him and the two unaddressed unsigned letters from someone's wife to her husband, Miller unblushingly stated they were to a client of his in Mexico, whose name he did not feel at liberty to divulge. He stated that his interest in Mexican affairs was purely altruistic. . . . When asked about Jose Sedano Mr. Miller declared that he was not in Mexico either; was, to the best of his knowledge and belief, "somewhere in California."

As for Espinosa, he was a known *villista.*

Agent Burleson further vented his frustration: "As stated, no real information could be obtained from any one of the three persons examined; and their reticence and the cock-and-bull story they did offer for our acceptance, tempted one to wish that the rack, the thumb-screw and the boot were still in vogue." He concluded: "It is believed that the real object of this projected expedition mentioned in the letters of Miller to 'someone in Mexico' and the reason for Howard's presence there (of which we are convinced) is that this law firm is trying to make some arrangement to bring out a quantity of bullion which Francisco Villa 'confiscated' and has hidden there. He, in person, or his supporters have made efforts in this direction before." While the Bureau might be morally certain that the trio was up to no good, there was no hard evidence against them. Gauldin and Espinosa were reluctantly released but were kept under observation.[19] Gauldin fit right in with the two lawyers; by 1919, he was described as "a crook, shyster lawyer, and partner of Harry C. Miller and G. Volney Howard."[20]

On May 24, the army in the Big Bend detained an unkempt and bedraggled trio traveling on foot: Volney Howard, José Sedaño, and José Sapién, "Villistas who crossed [the] river at Ruidosa, Texas" on their way back to El Paso. When questioned, "Mr. Howard stated that he was from El Paso, and was down in that section for the purpose of buying cattle; that 'Mr.' Sedano was his partner in this cattle acquiring enterprise, and that the other Mexican was their mozo, ('flunky'). Sedano stated that he was from El Paso, left there about a month ago, and had come down to Marfa with Mr. Howard to buy cattle. Howard gave as references in El Paso, Judge R. H. Crawford, Asst. U.S. Attorney, and Mr. Works [*sic*], Deputy U.S. marshal. It is undoubtedly most true that Mr. Howard is known to the above mentioned gentlemen, but in no way which would be cause for his giving them as references, were he not possessed of an amount of gaul [*sic*] which compels the reluctant admiration of all beholders."[21]

The army officer on the scene permitted Howard and Sedaño to continue their journey unmolested toward Valentine where they planned to catch the train but later had misgivings and asked the Texas Rangers to detain the trio. They did so on May 26 and delivered them to the military authorities in Marfa. Howard received permission to use the toilet alone; a small boy reported that he had seen the attorney "doing something" with a lot of papers. When a ranger rushed into the restroom he discovered that Howard had just burned a quantity of documents. Both Howard and Sedaño stoutly denied they had been in Mexico at all, Sedaño stating that Howard was his lawyer and would speak for him. The crafty Howard had also been speaking with Colonel George Langhorne, commanding the army in the Big Bend, and had told him in strictest confidence that he had indeed been in Mexico, and he also imparted some information of considerable military value. Howard was adept at hedging his bets.

The Bureau remained convinced that Howard and Sedaño had been to see Pancho Villa about bullion, but for lack of evidence they had to be released. Agent John Wren, who interrogated Howard, was understandably frustrated. Regarding Sedaño, he commented that "if Mr. Sedano could once be deported and delivered to the Carrancista authorities, it is believed that it would not be necessary to investigate him ever again and the file on him could be closed." The Bureau kept Sedaño under surveillance and planned to search his room at the Mesa Hotel.[22] As for Howard, once he returned to El Paso his law partner Harry Miller claimed that "he was in possession of information of inestimable value to the U.S. Government, but it was 'no use to try to talk to any Government employees in El Paso, and he was going to Washington with what he knew;' and he has left El Paso for the East."[23] Miller traveled to Washington, then to Philadelphia, from where he wired his partner Volney

Howard on June 6: "Tell Gauldin to disregard telegraphic request of 5th, and if money sent have it recalled; am en route New York arrange some means carrying out matters as arranged prior to my leaving, which were modified as stated in your letter. This imperative."[24] Miller was referring to a $700 loan he had taken out at the Border National Bank in El Paso, the guarantor of which was Fred J. Feldman, a local arms dealer. Feldman and Miller were suspected of smuggling ammunition to Villa.[25]

Miller's trip evidently had to do with Villa's bullion. Frank C. Jones, president of the El Paso Bank and Trust Company, informed the Bureau that Miller had called on him a month earlier asking if Jones could handle $3 million worth of bullion. Jones replied that he could if the bullion were brought into the United States legitimately; otherwise he wouldn't consider the proposition. Miller then stated that he had $3 million worth of Villa bullion in Mexico and was going to Washington to try to arrange with the authorities the crossing of the bullion. According to Jones, Miller was also going to assure the Wilson administration that Villa soon expected to control ports of entry along the border and that the United States could count on his full cooperation, "that he would deliver any and all Germans actively engaged in German espionage in Mexico near the border."[26]

In El Paso José Sedaño had a two-hour conversation with the assistant district intelligence officer, stating that he was Villa's representative and a general in the *villista* forces and producing a commission to that effect purportedly signed by Pancho Villa on May 14, 1918. Sedaño discoursed at length about the purity of Villa's actions and aims, stressing that the Mexican chieftain hoped for diplomatic recognition by President Wilson. Lastly, Sedaño gave the American officer his local address and offered his services in any capacity. When Agent Jones received a copy of this interview, he was furious. For starters, there was the sheer effrontery of Sedaño just being in the United States, since by his own admission he had entered illegally, and of him having the nerve to spout propaganda to an officer of the U.S. Army. And "his statement might possibly be somewhat impressive to one knowing nothing whatever of Mexican conditions, or the character of the leader and faction of which he is the self-proclaimed herald; but to those acquainted with these gentry it has the ring of the same old 'press agent' stuff which agents of every faction have handed out on this side of the River for the past five years, i.e. their own particular leader is the lily-white savior of his country, without fear and without reproach; they, and they only are disinterested patriots, while the opposing faction is everything that is evil, vile—criminals of the most abandoned character."

Jones mentioned that "Alonso Taylor, of Taylor Brothers, owners and proprietors of the Orndorff Hotel, El Paso and a general merchandise, feed and grain business and flour mill at Casas Grandes and Colonia Juarez, Chih., Mexico," had told him in confidence that Sedaño had recently tried to extort protection money from him, saying that Villa needed supplies and that a "contribution" of $300 in American money would be acceptable and relating at the same time the sad fate of those businessmen unwise enough to be unsympathetic to the Villa cause. Sedaño had similar conversations with E. P. Fuller, manager and part owner of the Santo Domingo Ranch in Chihuahua, and with the manager of the Erupción Mining Company in that state. Sedaño had brazenly called on Fuller at his office, 810 Mills Building, directly across the hall from the private office of the Bureau agent in charge, Gus Jones. These American businessmen, and others, were in an extremely difficult position, since anyone found to be contributing to the *villistas* was liable to have his property confiscated by the *carrancista* authorities.[27]

On October 20, 1918, Villa sent a form letter to the general managers of the American Smelting and Refining Company, the Mexico Northwestern Railroad, and the Potosí Mining Company informing them within the next ten days a representative of his would go to El Paso to discuss their operations in Chihuahua, "for they are not and can not be guaranteed by the so-called Government of Carranza and it is necessary that you have an understanding with me in this respect; otherwise you will have no right to make any claim for the damage suffered by your business during the coming year," and asking them to notify other businesses whose operations were currently suspended to do likewise.[28] Agent Jones reported that Villa had sent the letters by a courier, who for some reason was unable to complete his mission and handed them on to another party for delivery. "This party exhibited them to me; I photographed them and allowed the originals to be delivered to the addressees.... Arrangements have been made by me to cover the arrival of his agent."[29]

American companies might be caught between *carrancistas* and *villistas*, but Harry Miller had no qualms about doing business in Chihuahua. He proposed to Pancho Villa's representative in Washington, Miguel Díaz Lombardo, that a front man, César Fargas (who happened to be a confidential informant for Military Intelligence), build a tannery in the village of Villa Ahumada: "In this business I will be able to make considerable money without being known in it at all so the Carrancistas would not molest it, provided General Villa would consent to my having it." To Miller's delight, Pancho Villa gave him permission to build the tannery.[30]

Agent Jones not only had a visceral dislike of Sedaño but was concerned that his comings and goings with impunity would harm U.S. relations with the Carranza administration, which the United States recognized as the legitimate government of Mexico. In fact, Carranza consul Andrés García became aware of Sedaño's attempt to extort money from Alonso Taylor and had Taylor prepare an affidavit containing the details. García didn't mention this to Agent Jones, who considered García's actions "a willful failure to cooperate with this office in this matter."[31] And in discussing an incident in which two *villista* couriers who had entered Chihuahua through Columbus carrying "a quantity of papers" for Villa, including letters from persons in Santa Fe, had been killed by Carranza troops, Agent T. B. White learned that the documents had been turned over to Andrés García, and "Mr. Garcia will probably send them direct to the State Department at Washington, thru the Mexican Ambassador, as he appears reluctant to have any dealings with any local officials of the U.S. Government, and then complains of 'lack of cooperation' here."[32]

By late 1918, García had become somewhat more cooperative, but Agent Jones remained skeptical of the information he received from the consulate. On October 28, a secretary from the Mexican consulate called at the offices of the district intelligence officer and the Bureau, stating that several Mexicans, whose names he provided, were leaving El Paso that night for Alpine and that two additional Mexicans and George Holmes were leaving for Presidio, all with ammunition for Villa's forces. He "did not know what time the above named persons would leave, or from where, or when they would arrive at destination, but he presumed that they would leave by automobile." The army and customs inspectors in the Big Bend were immediately alerted. But Agent Jones noted on November 5 that "the information furnished to the Mexican Consulate was not entirely correct; because most of the persons mentioned are known to this office very well indeed, and as recently as the 3rd inst., the writer saw some of them here in El Paso."[33]

Concluding his scathing evaluation of Sedaño, a frustrated Jones stated that "in considering Mr. Sedano and his coming and goings, it should be borne in mind that he does not make a move except upon the advice of a firm of lawyers, attorneys at law, members of the Texas Bar, who are thoroughly familiar with U.S. Law and penalties imposed for its violation. Reference is, of course, made to Miller & Howard, and it would seem also as if there ought to be some means of discouraging these gentlemen in aiding and abetting Francisco Villa, even tho they do manage to keep 'Within the Law.'"[34]

Sedaño and his associates were nothing if not industrious. On June 15, 1918, Colonel Langhorne advised from Marfa that "a movement seems to be on foot to attempt to smuggle through this District arms, ammunition, horse shoes, horses, and perhaps men in violation of the Neutrality Laws, and every effort should be made to prevent this. The men who are supposed to be engaged in this are Dr. Orr, Presidio, J. M. Keedy, Presidio, Jose Sedano, Villista officer, who now has rank of general, Miller and Howard, lawyers at El Paso, Fletcher Rawls, Bob Carter of Polvo, Francisco Hernandez of Loma Pelona, and probably the Kilpatricks of Candelaria."[35]

Presumably to retrieve Villa's buried bullion, Sedaño had organized another filibustering expedition. However, Jones reported that Sedaño and his assistant Narciso Villanueva "have had another quarrel, and now the prospects of the expedition crossing into Mexico are rather remote[.] . . . It now appears that these two

Villa grafters have fallen down on the money they were trying to extract from Villa followers here and, in my opinion, the whole scheme has fallen down."[36] Still, Sedaño continued to stockpile equipment, arms, and horses for the expedition at a ranch near La Unión, New Mexico, while he recruited replacements in El Paso for some of the original filibusters who had deserted.[37]

The Mexican ambassador complained to the State Department that George Holmes, José Sedaño, and other *villistas* had mounted a small expedition that had crossed into Mexico around February 1 with the object of blowing up railroad tracks. The Carranza officials complained that the expedition had crossed "without in any way being molested by the American authorities of the military."[38] It turned out that the reason the American military had not taken action against the expedition was because the Carranza officials hadn't bothered to notify the Americans of the expedition until after the fact.[39] Agent Jones was particularly indignant. He stated that Andrés García had not deigned to reciprocate the three courtesy visits that Jones had made to his office. Moreover, "I desire to say, also, that not one iota of information was furnished this office by the Mexican Consulate concerning this, or any other, alleged expedition."[40]

George Holmes had not crossed with the expedition but had returned to El Paso. He now owned several ranches in the vicinity of San Elizario and, according to his foreman Pablo Casas, all the employees were ex-*villistas* whom Holmes had ordered "not to tell any one anything even though they were threatened with death." Not infrequently, couriers from Villa on their way to El Paso with messages for adherents such as Teodoro Kyriacopulos or Carlos Jáuregui stayed over at one of Holmes's ranches. The messages often urged Villa's partisans to obtain ammunition and conceal it at designated fords on the Rio Grande.[41] As a Bureau informant reporting on conditions in Presidio put it: "Pablo Baeza is a Villista as is very nearly every other Mexican on this side of the River between El Paso and Lajitas, Texas. It may be that they smuggle animals, they certainly carry information. The Villistas have a well-nigh perfect intelligence system. But it is almost impossible to detect them in this."[42]

The Department of Justice really wanted to get George Holmes. "I call your especial attention to the fact," the assistant attorney general wrote to the U.S. district attorneys in San Antonio and New Mexico, "that it is said that one George Holmes, is involved. As you are already aware, the activities of this man in the past have been the source of much trouble to this Government. It is requested that, if evidence is forthcoming, vigorous prosecution be made for violation of laws by this man or others."

But Holmes was nothing if not bold, and he could be very persuasive. In August he calmly strolled into the Bureau office and had a long conversation with Gus Jones. Holmes frankly admitted his friendship with Francisco Villa and stated openly that he "had helped him in the past, and would continue to help him whenever opportunity presented itself." But, Jones reported, "he desired to emphasize to me that he was *an American* first, last and all the time; that his connection with Villa in the past has been for business reasons and because of a real admiration for Villa, the man, but when it comes to a point where the welfare of his (Holmes') country was concerned, he would show very definitely on which side he was." Holmes also spoke of dissension in the *villista* ranks: "Holmes very frankly told me that the Villista cause in the United States 'was being injured greatly' by having such men as Harry C. Miller, G. Volney Howard and Jose Sedano pose as Villa's accredited representatives, when in reality, he (Holmes) knew positively that Francisco Villa had not instructed them to act for him in any way, or authorized them to represent him in the United States."

In addition, Holmes provided useful information regarding the activities of these alleged lowlifes. According to Holmes, Miller and Howard were members of Sedaño party that crossed into Mexico in late January. They proceeded about fifty miles south of the border when Miller contracted a violent attack of cold feet and refused to go any farther. Sedaño sent Miller back with a guide, and he and Howard continued on to Pancho Villa's camp, which was at that time near Magistral, Durango. At Sedaño's urging, Villa grudgingly agreed to meet with Howard, the audience lasting about an hour. Howard tried to convince Villa that the firm of Miller and Howard had great influence in Washington and pleaded to be appointed Villa's representative in the United States. Howard also asserted that he could "advantageously handle certain bullion that Villa had in his possession." Villa informed Howard that his representative was Miguel Díaz Lombardo and suggested that Howard address himself to Díaz Lombardo. Miller did in fact correspond with Díaz Lombardo and allegedly handled his revolutionary matters on the border. When writing to Miller and Howard, Díaz Lombardo addressed his letters to "G. Méndez Velarde, Centro Social Mexicano, El Paso." Méndez Velarde was described as "operating and editing a second-class newspaper, in Spanish, called "The New Life" [*La Vida Nueva*], and is an unostentatious admirer of and propagandists for Francisco Villa." The Bureau established a "confidential censorship of mail" going to this address.[43]

Villa had declined to enter personally into any negotiations with Miller and Howard and suggested that Howard return to the United States. Agent Jones noted that Sedaño and Howard had been apprehended by the U.S. Army as they crossed the Rio Grande in the Big Bend, and he stated that "Mr. Holmes advised me that he got the above verbatim from Sedano, and it is certainly borne out by data in our files." Most interestingly, Holmes confirmed what the Bureau already suspected, namely, that the *villistas* and the *felicistas* had quietly reached a tacit agreement. Both groups were fighting to depose Carranza but for public consumption, especially in the United States, they had to appear antagonistic, for the United States considered Villa nothing but a murderous bandit. Presumably to Jones's great satisfaction,

"Mr. Holmes went on to say that while he knows he has always been considered somewhat of a renegade and smuggler by the Government men, he was willing to tell me frankly every detail of his past connection with the Villas and their party, and that while he had assisted Villa, and hoped to again, he had never been engaged in any actual smuggling of arms and ammunition into Mexico; that he had been of financial help to Villa—had backed him to a degree which had brought about dire financial straights [*sic*] for himself, but that was all." But not surprisingly, Holmes asked that he be permitted to enter Mexico, promising to collect and return with intelligence of great value.

Jones's evaluation of his conversation with Holmes was positive: "I will say that I was much impressed with the apparent frankness and sincerity of Mr. Holmes' statement. I have known him personally for a good many years, and while I do not overlook his record on neutrality matter in connection with the Villa movement, I will 'give the Devil his due,' and say that I do not believe George Holmes is pro-German in any way, thought or form. On the other hand, I am satisfied that he [is] loyally American, as against the Huns." Jones was inclined to take a chance on Holmes's offer to collect intelligence about Villa, feeling that this was more important than strict enforcement of the neutrality laws. But Jones covered himself with his superiors by noting that "I am submitting this report *without recommendation* for such action as it may merit."[44]

Chief Bielaski of the Bureau sent a copy of Jones's report to Leland Harrison, counselor of the State Department, who was anything but enthusiastic, writing to Bielaski that "I presume that you have already instructed Agent Jones to keep Holmes carefully under surveillance inasmuch as Holmes is now indicating a desire to cross the Border and get into touch with Villa and that you have warned Jones that under no circumstances is he to intimate to Holmes that permission would be granted to the latter to go into Mexico. It might be well also to instruct Agent Jones to bring the matter to the attention of the proper officials along the Border with a view to preventing Holmes from going into Mexico under any circumstances. I have placed the name of Mr. Holmes on the passport refusal cards of this Department."[45] Chief Bielaski disagreed. He informed Harrison that he'd instructed Agent Jones to permit Holmes to travel to Mexico, "first taking steps, however, to cover very closely his arrival and departure. It was not thought that any serious damage could be done by his making the trip and we hope thereby to secure intelligence of value."[46]

Both Harrison and Bielaski anxiously awaited Agent Jones's report on Holmes's proposed trip. Jones advised that all preparations had been made for it, but unfortunately Villa had just launched a new offensive in southern Chihuahua in the vicinity of Jiménez and Parral, making it impossible for Holmes to contact him, so "the matter has been held in abeyance until Villa is somewhat more in 'retirement,' and can be located in some certain place. At such time as the journey can be made I shall notify you the day that Holmes crosses the Line."[47]

Agent Jones was able to put Holmes's *villista* connections to good use. He notified his chief on November 6 that he had personally accompanied Holmes and two Mexican guides to the Rio Grande on the night of November 3 and had watched them enter Mexico. Jones had gone to Holmes's ranch and had proposed to Holmes a hazardous mission. To Jones's relief Holmes, who was no doubt anxious to acquire merit with the Bureau, accepted the assignment.

On October 11, a *villista* chieftain, Epifanio Holguín, had kidnapped three American officials of the Erupción Mining Company, located twenty-six miles east of Villa Ahumada, Chihuahua, and took them to the camp of Pancho Villa, who then held them for ransom.[48] Villa had subsequently freed two of the captives, sending one to El Paso to present his demands. Having secured the approval of Military Intelligence and the general commanding the El Paso Patrol District, Jones was secretly sending George Holmes to Villa's camp to try to secure the release of Frank Knotts, the company's manager, and to gather whatever intelligence he could. Jones telegraphed his chief: "Utmost secrecy this matter necessary as Villa has threatened kill Knotts if Carranzistas [*sic*] learn his demand." And Jones declared that "I am further convinced that the only living American that could in any way exercise any influence over Francisco Villa looking to the release of this man is George Holmes. I will also state that in my opinion, Mr. Holmes has undertaken a very dangerous mission and is deserving of some commendation in that he has undertaken this trip without any promise of pay and for the reason that an American's life is at stake."[49]

According to Knotts, initially Villa was in a towering rage and threatened to hang his captives on the first tree he came to. But Villa eventually calmed down. He demanded a ransom of $300,000 "because he said that that was the amount of which his brother Hipolito had been robbed when here [presumably referring to the money Lázaro de la Garza had appropriated]. Nothing, however, seemed to hurt him more than the treatment accorded his wife; he said all her money was taken from her and the rings were torn from her fingers; Villa positively wept when he told me this." Knotts finally managed to talk Villa into reducing the ransom to $15,000, but Villa demanded that it be paid in American gold coin.

Holmes reported that by hard riding he reached Villa's headquarters on November 5, the day Villa had promised to kill Knotts if he didn't receive the ransom. "Of course, I needed no introduction to Villa, as I have known him for 15 or 20 years. He seemed to be very glad to see me and we had a conference lasting some two or three hours. I talked with him regarding the capture and holding of Mr. Knotts and told him that I had brought the money with me to pay the ransom if he still demanded it[.] . . . He told me that he regretted very much to have to hold Knotts, but in view of the fact that he needed financial assistance, he deemed it no more than right that the Erupcion Mining people should pay him a tribute for doing business in his territory in Mexico, as they paid taxes to the Carranza Government and received no protection whatever and the money he was asking for was merely an enforced loan and would be returned by him to the mining company within 60 days." Villa was angry that Holmes had brought currency instead of gold coin, but Holmes pointed out quite reasonably that he couldn't have brought gold coin because of the weight. In the course of their conversation Villa mentioned that his brother Hipólito was operating in the vicinity of Ojinaga. He also denied that he had anything to do with the Columbus raid, which of course was a bald-faced lie. The mercurial Villa was about to release Knotts when he suddenly changed his mind and demanded 3,000 pounds of flour and 600 pounds of *piloncillo* (Mexican sugar) before he would let the prisoner go.

Holmes returned to El Paso and reported on his mission. Even though the United States had in place a wartime embargo on exporting foodstuffs to Mexico, Jones and Zach Cobb decided that the paramount consideration should be saving Knotts's life, so the Erupción Mining Company quietly received an export permit for the flour and sugar. On November 13, a truck left El Paso with the goods, accompanied by George Holmes, and delivered them to the Bosque Bonito; the *villistas* received the merchandise and Knotts was liberated. However, Knotts's brother, T. H. Knotts of Des Moines, Iowa, told the newspaper there that he had paid the ransom—$15,000 and $3,000 worth of supplies. When this account was published, both Agent Jones and Frank Knotts publicly issued a Jesuitical denial, categorically denying that any ransom had been paid to the *villista* chieftain Epifanio Holguín. This was of course true—the ransom had been paid to Pancho Villa.[50]

In his statement to the Bureau, Knotts mentioned that "Villa says that when he gets back into power he is going to issue to each of his soldiers 'a pardon for 200 years and a premium for each Turk, Syrian or Arab they kill.' Second, 50 years and a premium to each soldier for every Chinaman they kill. This statement is made to show his contempt for the races above mentioned." Knotts also stated that "Harry C. Miller, the El Paso lawyer, was with Villa for two weeks; this was about six weeks ago."[51]

One curious result of Holmes's mission to Villa was that the Mexican chieftain wrote a letter on November 18 from his camp to the "Chief of the Department of Justice, El Paso, Texas." Delivered to Agent Jones by a *villista* courier, it read in translation: "Esteemed Sir: Mr. George M. Holmes has talked with me regarding some documents which are in my possession, and which refer to the relations between the Germans and the Carrancista Party; and which I do not send to you immediately, because they are safely put away at a place quite a distance from where I now am;

but I shall arrange to have them in my hands again, and I hope to be able to do this at no distant date."[52]

While Holmes had been intriguing, the focus of attention in El Paso had shifted from the Mexican Revolution to a terrifying epidemic—the influenza pandemic that ultimately killed an estimated 21 million people worldwide.[53] The epidemic struck the city in late September, and by October 8, some eighteen hundred cases were reported. Crowded and heavily Hispanic south El Paso was hard hit. An emergency hospital staffed by volunteers proved to be an effective response to this phase of the crisis. But it was at Fort Bliss where the epidemic struck hardest—by October 15, two thousand cases were reported, and the post was under a strict quarantine. By October 23, the city health officer reported some 5,000 cases, with a death toll of at least 400. By the end of November, the number of cases had dropped dramatically. Revolutionary plotting resumed in full force.[54]

Several respectable El Paso businessmen continued to deal with revolutionists. Haymon Krupp was one of them. He had profited by supplying Pancho Villa with shoes and uniforms, "and no doubt, [he] furnished him ammunition as well, but always managed to dodge a Federal prosecution." As a naturalized American, he was kept under Bureau surveillance during the war.[55] In early January 1918, his brother-in-law Victor Carusso was negotiating from his office at 429 First National Bank Building, El Paso, with Octavio Paz, a reputed agent of General Emiliano Zapata currently in Los Angeles and using the cover name of Mario Cartal, about a scheme to supply Zapata's forces by shipping merchandise down the Pacific coast of Mexico. Paz made the proposition to Carusso and Krupp, who suggested they go to Los Angeles to discuss the matter in person. They were exceedingly circumspect in their letters, assuming the authorities were reading their mail, as indeed they were. Thus we only have the broad outlines of this particular enterprise. Carusso, incidentally, mentioned that he had suffered severe financial reverses.[56] Underscoring Paz's connections with the Zapata, an alleged *zapatista* courier the *carrancistas* captured in Nuevo Laredo carried a letter signed by Paz.[57] Krupp and Carusso's connection with Paz lasted through 1918. The San Antonio office of the Bureau reported in December that the parties were plotting shipments of shoes and clothing to Zapata "via San Pedro [California], money and goods furnished by Hymon [*sic*] Krupp, El Paso."[58]

Haymon Krupp also received considerable attention from the Mexican government. The Mexican ambassador informed the State Department that Haymon Krupp and Company were among "the persons or commercial houses of the city of El Paso who are engaged in sending contraband of arms to the Villistas, thereby doing injury to the lives and interests of both American and Mexican citizens living in the parts where those bandits are operating." The Mexican consulate in the border city alleged that Krupp and Company "reaped its harvest at the time when the

Villistas had the upper hand in the neighboring state of Chihuahua. In return for the favors they received from the bandit, they now assume the shipments of munitions to him, which they bring in concealed in packages of the various merchandise they send to Mexico."[59] However, in November 1918, Pancho Villa was quoted as complaining that "he had made Krupp (of Haymon Krupp & Co. El Paso) rich, but now, if he ordered $100 worth of goods, they would not fill same."[60] It would appear that most of Krupp's wheeling and dealing had occurred in 1913–15.

One who was no longer wheeling and dealing was Ike Alderete. He had been having a run of bad luck. In September 1916, Ike had been severely injured when his automobile had been rear-ended by a car belonging to General Luis Terrazas. Alderete had sued but had lost the case. Lately, Ike had been operating a social club, the Sociedad Unión Fraternal, but the sheriff kept raiding the place, confiscating Ike's stock of liquor, and arresting Ike himself. This was bad enough, but then Ike had some really terrible luck. On June 22, 1918, as Ike was standing at the doorway of his club a crazed Mexican began shooting at some soldiers standing outside; two soldiers were wounded, and Ike was killed by a stray bullet in the head. After an impressive funeral he was buried in Evergreen Cemetery.[61]

Ike's brother, Frank, was still a player, though. Frank Alderete, "well, and rather unfavorably known to this office," called on Agent Jones to denounce the smuggling of arms and ammunition and to declare that he had seen José Acosta, head of the Carranza secret service in Juárez, carry large boxes out of the Popular Dry Goods Company almost on a daily basis, boxes he suspected contained ammunition. Further, Alderete confided that he had seen Mexicans whom he knew to be *carrancistas* go to the home of Jesse L. Mayer, an employee of the Popular Dry Goods Company, and haul away boxes. Jones commented: "Inasmuch as Frank Alderete has himself been under investigation by this office, and is an all-round Mexican crook, it would be rather obvious what his object might be in furnishing the above information. However, investigation will be made in order to ascertain how much truth there may be in his report."

Mayer was a longtime employee of the dry goods store, working in the men's furnishings department. He was arrested on the night of July 3 in downtown El Paso as he handed two Mexicans a package found to contain 1,700 rounds of small-arms ammunition. Mayer was the El Paso representative of a gang smuggling arms to the *carrancistas* in Juárez. They had allegedly crossed more than 100,000 rounds and hundreds of rifles. Mayer readily admitted being involved in the lucrative traffic for months, helpfully stating that he bought rifles for $56.50 and sold them to the smugglers for $80. Cartridges cost him $24 per thousand, and he sold them for $60.

The head of the Popular Dry Goods Company, Adolph Schwartz, was at pains to assure the Bureau that he was not engaged in illicit activities. Jones tended to discount Alderete's allegations but noted that Schwartz had been extremely profuse in his protestation that Mayer's involvement in arms smuggling was but "a sideline, something wholly apart from his connection with the Popular D. G. Co., whose officers were absolutely innocent of complicity in his sinister and unscrupulous transactions. In fact, Mr. Schwartz's conversation irresistibly brought to mind 'Methinks thou dost protest too much.'" Schwartz claimed he had warned Mayer against getting involved in arms trafficking. The warning was inspired by his having observed Mayer talking in the store with two Mexicans, one of whom was overheard saying that their purpose was to procure arms and ammunition and convey it to the Carranza forces in Juárez.[62]

It turned out that Mayer had purchased nine cases of .30-.30 ammunition from Feldman and Company, which firm had not obtained permits from the District Intelligence Office to make the sales to Mayer. In retaliation, Feldman was denied "any and all permits for ammunition." Fred J. Feldman hired a lawyer and pleaded his case to the district intelligence officer and to Agent Jones—if munitions had been sold in his store to irresponsible parties it was entirely without his personal knowledge. When the manager of Feldman's arms and ammunition department was questioned, he declared that Feldman had been engaged in ammunition smuggling as early as the fall of 1917. The authorities were less than pleased that Feldman had lied to them.[63]

Then there was Hipólito Villa's connection with Maurice Schwartz, Adolph's nephew. Schwartz showed the general commanding the El Paso Patrol District a confidential letter Hipólito had written him. Mentioning the "kind and spontaneous offers which some time or times you have made me, to the effect that you are willing to take care of my requests at all times," he asked Schwartz to send him from the Popular Dry Goods Company fifteen complete uniforms for his officers, for which of course he would pay. The Bureau and the Intelligence Office quickly formulated a plan: to let Hipólito's emissaries—Manuel G. González and Alfonso Gómez Morentín—buy the merchandise and leave, and then they would arrest them. Accordingly, on July 18, a Lieutenant Houghton pretended to be a store clerk, while Bureau agents Wren and White waited outside in an automobile. The lieutenant waited on the purchasers and even helped them load the goods into a waiting taxi. The Bureau agents followed them to the Smith Hotel, where they went to room 43, registered to Gómez Morentín. As they were leaving, the Bureau agents pounced, arresting the emissaries and searching them and the hotel room. The two *villistas* were escorted to the Bureau office, where "after a severe grilling" Gómez Morentín gave a statement describing his journey from Hipólito's encampment through the Big Bend to El Paso. He candidly admitted that "it is his business to purchase goods or to smuggle them across the river to the Villistas." At their arraignment their bond was fixed at $1,500 each, which was promptly posted. A federal grand jury indicted them on November 5 for attempted smuggling.[64] When the case came to trial on November 29, Gómez Morentín engaged in a bit of disinformation. He testified that he had been with Pancho Villa on the night of the Columbus raid and Villa had been nowhere near the place. As to the offense with which Gómez Morentín was charged, that of trying to export merchandise without a proper license, on the federal attorney's motion the jury brought in an instructed verdict of not guilty.[65]

Agent Gus Jones continued to expand his files on Mexicans worth watching. He sent his superiors a list of the six male and three female *carrancista* secret agents based in Juárez together with their physical description and habitual wearing apparel. Jones also included the names of the immigration and customs inspectors and the single military police plainclothesman in Juárez. Finally, he listed the names of owners of automobiles licensed as taxis in that city. Reflecting the close cooperation between the local offices of the Bureau and the District Intelligence Office, Jones received a list from that office of Mexicans residing in El Paso who had been active in Mexican politics during the past several years. And Jones received copies of intercepted and translated Mexican Army messages, including, for example, communications from General Francisco Murguía to his subordinate commanders.[66] Increasingly, it was the District Intelligence Office that ran most of the informers rather than the Bureau. Agent Jones thought well of them: "I will state that the under cover operatives working in Juarez for the District Intelligence office here are very capable and reliable men."[67]

However, on occasion the Bureau of Investigation and the District Intelligence Office worked at cross-purposes. For instance, both agencies were investigating Manuel Bonilla, a civil engineer who had been secretary of communications and public works in the Madero cabinet. They suspected Bonilla of helping to organize the El Paso *villista* junta. Postal censorship had intercepted a letter to him from someone in Havana. The Bureau was conducting an undercover investigation of Bonilla, but the Intelligence Office sent an officer in plain clothes to interview Bonilla. Agent Jones was not pleased: "In this connection I might say that it is unfortunate that we could not have known sooner that the District Intelligence Office was also conducting an investigation of this matter; because had we known, the degree of 'lost motion' consequent upon two separate investigations of the same case, conducted along different lines, could have been avoided, as we could have arranged our investigation to dovetail with theirs."[68]

Then there was the Carranza secret service. Agent Jones reported in June that "I will state that the under cover operatives of the Carranza Government here are causing us more trouble than any other faction."[69] As of April 1918, the Mexican Secret Service in the United States had five agents in El Paso, five in San Antonio, two in Del

Rio, three in Laredo, three in Eagle Pass, three in Brownsville, four in New Orleans, two in Washington, five in New York, five in Los Angeles, three in San Francisco, "and others scattered out in smaller places." These men received from $75 to $150 per month, and, except for railroad transportation, they paid their own expenses.[70] The Carranza secret agents focused on two things: combating "reactionaries," mainly *villistas* and *felicistas*, and smuggling ammunition to the Carranza garrison in Juárez. Regarding the garrison, the efforts of the Bureau of Investigation and the District Intelligence Office apparently had a significant effect by August. José Acosta, chief of the secret service in Juárez, which, by the way, wasn't so secret—the *El Paso Morning Times* repeatedly referred to Acosta as the "Chief of the Mexican Secret Service in Juarez"—met secretly with the garrison commander and other officers to discuss the increasing difficulty in crossing ammunition. The schemes suggested included filling several automobiles with society girls pretending to be going to a dance or a marriage in Juárez, or monitoring the schedule of American patrols on Córdova Island and smuggling when the coast was clear, or even "having society girls and women of the better class, who are never bothered on the bridge, bring what they could over in their hair under their hats." One officer suggested digging a tunnel under the boundary on Córdova Island, but Acosta vetoed this because it would be too difficult to keep the project secret.[71]

CHAPTER 19

Exile Futility

With respect to the 1918 crop of Mexican revolutionary juntas, the State Department's agents stated that "the greatest impetus, however, to the elements opposing Carranza has been the attitude assumed by him towards the United States during the present world war. His opponents have been firm in the belief, and their private correspondence shows it, that he is pro-German."[1] So the conservative exiles thought the United States would thus be supportive of their efforts to overthrow Carranza. The United States evidently wasn't, but as a recruiting ploy the exiles sometimes claimed that Washington would, at the very least, not interfere with their intrigues.[2] They engaged in interminable conspiratorial meetings and florid manifestos, but in the final analysis most of them were willing to fight to the last drop of somebody else's blood in order to gain power. As the colonel commanding Camp Eagle Pass, Texas, contemptuously put it: "I desire to remark that it is my firm belief that not a single one of these leaders could be pulled across the river under any circumstances by a six-mule team. I am firm in the belief that their only object, like the ordinary Phillipino [*sic*] Conspiracy, is the collection of funds to enable these leaders to live in idleness in the United States."[3]

In response to the Mexican ambassador's having notified the State Department about the activities on the border of some Mexican factions, Agent Gus Jones reported to the chief in June that "so far we have been unable to verify the fact that the Mexican reactionary element has formed any definite plans for the organization of an army movement against Ciudad Juarez." The ambassador alleged that a certain Romero would lead the movement, and that the "reactionaries" were merely awaiting the arrival of ex–federal generals Felipe Angeles, Juan José Rocha, and Guillermo Rubio Navarrete. However, as Jones explained, "so far as Juan Jose Rocha is concerned, you are no doubt aware that he is one of the best under cover Mexican Operatives connected with the United States Army Intelligence office and I presume that when the junta gathers he will be in a position to keep the Government informed as to their movements."[4] As had been the case for years, juntas in El Paso were penetrated with monotonous regularity.

A letter dated on May 7, 1918, from Villa's general Martín López at his encampment to George Holmes provides a fascinating glimpse into the workings of the *villista* network. Postal censorship intercepted the letter, photographed it, and returned it to the postal service for delivery. Major (and former Bureau agent in charge in San Antonio) Robert L. Barnes, intelligence officer for the Southern Department, urgently sent a copy to the Bureau's El Paso office. For reasons of security, General López addressed the letter to the trustworthy one-armed Italian *villista* partisan Pascual Cesaretti, instructing him to hand it personally to George Holmes at a saloon on the corner of Fourth and El Paso streets. Holmes was directed to deliver to Cesaretti the plans and sketches that a Mexican engineer, Louis R. Goldbaum, who was ostensibly a Carranza supporter, had over a period of months been assembling for Pancho Villa. Goldbaum's material dealt with the defenses of not only Ciudad Juárez but also El Paso, "for he informs us he has managed to get in the good graces of some of the military authorities of that City of El Paso, and for that reason can furnish all kinds of information relative to forces and movements, the leaving of troops, etc., etc, information that without costing us anything has helped us in obtaining good funds" (from the sale of this information to the Germans?). "From these funds, this same Cesaretti (Whom you may seek on El Paso Street South, across the street from the Star Theatre or for Isleta, which is where we frequently can pass somewhat [*sic*] of the ammunition and arms with which we can be greatly troubling the famous Carrancistas) will deliver to you $3470 of which you will give $1600 to Engineer Goldbaum and $700 to Cesaretti. Tell this same engineer that Mr. Buringh [unidentified] told me that by the man he sent with the plan of the Aviation there [El Paso] by way of Laredo he had already sent $2800, and he hopes he will advise him when he needs funds." López reminded Holmes that Cesaretti was only interested in money; "I do not," he stated, "believe him to be either friendly to the Germans nor ourselves." The $3,470 had been sent to Cesaretti the week before by a courier who entered the United States at Laredo. López instructed Holmes to destroy the letter and when replying not to "forget that every letter must be sent to me through Torreon, that they get them there and forward them to where we are camped." Finally, the general urged Holmes to send ammunition, of which the *villistas* were in desperate need.[5] Interestingly, the American charge d' affaires in Mexico City had reported in 1917 that German letters were being carried from Torreón and the surrounding Laguna district to El Paso by one "Pascual Caeserretti" [*sic*].[6]

The El Paso Bureau office presumably rejoiced when it was finally rid of José Sedaño. At the Bureau's urgent request, the Immigration Service took Sedaño into custody on a charge of having entered the United States illegally. But when his friend Teodoro Kyriacopulos posted a $500 bond for him, the agency released Sedaño pending a decision in his case. Sedaño promptly fled across the Rio Grande. Sedaño allowed as how he regretted that his friend Kyriacopulos would lose his bond money, but Sedaño had urgent business with Francisco Villa and couldn't await the outcome of his case. In September, Sedaño and five associates visited the Erupción mine, near Villa Ahumada, Chihuahua, and "helped themselves to provisions, etc. This would indicate that Sedaño has resumed his profession of brigand."[7] A subsequent report stated that Sedaño had joined a *villista* band headed by Epifanio Holguín but then left it to try to contact Villa himself. He was, however, reportedly captured by Carranza soldiers, who took him to the town of Satevó, where he was hanged the following day. Agent Jones commented that "efforts will be made to verify this report, and it will be remembered in this connection that this is not the first time that Jose Sedano has been reported hung, or otherwise made an end of. In fact, if his future duplicates his past, he will soon have died as many deaths as did his leader, Francisco Villa, during the days of the Pershing Expedition in Mexico."[8] And indeed the report of Sedaño's demise proved premature. A month later he still figured among Villa's officers.[9]

Sedaño's attorney Harry Miller traveled to Marfa in late August, allegedly to see about a gold mine he owned across the river in Mexico. Probably not coincidentally, the army and the Texas Rangers had received reports that substantial amounts of ammunition were being smuggled across the Rio Grande in that vicinity. Captain Carroll Bates, an ex–Texas Ranger, reported that 23,000 rounds had recently been smuggled near Terlingua, and when Carranza troops arrived on the scene all they found were the empty boxes. But it turned out that Bates had gotten his information indirectly from some Mexicans, and the report was unfounded. On August 26, customs inspectors detained Harry Miller, two other Anglos, and two Mexicans in Terlingua on suspicion of smuggling but had to release them for lack of evidence. Miller and his associates explained that they had gone to the Rio Grande to arrange for the crossing of livestock. It seems that Frank P. Jones, president of the El Paso Bank and Trust Company, was interested in acquiring some twenty-five hundred head of horses, mules, and cattle from Mexico and had secured the necessary import permits from the War Trade Board. Miller was retained as the representative of the *villistas* who were selling the livestock, and his associates were all involved in the transaction. Although Miller's business appeared legitimate, the Customs Service kept him under close surveillance.[10]

Miller seemed to be branching out in all directions. By September, he was a partner in Miller and Gauldin, 614 Martin Building, El Paso. Miller notified Gauldin that he had contracted to import bat guano from caves on the Mexican side of the Rio Grande in the Big Bend. To the jaundiced eye of the Bureau "It is very possible that if the opportunity affords, Miller will bring guano to this side and under cover of that activity cross ammunition to Mexico."[11]

Miller persuaded H. F. Work, a deputy U.S. Marshal based in El Paso, to secure a permit for importing bat guano, which was used in commercial fertilizer. The attorney indeed imported more than a ton of guano, storing it in the barn in Santa

Helena on the ranch of ex–Texas Ranger Captain Carroll Bates, whose brother L. E. Bates was a Bureau agent in El Paso. Carroll Bates agreed to cooperate in uncovering Miller's plans, which centered on importing Pancho Villa's bullion, by legal means if possible but by smuggling if necessary. The Bureau suspected that Miller intended to smuggle bullion in the sacks of guano. The authorities in the vicinity were alerted to this possibility and were dutifully performing the unenviable task of inspecting the sacks of guano, but realistically speaking, as a Bureau agent pointed out "there are so many chances for such a bunch to slip through our lines and do their smuggling and get away with it as the country affords such a good opportunity for smugglers to carry out their plans. Miller should be excluded from visiting this district if possible as it is impossible to watch all his movements. Miller has made one trip to El Paso since he has been down on the river, but has returned and was last heard of at Santa Helena, Tex., where he had made preparations to stay several weeks."[12] Miller made his headquarters at Captain Bates's ranch, a circumstance that made Colonel Langhorne suspect that Bates not only was in collusion with Miller but was getting inside information from Bates's brother, the Bureau agent in El Paso.[13] Agent Jones stoutly denied this.

In addition to carrying out his other nefarious activities, Miller had evidently been recruiting in El Paso for the Villa movement. A certain Florencio Villanueva claimed that he had gone to Harry Miller and told him he was a Villa sympathizer and wanted to join Villa, whereupon Miller gave him a revolver and $100 for traveling expenses.[14] On occasion, Miller received letters from Pancho and Hipólito Villa.[15]

Agent Jones instructed his colleague Agent John Wren to keep in touch with George Holmes and gather any information he might have concerning Villa's activities. Since Wren had known Holmes for years, Jones felt that Holmes would speak frankly with Wren. Holmes informed Wren that on the night of December 11–12, a group of Villa's followers had come to his house near San Elizario to bid him farewell, for they were crossing into Mexico to join Pancho Villa. Heading the group was General Felipe Angeles, Villa's former artillery commander. (Since Angeles didn't know the first thing about being a dairy farmer, his farm near Ysleta had failed, and he had sold out.[16] He had secured employment inspecting munitions in New York City for the French government. More recently he had been organizing Mexican exiles in New York in hopes of overthrowing Carranza.)

Besides Angeles, his expedition consisted of Alfonso Gómez Morentín (the *villista* operative), José Jaurrieta (until recently Villa's secretary), Miguel Chávez, (Holmes's guide in the Knotts affair), and Pascual Cesaretti (Holmes's mail contact). They were all armed and mounted. The Bureau subsequently learned that it was George Holmes who had purchased from Shelton-Payne the equipment for the Angeles expedition, but the agency had insufficient evidence to charge W. H. Shelton, who professed his innocence (the Bureau didn't believe him).[17] Since he hadn't heard from the expedition, Holmes assumed they had successfully crossed the Rio Grande. The *villistas* didn't exactly know where their leader was, but they expected to find him somewhere near Villa Ahumada.

It turned out that the attorney Harry C. Miller had advised Captain Carroll M. Counts, the district intelligence officer, that a party of *villistas* intended to cross into Mexico on the night of December 11 near Socorro. All Miller would say was that they were "important." Captain Counts believed this information to be reliable because Miller and the Villa faction had had a falling out, and Miller was now anxious to cause as much trouble for them as he could. Counts informed the commanding general of the El Paso district of Miller's information. The general had ordered that sentries be deployed in force between San Elizario and Socorro, a distance of about a mile and a half, and that no one be permitted to cross into Mexico. Despite these precautions, General Angeles and his companions had slipped across the Rio Grande, aided by a torrential rainstorm that lasted until about midnight.

Agent Wren spoke with Villa partisan Teodoro Kyriacopulos, with whom he was personally acquainted. Kyriacopulos not only confirmed Holmes's account but offered to give Wren any information of interest that came his way. The Greek also imparted a bit of news that must have cheered the El Paso Bureau agents—he had received reliable news in December that Villa had recently executed José Sedaño for having killed two old men who were informants of Villa's and whose sons were serving under him. Agent Wren stated that this was probable, because George Holmes claimed to have personal knowledge that Pancho Villa had placed Sedaño under arrest. George Holmes subsequently confirmed that Sedaño was indeed dead. Holmes got this information from a courier sent by Pancho Villa who declared that Villa himself had related that he had arrested Sedaño and had turned him over to a *villista* captain, a certain Baltasar Aros, because Sedaño had recently killed Aros's brother. Aros executed Sedaño near Villa Ahumada. Holmes continued to pass along to Agent Wren information as well as letters from Villa to Holmes.[18]

The falling out between the *villistas* and Harry Miller was a tale of greed and treachery. One of Agent Jones's confidential informants reported that the *villista* colonel Alfonso Gómez Morentín last entered Texas in late November at an isolated point in the Big Bend. His principal object in returning was to stand trial for a neutrality violation, being under a $1,500 bond to appear in federal court in El Paso. He was carrying certain letters from Pancho Villa to some of his most influential partisans in the United States, letters that went into detail concerning Villa's future military plans. En route from Pancho Villa's camp, Gómez Morentín passed through the encampment of Hipólito Villa, opposite Santa Helena, Texas. Hipólito advised Gómez Morentín that as soon as he crossed the Rio Grande to turn the documents over to César Fargas, who would not be searched between the river and Marfa since he was an informant for the U.S. Army in the Big Bend. César and his brother Juan had been confidential informants for some time. They were ex-*villistas*; Juan Fargas had been a captain and readily recounted the atrocities of Villa's that he had witnessed.[19] When Gómez Morentín was safely past Marfa, Fargas would return the papers to him and Gómez Morentín could deliver them. Gómez Morentín followed Hipólito's suggestion. Gómez Morentín and Fargas proceeded to El Paso separately. When Gómez Morentín asked Fargas for the documents, Fargas declared that he'd been arrested and jailed in Marfa but had managed to secrete the papers in the jail. After being questioned and released, he hadn't had the opportunity to return to the jail and retrieve them. Fargas told this to Gómez Morentín in the presence of attorney Harry C. Miller, who informed Gómez Morentín that it would take $1,000 to bribe the jailer and recover the papers. Miller and Fargas were aware that Gómez Morentín was carrying $1,000 to be delivered to Pancho Villa's wife, who was living in San Antonio. Gómez Morentín refused to pay, and he never got the documents. Although terrified of Villa's reaction, Gómez Morentín intended to explain to Villa how he'd been treated by "two supposedly faithful adherents and warm supporters of the Villa Cause."

Agent Jones took considerable satisfaction in this outcome: "The result of this attempted blackmail by Miller and Fargas is that they are now in disrepute with the loyal Villistas here, by which the Government will probably profit, as the anti-Miller-Fargas faction among the Villistas here will be eager to report everything possible regarding their future activity, and they will, in turn, tell the Government's employees all they can regarding the Villista Junta, etc. The majority of the local Villistas who are cognizant of this incident believe that Harry C. Miller has sold the documents to Andres G. Garcia, the Inspector General of Mexican Consulates in the U.S." However, further investigation established that both Fargas and Gómez Morentín had been detained by the army in Marfa and that Fargas had been held in the guardhouse, not the county jail. The intelligence officer in Marfa conducted a thorough search of the guardhouse and had in fact located the missing documents. They consisted of seven letters signed by Pancho Villa and addressed to his wife, Manuel Bonilla, Harry Miller, and Miguel Díaz Lombardo, translations of which were supplied to the Bureau.[20]

Jones had also acquired "by confidential means" two letters written by Gómez Morentín in El Paso. One was to Matías G. García "an old Mexican school teacher, and protégé of Francisco Villa, who lives in San Antonio, Texas, at the establishment maintained there for Luz Corral de Villa." The other letter was to his mother in Mexico City telling her to send his mail to 510 Prospect Avenue, El Paso, to be held until his return to the United States. The address was the home of Teodoro Kyriacopulos. Jones hoped to be able to prosecute Gómez Morentín, who had crossed into Mexico with General Felipe Angeles, for violation of the passport regulations should he ever return to the United States.[21]

George Holmes was apparently living up to his arrangement with the Bureau. He supplied several letters he'd recently received, one of them from Pancho Villa himself. And on December 24 he informed Agent Jones that he was leaving the next day for Candelaria, Texas, on the Rio Grande in the Big Bend, to confer with a *villista* colonel who was waiting for him in San Antonio, Chihuahua, across the river from Candelaria. Holmes wanted the federal authorities to know that he was going and that they were at liberty to cover his movements. He hoped to obtain firsthand information concerning Pancho Villa's future movements and plans. The El Paso District Intelligence Office telegraphed this information to their counterparts in the Big Bend so they could keep Holmes under surveillance.[22]

Pancho Villa launched a new offensive aimed at Ciudad Juárez in late November. He swept into the town of Villa Ahumada on the Mexican Central between Juárez and the city of Chihuahua at dawn on November 24. He had some five hundred men, and after a half an hour of fighting what was left of the hundred-man Carranza garrison surrendered. Villa took thirty-seven prisoners and marched them to the cemetery, where all but two died at the hands of a firing squad. The two wounded men played dead until they could escape the next day. Another wounded *carrancista* revived. An onlooker asked why the firing squad didn't put him out of his misery. The officer in charge replied that he had orders not to fire any more, and if he disobeyed he would incur the wrath of Villa. So he got a large rock and bashed the prisoner's brains out.[23] Uncharacteristically, Villa executed only two civilians—a saloon keeper known to be a crook and a wealthy rancher whom Villa personally disliked. The rebel chieftain assembled the townspeople and gave a rousing speech denouncing Carranza and his general Francisco Murguía and warning the crowd that he would be back, so they'd better decide whether they were with Villa or against him. The victorious Villa also seized fifteen tons of flour, a quantity of merchandise and clothing, and some cash extorted from businessmen. During the day more groups of his followers straggled into town, so that he now had some two thousand men in his command, including his brother Hipólito and General Martín López. But all this was of little consolation, for Villa had failed in his main objective.

He had planned to repeat the tactic that had been so spectacularly successful in November 1913—capture a southbound train, load his troops aboard, have the train return to Juárez, and take the town by surprise. But somebody bungled, and the crew of an approaching train was able to slam it into reverse and back away toward Juárez at full speed. On reaching the border town they gave the alarm, and Villa's element of surprise evaporated. A frustrated and furious Villa retreated from Villa Ahumada on November 25, heading westward in the direction of Casas Grandes. It should be noted that through a confidential informant Agent Jones sent into Villa's headquarters, the Bureau was aware of Villa's proposed strategy for capturing Ciudad Juárez as early as November 23.[24]

As usual, the Carranza army was reluctant to engage Villa. On November 26, *carrancista* cavalry reoccupied Villa Ahumada, but this proved to be a mixed blessing for the inhabitants. An eyewitness said that "as soon as the Carrancistas took possession of the town they at once killed all the milk-cows and chickens, and did more damage generally than the Villistas had done." Instead of pursuing Villa, General Francisco Murguía made a leisurely trip from the state capital up the central railroad, arriving in Villa Ahumada on November 28 with four trainloads of troops. "He stayed four days and kept his band playing the entire time. He had approximately two thousand men but did not attempt to send out any troops in pursuit of Villa." Murguía then proceeded on to Juárez, whose inhabitants had been panic stricken because "they fear Villa as the devil himself." Some had begun crossing to the safety of El Paso, whose inhabitants had been in a state of nervous anticipation at the prospect of getting to witness another Villa attack on Juárez.[25]

Murguía was in no hurry to press his campaign against Villa, for prolonging it was making him rich. He was using the time-honored technique of carrying phantom soldiers on the rolls and pocketing their salaries. The same informant declared that "Genl. Murguia has been rendering payroll vouchers to Mexico City for 19,000 officers and men, when he can not actually have more than 7,000, all told. He should, therefore, be about ready to retire." Another informant stated that Murguía was billing his government for 17,000 soldiers but actually had only 10,000 or less, and 20 percent of them lacked weapons. "Murguia's soldiers range from 12 years of age up. The majority of them are smaller than the guns they carry." Moreover, it was common knowledge that Murguía was sending much of the loot he acquired, especially cattle, to his ranch in Zacatecas.[26] And indeed, President Carranza soon ordered Murguía relieved, not only because he was ineffectual militarily but also because he was in a bitter feud with the governor of Chihuahua, General Ignacio Enríquez, a protégé of Carranza's.

Murguía's replacement as commander in northern Mexico was General Jesús Agustín Castro, who arrived in the city of Chihuahua and took command on December 13. Castro promised to protect the vital Mexican Central and to exterminate the *villistas*. Unlike Murguía, Castro was believed to be friendly toward Americans. And also unlike Murguía, Castro employed a female publicity agent to boost his image in the United States.[27] But information from confidential informants indicated that Villa still had hopes of capturing Juárez between September 12 and 17, presumably by surprise attack, as he had captured the city of Chihuahua on September 16, 1916.[28] But nothing happened.

Yet Villa and his men continued to make traveling by rail one of the most hazardous undertakings in Mexico. Sadly, accounts of *villistas* wrecking trains, slaughtering passengers and military escorts, and carrying off loot and women were commonplace. There was nothing the state authorities in Chihuahua could do to remedy the situation. When provisional governor Andrés Ortiz assumed office in December 1918, he reportedly found exactly $13.60 in the state treasury.[29]

The *villista* junta in El Paso remained optimistic about Villa's chances of making a comeback. The group received its mail addressed to Gumecindo Méndez Velarde, 511 South Oregon Street. The American authorities intercepted and translated much of it. The three directors of the junta were Manuel Bonilla, who was a civil engineer, and Federico Cervantes and Macrino J. Martínez, *villista* generals. They were in correspondence with Miguel Díaz Lombardo, Villa's representative in Washington, and with the directors of the Mexican Liberal Alliance in New York City—General Felipe Angeles, Antonio Villarreal, and Enrique Llorente—who had authorized them to organize a local junta. An organizational meeting was held on December 1 at the elementary school at Fifth and Tays streets. The stated purpose of the alliance was to unite all Mexican factions and to bring about peace in that country. Most of those attending were Villa sympathizers, including one who was an undercover operative of the District Intelligence Office and would keep that office abreast of developments.[30] The pro-Villa Spanish-language El Paso newspaper *La República* ran an article on December 16 stating that General Felipe Angeles would soon prepare a manifesto for the Mexican nation and that Angeles and Villa would soon confer.[31]

The *felicistas*, on the other hand, simply couldn't generate much traction in El Paso. Francisco Castro wrote to General Aureliano Blanquet, who used the pseudonym of "H. G. Soto," in Brooklyn that although Félix Díaz's new manifesto had been well received and he himself was very willing to help the cause, he felt not much could be accomplished in El Paso because the head of the local junta was very intimate with a *carrancista*.[32] Another El Paso *felicista* wrote to the general that he had managed to secure arms and equipment for a small group prepared to fight in Chihuahua. He had optimistically named them the "Benjamín Argumedo Brigade."[33] For his part, General Blanquet was most anxious to learn whether an El Paso *felicista* sympathizer had finally managed to mortgage his house for the $3,000 he had promised to contribute to the cause. He had not. Therefore when the *felicista* general Juan Montaño went from El Paso to New York to confer with Blanquet he had to report raising but little money for the purchase of munitions.[34]

It was the prominent local cattle dealer Charles Hunt who had offered to mortgage one of his properties. General Arnaldo Casso López introduced Hunt to General Juan Montaño, who hoped to secure a loan of $3,000.[35] But the $3,000 from Hunt fell through when Hunt backed out at the last minute. With that money the *felicistas* could have mounted two small expeditions. Mrs. Charles Hunt wrote to General Montaño asking whether the *felicistas* would like to take her entire interest in a piece of property she owned in El Paso for $5,000: "If your people are successful in carrying out your program with our little assistance and your purchasers wished to return us the property, I would gladly do it as it is a splendid piece of property for an apartment house. . . . Regards from Col. Hunt and myself."[36]

General Aureliano Blanquet, from New York, designated Juan José Rocha as military representative in El Paso of the *felicista* movement. They had hopes of organizing an expedition to capture Ciudad Juárez, provided of course they could raise the necessary funding to purchase ammunition and so forth, which seemed most unlikely. Still, they optimistically talked of raising $10,000 with which to suborn the Juárez garrison. Rocha duly reported these developments to the District Intelligence Office. (The State Department suspected that Rocha was a Military Intelligence informant; the army had not shared this information.)[37] Juan José Rocha, the former colonel in the federal army and now ostensibly a fervent *felicista*, was of course the prime informant of the District Intelligence Office, referred to as "Informant AR."[38]

Rocha, from his isolated residence at 212 Hadlock Place, wrote to Blanquet that his home was available for use by *felicista* leaders. Blanquet had recently withdrawn $4,000 from his bank account and presumably had sent it to General Montaño in El Paso.[39] Montaño had indeed received $3,300 for the proposed Chihuahua campaign. On September 24 a meeting was held in Rocha's home. He reported the names of those attending and stated that, because the *felicista* junta's plans changed almost every other day, no definite arrangements had been made. So, their activities were on hold pending further orders, since there was a possibility that Blanquet himself would come to El Paso to lead the attack on Juárez. The *felicistas* hoped to forge an alliance with Home Guard (Defensas Sociales) units in Chihuahua who were dissatisfied with the Carranza regime.[40]

Rocha advised that Marcelo Caraveo, the former *orozquista* and *huertista*, was now a *felicista* general, besieging the city of Puebla. He also reported that General Blanquet had instructed General Montaño

> not to attempt to send funds to the Carrancista General Lazaro Alanis [the former *orozquista* and *huertista*] in order that he might join the felicista movement; for, taking into consideration the antecedents of General Alanis, who has always been very changeable, it is feared that he might accept the money and might even be acting in accord with General Murguia in this

> matter—and at the end would *not* revolt against Carranza. General Blanquet instructed General Montano that he should try to effect a concentration of all the members of the Defensas Sociales (Home Guards) who have promised to join the Felicista movement, and have everything ready, so that, after a force is assembled, General Blanquet could come to El Paso and place himself at the head of the forces which are organized. General Blanquet delivered to General Montano one thousand dollars, in addition to another thousand which he sent by draft [from] New York.

Completely unaware of the traitor in their midst, the *felicista* junta received orders from General Blanquet that upon the capture of Juárez, Colonel Rocha should immediately go there, arrest the German consul and other German subjects, seize all the German consulate files and turn them over to the American government, to show the government and the people of the United States that the *felicistas* were truly pro-Ally in their actions, not just in words. And Rocha was designated as the liaison between the proposed *felicista* authorities in Juárez and the U.S. Army in El Paso. Rocha must have chuckled to himself when he reported these items. He also mentioned that on October 1, the *felicistas* had another meeting at his house, Colonel de la Cruz and General Albino Farías conferring with General Montaño regarding the organization of the movement in the state of Chihuahua.[41]

The chief of the Bureau commented that "our El Paso office advises us confidentially that Jose Juan [*sic*] Rocha is a confidential informant for the District Intelligence Office of the Army."[42] The State Department ascertained that Blanquet from New York, using the assumed name of Soto, had sent Montaño a check for two thousand pesos.[43] Bielaski sent Jones a copy of a letter from Montaño to one R. G. Soto; the letter was obtained in a "very confidential manner. Don't disclose the fact that we have this letter."

In El Paso, a *felicista* Committee of National Union was formed on June 1, 1918, to reestablish 1857 Constitution: the president was Fausto E. Miranda, and the members included Arnaldo Casso López, General of the Division, Brigadier General Genaro B. Trías, Brigadier General Juan Montaño, Samuel Caraveo, Colonel Juan José Rocha, and Jesús Acevedo, secretary. A total of fifty-three men, including the old *orozquista* José G. Rochín, signed as members of the committee.

While the *felicistas* in El Paso dithered, Villa's forces became more active across the Rio Grande from the Big Bend, the capture of the port of entry of Ojinaga being their principal objective. To meet this threat the Carranza army rushed all available ammunition from Juárez to Ojinaga, where General Francisco Murguía's brother General José C. Murguía was now in command. In addition, the Carranza consular agent in Presidio, Cosme Bengoechea, was suspected of smuggling ammunition to his colleagues across the river in Ojinaga. The military censor in El Paso had little difficulty in decoding and translating the telegrams passing between Ojinaga and Juárez.[44]

To prevent duplication of effort, the Bureau and the State Department had entered into a delimitation agreement (which may have been the first formal delimitation agreement in the U.S. intelligence community) by which State assumed responsibility for the surveillance of certain persons, whether Mexicans or Americans, involved in revolutionary intrigue. The State Department's counselor prepared a list of thirty-one people, among them General Felipe Angeles and John Hawes, that State was actively investigating.[45] At least this relieved some of the pressure on the overstretched Bureau office in El Paso.

Events would move to a climax in 1919.

CHAPTER 20

Villa's Eclipse

Pancho Villa continued to raise hell in Chihuahua. He let it be known that he was massing his followers by January 15, 1919, for an attack shortly thereafter against Ciudad Juárez.[1] While the federal army braced for that onslaught, Villa personally led a raid on January 22 against the installations of American-owned mining companies in Santa Eulalia, just ten miles northeast of the city of Chihuahua. The Carranza military was again caught flatfooted. At the head of some five hundred followers, Villa and his chief subordinate General Martín López swept into the mining town at 4:30 a.m. and easily overwhelmed the sixty-man Carranza garrison. Villa looted and wrecked the headquarters of the Potosí Mining Company, the reduction mill of the American Smelting and Refining Company, and the facilities of the Peñoles Company and the Buena Tierra Mining Company. Villa wreaked havoc and stole everything that was not nailed down, including fifty cases of dynamite and fifteen batteries, but he refrained from blowing up the mines themselves.

The triumphant chieftain soon rode away, taking with him six American hostages. "He also had taken a Mexican 'ore-thief' prisoner. Him he hung out of hand; which Mr. Quigley [general manager of the Potosí Mining Company] stated was worth to his company all of the 800 pesos taken, as the man had caused them a great deal of trouble." Villa lined up his American prisoners, harangued them at length on the necessity of their companies complying with the letters he had sent demanding "contributions," and gave them until March 1 to meet his demands; if not, the companies' properties would be utterly destroyed.[2] He then released the shaken Americans. The inhabitants of the state capital were also quite shaken, having awakened with Villa on their very doorstep. But instead of attacking Chihuahua, Villa headed south toward Parral, burning the bridges on the Mexican Central Railroad as he went.[3] American Smelting and Refining was a prime source of intelligence on Mexican affairs: "This firm extends every assistance to the Government in [the] way of valuable information gathered through its organization throughout Mexico. (Confidential)"[4]

Neither General Jesús Agustín Castro, Carranza's new commander in northern Mexico, nor Andrés Ortiz, newly appointed governor of Chihuahua, could do much, for they were on an official visit to Juárez at the time of Villa's latest outrage.

On January 21, the day before Villa's raid, they were given a luncheon by the Juárez Chamber of Commerce, a luncheon at which the El Paso Patrol District commander Brigadier General James J. Hornbrook and his staff were honored guests. There were the usual flowery speeches about friendship between Mexico and the United States and the bonds between the twin cities of Juárez and El Paso, and General Castro outlined his plan for the pacification of northern Mexico "but seemed to be quite sure there was very little for him to do in that line; all disturbances being of a purely sporadic nature, perpetrated by roving bands of irresponsible bandits, whom it would not be hard to round up and either exterminate or pacify." The following day the El Paso Chamber of Commerce hosted a luncheon for practically the same guests at the Paso Del Norte Hotel. In the afternoon General Hornbrook had Castro review the troops at Fort Bliss, and that night the personages again gathered for a banquet, this time at the University Club.[5] Presumably everyone maintained an embarrassed and discreet silence regarding Castro's confident assurances about exterminating bandits.

Despite General Castro's issuing a proclamation on February 10 to the citizens of Chihuahua apprising them of his aims, intentions, and principles, "the bandit Villa" continued to make the Carranza army's life miserable.[6] Hampered by shortages of soldiers, rations, and ammunition, Castro mounted no offensive operations against the elusive rebel chieftain, who menaced the Mexican Central between Juárez and the state capital.[7] Furthermore, communications between Juárez and Ojinaga were so precarious that on February 15, the Mexican consul in El Paso wired the Mexican ambassador asking him to solicit permission from the U.S. government for General Castro to ship 50,000 rounds of ammunition from Juárez to Ojinaga over American railroads. General Castro contented himself with reinforcing the garrisons in the larger towns.[8] From time to time the Carranza authorities optimistically trumpeted the elimination of prominent *villista* chieftains, as when Consul García assured the local newspapers that Martín López, Epifanio Holguín, and Ramón Vega were killed in a clash with Carranza troops near Ascención, Chihuahua, on March 18. But according to eyewitnesses the trio was alive and well.[9] As indeed was Pancho Villa, who took the city of Parral in southern Chihuahua by storm in April.[10]

World War I having come to an end on November 11, 1918, wartime censorship of telegrams and mail was discontinued, passport regulations were relaxed, and civilian employees of the Military Intelligence Office were dismissed owing to a lack of federal appropriations with which to pay them.[11] It thus became much easier to engage in revolutionary intrigue. And Villa continued to have many supporters on the U.S. side of the border, people such as George Holmes. Holmes cooperated with the Bureau to some extent, but he remained firmly committed to helping Pancho Villa.[12] His immediate objective was to procure and cross into Mexico all the ammunition and supplies possible so that they would be available whenever Villa launched his long-anticipated attack on Ciudad Juárez. The intelligence officer in the Big Bend detained several ammunition smugglers, "all connected with Holmes."[13] Holmes himself was once again arrested, on February 5, 1919, the result of the Bureau of Investigation and the District Intelligence Office uncovering an important part of his nefarious operations.

It seems that a Vickers machine gun, a quantity of ammunition, and seven rifles were stolen from the supply tent of the 9th U.S. Engineers at Camp Courchesne, in Smeltertown. Suspicion fell on the first sergeant of Company C, Ernest B. Stalder, whom the intelligence officer and Agent Jones interrogated. The sergeant eventually broke down and signed a statement. He said that Frank Miller (apparently no relation to attorney Harry Miller) approached him about obtaining some detonating caps; Stalder gave him two hundred, whereupon Miller allowed as how he was also in the market for arms and ammunition—he could get five cents a cartridge and $10 per service rifle, and he offered to split the profits and let the sergeant have free use of Miller's two cars. Stalder, in financial difficulties, accepted Miller's proposition. The previous November, Stalder had delivered to Miller from Camp Courchesne 500 dynamite caps and 500 detonators, each with four feet of copper wire attached. The authorities were still looking for these items.[14] With the help of two accomplices—Private John H. Minahan of the 7th U.S. Cavalry and Dick N. Harrell—Stalder on January 15 broke into the supply tent at Camp Courchesne and stole the Vickers machine gun, a tripod, an extra barrel, a box of spare parts, a water box and hose for cooling the machine gun, three cases (3,600 rounds) of service ammunition, and seven rifles. The thieves loaded these items into an auto and drove to El Paso, where they hid the goods.

The next day, in Shorty Ball's Thirst Parlor at the corner of North Kansas and East Second streets they met the purchaser, a man "about fifty years old, rather fat, smokes cigars incessantly"—George Holmes. Miller placed six hundred rounds of the stolen ammunition in Holmes's car. Holmes announced that he wanted rifles and wanted them badly but couldn't pay for any munitions until he returned in about a week from a trip to Mexico to see Pancho Villa. Sergeant Stalder kept asking Miller for his share of the money, and Miller kept answering that he would have to wait until Holmes returned. The sergeant was bitter because he never made a cent out of the deal.

Bureau agents and the intelligence officer, Captain Carroll M. Counts, arrested Miller. Agent Jones had known him for a number of years and stated that "I do not know of a more hardened criminal operating on the border than Frank Miller." The prisoner had nothing to say, and he was placed in solitary confinement in the stockade at Fort Bliss. The officers next arrested Dick Harrell, who confessed to his role in the affair, stating that he and Miller had driven to George Holmes's ranch near San Elizario with the rest of the stolen items. A search of Holmes's ranch yielded nothing, but the officers detained one Francisco López, who had a small ranch a mile from

Holmes's place and who had worked for Holmes and owed him money. After "severe grilling" López admitted having received the stolen machine gun, rifles, ammunition, and equipment. He reluctantly showed the officers where they were hidden.

Agent Jones had Harrell and López placed in the county jail, along with Salvador Cano, Holmes's chauffeur. Jones swore out complaints against George Holmes, Frank Miller, Sergeant Ernest Stalder, and Private John Minahan, charging them with theft of government property and conspiracy to export arms to Mexico. He filed a complaint against Dick Harrell charging him with aiding and abetting in these offenses. George Holmes was currently in Sierra Blanca on his way to the Rio Grande on horseback with two hundred cartridges. Jones sent a deputy U.S. marshal and a customs inspector there to arrest him and bring him to El Paso. On the evening of February 5, Holmes was arraigned before the U.S. commissioner, who set his bond at $10,000. Unable to post it, Holmes was remanded to the county jail. Frank Miller managed to post his $5,000 bond. Holmes's chauffer eventually gave a statement, declaring that Shorty Ball's Thirst Parlor was the headquarters for Holmes and his associates and that on another occasion he had on Holmes's instructions delivered a Browning automatic rifle and ammunition to Francisco López. The authorities managed to recover the Browning, some 2,000 rounds of ammunition, and some clothing at the ranch of another of Holmes's confederates, Pedro García, whose property on Córdova Island abutted the international boundary. They also seized three electrical blasting machines for setting off dynamite charges that Frank Miller had purchased in El Paso.

At their arraignment, Sergeant Stalder and Private Minahan stated that they intended to plead guilty; they were remanded in default of $2,500 bond each. Harrell was arraigned and jailed in default of a $1,000 bond. Harrell was convicted of stealing government property, and on May 3, 1919, he was sentenced to two years in the federal penitentiary in Atlanta. On January 16, 1920, his sentence was commuted to expire at once—Harrell was freed on compassionate grounds because his wife was seriously ill.[15] López was placed under a $1,000 bond as a material witness. Pedro García was jailed. As far as Agent Jones was concerned, "it is my intention if possible to keep George Holmes in the county jail; should he make a ten thousand dollar bail, which is now pending, it is my intention to file additional charges against him. I need not make any comment on George Holmes, except that he has been a prime mover in revolutionary affairs on the border for the past five years."[16] For his work on this case Agent Jones received a commendation from his superior, who praised him to the chief of the Bureau. Even Mexican consul Andrés García thanked Jones effusively, both personally and on behalf of his government.[17]

A commentary on the level of cooperation between county and federal officers is revealed by the following incident, A deputy sheriff named Ivy Finley happened to see Agent John Wren in the jail with Sergeant Stalder and asked what the soldier had done. When Wren replied that he had stolen a machine gun, Finley commented "I'll bet that George Holmes had something to do with it." Finley went on to say that several weeks previously he had served some court papers in San Elizario and had stopped by Holmes's house. While there, Finley asked whether Holmes had any dried meat, and Holmes hospitably told him to help himself. When Finley went into a back room to get some of the meat hanging on a wall, he stumbled over something bulky covered with a tarpaulin. He thought it might be some kind of machine gun and asked Holmes about it. Holmes replied that it was indeed a machine gun and that he had obtained it for Villa through some soldiers. Finley explained that he hadn't passed this information on to the Bureau because he had been busy, and anyway he knew the Bureau was watching Holmes.[18]

Holmes didn't like the county jail. He propositioned the jailer to let him escape, stating that he would soon receive a large sum of money. The jailer informed the Bureau and kept the agents apprised of Holmes's activities in jail. And Holmes was active, offering a trusty $1,000 to slip him a key to his cell and help him flee and plotting with two other prisoners, the wife of one of whom had smuggled three hacksaws into the facility.[19]

A local bootlegger, Ed Jones, also informed on Holmes in return for the Bureau's putting in a good word for Jones with the judge. He reported that one Ben Heckelmann, the bartender at Shorty Ball's place, was a good friend of Holmes and that Heckelmann used to steal cattle with him in south Texas. Heckelmann stated he was very sorry to see Holmes in trouble but that the Holmes crowd was expecting to receive about $20,000 from Francisco Villa's headquarters in Mexico. Further, he said that on the day of Holmes' arrest, February 5, Holmes sent a messenger to Villa informing him of his arrest. Villa dispatched a courier who arrived in El Paso on the morning of the February 12 and who told Heckelmann and Frank Miller that Villa would indeed send $20,000 for Holmes. Heckelmann and Frank Miller were very skittish about being under surveillance, to the point that before discussing these matters they checked all over Miller's house searching for a dictograph, and instead of talking in one of the rooms, they went into the bathroom.

According to Jones, when Villa attacked Juárez, the munitions and equipment that Holmes and company were accumulating, allegedly amounting to five or six carloads, would be supplied him. However, for political reasons General Felipe Angeles rather than Villa would nominally lead the attack. When Villa had captured the town, Holmes would take charge of the packing plant and handle the export of cattle from Mexico; Heckelmann would be his right-hand man at the plant, at a good salary. Shorty Ball would receive various concessions for saloons and gambling. Informant Jones stressed that the Holmes crowd had lots of spotters and requested that the Bureau not mention his name.[20]

Holmes made his influence felt even outside the jail. The Bureau was dismayed when notified that Francisco Villalobos, who "has long been a notorious character along the Border, and has been for some years a henchman of George M. Holmes," had posted bond for Francisco López, the crucial material witness in the Holmes case. This was a maneuver to spirit López to Mexico so he couldn't testify at the upcoming trial, scheduled for the April term of the federal court. On Agent Jones's instructions, Agent Wren had a serious talk with López, strongly suggesting that he remain in El Paso. But just to be sure he did, Wren got authorization from the assistant U.S. attorney to file a charge of conspiracy against López, who was slapped with a new $2,500 bond, which he couldn't post, and he was speedily remanded to the county jail. Agent Jones wrote: "I do not believe that Holmes' allies and supporters will be able to make this bond. However, in case it is made, it is my intention to file another charge against Lopez. There is practically no doubt, in my mind, that if any of the local Villistas are successful in obtaining the release of any of the committed witnesses in the Holmes Case, such witnesses will be persuaded to leave the country, the method employed being either threats, intimidation or bribery."[21]

Holmes was still scheming to get out of jail somehow. He discussed plans for escaping with several people, among them deputy sheriff Ivy Finley. Holmes also considered the idea of feigning illness so that he could be taken to the county hospital, from where he could flee in an automobile.[22] The Bureau certainly took Holmes seriously. Agent Jones was even called to San Antonio to confer with his division superintendent and to Waco to confer with the U.S. attorney and the U.S. marshal for the Western District of Texas. The purpose of this trip was to discuss the advisability of removing George Holmes and his codefendants from El Paso "to an inland point within the Western District of Texas. This, for the reason as will be noted in previous reports, that a scheme had been uncovered looking to an attempted jail delivery and the release of these parties by Villista sympathizers in El Paso and vicinity."[23]

While trying to keep George Holmes locked up, the Bureau was also gathering intelligence on General Felipe Angeles, who had stopped by Holmes's house to say farewell and had entered Mexico on the night of December 11, 1918. His mission was to build support for the Mexican Liberal Alliance (Alianza Liberal Mexicana). He had been instrumental in forming the Liberal Alliance in New York City on November 9, 1918. The principal reason for establishing such an organization was the hope that Mexican politicians and intellectuals could unite in opposition to Carranza, bring about peace in Mexico, and thus lessen the possibility of intervention by a militarily powerful United States. That specter loomed even more menacingly in 1919, when Senator Albert Fall of New Mexico led a drive to have the United States withdraw its diplomatic recognition of Carranza, a drive that had the enthusiastic support of powerful American corporations and individuals with economic interests in Mexico.

The Liberal Alliance called for abolishing the radical Constitution that the Carranza regime had enacted in 1917 and restoring the venerable 1857 Constitution. The Liberal Alliance's objectives were spelled out in the obligatory manifesto, largely formulated by General Antonio Villarreal, originally a *magonista* and one of the few leftists in the organization. However, the organization faced the same problems that had sunk previous attempts to forge a coalition to depose Carranza—vicious infighting between factions and individuals, many of whom were either conservatives or reactionaries.

The Liberal Alliance's executive committee in New York was composed of directors General Felipe Angeles, General Antonio Villarreal, and Enrique Llorente; treasurer Federico González Garza; and secretaries Enrique Santibañez, N. Icaza Morán, and General J. F. del Valle.[24] Among the members were figures such as Miguel Díaz Lombardo and Jesús Flores Magón. The organization established branches in several other American cities, including El Paso. There the executive committee consisted of Manuel Bonilla, General Federico Cervantes, General Macrino Martínez, Miguel Baca Ronquillo, G. Méndez Velarde, Eduardo Angeles, and Manuel David Camarena—*villistas* predominated. When the Liberal Alliance's manifesto was communicated to Pancho Villa, he and his subordinates heartily endorsed it, promulgating it as their *Plan de Rio Florido*.[25] Not unnaturally, the heavy *villista* influence in the Liberal Alliance produced considerable skepticism as to just how broadly based the organization really was.

Once he had crossed into Mexico, Angeles had a statement published on January 1, 1919, in the El Paso *villista* newspaper *La Patria*, edited by Silvestre Terrazas.[26] In the manifesto, which called for the reestablishment of the 1857 Constitution, Angeles proclaimed himself leader of the movement, naming Pancho Villa as commander of the cavalry and announcing that the *villista* chieftains Hipólito Villa, Martín López, and Epifiano Holguín had recognized Angeles as their leader. Unfortunately for Angeles, many people regarded him as a mere figurehead, with Villa as the real power. Agent Jones was of the opinion that "it would appear to be Francisco Villa's plan that Angeles shall be the sugar-coating of the Villa-recognition pill, which he hopes the United States and Allies will be induced to swallow as a possible solution of the 'Mexican Problem.'"[27] Then Angeles issued a lengthy manifesto setting forth his objectives, which was published in *La Patria* on February 5. The date was chosen because of its symbolism—the 1857 Constitution had been promulgated on February 5.[28]

In an effort to generate some degree of unity among Mexican refugees, a mass meeting was held in Liberty Hall, the auditorium of the El Paso County courthouse, on January 5. Some six to seven hundred persons attended, including of course an employee of the Bureau, who reported on the proceedings. A succession of speakers pledged to lay aside their former alliances and work for a single object, the pacification of Mexico. By standing vote those present elected officers for the as-yet-untitled organization: General Manuel Landa, General Federico Cervantes, Rafael Uro, Hilario Lozoya, Vicente Vergara, and J. M. Gutiérrez Fernández. The Bureau's analysis was that "from the line-up Sunday, there does seem to be an understanding between Felicistas and Villistas, because representatives of both factions certainly had a hand in the affair of last Sunday. Judging from past events in Mexico, this amicable understanding can not last; but for the present, it is quite interesting, and will be watched by this Office."[29] The role of General Federico Cervantes, one of the principal speakers at the meeting, was noteworthy. He was a devoted follower of Felipe Angeles, a director of the Asociación Unionista Mexicana, and an organizer of the El Paso branch of the Mexican Liberal Alliance.[30] Agent Jones commented that "it will be gathered from this that there are wheels within wheels in revolutionary circles along the Border."[31]

At a subsequent mass meeting of the Mexican Liberal Alliance (covered by an informant of the District Intelligence Office and an undercover Bureau employee), General Federico Cervantes was again one of the principal speakers, as was Colonel Juan José Rocha (the *felicista* stalwart who was also Informant AR for the District Intelligence Office). Indicating the audience's sympathies, "the mention of Santa Ana's [*sic*] name was received in silence; Juarez' with unanimous applause; Porfirio Diaz' also with great applause; Madero's with applause only from the Villistas present, and some Angelistas; Huerta's in silence except by the Villistas and Angelistas, who applauded the epithets applied, and the vilification of Carranza met with the loudest and longest applause of all." In evaluating the meeting, Agent Jones was of the opinion that "the foregoing shows that this Alliance has thrown off the veil of non-partisanship with which it seems they intended to mask their propaganda; and has come out frankly as sponsoring the Angeles-Villa movement, this combination being backed by both Felicistas and Villistas, 'Confusion to Carranza!' being the common battle-cry."[32] Jones also stated that "we do not believe the sort of Mexicans who seem to make up the Felicista party will ever really accept a man of Francisco Villa's stamp, but we believe they plan to use him and his forces to assist them in ousting Carranza; that accomplished, to eliminate Villa. And, it will be understood that he does not eliminate easily; therefore the present movement does not promise very much by way of ultimate pacification of Mexico." Stating the obvious, Jones commented that "if the plans of the Mexican Liberal Alliance are carried out, it would seem as if El Paso, Texas, is likely to be the storm center of the new revolutionary plots and counterplots." As matters developed, the Asociación Unionista Mexicana decided to have nothing to do with the Mexican Liberal Alliance because it was a "political organization." To commemorate the 1857 Constitution the Asociación Unionista held its own celebration, to which American military and civilian officials, including the Bureau contingent, were cordially invited. Taking a prominent role in these festivities was Colonel Juan José Rocha. Agent Jones mused: "This goes to show how involved Mexican revolutionary matters have become here."[33] Carranza's followers could take great satisfaction in watching their adversaries squabble bitterly among themselves, and not only in El Paso. In Los Angeles, exiled attorney Jorge Vera Estañol organized the National Alliance (Alianza Nacionalista) in an effort to unite exiles to restore the 1857 Constitution. The National Alliance, whose president was the *orozquista, vazquista, huertista* and now *felicista* General David de la Fuente, had no connection with the Mexican Liberal Alliance.[34]

Providing a gauge of the progress of the local *felicista* junta was George Holmes, who informed the Bureau that about January 2 a *felicista* filibustering expedition of twenty men under General Evaristo Pérez, a former *orozquista*, had crossed the border. They had publicly declared themselves *felicistas* because that was who had financed them, but in reality they were independents who planned to join Pancho Villa. Then in April, "there are two distinct expeditions being planned, one of which is being organized by Gen. [Arnaldo] Casso Lopez [the head of the local *felicista* movement] and the other by Fausto Miranda, local Mexican lawyer. There seems to be some friction between these two leaders, and although their expeditions are to accomplish the same results, they are nevertheless being organized independent [*sic*] of each other."[35] Even if these small expeditions made it into Chihuahua they would have virtually no impact on the military situation there.

The *felicistas* were a lot better at talking than fighting. They professed great indignation at the promulgation of the Carranza regime's radical 1917 Constitution. A galaxy of conservative and reactionary Mexicans had attended organizational meetings in New York City. Among these personages were General Manuel Mondragón and General Aureliano Blanquet, as well as Luis Terrazas, his son-in-law Enrique Creel, David de la Fuente, Jesús Flores Magón, and Ricardo Gómez Robelo.[36] But militarily things didn't go all that well. Félix Díaz had support in southern Mexico, but in April 1919, General Aurelio Blanquet, his best commander, was killed in the state of Veracruz when his horse fell down a ravine. Carranza troops decapitated the corpse and took Blanquet's head off in triumph to the state capital.[37]

In El Paso the Asociación Unionista managed to elect a board of directors at a meeting on February 23 at the Fraternal Hall. And a leading *felicista*, Nemesio García Naranjo, came from San Antonio to address the organization at its meeting on March 2, a meeting attended by more than one thousand persons. Informant AR of course both participated in and reported on the meetings, and Agent Jones concluded that "it would now seem as if this 'Mexican Unionist Association,' although composed of Mexicans from different factions, is dominated by representatives of the Felicista Party, and this office, as well as the District Intelligence Office, is of the opinion that it was organized principally to neutralize the efforts of the Mexican

Liberal Alliance, which is Villista-Angelista although the ostensible object of both organizations is the union of all Mexicans." The members of the local committee of the National Union were also members of the Mexican Unionist Association, founded by García Naranjo to support Félix Díaz.[38] "Its members are at present doing everything they can to secure the recognition of the Diaz forces as belligerents." Further, "This union between the two organizations will merely mean, as this office understands the situation, as far as it *can* be understood, that the Mexican Unionist Association will now be openly Felicista instead of camouflaging."[39]

The Bureau and the Intelligence Office were able continually to monitor the exile community not only with operatives but also through the voluminous correspondence furnished by the military censor and by informants.[40] An intercepted letter from Hipólito Villa's wife, Mabel Silva de Villa, to her husband revealed that she was desperately unhappy with Hipólito and with things in general. A very attractive woman, Mabel had caught the eye of Hipólito when she was a cashier at an El Paso movie theater.[41] The Bureau kept an eye on her so that if she became sufficiently sorry for herself she might be properly approached by the right kind of undercover informant and provide useful information about *villista* activities. The Bureau also obtained yet another *villista* code in April 1919, and on May 21, 1919, the agency produced a lengthy "Resume of the General Mexican Situation as It Has Existed in the San Antonio Division during the Six Months, Beginning, Approximately, with December, 1918." In addition, the Bureau compiled a list of the more prominent *villistas* in El Paso and vicinity.[42] Agent Jones added that "We have no list of the membership of the "Villista Junta" as such, because we are not quite sure whether the Mexican Liberal Alliance or the Association [*sic*] Unionista Mexicana would be termed the Villa Junta, as there are members of both who are Villistas, and also members of each who are not Villistas, but we can safely state that names given above are of those who are Villa sympathizers, active or quiescent."[43]

For example, in discussing an intercepted letter from Ramon Prida in New York City to Manuel Bonilla in El Paso, Agent Jones commented that "the above letter, and others of a similar nature, have been incorporated and translated, in order to show the apparent impossibility of any Mexican factions cooperating, or working in accord for anything. Also, it would appear from recent intercepted letters that the adherents and admirers of Felipe Angeles are far from looking favorably upon Francisco Villa."[44]

In this connection, *villista* adherents Fernando Liceaga, Rafael Iturbide, and Manuel de Icaza blew into town, and Liceaga was very anxious to talk with George Holmes, who was still in jail. The Bureau was most accommodating, not only permitting such a visit but furnishing Liceaga with an escort—in the person of Colonel Rocha (Informant AR). Holmes was overjoyed to see Rocha, which made Liceaga that much more confident that Rocha was trustworthy. Holmes informed them that General Angeles was anxiously awaiting the arrival of an expedition composed of his supporters. Holmes pointed out that unfortunately he himself wasn't in a position to be of much assistance, but he referred them to certain *villista* sympathizers in El Paso and Sierra Blanca who could help them obtain horses, arms, ammunition, and guides. Of these the most important was Manuel González Jr., who was reportedly filling in for Holmes as Villa's local purchasing agent for arms and ammunition. Informant AR said González had accumulated about 5,000 rounds, which he had purchased from American soldiers in small amounts.[45]

The proposed expedition took shape under the leadership of General Federico Cervantes, who was a devoted follower of General Angeles. Cervantes had been eking out a living in El Paso as a jitney driver and was mortified that he had not for financial reasons been able to leave his family and accompany his revered commander into Chihuahua. But he had promised to join Angeles within three months. It was Cervantes who had summoned Liceaga, Iturbide, and Icaza to El Paso in order to participate in the mission.[46] As Cervantes and his associates made their preparations, Colonel Rocha was constantly in touch; for example, he let Cervantes keep on his property the seven horses the conspirators purchased at a sale of condemned U.S. Army livestock. Cervantes decided to disregard George Holmes's recommendation that they cross the Rio Grande at the Bosque Bonito. Instead, Cervantes planed to cross the river near Socorro, downriver from El Paso.[47]

Not only did the American authorities know the conspirators' plans in detail, but so did Andrés García. He went to the Bureau office and informed the agents that he had a spy in Cervantes's expedition, one José Velázquez de la Rosa, a former *villista* lieutenant colonel who was on García's payroll at $75 a month. Moreover, to the Bureau's delight García said he would allow his operative to testify in federal court. "This will be of material assistance to us, in case that we are able to so conclude this investigation as to prosecute, because the District Intelligence Officer is endeavoring to so handle it that A. R.'s connection with the D. I. O. will not become known. This is rather imperative, because to uncover A. R. for use as a witness would put an end to his service as Informant for the D. I. O., and also would be likely to result in exceedingly unpleasant consequences for A. R. personally, because none of the various Mexican factions here would be favorably impressed with A. R's work for the D. I. O."[48]

The expedition prepared to cross the Rio Grande on March 18, 1919, at Socorro, unaware that the Americans were waiting to pounce. Assisting the team from the District Intelligence Office and the Bureau of Investigation were Informant AR and Consul García's operative. The officers tracked the seven horses when they were taken to Socorro. They followed Liceaga and Icaza in automobiles and established a roadblock; when the pair tried to speed around the roadblock Agent Wren blasted one of their tires with a sawed-off shotgun and fired again in the air. The Mexicans, attired for the field in riding breeches and leggings, surrendered, and the weapons, ammunition, and equipment in the car were confiscated. Wren, by the way, was the only member of the whole American contingent who spoke Spanish.

The officers then telephoned the detachment of the 7th U.S. Cavalry stationed in Ysleta, and six troopers were detailed to assist them. As the soldiers neared Socorro the *carrancista* agent led them to a spot where the six "enlisted men" of the Cervantes expedition waited. The officers apprehended them and seized a quantity of arms and ammunition concealed in the brush nearby. General Cervantes and several others were arrested as they arrived. One tried to resist and suffered a slight flesh wound in the leg. An army truck transported the eighteen dejected prisoners to the Fort Bliss stockade for safekeeping. Bureau agents and the district intelligence officer obtained a search warrant and ransacked Cervantes's apartment at the Ashley Hotel, 607½ South El Paso Street, removing a number of documents. Under the same warrant they examined the trunks of Liceaga and Iturbide at the same hotel, seizing a quantity of letters and other papers.[49] Alfonso Gómez Morentín, the *villista* colonel, tried to put a good face on the capture of Cervantes and company, pointing out that the *carrancistas* knew exactly when they were coming and where they were crossing and would have shot them all had they made it across the Rio Grande.[50]

Bureau agents had the most important prisoners brought to their office in the Mills Building for interrogation. Several of them gave statements. The Bureau then filed complaints against sixteen of the men. At the preliminary hearing the bonds for Cervantes, Liceaga, Iturbide, and Icaza were set at $5,000 each and at $3,000 for the rest. Only one of them could post bail. Agent Wright commented that Cervantes, Liceaga, Iturbide, and Icaza "are of an entirely different class from the rest of the defendants. They are of the better class Mexican, in which the Spanish blood predominates, are well educated, well bred, and men of intelligence. . . . The other defendants, including 'Colonel' Magdaleno Flores, are of the lower class, practically undiluted Indian extraction, ignorant and of very little, if any, education."[51] Cervantes later complained that the authorities treated them roughly, particularly those of Indian appearance.

Only Cervantes and five of his more important companions were tried. The Liberal Alliance obtained defense attorneys, one of them being Volney Howard. (Despite his reputation, Howard wasn't entirely a reprobate. He managed State Senator Claude Hudspeth's successful campaign for Congress in 1918. But, on February 17, 1924, Volney Howard committed suicide at a friend's house near El Paso.)[52] As Consul García had promised, Velázquez de la Rosa testified for the prosecution. The defense attorneys tried to secure a continuance until the next term of court and have the defendants released on bond, but to no avail. On April 16, 1919, the accused were found guilty of conspiracy. Three days later each was sentenced to two years in Leavenworth. According to Cervantes, the judge was sympathetic and told them privately that he had instructions from his government, at the request of the Mexican government, to hand down harsh sentences.[53] Cervantes, incidentally, had an article entitled in translation "Francisco Villa and the Revolutionary Cause" published in the April 29, 1919, issue of *La Patria* newspaper. That newspaper, generally considered to be the "official" *villista* organ in El Paso, launched a petition drive to obtain clemency for Cervantes and his companions.[54] The drive was unsuccessful.

Another trial soon titillated the public. The Bureau worked hard to prepare the case against George Holmes and his associates for conspiracy to steal government property and export arms to Mexico, the charge stemming from the theft of the munitions from the 9th Engineers. On April 7, a federal grand jury returned true bills against Holmes, Ernest Stalder, John Minahan, Frank Miller, and Dick Harrell. When their trial began on April 17, Stalder, Minahan, and Harrell pleaded guilty. George Holmes and Frank Miller pleaded not guilty, and their attorneys immediately requested a continuance on the ground that the witnesses for the defense couldn't be located. The judge granted the motion, postponing the trial until April 28. In the meantime the Bureau located one C. E. Summers, whom the defense attorneys alleged was a material witness for their side. Summers, however, signed an affidavit denying that he knew anything about the case or had even spoken with the defendants. He further stated that he wouldn't testify to anything that was alleged by the defense attorneys. The assistant U.S. attorney was not amused by this perjured application for a continuance and planned to file perjury charges against George Holmes and Frank Miller. Learning that George Holmes had sent two of the witnesses away to Mexico, the Bureau was so determined to locate them that Agent Wren was dispatched to the Big Bend with instructions to cross into Mexico if necessary. He did so, returning from Mexico after a week with the two missing witnesses.[55]

Agent Jones gleefully reported that "when this case was called for trial this morning [April 28], the attorneys for the defense renewed their Motion for Continuance, and were very much surprised when we presented them with their missing witnesses." Jones continued: "After using every underhand method and devious wile known to an unscrupulous brain, trained in law, even to the introduction of perjured testimony, the defense completed its case." The jury was out for all of fifteen minutes on April 30 before finding George Holmes and Frank Miller guilty on all counts.[56]

On May 3, the judge sentenced Holmes and Miller to five years in a federal penitentiary and a $500 fine each; Stalder, Minahan, and Harrell each received two years in the penitentiary. Holmes was unable to make bond while he appealed his sentence. And there was allegedly an attempt to bribe one of the other defendants not to testify against Holmes.[57] In the unlikely event that Holmes's conviction was reversed, Agent

Jones planned to charge him with financing and outfitting the Angeles expedition. Jones was able to state triumphantly that "George M. Holmes has been the subject of a great many reports by the writer, and other agents of this Bureau; in fact, during the past three years his name has figured more prominently in the files of this office than that of any other one person. His arrest, conviction and sentence will have a most salutary effect in this section of the Border country, and it is the result of several years [of] persistent effort on the part of Agents of the Department. FILE CLOSED."[58]

Even without George Holmes's help, Pancho Villa was doing well. He had been building up his forces in Chihuahua during the spring, and by early June was able virtually to isolate the state capital by destroying rail lines and cutting telegraph wires, his object being not to attack the city but to destroy *carrancista* morale and hopefully induce the garrison to surrender. "It is known that the Federal commanders in Chihuahua City have no confidence in the loyalty of their troops; and this is said to be the reason they will not send out detachments into the field in pursuit of Villa."[59]

But as far as the Carranza regime was concerned, Pancho Villa's rampage was entirely the fault of the United States. General Cándido Aguilar, governor of Veracruz and Carranza's son-in-law, issued a statement alleging that the Mexican government couldn't eliminate Villa because of the United States' selfish wartime restrictions on the export of war materiel. The bandits, on the other hand, he complained, were able to smuggle in whatever they needed. Aguilar asserted that the United States couldn't demand pacification of the border and at the same time deny the Mexican government the means to accomplish this.[60] Of course graft, corruption, incompetence, and cowardice on the part of the Carranza military weren't factors in the success of Villa's continuing campaign.

That campaign was classic Villa: having pinned down the Carranza garrison in the city of Chihuahua, he launched an attack against Ciudad Juárez. This was a foolhardy move, since it would provoke some kind of response by the United States. Besides, even if Villa succeeded in capturing Juárez it would do him little good, since the United States would immediately close the port of El Paso. General Felipe Angeles, who had hoped to control Villa and have him adhere to the rudiments of civilized warfare, was depressed not only because he had failed to influence Villa but also because not a single one of the leading Mexican intellectual and political exiles in the United States had had the courage to join Angeles in Mexico. Angeles had been arguing with Villa about the conduct of the campaign and strongly advised against such an attack, but Villa wouldn't listen and moved his troops up the Mexican Central toward the border town. His adherents in El Paso confidently predicted that Juárez would fall without a fight.

As Villa moved toward Juárez many of the town's inhabitants fled to El Paso. By June 11, Villa had isolated the town. The federal garrison skirmished with the advancing *villistas* and nervously awaited the main assault. Ironically, the commander of the Juárez garrison was Brigadier General Francisco González, graduate of Notre Dame and St. Louis universities in the United States and brother of the late Abraham González, the *maderista* leader who had originally recruited Villa back in 1910.[61]

The U.S. Army closely monitored Villa's advance. The commander of the El Paso Patrol District, Brigadier General James B. Irwin, was tight lipped about his orders, stating only that "adequate measures" were being taken to protect El Paso. One battalion of the 19th U.S. Infantry was deployed along the river. As a precaution, the other battalion of the 19th Infantry was dispatched from Douglas, and the entire 24th Infantry was rushed from Columbus to El Paso in three special trains, arriving on June 13. A battery of the 82nd Field Artillery was emplaced near the Stanton Street bridge, and other batteries had been unlimbered on the mesa near Fort Bliss, their guns trained on Juárez.

At 12:10 a.m. on June 15, Villa launched a full-scale assault beginning along the river, the same tactic Orozco had used in 1911. His men battled their way into the business district, driving the federal garrison into Fort Hidalgo. But the *villistas* then began engaging in widespread looting, especially of cantinas, and the ensuing disorganization enabled the federals to launch a strong counterattack led by Colonel José Gonzalo Escobar.

Meanwhile, hordes of *juarenses* stampeded across the international bridges, led by the Chinese community, who had no desire to experience Villa's tender mercies. The U.S. Army had to establish temporary stockades for those Juárez townspeople without passports. The Juárez authorities also transferred all their valuable records to El Paso for safekeeping. Merchants had already loaded their goods into boxcars and had arranged for the cars to be pulled across the river to El Paso. While *juarenses* sought the safety of El Paso, El Pasoans sought the best vantage points from which to view the battle. The military had considerable difficulty trying to keep them away from the river.

During the fighting bullets inevitably landed in El Paso, especially near the American end of the Stanton Street bridge. The Carranza commander, General Francisco González, appeared at the Mexican end of the bridge and requested a parley, expressing his apologies on behalf of his government for the rounds landing the El Paso and assuring the American authorities that he had ordered his men not to fire into the United States. González informed the Americans that the *villistas* had been repulsed and the *carrancistas* were again in complete control of the town.

But just when everyone hoped Villa would withdraw, he launched a new attack that afternoon. Swarms of El Pasoans blocked the streets as they jostled for good vantage points. Some even climbed on top of the tanks at the city gas plant.

Binoculars were at a premium; sometimes their owners were forced to share them with those less fortunate. As his followers fought their way into the center of Juárez toward imminent victory, another shower of bullets landed in El Paso, killing a soldier and two civilians and wounding several other persons.

General Irwin had had it with Pancho Villa's antics. Irwin issued a statement that that on account of the *villistas*' firing into El Paso, which three reputable El Paso citizens had signed affidavits attesting to, and on account of the wounding of a Hispanic girl and two U.S. soldiers by *villista* gunfire, under authority given him in a telegram from the Southern Department on June 12, he was ordering troops into Juárez to disperse the *villistas* but *not* to undertake an invasion of Mexico. As soon as the safety of El Pasoans was secured, the troops would withdraw.

A force of some thirty-six hundred U.S. soldiers began crossing into Ciudad Juárez at 11 p.m. on June 15. Two armored cars led the 24th Infantry across the Santa Fe Street bridge into the downtown area. The *carrancistas* withdrew, to prevent any clash with the American troops; the *villistas* just ran. When the American infantry reached the center of town, the 5th and 7th Cavalry regiments and the 7th Field Battalion of the Signal Corps began crossing on a pontoon bridge hurriedly built by the 8th Engineers. When these units were across, the order was given for the artillery to swing into action. At 12:30 a.m., the 82nd Field Artillery opened a devastating barrage of shrapnel shells against a *villista* concentration at the grandstand of the Juárez racetrack. Villa's men fled in panic. From his office on the tenth floor of the Mills Building, General Irwin watched the progress of his troops, marked by flares. By noon on June 16 the Americans had inflicted a decisive defeat on Villa. Yet the victory was incomplete—the cavalry had planned to execute a pincer movement and cut off Villa's retreat, but the troopers got bogged down in the network of irrigation ditches around Juárez and were unable to make the glorious mounted charge they had been dreaming of.[62] The U.S. Army had accomplished its mission at the cost of two soldiers killed and ten wounded. The troops returned to El Paso in triumph to the cheers of the citizenry. And on June 17, the first five of twelve army aircraft sent from San Antonio began arriving, marking the beginning of El Paso as the principal base for aerial surveillance of the border.[63]

CHAPTER 21

The New Strongman

In the aftermath of the battle, El Pasoans swarmed into Juárez for souvenirs, many of these souvenir hunters hoping to make a quick profit by selling their artifacts, thinking they had added value because this time American troops had been involved in the battle.[1] To hear General González tell it, the Americans had not even been needed: "I did not and do not think the crossing of the American forces was necessary for the defeat of the Villa forces as my forces defended the town most bravely."[2] (Villa's colleague General Felipe Angeles was of the opinion that if the United States had not intervened, Villa would have captured Juárez in another hour or two.)[3] Predictably, although the American operation had saved his largest border town, Carranza denounced it as a gross violation of Mexican sovereignty.[4]

To emphasize that it had been Mexican valor that had saved Juárez, Colonel José Gonzalo Escobar, who had distinguished himself in the fighting, was promoted to brigadier general. Of course the reason Escobar was even around to be promoted was because of the Americans. At 6:15 on June 15 he had showed up on horseback at the Stanton Street bridge with a serious chest wound saying he needed a little help. He then toppled off his horse, was rushed by ambulance to Hotel Dieu hospital where he received medical attention, and convalesced into August at 1819 Montana Street in El Paso.[5] The Juárez garrison also received a bonus for gallantry: all officers got cash in varying amounts up to $400 for colonels, while the soldiers got new uniforms (made in El Paso). Both the Juárez citizenry and the national government presented medals to the city's defenders.[6]

During the morning of the sixteenth, the commander of the Southern Department, General De Rosey M. Cabell, arrived from Fort Sam Houston and conferred with General González, who requested that the American troops be immediately recalled from Mexican territory. The mission having been accomplished, the American general so ordered, and by nightfall on the sixteenth all American soldiers were back across the Rio Grande.

On the evening of June 19, a *villista* messenger in the person of Alfonso Gomez Morentín delivered to General Irwin a note from Felipe Angeles inquiring why American troops had fired on the *villistas* when they had made every effort to prevent bullets from landing in El Paso. Irwin and Agent Jones interpreted this as a trial balloon to determine whether there was any hope of the United States recognizing the Villa movement diplomatically. There wasn't. Irwin informed Gómez Morentín that he had no intention of answering Angeles's note and that the United States recognized only the Carranza regime as the legitimate government of Mexico. Agent Jones personally escorted Gómez Morentín to the border.[7]

Villa issued a public statement on June 25 claiming that his men had had strict orders not to fire into El Paso and accusing the Carranza garrison of having been the ones to do so in order to provoke American intervention.[8] Villa's sympathizers in El Paso kept trying to polish his image. Carlos Jáuregui, who was currently a truck driver in the city, and Frank Thayer, who frequented hotel lobbies looking for a lucrative deal, both of whom we have encountered before, asked an unnamed American with extensive interests in Chihuahua to carry certain letters for them to Villa. The letters urged Villa not to retaliate against Americans for his recent defeat by U.S. forces and stated that the writers had positive proof that it had been the *carrancistas* who had fired into El Paso to provoke American intervention and thus avoid defeat at Villa's hands. The American prudently declined their request.[9]

In July, the Bureau was told a most interesting story involving letters from Villa. A. J. McQuatters, president and general manager of the Alvarado Mining and Milling Company in Parral, Chihuahua, related that sometime in April 1919 none other than our old friend Todd McClammy had approached him in Los Angeles and had shown him a letter written to McClammy, who had smuggled ammunition for Pancho Villa, signed by Villa himself.[10] In it Villa mentioned certain silver bullion belonging to the Alvarado Company that he had appropriated, and he stated that he, Villa, authorized McClammy to negotiate with McQuatters regarding the return of the bullion to the Alvarado Company. Then in May in El Paso, McClammy showed McQuatters another letter signed by Villa in which the Mexican chieftain conferred full authority on McClammy and Juan Vargas to act for him in the bullion matter. Vargas, described as Villa's confidential agent, was constantly traveling between the United States and Villa's camp in Mexico. As the negotiations progressed, McClammy presented to McQuatters yet another letter from Villa stating that if McQuatters would deliver $4,500 to McClammy, acting as Villa's agent, the bullion would be returned, delivery to be made at the company's plant in Parral. The $4,500, however, was but earnest money, a down payment against the total amount that Villa demanded for the bullion. To prove his close association with Villa, Vargas produced a small photograph, taken recently in San Andrés, Chihuahua, showing himself and Villa seated together informally on the ground and smiling happily. McQuatters duly paid McClammy and Vargas the $4,500 on the understanding that they were to leave immediately for Villa's camp to conclude the final details for the delivery of the bullion, and then they left.

As we have seen, Villa captured the town of Parral in April. He made fresh demands on the Alvarado Mining and Milling Company and other foreign-owned enterprises there, demands that were very much at variance with the agreement concluded with McClammy and Vargas. When Villa made no move to return the bullion, McQuatters took the potentially hazardous decision to travel to Villa's camp and resolve the matter in person. He located Villa in Pilares de Concho, about ten miles from Parral. Villa received him civilly, they having met before, but when McQuatters explained his mission and mentioned the $4,500 payment, Villa went into one of his famous rages and demanded to see the letter he'd purportedly signed. McQuatters had it with him and showed it to Villa, who emphatically declared that he knew nothing about it, "that he knew J. Tod [*sic*] McClammy and Juan Vargas quite well, and did not care for either; had not seen McClammy for three years and Vargas for a year and a half; however, desired most earnestly to see both [of] them, and when he did they would regret it, but not for long."

A chagrined McQuatters returned to El Paso and related his tale of woe to Agent Jones, who had to inform him that no federal statutes had been violated by McClammy's scam. But Jones had investigated both McClammy and Juan Vargas in the past and knew that Vargas "was exceedingly handy with a pen and could imitate Villa's signature so perfectly that even persons very familiar with it would be deceived." In fact, Vargas had once demonstrated this talent in the Bureau office to agents Jones and Wren. Jones had also seen the photograph of Vargas and Villa, which was a fake. Besides being an accomplished forger, Vargas was an expert photographer, having once been employed at the local studio of Fred J. Feldman. The photograph, taken at Washington Park, was of Vargas and a Mexican jitney driver skillfully made up to accentuate a superficial resemblance to Villa. In addition, Vargas had retouched the photo to enhance the resemblance.

At Jones's suggestion McQuatters filed a complaint in state court against McClammy and Vargas for obtaining money under false pretenses. McClammy was arrested, but Vargas was nowhere to be found. McClammy claimed that he was Vargas's victim, having been deceived by the letters and photograph. Jones didn't buy it, believing that the scheme was McClammy's and that Vargas provided the technical expertise. McClammy was currently at liberty, McQuatters having dropped his complaint on McClammy's promise to make restitution of the $4,500. As for Vargas, there was a state warrant for his arrest. However, McClammy located him in the Fisher Hotel, gave him a good pistol-whipping, stole his money, and ran him out of town.[11]

From Mexicali, Vargas later wrote several plaintive letters to the district intelligence officer giving his version of the affair, denying any involvement in defrauding McQuatters and blaming "J. Tod [*sic*] McClammy, an American of unsavory reputation, and [who] according to his own account is constantly selling bars of silver for Villa." Vargas reluctantly agreed to return to El Paso and be jailed while waiting to testify against McClammy. He recounted the extortion scheme to a state grand jury, admitting that he had forged the Villa letters. The grand jury indicted him and McClammy for having obtained money from McQuatters under false pretenses and in a separate indictment charged McClammy with the assault and robbery of Vargas in the Fisher Hotel. McClammy posted a $5,000 bond, but Vargas went to jail in default of bond. McClammy was tried in December 1919. The jury found him not guilty.[12] The foregoing is but another example of El Paso's being a veritable mecca for hustlers, swindlers, and confidence men of every stripe eager to cash in on the opportunities arising from the Mexican Revolution.

On the other hand, some players wanted out. Hipólito Villa in July 1919 applied to the Immigration Service for permission to enter the United States, his ostensible reason being to enter a sanitarium in San Antonio, where his wife currently resided. He had left the United States surreptitiously in 1917, after having promised to stay away from the border, and had been assisting his brother Pancho ever since. Hipólito held the region south of the Big Bend for Pancho, controlling the export of cattle and purchasing ammunition from Carranza soldiers, ammunition that he then shipped to Pancho. There were no federal neutrality charges pending against Hipólito, but if admitted into the United States he would probably be charged with violating the passport law; otherwise it would set a bad precedent. Hipólito was now in bad shape mentally and physically. Paralyzed in both legs and semi-conscious, he'd been transported by oxcart from Villa Ahumada to a hamlet on the Mexican side of the Big Bend. Agent Jones reported succinctly: "Villa denied admission by Immigration. Is crazy and will not live long."[13] This proved to be premature, for Hipólito regained his reason and his health and lived for decades thereafter, dying in 1964.

In El Paso, meanwhile, the deck of exile organizations was reshuffled. A new organization appeared, the Mexican Peace Committee, the successor to both the Liberal Alliance and the Asociación Unionista. Its stated goal was of course to unite Mexican refugees in order to restore peace and stability to Mexico. "A meeting in El Paso was recently addressed by David de la Fuente, a Felicista, who left here for San Antonio for the same purpose. The 'charter members' and organizers here are Manuel Bonilla, Carlos A. Nieto, Jose Luis Velasco ('La Republica' fame), Sylvester [*sic*] Terrazas (editor of 'La Patria'); all recognized as the leading spirits among the Villistas in this section."[14] On August 20, Chairman Manuel Bonilla and Secretary Carlos A. Nieto issued a manifesto, in English, expounding the principles of the Mexican Peace Committee. Agent Jones commented rather cynically that "truly it would seem to be the sincere belief of Sr. Bonilla and associate refugees that 'the pen *is* mightier than the sword." Bonilla soon left El Paso with his family for San

Diego and Los Angeles saying he planned to remain there indefinitely attending to his private business interests and organizing new branches of the Mexican Peace Committee. The Liberal Alliance had not prospered in Los Angeles.[15]

While Mexican refugees were organizing against Carranza, he was organizing against them. In the summer of 1919, Consul Andrés García informed the district military intelligence officer that Carranza had authorized him to establish an intelligence service on both sides of the border to work with American agents to suppress neutrality violations, especially the smuggling of arms and ammunition. García stated that he was going to have an agent in every border town from Presidio to El Paso and promised to furnish to Military Intelligence with all information that could prove useful for prosecutions. On September 26, the director of Military Intelligence notified the Bureau of García's operation, stated that Mexican agents had supplied a great deal of valuable intelligence, and expressed the belief that García was sincere in his offer, "the idea being to curb Villista activities in the United States by gathering evidence that could not be obtained by agents of this Government." García claimed to have unlimited funds for this work and had offered "to employ as agent any person the Military Intelligence Officer believes would render valuable services." The director of Military Intelligence added that through a confidential source it had been learned that García had forty-two men in his network, located in New York, Washington, San Antonio, Presidio, and El Paso. Their exact names and the number at each location hadn't yet been determined. The director suggested that García's primary object no doubt was exactly as he had stated, but his agents "may also be used in gathering information detrimental to this Government."[16]

The Bureau must have been less than pleased at García's arrangement with Military Intelligence, especially with the part about unlimited funds and the offer to employ as agents whomever Military Intelligence wanted, since this was reminiscent of the palmy days of 1912 when the Bureau had essentially the same arrangement with the Madero administration. But this sheds light on why it was the Military Intelligence officer rather than Agent Jones who was running important agents such as Informant AR. Another view came from the Bureau agent in Brownsville, who pointed out that García's plan was redundant given the fact that the local Mexican consul already had a secret agent in the person of Henry Gray, the American who had been in the revolutionary game for years and who daily conferred with the Brownsville Military Intelligence officer and often accompanied him on trips as far upriver as Rio Grande City. "Therefore," the agent concluded, "it would be absolutely a useless expenditure of money for the Mexican Government to appoint other operatives to keep track of Military Movements on this side of the Rio Grande from Brownsville to Rio Grande City, Texas, a distance of over 100 miles."[17]

Consul García wasn't the only one who was organizing. Carlos Jáuregui and Frank Thayer were working on a silver bullion deal in the Big Bend. The smuggling of bullion had been disrupted by things such as Hipólito Villa's illness and the redeployment of *villistas* for the attack on Juárez. But by October, the scheme was again in play. The Bureau noted that "Frank Thayer, well and unfavorably known to this office, has been making frequent trips to Marfa and vicinity and back to El Paso, in connection with 'the purchase of some goats;' also that Carlos Jauregui has been for the past three months in the Big Bend Section." The *villista* Teodoro Kyriacopulos was also involved. He and Thayer hired another *villista*, one Juan José Aguilar, to assist them, cautioning him never to be seen talking with either of them because they were being closely watched by secret service men. What Kyriacopulos and Thayer didn't know was that Aguilar had agreed to serve as a confidential informant for the District Intelligence Office and the Bureau.

Thayer told Aguilar to hold himself in readiness to accompany Thayer to the Big Bend on short notice and promised that if the smuggling operation succeeded he'd pay Aguilar $1,500 plus expenses. Carlos Jáuregui had been negotiating with certain *villistas* in Mexico to deliver a large quantity of buried bullion to him and Thayer for transportation into the United States. Thayer, Jáuregui, and Kyriacopulos would be responsible for getting the bullion to El Paso, while an unnamed official in the Rio Grande Bank and Trust Company would market the ingots.

Captain Counts and Agent Jones decided to have Aguilar alert the customs supervisor in the Big Bend about the proposed smuggling operation. Aguilar and Thayer left El Paso by train on October 7. Thayer took elaborate precautions. He and Aguilar separated once they reached Marfa. That night Aguilar took a stroll out of town, and Thayer picked him up in an automobile. They continued on to the village of Lajitas on the Rio Grande where they conferred with Jáuregui. They expected to receive the bullion within a day or two.

Complicating matters, there was another group after the same bullion. Harry Miller, attorney at law in El Paso, and Dr. R. H. Ellis of the town of Terlingua headed these would-be smugglers. Agent Jones wrote: "These gentlemen are employing Cesar Fargas as intermediary and ambassador. Fargas is also being used as an undercover informant by the Intelligence Office and this office, and should this last mentioned clique obtain the coveted bullion instead of Messrs Thayer et al, we shall still be in position to know of their movements and apprehend them at the proper time."[18] The whole thing was beginning to resemble an Alec Guinness comedy. Unfortunately, the outcome is unknown.

Meanwhile, General Felipe Angeles's fortunes continued to decline. Unable to influence Pancho Villa as he'd hoped, Angeles finally broke with the Mexican chieftain. With a literal handful of followers he took refuge in a cave in southern

Chihuahua. He was betrayed into the hands of Carranza forces on November 19, was taken to the city of Chihuahua, and was tried for treason by court martial. The outcome was a foregone conclusion, and on November 26, Angeles was executed by a firing squad. Some five thousand persons attended the funeral of General Felipe Angeles, one of the most honorable figures in the Mexican Revolution.[19]

George Holmes's legal troubles intensified. He not only had been convicted of stealing government property, for which, as we've seen, he had been sentenced to five years in the penitentiary, but he was also being tried on a perjury charge; the case was continued until December. His friends and family desperately tried to raise the $10,000 of his appearance bond, and they tried to mobilize all the political influence they could, writing to Senator Albert Fall to intercede on Holmes's behalf. But on December 10 Holmes was found guilty. He was sentenced to a $100 fine and three years in Leavenworth, to be served concurrently with his five-year sentence. The army considered George Holmes important enough to comment on his convictions in its weekly border intelligence summary.[20] His partisans immediately began preparing an appeal, hoping that both cases would be decided at the same time.[21]

Holmes appealed his convictions all the way to the U.S. Supreme Court, which in October 1920 refused to review his case. It didn't matter, though, for Holmes never saw the inside of a federal prison. While his appeal was pending he was freed on a $15,000 bond, for which Pancho Villa provided the money. Holmes jumped bond and fled to Mexico, staying for a time with Villa in Canutillo, Durango. Holmes acquired substantial properties in Chihuahua, reportedly owning fourteen mines and some 485,000 acres, though how he did so is unclear. On February 15, 1927, he left Ciudad Juárez for his mines, expecting to return in April with a shipment of rich ore concentrate. But on March 16, 1927, he was killed in the Sierra Madre of western Chihuahua. It seems that Holmes had engaged in "inappropriate behavior"—he had tried to buy a twelve-year-old girl, presumably for what the politically correct would term "intergenerational intimacy." When the girl's mother objected, Holmes evicted the family, claiming he owned the house in which they were living. Two of the girl's uncles then killed Holmes. One of the major players in our story thus made a disgustingly sordid exit.[22]

Villa's failed attack on Ciudad Juárez was a major turning point: the battle of Juárez was his last hurrah, militarily speaking. Of course support remained for Villa, some of it even within the Carranza forces. *Villista* sympathizers in the Chihuahua garrison plotted a mutiny for August 8 to turn the city over to Villa. Unfortunately for the plotters, one of them revealed the conspiracy. A court martial convicted eleven officers. Two colonels and three captains were shot and the rest received prison sentences.[23] Villa's decline accelerated when thereafter he lost his three principal subordinates. Martín López was killed in action, while Ramón Vega and Epifanio Holguín abandoned the cause and secured amnesty from the government.[24]

Other rebels not only secured amnesty but cut advantageous deals with the government. General Emilio Campa, the former *magonista* and *vazquista*, became a *carrancista* general, as did his colleague Lázaro Alanís. The latter, however, was not entirely trusted by the Carranza authorities, who suspected him of being in sympathy first with the *felicistas* and then with Villa.[25]

General Marcelo Caraveo, successively *orozquista* and *huertista*, left his El Paso exile in 1916 and returned to Mexico to fight on behalf of Félix Díaz, yet another losing cause. But by 1928, he had risen to general of division, the highest rank in the Mexican Army. And on October 3, 1928, he was inaugurated as governor of Chihuahua. But Caraveo miscalculated disastrously—in 1929 he joined the unsuccessful rebellion led by General José Gonzalo Escobar, the hero of the 1919 battle of Juárez, and once again fled into exile in El Paso. In 1935, he received permission from the government to return to Mexico but declined to do so. When his friend Adolfo Ruiz Cortines became president in 1952, Caraveo secured appointment as chief of customs in Juárez, the position he held when he died in an El Paso hospital in 1955.[26]

His *orozquista* and *huertista* colleague General Rodrigo Quevedo, another military mediocrity, proved quite adept at treading the corridors of power in postrevolutionary Mexico. The nadir of his career was in 1914, when he was captured as a filibuster and interned in Fort Bliss and Fort Wingate.[27] But by 1932 his fortunes had improved dramatically—on October 3, 1932, he was installed as governor of Chihuahua, serving until 1936. Thereafter he held important military positions—commander of the 25th Military Zone in Puebla, commander of the 6th Military Zone in Coahuila, and inspector general of the Mexican Army. In the latter capacity he had the satisfaction in January 1942 of making a formal visit to Fort Bliss, where he had once languished as a prisoner. He achieved dubious immortality when the town of Palomas was renamed for him; everybody still calls it Palomas.[28]

Since Juárez was firmly in *carrancista* hands, anti-Carranza elements in El Paso became disheartened. Nevertheless, they made feeble attempts to organize. In September 1919, Manuel Bonilla, the local *villista* leader, convened a meeting of dissidents. According to the Mexican embassy, David de la Fuente, Manuel Bonilla, José Luis Velasco, Silvestre Terrazas, José Nieto, and Rocha Chabre met, on instructions from Jorge Vera Estañol, to try to form a national opposition movement composed of all dissident factions to work against the Carranza regime.[29] As usual, unity proved impossible, for the factions led by Félix Díaz and Manuel Peláez refused to participate. General Juan Montaño, who had accompanied the unfortunate *felicista* General Aureliano Blanquet into Mexico in 1919, was in El Paso on September 23 trying to organize another expedition and to buy munitions for that failing movement.

Carranza's intelligence service routinely intercepted the dissidents' correspondence. And to counter the efforts of their political enemies, the Carranza regime established a newspaper, *El Nacional*.[30]

With Villa in dramatic decline, and Prohibition taking hold in the United States, there occurred a notable shift in the nature of smuggling. Contraband ammunition was still carried over to Juárez, sometimes in secret compartments in automobile gas tanks, and the smugglers loaded up with liquor, mainly tequila, for the return trip. The smuggling fraternity continued to impress the authorities with their ingenuity. One well-dressed young woman was caught bringing over a quart of tequila in a rubber hot-water bottle held in place by a cloth tied with string around her waist. Officers discovered a much more imaginative arrangement—an aerial tramway across the Rio Grande. On the Mexican bank were two crossed poles that were set upright at night, connected by a wire, kept underwater by day, tied to a tree on the American bank. A pulley arrangement enabled containers of liquor to slide easily across the river. Unfortunately for the smugglers, customs line riders stumbled across the wire and cut it. Demonstrating even more creativity, a gang trained a large dog to swim the Rio Grande with a bag fastened around his shoulders and neck holding four bottles of tequila. Mexican customs officers eventually managed to shoot the dog.[31] Almost literally every other day the El Paso newspapers reported another smuggling incident, usually involving either liquor or narcotics. At the October 1919, term of the federal court there were 169 indictments, shattering the previous record.[32]

The Krakauer family did quite well out of the Revolution. The patriarch, Adolph, died in 1914, and his son Robert, vice president of Krakauer, Zork and Moye, handled much of the firm's munitions business. In 1915, he built himself a mansion, at 1519 Hill Terrace.[33] Robert Krakauer remained prominent in both social and business circles, serving as president of the Rotary Club, the country club, and the El Paso Ranger Oil Company. He was also one of the organizers of the Hueco Basin Oil Company.[34] But just when it seemed everything was going his way, he ceased to be a player. On September 7, 1919, as Krakauer and his wife were unloading their shotguns at the Krakauer ranch east of Clint one of the weapons accidentally discharged, killing him instantly. His funeral was one of the largest in the history of El Paso.[35] Ironically, firearms, which had been so lucrative for Robert Krakauer, proved to be his undoing.

Senator Fall of New Mexico, never an admirer of Venustiano Carranza and always an advocate of U.S. intervention in Mexico, launched an intensified campaign against the Mexican president in 1919. Fueling Fall's campaign were American concerns over the radical Mexican Constitution of 1917's threat to foreign-owned property and over Washington's outrage at the Carranza authorities' arrest of the U.S. consular agent in Puebla. Fall and his allies hoped to bring about U.S. military intervention in Mexico.[36] Not only did Fall introduce a resolution calling for the

United States to withdraw its diplomatic recognition of Carranza, a move that would have enormously encouraged Carranza's enemies, but Fall also headed a Senate subcommittee created to review conditions in Mexico and U.S.-Mexican relations. Fall used El Paso as his base of operations and quickly assembled a staff that included El Paso attorney and judge Dan M. Jackson, who resigned his wartime commission as a major in the Judge Advocate General's office to become the committee's secretary; federal Bureau of Investigation special agent in charge of the El Paso office Gus Jones, who received a furlough from the agency to become a committee investigator; William Martin Hanson, senior Texas Ranger captain, who was granted a leave of absence to be the committee's chief investigator; Captain George Hyde, representing Military Intelligence; and Henry O. Flipper, the committee's interpreter and translator. Flipper was an interesting character with wide border experience. He was the first black graduate of West Point, and he had worked for the Sierra Mining Company in El Paso from 1912 to 1919, during which time he'd kept Fall abreast of conditions in Mexico. Fall's subcommittee heard testimony in several cities from December 1, 1919 to June 5, 1920, producing a massive *Investigation of Mexican Affairs*.[37]

Fall used the subcommittee to try to demonstrate that Carranza caused most of the trouble between the United States and Mexico.[38] As might be expected, Carranza's intelligence service was most interested in the committee's activities. Jesús María Arriola, the onetime head of Mexican intelligence, had continued working as an agent in Los Angeles. Being a remarkably indiscreet sort of spy, he took from his black briefcase with a false bottom his commission as special agent of the secretary of foreign relations dated on November 19, 1919, and showed it to a local Bureau agent, confiding that he was being paid a handsome $20 a day plus expenses. Furthermore, he stated that all Mexican secret service agents in the United States had been instructed to take note of all Mexicans appearing before the Fall committee. Arriola also confidentially revealed the names of two of his agents specifically hired to monitor such Mexicans. The Bureau was presumably grateful for Arriola's information, since it was already keeping him under surveillance and obtaining copies of all telegrams he sent.[39] On orders from the secretary of foreign relations, Arriola assumed charge of the Mexican consulate in San Diego in April 1920 with instructions to combat dissident Mexican exiles.[40]

As it happened, Fall's vendetta against Carranza failed, not because of Fall's efforts but because of developments in Mexico. By 1919, Carranza had amassed a host of enemies, for ideological and personal reasons. And more and more Mexicans were disgusted by the rampant corruption that characterized his regime. Their dissatisfaction increased when it became evident that Carranza, barred by the Constitution from serving another term, planned to remain the power behind the throne by engineering the election in 1920 of a figurehead president, his follower Ignacio Bonillas, the Mexican ambassador to the United States. But ominously, on June 1, 1919, General Alvaro Obregón, who had been instrumental in elevating Carranza to power and keeping him there, issued a manifesto in Nogales announcing his own candidacy for the presidency.[41]

Obregón's emergence as a presidential contender shifted the focus of revolutionary intrigue on the border away from Chihuahua and Pancho Villa, who was still in the field although the governor of Chihuahua had in December 1919,offered a $25,000 reward for him dead or alive.[42] The center of attention on the border was no longer El Paso and Villa but rather Sonora and Obregón. By the spring of 1920, Carranza's regime was tottering, especially since on April 23, Obregón's Sonoran allies promulgated the indispensable revolutionary manifesto, the *Plan de Agua Prieta*.[43] Thereafter Carranza's rule collapsed with breathtaking rapidity, recalling Porfirio Díaz's downfall in 1911. The rebellion was not so much a revolution as a triumphal march from Sonora to Mexico City, with Carranza's erstwhile supporters abandoning him in droves to get on the winning side. By the end of May, Carranza had been not only overthrown but assassinated. His death ushered in a new era, one in which General Alvaro Obregón, using some of the same techniques that Porfirio Díaz had employed, served as the new president and strongman of Mexico. The year 1920 was also a watershed in that it was the last time a Mexican regime was overthrown by force.

Obregón's triumph marked the beginning of what has been called the "Northern Dynasty," when strongmen from Sonora controlled Mexico from 1920 to 1935. The assassinated Venustiano Carranza's exiled partisans engaged in unsuccessful intrigues against the Sonorans. Among these exiles was Andrés García, who spent the decade of the 1920s in El Paso, this time as one of those forlorn refugee conspirators he had so successfully combated earlier.[44]

One of the results of Carranza's elimination was that it provided Pancho Villa with a face-saving way of requesting amnesty from the provisional government as it enabled him to argue that his quarrel had been solely with Carranza. A mutually advantageous arrangement resulted; the government was anxious for Villa to quit shooting up the place, and it therefore cut him a cushy deal. In July 1920, Villa received not just amnesty but an hacienda, Canutillo, in Durango, and a nice cash subvention. In return, he pledged to retire from public life.[45] The elimination from the political scene of both Villa and Carranza within two months was a deathblow to revolutionary plotting in El Paso, since their partisans constituted most of the plotters.

Villa kept his word, but in 1923, with the de la Huerta rebellion brewing, the government evidently decided that Villa was just too dangerous to be permitted to live. He was assassinated in Parral, Chihuahua, on July 20, 1923. Three years later, somebody desecrated his grave, exhuming the body and making off with Villa's head.

The culprit was strongly suspected to be none other than the veteran mercenary Emil Holmdahl, who just happened to be in Parral at the time. The resourceful Holmdahl managed to convince the authorities of his innocence, mainly by drinking without ill effect a jar of clear liquid that the Mexicans were convinced was embalming fluid and Holmdahl insisted was mineral water.[46] The whereabouts of Pancho Villa's head remains one of the mysteries of the Mexican Revolution.

Conclusion

El Paso played a key role in the Mexican Revolution. In fact, even before the revolution the city was a center of *magonista* intrigue. But it was the 1910–20 decade that solidified the city's status as the most strategic spot on the Mexican border. Access to El Paso was crucial during both the Madero and Orozco phases of the revolution. The ensuing Constitutionalist phase encompassed the entire northern tier of Mexican states, but again El Paso was the key to control of the border. And Pancho Villa's military career waxed and waned according to his ability to supply his forces through El Paso.

Conversely, the Mexican Revolution played a key role in the development of El Paso, a city basking in the prestige arising from the 1909 Taft-Díaz meeting. For one thing, the revolution produced a vastly increased military presence. From a 350-man garrison in 1910, Fort Bliss and its surrounding camps expanded to house more than 40,000 troops by the fall of 1916, making it the most important military post in the country. The revolution transformed El Paso into the "army town" that it still is. The considerable amounts of money that the army spent in El Paso became a mainstay of the city's economy.

That economy underwent other significant changes during the revolutionary decade. With the disruption of normal commercial relations with Mexico, El Paso merchants proved quite adept at adjusting to changing market conditions. The munitions traffic, both legitimate and contraband, assumed major proportions, and firms such as Krakauer and Sheldon-Payne profited enormously. Other businessmen such as Haymon Krupp did quite well by supplying dry goods as well as munitions. And there was a ready market for the loot being brought to the border by revolutionists, such as the Laguna cotton crop and the tens of thousands of head of livestock that revolutionary leaders exported to pay for arms purchases. El Paso banks handled impressive amounts arising from these transactions, to say nothing of the funds deposited by wealthy Mexican refugees.

But there was also a secret struggle that took place in the city, pitting American authorities against Mexican factions and the common criminal element. Perhaps the most striking aspect of this secret war was the degree to which U.S. and Mexican intelligence agencies cooperated. Not only did armed Mexican consuls and military officers participate in raids against the *magonistas*, but the Madero government enjoyed astounding latitude in conducting operations against its enemies. The activities of Madero's operatives and federal Bureau of Investigation agents in 1912 were intertwined to an unprecedented extent. In fact, never before or since has a foreign intelligence service been permitted to operate as blatantly in the United States. So, for example, with the Bureau's approval, armed Mexican agents were allowed to search American citizens on American soil.

Without the considerable assistance of the Mexicans, the Bureau of Investigation simply could not have performed its function adequately. But the Bureau had an enormous advantage over its Mexican counterparts in that it had a nationwide structure controlled from Washington, D.C., enabling the agency to react to situations. By contrast, the Mexican intelligence service was highly decentralized, the historic pattern being for each consul to recruit and run his own secret agents. In practice this meant that some consuls were much more effective than others. But what they all had in common was a resistance to any attempt to centralize the collection of intelligence. Moreover, both in the case of *villistas* and *carrancistas*, intelligence services had to be created from scratch.

The intelligence war often turned on the selective application of the neutrality laws. American authorities would assist one Mexican faction against another, and one Mexican faction would try to manipulate the Bureau against its enemies. This struggle had a decisive effect on the flow of war materiel into Mexico, best illustrated by the way Orozco's rebellion was choked off. In the intelligence war treachery was elevated to an art form. It seemed as though every conspiracy—and conspiracy was a staple of everyday life—was thoroughly penetrated by informers of one type or another. The machinations from 1916 on of conservative Mexican exiles trying to overthrow Carranza resembled White Russians in Paris in the 1920s busily hatching grandiose schemes for overthrowing the Soviet government, blissfully unaware that their plans were invariably being revealed to Soviet intelligence.

What the El Paso experience illustrates is the complexity of factionalism. Of necessity, just for manageability, people are described as being *villistas*, *carrancistas*, and so on. Yet the element of ideology has been overemphasized. As we have seen, people frequently changed their allegiance—many were much more interested in the cash than in the cause. Thus it is necessary to specify at what phase of a person's career he belonged to a particular faction, José Inés Salazar being a prime example. Factional infighting invariably derailed plans for exile unity.

Information was a prized commodity, and even today it is sometimes difficult to sift fact from rumor, misinformation, or disinformation. El Paso presents similarities to Berlin at the height of the Cold War, a city infested with refugees, secret agents, double agents, smugglers, gunrunners, propagandists, adventurers, confidence men, and other exotic types. The cast of characters during the revolution boasted a number of larger-than-life figures such as Sam Dreben, Victor Ochoa, Giuseppe Garibaldi, Benjamin Viljoen, George Holmes, and Emil Holmdahl. And a variety of Mexican revolutionary personages—Madero, Villa, Orozco, Obregón, Carranza, to name a few—graced the city with their presence.

In its efforts to monitor revolutionary activities, the Bureau utilized a number of techniques. To supplement its meager budget, the agency relied heavily on informants, primarily Mexicans. This sometimes proved counterproductive, for juries tended to discount the testimony of Mexican witnesses. The Bureau also relied heavily on Western Union and the U.S. Postal Service for copies of telegrams and for mail covers. Moreover, Bureau agents were not averse to conducting "black bag" operations to obtain evidence. In a preview of things to come, the Bureau utilized the latest technology, clandestine listening devices. Bureau agents were not immune to corruption. In the course of the revolutionary decade two of the best special agents in charge, Louis Ross and Edward Stone, were dismissed for criminal activities. El Paso continues to ruin FBI careers. In 2006 the special agent in charge was convicted of having ties to a Juárez gambling figure connected with a drug cartel. And El Paso continues to attract the FBI's attention. The agency is currently—2009—conducting in El Paso what is arguably on of the largest public corruption investigation is in the United States.

With regard to corruption, now as then, there was just too much money involved in smuggling. From one perspective the revolutionary decade can be viewed as a chapter in the history of smuggling along the border. Historically, smuggling in El Paso has been viewed as a quasi-respectable profession. Smuggling has been a constant, the only difference being what is being smuggled and in which direction. Prior to the revolution the commodities smuggled into the United States were cattle and Chinese laborers. With the outbreak of the revolution, the focus shifted to running guns and ammunition into Mexico. As the revolution wound down and Prohibition was enacted, the focus shifted again, this time to smuggling liquor into the United States. And of course today smuggling remains a major factor along the border, the principal commodities being drugs and human beings going north and weapons going south. Once again El Pasoans are nervous about conditions in Ciudad Juarez, this time because drug-related killings have spiraled out of control.

El Paso as a case study not only sheds light on the Mexican Revolution but illustrates what can be learned by investigating revolutionary intrigue in San Antonio, Brownsville, Laredo, Douglas, Los Angeles, New York, and Washington, D.C., for the entire decade, a project that the present authors have under way. What happened in the United States had a decisive effect on the course of the revolution in Mexico.

Abbreviations

ABFP — Albert Bacon Fall Papers University of New Mexico, Albuquerque, N.Mex.

ABFFP — Albert Bacon Fall Family Papers, Rio Grande Historical Collections, New Mexico State University, Las Cruces, N.Mex.

AREM — Archivo Histórico Diplomático Mexicano de la Secretaría de Relaciones Exteriores, México, D.F.

AEMEUA — Archivo de la Embajada de México en Estados Unidos de América

BI — Federal Bureau of Investigation

DDIA — *Douglas Daily International-American*

DF — Decimal Files, Internal Affairs of Mexico, 1910–29

DHRM — Isidro Fabela et al., eds. *Documentos históricos de la Revolución Mexicana.* 28 vols. México, D.F.: Editorial Jus, 1960–76

ECLP — Enrique C. Llorente Papers, Manuscript Division, New York Public Library, New York City

EPDT — *El Paso Daily Times*

EPH — *El Paso Herald*

EPHP — *El Paso Herald Post*

EPMT — *El Paso Morning Times*

EPT — *El Paso Times*

FRC-D — Federal Records Center, Denver, Colo.

FRC-FW — Federal Records Center, Fort Worth, Tex.

FRC-L — Federal Records Center, Laguna Niguel, Calif.

LWT — *Laredo Weekly Times*

MID Military Intelligence Division

NARA National Archives and Records Administration, Washington, D.C.

NDH *Nogales Daily Herald*

NMF Numerical and Minor Files of the Department of State, 1906–10

OMF Old Mex 232 Files

ONI Office of Naval Intelligence

PGA General Pablo González Archive

RDJ Records of the Department of Justice

RDS Records of the Department of State

RFBI Records of the Federal Bureau of Investigation

RG Record Group

RSS Records of the United States Secret Service

RUSACC Records of United States Army Continental Commands, 1821–1920

VCA President Venustiano Carranza Archive, Centro de Estudios de Historia de México, Departamento Cultural de Condumex, México, D.F.

VOP Victor Ochoa Papers, National Museum of American History, Kenneth E. Behring Center, Smithsonian Institution, Washington, D.C.

Notes

Preface

1. *Revoltosos: Mexican Rebels in the United States, 1903–1923* (College Station: Texas A&M University Press, 1981).

2. "Exiles and Intrigue: Francisco I. Madero and the Mexican Revolutionary Junta in San Antonio, 1910–1911" (MA thesis, Trinity University, 1975).

3. *Mexican Exiles in the Borderlands, 1910–1913* (El Paso: Texas Western Press, 1979).

4. "Border Revolution: The Mexican Revolution in the Ciudad Juárez/El Paso Area, 1906–1915" (MA thesis, University of Texas at El Paso, 1975). See also his article "The Mexican Revolution in the Ciudad Juárez-El Paso Area, 1910–1920, *Password* 24, no. 2 (1979): 55–69.

5. "The Mexican Secret Service in the United States, 1910–1920," *The Americas* 59, no. 1 (2002): 65–85, and "Andrés G. García: Venustiano Carranza's Eyes, Ears, and Voice on the Border," *Mexican Studies/Estudios Mexicanos* 23, no. 2 (2007): 355–86.

6. Victoria Lerner Sigal, "Espionaje y Revolución Mexicana," *Historia Mexicana* 44, no. 4 (1995): 617–42, and "Espías mexicanos en tierras norteamericanas (1914–1915)," *New Mexico Historical Review* 69, no. 3 (1994): 230–47; Friedrich Katz, "El espionaje mexicano en Estados Unidos durante la Revolución," *Eslabones: Revista Semestral de Estudios Regionales* 2, no. 2 (1991): 8–15; Jacinto Barrera Bassols, "El espionaje en la frontera Mexico-Estados Unidos (1905–1911)," *Eslabones: Revista Semestral de Estudios Regionales* 2, no. 2 (1991): 23–28.

7. *Ringside Seat to a Revolution: An Underground Cultural History of El Paso and Juárez, 1893–1923* (El Paso: Cinco Puntos Press, 2005).

8. "July 26, 1908, Attorney General Bonaparte ordered the special agent force to report to Chief Examiner Stanley W. Finch. This order is considered the formal beginning of the agency that became the FBI in 1935. In March 1909, Attorney General George W. Wickersham named this force the Bureau of Investigation (BOI)" (Federal Bureau of Investigation, http://www.fbi.gov/libref/historic/history/historicdates.htm).

9. DF, microcopy no. 274, RDS, RG 59, NARA.

10. OMF, microcopy, Investigative Records, 1908–22, RFBI, RG 65, NARA. These twenty-four rolls have been numbered by the National Archives as 851–74. We refer to the original FBI roll numbers (1–24), using BI, preceded by the roll number, as a short form for OMF. Recently, the National Archives has made available additional FBI documentation in the Old Mex, Old German, and Miscellaneous Files. These documents are cited by file number.

11. See C. L. Sonnichsen, *Pass of the North: Four Centuries on the Rio Grande* (El Paso: Texas Western Press, 1968), 387–405; W. H. Timmons, *El Paso: A Borderlands History* (El Paso: Texas Western Press, 1990), 209–27; Mardee Belding de Wetter, "Revolutionary El Paso: 1910–1917," *Password* 3, no. 2 (1958): 46–59, no. 3 (July 1958): 107–19, no. 4 (October 1958):

145–58. The El Paso/Juárez Historical Museum has published several works by local historian Fred Morales, among them *Córdova Island* (2002), *The Mexican Revolution Trail of El Paso and Juárez* (2003), *Francisco Villa* (2006), and *Smeltertown* (2004).

12. White report, June 25, 1918, 20BI.

Chapter 1

1. President Theodore Roosevelt had met Panamanian president Manuel Amador Guerrero in Panama City, Panama, in August 1906. *EPMT*, October 17, 1909, published a list of meetings of American presidents with several Central American presidents prior to 1909.

2. NMF, file no. 20292/91–93, microcopy M-862, RDS, RG 59, NARA.

3. See, for example, Charlotte Crawford, "The Border Meeting of Presidents Taft and Diaz," *Password* 3, no. 3 (1958): 86–96; Robert Bruce Crippen, "Celebration on the Border: The Taft-Diaz Meeting, 1909," *Password* 29, no. 3 (1984): 114–22; W. H. Timmons, "Taft-Diaz Meeting," *The New Handbook of Texas*, 6 vols. (Austin: Texas State Historical Association, 1996), 6:193; Peter V. N. Henderson, *In the Absence of Don Porfirio: Francisco León de la Barra and the Mexican Revolution* (Wilmington, Del.: Scholarly Resources, 2000), 19. Henderson's scholarly biography of Ambassador de la Barra states that the ambassador believed he had arranged the meeting. De la Barra indeed aided and abetted the presidential summit, but it is clear that the initiative came from Díaz. A somewhat oblique reference in Henry F. Pringle's excellent biography of Taft suggests Díaz's role. In a letter to his wife, Helen, dated October 17, 1909, the day following the meeting, Taft explained that he had "received a communication, perhaps directly from the old man, of an informal character, saying how glad he would be to have such a meeting brought about" (*Life and Times of William Howard Taft: A Biography*, 2 vols. [New York: Farrar and Rinehart, 1938], 1:462). The Díaz letter itself cannot be found either in the State Department files on the meeting or in the William Howard Taft Papers. The State Department files on the Taft-Díaz summit are NMF, file no. 20292. Logically, the letter should be filed in the beginning of file no. 20292/2–4, but the attached buck slip reads: "The Department has not been furnished with a copy of President Diaz's note of June 16th sent through Judge Wilfley." That Judge L. R. Wilfley transmitted Díaz's letter is clear from his letter to Taft dated June 18, 1909, from Mexico City. Wilfley's letter was typed, but the postscript in Wilfley's handwriting reads: "P.S. Since writing this letter President Diaz sent me the enclosed note and asked me to transmit it to you" (file no. 4178, reel 35, William Howard Taft Papers, Executive Office Correspondence [Presidential Series no. 1], Library of Congress. Confirmation of the Díaz letter is also found in file no. 4178, in Taft's response of June 25, 1909, to Díaz's letter.

4. Taft to Wilfley, January 21, 1910. The voluminous correspondence between Taft and Wilfley is in the above-cited file no. 4178, Taft Papers.

5. Pringle, *Life and Times of William Howard Taft*, 2:700. For a detailed study of American investment in Mexico, see John Mason Hart, *Empire and Revolution: The Americans in Mexico since the Civil War* (Berkeley: University of California Press, 2002).

6. *EPMT*, July 10, 11, 1909.

7. See *New York Times*, July 25, 1909.

8. See Victor Macías-González, "The Mexican Aristocracy and Porfirio Díaz, 1876–1911" (PhD diss., Texas Christian University, 1999), ch. 5.

9. Macías-González, "Mexican Aristocracy," ch. 5.

10. Archibald Butt, *Taft and Roosevelt: The Intimate Letters of Archie Butt, Military Aide*, 2 vols. (Port Washington, N.Y.: Kennikat Press, 1971), 2:183–84.

11. See M. Huntington Wilson, *Memoirs of an Ex-Diplomat* (Boston: Bruce Humphries, 1945), 180.

12. Memorandum, Mexican embassy, August 21, 1909, NMF, file no. 20292/8.

13. Wilson to Phillips, August 27, 1909, NMF, file no. 20292/7.

14. The Chamizal was the subject of lengthy diplomatic negotiations between the two countries, and the issue was not resolved until 1963. See Sheldon B. Liss, *A Century of Disagreement: The Chamizal Conflict, 1864–1964* (Washington: University Press of Washington, D.C., 1965), 8–16. See also Fred Morales, *Córdova Island* (El Paso: El Paso/Juárez Historical Museum, 2002), 3–4.

15. Mexican embassy memorandum, August 21, 1909, NMF, file no. 20292/8.

16. Henderson, *In the Absence of Don Porfirio*, 49.

17. Carpenter to Phillips, August 31, 1909, NMF, file no. 20292/13; Wilson, in a letter to American embassy dated September 22, 1909, requested that the ambassador explain to the foreign minister that Secretary of State Knox "cannot after all" attend the summit (NMF, file no. 20292/38).

18. Kinne, general secretary, [Committee for the] International Meeting of Presidents Taft and Díaz, September 7, 1909, NMF, file no. 20292/27; Phillips to Kinne, September 16, 1909, NMF, file no. 20292/28.

19. *EPMT*, March 19, 1913.

20. Oscar J. Martínez, *Border Boom Town: Ciudad Juárez since 1848* (Austin: University of Texas Press, 1978) 45; Fred M. Morales, "Chihuahuita: A Neglected Corner of El Paso," *Password* 36, no. 1 (1991): 23–34.

21. The offer of the El Paso Chamber of Commerce building was made in a telegram from John Wyatt, who chaired the General Arrangements Committee, to Fred Carpenter, the president's secretary. Carpenter referred Wyatt's telegram to the State Department (Carpenter to Wyatt, September 5, 1909, NMF, file no. 20292/68–69).

22. Sweeney to Knox, August 2, 1909, NMF, file no. 20292/5; de la Barra to Adee, August 7, 1909, NMF, file no, 20292/6; Adee to Sweeney, August 18, 1909, NMF, file no. 20292/7; Adee telegram to Sweeney, August 16, 1909, NMF, file no. 20292/?.

23. Wotherspoon to Knox, August 28, 1909, NMF, file no. 20292/14.

24. Undecipherable to Taft, August 20, 1909, NMF, file no. 20292/12; Fornaro to Taft, August 31, 1909, NMF, file no. 20292/12; Lovell to Taft, September 4, 1909, NMF, file no. 20292/25.

25. Thompson to secretary of state, September 1, 1909, NMF, file no. 20292/10; Adee to American embassy, September 2, 1909, NMF, file no. 20292/11.

26. Adee to Wyatt, September 8, 1909, NMF, file no. 20292/17; Wyatt to Adee, September 9, 1909, NMF, file no. 20292/21.

27. Vice consul to acting secretary of state, August 25, 1909, NMF, file no. 20292/21; Adee to Edwards, September 15, 1909, NMF, file no. 20292/21.

28. Wyatt to acting secretary of state, August 13, 1909, NMF, file no. 20292/27; Adee to Wyatt, September 14, 1909, NMF, file no. 20292/27.

29. Sweeney to Adee, September 14, 1909, NMF, file no. 20292/28–29; Adee to Sweeney, September 15, 1909, NMF, file no. 20292/28–29.

30. Myer to adjutant general, September 18, 1909, no. 31261, Department of Texas, NMF, file no. 20292/33–37.

31. Sweeney to Adee, September 28, 1909, NMF, file no. 20292/59½.

32. Edwards to secretary of state, September 24, 1909, NMF, file no. 20292/40.

33. Adee to American embassy, September 26, 1910, NMF, file no. 20292/42.

34. Adee to American embassy, September 30, 1909, NMF, file no. 20292/47.

35. Thompson to secretary of state, September 28, 1909, NMF, file no. 20292/46.

36. Thompson to secretary of state, September 30, 1909, NMF, file no. 20292/58, and October 1, 1909, NMF, file no. 20202/57.

37. Adee memorandum, October 1, 1909, NMF, file no. 20292/67; Phillips to Adee, October 1, 1909, NMF, file no. 20292/66; Adee to Edwards, October 1, 1909, NMF, file no. 20292/58B; Adee to Sweeney, October 1, 1909, NMF, 20292/58C.

38. Adee to Campbell, October 1, 1909, NMF, file no. 20292/52; Campbell to Adee, October 9, 1909, NMF, file no. 20292/75.

39. Adee to American embassy, October 2, 1909, NMF, file no. 20292/58.

40. Phillips to Adee, October 2, 1909, NMF, file no. 20292/70.

41. Wilkie to secretary of state, October 7, 1909, NMF, file no. 20292/73.

42. Adee to Wilkie, October 7, 1909, NMF, file no. 20292/75.

43. The first out-of-town newsman to arrive was Otto Praeger, the Washington correspondent for the *Dallas News* (*EPMT*, October 10, 13, 1909).

44. *EPMT*, October 12, 14, 1909.

45. *EPMT*, October 13, 1909.

46. Charles H. Harris III and Louis R. Sadler, *Bastion on the Border: Fort Bliss, 1854–1943*, Historic and Natural Resources Report no. 6 (Ft. Bliss, Tex.: Cultural Resources Management Branch, Directorate of Environment, United States Army Air Defense Artillery Center, 1993), 7; post returns, Fort Clark, Tex., October, 1909, and post returns, Fort Sam Houston, Tex., October, 1909, RG 407, NARA; *EPMT*, October 14, 1909.

47. A plaque at the southeast corner of Main and Oregon streets commemorates the spot where Taft alighted from his private railroad car, the Mayflower (*El Paso: A Centennial Portrait* [El Paso, Tex.: El Paso County Historical Society, 1972], 285).

48. *EPMT*, October 16, 18, 1909.

49. According to Doctor John G. Sotos, Taft had "obstructive sleep apnea" and suffered from excessive daytime somnolence, snoring, and systemic hypertension. Taft's hypersomnolence was "severe and obvious" ("Taft and Pickwick: Sleep Apnea in the White House," *Chest: Journal of the American College of Chest Physicians* 124, no. 3 [2003]: 1133–42).

50. For a Mexican perspective on what they might have discussed, see Francisco R. Almada, "La entrevista Díaz-Taft," *Boletín de la Sociedad Chihuahuense de Estudios Históricos* 9, no. 6 (1955): 862–64. Almada suggests that Taft wanted an American coaling station at Magdalena Bay in Baja California and that the chief executives differed regarding the Santos Zelaya administration in Nicaragua. It seems more likely that Díaz requested American help in suppressing Mexican exile activity along the border.

51. The chamber of commerce had the chair repaired and for decades kept it in its office. For a photograph of the notorious chair, see Crawford, "Border Meeting," 88.

52. John Hays Hammond, *The Autobiography of John Hays Hammond*, 2 vols. (New York: Arno Press, 1974), 2:565–66.

53. Thompson to secretary of state, September 27, 1909, NMF, file no. 20292/46.

54. Thompson to secretary of state, September 27, 1909, NMF, file no. 20292/45.

55. Adee to Sweeney, September 27, 1909, NMF, file no. 20292/42.

56. Wilkie to secretary of state, October 12, 1909, NMF, file no. 20292/82.

57. Charles H. Harris III and Louis R. Sadler, *The Texas Rangers and the Mexican Revolution: The Bloodiest Decade, 1910–1920* (Albuquerque: University of New Mexico Press, 2004), 76.

58. Frederick Russell Burnham, http://en.wikipedia.org/wiki/Frederick_Russell_Burnham.

59. Hammond, *Autobiography*, 2:565–66; Crawford, "Border Meeting," 88.

60. Hammond, *Autobiography*, 2:565.

61. Hammond, *Autobiography*, 2:566; *EPMT*, October 17, 1909.

62. Hammond, *Autobiography*, 2:565–66; Hughes to adjutant general, report on the operations of Company A, September 1, 1909–June 29, 1911, Texas Ranger Records, Texas National Guard Archives, Camp Mabry, Austin, Tex. Burnham would publish two autobiographies: *Scouting on Two Continents* (Garden City, N.Y.: Garden City Publishing, 1926) and *Taking Chances* (Los Angeles: Haynes Corporation, 1944). In the first one, the foreword for which was written by John Hays Hammond, Burnham does not mention the assassination attempt. The second autobiography, published thirty-five years after the event, does recount the attempt. He states: "Within a few feet of one of the Presidents one of the suspects was stopped with a loaded gun in his hand." He describes the weapon as a gun with the barrel sawed off short with a lead pencil in the barrel (the pencil was "protruding . . . between the trigger and middle fingers"). When questioned, "the man claimed to be a refugee newspaper man fearing for his own life, but that he needed a copy of the meeting of the Presidents to sell to the press" (262–63).

63. Don Wilkie as told to Mark Lee Luther, *American Secret Service Agent* (New York: Burt, 1934), 155–74. Don Wilkie was the son of John Wilkie, the head of the U.S. Secret Service in 1909. Don Wilkie was also a U.S. Secret Service agent and during World War I served overseas as a special agent of the Office of Naval Intelligence.

Chapter 2

1. Ward S. Albro, *Always a Rebel: Ricardo Flores Magón and the Mexican Revolution* (Fort Worth: Texas Christian University Press, 1992), 3–35.

2. Eugenio Martínez Núñez, *Juan Sarabia, apóstol y mártir de la Revolución Mexicana* (México, D.F.: Talleres Gráficos de la Nación, 1965), 149–84.

3. They included *La Bandera Roja*, *La Democracia*, and *El Clarín del Norte* (W. Dirk Raat, *Revoltosos: Mexican Rebels in the United States, 1903–1923* [College Station: Texas A&M University Press, 1981], 95).

4. Raat *Revoltosos*, 95–96.

5. Raat, *Revoltosos*, 26.

6. Albro, *Always a Rebel*, 52–53.

7. In 1907, Enrique Creel, who headed the Mexican government's campaign against dissidents, hired Thomas Furlong, whose detective agency worked against the *magonistas* for the next four years (Thomas Furlong, *Fifty Years a Detective* [St. Louis, Mo.: C. E. Barnett, 1912], 137–48).

8. Raat, *Revoltosos*, 33–35.

9. Richard Estrada, "Border Revolution" (MA thesis, University of Texas at El Paso, 1975), 33–39.

10. Estrada, "Border Revolution," 40–41.

11. Raat, *Revoltosos*, 119.

12. Albro, *Always a Rebel*, 66.

13. Villarreal, as "Pedro N. González," had been indicted in Del Rio on October 12, 1906, for "conspiring to set on foot a military expedition against Mexico" (*U.S. v. Pedro N. González, C. V. Márquez, Demetrio Castro and Trinidad García*, no case number, U.S. Commissioner, Del Rio, Tex., FRC-FW; see also *U.S. v. Trinidad García*, no. 1, U.S. District Court, Del Rio, Tex., FRC-FW).

14. Albro, *Always a Rebel*, 67; Raat, *Revoltosos*, 132–34; *EPMT*, October 20, 21, 23, 1906; Estrada, "Border Revolution," 42–43.

15. Albro, *Always a Rebel*, 69–70; Raat, *Revoltosos*, 133–36; *DDIA*, February 14, 1907.

16. *DDIA*, July 1, 2, 3, 5, 6, 10, 11, 12, 13, 15, 16, 17, 19, 25, 1907.

17. Albro, *Always a Rebel*, 84–89, 96–98. See also Colin M. MacLachlan, *Anarchism and the Mexican Revolution: The Political Trials of Ricardo Flores Magón in the United States* (Berkeley: University of California Press, 1991).

18. Raat, *Revoltosos*, 175–80.

19. See Juan Gómez-Quiñones, "Piedras contra la Luna, México en Aztlán y Aztlán en México: Chicano-Mexican Relations and the Mexican Consulates, 1900–1920," in *Contemporary Mexico: Papers of the IV International Congress of Mexican History*, ed. James W. Wilkie, Michael C. Meyer, Edna Monzón de Wilkie (Berkeley: University of California Press and México, D.F.: El Colegio de México, 1976), 494–523.

20. The letter reads: "What steps you may be empowered to take, under the law, in case a suspicious band . . . armed or unarmed, should attempt to cross the border into Mexico with a . . . revolutionary intention, and how far your authority as a military commander may extend under the neutrality laws without the call of the civil authorities, either state or federal or both, I am directed by the Acting Secretary [Robert Shaw Oliver] to advise you as follows: The President authorizes you to take the necessary action to carry out Section 5267 of the Revised Statutes, should it become necessary to do so, the necessity, of course to be determined by you. Since the law warrants ultimate action, there would appear to be no objection to information being allowed to spread along the Texas border to the effect that the United States is prepared by means of its military force to enforce the neutrality laws and to protect the territory of a foreign state, with which the United States is at peace, from an invasion by an armed party from the territory of the United States, should such invasion be threatened. While under the orders of the President, no call for action by the civil authorities is necessary, the knowledge of any facts which seem to indicate that acts forbidden by the statute cited are in actual contemplation should at once be communicated by you to the United States marshal or the United States attorney with a view to his taking the proper steps toward bringing the offending parties to justice. In

this connection, the acting Secretary of War directs that the instructions conveyed by this letter be considered confidential and they be divulged only in case circumstances should warrant such action. Please acknowledge receipt of this letter" (adjutant general to commanding general, Department of Texas, September 28, 1907, NMF, [confidential] file no. 5028, microcopy M-862, RDS, RG 59, NARA).

21. Dorothy Pierson Kerig, *Luther T. Ellsworth: U.S. Consul on the Border During the Mexican Revolution* (El Paso: Texas Western Press, 1975), 5–6.

22. Raat, *Revoltosos*, 32–33.

23. Albro, *Always a Rebel*, 109.

24. Raat, *Revoltosos*, 100.

25. Estrada, "Border Revolution," 45.

26. *U.S. v. Leocardio B. Treviño, Prisciliano G. Silva, José María G. Ramírez, Benjamín G. Silva*, no. 86, U.S. Commissioner, El Paso, Tex., and no. 1359, U.S. District Court, El Paso, Tex., FRC-FW.

27. Lomelí to foreign secretary, June 26, 1908, L-E 821, leg. 1, exps. 18–19, AREM.

28. Estrada, "Border Revolution," 46.

29. Albro, *Always a Rebel*, 107.

30. *U.S. v. Ricardo Flores Magón, Antonio I. Villarreal, Enrique Flores Magón, Práxedis G. Guerrero*, no. 1360, U.S. District Court, El Paso, Tex., FRC-FW; *U.S. v. Ricardo Flores Magón, Antonio I. Villarreal, Enrique Flores Magón, Antonio de P. Araujo, Encarnación Díaz Guerra*, no. 1375, U.S. District Court, El Paso, Tex., FRC-FW; *U.S. v. Enrique Flores Magón and Práxedis G. Guerrero*, no. 1361, U.S. District Court, El Paso, Tex., FRC-FW.

31. See U.S. Commissioner's nos. 88, 100, 101, 117, 156, El Paso, Tex., and U.S. District Court nos. 1362–69, 1371–74, 1376, 2007, El Paso, Tex., FRC-FW.

32. See, for example, Ellsworth to secretary of state, September 30, 1909, and Priest to secretary of state, September 28, 1909, file no. 90755–158, RDJ, RG 60, NARA.

33. Estrada, "Border Revolution," 50–51. Mexican soldiers finally killed him in Sonora in February 1918 (*EPMT*, February 8, 1918).

34. Leon C. Metz has chronicled the exploits of several of these notorious badmen. See, for example, his *Dallas Stoudenmire: El Paso Marshal* (Norman: University of Oklahoma Press, 1969) and *John Wesley Hardin: Dark Angel of Texas* (Norman: University of Oklahoma Press, 1998).

35. Clyde Wise Jr., "The Effects of the Railroads upon El Paso," *Password* 5, no. 3 (1960): 91.

36. In the 1910 census, El Paso's population was 39,279 while that of Ciudad Juárez was 10,621 (David Lorey, ed. *United States-Mexican Border Statistics since 1900* [Los Angeles: UCLA Latin American Center Publications, 1990], 33).

37. The railroads were the Atchison, Topeka, and Santa Fe, El Paso and Southwestern, Texas and Pacific, Denver and Rio Grande, Kansas City Southwestern, and El Paso and Northeastern. See Edward A. Leonard, *Rails at the Pass of the North* (El Paso: Texas Western Press, 1981).

38. Oscar J. Martínez, *Border Boom Town: Ciudad Juárez since 1848* (Austin: University of Texas Press, 1978), 36, 38.

39. I. J. Bush, *Gringo Doctor* (Caldwell, Idaho: Caxton Printers, 1939), 152.

40. *EPMT*, April 2, 1910.

41. U.S. Senate, *Revolutions in Mexico: Hearing before a Subcommittee of the Committee on Foreign Relations, United States Senate*, 62nd Cong., 2nd sess. (Washington, D.C.: Government Printing Office, 1913), 108–16, 125–27.

42. John Mason Hart, *Empire and Revolution: The Americans in Mexico since the Civil War* (Berkeley: University of California Press, 2002), 209.

43. John H. McNeely, *The Railways of Mexico: A Study in Nationalization* (El Paso: Texas Western College Press, 1964), 20–21; U.S. Senate, *Revolutions in Mexico*, 153; Hart, *Empire and Revolution*, 520.

44. See *EPMT*, May 25, 1910, for a map of the MNW.

45. *EPMT*, May 20, June 6, 24, 1910; Hart, *Empire and Revolution*, 120, 133, 186, 196, 250, 296–97.

46. U.S. Senate, *Revolutions in Mexico*, 153–56.

47. *EPMT*, April 27, 1910.

48. *EPMT*, May 2, 22, 24, 1910; U.S. Senate, *Revolutions in Mexico*, 153.

49. *EPMT*, May 18, 20, 22, 1910.

50. *EPMT*, January 15, 1910.

Chapter 3

1. W. Dirk Raat, *Revoltosos: Mexican Rebels in the United States, 1903–1923* (College Station: Texas A&M University Press, 1981), 209.

2. Lomelí to foreign secretary, November 25, 1910, in *DHRM*, 5:101–3.

3. Francisco R. Almada, *Vida, proceso y muerte de Abraham González* (México, D.F.: Talleres Gráficos de la Nación, 1967), 32.

4. U.S. Senate, *Revolutions in Mexico: Hearing before a Subcommittee of the Committee on Foreign Relations, United States Senate*, 62nd Cong., 2nd sess. (Washington, D.C.: Government Printing Office, 1913), 35, 130–32; William H. Beezley, *Insurgent Governor: Abraham González and the Mexican Revolution in Chihuahua* (Lincoln: University of Nebraska Press, 1973), x, 41.

5. Beezley, *Insurgent Governor*, 44.

6. Beezley, *Insurgent Governor*, 38, 45.

7. BI report, February 21, 1911, OMF, BI roll 1, Investigative Records, 1908–22, RFBI, RG 65, NARA (OMF hereafter cited as BI preceded by roll number); Beezley, *Insurgent Governor*, 45, 46.

8. I. J. Bush, *Gringo Doctor* (Caldwell, Idaho: Caxton Printers, 1939), 178.

9. Friedrich Katz, *The Life and Times of Pancho Villa* (Stanford, Calif.: Stanford University Press, 1998), 5; Michael C. Meyer, *Mexican Rebel: Pascual Orozco and the Mexican Revolution, 1910–1915* (Lincoln: University of Nebraska Press, 1967), 6.

10. On average, one mounted customs inspector was responsible for about 150 miles of riverfront in the rugged Big Bend region of the Texas border. See Michael Dennis Carman, *United States Customs and the Madero Revolution* (El Paso: Texas Western Press, 1976).

11. Charles H. Harris III and Louis R. Sadler, *Bastion on the Border: Fort Bliss, 1854–1943*, Historic and Natural Resources Report no. 6 (Fort Bliss, Tex.: Cultural Resources Management Branch, Directorate of Environment, United States Army Air Defense Artillery Center, 1993), 14.

12. Lomelí to foreign secretary, November 24, 28, 1910, *DHRM*, 5:106–8, 132–33.

13. De la Barra to foreign secretary, *DHRM*, 5:108–9; *EPMT*, September 14, 1918.

14. Guy reports, January 28, 30, 1915, 5BI.

15. *EPMT*, January 6, 1912. See Erika Lee, "Enforcing the Borders: Chinese Exclusion along the U.S Borders with Canada and Mexico, 1882–1924," *Journal of American History* 89, no. 1 (2002): 54–86, and Lawrence Douglas Taylor Hansen, "The Chinese Six Companies of San Francisco and the Smuggling of Chinese Immigrants across the U.S.-Mexico Border, 1882–1930," *Journal of the Southwest* 48, no. 1 (2006): 37–61.

16. BI reports, December 1, 7, 12, 27, 1910, 1BI.

17. BI report, December 31, 1910, 1BI.

18. Lomelí to foreign secretary, November 18, 1910, L-E 612 (5), exp. 74, and January 4, 1911, L-E 623 (2), exp. 243, AREM; Gamboa to consul, November 23, 1910, L-E 612 (5), exp. 75, AREM; Lomelí to foreign secretary, November 25, 1910, L-E 678 (3), exp. 20, AREM. See also, for example, Smith to Lomelí, November 21, 28, 29, 30, December 2, 3, 4, 7, 1910, L-E 678 (2), exps. 1, 61, 67–73, AREM. Australian Billy Smith's real name was Charles Mathews.

19. Lomelí to foreign secretary, January 20, 1911, *DHRM*, 5:174–76.

20. Creel to Lomelí, February 10, 1911, *DHRM*, 5:234–35.

21. BI report, December 21, 1910, and Scully report, April 24, 1912, 1BI.

22. U.S. Senate, *Revolutions in Mexico*, 759–60.

23. Joseph E. Persico, "The Great Gun Merchant," *American Heritage* 25, no. 5 (1974): 52–55, 89.

24. See, for example, BI reports March 4, 11, 24, May 2, 3, 10, 17, 19, 20, 22, 26, 31, 1911, 1BI.

25. Mexican embassy, Washington, D.C., to foreign secretary (confidential), February 26, 1911, *DHRM*, 5:256–57; Berta Ulloa, comp., *Revolución Mexicana, 1910–1920*, 2nd ed. (México, D.F.: Secretaría de Relaciones Exteriores, 1985) 65, 70, 71–72, 74, 75.

26. BI report, March 29, 1911, 1BI; Ulloa, *Revolución Mexicana*, 73, 78, 79, 83, 96.

27. *New Yorker Unlimited: The Memoirs of Edward Laroque Tinker* (Austin: University of Texas at Austin Press and the Encino Press, 1970).

28. *Who Was Who in America*, vol. 1 (Chicago: A. N. Marquis, 1942), 587; Ulloa, *Revolución Mexicana*, 70, 75, 78, 79, 81, 83; "Intriguers and Mexico," *The Nation*, July 2, 1914; U.S. Senate, *Investigation of Mexican Affairs*, 2 vols., Senate doc. no. 285, 66th Cong., 2nd sess. (Washington, D.C.: Government Printing Office, 1920), 2411–19, 2520–74.

29. José Vasconcelos, *Ulises criollo: La vida del autor escrita por él mismo*, 9th ed. (Mexico, D.F.: Ediciones Botas, 1945), 356–58.

30. BI reports, December 9, 21, 27, 28, 1910, 1BI. See also U.S. Senate, *Revolutions in Mexico*, 743–97.

31. Nolte to attorney general, April 25, 1911, in Wickersham to secretary of state, April 29, 1911, DF, file no. 812.00/1548, microcopy no. 274, RDS, RG 59, NARA.

32. De la Barra telegrams, December 6, 8, 1910, *DHRM*, 5:119–21.

33. U.S. Senate, *Revolutions in Mexico*, 751–52; *EPH*, December 7, 1910; Francisco Vázquez Gómez, *Memorias políticas* (México, D.F.: Imprenta Mundial, 1933), 71.

34. BI report, January 30, 1911, 1BI.

35. BI reports, February 1, 15, 16, March 1, 3, 10, April 6, 18, 1911, 1BI; Ulloa, *Revolución Mexicano*, 85.

36. *EPMT*, September 15, 1905, July 10, 1910; Beezley, *Insurgent Governor*, 47. For details of Caracristi's subsequent career, see Charles H. Harris III and Louis R. Sadler, *The Texas Rangers and the Mexican Revolution: The Bloodiest Decade, 1910–1920* (Albuquerque: University of New Mexico Press, 2004), 178–80, 364.

37. U.S. House, *Hearings before the Committee on Expenditures in the Treasury Department: Subject of Hearing—Charges against Collector R. W. Dowe, August 17, 1911*, 62nd Cong., 1st sess. (Washington, D.C.: Government Printing Office, 1911), esp. 25.

38. Ulloa, *Revolución Mexicana*, 54–55, 60, 61, 75, 84.

39. McCloskey to Fall, September 3, 1912, no. 583, roll 6, ABFP; Ulloa, *Revolución Mexicana*, 261. McCloskey, incidentally, was a Mexican government agent in 1913–14, monitoring vessels in Key West suspected of smuggling arms to the southern state of Campeche.

40. Ulloa, *Revolución Mexicana*, 69, 92. Adams would become a Mexican government agent again in 1913 (Elías to foreign secretary, April 1, 1913, *DHRM*, 14:169–72).

41. Foster to Creel, February 1, 1911, L-E 627, leg. 1, exps. 170–74, AREM.

42. See his reports in L-E 679, leg. 2, exps. 77, 78, 94–95, 102, 129, 146–51, 154, 157–60, 165–66, 168, AREM.

43. See their reports in L-E 679, leg. 2, exps. 4–9, 17, 20–21, 28–34, 36–38, 40–45, 55–62, 69–73, 74–76, 82–85, 97–98, 103–5,129–37, 138–39, 142–45, 152–53, 155–56, 169–70, 179, AREM.

44. Arguably the best treatment of this subject, although based only on U.S. sources, is Kenneth J. Grieb, "Standard Oil and the Financing of the Mexican Revolution," *California Historical Society Quarterly* 49, no. 1 (1970): 59–71. See also John Skirius, "Railroad, Oil and Other Foreign Interests in the Mexican Revolution, 1911–1914," *Journal of Latin American Studies*, 35, no. 1 (2003): 25–51.

45. "Your Informants" to [Torres], April 19, 1911, L-E 679, leg. 2, exps. 69–73, AREM; April 22, 1911, L-E 679, leg. 2, exps. 103–5, AREM; April 25, 1911, L-E 679, leg. 2, exps. 130–37, AREM; April 27, 1911, L-E 679, leg. 2, exps. 152–53, AREM; April 28, 1911, L-E 679, leg. 2, exps. 155–56, AREM.

46. BI reports, April 18, 24, 26, 27, 29, 1911, 1BI.

47. BI report, April 27, 1911, 1BI.

48. Wickersham to secretary of state, May 2, 1911, with enclosures, DF, file no. 812.00/1593.

49. Archbold to Knox, May 15, 1911, DF, file no. 812.00/1796.

50. BI report, January 10, 1911, 1BI.

51. "Your Informants" to Torres, April 3, 1911, L-E 679, leg. 2, exps. 4–6, AREM.

52. BI reports, January 12, 13, 1911, 1BI.

53. BI reports, January 21, 23, 1911, 1BI. Phillips apparently operated a private detective agency in Washington, D.C. (de la Barra to foreign secretary, December 2, 1910, *DHRM*, 5:112).

54. BI reports, February 4, 6, 10, 1911, 1BI.

55. BI report, February 14, 1911, 1BI.

56. BI reports, February 28, March 2, 3, 1911, 1BI; Thompson report, September 7, 1912, 3BI; *Annual Report of the Attorney General of the United States for the Year 1916* (Washington, D.C.: Government Printing Office, 1916), 347.

57. Vázquez Gómez, *Memorias políticas*, 72; Casasús to foreign secretary, February 6, 7, 1911, *DHRM*, 5:227–31.

58. Lomelí to foreign secretary, February 14, 1911, *DHRM*, 5:244–45; BI reports, February 17, 20, 21, 1911, 1BI; *U.S. v. Francisco I. Madero, Abraham González, Martín Casillas*, no. 771, U.S. Commissioner, El Paso, Tex., FRC-FW. The Mexican government's case against Madero was summarized in a study by Roberto A. Esteva Ruiz for the foreign secretary, January 4, 1911, *DHRM*, 5:141–46.

59. Timothy Turner, *Bullets, Bottles, and Gardenias* (Dallas, Tex.: South-West Press, 1935), 26–27.

60. J. F. Neville, an *El Paso Herald* reporter, also acted as a courier, as did a Mrs. Victoria Sloat (BI reports, February 24, 28, 1911, 1BI).

61. Torres to foreign secretary, March 22, 1911, L-E 679, leg. 3, exp. 128, AREM.

62. U.S. Senate, *Revolutions in Mexico*, 102–8; BI report, March 3, 1911, 1BI. The most detailed account of the Converse and Blatt affair is in U.S. House, *Claims Growing Out of Insurrection in Mexico*, House doc. no. 1168, U.S Congressional serial set, vol. 6586, 62nd Cong., 3rd sess. (Washington, D.C.: Government Printing Office, 1912), 8–12, 20, 47–186.

63. Lawrence D. Taylor has written extensively on foreign mercenaries in the revolution: "The Great Adventure: Mercenaries in the Mexican Revolution, 1910–1915," *The Americas* 43, no. 1 (1986): 25–45; *La gran aventura en México: El papel de los voluntarios extranjeros en los ejércitos revolucionarios, 1910–1915*, 2 vols. (México, D.F.: Consejo Nacional Para la Cultura y las Artes, 1993); "The Border as a Zone of Conflict: Foreign Volunteers in the Mexican Revolution and the Issue of American Neutrality, 1910–1912," *Journal of Borderlands Studies* 20, no. 1 (2005): 91–113.

64. Turner, *Bullets, Bottles, and Gardenias*, 29.

65. Letcher to secretary of state, April 19, 1911, DF, file no. 812.00/1493, and June 1, 1911, DF, file no. 812.00/2111, RDS; Turner, *Bullets, Bottles, and Gardenias*, 28–30; Bush, *Gringo Doctor*, 196.

66. Turner, *Bullets, Bottles, and Gardenias*, 29.

67. U.S. House, *Claims Growing Out of Insurrection in Mexico*, 77–78, 605. Brown was released in April 1911 (*EPMT*, April 24, 1911).

68. Turner, *Bullets, Bottles, and Gardenias*, 29, 35.

69. Bush, *Gringo Doctor*, 195.

70. Bush, *Gringo Doctor*, 196. In his autobiography O'Reilly was not bashful about his accomplishments (*Roving and Fighting: Adventure Under Four Flags* [New York: Century, 1918]). See also Lowell Thomas, *Born to Raise Hell: The Life Story of Tex O'Reilly, Soldier of Fortune, As Told to Lowell Thomas* (Garden City, N.Y.: Doubleday, Doran, 1936), and *EPMT*, April 19, 1915.

71. Bush, *Gringo Doctor*, 195–96; Ellsworth to secretary of state, May 5, 1911, DF, file no. 812.00/1689; BI reports, March 11, 21, 1911, 1BI.

72. Ira J. Bush, "The Battle of Casas Grandes," *Sports Afield*, August 1912, 116–20. The official Mexican Army report of the engagement is in *DHRM*, 5:270–80.

73. Letcher to secretary of state, April 19, 1911, DF, file nos. 812.00/1493, 812.00/2108.

74. Giuseppe Garibaldi, *A Toast to Rebellion* (Garden City, N.Y.: Garden City Publishing, 1935), 240.

75. Garibaldi, *A Toast to Rebellion*, 298–99.

76. Turner, *Bullets, Bottles, and Gardenias*, 25, 35, 43–44.

77. BI reports, March 29, April 17, 1911, 1BI.

78. Ellsworth to secretary of state, April 18, 1911, DF, file no. 812.00/1427; Letcher to assistant secretary of state, April 15, 1911, DF, file no. 812.00/1455.

79. Garibaldi, *A Toast to Rebellion*, 218–23.

80. Turner, *Bullets*, 24, 64.

81. Garibaldi, *A Toast to Rebellion*, 303.

82. Bush, *Gringo Doctor*, 191.

83. Brian M. Du Toit, *Boer Settlers in the Southwest* (El Paso: Texas Western Press, 1995), 4, 9, 10.

84. Du Toit, *Boer Settlers in the Southwest*, 10; Rayne Kruger, *Good-Bye Dolly Gray: The Story of the Boer War* (New York: Lippencott, 1960), 202.

85. Thomas Packenham, *The Boer War* (New York: Random House, 1979), 101.

86. Du Toit, *Boer Settlers in the Southwest*, 10, 12. For more on Viljoen's military exploits, see Packenham, *Boer War*, 138–44, 449ff., 522, and Peter Trew, *The Boer War Generals* (n.p.: Wrens Park Publishing, 2001), 35, 37, 111, 116, 140, 149, 153–54, 158, 159, 161, 165.

87. Packenham, *Boer War*, 455.

88. *My Reminiscences of the Anglo-Boer War* (London: Hood, Douglas and Howard, 1903).

89. Du Toit, *Boer Settlers in the Southwest*, 12–13, 55.

90. Du Toit, *Boer Settlers in the Southwest*, 12, 18, 21, 26, 27, 39; Dale C. Maluy, "Boer Colonization in the Southwest," *New Mexico Historical Review* 52, no. 2 (1977): 93–109.

91. Du Toit, *Boer Settlers in the Southwest*, 38, 39, 42, 43, 48, 57–58.

92. Du Toit, *Boer Settlers in the Southwest*, 1, 63.

93. Bush, *Gringo Doctor*, 195.

94. BI reports, March 20, 29, 30, April 1, 1911, 1BI.

95. BI reports, March 17, 18, 1911, 1BI.

96. *EPMT*, April 6, 1911.

97. Lomelí to foreign secretary, *DHRM*, 5:111–14; Smith to Lomelí, December 2, 3, 1910, L-E 678 (2), exps. 70, 71, AREM.

98. U.S. Senate, *Revolutions in Mexico*, 703–4.

99. BI report, April 18, 1911, 1BI; "Your Informants" to Torres, April 25, 1911, L-E 679, leg. 2, exps. 130–37, 138–39, 142–45, AREM.

100. BI report, May 9, 1911, 1BI.

101. BI reports, April 6, 12, 29, 1911, 1BI.

102. BI report, April 24, 1911, 1BI; "Your Informants" to Torres, April 15, 21, 1911, L-E 679, leg. 2, exps. 36–38, 97–98, AREM.

103. BI report, April 19, 1911, 1BI; "Your Informants" to Torres, April 3, 1911, L-E 679, leg. 2, exps. 4–6, AREM.

104. BI report, May 9, 1911, 1BI.

105. BI report, May 16, 1911, 1BI.

106. BI report, April 10, 1911, 1BI.

107. BI reports, March 24, April 24, 1911, 1BI.

108. BI report, May 13, 1911, 1BI.

109. Williams to adjutant general, May 9, 1911, DF, file no. 812.00/2034.

110. Williams to adjutant general, May 9, 1911, DF, file no. 812.00/2034.

111. BI report, April 24, 1911, 1BI; Garibaldi, *A Toast to Rebellion*, 275–78; Turner, *Bullets, Bottles, and Gardenias*, 46–49.

112. Ellsworth to secretary of state, April 24, 1911, DF, file no. 812.00/1517.

113. BI report, May 12, 1911, 1BI.

114. "Your Informants" to Torres, April 26, 29, 1911, L-E 679, leg. 2, exps. 142–45, 167–70; Arriola to Torres, April 26, 1911, L-E 679, leg. 2, exps. 146–51, AREM.

115. BI reports, May 2, 4, 1911, 1BI.

116. BI report, April 26, 1911, 1BI.

117. *EPMT*, April 28, 1911.

118. "Your Informants" to Torres, April 30, 1911, L-E 679, leg. 2, exp. 179, AREM.

119. BI report, May 8, 1911, 1BI.

120. BI report, May 2, 1911, 1BI.

121. BI reports, May 8, 9, 1911, 1BI.

122. Meyer, *Mexican Rebel*, 28–29.

123. Torres to foreign secretary, May 7, 1911, *DHRM*, 5:364.

124. "Your Informants" to Torres, April 24, 1911, L-E 679, leg. 2, exps. 129–34, AREM.

125. An interesting account of the campaign culminating in the battle is Pedro Siller and Miguel Angel Berumen, *1911: La batalla de Ciudad Juárez* (El Paso, Tex.: Berumen y Muñoz Editores, 2003).

126. Meyer, *Mexican Rebel*, 29–30.

127. Steever to adjutant general, May 10, 1911, DF, file no. 812.00/1910; Hillebrand to Nolte, May 12, 1911, 1BI.

128. Duncan to adjutant general, May 9, 1911, DF, file no. 812.00/2034; Steever to adjutant general, May 10, 1911, DF, file nos. 812.00/1908, 812.00/2034; Ellsworth to secretary of state, April 18, 1911, DF, file no. 812.00/1427; Torres to foreign secretary, May 10, 1911, *DHRM*, 5:375–77; Lomelí to foreign secretary, May 26, 1911, *DHRM*, 5:409–15.

129. BI report, May 10, 1911, 1BI.

130. BI report, April 26, 1911, 1BI.

131. Oliver to secretary of state, May 20, 1911, DF, file no. 812.00/1899.

132. Thompson reports, May 16, 1911, 1BI; "Persons Killed and Wounded on American Side, Juarez battle," May 23, 1911, 1BI. For a detailed account of the casualties see U.S. House, *Claims Growing Out of Insurrection in Mexico*, 187–460.

133. Steever to adjutant general, May 11, 1911, DF, file no. 812.00/1908.

134. *EPMT*, March 25, 1911.

135. Duncan to secretary of war, undated, DF, file no. 812.00/1908; memorandum for adjutant general, May 10, 1911, DF, file no. 812.00/2034; Oliver to secretary of state, May 22, 1911, DF, file no. 812.00/1961; Bush, *Gringo Doctor*, 202.

Chapter 4

1. Steever to adjutant general, May 13, 1911, DF, file no. 812.00/1908, microcopy no. 274, RDS, RG 59, NARA. Madero's soldiers added to the discord by demanding food and better clothing (BI report, May 19, 1911, OMF, BI roll 1, Investigative Records, 1908–22, RFBI, RG 65, NARA [OMF hereafter cited as BI preceded by roll number]).

2. Arriola to foreign secretary, May 12, 1911, *DHRM*, 5:383; Torres to foreign secretary, May 14, 1911, *DHRM*, 5:387–88.

3. Steever to adjutant general, May 13, 1911, DF, file no. 812.00/1908.

4. Lancaster report, May 18, 1911, 1BI; Eberstein report, May 13, 1911, 1BI; Lancaster report, May 16, 1911, 1BI; BI report, May 19, 1911, 1BI; Arriola to foreign secretary, May 13, 1911, *DHRM*, 5:385.

5. Steever to adjutant general, May 18, 1911, DF, file no. 812.00/2034. Villa's intention was allegedly to kill Garibaldi (Pascual Ortiz Rubio, *La Revolución de 1910: Apuntes Históricos*, 2nd ed. [México, D.F.: Ediciones Botas, 1937], 346–47).

6. "Your Informants" to Torres, April 30, 1911, L-E 679, leg. 2, exp. 179, AREM.

7. Eberstein report, May 13, 1911, 1BI.

8. BI report, Agent 19, May 16, 1911, 1BI.

9. BI report, Agent 19, May 18, 1911, 1BI.

10. BI report, Agent 53, May 18, 1911; Lancaster reports, May 18, 25, 1911, 1BI; *EPMT*, January 13, 1912.

11. Lancaster report, May 18, 1911, 1BI.

12. *EPT*, January 23, 1955; Leon C. Metz, *Dallas Stoudenmire: El Paso Marshal* (Norman: University of Oklahoma Press, 1993), 113.

13. Steever to adjutant general, May 23, 1911, DF, file no. 812.00/1972.

14. *EPH*, May 19, 20, 1911.

15. *EPH*, May 29, 31, 1911; Ellsworth to secretary of state, June 17, 1911, DF, file no. 812.00/2167.

16. Dunne to Díaz, February 4, 1911, *DHRM*, 5:220–22.

17. Smith was a colorful character. A native of Adelaide and a gifted athlete, he had lived in El Paso for years, and had been chief of city detectives. It was he whom the Mexican consul

had enlisted to shadow Antonio Villarreal in November 1910. In September 1911, Smith would receive a commission as a Texas Ranger captain and work as a detective for the Texas adjutant general until 1912 (Texas Rangers, Service Records, microfilm, Archives Division, Texas State Library, Austin).

18. *EPH*, May 29, 1911.

19. Juan Sánchez Azcona, *Apuntes para la historia de la Revolución Mexicana* (México, D.F.: Instituto Nacional de Estudio de la Revolución Mexicana, 1961), 311–12; Ortiz Rubio, *La Revolución de 1910*, 368–69.

20. Ellsworth to secretary of state, October 6, 1911, DF, file no. 812.00/2408.

21. *EPMT*, January 5, 1912; *EPH*, February 10, 1912.

22. *EPH*, May 30, 31, 1911; Ellsworth to secretary of state, June 3, 1911, DF, file no. 812.00/2064.

23. Lancaster report, June 29, 1911, 2BI; Ross report, May 13, 1912, 2BI.

24. *EPH*, May 12, 1911.

25. Francisco Vázquez Gómez, *Memorias políticas* (México, D.F.: Imprenta Mundial, 1933), 270–71.

26. The text of his resignation message is in *DHRM*, 5:402–3.

27. Madero's manifesto to the nation is in *DHRM*, 5:406–9.

28. De la Barra's manifesto to the nation on assuming the office of provisional president is in *DHRM*, 5:404–6.

29. The standard biography of de la Barra is Peter V. N. Henderson, *In the Absence of Don Porfirio: Francisco Leon de la Barra and the Mexican Revolution* (Wilmington, Del.: Scholarly Resources, 2000).

30. Brown to Fall, July 26, 1913, roll 30, ABFP.

31. Edwards to secretary of state, May 19, 1911, DF, file no. 812.00/1927.

32. *EPMT*, September 6, 1911.

33. *EPMT*, December 7, 16, 1911; Lowell L. Blaisdell, "Harry Chandler and Mexican Border Intrigue, 1914–1917," *Pacific Historical Review* 35, no. 4 (1966): 387, 389 n. 21; Blanford reports, February 16, 19, 1915, 7BI; Webster reports, February 16, March 13, 17, 1915, 7BI; Brian M. Du Toit, *Boer Settlers in the Southwest* (El Paso: Texas Western Press, 1995), 67; *EPMT*, January 14, 1917.

34. BI reports, May 19, 26, 1911, 1BI.

35. BI report, May 29, 1911, 1BI.

36. Eberstein report, May 25, 1911, 1BI.

37. See Lowell L. Blaisdell, *The Desert Revolution: Baja California, 1911* (Madison: University of Wisconsin Press, 1962).

38. Lancaster report, June 21, 1911, 2BI; John Mason Hart, *Empire and Revolution: The Americans in Mexico since the Civil War* (Berkeley: University of California Press, 2002), 524.

39. Ross report, July 3, 1911, 2BI.

40. Thompson report, June 28, 1911, 2BI.

41. Thompson report, June 16, 1911, 2BI.

42. Ross report, August 10, 1911, 1BI.
43. Lancaster report, July 3, 1911, 2BI.
44. BI report, July 14, 1911, 1BI; Ross report, July 15, 1911, 1BI; Wren report, February 9, 1917, 13BI.
45. Ross report, July 24, 1911, 1BI.
46. Ross report, July 24, 1911, 1BI.
47. Ross report, July 29, 1911, 1BI.
48. Ross report, July 29, 1911, 1BI.
49. Ross report, July 31, 1911, 1BI.
50. Ross report, August 1, 1911, 1BI.
51. Lancaster report, June 30, 1911, 2BI; Ross report, August 2, 1911, 1BI.
52. Hebert report, August 2, 1911, 1BI.
53. Ross report, August 3, 1911, 1BI.
54. *U.S. v. Calixto Guerra*, no. 1368, U.S. District Court, El Paso, Tex., FRC-FW; the case was transferred to the district court in Del Rio (*U.S. v. Calixto Guerra*, no. 20, U.S. District Court, Del Rio, Tex FRC-FW); Ross report, August 4, 1911, 1BI; Thompson report, August 6, 1911, 1BI.
55. Ross report, August 5, 1911, 1BI.
56. *EPH*, June 22, 1911; Ross report, August 9, 1911, 1BI.
57. Edwards to secretary of state, August 10, 1911, DF, file no. 812.00/2270.
58. Ross report, August 11, 1911, 1BI.
59. Ross report, August 31, 1911, 1BI.
60. Ross report, September 2, 1911, 1BI.
61. Ross report, September 4, 1911, 1BI.
62. Ross report, September 2, 1911, 1BI.
63. Ross report, September 4, 1911, 1BI.
64. Ross report, September 5, 1911, 1BI.
65. Ross report, September 5, 1911, 1BI.
66. Ross report, September 5, 1911, 1BI.
67. BI reports, April 19, 20, 1911, 1BI; Lancaster report, June 30, 1911, 2BI.
68. Ross report, September 8, 1911, 1BI.
69. Ross reports, September 5, 6, 1911, 1BI.
70. Thompson report, September 7, 1911, 1BI.
71. BI report, December 13, 1909, 1BI.
72. See also Ellsworth to secretary of state, October 24, 1911, DF, file no. 812.00/2446.
73. Wilbur report, October 20, 1911, 1BI.

74. Ellsworth to secretary of state, July 19, 1911, DF, file no. 812.00/2237. See also Wilbur report, August 26, 1911, 1BI; Thompson reports, July 12, 16, 21, 27, 1911, 1BI; Hebert report, July 16, 1911, 1BI.

75. See, for example, Miller report, June 13, 1919, 20BI.

76. Lancaster report, Sep 1, 1911, 1BI.

77. Thompson report, October 22, 1911, 2BI.

78. Thompson report, October 24, 1911, 1BI; *EPMT*, October 3, 1911.

79. Lancaster report, September 9, 1911, 1BI; Charles H. Harris III and Louis R. Sadler, "The 1911 Reyes Conspiracy: The Texas Side," *Southwestern Historical Quarterly* 83, no. 4 (1980): 325–48; E. V. Niemeyer Jr., *El General Bernardo Reyes*, trans. Juan Antonio Ayala (Monterrey, México: Universidad de Nuevo León, 1966), 204–20; Vic Niemeyer, "Frustrated Invasion: The Revolutionary Attempt of General Bernardo Reyes from San Antonio in 1911," *Southwestern Historical Quarterly* 67, no. 2 (1963): 213–25.

80. Lancaster reports, September 12, 16, 18, 1911, 1BI.

81. Ross reports, September 15, October 20, 1911, 1BI.

82. Ross report, September 20, 1911, 1BI. See also Ross reports, October 1, 2, 1911, 2BI.

83. Rogers to Nolte, September 16, 1911, in Thompson report, September 22, 1911, 1BI.

84. Ross reports, September 16, 20, November 25, 1911, 1BI, and November 23, 1911, 2BI.

85. *EPMT*, September 12, 1911.

86. Ross report, October 1, 1911, 2BI.

87. Hebert report, October 25, 1911, 1BI; Ross reports, November 2, 14, 1911, 2BI.

88. *EPMT*, December 23, 25, 1913.

89. *EPMT*, November 21, 1911.

90. Ross report, November 20, 1911, 2BI. See also Stimson to secretary of state, November 21, 1911, DF, file no. 812.00/2520.

91. See, for example, Ross report, November 18, 1911, 2BI.

92. Ross report, November 21, 1911, 2BI.

93. The captain was Juan José Alvarez (Ross report, November 22[?], 1911, 2BI).

94. *U.S. v. Gen. Bernardo Reyes, Amador Sánchez, Antonio Magnón, José Sánchez, Severo Villarreal*, nos. 552, 893, U.S. District Court, Laredo, Tex., FRC-FW; *U.S. v. Miguel Quiroga*, no. 93, U.S. Commissioner, San Antonio, Tex., FRC-FW; *U.S. v. Ismael Reyes Retana*, no. 2060, U.S. District Court, Brownsville, Tex., FRC-FW.

95. Charles H. Harris III and Louis R. Sadler, *The Texas Rangers and the Mexican Revolution: The Bloodiest Decade, 1910–1920* (Albuquerque: University of New Mexico Press, 2004), 80–81.

96. Chamberlain report, November 30, 1911, 3BI.

97. Ross reports, November 27, 1911, January 17, 1912, 2BI.

98. Harris and Sadler, *The Texas Rangers*, 82–83.

99. *EPH*, December 2, 1911; *EPMT*, December 3, 7, 10, 1911; Ellsworth to secretary of state, December 11, 1911, DF, file no. 812.00/2629; *U.S. v. Rafael Limón Molina*, no. 983, U.S.

Commissioner, El Paso, Tex., and no. 1564, U.S. District Court, El Paso, Tex., FRC-FW. See also Llorente to foreign secretary, December 30, 1911, L-E 817 (1), exp. 232, AREM.

100. *U.S. v. Rafael Limón Molina, Manuel Garza Aldape, Bernardo Reyes, E. M. Franco, R. A. Dorame, Fernando Palomares, Ricardo Flores Magón, José Santana Gómez, José Navarrete, Juan Hidalgo, José Aguilar, Silvestre Lomas*, no. 983, U.S. Commissioner, El Paso, Tex., and no. 1564, U.S. District Court, El Paso, FRC-FW.

101. *EPMT*, September 20, 1911.

102. *EPMT*, November 20, 21, December 10, 1911.

103. *EPMT*, October 19, 20, 21, 1911.

104. *EPMT*, November 29, December 23, 24, 1911.

105. John Anthony Caleca, "The Vasquez Gomez Brothers and Francisco I. Madero: Conflict Within the Mexican Revolution, 1909–1913" (MA thesis, University of Nebraska, 1970), 74–103.

106. Wickersham to president, March 3, 1912, DF, file no. 812.00/3063.

107. Thompson reports, January 3, 1912, 2BI; Thompson reports, March 3, 9, 12, 1912, 1BI; Chamberlain report, January 11, 1912, 3BI; Francisco R. Almada, *La Revolución en el Estado de Chihuahua*, 2 vols. (México, D.F.: Talleres Gráficos de la Nación, 1967), 1:272.

108. Wickersham to secretary of state, February 1, 1912, DF, file no. 812.00/2713; Stimson to secretary of state, February 1, 1912, DF, file nos. 812.00/2711, 812.00/2716; Edwards to secretary of state, February 1, 1912, DF, file no. 812.00/2717, and February 6, 1912, DF, file no. 812.00/2766; *EPMT*, February 1, 2, 1912.

109. *EPMT*, January 13, 1912.

110. *EPMT*, February 6, 1912.

111. *EPMT*, February 9, 1912.

112. Letcher to secretary of state, February 2, 1912, DF, file no. 812.00/2725. See also Letcher to secretary of state, February 13, 1912, DF, file no. 812.00/2844.

113. *EPMT*, February 6, 1912.

114. *EPMT*, February 1, 1912.

115. See, for example, Llorente reports, January 31, 1912, L-E 817 (1), exps. 203, 204, AREM.

116. Wickersham to secretary of state, February 2, 1912, DF, file no. 812.00/2724; Ross to Finch, February 3, 1912, DF, file no. 812.00/2743.

117. Stimson to secretary of state, February 5, 1912, DF, file no. 812.00/2738.

118. El Paso Chamber of Commerce to president, February 1, 1912, DF, file no. 812.00/2730.

119. Edwards to secretary of state, February 15, 1912, DF, file no. 812.00/2802; Stimson to secretary of state, February 16, 1912, DF, file nos. 812.00/2807, 812.00/2811; *EPMT*, February 17, March 9, 1912. Lieutenant Fields was convicted by the court martial (U.S. House, *Claims Growing Out of Insurrection in Mexico*, House doc. no. 1168, U.S. Congressional serial set, vol. 6586, 62nd Cong., 3rd sess. [Washington, D.C.: Government Printing Office, 1912], 116).

120. Stimson secretary of state, February 23, 1912, DF, file no. 812.00/2859.

Chapter 5

1. Memorandum, Office of the Army Chief of Staff, February 24, 1912, DF, file no. 812.00/2902, microcopy no. 274, RDS, RG 59, NARA.

2. Stimson to secretary of state, February 27, 1912, DF, file no. 812.00/2917; *EPMT*, February 26, 1912.

3. *EPMT*, February 28, 1912; Edwards to secretary of state, February 27, 1912, DF, file no. 812.00/2930; Stimson to secretary of state, February 26, 1912, DF, file no. 812.00/2904, and February 27, 1912, DF, file no. 812.00/2935; Wilson to secretary of state, February 26, 1912, DF, file no. 812.00/2906.

4. *EPMT*, March 1, 2, 1912.

5. Lancaster report, November 30, 1911, OMF, BI roll 4, Investigative Records, 1908–22, RFBI, RG 65, NARA (OMF hereafter cited as BI preceded by roll number); Ross report, August 1, 1912, 4BI.

6. Michael C. Meyer, *Mexican Rebel: Pascual Orozco and the Mexican Revolution, 1910–1915* (Lincoln: University of Nebraska Press, 1967), 52–61.

7. Acting secretary of treasury to secretary of state, February 29, 1912, DF, file no. 812.00/3029.

8. "Summary of Military Events September 4 to 10th, 1913," Military Intelligence Division, file no. 5761-836, RG 165, NARA; Letcher to secretary of state, April 19, 1912, DF, file no. 812.00/3730.

9. Wilson to secretary of state, March 5, 1912, DF, file no. 812.00/3054.

10. Wilson to secretary of state, March 6, 1912, DF, file no. 812.00/3066; Stimson to secretary of state, March 13, 1912, DF, file no. 812.00/3193.

11. Stimson to secretary of state, March 11, 1912, DF, file no. 812.00/3138.

12. Stimson to secretary of state, March 9, 1912, DF, file no. 812.00/3115.

13. Lancaster to Finch, March 5, 1912, DF, file no. 812.00/3142.

14. See, for example, U.S. Senate, *Revolutions in Mexico: Hearing before a Subcommittee of the Committee on Foreign Relations, United States Senate*, 62nd Cong., 2nd sess. (Washington, D.C.: Government Printing Office, 1913), 44, 65.

15. U.S. Senate, *Revolutions in Mexico*, 296–97; *EPMT*, March 28, 1912.

16. Elton Atwater, *American Regulation of Arms Exports* (Washington, D.C.: Carnegie Endowment for International Peace, 1941), 51–55, 58–59. See also Harold Eugene Holcombe, "United States Arms Control and the Mexican Revolution, 1910–1924" (PhD diss., University of Alabama, 1968).

17. John H. McNeely Jr., "The Mills Building: El Paso Landmark," *Password* 30, no. 4 (1985): 193–96; *EPMT*, June 2, 1918.

18. Ellsworth to secretary of state, March 27, 1912, DF, file no. 812.00/3435; Letcher to secretary of state, August 19, 1912, DF, file no. 812.00/4781.

19. "Revolutionary Information," April 4, 1912, 1BI.

20. Geck report, April 4, 1912, 1BI; Almada, *La Revolución en el estado de Chihuahua*, 2 vols. (México, D.F.: Talleres Gráficos de la Nación, 1967), 1:304.

21. Ross resided with his wife at 518 Buchanan Street.

22. Ross report, September 21, 1912, 3BI.
23. U.S. Senate, *Revolutions in Mexico*, 152.
24. U.S. Senate, *Revolutions in Mexico*, 169.
25. U.S. Senate, *Revolutions in Mexico*, 437.
26. *EPH*, February 22, 1912.
27. *EPH*, February 22, 1912; *EPMT*, August 21, 1912.
28. *EPMT*, June 3, 1913.
29. Ellsworth to secretary of state, August 28, 1912, DF, file no. 812.00/4776.
30. *EPH*, June 20, 1912.
31. Thompson to Bielaski, November 20, 1912, 3BI.
32. *EPH*, July 20, 1912.
33. Offley report, May 26, 1913, 3BI.
34. Cobb to Polk, April 24, 1917, 12BI; Harry Thayer Mahoney and Marjorie Locke Mahoney, *Espionage in Mexico: The 20th Century* (San Francisco: Austin and Winfield, 1997), 70.
35. Hagadorn to adjutant general, January 21, 1912, General Correspondence, Department of Texas, 1870–1913, file no. 40695F/W40260, Records of Named Departments, RUSACC, RG 393, NARA.
36. Thompson report, May 2, 1913, 3BI.
37. Sommerfeld file, MID, file no. 9140-1754, RWDGSS; U.S. Senate, *Revolutions in Mexico*, 387–447; Michael C. Meyer, "Villa, Sommerfeld, Columbus y los alemanes," *Historia Mexicana* 28, no. 4 (1979): 546–66; *EPH*, December 22, 1910.
38. García to Llorente, April 11, 1912, and Llorente to foreign secretary, April 12, 1912, L-E 748 (4), exps. 1–3, AREM.
39. *EPMT*, February 28, 1915. The *orozquistas* too were anxious to employ airpower against the enemy. They purchased an airplane in France, had it shipped to El Paso, and were devastated when the United States prohibited its export to Mexico (Henry F. Pringle, *The Life and Times of William Howard Taft: A Biography*, 2 vols. [New York: Farrar and Rinehart, 1939], 2:706).
40. Llorente and his wife rented the house of Mrs. A. L. Justice at 1117 Magoffin Avenue. *EPMT*, December 9, 1911, January 19, 1912.
41. U.S. Senate, *Revolutions in Mexico*, 284.
42. *EPH*, February 29, 1912; U.S. Senate, *Revolutions in Mexico*, 387–97, 411.
43. "Revolutionary Information," April 22, 1912, 1BI.
44. Lancaster report, March 1, 1912, 2BI.
45. *EPMT*, March 12, 21, 22, 24, May 6, 1912.
46. The other members of the team were Angel Schiavo and José Borja Ramos (Ross report, July 3, 1912, 2BI).
47. *U.S. v. Peter S. Aiken*, no. 1553, U.S. District Court, El Paso, Tex., FRC-FW; Ross report, September 13, 1912, 2BI.

48. Ross reports, May 3, 1912, with Aiken's statement attached, 2BI, and May 10, 1912, 2BI.

49. *EPMT*, April 11, 12, 15, 16, 1912. There was some controversy over whether Fountain had become a naturalized Mexican citizen (Fall to Fountain, April 16, 1912, ABFFP).

50. Ross report, May 8, 1912, 2BI; *EPMT*, May 4, 1912.

51. Harris reports April 2, 8, 12, 1912, 1BI. Jack Noonan, a native of Troy, New York, had participated in the Yukon gold rush and had distinguished himself as a member of Madero's foreign legion during the battle of Juárez. By 1916, he had become a U.S. Customs inspector at Nogales, Arizona (*EPMT*, April 19, 1915, December 18, 1916).

52. Ross report, June 14, 1912, 2BI; Barnes report, June 21, 1912, 2BI.

53. Ross report, June 19, 1912, 2BI; Barnes report, June 21, 1912, 2BI; Ellsworth to secretary of state, September 30, 1912, DF, file no. 812.00/5151; U.S. Senate, *Revolutions in Mexico*, 447, 505–28.

54. Ross report, June 14, 1912, 2BI.

55. Ross report, June 20, 1912, 2BI.

56. U.S. Senate, *Revolutions in Mexico*, 624–27.

57. Thompson report, May 31, 1912, 2BI; Hebert report, May 31, 1912, 2BI. Giuseppe Garibaldi fought as a general in the Greek Army in the Balkan War. In 1914, he helped raise an Italian legion that fought for France. When Italy entered the war on the Allied side in 1915, he fought as an Italian general. He opposed Mussolini and lived as a voluntary exile in the United States from 1924 to 1940, when he made his peace with the Italian dictator. Garibaldi died in Rome on May 19, 1950, at the age of seventy (*New York Times*, May 20, 1950).

58. U.S. Senate, *Revolutions in Mexico*, 582–91. Jones worked from April 1 until July 17, 1912.

59. *EPMT*, February 11, 13, 1912; Llorente report, December 18, 1911, L-E 811 (1), exp. 13, AREM.

60. Ross reports, March 1, 9, 1912, 2BI.

61. Stimson to secretary of state, April 6, 1912, DF, file no. 812.00/3514; Ross report, April 6, 1912, 1BI.

62. Ross report, June 14, 1912, 2BI; *U.S. v. John D. Dixon*, no. 1097, U.S. Commissioner, and no. 1598, U.S. District Court, El Paso, Tex., FRC-FW.

63. Ross report, April 22, 1912, 1BI.

64. Ross report, April 24, 1912, 1BI.

65. BI report, March 28, 1912, DF, file no. 812.00/3628.

66. BI report, May 8, 1912, DF, file no. 812.00/3865.

67. U.S. Senate, *Revolutions in Mexico*, 401.

68. *EPH*, February 21, 23, 26, 1912; *EPMT*, February 22, 23, 25, 1912.

69. Thompson to Bielaski, June 20, 1912, with Molina's notes attached, 2BI.

70. *EPMT*, March 17, 20, 21, 1912.

71. *EPMT*, October 6, 1912; BI report, Agent 53, May 18, 1911, 1BI; Breniman report, September 13, 1912, 3BI; Ellsworth to secretary of state, October 9, 1912, DF, file no. 812.00/5231.

72. Barnes report, April 2, 1913, 3BI.

73. James Burks, "Colonel James C. Bulger," *The Recount* 5, no. 1 ([1960]). See also *EPMT*, January 8, 9, November 11, 1916.

74. BI report, May 8, 1912, DF, file no. 812.00/4013.

75. BI report, May 31, 1913, DF, file no. 812.00/7789; Beckham report, December 5, 1914, 5BI; Pinckney report, April 27, 1915, 5BI; *EPMT*, March 14, 1916.

76. See, for example, "Revolutionary Information," March 4, 5, 6, 8, 16, 22, 23, 24, 26, 27, 28, 29, April 2, 4, 8, 10, 22, 28, 1912, 1BI. For Thiel's reports to the Mexico Northwestern Railway see "Revolutionary Information," October 22, 1912, John H. McNeely Collection, Box 13, packet misc. 1912–14, Records of the Mexico Northwestern Railway, Special Collections, University of Texas at El Paso; for Thiel's reports to the Mexican government see *DHRM* 7: 371–75, 391–94, 416–18.

77. Lancaster to Finch, "Personal and Confidential," March 23, 1912, 1BI.

78. Charles H. Harris III and Louis R. Sadler, "The 'Underside' of the Mexican Revolution: El Paso, 1912," *The Americas* 39, no. 1 (1982): 74–75.

79. Ross report, May 10, 1912, 2BI.

80. "Revolutionary Information," April 4, 1912, 1BI; *EPMT*, April 3, 4, 5, 6, 1912.

81. Felix Sommerfeld estimated that Roberts had twelve to sixteen men (U.S. Senate, *Revolutions in Mexico*, 401).

82. Ross report, June, 13, 1912, 2BI.

83. Ross report, May 18, 1912, 2BI.

84. Ross reports, May 10, 29, 1912, 2BI.

85. *EPMT*, February 25, 1912; Ross reports, April 8, 10, 13, 1912, 1BI. For Molina's cooperation with the U.S. Secret Service, see Tyrrell to chief, July 6, 8, 15, 1912, Daily Reports of Agents, 1875 thru 1936, microcopy, RSS, RG 87, NARA.

86. Ross report, May 16, 1912, 2BI.

87. Thompson to Finch, April 21, 1912, 1BI.

88. See, for example, *EPMT*, March 26, April 8, 1912.

89. *EPMT*, April 11, 1912.

90. Ellsworth to secretary of state, April 12, 1912, DF, file no. 812.00/3594, and April 18, 1912, DF, file no. 812.00/3696; *EPH*, April 10, 1912; *EPMT*, April 11, 1912; U.S. Senate, *Revolutions in Mexico*, 454.

91. *EPMT*, April 16, 1912.

92. U.S. Senate, *Revolutions in Mexico*, 689–91.

93. *EPMT*, July 2, August 24, 1912.

94. Barnes report, July 17, 1912, 4BI.

95. J. Morgan Broaddus Jr., *The Legal Heritage of El Paso* (El Paso: Texas Western Press, 1963), 223.

96. Lea to Sulzer, June 19, 1912, DF, file no. 812.00/4269; Ross report, June 30, 1912, 2BI; Knox to Sulzer, July 11, 1912, DF, file no. 812.00/4397; *EPH*, July 26, 1912.

97. Ross report, April 6, 1912, 1BI.

98. Ross reports, April 1, 4, 1912, 1BI.

99. BI report, May 11, 1912, DF, file no. 812.00/4013.

100. Ross reports, May 11, 14, 16, 18, 1912, 2BI.

101. Ross report, May 2, 1912, 2BI. Mebus was a Bureau of Investigation agent 1916–17 and an El Paso city detective by 1918 (*EPMT*, January 3, 18, 20, 25, 30, 1918).

Chapter 6

1. U.S. Senate, *Revolutions in Mexico: Hearing before a Subcommittee of the Committee on Foreign Relations, United States Senate*, 62nd Cong., 2nd sess. (Washington, D.C.: Government Printing Office, 1913), 185.

2. Krakauer, Zork and Moye Archive, Special Collections, University of Texas at El Paso. This archive has been purged of all documents dealing with arms sales to Mexicans (Floyd S. Fierman, "Insights and Hindsights of Some El Paso Jewish Families," *El Paso Jewish Historical Review* 1, no. 2 [1983]: 162).

3. U.S. Senate, *Revolutions in Mexico*, 127, 163; *EPMT*, January 28, 1912.

4. U.S. Senate, *Revolutions in Mexico*, 124.

5. U.S. Senate *Revolutions in Mexico*, 123.

6. See, for example, Ross reports, May 10, 11, 13, 1912, OMF, BI roll 2, Investigative Records, 1908–22, RFBI, RG 65, NARA (OMF hereafter cited as BI preceded by roll number).

7. Ross report, May 13, 1912, 2BI; Thompson report, June 4, 1912, 2BI; U.S. Senate, *Revolutions in Mexico*, 108–16; *U.S. v. Robert Krakauer, Cástulo Herrera, Pascual Arellano, Adolph Krakauer, Victor L. Ochoa, alias Wallace, alias Perkins, S. Domínguez, S. Gutiérrez, Francisco Navarro, Julius Krakauer*, no. 1626, U.S. District Court, El Paso, Tex., FRC-FW.

8. Barnes report with Krakauer's letter attached, June 20, 1912, 2BI.

9. Ross reports, June 11, 18, 1912, 2BI.

10. Ross reports, May 31, June 1, 15, 1912, 2BI. For details about Krakauer's complaints, see Krakauer to Steever, July 24, 1912, and Krakauer to Fall, July 25, 26, 1912, ABFFP.

11. Thompson report, May 31, 1912, 2BI; Ross report, May 31, 1912, 2BI.

12. Ross reports, April 5, 14, 1912, 1BI.

13. Thompson report, July 11, 1912 3BI; Barnes report, July 13, 1912, 3BI.

14. "Distribution of Troops on Patrol Duty," May 3, 1912, DF, file no. 812.00/3962, microcopy no. 274, RDS, RG 59, NARA.

15. Edwards to secretary of state, May 26, 1912, DF, file no. 812.00/4028.

16. Ross report, May 2, 1912, 2BI.

17. Thompson report, June 5, 1912, 2BI.

18. Ross report, June 14, 1912, 2BI.

19. Thompson reports, June 7, 8, 1912, 2BI; Barnes report, June 8, 1912, 2BI; Ross reports, June 8, 10, 1912, 2BI; *U.S. v. Cástulo Herrera, alias George Valencia, Ignacio Gutiérrez, Eduardo Ochoa, alias A. González Jesus de la Torre, Ignacio Núñez*, no. 1161, U.S. Commissioner, District of

New Mexico, and no. 85, U.S. District Court, Santa Fe, N.Mex. (see also nos. 1204, 1251, 1604, U.S. Commissioner, and no. 1654, U.S. District Court, Santa Fe, N.Mex.), FRC-D.

20. Ross report, June 15, 1912, 2BI.

21. Ross report, May 22, 1912, 2BI.

22. Ross reports, May 30, 31, 1912, 2BI; Thompson report, May 31, 1912, 2BI; *U.S. v. Floyd S. Sitler*, no. 1595, U.S. District Court, El Paso, Tex., FRC-FW.

23. *EPMT*, April 11, 1912; *U.S. v. James McKay*, no. 1555, U.S. District Court, El Paso, Tex., FRC-FW.

24. Ross reports, April 13, 20, 22, 1912, 1BI; *U.S. v. Cástulo Herrera, Savino* [*sic*] *Guaderrama, Avelino* [sic] *Guaderrama*, no. 1070, U.S. Commissioner, El Paso, Tex., FRC-FW; *EPMT*, April 21, 28, 30, 1912.

25. Thompson report, July 26, 1912, 3BI, Ross report, July 27, 1912, 3BI; Ellsworth to secretary of state, July 29, 1912, DF, file no. 812.00/4533; *EPMT*, July 26, 1912; *U.S. v. Savino Guaderrama, Isabel Rangel, José Cerros*, no. 1135, U.S. Commissioner, El Paso, Tex., and *U.S. v. Savino Guaderrama, Avelino Guaderrama, Longino González, Isabel Larrazola*, no. 1629, U.S. District Court, El Paso, Tex., FRC-FW.

26. "Victor Ochoa's Biographical Sketch," http://www.smithsonianeducation.org/seitech/impacto/graphic/victor/man.html. Another source states that he was born in the city of Chihuahua in 1861 (*EPDT*, January 12, 1894). The Victor L. Ochoa Papers, in the National Museum of American History, Kenneth E. Behring Center, Smithsonian Institution, Washington, D.C., consist largely of newspaper clippings, often undated, about his career as well as of sketches and correspondence concerning his inventions and a number of photographs.

27. A. Gabriel Meléndez, *Spanish-Language Newspapers in New Mexico, 1834–1958* (Tucson: University of Arizona Press, 2005), 64, 87–89; David Romo, *Ringside Seat to a Revolution: An Underground Cultural History of El Paso and Juárez, 1893–1923* (El Paso, Tex.: Cinco Puntos Press, 2005), 48.

28. Paul J. Vanderwood, *The Power of God Against the Guns of Government* (Stanford, Calif.: Stanford University Press, 1998), 291–92.

29. *EPH*, December 1, 1893, January 13, 1894; *EPDT*, January 7, 8, 9, 10, 11, 12, 13, 14, 15, 16, 17, 18, 1894.

30. *EPDT*, January 17, 1894.

31. Francisco R. Almada, *Diccionario de historia, geografía y biografía chihuahuense*, 2nd ed. (Chihuahua, México: Universidad de Chihuahua, 1968), 446; I. J. Bush, *Gringo Doctor* (Caldwell, Idaho: Caxton Printers, 1939), 110; *EPDT*, January 21, 22, 23, 24, 25, 26, 27, 28, 29, 30, 31, 1894.

32. *EPDT*, February 1, 2, 1894.

33. *U.S. v. Victor Ochoa*, no. 893, U.S. District Court, El Paso, Tex., FRC-FW; *EPH*, October 15, 1894.

34. *EPH*, October 15, 24, 1894; Bob Alexander, *Lawmen, Outlaws, and S.O.B.s: Gunfighters of the Old Southwest* (Silver City, N.Mex.: High-Lonesome Books, 2004), 175–76.

35. *U.S. v. Victor Ochoa*, no. 893, U.S. District Court, El Paso, Tex., FRC-FW; *Annual Report of the Attorney General of the United States for the Year 1906* (Washington, D.C.: Government Printing Office, 1906), 70.

36. Romo, *Ringside Seat*, 45–49; In April 1912, his business address was the "V. L. Ochoa Pen Co., Inc., 297 Main St., Paterson, N.J."

37. *EPMT*, November 11, 1911; *Paterson Morning Call*, October 4, 1911, VOP. Ochoa was not averse to suing people. He filed a $100,000 suit against one E. J. Ridgway, also for libel (undated newspaper clipping, VOP).

38. Madero to Ochoa, November 3, 1911, VOP; Ross report, April 17, 1912, 1BI.

39. Ellsworth to secretary of state, May 7, 1912, DF, file no. 812.00/3860.

40. Barnes report, June 19, 1912, 2BI.

41. Ross report, May 13, 1912, 2BI.

42. Ross report, June 19, 1912, 2BI.

43. Ross report, June 20, 1912, 2BI; Barnes report, June 20, 1912, 2BI; Thompson report, June 21, 1912, 2BI.

44. Ross report, June 26, 1912, 2BI.

45. Ross report, June 1, 1912, 2BI.

46. Barnes report, June 19, 1912, 2BI.

47. Ross report, June 19, 1912, 2BI.

48. Barnes reports, June 21, 22, 23, 29, 1912, 2BI.

49. Barnes reports, June 22, 23, 24, 1912, 2BI.

50. Ross report, June 26, 1912, 2BI.

51. Barnes reports, June 21, 22, 23, 1912, 2BI.

52. Barnes reports, June 23, 24, 25, 26, July 3, 1912, 2BI.

53. Ross report, July 2, 1912, 2BI. See also Romo, *Ringside Seat*, 47, 49.

54. Ross report, July 2, 1912, 2BI.

55. *EPMT*, July 21, 1912.

56. Ross report, July 6, 1912, 3BI; *U.S. v. Victor L. Ochoa, Flavio Sandoval, José Trujillo, T. C. Cabney*, no. 1126, U.S. Commissioner, El Paso, Tex., and no. 1630, U.S. District Court, El Paso, Tex., FRC-FW. See also. *U.S. v. Victor L. Ochoa*, no. 1625, U.S. District Court, El Paso, Tex., FRC-FW.

57. Ross report, July 8, 1912, 3BI.

58. Ross report, July 9, 1912, 3BI.

59. Ross report, July 12, 1912, 3BI.

60. Ross report, July 1, 1912, 1BI.

61. *EPMT*, May 9, 1912.

62. Letcher to secretary of state, April 24, 1912, DF, file no. 812.00/3710; Hanna to secretary of state, April 26, 1912, DF, file no. 812.00/3727.

63. *EPMT*, July 5, 1912.

64. These included an American, John Barbrick. See Letcher to secretary of state, July 16, 1912, DF, file no. 812.00/4553.

65. Thompson reports, May 4, 12, 1912; Ross reports, May 4, 5, 1912; Hebert report, May 5, 1912, 2BI; Letcher to secretary of state, May 10, 1912, DF, file no. 812.00/3930.

66. Ross report, June 10, 1912, 2BI.

67. Ross report, June 17, 1912, 2BI.

68. *EPMT*, August 22, 1912; Ganor report, November 24, 1912, 3BI.

69. Ganor reports, May 25, July 9, 1912, 2BI.

70. Edwards to secretary of state, May 8, 1912, DF, file no. 812.00/3841. See also U.S. Senate *Revolutions in Mexico*, 596–602.

71. Ellsworth to secretary of state, May 1, 1912, DF, file no. 812.00/3912; U.S. Senate, *Revolutions in Mexico*, 165.

72. U.S. Senate, *Revolutions in Mexico*, 314–16.

73. Edwards to secretary of state, November 20, 1912, DF, file no. 812.00/5583.

74. *EPH*, February 28, 29, March 4, 1912.

75. *EPMT*, March 31, 1912.

76. Ellsworth to secretary of state, September 26, 1912, DF, file no. 812.00/5128; *EPMT*, March 31, 1912. The standard biography of Dreben is Art Leibson, *Sam Dreben: "The Fighting Jew"* (Tucson, Ariz.: Westernlore Press, 1996).

77. *EPMT*, June 24, 1912; Barnes report, June 26, 1912, 2BI.

78. Harris report, August 7, 1912, 3BI. See also the memorandum by Captain W. A. Burnside, the U.S. military attaché in Mexico, who had personal dealings with Barbrick (July 17, 1912, DF, file no. 812.00/4511). In January 1913, Barbrick worked in New Orleans for the U.S. Senate committee investigating American involvement in the Mexican Revolution. See U.S. Senate, *Revolutions in Mexico*, 841, 883–95.

79. Ross report, June 28, 1912, 2BI; Thompson report, July 11, 1912, DF, file no. 812.00/4475; BI report, July 26, 1912, DF, file no. 812.00/4627.

80. Ross report, June 29, 1912, 2BI.

81. Ross report, July 6, 1912, 2BI.

82. Ross report, July 12, 1912, 3BI.

83. Harris reports, July 31, August 2, 1912, 3BI.

84. Hebert report, September 9, 1912, 3BI; Ross reports, September 8, 11, 1912, 3BI.

85. Barnes report, September 28, 1912, 2BI.

86. Dale L. Walker, "Tracy Richardson . . . Machine Gun for Hire," *El Paso Magazine* 4, no. 3 (1973): 6.

87. *EPH*, March 29, 1912.

88. He was reportedly recruited by General David de la Fuente.

89. Gresh report, October 24, 1912, 3BI. See also Gresh report, October 26, 1912, 3BI.

90. Blanford report, September 17, 1914, 8BI.

91. Walker, "Tracy Richardson," 6–7, 15.

92. Ross report, July 6, 1912, 3BI.
93. Ross report, July 2, 1912, 2BI.
94. Ross report, July 13, 1912, 3BI.
95. Ross reports, July 18, 1912, 4BI, and July 19, 1912, 2BI.
96. Ross report, July 18, 1912, 4BI.
97. Ross reports, May 25, 1912, 2BI, and July 19, 1912, 4BI.
98. Ross reports, July 18, 19, 1912, 4BI.
99. Ross reports, July 3, 1912, 2BI, and July 13, 1912, 3BI.
100. Ross reports, May 10, 1912, 2BI, and July 18, 1912, 4BI.
101. Ross report, July 18, 1912, 4BI.
102. Thompson report, May 17, 1912, 2BI.
103. Ross report, July 20, 1912, 3BI. See also Thompson report, July 22, 1912, 3BI.
104. Thompson report, July 22, 1912, 3BI; *EPMT*, July 21, 1912.
105. *EPMT*, July 31, 1912.
106. Thompson reports, July 31, 1912, 3BI, and July 31, 1912, 4BI; Ross report, July 31, 1912, 4BI. See also Thompson reports, July 22, 1912, 3BI, and July 22, 1912, 4BI; Ross report, July 24, 1912, 3BI; Ellsworth to secretary of state, August 1, 1912, DF, file no. 812.00/4563; *U.S. v. Victor L. Ochoa*, no. 1126, U.S. Commissioner, El Paso, Tex., FRC-FW; *U.S. v. Victor L. Ochoa*, no. 1625, U.S. District Court, El Paso, Tex., FRC-FW. The case was dismissed in April 1913.
107. Ross report, August 28, 1912, 2BI.
108. Ross report, July 24, 1912, 3BI.
109. Ross report, July 27, 1912, 3BI.
110. Ross report, August 9, 1912, 3BI.

Chapter 7

1. Llorente to Madero, July 12, 1912, enclosing reports to Molina from his operatives "J. Sterling" and Manuel González, L-E 816 (7), exps. 18–22, AREM; Hebert report, July 12, 1912, OMF, BI roll 3, Investigative Records, 1908–22, RFBI, RG 65, NARA (OMF hereafter cited as BI preceded by roll number).
2. Ross report, July 9, 1912, 3BI. See also Barnes report, July 13, 1912, 3BI.
3. Ross report, July 10, 1912, 3BI; Barnes reports, July 10, 12, 13, 1912, 3BI; Thompson reports, July 11, 1912, 3BI, and August 15, 1912, 2BI; Ellsworth to secretary of state, July 12, 1912, DF, file no. 812.00/4431, microcopy 274, RDS, RG 59, NARA; *EPMT*, July 10, 11, 13, 1912.
4. Ross report, July 13, 1912, 3BI.
5. Ross report, July 6, 1912, 2BI.
6. Thompson reports, July 18, 19, 1912, 4BI.
7. Ross report, July 3, 1912, 2BI.

8. Scully report, April 12, 1912, 1BI; Offley report, April 12, 1912, 1BI; Dannenberg report, April 17, 1912, 1BI.
9. Thompson report, September 7, 1912, 3BI; Ellsworth to secretary of state, September 25, 1912, DF, file no. 812.00/5127; U.S. Senate, *Revolutions in Mexico: Hearing before a Subcommittee of the Committee on Foreign Relations, United States Senate*, 62nd Cong., 2nd sess. (Washington, D.C.: Government Printing Office, 1913), 458–72.
10. Thompson report, September 13, 1912, 3BI; Phillips reports, February 15, 20, 1915, 7BI; Offley reports, February 27, March 9, 11, 13, 1915, 7BI; Scully report, March 1, 1915, 7BI.
11. *EPMT*, August 1, 1912.
12. Lancaster report, July 23, 1912, 3BI; Ross reports, July 22, 24, 1912, 2BI; Ross report, July 24, 1912, 3BI; Thompson report, July 25, 1912, 3BI; *EPMT*, July 23, 24, 1912.
13. BI report, January 12, 1913, DF, file no. 812.00/5923.
14. Thompson reports, July 29, 1912, 3BI, and August 15, 1912, 2BI; *EPMT*, July 26, 1912.
15. Barnes report, July 13, 1912, 3BI; Ross reports, July 27, 1912, 3BI, and July 30, 1912, 4BI.
16. See Clifford Wayne Trow, "Senator Albert B. Fall and Mexican Affairs, 1912–1921" (PhD diss., University of Colorado, 1966).
17. Harriet Howze Jones, "Heritage Homes of El Paso: The A. B. Fall House," *Password* 22, no. 3 (1977): 124–26.
18. Trow, "Senator Albert B. Fall," 55.
19. Ross report, August 24, 1912, 2BI. See also BI report, May 30, 1912, DF, file no. 812.00/4151.
20. Edwards to secretary of state, August 21, 1912, DF, file no. 812.00/4715.
21. Ross report, September 3, 1912, 3BI; Ellsworth to secretary of state, September 6, 1912, DF, file no. 812.00/4860, and September 7, 1912, DF, file no. 812.00/4876.
22. Letcher to secretary of state, August 15, 1912, DF, file no. 812.00/4695; BI reports, August 23, 1912, DF, file no. 812.00/4811, and September 3, 1912, DF, file no. 812.00/4915.
23. Schuster allegedly claimed that he himself had lost $100,000 that Orozco had promised him if he'd been able to arrange a peace settlement (U.S. Senate, *Revolutions in Mexico*, 439–42).
24. Ellsworth to secretary of state, September 12, 1912, DF, file no. 812.00/4938, and October 8, 1912, DF, file no. 812.00/5232.
25. Harris reports, January 19, 20, 1913, 3BI.
26. State Department memorandum, July 8, 1912, DF, file no. 812.00/7956 (Saenz had given Martínez's address as 1508 Wyoming); Lancaster report, July 5, 1912, 3BI; Thompson report, August 12, 1912, 7BI.
27. Thompson report August 13, 1912, 2BI.
28. Thompson report, August 16, 1912, 2BI; Ross report, September 7, 1912, 3BI.
29. Thompson report, August 19, 1912, 2BI.
30. Hebert report, July 6, 1912, 3BI.
31. Hebert report, July 8, 1912, 3BI.
32. Barnes report, July 9, 1912, 3BI.

33. Thompson report, August 10, 1912, 3BI.

34. Ellsworth to secretary of state, October 9, 1912, DF, file no. 812.00/5231; BI report, October 8, 1912, DF, file no. 812.00/5309; *EPMT*, October 8, 1912.

35. Breniman report, November 15, 1912, 3BI.

36. Ross reports, August 2, 3, 1912, 3BI; Barnes report, August 26, 1912, 2BI.

37. Thompson report, August 9, 1912, 2BI; *U.S. v. Lázaro Alanís, Ines Salazar, Roque Gómez, Concepción Tovar, Marcial Andujos*, nos. 1158 and 1268, U.S. Commissioner, Santa Fe, N.Mex., FRC-D; *U.S. v. Lázaro Alanís, Ines Salazar, Roque Gómez, Concepción Tovar, Marcial Andujos*, nos. 1158 and 1167, U.S. Commissioner, El Paso, Tex., FRC-FW; *U.S. v. Lázaro Alanís, Ines Salazar, Roque Gómez, Concepción Tovar, Marcial Andujos*, no. 84, U.S. District Court, Santa Fe, N.Mex., FRC-D; Thompson reports, August 12, 14, 1912, 2BI; Ross report, August 14, 1912, 2BI; Barnes report, August 16, 1912, 2BI; Blanford report, May 1, 1913, 3BI; *EPMT*, August 13, 1912.

38. Thompson report, July 26, 1912, 3BI; Ross report, July 27, 1912, 3BI.

39. Ross report, July 31, 1912, 4BI.

40. Ross report, August 2, 1912, 3BI; *U.S. v. Savino* [sic] *Guaderrama*, no. 11629, U.S. District Court, El Paso, Tex., FRC-FW.

41. Ross reports, August 8, 1912, 2BI, and August 8, 1912, 3BI.

42. Ross report, August 9, 1912, 2BI.

43. Ross report, August 17, 1912, 2BI.

44. Barnes report, August 20, 1912, 2BI.

45. Holliday to Adee, August 14, 1912, DF, file no. 812.00/4635.

46. Thompson report, August 16, 1912, 2BI.

47. *EPMT*, August 21, 22, 1912.

48. Letcher to secretary of state, July 31, 1912, DF, file no. 812.00/4541.

49. Thompson report, August 21, 1912, 2BI.

50. U.S. Senate, *Revolutions in Mexico*, 389–90, 455; *EPMT*, September 4, 5, 1912.

51. Thompson report, August 19, 1912, 2BI.

52. Thompson report, August 21, 1912, 2BI.

53. U.S. Senate, *Revolutions in Mexico*, 624–31.

54. Wilson to Lascuráin, July 17, 1912, DF, file no. 812.00/4511, and July 29, DF, file no. 812.00/4567.

55. U.S. Senate, *Revolutions in Mexico*, 431.

56. Ross report, July 20, 1912, 3BI.

57. Ross report, May 18, 1912, 2BI.

58. Ross report, May 10, 1912, 2BI.

59. *U.S. v. Jesús Morales Guevara*, no. 1080, U.S. Commissioner, El Paso, Tex., FRC-FW.

60. Ross reports, May 18, 20, 1912, 2BI; Thompson report, May 22, 1912, 2BI.

61. Ross reports, July 9, 1912, 4BI, and July 12, 1912, 3BI; U.S. Senate, *Revolutions in Mexico*, 505–28; Ellsworth to secretary of state, September 30, 1912, DF, file no. 812.00/5151. See also the testimony of R. H. G. McDonald and D. J. Mahoney in U.S. Senate, *Revolutions in Mexico*, 680–86.

62. *EPH*, September 28, 1912; *U.S. v. E. L. Charpentier, D. J. Mahoney, Robert McDonald, A. Monahan* "and other evil minded persons," no. 1607, U.S. District Court, El Paso, Tex., FRC-FW (A. Monahan was in fact J. H. Noonan); Thompson report, February 6, 1913, 3BI.

63. Thompson reports, July 3, 5, 1912, 2BI.

64. Thompson report, August 21, 1912, 2BI.

65. Ross report, August 22, 1912, 2BI. See also his report August 27, 1912, 2BI.

66. Ross report, August 29, 1912, 2BI.

67. Thompson report, November 7, 1912, 3BI.

68. Agustín Estrada, Gonzalo C. Enrile, David de la Fuente, Magdaleno Juárez, Benito R. Sicardo, Felipe S. López, Pascual Orozco Sr., and José M. Córdova. For a partial chronology of these arrests, see U.S. Senate, *Revolutions in Mexico*, 623–24, 632–44.

69. BI report, November 9, 1912, DF, file no. 812.00/5562; Blanford report, August 9, 1913, 3BI.

70. *U.S. v. Arnulfo Chávez, alias Arnuto Chávez*, no. 1081, U.S. Commissioner, and no. 1590, U.S. District Court, El Paso, Tex., FRC-FW.

71. Thompson reports, October 4, 7, 8, 1912, 2BI; *EPMT*, October 7, 1912.

72. Thompson report, October 16, 1912, 2BI.

73. Thompson report, October 18, 1912, 2BI.

74. Thompson report, October 30, 1912, 3BI; Breniman report, October 31, 1912, 3BI. The brothers sold ten cases of these rifles to the Wyith Hardware Company of Saint Joseph, Missouri (Ross to Bielaski, August 28, 1912, 2BI; Breniman report, November 16, 1912, 3BI). What became of the rest of the munitions is unknown.

75. Thompson report, October 14, 1912, 2BI.

76. Thompson report, October 14, 1912, 2BI; Breniman report, October 26, 1912, 3BI.

77. Thompson report, October 31, 1912, 3BI.

78. Dudley to Fall, October 1, 1912, roll 30, ABFP.

79. Thompson report, August 28, 1912, DF, file no. 812.00/4915.

80. Allegedly Floyd S. Sitler was used as the actual smuggler (Gresh reports, October 22, 1912, 2BI, and October 31, 1912, 3BI).

81. For a discussion of this *orozquista* operation see Charles H. Harris III and Louis R. Sadler, "The 'Underside' of the Mexican Revolution: El Paso, 1912," *The Americas* 39, no. 1 (1982): 62–64.

82. U.S. Senate, *Revolutions in Mexico*, 528–41; Blanford reports, June 6, 9, 22, 1913, 3BI; Breniman report, June 10, 1913, 3BI; Thompson to Bielaski, September 13, 1912, 3BI.

83. Blanford report, April 9, 1914, 5BI.

84. U.S. Senate, *Revolutions in Mexico*, 648–52, 654.

85. Thompson report, September 8, 1912, 3BI.

86. *U.S. v. Juan Pedro Didapp, alias José Hackin*, no. 2080, U.S. District Court, El Paso, Tex., FRC-FW.

87. Ross report, September 24, 1912, 3BI. The other Mexican agent was John Neville (*EPMT*, September 23, 1912; *EPH*, September 24, 1912). Didapp claimed he'd come to El Paso to testify before the Senate committee's members Smith and Fall.

88. Thompson report, October 14, 1912, 2BI; Adkins to secretary of the treasury, October 14, 1912, file no. 90755-1857, RDJ, RG 60, NARA.

89. *EPMT*, October 14, 1912.

90. Breniman report, October 23, 1912, 2BI; *EPMT*, November 3, 1912.

91. *EPMT*, October 191, 1912.

92. See, for example, Ross reports to Llorente, October 18, 19, November 6, 1912, ECLP.

93. Gresh report, October 24, 1912, 3BI.

94. Breniman reports, October 25, 30, November 3, 4, 24, 1912, 3BI.

95. Hall had informants not just on the border but among the rebels still holding out in Chihuahua. See, for example, BI report, December 21, 1912, DF, file no. 812.00/5792.

96. Blanford report, September 16, 1913, 4BI.

97. *EPMT*, February 5, 1913.

98. *EPMT*, January 14, 15, 16, 17, 1913.

99. *EPMT*, February 17, 1913.

100. *EPMT*, February 18, 19, 1913.

101. *EPMT*, February 23, 1913.

102. *EPMT*, February 27, 28, March 1, 1913.

103. He wasn't convicted, for on September 10, 1918, he became a special agent of the federal Bureau of Investigation, and on February 19, 1921, he was commissioned as a Texas Ranger (serving only until March 14).

104. *EPMT*, March 28, 29, 31, April 5, June 1, 1913.

105. See, for example, Thompson report, July 11, 1912, 3BI.

106. Ellsworth to secretary of state, August 26, 1912, DF, file no. 812.00/4751.

107. Dye to secretary of state, September 29, 1912, DF, file no. 812.00/5104.

108. *EPMT*, September 29, October 9, 27, 1912; Thompson to Bielaski, January 23, 1913, DF, file no. 812.00/5961; Thompson report, September 27, 1912, 3BI.

109. Steever to adjutant general, War Department, November 21, 22, 1912, Record Cards, 1909–12, Department of Texas, no. 42601, Records of Named Departments, RUSACC, RG 393, NARA; Breniman reports, November 23, 29, 1912, 3BI; Oliver to secretary of state, November 22, 1912, DF, file no. 812.00/5565.

110. Ross report, September 7, 1912, 3BI; del Toro to foreign secretary, September 19, 1912, *DHRM* 14: 68–73.

111. Ross report, August 27, 1912, 2BI.

112. Ross report, September 15, 1912, 3BI.

113. It was reported that Bill Russell, superintendent of the mines at Shafter and a diehard Orozco partisan, hid the Mexican rebel and helped him escape (Blanford report, October 4, 1914, 8BI).

114. Those arrested were Rafael Flores, José Rochín, Miguel Caballero, Cristóforo Caballero, and José Córdova.

115. *U.S. v. Pascual Orozco, Sr.*, no. 1559, U.S. District Court, El Paso, Tex., FRC-FW.

116. Thompson report, September 17, 1912, 3BI; Ross report, September 17, 1912, 3BI.

117. *EPMT*, September 22, 1912.

118. Ross report, September 24, 1912, 3BI; U.S. Senate, *Revolutions in Mexico*, 499–505; *EPMT*, September 24, 1912.

119. Thompson report, October 21, 1912, 2BI.

120. Thompson report, October 21, 1912, 2BI.

121. Breniman report, October 24, 1912, 2BI. See also U.S. Senate, *Revolutions in Mexico*, 472–81.

122. Gresh report, October 24, 1912, 3BI.

123. José R. Rochín, who'd been arrested at Presidio along with Orozco, was also serving a forty-day sentence for an alleged crime committed in Chihuahua (Breniman report, November 16, 1912, 3BI).

124. U.S. Senate, *Revolutions in Mexico*, 665–69; Ellsworth to secretary of state, August 29, 1912, DF, file no. 812.00/4780, October 9, 1912, DF, file no. 812.00/5231, and October 15, 1912, DF, file no. 812.00/5278; Thompson report, November 8, 1912, 3BI.

125. Breniman report, November 1, 1912, 3BI.

126. *U.S. v. Ricardo Gómez Robelo*, no. 128, U.S. Commissioner, and no. 2080, U.S. District Court, El Paso, Tex., FRC-FW.

127. Ross report, September 15, 1912, 3BI.

128. Ross report, September 28, 1912, 3BI.

129. *EPMT*, October 9, 10, 1912; Ellsworth to secretary of state, October 11, 1912, DF, file no. 812.00/5235, and October 12, 1912, DF, file no. 812.00/5248.

130. *EPMT*, October 17, 1912; *U.S. v. Lázaro Alanís, Inés Salazar, Roque Gómez, Concepción Tovar, Marcial Andujos*, no. 1158 (see also nos. 1167 and 1168), U.S. Commissioner, and no. 84, U.S. District Court, Santa Fe, N.Mex., FRC-D.

131. Blanford report, November 29, 1912, 3BI; Breniman reports, November 14, 16, 17, 25, 1912, 3BI.

132. Other members were Crisóforo Caballero, Rafael Flores, Miguel Caballero Aldaz, Primitivo Enríquez, José Rochín, Amado González, Avelino González, and Melecio Parra.

133. Ross report, September 28, 1912, 3BI.

134. Ross report, October 7, 1912, 2BI.

135. Ross report, October 7, 1912, 2BI.

136. Breniman reports, October 27, November 13, 1912, 3BI.

137. Gresh report, October 30, 1912, 3BI; Breniman report, November 4, 1912, 3BI.

138. Breniman report, November 12, 1912, 3BI.

139. *U.S. v. David de la Fuente*, no. 128, U.S. Commissioner, and no. 2080, U.S. District Court, El Paso, Tex., FRC-FW; de la Fuente habeas corpus proceedings, no. 994, U.S. Supreme Court; Pascual Orozco Sr., ex parte application for habeas corpus, no. 1307, U.S; District Court, El Paso, Tex., FRC-FW; Oliver to secretary of state, November 23, 1912, DF, file no. 812.00/5581; Wickersham to secretary of state, December 16, 1912, DF, file no. 812.00/5696.

140. Barnes reports, December 23, 26, 1912, 3BI; Ellsworth to secretary of state, December 17, 1912, DF, file no. 812.00/5731, and December 27, 1912, DF, file no. 812.00/5793; *San Antonio Light*, December 22, 1912.

141. Breniman reports, November 8, 10, 1912, 3BI.

142. The standard biography of Holmdahl is Douglas V. Meed, *Soldier of Fortune: Adventuring in Latin America and Mexico with Emil Lewis Holmdahl* (Houston, Tex.: Halcyon Press, 2003).

143. Thompson report, November 16, 1912, 3BI. Cáceres had been one of General David de la Fuente's most important subordinates and later served under General José Inés Salazar.

144. Breniman report, November 8, 1912, 3BI.

145. Breniman reports, November 10, 14, 1912, 3BI.

146. Breniman report, November 11, 1912, 3BI; Blanford reports, November 11, 12, 1912, 3BI.

147. Thompson report, November 14, 1912, 3BI.

148. Blanford reports, November 14, December 11, 1912, 3BI; Breniman report, November 16, December 4, 1912, 3BI; Thompson report, November 18, 1912, 3BI.

149. BI report, December 5, 1912, DF, file no. 812.00/5773.

150. Blanford report, December 18, 1912, 3BI.

151. Blanford report, December 17, 1912, DF, file no. 812.00/5773.

152. Blanford report, December 20, 1912, 3BI.

153. Blanford report, December 17, 1912, 3BI; Thompson report, December 19, 1912, 3BI.

154. Blanford report, December 20, 1912, 3BI.

155. Blanford reports, December 23, 24, 1912, 3BI.

156. Blanford report, December 28, 1912, 4BI.

157. Blanford report, December 30, 1912, 4BI.

158. Palmer report, January 7, 1913, 3BI.

159. Edwards to secretary of state, November 26, 1912, DF, file no. 812.00/5594.

160. Edwards to secretary of state, December 3, 1912, DF, file no. 812.00/5636.

161. Oliver to secretary of state, November 29, 1912, DF, file no. 812.00/5617.

162. Thompson report, December 5, 1912, DF, file no. 812.00/5713.

163. Taft to Wickersham, December 12, 1912, DF, file no. 812.00/5697. For an account of the incident in which a soldier shot at an automobile, see U.S. Senate, *Revolutions in Mexico*, 722–24.

Chapter 8

1. *U.S. v. Emilio Vázquez Gómez, Paulino Martínez, alias Luis González, Dr. Policarpo Rueda, alias F. P. Rice, alias J. P. Weel, Francisco I. Guzmán, Felipe Fortuno Miramón, Manuel L. Márquez, Dr. Luis J. Snowball, alias L. J. Stone, alias Luis J. Straight, Manuel Garza Aldape, Miguel Garza Aldape, J. A. Fernández, Ramón Vázquez, Teodoro G. Rodríguez, alias Francisco Rodríguez, Antonio M. Franco, Candelario Inzunza, José Villa, Joaquín Esquer y Barbecho, Belisario García, Camilo Garcelum* [sic], *Camilo Gastelum, Teodoro Valenzuela, alias Francisco Valenzuela, Porfirio Gómez, Manuel Mascarenas Jr., Juan Reyes, J. Garcia, Dr. José S. Saenz, David de la Fuente, Ricardo Gómez Robelo, Delio Moreno Cantón, Juan Pedro Didapp, alias José Hackim, J. Cantú Cárdenas, Emilio L. Llanes, José Cavazos Eschavarria* [sic], *Felipe L. López, Luis Martínez, Herminio R. Ramírez, Emiliano Zapata, Francisco M. Herrera, Francisco R. Pradillo, Alberto Salas, Melchor Camacho*, No. 2080, U.S. District Court, San Antonio, Tex.; *U.S. v. Dr. Luis J. Snowball, alias L. J. Stone, alias Luis J. Straight*, no. 125, U.S. Commissioner, San Antonio, Tex., FRC-FW; Thompson to Bielaski, January 9, 1913, DF, file no. 812.00/5847, microcopy 274, RDS, RG 59, NARA; BI report, January 10, 1913, 812.00/5923.
2. Letcher to secretary of state, January 21, 1913, DF, file no. 812.00/5912; Stimson to secretary of state, January 29, 1913, DF, file no. 812.00/5960.
3. Edwards to secretary of state, January 25, 1913, DF, file no. 812.00/5964, and January 29, 1913, DF, file no. 812.00/5963.
4. Thompson reports, January 10, 13, 24, 1913, OMF, BI roll 3, Investigative Records, 1908–22, RFBI, RG 65, NARA (OMF hereafter cited as BI preceded by roll number); Blanford reports, January 10, 11, 12, 13, 15, 16, 1913, 3BI.
5. Blanford reports, January 23, 1913, 3BI, and December 2, 1913, 4BI; Breniman report, February 1, 1913, 3BI; Wren report, November 3, 1913, 4BI; Weiskopf report, May 23, 1917, 16BI.
6. *U.S. v. Enrique Llorente*, no. 1650, U.S. District Court, El Paso, Tex., FRC-FW.
7. *EPMT*, February 7, 8, 9, 10, 11, 1913.
8. Thompson reports, February 6, 8, 1913, 3BI.
9. Blanford report, April 21, 1913, 3BI; see also *EPMT*, April 19, 20, 1913.
10. The defendants were Jesús Guaderrama, Ricardo Flores Magón, Enrique Flores Magón, Antonio I. Villarreal, Práxedis G. Guerrero, Demetrio Ponce, Alberto Echeverría, Jesús de la Torre, Nemecio Padilla, Enrique Esparza, Agustín Gallo, Sabino Guaderrama, Isabel Larrazola, Fred Freepartner, W. E. Mason, Joe de Lauter, Lou Mullady, José Marquez, and Macho Luz (*EPMT*, April 15, 22, 1913).
11. Thompson report, January 24, 1913, 3BI.
12. Blanford report, January 23, 1913, 3BI; Breniman report, January 27, 1913, 3BI.
13. BI report, February 1, 1913, DF, file no. 812.00/6260.
14. Blanford reports, January 24, 25, 1913, 3BI; Breniman reports, January 27, 28, 30, 1913, 3BI; Thompson report, January 27, 1913, 3BI.
15. Thompson report, January 30, 1913, 3BI; Breniman report, January 30, 1913, 3BI; Barnes report, February 17, 1913, 3BI; *EPMT*, February 16, 17, 1913.
16. Generals Emilio P. Campa and Antonio Rojas, colonels José Pérez Castro, Lázaro Alanís, Roque Gómez, Máximo Castillo, and Lino Ponce, lieutenant colonels Silvestre Quevedo

and Rodrigo Quevedo, and a number of majors, among them Enrique Portillo (Vázquez Gómez proclamation, February 15, 1913, DF, file no. 812.00/6534).

17. Salazar to secretary of state, February 25, 1913, DF, file no. 812.00/6534, and decree no. 1, February 24, 1913, DF, file no. 812.00/6534.

18. De la Fuente to secretary of state, February 22, 1913, DF, file no. 812.00/6689.

19. Salazar to Bryan, March 13, 1913, DF, file no. 812.00/6788, and March 21, 1913, DF, file no. 812.00/6863; telegrams, March 19, 1913, DF, file no. 812.00/6851.

20. General Lauro Villar's official report of the engagement, February 9, 1913, *DHRM*, 9:36–47.

21. The best treatment of Huerta's career is Michael C. Meyer, *Huerta: A Political Portrait* (Lincoln: University of Nebraska Press, 1972). See also George Jay Rausch Jr., "Victoriano Huerta: A Political Biography" (PhD diss., University of Illinois, 1960), and Kenneth J. Grieb, *The United States and Huerta* (Lincoln: University of Nebraska Press, 1969).

22. See Huerta to Taft, February 18, 1913, DF, file no. 812.00/6250; Wilson to secretary of state, February 20, 1913, DF, file no. 812.00/6288.

23. De la Barra to Mexican embassy, February 23, 1913, DF, file no. 812.00/7239.

24. Holland to secretary of state, February 21, 1913, DF, file no. 812.00/6302.

25. Breniman report, December 24, 1913, 4BI. The Constitutionalist consular agent in El Paso was Manuel Urquidi (Ellsworth to secretary of state, April 24, 1913, DF, file no. 812.00/7297).

26. Bowman to secretary of state, February 28, 1913, DF, file no. 812.00/6435.

27. Letcher to secretary of state, February 10, 1913, DF, file no. 812.00/6084.

28. Letcher to secretary of state, February 22, 1913, DF, file no. 812.00/6308, February 23, 1913, DF, file no. 812.00/6309, and February 24, 1913, DF, file no. 812.00/6343; *EPMT*, February 26, 1913.

29. Stephens to secretary of state, March 15, 1913, DF, file no. 812.00/6727.

30. Wilson to secretary of state, March 2, 1913, DF, file no. 812.00/6448.

31. Letcher to secretary of state, March 1, 1913, DF, file no. 812.00/6456.

32. Letcher to secretary of state, March 19, 1913, DF, file no. 812.00/6774.

33. Letcher to secretary of state, March 24, 1913, DF, file no. 812.00/6952; Francisco R. Almada, *Vida, proceso y muerte de Abraham González* (México, D.F.: Talleres Gráficos de la Nación, 1967), 148–49.

34. For the "throwing under the train" story, see *EPMT*, March 31, 1913.

35. Ellsworth to secretary of state, March 31, 1913, DF, file no. 812.00/6695; *EPMT*, March 29, 1913.

36. Edwards to secretary of state, February 24, 1913, DF, file no. 812.00/6346, and February 25, 1913, DF, file no. 812.00/6377; Vargas to Carranza, June 2, 1913, 339, VCA.

37. Breckenridge to secretary of state, August 21, 1913, DF, file no. 812.00/8521.

38. Bravo to foreign secretary, March 4, 1913, *DHRM* 14:108–10; Garza Estrada to Carranza, June 7, 1913, 400, VCA.

39. *EPMT*, November 8, 1913.

40. BI report, June 13, 1913, DF, file no. 812.00/7867; Carranza to Aguirre Benavides, May 20, 1913, 227, VCA; Acevedo to Carranza, December 19, 1913, 666, VCA.

41. Elías to [secretaría de] relaciones [exteriores], April 28, 1913, *DHRM* 14:206.

42. Wilson to secretary of state, February 19, 1913, DF, file no. 812.00/6271; Stimson to secretary of state, February 23, 1913, DF, file no. 812.00/6310, and February 24, 1913, DF, file no. 812.00/6333; Nagel to secretary of state, February 24, 1913, DF, file no. 812.00/6317.

43. Edwards to secretary of state, March 6, 1913, DF, file no. 812.00/6499; *EPMT*, March 11, 1913.

44. Breniman reports, March 11, 13, 26, 1913, 3BI; *EPMT*, March 10, 23, 31, 1913.

45. *EPMT*, April 1, 1913.

46. Breniman report, April 2, 1913, 3BI.

47. Antimaco Sax, *Los mexicanos en el destierro* (San Antonio, Tex.: International Printing, 1916), 68–69.

48. García to Zapata, *DHRM* 14:140; John Womack Jr., *Zapata and the Mexican Revolution* (New York: Knopf, 1969), 162, 175.

49. Fred Morales, *Smeltertown* (El Paso: El Paso/Juárez Historical Museum, 2004), 21; Blanford report, February 20, 1913, 3BI.

50. Rodolfo Uranga, "Como vivió Francisco Villa desterrado en Estados Unidos," *La Prensa*, December 28, 1930.

51. Blanford reports, February 20, 21, 1913, 3BI; *EPH*, February 19, 20, 1913.

52. Breniman report, March 9, 1913, 3BI; BI report, March 11, 1913, DF, file no. 812.00/6731.

53. Blanford reports, February 22, 23, 1913, 3BI.

54. Blanford report, February 27, 1913, 3BI.

55. Friedrich Katz, *The Life and Times of Pancho Villa* (Stanford, Calif.: Stanford University Press, 1998), 206.

56. Blanford report, February 28, 1913, 3BI.

57. Breniman report, March 14, 1913, 3BI.

58. By August the Constitutionalist junta had rented offices in the Mills Building (Scott to commanding general, August 8, 1913, DF, file no. 812.00/8679).

59. García to Carranza, May 15, 1913, 175, VCA.

60. They were Dr. Samuel Navarro, the head of the junta, who had been a major and surgeon in the Juárez garrison but had deserted and fled to El Paso, attorney Gunther R. Lessing, Crispín Juárez, M. B. Mercado, Roberto V. Pesqueira, Juan N. Medina, Aureliano González, Juan Amador, Teodoro Kyriacopulos, Bernardo Anaya, Roque González Garza, Paulino Martínez, Alberto Madero, Luis Hernández, Antonio de Zamacona, Juan Ortega, Juan Anaya, and Román González (Blanford report, May 2, 1913, 3BI). See also de la Cueva to Bryan, April 11, 1913, DF, file no. 812.00/7106; subsecretary to foreign secretary, June 10, 1913, L-E 766 (24), exp. 10, AREM; Fernández to foreign secretary, April 6, 7, 1913, *DHRM*, 14:156–59; Elías to foreign secretary, May 14, 1913, *DHRM*, 14:229.

61. Breniman reports, March 9, 11, April 15, 1913, 3BI.

62. *EPMT*, April 1, 1913.

63. *EPMT*, April 6, 17, 1913.

64. Diebold to foreign secretary, May 14, 1913, L-E 766 (24), exps. 1–8, AREM.

65. *EPMT*, July 21, 1913; Blanford report, February 9, 1914, 5BI. Llorente's commission as "Encargado del Departamento de Agencias Comerciales en la Sria de Relaciones Exteriores," was signed by Venustiano Carranza on May 1, 1914. His salary, incidentally, was seven pesos a day (ECLP).

66. Hopkins to Carranza, May 13, 1913, 157, VCA; Michael M. Smith, "*Carrancista* Propaganda and the Print Media in the United States: An Overview of Institutions," *The Americas* 52, no. 2 (1995): 160.

67. Hopkins to Carranza, November 6, 1913, *DHRM*, 14:380–81; Hopkins to Carranza, November 7, 1913, *DHRM*, 14:382–84; Hopkins to Carranza, November 14, 1913, *DHRM*, 14:384–85.

68. *New York Herald*, July 1, 2, 3, 4, 5, 1914; José Vasconcelos, *La tormenta*, 7th ed. (México, D.F.: Ediciones Botas, 1948), 100–101.

69. Blanford report, June 8, 1913, 3BI.

70. Blanford report, June 22, 1913, 3BI; Breniman report, August 8, 1913, 3BI.

71. Neunhoffer report, August 5, 1916, 15BI; Blanford to Barnes, August 7, 1915, 15BI; Barnes report, August 12, 1916, 15BI; Hopkins report, March 15, 1917, Old German Files, 1909–21, case no. 8000-2633, microfilm publication no. M1085, Investigative Records, 1908–1922, RFBI, RG 65, NARA.

72. Breniman report, March 26, 1913, 3BI.

73. *EPMT*, March 25, 1913; Barnes report, April 2, 1913, 3BI. He had gone there from Houston, and a glimpse of his background is provided by one describing "the man signing himself Paul Mason, Colonel" as "the Swede [who] was one time cook at Jap. Restaurant on Congress St" (Thompson report, March 26, 1913, 3BI). See also Spates reports, August 2, 12, 1913, 3BI, and August 15, 1913, 4BI; Barnes reports, April 2, 1913, 3BI, and July 6, 1914, 7BI; Flores to attorney general, August 15, 1913, 4BI.

74. Blue to secretary of state, June 28, 1913, DF, file no. 812.00/7927; Matthews report, July 11, 1913, 3BI.

75. Blanford reports, March 1, 3, 1913, 3BI; Breniman report, March 12, 1913, 3BI.

76. *EPMT*, February 26, 1913.

77. *EPMT*, March 1, 2, 3, 8, 9, 10, 23,1913.

78. *EPMT*, August 29, September 19, 1912, March 4, 5, 1913.

79. *EPMT*, March 8, 1913.

80. Diebold to foreign secretary, September 25, 1913, L-E 778 (3), exps. 1–4, AREM.

81. *EPMT*, April 11, 1913.

82. Breniman report, March 8, 1913, 3BI.

83. Breniman report, March 13, 1913, 3BI.

84. Peña y Reyes to Diebold, May 1, 1913, L-E 778 (7), exp. 2, AREM.

85. Blanford report, July 2, 1913, 3BI.

86. Thompson report, June 13, 1913, 3BI.

87. *United States, Plaintiff in Error v. Arnulfo Chávez alias Arnuto Chávez, defendant in error,* no. 863, U.S. Supreme Court; *United States, Plaintiff in Error v. José Mesa, defendant in error;* no. 864, U.S. Supreme Court; Thompson report, May 9, 1913, 3BI; Adkins to secretary of state, May 26, 1913, DF, file no. 812.00/7622.

88. Assistant attorney general to Camp, July 8, 1913, 3BI.

89. Thompson report, June 30, 1913, 3BI.

90. Thompson report, August 16, 1913, 4BI. In April, the Huerta officials in Texas notified the Bureau that Shelton-Payne was shipping ammunition and carbines to Del Rio paid for by Roberto V. Pesqueira, Carranza's representative in Washington (Elías to Thompson, April 30, 1913, L-E 775 [20], exp. 2, and Peña y Reyes to Elías, May 19, 1913, L-E 775 [20], exp. 3, AREM).

91. Elton Atwater, *American Regulation of Arms Exports* (Washington, D.C.: Carnegie Endowment for International Peace, 1941), 58–59, 62–69.

92. BI reports, May 23, 26, 1913, DF, file no. 812.00/7632.

93. *EPMT*, August 10, December 17, 1913.

94. Edwards to secretary of state, April 29, 1913, DF, file no. 812.00/7305, May 1, 1913, DF, file no. 812.00/7332, and May 5, 1913, DF, file no. 812.00/7387.

95. *EPMT*, June 17, 1913, January 17, 1914; *EPH*, June 21, 1913.

96. Letcher to secretary of state, June 25, 1913, DF, file no. 812.00/7892; BI report, June 9, 1913, DF, file no. 812.00/7867; Edwards to secretary of state, July 5, 1913, DF, file no. 812.00/7970.

97. *EPMT*, July 31, 1913.

98. Letcher to secretary of state, July 29, 1913, DF, file no. 812.00/8220.

99. Blanford report, November 10, 1913, 4BI. Consul Diebold reported that a telegrapher in Juárez was passing information to the Constitutionalists (Diebold to foreign secretary, September 20, 1913, L-E 778 [4], exps. 1–2, AREM).

100. Blanford report, July 6, 1913, 3BI. Two men caught attempting to cut through the barbed wire entanglements were summarily executed by the Huerta soldiers (*EPMT*, July 17, 1913).

101. Blanford reports, July 22, 30, 1913, 3BI.

102. Blanford report, July 17, 1913, 3BI; Cootes to commanding general, July 17, 1913, DF, file no. 812.00/8521; *EPMT*, July 16, 1913.

103. The four Mexicans couldn't pay their $1,000 bond each either and also went to jail. Blanford reports, July 19, 23, 25, 1913, 3BI; Thompson report, July 20, 1912, 3BI; *EPMT*, July 18, 19, 20, 22, 23, 24, 26, 31, 1913; *U.S. v. Powell Roberts, Manuel Mendoza, Francisco Camacho, Pablo Carbajal, Paulino Q. Díaz*, no. 1227, U.S. Commissioner, El Paso, Tex., FRC-FW; *U.S. v. J. B. Badger*, no. 1229, U.S. Commissioner, El Paso, Tex., FRC-FW; *U.S. v. G. Padres, Powell Roberts, J. B. Badger*, nos. 1680 and 1681, U.S. District Court, El Paso, Tex., FRC-FW.

104. Blanford reports, July 19, 22, 23, 1913, 3BI.

105. In 1917, Padres was elected to the Mexican Congress ("Intelligence Report, Nogales, Arizona," March 16, 1917, MID, file no. 8536-176, NARA).

106. Blanford reports, July 23, 1913, 3BI, and October 21, 1913, 4BI.

107. Breckenridge to secretary of state, August 25, 1913, DF, file no. 812.00/8719.

108. *EPMT*, July 24, 1913.

109. Blanford report, December 7, 1913, 4BI.

110. Franco reports, August 21, 25, September 26, 27, October 2, 13, 1913, 4BI; Blanford reports, August 25, September 2, 18, 1913, 4BI; Wren reports, November 3, 4, 1913, 4BI.

111. Blanford report, September 24, 1913, 4BI.

112. Breckenridge to secretary of state, September 8, 1913, DF, file no. 812.00/8737, and September 12, 1913, DF, file no. 812.00/8850; Post to secretary of state, September 19, 1913, 812.00/8916; Dunsmore to secretary of state, September 27, 1913, 812.00/8996, RDS.

113. Edwards to secretary of state, September 9, 1913, 812.00/8874, RDS.

114. *EPMT*, October 9, November 8, 1913.

115. *EPMT*, October 16, 17, 18, 22, 24, December 25, 1913.

116. *EPMT*, October 13, 18, 1913.

117. *EPMT*, October 26, 1913.

118. Blanford report, October 21, 1913, 4BI.

119. Blanford report, August 25, 1913, 4BI.

120. Franco report, August 29, 1913, 4BI; Blanford report, December 29, 1913, 4BI; Wren report, December 31, 1913, 4BI.

121. Thompson reports, July 18, 1913, 3BI, August 28, 1913, 4BI.

122. Breniman report, September 30, 1913, 4BI. For a detailed listing of the ammunition Winchester and Remington shipped to Krakauer and Shelton-Payne in 1912 and 1913, see Breniman report, December 12, 1913, 4BI.

123. Blanford report, September 27, 1913, 4BI; Breniman report, December 24, 1913, 4BI.

124. Thompson report, September 15, 1913, 4BI.

125. Breniman report, September 30, 1913, 4BI.

126. Thompson report, October 2, 1913, 4BI.

127. Barnes report, October 25, 1913, 4BI; *U.S. v. Shelton-Payne Arms Co., Douglas Hardware Co., W. H. Shelton, John Henry Payne, W. F. Fisher*, no. C-676, U.S. District Court, Phoenix, Ariz., FRC-L; *U.S. v. L. D. McCartney, Shelton-Payne Arms Co., W. H. Shelton, John Henry Payne, J. N. Gonzales*, no. C-677, U.S. District Court, Phoenix, Ariz., FRC-L; *U.S. v. Krakauer, Zork and Moye, Julius Krakauer, L. D. McCartney*, no. C-679, U.S. District Court, Phoenix, Ariz., FRC-L; *U.S. v. Phelps-Dodge Mercantile Co., Douglas Hardware Co., W. H. Brophy, R. P. de Negri, F. E. Coles, W. F. Fisher, Pedro Bracamonte, M. M. Martínez, J. L. Perez*, no. C-525, U.S. District Court, Phoenix, Ariz., FRC-L.

Chapter 9

1. Miguel A. Sánchez Lamego, *Historia militar de la Revolución Constitucionalista*, 5 vols. (México, D.F.: Talleres Gráficos de la Nación, 1957), 3:226–29.

2. Diebold to foreign secretary, November 17, 1913, L-E 778 (1), exps. 18–22, AREM. For Diebold's detailed account of the capture of Juárez see L-E 778 (1), exps. 24–33, AREM.

3. Blanford report, November 17, 1913, OMF, BI roll 4, Investigative Records, 1908–22, RFBI, RG 65, NARA (OMF hereafter cited as BI preceded by roll number); *EPMT*, November 15, 16, 17, 18, 1913; *EPH*, November 15, 1913.

4. "Report of General Conditions," September 26, 1913, DF, file no. 812.00/9044, microcopy 274, RDS, RG 59, NARA; *EPH*, September 16, 1913.

5. *EPMT*, November 18, 19, 20, December 2, 3, 1913.

6. *EPMT*, December 8, 22, 24, 1913. Regarding foreign fighters, Villa wasn't as particular as Carranza. Not until February 1914 did Villa discharge the fifteen foreign soldiers of fortune then serving under him, giving each one fifty pesos in Constitutionalist currency, which was virtually worthless (*EPMT*, February 24, 27, March 1, 1914).

7. Ivor Thord-Gray, *Gringo Rebel: Mexico, 1913–1914* (Coral Gables, Fla.: University of Miami Press, 1960), 20.

8. Thord-Gray, *Gringo Rebel*, 19–29.

9. *EPMT*, November 24, 25, 26, 28, 1913.

10. Wren report, December 3, 1913, 4BI.

11. Thord-Gray, *Gringo Rebel*, 30–51, 54–61.

12. *EPMT*, December 5, 7, 1913; Thord-Gray, *Gringo Rebel*, 71–455. For comments about Thord-Gray from someone who knew him during this phase of his career, see Turner, *Bullets, Bottles, and Gardenias* (Dallas: South-West Press, 1935), 103–4, 106–8, 110, 140–41, 155, 157.

13. *EPMT*, August 27, 1916, May 11, 1918.

14. Thord-Gray file, Confidential General Correspondence, 1913–24, file no. 21000/514, Records of the Office of the Chief of Naval Intelligence, RG 38, NARA.

15. Friedrich Katz, *The Life and Times of Pancho Villa* (Stanford, Calif.: Stanford University Press, 1998), 225–27, 300, 859 n. 69.

16. *EPMT*, November 27, 1913.

17. Sánchez Lamego, *Historia Militar*, 3:244.

18. Thord-Gray file.

19. Thompson report, November 29, 1913, 4BI.

20. *EPH*, November 19, 1912.

21. Thompson report, December 2, 1913, 4BI; Breniman report, December 3, 1913, 4BI.

22. Thompson report, December 13, 1913, 4BI.

23. Breniman report, December 12, 1913, 4BI.

24. Blanford report, December 23, 1913, 4BI.

25. Blanford report, December 4, 1913, 4BI.

26. Barnes report, December 20, 1913, 4BI. The members of the junta were Paulino Martínez, José Hernández, A. C. Carascosa, A. Molinar, Felipe Cáceres, Roque Gómez, and Silvestre Caraveo.

27. *EPMT*, December 18, 19, 20, 1913; Blanford report, December 31, 1913, 4BI.

28. *EPMT*, November 11, December 6, 1913.

29. *EPMT*, December 3, 1917.

30. *EPH*, February 28, 1912.

31. Castillo continued to make a nuisance of himself by raiding ranches and settlements in northwestern Chihuahua, but he lacked a power base (*EPMT*, January 16, 19, 27, February 12, 13, 1914). In February 1914, Castillo was captured in New Mexico and interned in Fort Bliss (*EPMT*, February 18, 1914).

32. *EPMT*, December 15, 16, 1913, January 1, 3, 1914; Blanford report, December 31, 1913, 4BI; Wren report, January 6, 1914, 4BI.

33. Breniman report, January 1, 1914, 4BI.

34. *EPMT*, January 11, 1914.

35. Blanford report, January 1, 1914, 4BI.

36. Blanford report, January 1, 1914, 4BI.

37. Pendleton reports, January 4, 7, 8, 9, 1914, 5BI; Blanford report, January 8, 1914, 5BI. Solomon was connected with the firm of E. M. Solomon and Company, 203–5 Godchaux Building, New Orleans (Ibs report, January 30, 1917, 16BI).

38. Pendleton report, January 14, 914, 5BI; Blanford report, January 28, 1914, 5BI.

39. Pendleton reports, January 30, 31, 1914, 5BI, and February 1, 1914, 9BI.

40. Blanford report, February 1, 1914, 5BI; Carranza to Castillo Brito, May 14, 1913, *DHRM*, 14:232–33; Berta Ulloa, comp., *Revolución Mexicana, 1910–1920*, 2nd ed. (México, D.F.: Secretaría de Relaciones Exteriores, 1985), 88, 95, 164, 186, 223, 260, 261, 262, 270, 272; *EPMT*, August 6, 7, 1913.

41. Wren reports, January 9, 15, 1914, 9BI; Blanford report, January 15, 1914, 9BI; *EPMT*, January 11, 14, 1914.

42. Daniel report, January 12, 1914, 9BI; Wren report, January 13, 1914, 9BI.

43. Daniel report, January 12, 1914, 9BI.

44. *EPMT*, January 14, 1914.

45. Daniel report, January 14, 1914, 9BI; Barnes reports, January 22, 29, 1914, September 12, 1914, 4BI; Blanford report, October 4, 1914, 8BI.

46. Barnes reports, January 5, 9, 22, February 17, 27, 1914, 4BI; Daniel report, February 11, 1914, 4BI; Fernández Arteaga to Carranza, February 25, 1914, L-E 760 (22), exp. 226, AREM. The Orozcos first resided at 601 and 611 Boulevard Street and then moved to "a very fine residence" at 2429 South Presa Street. The post office maintained a mail cover, a list of the letters the Orozco family received.

47. Blanford reports, January 17, 1914, 9BI, and January 18, 1914, 4BI; Barnes report, September 12, 1914, 8BI.

48. L-E 793 (1), AREM; Blanford report, December 3, 1914, 5BI.

49. [Diebold] to Castro, April 6, 1914, L-E 793 (1), AREM. See also Larry D. Ball, *Elfego Baca in Life and Legend* (El Paso: Texas Western Press, 1992), 68; Fall to Garrison, March 4, 1914, ABFFP; Fall to Wilson, March 6, 1914, ABFFP; Fall to Bryan, March 6, 1914, ABFFP.

50. "Elfego Baca vs. The 80 Cowboys," *Albuquerque Journal*, October 8, 2000.

51. Baca to Elías, June 11, 1914, and Elías to Baca, June 17, 1914, L-E 812 (1), exps. 144, 145.

52. Blanford reports, April 27, May 9, 1914, 8BI.

53. Barnes report, March 18, May 9, 1914, 8BI.

54. Blanford report, May 11, 1914, 8BI.

55. Blanford report, May 12, 1914, 8BI.

56. Blanford reports, May 13, 15, 1914, 8BI.

57. Barnes report, September 12, 1914, 8BI.

58. Blanford reports, September 17, 18, 19, 22, 24, 25, October 4, 1914, 8BI; Hilliard report, September 19, 1914, 8BI. See also Barnes report, October 3, 1914, 8BI, and Allen report, October 3, 1914, 8BI.

59. Blanford reports, October 13, 14, 1914, 8BI; Barnes to Goens, November 12, 1914, 8BI.

60. Blanford report, November 25, 1914, 5BI; Beckham report, November 27, 1914, 5BI.

61. Beckham report, January 4, 1915, 5BI.

62. Ralph H. Vigil, "Revolution and Confusion: The Peculiar Case of José Inés Salazar," *New Mexico Historical Review* 53, no. 2 (April 1978): 152–54, 164–67; Ball, *Elfego Baca*, 120. Senator Fall said that he indirectly assisted Baca in his trial at Santa Fe ([Fall] to Elfego Baca, January 15, 1916, ABFFP).

63. In October 1914, Sabino Guaderrama and two accomplices were charged with having sold ammunition in boxes in which they'd substituted sand and bricks for cartridges (*EPMT*, October 21, 1914).

64. Blanford report, January 16, 1914, 5BI; Wren report, January 16, 1914, 4BI.

65. Blanford report, January 17, 1914, 5BI. José Guaderrama was the father of three daughters and nine sons: Manuel, Jesús, Abelino, Juan, Sabino, Angel, David, Adolfo, and José (*EPMT*, December 31, 1915).

Chapter 10

1. Blanford report, February 1, 1914, OMF, BI roll 5, Investigative Records, 1908–22, RFBI, RG 65, NARA (OMF hereafter cited as BI preceded by roll number); "Lista de consignaciones hechas al gran jurado por violaciones a las leyes de neutralidad americanas," L-E 787, leg. 27, exps. 1–2, AREM.

2. *EPMT*, January 15, 25, February 3, 8, 1914.

3. Elton Atwater, *American Regulation of Arms Exports* (Washington, D.C.: Carnegie Endowment for International Peace, 1941), 68; *DHRM*, 15:26; Blanford report, July 3, 1914, 5BI.

4. Pendleton report, February 5, 1914, 9BI.

5. Blanford report, April 7, 1914, 9BI.

6. *EPMT*, February 4, 5, 6, 7, April 17, 1914.

7. Allegedly, at the beginning of the Constitutionalist revolution some federal artillery shells were loaded with inferior powder and even with sawdust, the result of collusion between crooked contractors and some federal commanders (*EPMT*, March 14, 1914).

8. *EPMT*, February 6, 7, 27, March 2, 3, 8, 12, 16, 19, 21, 1914; Múzquiz to Carranza, December 31, 1913, 717, VCA.

9. *EPMT*, September 24, 1916.

10. See, for instance, Madero to Madero, February 4, 1914, L-E 760 (22), exp. 158, AREM; Levy to Colla [*sic*], February 4, 1914, L-E 760 (22), exp. 159; Merifield to Villa, February 5, 1914, L-E 760 (22), exp. 162, 164; Berger to Villa, February 8, 1914, L-E 760 (22), exp. 173; Hopkins to Madero, February 9, 1914, L-E 760 (22), exp. 173, AREM.

11. For example, Donald J. Stoker Jr. and Jonathan A. Grant, eds., *Girding for Battle: The Arms Trade in a Global Perspective, 1815–1940* (Westport, Conn.: Praeger, 2003), do not even mention the Mexican Revolution.

12. Baker reports, May 18, 22, 1914, 6BI; Tucker report, December 16, 1914, 7BI; Scully report, December 16, 1914, 7BI. See also Sommerfeld to Villa, February 17, 1914, L-E 760 (22), exp. 195, 199, 207, 209, AREM.

13. Not surprisingly, in his memoirs Flint mentions nothing about his Mexican business dealings (*Memories of an Active Life: Men and Ships and Sealing Wax* [New York, Putnam, 1923]); http://www-03.ibm.com/ibm/history/exhibits/builders/builders_flint.html; *New York Herald*, July 8, 1914.

14. *EPMT*, May 18, 1914.

15. Baker reports, June 4, 13, 23, 26, 27, July 7, 17, 21, 24, 28, 31,1914, 6BI; Clabaugh reports, June 6, August 3, 1914, 6BI; invoice and attached documents, July 25, 1914, 9BI; Barnes reports, July 31, September 7, 1914, 6BI; statement of I. M. Petersen, July 31, 1914, 9BI; Pendleton reports, August 1, 3, 1914, 7BI; Offley report, August 7, 1914, 6BI; Pabst to Barnes, August 6, 1914, 6BI; Zubarán to Burns, August 13, 1914, 9BI; Burns to Zubarán, August 14, 15, 22, 1914, 9BI; Barnes to Guy, September 6, 1914, 6BI; I. M. Peters to collector of customs, October 22, 1914, 9BI; Anderson to Leckie, October 23, 1914, 9BI; *EPMT*, May 18, 1914.

16. Llorente to Villa, February 10, 1915, ECLP.

17. Carothers to secretary of state, October 17, 1916, DF, file no. 812.00/19596, microcopy 274, RDS, RG 59, NARA; Blanford report, June 17, 1916, 7BI.

18. *EPMT*, February 24, 1914. He succeeded one Gabino Vizcarra.

19. *New York Herald*, July 1, 1914.

20. *EPMT*, April 9, 11, 14, 15, 17, 18, 19, 25, 26, 28, May 6, 13, 14, 15, 18, 21, 26, July 9, August 25, 1914; Diebold to foreign secretary, April 9, 1914, L-E 797, leg. 1, exp. 9–10, and May 6, 1914, L-E 797, leg. 1, exp. 4, AREM.

21. Chief to Barnes, June 8, 1914, 5BI. See also Pendleton report, July 4, 1914, 5BI.

22. Blanford report, June 23, 1914, 5BI; *EPMT*, January 25, February 8, 1914.

23. BI report, September 30, 1913, DF, file no. 812.00/9247.

24. Blanford report, January 28, 1914, 5BI.

25. Villa to Carranza, December 22, 1913, 686, VCA; Castro to Diebold, March 14, 1914, L-E 793 (d1), AREM; *EPH*, August 18, 1914.

26. Blanford report, January 17, 1914, 5BI; Wren report, January 18, 1914, 5BI.

27. Blanford report, July 20, 1914, 6BI; Bowen report, July 23, 1914, 6BI.

28. Ramos [to Carranza], December 17, 1913, 655, VCA; Michael M. Smith, "Andrés G. García: Venustiano Carranza's Eyes, Ears, and Voice on the Border," *Mexican Studies/Estudios Mexicanos* 23, no. 2 (2007): 362.

29. Ramos to Llorente, March 4, 1915, ECLP; *EPMT*, October 20, 1914.

30. *EPMT*, February 22, 1914.

31. Blanford reports, February 19, 21, 23, 1914, 5BI; Mock report, April 11, 1918, 20BI.

32. Blanford reports, February 21, March 23, 1914, 5BI.

33. In June 1914, General Salvador Alvarado jailed Holmdahl in Hermosillo and deported him ten days later for allegedly being a spy for the American government (*EPMT*, July 9, 11, 1914; Barnes to Bielaski, March 8, 1917, 16BI).

34. Blanford report, October 7, 1914, 6BI.

35. See, for example, *U.S. v. Domingo Flores*, no. 1284, U.S. Commissioner, El Paso, Tex., FRC-FW.

36. The cipher is included in Bowen report, September 10, 1914, 7BI; Blanford report, January 5, 1915, 5BI.

37. Blanford report, February 14, 1914, 5BI; Mexican consul, San Antonio, to consul, El Paso, January 27, 1914, L-E 796 (10), exp. 2; Diebold to foreign secretary, January 25, 1914, L-E 796 (10), exp. 4; Fernández MacGregor to Diebold, February 12, 1914, L-E 796 (10), exp. 5, AREM.

38. Blanford report, January 20, 1914, 4BI.

39. *U.S. v. Jesús Chávez*, no. 1305, U.S. Commissioner, El Paso, Tex., FRC-FW.

40. *EPH*, March 23, 25, 1914.

41. Blanford reports, February 1, 19, 1914, 5BI; Diebold to foreign secretary, February 21, 1914, L-E 784 (2), exp. 49, and March 2, 1914, L-E 784 (2), exp. 64, AREM.

42. Chief to Blanford, February 9, 1914, 9BI.

43. Diebold to Blanford, February 11, 1914, 5BI; [Blanford] to Diebold, February 11, 1914, 5BI. The chief of the Bureau also replied to Diebold, pointing out that as long as the laws weren't violated those keeping the consul under surveillance couldn't be required to cease their activities and that as long as Diebold didn't violate the laws the Bureau would take no action against him (chief to Diebold, February 26, 1914, 5BI).

44. Barnes report, February 14, 1914, 5BI; *EPMT*, February 12, 13, 14, 16, 1914.

45. Blanford report, February 19, 1914, 5BI.

46. Blanford report, January 18, 1914, 4BI.

47. Blanford reports, February 1, 20, 1914, 5BI.

48. The brothers lived in El Paso at 1106 East Fourth Street and maintained a real estate office at 103 Mesa Avenue.

49. Blanford report, March 16, 1914, 5BI.

50. Blanford reports, March 3, 1914, 5BI.

51. Blanford reports, February 20, 21, 1914, 5BI.

52. Blanford report, February 23, 1914, 9BI; chief to Blanford, March 3, 1914, 9BI.

53. Blanford reports, March 23, 1914, 9BI, and April 10, 1914, 5BI.

54. Diebold to foreign secretary, May 1, 1914, L-E 787 (7), AREM; Quevedo to Diebold, April 14, 1914, L-E 787 (7), AREM.

55. Blanford report, February 22, 1914, 5BI.

56. Blanford report, February 20, 1914, 5BI.

57. Blanford reports, February 19, 21, 1914, 5BI.

58. Blanford report, February 21, 1914, 5BI.

59. Blanford report, February 28, 1914, 5BI.

60. Blanford report, February 23, 1914, 6BI.

61. Blanford reports, February 23, 1914, 6BI, and March 3, 1914, 9BI.

62. To evade being arrested at the Union Depot, some *huertistas* had taken the interurban to Ysleta or had gone farther down the line, for example to Sierra Blanca, to board the train for Eagle Pass (Blanford report, April 2, 1914, 5BI).

63. Blanford report, March 10, 1914, 5BI.

64. *U.S. v. M. E. Diebold, E. de la Sierra, R. Saldana, Alfredo Margáin*, no. 1306, U.S. Commissioner, El Paso, Tex., FRC-FW; *U.S. v. Miguel E. Diebold, Enrique de la Sierra, F. de J. Saldaña, M. S. Marmol*, no. 1708, U.S. District Court, El Paso, Tex., FRC-FW.

65. Blanford reports, March 10, 11, 1914, 5BI; Diebold to foreign secretary, March 10, 1914, L-E 784 (2), exp. 76, AREM.

66. Blanford report, March 11, 1914, 5BI.

67. Blanford reports, March 12, 14, 1914, 5BI. See also unsigned memorandum on this case, March 28, 1914, L-E 784 (2), exp 105, AREM.

68. Blanford reports, March 16, April 5, 1914, 5BI.

69. Blanford reports, March 21, 23, 1914, 5BI.

70. Blanford report, March 30, 1914, 5BI.

71. Blanford report, April 2, 1914, 5BI.

72. Blanford reports, April 3, 4, 1914, 5BI.

73. Blanford report, April 9, 1914, 5BI.

74. Blanford report, April 10, 1914, 5BI.

75. Blanford reports, April 13, 14, 1914, 5BI.

76. Blanford report, April 15, 1914, 5BI.

77. Blanford report, April 20, 1914, 5BI.

78. Blanford report, April 24, 1914, 5BI.

79. Memorandum from the solicitor, Department of State, to the Department of Justice, May 6, 1914, 6BI; Atwater, *American Regulation*, 69–72.

80. Blanford reports, April 24, 27, 1914, 5BI.

81. Blanford report, April 7, 1914, 5BI.

82. Blanford report, April 27, 1914, 5BI. By 1918, Blanford was special agent in charge in San Francisco.

83. On one occasion, the 321 officers received $5 each and the 3,057 enlisted men got $2 (Diebold to Blanquet, April 13, 1914, L-E 793 [1], AREM).

84. Diebold to foreign secretary, April 6, 1914, L-E 793 (1), AREM; *EPH*, April 27, 1914; *EPMT*, April 28, May 6, 1914; *EPH*, April 27, 1914.

85. Elías to foreign secretary, June 15, 1914, L-E 784, leg. 15, exps. 185–87, AREM.

86. Blanford report, June 23, 1914, 5BI; McCluer report, July 25, 1914, 7BI.

87. Blanford report, April 3, 1914, 5BI.

88. U.S. Senate, *Investigation of Mexican Affairs*, 2 vols., Senate doc. no. 285, 66th Cong., 2nd sess. (Washington, D.C.: Government Printing Office, 1920), 2626–30; Blanford reports, May 31, 1913, 3BI, and April 10, 1914, 5BI; Texas Ranger Service Records, Texas State Library, Austin, Texas; *EPT*, March 30, 1931.

89. Blanford report, April 21, 1914, 5BI.

90. Blanford report, June 23, 1914, 5BI.

91. Blanford report, June 27, 1914, 5BI.

92. Blanford report, October 6, 1914, 5BI.

93. Blanford report, October 16, 1914, 5BI.

94. Blanford report, October 17, 1914, 5BI.

95. Blanford report, October 23, 1914, 7BI.

96. *EPMT*, November 23, 24, 1914.

97. Blanford report, December 24, 1914, 5BI.

98. *EPMT*, March 21, 30, May 13, 1914.

99. Blanford report, June 27, 1914, 6BI.

100. Elías to foreign secretary, July 1, 1914, *DHRM*, 15:116–19.

101. Barnes report, July 23, 1914, 6BI, and August 3, 1914, 7BI; Blanford reports, July 15, 1914, 7BI, and July 23, 1914, 12BI; McCluer report, July 23, 1914, 13BI.

102. McCluer report, July 29, 1914, 7BI.

103. Blanford report, August 5, 1914, 7BI.

104. Barnes to Blanford, November 12, 1914, 8BI; Barnes memorandum, November 21, 1914, 5BI.

105. Blanford report, August 21, 1914, 8BI; Barnes reports, August 25, 26, 1914, 8BI.

106. Blanford reports, September 3, 4, 1914, 8BI.

107. Burkhart to Barnes, September 7, 1914, 8BI.

Chapter 11

1. Villa to Carranza, September 22, 1914, *DHRM*, 15:179; Villa's manifesto to the nation, September 23, 1914, *DHRM*, 15:185–86.

2. See, for example, Diebold to foreign secretary, July 1, 1914, *DHRM*, 15:110–16.

3. Blanford report, October 6, 1914, OMF, BI roll 5, Investigative Records, 1908–22, RFBI, RG 65, NARA (OMF hereafter cited as BI preceded by roll number).

4. *Worley's Directory of El Paso, Texas, 1915* (Dallas: John F. Worley, 1915), 390; *U.S. v Agustín Pantoja*, no. 1352, U.S. Commissioner, El Paso, Tex., FRC-FW; *U.S. v Bernardo Bernal*, no. 1353, U.S. Commissioner, El Paso, Tex., FRC-FW.

5. Blanford reports, October 22, 23, 1914, 5BI.
6. Blanford to McCluer, October 30, 1914, 7BI.
7. Blanford report, November 6, 1914, 5BI.
8. Blanford to Barnes, November 27, 1914, 5BI; *EPMT*, October 28, 1914.
9. Blanford reports, November 6, 25, 1914, 5BI.
10. Blanford report, October 29, 1914, 5BI.
11. Lessing to attorney general, October 28, 1914, 5BI; acting chief to Barnes, November 3, 1914, 5BI; Barnes to Bielaski, November 21, 1914, 5BI.
12. McCluer report, November 3, 1914, 7BI; Blanford report, November 12, 1914, 5BI; Breniman reports, November 15, 16, 1914, 5BI.
13. Breniman to Camp, March 6, 1917, 16BI.
14. McCluer report, November 4, 1914, 5BI; Blanford reports, November 5, 6, 1914, 5BI; *U.S. v. Victor L. Ochoa, Tandy Sanford, John Sanford, Fred Mendenhall, Rafael Díaz, R. H. G. McDonald, José Orozco, Francisco Rojas, Vicente Carreón*, no. 1359, U.S. Commissioner, El Paso, Tex., FRC-FW; *U.S. v. E. L. Holmdahl*, no. 1363, U.S. Commissioner, El Paso, Tex., FRC-FW; *U.S. v. Victor L. Ochoa*, no. 1810, U.S. District Court, El Paso, Tex., FRC-FW; *U.S. v. E. L. Holmdahl*, no. 1811, U.S. District Court, El Paso, Tex., FRC-FW; *U.S. v. R. H. G. McDonald*, nos. 294 and 300, U.S. Commissioner, Santa Fe, N.Mex., FRC-D.
15. Blanford reports, November 6, 8, 1914, 5BI.
16. Blanford reports, November 10, December 2, 8, 14, 17, 21, 1914, 5BI.
17. Blanford report, November 12, 1914, 7BI.
18. Blanford reports, November 12, 15, December 14, 1914, 5BI.
19. Blanford report, November 20, 1914, 5BI. The defendants' attorney was Juan Larrazolo.
20. Fred Mendenhall was released, as were the Sanfords. The U.S. attorney directed the filing of a complaint against Jorge Orozco, but when it was learned he had gone to Los Angeles the matter was dropped (Blanford reports, November 20, 24, 25, December 17, 1914; Guy report, January 17, 1915, 5BI).
21. See his *Venustiano Carranza's Nationalist Struggle, 1893–1920* (Lincoln: University of Nebraska Press, 1983).
22. *EPMT*, January 25, 1914, March 22, 1916. See Charles C. Cumberland, "The Sonora Chinese and the Mexican Revolution," *Hispanic American Historical Review* 40, no. 2 (1960): 191–211.
23. Friedrich Katz, *The Life and Times of Pancho Villa* (Stanford, Calif.: Stanford University Press, 1998), 597, 604, 626.
24. Mike Downs, *The Adventurers' Golden Jubilee, 1964: A History of the Adventurers' Club of New York* (New York: The Adventurers' Club, 1965), 1–5.
25. Other members were Frank Thayer, Major W. H. H. Llewellyn, J. G. Adams, T. J. Garside, Gerald Brandon, Serge McFall, George Clements, George F. Weeks, Homer Scott, James I. Redding, Edmund Behr, Lieutenant W. M. Mondisette, and Lieutenant C. I. Michaelis (*EPMT*, April 14, 16, 19, 21, 1915).
26. Assistant attorney general to secretary of war, February 18, 1915, file no. 90755-2403, RDJ, RG 60, NARA; Guy report, January 22, 1915, 5BI; Beckham report, February 17, 1915, 5BI. Ochoa was also tried for allegedly embezzling $800 given him by a *villista* colonel in

exchange for *villista* currency that he never received. Ochoa denied any criminal intent, alleging that the $800 was paid in settlement of a debt. The trial ended in a hung jury (*EPMT*, January 9, 20, 29, 30, 31, 1915).

27. A start is Richard A. Banyai, *Money and Finance in Mexico during the Constitutionalist Revolution, 1913–1917* (Taipei: Tai Wan Enterprises, 1976).

28. Carranza to Múzquiz, December 23, 1913, *DHRM*, 14:424.

29. See a letter from Major Reinaldo Salazar in El Paso to General Plutarco Elías Calles in Agua Prieta, Sonora, March 31, 1915, in Pinckney report, April 1, 1915, 8BI; Breniman to Guilfoyle, April 3, 1915, 8BI; Lansing to Llorente, February 26, 1915, ECLP; Ramos to Llorente, March 7, 1915, ECLP; Llorente to Ramos, March 12, 1915, ECLP.

30. Ramos to Llorente, March 4, 1915, ECLP.

31. Llorente to Bryan, March 8, 1915, DF, file no., 812.00/14532, microcopy 274, RDS, RG 59, NARA, and March 9, 1915, DF, file no. 812.00/14571; Lansing to Llorente, March 25, 1915, DF, file no. 812.00/14641, and June 4, 1915, DF, file no. 812.00/15091.

32. Guy reports, January 19, 20, 1915, 5BI.

33. Guy reports, January 19, 20, 26, 31, February 5, 6, 1915, 5BI, and February 13, 1915, 8BI.

34. Arredondo to Bryan, May 6, 1915, DF, file no. 812.00/14988.

35. The agent was allegedly José Fabián (Guy report, March 18, 1915, 6BI).

36. Guy reports, February 16, 17, 1915, 5BI; Llorente to Bryan, February 22, 1915, DF, file no. 812.00/14433.

37. Guy report, February 16, 1915, 5BI.

38. Guy report, February 21, 1915, 5BI.

39. *EPMT*, June 22, 26, 1915.

40. *U.S. v. Sabino Guaderrama*, no. 1376, U.S. Commissioner, El Paso, Tex., FRC-FW.

41. Guy reports, January 26, 28, 1915, 5BI; *EPMT*, January 24, 26, 1915.

42. Cobb to Davis, June 5, 1915, DF, file no. 812.00/15265, and Cobb to secretary of state, June 19, 1915, DF, file no. 812.00/15266.

43. Olin to Sommerfeld, February 19, 1915, 12BI. For details regarding the financing of this arms deal, see U.S. Senate, *Brewing and Liquor Interests and German and Bolshevik Propaganda*, Senate document no. 62, 66th Cong., 1st sess. (Washington, D.C.: Government Printing Office, 1919), 2167–74.

44. Chart, April 6–May 24, 1915, 12BI.

45. Cobb to Davis, April 16, 1915, DF, file no. 812.00/15118; Cobb to Bryan, April 27, 1915, DF, file no. 812.00/15132.

46. Guy reports, January 22, March 10, 12, 1915, 9BI; Breniman report, April 3, 1915, 5BI; Beckham report, May 14, 1915, 9BI.

47. Blanford report, December 24, 1914, 5BI; Guy report, December 30, 1914, 5BI.

48. Guy report, January 12, 1914, 5BI.

49. Breniman reports, March 21, 28, 30, 31, April 1, 8, 11, 1915, 5BI; Guy report, March 21, 1915, 5BI; weekly report, March 31, 1915, DF, file no. 812.00/14791.

50. *EPMT*, April 3, 5, 1916. The April 5 article includes a photo of McDonald.

51. *U.S. v. Victor L. Ochoa, E. L. Holmdahl*, no. 1781, U.S. District Court, El Paso, Tex., FRC-FW.

52. Breniman reports, April 6, 8, 11, 1915, 5BI. As Ochoa and Holmdahl were already under bond, the U.S. attorney had their bond increased from $1,500 to $2,500 each, which they furnished (Pinckney report, April 13, 1915, 5BI).

53. *EPH*, April 16, 1915. Those indicted were Victor Ochoa, José Orozco, Jorge Orozco, Emil Holmdahl, Cristóbal Limón, Fred Mendenhall, and Vicente Carreon.

54. Pinckney report, April 16, 1915, 5BI; Blanford report, April 18, 1915, 5BI.

55. Barnes to Pinckney, April 14, 1915, 5BI; Pinckney report, April 16, 1915, 5BI; Blanford report, April 18, 1915, 5BI.

56. Breniman report, April 6, 1915, 5BI.

57. Blanford report, April 18, 1915, 5BI; Pinckney to Bielaski, May 1, 1915, 5BI.

58. Pinckney report, April 27, 1915, 5BI; Blanford report April 28, 1915, 5BI; *EPMT*, April 29, 30, 1915.

59. *EPH*, April 30, 1915; Pinckney reports, April 27, 28, 1915, 5BI; Beckham report, May 10, 1915, 9BI.

60. Pinckney to Bielaski, May 1, 1915, 5BI.

61. *EPMT*, April 27, 1915.

62. Pinckney report, April 27, 1915, 5BI; Beckham report, May 10, 1915, 9BI; *EPMT*, May 30, 1915.

63. Pinckney reports, April 23, 25, 27, 1915, 5BI.

64. Pinckney report, April 27, 1915, 5BI; Blanford report, April 28, 1915, 5BI; *EPMT*, April 29, 30, 1915.

65. Guy report, April 1, 1915, 8BI; Breniman report, March 1, 1915, 8BI.

66. Pinckney reports, April 2, 5, 1915, 8BI.

67. A translation of Thompson's message is in Guy report, January 23, 1915, 6BI. See also Barnes to Guy, January 25, 1915, 6BI.

Chapter 12

1. Pinckney to Bielaski, May 1, 1915, OMF, BI roll 5, Investigative Records, 1908–22, RFBI, RG 65, NARA (OMF hereafter cited as BI preceded by roll number).

2. Cobb to Bryan, April 27, 1915, DF, file no. 812.00/15132, microcopy 274, RDS, RG 59, NARA; Garrison to secretary of state, May 26, 1915, DF, file no. 812.00/15091.

3. Beckham reports, April 26, 28, 1915, 9BI.

4. See, for example, Llorente to Scott, April 23, 1915, ECLP; Lansing to Llorente, May 6, 1915, ECLP.

5. He was John McGinnis, Elfego Baca's former son-in-law (Beckham report, May 16, 1915, 9BI).

6. Pinckney report, April 23, 1915, 9BI; Beckham report, April 28, 1915, 9BI; Llorente to Bryan, April 23, 1915, DF, file no. 812.00/14955.

7. Henry Landau, *The Enemy Within: The Inside Story of German Sabotage in America* (New York: Putnam, 1937), 48; Franz von Rintelen, *The Dark Invader: Wartime Reminiscences of a German Naval Intelligence Officer* (London: Peter Davies, 1933), 175–77, 182–84, 223–24, 265, 272–73.

8. Michael C. Meyer, "The Mexican-German Conspiracy of 1915," *The Americas* 23, no. 1 (1966): 83–84.

9. Medina Barrón to Moheno, February 4, 1915, 9BI.

10. Offley reports, March 11, 13, 1915, 7BI.

11. Cantrell report, July 15, 1915, 9BI; Horn to Barnes, July 24, 1915, 4BI.

12. Guy report, April 14, 1915, 7BI; Blanford report, February 1, 1916, 7BI; Cantrell report, July 10, 1915, 9BI; Molina report, July 19, 1915, 9BI.

13. Offley to Bielaski, April 15, 1915, 4BI. See also Childers report, April 29, 1915, 8BI, and Emanuel Victor Voska, *Spy and Counterspy* (New York: Doubleday, 1940), 192–96, 251.

14. Perasler[?] report, April 17, 1915, 7BI.

15. Offley to Bielaski, June 29, July 7, 1915, 8BI; Cantrell report, July 10, 1915, 9BI.

16. Childers report, May 12, 1915, 8BI.

17. Beckham report, May 14, 1915, 9BI.

18. Stone report, July 9, 1915, 9BI. See also chief to Barnes, August 26, 1915, 7BI, and Baker report, January 8, 1916, 8BI.

19. Scully report, February 8, 1916, 10BI.

20. Offley to Bielaski, May 13, 1915, 8BI; Childers report, May 15, 1915, 8BI.

21. Beckham report, May 19, 1915, 9BI.

22. The firm's name was Cal Hirsch and Sons, Iron and Metal Company, located at 315 South Broadway, St. Louis, Missouri. In 8BI, there forty-two telegrams exchanged in April between the home office and the El Paso branch and twenty-six telegrams in May between Hirsch and Hipólito Villa, who ran his brother's commercial agency in Juárez. For July there are twenty-five Hirsch telegrams; for August, thirty-nine. See also Breniman reports, January 20, 29, 1916, 8BI, and Barnes to Pinckney, April 26, 1916, 8BI.

23. For Krupp's career see Floyd S. Fierman, "Haymon Krupp, Economic Adventurer in the Southwest," *Password* 26, no. 2 (1981): 51–77.

24. Harris to Hirsch, April 8, 1915, 8BI; Cal Hirsch to Harris, May 21, 1915, 8BI; Brennan report, January 29, 1916, 8BI.

25. Beckham report, May 23, 1916, 9BI.

26. Arredondo to Carranza, October 2, 1915, *DHRM*, 16:246.

27. Blanford report, June 30, 1915, 6BI.

28. Stone to Barnes, January 3, 1916, 9BI.

29. Beckham reports, July 5, 1915, January 13, 1916, 8BI; Hazen report, July 6, 1915, 8BI; Guy report, July 7, 1915, 8BI; Offley to Horn, July 25, 1915, 8BI; Stone report, January 14, 1916, 8BI; Barnes to Stone, January 10, 1916, 8BI; Beckham report, December 29, 1915, 9BI. Cobb reported that fourteen machine guns were in Zozaya's warehouse as of June 11 (Cobb to

secretary of state, June 11, 1915, DF, file no. 812.00/15199). See also Cobb to secretary of state, June 14, 1915, DF, file no. 812.00/15217.

30. Beckham reports, May 15, 24, June 6, 13, July 5, 1915, 9BI; Wright report, July 19, 1915, 5BI.

31. Cantrell report, July 7, 1915, 9BI.

32. Beckham report, May 21, 1915, 9BI.

33. Beckham reports, June 1, 1915, 5BI, and June 1, 1915, 9BI.

34. Beckham report, May 21, 1915, 9BI; Llorente to Bryan, April 23, 1915, DF, file no. 812.00/14955. Llorente was head of the Agencia Confidencial Del Gobierno Provisional de Mexico (Llorente to Bustamante, June 16, 1915, 11BI).

35. See, for example, Cobb to secretary of state, May 12, 1915, DF, file no. 812.00/15008.

36. Beckham reports, May 19, June 6, 1915, 9BI.

37. Beckham report, May 24, 1915, 9BI; Beckham report, August 10, 1915, 8BI.

38. *EPMT*, November 1, 1916.

39. Beckham report, June 6, 1915, 9BI.

40. Guy reports, December 29, 1915, 9BI, and January 18, 1916, 8BI; *EPMT*, May 13, 1915; Baca to Fall, June 6, 1915, ABFFP.

41. Cobb to secretary of state, June 25, 1915, DF, file no. 812.00/15308.

42. *EPMT*, June 12, 27, 1915.

43. Offley to Bielaski, May 27, 1915, 8BI; Cantrell report, June 21, 1915, 8BI.

44. Chief to Offley, June 25, 1915, 8BI.

45. Bielaski to Barnes, June 26, 1915, 8BI.

46. Those listed were Ignacio Alcocer, General A. Bravo, Hilario Lozoya, Vicente Calero, José Alessio Robles, Santiago Mendoza, Leopoldo Zea, Carlos Gorostieta, Ricardo Aguilar, Pedro García, "and about 20 officials whose names couldn't be secured."

47. Barnes to Beckham, June 28, 1915, 8BI; *EPMT*, May 15, 1915.

48. They were General José Delgado, General Carlos Aguilar, and José María Lozano (Pendleton report, June 29, 1915, 8BI).

49. John F. Chalkley, *Zach Lamar Cobb: El Paso Collector of Customs and Intelligence During the Mexican Revolution, 1913–1918* (El Paso: Texas Western Press, 1998), 21–27.

50. For Cobb's role in these events, see Chalkley, *Zach Lamar Cobb*, 29–34.

51. Beckham report, June 29, 1915, 8BI.

52. It turned out that only one automobile awaited Huerta; the others belonged to newsmen covering Huerta's arrival and to R. P. Dorman, of the photographic firm of Aultman and Dorman, who was photographing it.

53. Michael C. Meyer, *Mexican Rebel: Pascual Orozco and the Mexican Revolution 1910–1915* (Lincoln: University of Nebraska Press, 1967), 128. As of 1918, Zozaya was president of Trueba-Zozaya-Seggerman, Inc., wholesale grocers—importers and exporters—in El Paso (*EPMT*, December 2, 1918).

54. *EPMT*, June 28, 29, 1915; Pinckney report, July 15, 1915, 9BI.

55. Pinckney report, July 6, 1915, 9BI; Beckham report, July 6, 1915, 9BI; Pinckney report, July 10, 1915, 8BI; *EPMT*, July 5, 1915.
56. Beckham report, July 15, 1915, 9BI; *EPMT*, July 13, 1915, January 29, 1917.
57. Bielaski to Barnes, June 28, 1915, 8BI.
58. *EPH*, June 30, 1915; *EPMT*, June 29, 30, 1915; Beckham report, July 1, 1915, 9BI.
59. *EPMT*, July 2, 3, 7, 1915.
60. *EPMT*, July 4, 1915.
61. *EPMT*, July 1, 3, 1915; Pinckney to Bielaski, July 1, 1915, 4BI.
62. *EPMT*, July 2, 1915.
63. Pinckney report, June 30, 1915, 8BI.
64. Pinckney report, June 29, 1915, 8BI.
65. *EPMT*, July 4, 1915.
66. Beckham to Bielaski, July 3, 1915, 9BI.
67. Beckham report, July 5, 1915, 9BI.
68. Pinckney reports, July 6, 8, 1915, 8BI; Barnes to Horn, July 15, 1915, 5BI; Pinckney report, July 16, 1915, 9BI. See also *EPMT*, September 20, 1915.
69. *U.S. v. Victoriano Huerta, Pascual Orozco, Enrique Gorostieta, Sr., Ricardo Gómez Robelo, José Elgisero [Elguero], Eduardo Cauz, José Alessio Robles, Alberto Quiroz, José Delgado, Rafael Pimienta, José B. Ratner, Ignacio L. Bravo, Mauro Huerta*, no. 316, U.S. Commissioner, San Antonio, Tex., FRC-FW. See also nos. 1446, 1449, 1468, and 1536, U.S. Commissioner, El Paso, Tex., FRC-FW.
70. Enrique Gorostieta, Eduardo Cauz, José Delgado, José B. Ratner, and Ignacio L. Bravo (*EPMT*, July 4, 1915).
71. *EPMT* July 4, 5, 6, 1915.
72. Pinckney report, July 8, 1915, 8BI.
73. Pinckney reports, July 9, 12, 1915, 8BI; Pinckney report, July 16, 1915, 9BI; Stone report, July 28, 1915, 8BI.
74. *EPMT*, July 7, 10, 12, 1915; Pinckney reports, July 9, 12, 1915, 8BI.
75. See also *EPMT*, July 10, 1915. On February 17, 1915, José Zozaya had telegraphed from El Paso to Pascual Orozco, 415 Elmira, San Antonio: "Tom Lea elected. We are delighted" (Barkey report, September 16, 1915, 8BI).
76. *EPMT*, February 26, 27, 28, March 3, 5, June 9, 10, 15, 16, 23, 25, December 22, 1915, February 5, 1916; Cobb to secretary of state, July 13, 1915, DF, file no. 812.00/15431; undated newspaper clipping, VOP.
77. Guy reports, November 6, 7, 9, 12, 13, 15, 1915, 8BI; Pinckney reports, November 10, 11, 17, 1915, 8BI; Stone report, December 1, 1915, 8BI; Stone report, December 27, 1915, 7BI; Stone report, December 27, 1915, 9BI. José Orozco, in the county jail at the time, gave the most detailed account.
78. They arrived on July 21 (Beckham report, July 22, 1915, 9BI). Orozco's family, incidentally, moved to 1218 Montana (Offley memo, July 17, 1915, 9BI).

79. Stone report, July 27, 1915, 8BI.

80. Pinckney report, July 12, 1915, 9BI.

81. Beckham report, July 19, 1915, 9BI.

82. Beckham report, July 21, 1915, 9BI.

83. Beckham report, July 24, 1915, 8BI.

84. Beckham report, July 29, 1915, 8BI.

85. Stone reports, August 14, 27, 1915, 8BI; Beckham reports, August 27, September 1, 1915, 8BI; *EPMT*, August 26, 27, 1915.

86. *EPMT*, August 28, 1915.

87. *EPMT*, September 17, 1915.

88. Beckham reports, July 21, 23, 1915, 5BI; Pinckney report, July 22, 1915, 5BI; Stone report, July 23, 1915, 5BI; *EPMT*, August 4, 1915.

89. *EPMT*, July 5, 1915.

90. Beckham report, September 4, 1915, 8BI; Barnes to Stone, January 6, 1916, 8BI; *U.S. v. Victoriano Huerta, Alberto Quiroz, Roque Gómez, Francisco Escandón, Albino Frías, Vicente Calero, Luis Fuentes, Aristarco Carrascosa, Rafael Pimienta, Enrique Gorostieta, Jr., Jesús Valverde, alias Jesús Velarde, José C. Zozaya, José B. Ratner, José C. Delgado, Jesús Guaderrama, Pascual Orozco, Crisóforo Caballero*, no. 2185, U.S. District Court, San Antonio, Tex., FRC-FW (the case was dismissed in January 1919 on the motion of the U.S. attorney); White report, January 13, 1919, 20BI.

91. *EPMT*, August 31, September 1, 2, 3, 4, 5, 1915; Cobb to secretary of state, August 30, 1915, DF, file no. 812.00/15971, August 31, 1915, DF, file no. 812.00/1982, September 2, 1915, DF, file no. 812.00/16008, and DF, file no. 812.00/16046.

92. Martin Blumenson, *The Patton Papers: 1885–1940* (Boston: Houghton Mifflin, 1972), 298; Bob Alexander, *Fearless Dave Allison: A Transitional Lawman on a Transitional Frontier* (Silver City, N.Mex.: High-Lonesome Books, 2003), 188–204.

93. Rogers to attorney general, September 9, 1915, file no. 90755 A-210, RDJ, RG 60, NARA; "The Last Days of Pascual Orozco," E. A. "Dogie" Wright Papers, Center for American History, University of Texas at Austin; Blumenson, *Patton Papers*, 298; Meyer, *Mexican Rebel*, 131–33; *EPMT*, August 31, September 1, 1915.

94. Beckham report, September 2, 1915, 8BI. See also John D. Voliva, "The Guns of Green River Canyon," *Arms Gazette*, October 1976, 12–15.

95. Beckham report, September 4, 1915, 8BI.

96. *EPMT*, October 8, 9, 1915.

97. Stone report, September 2, 1915, 8BI; *EPMT*, September 2, 1915; Cobb to secretary of state, September 3, 1915, DF, file no. 812.00/16015, and September 4, 1915, DF, file no. 812.00/16016.

98. Beckham report, September 4, 1915, 8BI.

99. Meyer, *Mexican Rebel*, 133–34; *EPMT*, September 3, 4, November 3, 5, 1915.

Chapter 13

1. Stone report, December 23, 1915, OMF, BI roll 9, Investigative Records, 1908–22, RFBI, RG 65, NARA (OMF hereafter cited as BI preceded by roll number).
2. *EPMT*, July 4, 1915.
3. Guy report, December 11, 1915, 6BI.
4. Stone report, January 14, 1916, 8BI.
5. *EPH*, November 9, 1915.
6. Blanford report, March 3, 1914, 9BI. Williams had previously been the chief special agent for the Santa Fe railroad in Albuquerque.
7. Breniman report, November 5, 1915, 8BI.
8. Stone reports, January 12, 1916, 8BI, and December 9, 1916, 15BI; Hopkins report, August 28, 1916, 13BI.
9. Guy report, December 15, 1915, 6BI.
10. In December 1915, though, Carusso sued Hipólito Villa for allegedly swindling him (*EPMT*, December 25, 1915; Cobb to secretary of state, December 23, 1915, DF, file no. 812.00/17004, microcopy 274, RDS, RG 59, NARA).
11. Pinckney report, November 30, 1915, 6BI; Guy report, December 9, 1915, 6BI; Stone reports, December 9, 20, 1915, 7BI; Brennan report, January 25, 1916, 12BI; Pinckney report, January 10, 1916, 8BI.
12. *EPH*, November 22, 1915; *EPMT*, November 22, 1915.
13. Carothers to secretary of state, July 19, 1915, DF, file no. 812.00/15490, and July 22, 1915, DF, file no. 812.00/15518.
14. The price was $53,000 per 1 million cartridges. In a separate transaction González bought 400 Marlin rifles and 1,000 carbines for $22,000 (Webster reports, September 18, 1915, 5BI, and September 21, 1915, 9BI; see also Cobb to secretary of state, July 22, 1915, DF, file no. 812.00/15519, and July 23, 1915, DF, file no. 812.00/15528).
15. Cobb to secretary of state, August 5, 1915, DF, file no. 812.00/15651.
16. Cobb to secretary of state, October 16, 1915, DF, file no. 812.00/16503.
17. Cobb to secretary of state, October 27, 1915, DF, file no. 812.00/16612, November 4, 1915, DF, file no. 812.00/16702, and November 5, 1915, DF, file no. 812.00/16710; Lansing to collector, November 5, 1915, DF, file no. 812.00/16701.
18. Breniman reports, September 25, October 14, 15, 1915, 5BI.
19. Breniman reports, October 16, 17, 1915, 8BI; *EPMT*, October 15, 16, 17, December 21, 1915.
20. Breniman report, October 21, 1915, 5BI; *EPMT*, October 19, 20, 21, 28, 1915. The assistant U.S. attorney thought it advantageous to request pardons for Orozco and Holmdahl because they had information of value in the Huerta case (Cobb to secretary of state, November 4, 1915, DF, file no. 812.00/16699, and November 18, 1 DF, file no. 915, 812.00/16849; Gregory to secretary of state, December 22, 1916, DF, file no. 812.00/20154).
21. Wilson to Lansing, August 7, 1915, and Lansing to Wilson, August 9, 1915, DF, file no. 812.00/15751½.

22. *EPMT*, December 27, 1915.

23. *EPMT*, October 24, 26, 29, 30, 31, November 23, 30, 1915; Peters to secretary of state, October 14, 1915, DF, file no. 812.00/16483.

24. *EPMT*, November 18, 21, 23, 24, December 16, 18, 1915, February 8, 9, 12, 1916; Cobb to Lansing, December 13, 1915, DF, file no. 812.00/16952.

25. Elton Atwater, *American Regulation of Arms Exports* (Washington, D.C.: Carnegie Endowment for International Peace, 1941), 72–75.

26. Wilson to secretary of the treasury, October 19, 1915, 5BI; Blanford to Isaacs, October 20, 1915, 5BI; Barnes to Breniman, October 24, 1915, 8BI; *EPMT*, October 21, 1915.

27. *EPH*, November 5, 1915.

28. Spencer report, April 13, 1916, 12BI; González to Villa, February 12, 1917, 7BI; Stone report, February 13, 1917, 7BI.

29. *EPMT*, December 8, 9, 10, 1918; Cobb to Shaw, December 13, 1918, 18BI; Harrison to Bielaski, December 14, 1918, 18BI; acting chief to Jones, January 4, 1919, 18BI; Keep report, January 16, 1919, 18BI; Wren report, January 22, 1919, 18BI; Jones report, January 23, 1919, 18BI; Kosterlitzky reports, January 31, February 5, 1919, 18BI; Turner report, March 29, 1919, 18BI; Keep to Allen, April 2, 1919, 18BI.

30. Carothers to secretary of state, October 17, 1916, DF, file no. 812.00/19596; Villa to de la Garza, March 11 and April 29, 1919, de la Garza Archive, Nettie Lee Benson Latin American Collection, University of Texas at Austin.

31. Webster report, February 21, 1916, 6BI.

32. *EPMT*, January 3, 1935.

33. Breniman to Barnes, October 17, 1915, 9BI; Navarro to de la Garza, October 15, 1915, de la Garza Archive; Michael M. Smith, "Andrés G. García: Venustiano Carranza's Eyes, Ears, and Voice on the Border," *Mexican Studies/Estudios Mexicanos* 23, no. 2 (2007): 364–65.

34. Guy report, December 22, 1915, 10BI; Blanford report, March 30, 1916, 6BI; *EPMT*, October 25, 30, November 27, 1918; *EPH*, April 12, 1926.

35. Federico Cervantes, *Felipe Angeles en la Revolución: Biografía (1869–1919)*, 3rd ed. (Mexico D.F.: n.p., 1964), 216, 227–28. Maytorena reportedly advanced General Angeles $15,000 to buy the farm (Guy Waddington McCreary, *From Glory to Oblivion: The Real Truth About the Mexican Revolution* [New York: Vantage Press, 1974], 208).

36. Cobb to secretary of state, November 15, 1915, DF, file no. 812.00/16790.

37. *EPMT*, November 10, 14, 1915; Cobb to Lansing, November 9, 1915, DF, file no. 812.00/16750, and December 21, 1915, DF, file no. 812.00/16982.

38. Stone report, December 21, 1915, 6BI.

39. *EPMT*, March 5, 1916.

40. Stone to Barnes, December 20, 1915, 7BI; Cobb to secretary of state, December 4, 1915, DF, file no. 812.00/16908, December 19, 1915, DF, file no. 812.00/16973, and December 20, DF, file no. 1915, 812.00/16976; Carothers to secretary of state, December 20, 1915, DF, file no. 812.00/16977, and December 22, 1915, DF, file no. 812.00/16989, and DF, file no. 812.00/16992; Alvaro Obregón, *Ocho mil kilómetros en campaña*, 3rd ed. (México, D.F.: Fondo de Cultura Económica, 1960), 473–77; weekly report, December 31, 1915, DF, file no. 812.00/17048; Smith, "Andrés G. García," 366. Those signing the amnesty agreement are listed.

41. García to de la Garza, December 21, 1915, and Carranza to de la Garza, December 22, 1915, de la Garza Archive.

42. *EPMT*, December 28, 29, 31, 1915, January 2, 1916.

Chapter 14

1. *EPMT*, January 8, 1916.

2. *EPMT*, January 10, 1916.

3. Stone report, October 5, 1916, OMF, BI roll 11, Investigative Records, 1908–22, RFBI, RG 65, NARA (OMF hereafter cited as BI preceded by roll number).

4. Guy report, January 6, 1916, 8BI; Stone reports, January 4, 7, 8, 10, 1916, 8BI; Pinckney report, January 10, 1916, 8BI; Guy report, February 24, 1916, 9BI; *EPMT*, October 7, 1915.

5. Indictments were returned in San Antonio on January 12, 1916, in *U.S. v. Victoriano Huerta, Alberto Quiroz, Roque Gómez, Francisco Escandón, Albino Frías, Vicente Calero, Luis Fuentes, Artistarco Carrascosa, Rafael Pimienta, Enrique Gorostieta, Jr., Jesús Valverde alias Jesús Velarde, José C. Zozaya, José B. Ratner, José C. Delgado, and Jesús Guaderrama* (no. 2185, U.S. District Court, San Antonio, Tex., FRC-FW), charging them with conspiring on February 1, 1915, to organize a military expedition against Mexico; Stone report, January 18, 1916, 8BI.

6. Stone reports, January 1, 1916, 9BI, and January 4, 1916, 8BI; Barnes report, January 4, 1916, 8BI.

7. Stone to Camp, January 6, 8, 1916, 8BI; Beckham report, January 14, 1916, 8BI; *EPMT*, January 8, 10, 14, 1916; Michael C. Meyer, *Huerta: A Political Portrait* (Lincoln: University of Nebraska Press, 1972), 228–29; George J. Rausch Jr., "The Exile and Death of Victoriano Huerta," *Hispanic American Historical Review* 42, no. 2 (1962): 150–51.

8. Eileen Welsome, *The General and the Jaguar: Pershing's Hunt for Pancho Villa* (New York and Boston: Little, Brown, 2006), 64–69; Hilliard reports, February 2, 8, 1916, 9BI.

9. *EPMT*, January 14, 1916; Pershing to commanding general, January 15, 1916, DF, file no. 812.00/17158, microcopy 274, RDS, RG 59, NARA; weekly report, January 20, 1916, DF, file no. 812.00/17152.

10. *EPMT*, January 14, 1916.

11. *EPMT*, January 24, 1916.

12. *EPMT*, February 12, 1916; Cobb to secretary of state, January 13, 1916, DF, file no. 812.00/17090.

13. *EPMT*, February 1, 2, 1916.

14. *EPMT*, January 23, 1916. This was the second tragedy the Guaderrama family suffered in less than a month. Sabino's brother Manuel, age thirty-seven, had died on December 30, 1915, when an automobile driven by their brother David overturned in Arizona (*EPMT*, December 31, 1915, January 2, 1916).

15. Guy reports, January 23, 1916, 9BI, and March 10, 1916, 11BI; Stone report, March 13, 1916, 7BI. The other two secret agents were Samuel R[uiz] Sandoval and Pedro N. Fuente (consul to Arriola, July 31, 1916, 27-22-6, AREM).

16. Guy report, January 22, 1916, 9BI.

17. "To the Nation," February 23, 1916, 10BI; *DHRM*, 17:62–66.

18. Carothers to secretary of state, March 3, 1916, 11BI.

19. Pendleton report, April 4, 1916, 6BI.

20. Cobb to secretary of state, March 6, 1916, 7BI, and DF, file no. 812.00/17355.

21. Cobb to secretary of state, March 7, 1916, 7BI.

22. Barnes to Bielaski, March 9, 1916, 7BI; Cobb to secretary of state, March 9, 1916, 6BI; Carothers to secretary of state, March 11, 1916, 6BI; Herbert Molloy Mason Jr., *The Great Pursuit* (New York: Random House, 1970), 3–21.

23. Charles H. Harris III and Louis R. Sadler, "Pancho Villa and the Columbus Raid: The Missing Documents," *New Mexico Historical Review* 50, no. 4 (1975): 335–46.

24. "Translation of Documents of Villa Govt.," April 1, 1916, 6BI.

25. Clifford Wayne Trow, "Senator Albert B. Fall and Mexican Affairs, 1912–1921" (PhD diss., University of Colorado, 1966), 135–37. The best account of the Punitive Expedition is Frank Tompkins, *Chasing Villa: The Last Campaign of the U.S. Cavalry*, 2nd ed. (Silver City, N.Mex.: High-Lonesome Books, 1996).

26. Clarence C. Clendenen, *Blood on the Border: The United States Army and the Mexican Irregulars* (London: Macmillan, 1969), 213–14; *EPMT*, March 12, 1916.

27. Charles H. Harris III and Louis R. Sadler interview with E. "Bud" Flanagan, assistant to Julius Krakauer, February 14, 1970.

28. *EPMT*, March 10, 11, 12, 1916.

29. *EPMT*, March 15, 18, 24, 1916.

30. Barnes report, March 19, 1916, 6BI.

31. Guy report, March 13, 1916, 6BI; Stone reports, March 18, 22, 1916, 7BI; *EPMT*, March 25, 26, 1916. The suspects included Colonel Samuel Rodríguez and Colonel Manuel C. Sánchez, Lieutenant Colonel Emilio Galván, and a number of ex-soldiers.

32. *EPMT*, April 6, 8, 11, 1916. Others held included Jose Rochín, Samuel Caraveo, and Prudencio Miranda.

33. *EPMT*, August 4, 1916. Hall was commissioned as a captain in the army in 1918.

34. Pendleton report, April 29, 1916, 12BI; Barnes to Stone, August 12, 1916, 12BI; *EPMT*, March 26, 1916. Other El Paso attorneys had declined to represent Medinaveitia (*EPMT*, March 23, 1916).

35. 1920 United States Federal Census; http//www. ancestry.com (public member tree); Friedrich Katz, *The Life and Times of Pancho Villa* (Stanford, Calif.: Stanford University Press, 1998), 656.

36. Stone reports, March 18, April 6, 7, 1916, 7BI; Wren report, June 15, 1916, 12BI; *EPMT*, October 28, 1916.

37. Berliner reports, May 26, 29, 30, 1916, 12BI; Melrose report, June 8, 1916, 7BI; Gatens report, November 22, 1917, 13BI.

38. Grinstead to district commander, October 27, 1916, file no. 8532-49, MID; Pinckney report, May 5[?], 1916, 5BI.

39. *EPMT*, May 31, 1916; *La Prensa*, May 7, 1916.

40. García to González, March 9, 1915, roll 12, PGA.

41. Michael M. Smith, "*Carrancista* Propaganda and the Print Media in the United States: An Overview of Institutions," *The Americas*, 52, no. 2 (1995): 163.

42. *EPMT*, July 18, 20, 25, 1916; *EPH*, July 14, 1916.

43. John Middagh, *Frontier Newspaper: The El Paso Times* (El Paso: Texas Western Press, 1958), 185–88.

44. *EPMT*, July 25, 1916; Heyman report, February 12, 1918, 20BI. See also Smith report, February 4, 1918, 20BI. One of *carrancista* Andrés García's operatives claimed to have discovered proof that during the time well-known journalist Timothy Turner worked for the *El Paso Morning Times*, he had received a monthly payoff of $150 from Pancho Villa (Smith, "*Carrancista* Propaganda," 166).

45. *EPMT*, May 31, 1916.

46. *EPMT*, June 14, 1916.

47. *EPMT*, March 13, 1916.

48. *EPMT*, March 25, 26, 1916.

49. Barnes to Bielaski, March 24, 1916, 6BI.

50. Barnes report, March 21, 1916, 9BI; Blanford reports, March 22, 23, 1916, 6BI; Stone report, March 23, 1916, 12BI; Barnes to Bielaski, March 24, 1916, 6BI.

51. Barnes to Bielaski, March 26, 1916, 6BI.

52. Barnes report, March 31, 1916, 9BI.

53. Breniman report, March 30, 1916, 6BI. See also Barnes report, March 31, 1916, 6BI.

54. Breniman report, April 4, 1916, 6BI; Barnes reports, April 4, 19, 1916, 6BI; Stone reports, April 6, 19, 1916, 7BI; Stone report, April 19, 1916, 12BI; Stone report, April 20, 1916, 11BI; Pinckney reports, April 20, 1916, 6BI, May 5[?], 1916, 5BI, and May 5, 1916, 12BI.

55. Barnes report, April 15, 1916, 12BI; Pinckney reports, April 17, 19, 1916, 6BI.

56. See, for example, Stone reports, April 22, 1916, 5BI, and April 22, 1916, 6BI.

57. Stone reports, April 10[?], 20, 1916, 7BI; Pinckney report, May 3, 1916, 6BI.

58. Pinckney reports, May 5, 6, 1916, 12BI.

59. Jones report, November 2, 1917, 17BI; Berliner report, May 21, 1916, 12BI; Cobb to secretary of state, February 13, 1917, 6BI.

60. Pinckney reports, June 1, 3, 1916, 12BI; Berliner reports, May 31, June 3, 9, 10, 1916, 12BI; Stone reports, June 2, 1916, 12BI, and June 15, 1916, 13BI. Martin was "well and unfavorably known since coming here as a bookmaker and racetrack tout during the 1912–1913 racing season at Juarez." In 1919, Martin received the gambling concession in Juárez (Jones reports, November 20, 1919, 18BI, and November 28, 1919, 20BI).

61. Wren report, June 19, 1916, 12BI; Mennet report, October 24, 1916, 12BI.

62. Stone reports, April 24, 25, 1916, 7BI.

63. Stone report, April 30[?], 1916, 7BI.

64. Pinckney report, May 10, 1916, 12BI.

65. Barnes report, May 10, 1916, 9BI.

66. Pinckney to Barnes, May 13, 1916, 9BI; Barnes to Pinckney, May 16, 1916, 9BI.
67. Stone reports, June 2, November 8, 1916, 14BI.
68. Cobb to secretary of state, October 27, 1916, DF, file no. 812.00/19666.
69. Stone reports, April 6, 13, 1916, 12BI, and April 6, 7, 1916, 7BI; Barnes report, April 12, 1916, 6BI.
70. Chief to Barnes, July 10, 1916, 7BI.
71. Blanford report, March 27, 1916, 6BI; Stone reports, March 29, 30, 1916, 7BI. The Villa party left for New Orleans on March 30 (Barnes to FCP, March 31, 1916, 9BI; Barnes report, April 6, 1916, 6BI).
72. The works dealing with Terrazas shed little light on his activities during the revolution. See, for example, José Fuentes Mares, . . . *Y México se refugió en el desierto: Luis Terrazas, historia y destino* (México D.F.: Editorial Jus, 1954), 239–57, 263–70.
73. Pinckney report, May 3, 1916, 12BI. Military Intelligence, incidentally, used Orson P. Brown, leader of the Mormons in Chihuahua, as an informant. Brown worked for General George Bell Jr. (Jones report, December 26, 1917, 17BI).
74. Stone report, April 23, 1916, 11BI.
75. Stone reports, May 25, June 8, 1916, 12BI; Mock report, November 15, 1916, 12BI.
76. Pinckney report, April 24, 1916, 11BI; Stone report, April 26, 1916, 12BI.
77. Barnes report, March 27, 1916, 12BI.
78. Stone report, April 23, 1916, 12BI.
79. *EPMT*, May 30, 1916.
80. Stone reports, March 23, April 20, 1916, 5BI; Barnes reports, April 15, 19, 1916, 5BI; *EPMT*, April 11, 13, May 17, 18, 20, 21, 27, 1916.
81. Beckham report, May 29, 1915, 9BI.
82. *EPMT*, June 26, 27, 1916; *EPH*, June 27, 1916.
83. Stone report, June 30, 1916, 7BI.
84. Stone report, May 18, 1916, 12BI; Pinckney reports, May 23, 24, 1916, 12BI; *EPMT*, May 18, 19, 1916.
85. Berliner reports, May 25, 26, 31, 1916, 12BI; *EPMT*, April 13, May 24, September 21, 27, 1916, February 28, 1917.
86. Martin Blumenson, ed., *The Patton Papers: 1885–1940* (Boston: Houghton Mifflin, 1972), 330–36.
87. *EPMT*, July 13, 1916.
88. Elton Atwater, *American Regulation of Arms Exports* (Washington, D.C.: Carnegie Endowment for International Peace, 1941), 72–80.
89. Arthur S. Link, ed. *The Papers of Woodrow Wilson*, 69 vols. (Princeton, N.J.: Princeton University Press, 1966–94), 37:22–24, 38; Carothers to secretary of state, May 12, 1916, DF, file no. 812.00/18135.
90. *EPH*, April 29, 1916; *EPMT*, May 4, 9, 1916; Charles H. Harris III and Louis R. Sadler, *The Texas Rangers and the Mexican Revolution* (Albuquerque: University of New Mexico Press, 2004), 210–303.

91. *EPMT*, May 10, 13, 1916.

92. Barnes to Pinckney, May 13, 1916, 13BI. See also Barnes circular letter, June 9, 1916, 13BI, and Stone report, June 12[?], 1916, 14BI.

93. Barnes to special agents, local officers, special employees, informants, June 30, 1916, 12BI.

94. Wren report, November 4, 1916, 15BI.

95. Stone report, June 23, 1916, 13BI; Stone report, June 2, 1916, 14BI; Barnes to Pinckney, May 6, 1916, 14BI.

96. See, for example, Stone reports, June 22, 30, July 3, 26, 1916, 14BI.

97. "Special Report for Joe Solanos," in Stone report, June 27, 1916, 13BI; Stone to Barnes, July 4, 1916, 13BI.

98. For photographic copies of the correspondence see Stone to Barnes, June 17, 1916, 13BI, and Minck report, June 18, 1916, 13BI.

99. Stone to Barnes, June 27, 1916, 14BI; Minck report, June 13, 1916, 13BI; Stone to Barnes, June 17, 1916, 13BI; Barnes report, June 27, 1916, 13BI; Fletcher report, June 27, 1916, 13BI; Stone reports, June 30, July 1, 3, 1916, 13BI; Stone report, August 19, 1916, 11BI.

100. Stone report, August 9, 1916, 14BI. For a detailed account of these operations see Charles H. Harris III and Louis R. Sadler, *The Border and the Revolution: Clandestine Activities of the Mexican Revolution, 1910–1920*, 2nd ed. (Silver City, N.Mex.: High-Lonesome Books, 1990), 6–23.

101. Stone reports, July 1, 6, 14, August 14, 25, 1916, September 8, 11, 13, 14, 1916, 14BI; Stone report, September 18, 1916, 13BI.

102. Stone report, July 3, 1916, 14BI.

103. *EPMT*, June 6, 7, 8, 1916.

Chapter 15

1. The official account of the army's investigation of the Carrizal clash is in Arthur S. Link, ed., *The Papers of Woodrow Wilson*, 69 vols. (Princeton, N.J.: Princeton University Press, 1966–94), 38:378–86.

2. Carothers to secretary of state, June 25, 1916, DF, file no. 812.00/18564, microcopy 274, RDS, RG 59, NARA; Cobb to secretary of state, June 25, 1916, DF, file no. 812.00/18562.

3. *EPMT*, June 19, 1916.

4. *EPMT*, June 27, 30, 1916, OMF, BI, roll 12, Investigative Records, 1908–22, RFBI, RG 65, NARA (OMF hereafter cited as BI preceded by roll number); Barnes to Bielaski, June 8, 13, 1916, 12BI.

5. Barnes to Stone, June 22, 1916, 11BI.

6. Stone report, June 22, 1916, 14BI; Berliner reports, June 23, 25, 27, 1916, 14BI; Barnes report, June 28, 1916, 14BI; *EPMT*, June 24, 1916; Michael M. Smith, "Andrés G. García: Venustiano Carranza's Eyes, Ears, and Voice on the Border," *Mexican Studies/Estudios Mexicanos* 23, no. 2 (2007): 368, 371, 373–74.

7. *EPMT*, July 19, 20, 21, 22, 23, 31, August 9, 11, 21, 22, 23, 25, 27, 28, 31, September 9, 11, 1916.

8. Carothers to secretary of state, October 17, 1916, DF, file no. 812.00/19596. In June 1918, Sommerfeld was arrested in New York City as an enemy alien and was interned in Fort Oglethorpe, Georgia (*EPMT*, June 21, 1918).

9. Francisco R. Almada, *Vida, proceso y muerte de Abraham González* (México, D.F.: Talleres Gráficos de la Nación, 1967), 31.

10. Pinckney report, July 15, 1916, 7BI; chief to Offley, July 19, 1916, 7BI; Berliner report, July 15, 1916, 9BI.

11. García to Robles, September 6, 1916, *DHRM*, 17:127–28; Soriano Bravo to Aguilar, October 10, 1916, *DHRM*, 17:141–42. See also the protest by Emilio G. Sarabia et al., November 2, 1916, *DHRM*, 17:170–71.

12. His enemies alleged that he had been born in Fabens and was an American citizen.

13. Arriola to Arredondo, July 24, 1916, and Arriola's undated "Observaciones prácticas para el uso de los Agentes del 'Mexican Bureau of Investigation,'" AEMEUA, leg. 499 (12), AREM.

14. Michael M. Smith, "The Mexican Secret Service in the United States, 1910–1920," *The Americas* 59, no. 1 (2002): 69–72; Lee report, June 13, 1916, 12BI; Spencer report, June 18, 1916, 12BI; Barnes to Bielaski, June 13, 1916, 7BI; Beakley report, June 21, 1916, 13BI; Barnes report, June 24, 1916, 13BI; Arriola, circular no. 1, July 21, 1916, AEMEUA, leg. 499 (12), AREM.

15. Lawrence report, June 12, 1916, 13BI; Pendleton report, June 19, 1916, 13BI; Devlin report, June 17, 1916, 13BI; Stoy report, June 20, 1916, 10BI; Webster report, June 23, 1916, 12BI; Barnes report, June 24, 1916, 12BI; Pendleton report, June 24, 1916, 12BI; Blanford report, July 14, 1916, 12BI.

16. Barnes report, June 24, 1916, 13BI; Minck report, June 21, 1916, 13BI; Wren report, June 29, 1916, 7BI.

17. Minck report, June 25, 1916, 13BI; Stone reports, June 25[?], 30, July 1, 1916, 13BI; Stone to Barnes, July 23, 1916, 13BI; Minck report, August 8, 1916, 15BI.

18. Neunhoffer report, June 25, 1916, 13BI; Breniman report, June 25, 1916, 13BI.

19. Smith, "Mexican Secret Service," 75.

20. Arriola to Aguilar, October 29, 1916, AEMEUA, leg. 499 (12), AREM.

21. Smith, "Mexican Secret Service," 72–73; Minck reports, June 28, July 28, 1916, 13BI; Barnes report, June 28, 1916, 13BI; Stone report, July 1, 1916, 13BI.

22. Breniman report, September 30, 1916, 13BI; Stone report, October 5, 1916, 13BI.

23. Weekly report, June 21, 1916, 12BI; Barnes to Bielaski, including the code, June 13, 1916, 7BI.

24. Smith, "Mexican Secret Service," 72.

25. Foreign secretary to Beltrán, June 5, 1916, 13BI; Breniman, October 13, 14, 1916, 13BI.

26. Lawrence report, June 12, 1916, 13BI.

27. Arredondo to Lansing, December 27, 1916, DF, file no. 812.00/20190; Arriola to Aguilar, October 29, 1916, AEMEUA, leg. 499 (12), AREM.

28. Agent X reports, February 5, 1917, L-E 721 (1), and May 21, 1917, L-E 723 (1), AREM.

29. Minck reports, June 28, 30, July 5, 1916 8BI; Breniman report, June 23[?], 1916, 8BI; Breniman report, June 30, 1916, 14BI; Jones report, July 2, 1916, 14BI; Stone report, July 3, 1916, 14BI; Stone to Barnes, July 4, 1916, 14BI.

30. Blanford report, July 3, 1916, 14BI; Webster report, July 10, 1916, 7BI. The forty-two translated telegrams, from 1914, are in Webster report, July 14, 1916, 7BI; see also *EPMT*, February 19, 1917.

31. García to Carranza, August 15, 1916, 18-2-88 (1), AREM.

32. Minck reports, July 28, 1916, 15BI, and September 17, 1916, 13BI.

33. Stone report, July 3, 1916, 5BI.

34. Stone reports, June 12, 13, 1916, 12BI, June 13, 1916, 8BI, and June 13 1916, 7BI.

35. Jones reports, July 2, 23, 1916, 13BI.

36. The correspondence, spanning 1914–16, is included in Barnes to Bielaski, September 9, 1916, 11BI.

37. Mock report, September 5, 1916, 7BI; Hugh Lennox Scott, *Some Memories of a Soldier* (New York: Century, 1928), 517.

38. Jones reports, September 6, 8, 1916, 15BI; Minck reports, September 6, 10, 1916, 15BI; Stone reports, September 8, 11, 1916, 15BI; Mock report, September 19, 1916, 15BI.

39. Minck report, August 10, 1916, 14BI.

40. Weiskopf report, August 6, 1916, 15BI; Minck report, August 6, 1916, 15BI; Stone reports, August 11, 15, 19, 21, 1916, 15BI; *EPMT*, August 6, 7, 14, 18, 22, 1916.

41. Minck report, July 28, 1916, 8BI; Stone reports, August 23, 24, 25, 31, 1916, 15BI; Mock report, September 19, 1916, 15BI; *EPMT*, August 12, 24, 1916.

42. Stone report, August 31, 1916, 15BI; Minck report, September 6, 1916, 15BI; *EPMT*, August 26, 1916.

43. Agent X report, May 15, 1917, L-E 723 (1), AREM.

44. González to Villa, February 12, 1917, 7BI.

45. Jones report, August 12, 1918, 18BI.

46. Barnes report, August 30, 1916, 7BI.

47. Friedrich Katz, *The Life and Times of Pancho Villa* (Stanford, Calif.: Stanford University Press, 1998), 677; Minck report, September 13, 1916, 15BI; Jones report, September 7, 1916, 13BI; Minck report, September 8, 1916, 13BI; Breniman report, September 24, 1916, 13BI; Wren report, October 7, 1916, 13BI; Pendleton reports, October 2, 3, 4,5, 6, 1916, 13BI; *EPMT*, September 2, 3, 6, 7, 9, 14, 21, 27, 1916.

48. *U.S. v. Manuel Ochoa, José de Luna*, no. 1628, U.S. Commissioner, and *U.S. v. George M. Holmes, José de Luna, Manuel Ochoa, José Castillo, Pablo Carbajal*, no. 1979, U.S. District Court, El Paso, Tex., FRC-FW; *U.S. v. George M. Holmes, José de Luna, Manuel Ochoa, José Castillo, Pablo Carbajal*, no. 2053, U.S. District Court, El Paso, Tex., FRC-FW.

49. See the almost daily reports of Agent X and the less frequent ones of Agent H, Agent Dormilonas, and Agent Esparza, in L-E 721 and L-E 724, AREM. They identified Manuel Ochoa as the head of the *legalistas* in El Paso, along with Rodolfo Farías, Enrique Bordes Mangel, Juan José Rocha, José Kasparowitz, and Juan Valencia (Folsom to García, September 20, 1916, L-E 725, leg. 1, exps. 64–65, AREM; Agent X reports, November 13, December 18, 1916, L-E 724 [1], AREM).

50. Jones report, September 11, 1916, 12BI; Stone report, October 21, 1916, 15BI; *EPMT*, October 9, 14, 1916; acting attorney general to secretary of state, October 30, 1916, DF, file no. 812.00/19730.

51. Folsom to García, September 20, 1916, L-E 725, leg. 1, exps. 64–65; Arredondo to García, September 14, 1916, L-E 725, leg. 1, exp. 63; Aguilar to García, September 21, 1916, L-E 725, leg. 1, exp. 79; Soriano Bravo to Aguilar, October 9, 1916, L-E 725, leg. 1, exp. 103; Agent X reports, November 13, December 18, 1916, L-E 724 (1), AREM.

52. Stone reports, September 13, 16, 18, 1916, 14BI.

53. Informant "Mes" [aka Solanos] report, December 6, 1916, 14BI; Stone report, December 20, 1916, 15BI.

54. Stone reports, September 19, 1916, 13BI, and November 4, 1916, 12BI; *EPMT*, September 17, 18, 19, 20, 21, 22, 23, 24, 25, 28, October 23, 1916.

55. Stone report, November 2, 1916, 12BI.

56. Stone reports, September 20, 1916, 14BI, and October 4, 1916, 13BI; Jones report, September 22, 1916, 13BI.

57. *EPMT*, September 23, 28, 1916.

58. Chief to Pendleton, March 8, 1917, 13BI.

59. Stone report, September 21, 1916, 13BI; Wren report, September 23, 1916, 13BI.

60. Falvey to Bielaski, September 18, 1916, 13BI; Stone report, September 21[?], 1916, 13BI; Breniman report, September 24[?], 1916, 13BI; Pendleton reports, October 2, 3, 4, 5, 1916, 13BI; Wren report, October 7, 13BI.

61. Link, ed., *Papers of Woodrow Wilson*, 38:547.

62. Stone report, October 12, 1916, 14BI.

63. Stone report, November 8, 1916, 14BI.

64. Stone reports, November 25, December 17, 21, 28, 1916, 14BI.

65. Mock report, November 10, 1916, 15BI.

66. *EPMT*, May 24, 1916. For Avila's career see Francisco R. Almada, *Diccionario de historia, geografía y biografía chihuahuense,* 2nd ed. (Chihuahua: Universidad de Chihuahua, 1968), 53.

67. Soriano Bravo to Aguilar, February 9, 1917, L-E 799, leg. 7, exps. 96–98, AREM. See also Agent X report, November 11, 1916, L-E 724 (1), AREM, and García to Aguilar, March 2, 1917, 3-16-12, exp. 14, AREM.

68. Agent X report, November 10, 1916, L-E 724 (1), AREM; *NDH*, November 14, 1916.

69. *EPMT*, November 12, 13, 14, 15, 16, 1916; Stone report, January 29, 1917, 15BI.

70. *EPMT*, November 24, December 6, 1916.

71. Stone report, November 11, 1916, 14BI.

72. Stone report, November 14, 1916, 14BI.

73. Pendleton reports, November 17, 1916, 14BI, and November 18, 1916, 13BI; Stone reports, November 20, 21, 27, 1916, 14BI; Stone report, December 4, 1916, 15BI.

74. Beckham report, December 19, 1916, 13BI.

75. Intelligence officer to commanding general, December 19, 1916, 13BI.

76. Weekly report, December 22, 1916, DF, file no. 812.00/20192.

77. Stone reports, December 11, 23, 1916, 14BI; Informant "Mes" [aka Solanos] report, December 22, 1916, 14BI.

78. Informant "Mes" [aka Solanos] reports, December 28, 1916, 14BI, December 29, 1916, 12BI, and January 8, 1917, 13BI; *EPMT*, December 26, 1916.

79. Stone reports, October 10, 13, 1916, 12BI; Mock report, October 10[?], 1916, 12BI.

80. Chief to Barnes, October 23, 1916, 13BI. See also Bielaski to Breniman, October 15, 1916, 7BI, and Breniman report, October 17, 1916, 13BI.

81. Barnes to Bielaski, November 27, 1916, 10BI.

82. Breniman to Bielaski, November 16 1916, 13BI; Seman report, November 22, 1916, 13BI; Barnes reports, November 23, December 2, 1916, 13BI.

83. Chief to Offley, October 10, 1916, 7BI; Breniman report, October 13, 1916, 7BI; Offley report, October 14, 1916, 12BI; Underhill reports, October 14, 20, 1916, 12BI.

84. Rathbun report, October 18, 1916, 12BI; Allen report, October 31, 1916, 10BI.

85. Ross report, November 11, 1916, 12BI.

86. Guy report, November 14, 1916, 7BI.

87. Weiskopf report, November 12, 1916, 7BI.

88. Beckham report, December 21, 1916, 13BI; Stone reports, December 10, 17, 23, 1916, 12BI; Barnes report, December 16, 1916, 12BI; Wren report, December 20, 1916, 12BI; Stone report, December 23, 1916, 7BI; Pendleton report, December 27, 1916, 4BI; Smith, "Mexican Secret Service," 74–75, 77.

89. Stone to Barnes, November 25, 1916, 13BI; Stone report, December 23, 1916, 12BI.

90. Stone reports, November 7, 9, December 30, 1916, 12BI; Carothers to secretary of state, November 7, 1916, DF, file no. 812.00/19846; Cobb to Polk, November 13, 1916, DF, file no. 812.00/19914; Jones report, January 6, 1917, 16BI; Díaz report, March 8, 1917, 15BI. There is a photograph of Thayer in Stone to Barnes, June 21, 1917, 12BI.

91. González to Villa, February 12, 1917, 7BI.

92. Stone reports, December 23, 30, 1916, 12BI; Wren report, December 28, 1916, 12BI. Thayer's forged letter from Villa to Lázaro de la Garza is quoted in Stone report, March 19, 1917, 7BI.

93. Informant J report, January 29, 1917, 12BI.

94. Stone report, December 26, 1916, 7BI.

95. Stone reports, December 30, 1916, February 15, 1917, 7BI.

96. Charles H. Harris III and Louis R. Sadler, *Bastion on the Border: Fort Bliss, 1854–1943*, Historic and Natural Resources Report No. 6 (Fort Bliss, Tex.: Cultural Resources Management Branch, Directorate of Environment, United States Army Air Defense Artillery Center, 1993), 71–94; *EPMT*, August 29, 1916.

97. Minck report, July 26, 1916, 13BI.

98. Harris and Sadler, *Bastion on the Border*, 74–81, 83.

99. *EPMT*, December 25, 28, 29, 1916.

Chapter 16

1. Lea to attorney general, April 21, 1917, Hopkins to attorney general, January 29, 1917, Pershing to attorney general, March 14, 1917, and Bell to War Department, January 28, 1917, in "Application for Executive Clemency in behalf of Emil L. Holmdahl," file no. 31-305, Records of the Office of the Pardon Attorney, RG 204, NARA.
2. Hudspeth to Underwood, January 21, 1917, "Application."
3. Hudspeth to Sheppard, January 21, 1917, "Application."
4. Sheppard to Finch, January 31, 1917, with petition enclosed, Hudspeth to Underwood, January 21, 1917, and Underwood to Gregory, February 1, 1917, "Application."
5. Douglas V. Meed, *Soldier of Fortune: Adventuring in Latin America and Mexico with Emil Lewis Holmdahl* (Houston: Halcyon Press, 2003), 155–61.
6. *EPMT*, February 15, 1917, OMF, BI roll 16, Investigative Records, 1908–22, RFBI, RG 65, NARA (OMF hereafter cited as BI preceded by roll number); Jones report, January 27, 1917 16BI; Barnes reports, February 2, 19, 1917, 16BI; Barnes to Stone, February 8, 1917, 16BI; Holmdahl to attorney general, February 2, 1917, 16BI.
7. Camp to Finch, February 5, 1917, and Breniman to Camp, March 6, 1917, "Application."
8. Barnes to Bielaski, March 8, 1917, 16BI; Barnes report, March 26, 1917, 16BI.
9. Barnes to Blanford, February 8, 1917, 16BI; Barnes report, February 16, 1917, 16BI; Stone to Barnes, February 16[?], 19, 1917, 16BI; Smith to Whom It May Concern, February 28, 1917, 16BI; Breniman to Camp, March 6, 1917, 16BI; Barnes to Bielaski, March 12[?], 1917, 16BI; Utley report, March 14, 1917, 16BI; Bielaski to Barnes, March 20, 1917 16BI; Barnes to Stone, March 22, 1917, 16BI; Stone report, March 26, 1917 16BI; "Memorandum for the Pardon Attorney," March 22, 1917, 16BI; "Application."
10. Robertson to McLemore, May 31, June 6, 1917, "Application."
11. Gregory to Robertson, July 12, 1917, and Robertson to Gregory, July 12, 1917, "Application."
12. Meed, *Soldier of Fortune*, 160–66.
13. Finch, "Memorandum for the Attorney General," July 13, 1917, "Application."
14. *EPMT*, October 16, 1919; *Annual Report of the Attorney General of the United States for the Year 1917* (Washington, D.C.: Government Printing Office, 1917), 515, 519.
15. American Protective League report, November 7, 1917, 16BI; undated column by Virginia Turner, VOP; [Ochoa] to Naval Consulting Board, August 15, September 10, 1917, VOP; Anderson to Ochoa, December 3, 1917, VOP; Committee of Examiners to Ochoa, August 29, 1917, VOP; *El Paso City Directory* (El Paso: Hudspeth Directory Co., 1920), 711; *EPT*, September 20, 1921; *U.S. v. Victor Ochoa*, no. 3972, U.S. District Court, El Paso, Tex., FRC-FW.
16. Undated clippings, VOP; Melcord to Ochoa, November 12, 1941, VOP; Ochoa to Ochoa, undated, and March 18, 1942, VOP; David Romo, *Ringside Seat to a Revolution: An Underground Cultural History of El Paso and Juárez, 1893–1923* (El Paso, Tex.: Cinco Puntos Press, 2005), 51, 251.
17. Stone report, December 4, 1916, 14BI.
18. Funston to adjutant general, January 4, 191, 7BI.
19. Barnes to Stone, January 18, 1917, 7BI.

20. Funston to adjutant general, January 4, 1917, 14BI; Barnes to Stone, January 8, 1917, 14BI; Stone to Barnes, February 7, 1917, 5BI. The firm of Krakauer admitted smuggling a whole boxcar load of ammunition in 1915.

21. Jones report, September 6, 1917, 22BI; Webb report, July 7, 1917, 22BI.

22. See, for example, chief to Barnes, January 10, 19, February 27, 1917, 12BI; Pendleton reports, January 20, 26, 1917, 12BI; Jones reports, January 22, February 3, 8, 11, 12, 23, 25, 26, 27, 28, 1917, 12BI; Barnes reports, February 17, 28, March 6, 1917, 12BI; chief to Stone, February 20, 1917, 12BI, assistant attorney general to Western Cartridge Company, February 2, 1917, 12BI; Bielaski to Stone, February 24, 1917, 12BI; Stone reports, February 24, 28, 1917, 12BI; Gatens report, March 5,1917, 12BI; chief to Cartwell, March 16, 1917, 12BI; Spencer report, March 21, 1917, 12BI; Mohr to Pan American Importation and Exportation Company, February 5, 1917, 5BI; Stone report, February 6, 1917, 5BI; National Arms Company to Mohr, February 7, 1917, 5BI; Informant "Mes" [aka Solanos] report, February 16, 1917, 5BI.

23. Jones reports, January 30, February 28, March 9, 1917, 12BI; chief to Brennan, March 16, 1917, 12BI; Gatens report, March 19, 1917, 12BI.

24. Western Cartridge Company to Department of Justice, March 27, 1917, 12BI; Stone report, April 15, 1917, 12BI; Jones report, November 2, 1917, 12BI.

25. Chief to Barnes, January 4, 1917, 14BI.

26. Chief to Barnes, February 19, 1917, 14BI.

27. Jones report, April 30, 1917, 16BI.

28. Jones report, January 6, 1917, 7BI.

29. Michael M. Smith, "The Mexican Secret Service in the United States, 1910–1920," *The Americas* 59, no. 1 (2002): 78; Arriola to Aguilar, March 23, 1917, 1-6-12, AREM.

30. Bielaski to Offley, January 27, 1917, 12BI; Offley report, January 28, 1917, 12BI; Adams reports, January 30, 31, February 1, 1917, 12BI, and February 3, 5, 6, 7, 8, 12, 14,19, 20, 27, 1917, 16BI; Cobb to Polk, January 9, 1917, DF, file no. 812.00/20406, microcopy 274, RDS, RG 59, NARA, and January 11, 1917, DF, file no. 812.00/20384. Carusso's brother-in-law and partner Haymon Krupp was subsequently reported to be furnishing funds and merchandise to the followers of General Félix Díaz (Breniman report, November 26, 1917, 9BI).

31. Stone to Barnes, January 10, 1917, 12BI; Needham report, January 27, 1917, 12BI; Breniman report, January 29, 1917, 10BI; Stone to Barnes, January 11, 1917, 12BI; Informant "Mes" [aka Solanos] report, January 13, 1917, 12BI.

32. García to Bonillas, April 28, 1917, 7BI.

33. Brennan to Barnes, January 16[?], 1917, 13BI.

34. Stone reports, January 19, 23, 1917, 12BI; Jones reports, April 21, 22, 1917, 12BI.

35. Jones report, January 30, 1917, 12BI. See also his February 4, 1917, report, 12BI.

36. Jones report, February 11, 1917, 12BI.

37. Jones report, January 11, 1917, 14BI; Barnes report, January 23, 1917, 15BI; Stone report, January 23, 1917, 15BI.

38. Cobb to Polk, March 27, 1917, 7BI.

39. Cobb to secretary of state, April 16, 18, 19, 1917, 12BI; Harrison to Bielaski, April 19, 1917, 12BI; Gatens report, April 20, 1917, 12BI; *EPH*, April 18, 1917.

40. Stone report, April 24, 1917, 12BI.

41. See Barbara W. Tuchman, *The Zimmermann Telegram* (New York: Viking Press, 1958).

Chapter 17

1. Gatens report, April 5, 1917, OMF, roll 5, Investigative Records, 1908–22, RFBI, RG 65, NARA (OMF hereafter cited as BI preceded by roll number).

2. Offley report, April 7, 1917, 17BI.

3. *EPMT*, May 19, July 13, 1918, February 22, May 26, 1919, 20BI; Jones report, April 20, 1918, 20BI.

4. *EPMT*, September 10, 11, 15, 1918, July 18, 1919.

5. *U.S. v. Henry Beach and Clarence A. Toenniges*, no. 2060, U.S. District Court, El Paso, Tex., FRC-FW; *U.S. v. Henry Beach, Amelia Toenniges, Clarence A. Toenniges, and Josephine Toenniges*, no. 2072, U.S. District Court, El Paso, Tex., FRC-FW.

6. *U.S. v. August Winter*, no. 2197, U.S. District Court, El Paso, Tex., FRC-FW.

7. Harris reports, April 2, 9, 10, 1917, 16BI.

8. Weekly report, October 13, 1917, 10014-13, MID.

9. *EPMT*, December 22, 24, 1917.

10. Weekly report, January 12, 1918, 10014-31, MID. There is a photograph that was taken in the morgue of Feige's corpse in Old German Files, 1909–21, file no. 29822, microfilm publication no. M1085, Investigative Records, 1908–22, RFBI, RG 65, NARA.

11. Henry Landau, *Enemy Within: The Inside Story of German Sabotage in America* (New York: Putnam, 1937), 114 passim; Charles H. Harris III and Louis R. Sadler, "The Witzke Affair: German Intrigue on the Mexican Border, 1917–18," *Military Review* 59, no. 2 (1979): 36–50.

12. Enrique Moral, Carlos Austin, Arturo González, and one Gutiérrez.

13. Chief to Stone, May 2, 1917, 16BI; Stone to Bielaski, May 6, 1917, 16BI; assistant attorney general to secretary of state, May 17, 1917, 16BI.

14. Stone reports, March 27, 1917, 12BI, and April 9, 15, 16, 17, 1917, 16BI; Stone to Bielaski, April 9, 1917, 16BI; Barnes report, April 3, 1917, 7BI; Munson report, April 10, 1917, 12BI.

15. See, for example, Parker report December 4, 1917, 19BI; Jones report, December 1, 1917, 19BI; Pendleton report, November 21, 1917, 19BI; chief to Pendleton, December 5, 1917, 19BI; Jones report, February 19, 1917, 6BI.

16. Jones report, February 11, 1917, 6BI.

17. See, for example, Stone report, March 17, 1917, 5BI; Weiskopf report, March 22, 1917, 12BI.

18. *EPMT*, January 9, 1917; Needham report, January 19, 1917, 16BI; Barnes report, February 2, 1917, 13BI. See also chief to Barnes, February 28, 1917, 13BI.

19. Beckham report, January 27, 1917, 7BI; Stone to Barnes, February 6, 1917, 7BI; Green report, November 30, 1917, 15BI; *EPMT*, January 7, 1917; MID report, October 8, 1917, 8532-260, MID. Hawes's office was room 1000, 66 Broadway.

20. Barnes report, January 25, 1917, 7BI; Beckham report, January 25, 1917, 7BI.

21. Beckham report, January 27, 1917, 7BI; Utley report, May 1, 1917, 6BI; Carothers to secretary of state, April 5, 1917, 11BI; Stone report, January 26, 1917, 15BI; chief to Offley, February 7, 1917, 15BI. See also González to Villa, February 12, 1917, *DHRM*, 17:242–47.

22. Barnes report, January 16, 1917, 10BI, and January 20, 1917, 7BI.

23. Needham report, April 30, 1917, 6BI; Barnes to Bielaski, April 30, 1917, 6BI. Translations of some of these documents are attached to Needham reports, May 2, 3, 1917, 6BI.

24. Carothers to secretary of state, March 25, 1917, 11BI.

25. Stone report, January 16, 1917, 7BI; Informant J [aka Fernando Palacios] reports, January 20, 1917, 12BI, and January 24, 1917, 7BI; López report, January 30, 1917, 10BI; Stone to Barnes, January 20, 1917, 13BI. An extensive list of prominent *villistas* in El Paso is in ESB to CA, February 9, 1917, L-E 799, leg. 7, exps. 96–98, AREM.

26. Informant "Mes" [aka Solanos] reports, February 1, 2, 1917, 13BI, and February 16, 1917, 16BI. Hunt, representing large ranchers in Chihuahua, had earlier arranged to make a trip to Veracruz to see Venustiano Carranza and had asked Senator Fall for a letter of introduction to the First Chief (Hunt to Fall, October 4 and 9, 1915, ABFFP).

27. Clifford Waye Trow, "Senator Albert B. Fall and Mexican Affairs, 1912–1921" (PhD diss., University of Colorado, 1966), 92.

28. Soriano Bravo to Aguilar, March 10, 1917, *DHRM*, 17:261–61; Stone reports, January 26, February 6, 7, 1917, 15BI; Hunt to Villa, January 17, 1917, 16BI; Michael M. Smith, "The Mexican Secret Service in the United States, 1910–1920," *The Americas* 59, no. 1 (2002): 77–79; Trow, "Senator Albert B. Fall," 183–89; Agent "Equis" reports, February 28, March 17, 23, 25, 26, June 29, 1917, L-E 723 (1), AREM; Weiskopf reports, March 30, 31, April 2, 1917, 16BI; Barnes report, March 31, 1917, 16BI; Informant "Mes" [aka Solanos] report, May 27, 197, 16BI; report from "Thirty" [Mora brothers of Juárez] to Stone, April 24, 1917, 11BI. The Mora brothers, together with Informant "Mes," were Stone's principal sources of intelligence on developments in Chihuahua. See, for example, their reports to him March 27, April 4, 7, 10, 11, 15, 19, 23, 24, 27, May 2, 1917, 11BI, and April 21, 1917, 12BI.

29. Barnes report, January 25, 1917, 7BI.

30. Chief to Barnes, January 26, 1917, 12BI; Barnes report, January 29, 1917, 12BI; Stone report, January 29, 1917, 12BI.

31. Barnes report, January 30, 1917, 7BI. Those reportedly meeting were General Felipe Angeles, Miguel Díaz Lombardo, Enrique Llorente, Lázaro de la Garza, and Roque González Garza.

32. Wren report, February 21, 1917, 6BI.

33. Agent X reports, May 1, 6, 14, 1917, L-E 723 (1), AREM.

34. Breniman report, January 29, 1917, 10BI. Medina was at one time military commander in Juárez.

35. Stone report, June 13, 1917, 7BI; Díaz report, August 26, 1917, 12BI.

36. Cobb to Polk, September 29, 1916, DF, file no. 812.00/20254, microcopy 274, RDS, RG 65, NARA.

37. Silva to Villa, February 4, 1917, 7BI; García to Bonillas, April 28, 1917, 7BI; Stone reports, May 17, 1917, 7BI, and February 7, 1917, 16BI; Agent X reports for January and February 1917, L-E 721, AREM.

38. Stone reports, February 26, 1917, 7BI, and March 3, 1917, 5BI; Michael M. Smith, "Andrés G. García: Venustiano Carranza's Eyes, Ears, and Voice on the Border," *Mexican Studies/Estudios Mexicanos* 23, no. 2 (2007): 374–75.

39. Bonillas memorandum, March 26, 1916, 21BI. In 1918, Macrino Martínez applied to the Carranza government for amnesty (Chiapa report, January 21, 1918, L-E 858, exp. 37, AREM).

40. Stone report, May 17, 1917, 7BI.

41. Stone report, July 20, 1917, 14BI; Carothers to secretary of state, January 8, 1917, DF, file no. 812.00/20256.

42. Cobb to secretary of state, January 30, 1917, DF, file no. 812.00/20456; Carothers to secretary of state, April 5, 1917, 11BI.

43. Baldwin reports, February 5, 8, 1917, 12BI; Wren report, February 21, 1917, 6BI.

44. Stone report, February 13, 1917, 12BI; Barnes to Stone, February 18[?], 1917, 12BI; Agent "Equis" report, February 10, 1917, L-E 725, leg. 1, exp. 65, AREM; [consul] to Murguía, February 15, 1917, L-E, 799, leg. 7, exp. 66, AREM.

45. Stone reports, February 21, March 1, 5, 1917, 12BI; Barnes report, February 28, 1917, 12BI; Informant "Mes" [aka Solanos] reports, March 4, 5, 6, 1917, 12BI; Utley report, March 5, 1917, 6BI.

46. Soriano Bravo to foreign secretary, April 14, 1917, L-E 799, leg. 7, exp. 87, AREM.

47. Smith, "Mexican Secret Service," 78.

48. District intelligence officer to inspector general, March 15, 1918, 17BI; Arriola to García, May 27, 1917, *DHRM*, 17:275–77. A list of those arrested is also in Arriola to García, May 22, 1917, L-E 799, leg. 7, exp. 71, AREM. See also García to Arriola, May 24, 1917, L-E 841, leg. 4, exp. 72, AREM; Jones report, May 22, 1917, 17BI; *U.S. v. George M. Holmes*, no. 121, U.S. Commissioner, El Paso, Tex., FRC-FW.

49. Stone reports, March 20, 29, 1917, 7BI; Cobb to secretary of state May 19, 23, 1917, 7BI; Jones report, December 21, 1917, 7BI; Informant "Mes" [aka Solanos] report, March 22, 1917, 12BI; Jones report, March 25, 1917, 6BI; Barnes report, March 26, 1917, 6BI; *EPMT*, May 24, 26, June 1, 1917.

50. Jones report, March 21, 1917, 12BI.

51. Wren report, April 25, 1917, 12BI.

52. Cobb to secretary of state, April 27, 1917, 12BI.

53. Stone report, April 28, 1917, 12BI; Jones report, December 18, 1917, 7BI.

54. Barnes report, June 18, 1917, 7BI.

55. Joe Solanos report, July 8, 1917, 7BI.

56. Díaz reports, February 8, 1917, 13BI, and February 9, 1917, 12BI; Stone report, February 7, 1917, 16BI; González to Villa, February 12, 1917, *DHRM*, 17:242–47.

57. Cobb to secretary of state, February 13, 1917, 6BI; Stone reports, March 10, 1917, 7BI, and March 13, 1917, 7BI; Gershon reports, March 18, 20, 1917, 12BI.

58. Ernst Otto Schuster, *Pancho Villa's Shadow: The True Story of Mexico's Robin Hood As Told by His Interpreter* (New York: Exposition Press, [1947]), 133; Clifford Alan Perkins, *Border Patrol: With the U.S. Immigration Service on the Mexican Boundary 1910–34* (El Paso, Tex.: Texas Western Press, 1978), 40–41.

59. Chief to Barnes, March 24, 1917, 13BI; Stone to Barnes, March 30, 1917, 13BI; Barnes report, May 9, 1917, 6BI.

60. Carothers to secretary of state, April 5, 1917, 11BI.

61. Barnes to Bielaski, April 18, 19, 1917, 13BI; Barnes to Stone, April 23, 24, 26, 1917, 13BI; Ramón report, April 24, 1917, Stone report, April 28, 1917, 13BI; Bielaski to Barnes, April 18, 1917, 6BI.

62. Cobb to secretary of state, April 27, 1917, 12BI.

63. Agent X report, April 30, 1917, L-E 723 (1), AREM; Stone report, April 28, 1917, 7BI; Informant "Mes" [aka Solanos] report, April 29, 1917, 13BI.

64. Stone report, April 30, 1917, 13BI.

65. Stone report, April 28, 1917, 7BI.

66. Chief to Barnes, May 10, 1917, 13BI.

67. Informant "Mes" [aka Solanos] report, May 3[?], 1917, 13BI; Stone report, May 5, 1917, 7BI.

68. Barnes to Stone, May 2, 1917, 1 3BI.

69. *EPMT*, April 26, May 1, 2, 6, 1917; Weiskopf report, May 3[?], 1917, 13BI.

70. Needham report, May 6, 1917, 5BI.

71. Thomas to Villa, May 8, 1917, 13BI; Barnes to Bielaski, May 12, 1917, 13BI.

72. Stone to Barnes, August 2, 1917, 17BI; Barnes report, August 6, 1917, 18BI.

73. Chief to Barnes, May 18, 1917, 13BI; Barnes to Stone, May 21, 23, 24, 1917, 13BI; Needham report, May 24, 1917, 13BI; Weiskopf report, May 25[?], 1917, 13BI.

74. In May 1916, Kyriacopulos obtained a $900 judgment against Pancho Villa, to whom he claimed he had loaned $5,000 that Villa refused to repay (*La Prensa*, May 7, 1916).

75. Stone reports, June 8, 12, 1917, 13BI; Ramos report, June 11, 1917, 13BI.

76. Barnes to Bielaski, June 10, 1917, 13BI.

77. Carothers to secretary of state, May 1, 1917, 12BI; chief to Pendleton, May 12, 1917, 7BI.

78. Needham report, May 4, 1917, 6BI.

79. Needham report, May 3, 1917, 6BI; Stone report, May 5[?], 1917, 7BI.

80. Barnes report, October 25, 1917, 12BI.

81. Informant "Mes" [aka Solanos] reports, May 5, 8, 1917, 6BI, and May 26, 27, 12BI; Weiskopf reports, March 24, April 9, 1917, 16BI, and May 14, 1917, 7BI; Breniman report, March 3, 1917, 16BI; Jones reports, April 7, 15, 16BI; Matthews to Rogers, February 28, 1917, 16BI; Utley report, March 5, 1917, 16BI. On Dawkins Kilpatrick, see Glenn Justice, *Little Known History of the Texas Big Bend: Documented Chronicles from Cabeza De Vaca to the Era of Pancho Villa*. 2nd ed. (Odessa, Tex.: Rimrock Press, 2001), 111, 112, 118, 121–23, 127, 163, 167, 170.

82. Informant "Mes" [aka Solanos] report, May 25, 1917, 7BI; *EPMT*, May 25, 1917.

83. Barnes to Bielaski, May 20, 1917, 7BI; Informant "Mes" [aka Solanos] report, June 1, 1917, 7BI; Jones report, June 1, 1917, 7BI; Barnes to Stone, June 7, 1917, 7BI; *EPMT*, May 31, June 1, 1917.

84. Wren report, August 12, 1917, 5BI; Stone report, August 5, 1917, 5BI; *EPMT*, August 14, 19, 1917. Kingsbery's fears were apparently well founded. On July 13, 1918, he went missing. Mexican

officials later claimed he'd been killed by bandits—on the U.S. side of the border, of course (*EPMT*, July 30, October 2, 1918).

85. *EPMT*, August 7, 8, 1917.

86. This account of the Stone affair is based on the following reports in Miscellaneous Files, 1909–21, file no. 12603, Investigative Records, 1908–1922, RFBI, RG 65, NARA: Jones report, August 8, 1917; Barnes to Jones, August 6, 1917; Barnes to Bielaski, August 6, 10, 1917; Barnes to Crawford, August 6, 1917; Jones to Barnes, August 24, 1917; Utley to Barnes, August 10, 1917; Stone to Bielaski, August 23, 1917; Jones to Barnes, September 21, 1917.

87. *EPMT*, April 11, 1918; *EPH*, April 20, 21, 1918; *Annual Report of the Attorney General of the United States for the Fiscal Year 1923* (Washington, D.C.: Government Printing Office, 1923), 415.

88. Barnes report, August 30, 1917, Old German Files, 1909–21, file no. 59872.

89. For example, Jones had an informant employed in the telegraph office in Juárez (Jones report, May 26, 1917, 17BI).

90. 27-22-6, AREM.

91. Smith, "Mexican Secret Service," 75.

92. Smith, "Mexican Secret Service, 76.

93. Soriano Bravo to Arriola, December 12, 1916, AEMEUA, leg. 499 (12), and Gómez memo, February 28, 1916, 11-18-197-202, AREM. See also Smith, "Mexican Secret Service," 74.

94. Soriano Bravo to Aguilar, February 9, 1917, L-E 799, leg. 7, exp. 96–98, AREM.

95. Arriola to Aguilar, March 23, 1917, 106-12, AREM; Agent H report, June 14, 1917, L-E 723 (1), AREM.

96. Soriano Bravo to García, June 7, 1917, Arriola to Soriano Bravo, June 9, 1917, and Soriano Bravo to Garza Pérez, June 10, 1917, 27-22-6, AREM.

97. Cobb to secretary of state, November 15, 1915, DF, file no. 812.00/16790. See, for example, Agent X's reports for August 16, September 9, 1916, January 27, February 18, 19, 21, 22, 24, 25, 28, March 17, 18, 19, 21, 22, 23, 24, 25, 26, June 30, July 1, 1917, and reports from Agent Dormilonas, Agent G, and Agent H, in L-E 723 (1), AREM.

98. Agent X reports, February 23, 1917, L-E 721 (1), and March 9, 1917, L-E 723 (1), AREM; Soriano Bravo to foreign secretary, March 16[?], 1917, L-E 799 (1), AREM.

99. For examples of this controversy see García to Garza Pérez, July 12, 1917, Arriola to Aguilar, March 23, 1917, and García to Aguilar, May 21, 1918, 1-6-12, AREM; Arriola to foreign secretary, August 10, 1917, L-E 837 (11), and Arriola to Garza Pérez, August 15, 1917, L-E 837 (12), AREM.

100. García to Garza Pérez, December 20, 1917, 3-16-12, exp. 1, AREM.

101. Smith, "Mexican Secret Service," 76–80. Arriola was retained as a secret agent, however, being assigned to the consulate in San Francisco (Smith, "Mexican Secret Service," 80).

102. Jones report, September 3, 1917, 12BI.

103. Jones reports, October 3, November 24, 1917, 7BI; Weiskopf reports, September 23, 28, October 3, 4, 19, 20, November 4, 25, 29, 30, December 5, 7, 8, 1917, 7BI; Jones report, November 14, 1917, 13BI, and December 14, 1917, 9BI; Weiskopf report, December 5, 1917, 17BI; Utley report, January 12, 1918, 19BI.

104. Included in Jones report, November 27, 1917, 7BI, and Utley report, December 1, 1917, 7BI.

105. Barnes to Bielaski, September 17, 1917, 13BI.

106. MID report, October 20, 1917, 11BI.

107. Utley report, November 23, 1917, 7BI.

108. Breniman to Offley, November 6, 1917, 7BI.

109. Villa to Villa, October 6, 1917, *DHRM*, 17:436.

110. Breniman to Jones, October 27, 1917, 13BI; Weiskopf report, October 31, 1917, 7BI.

111. Breniman to Jones, October 29, 1917, 13BI; Breniman to Bielaski, November 9, 1917, 13BI; chief to Harrison, November 10, 1917, 13BI.

112. Langhorne to commanding officer, November 9, 1917, 13BI.

113. Jones reports, November 13, 1917, 13BI, and November 28, 1917, 7BI; Breniman report, November 2, 1917, 18BI.

114. Jones reports, November 14, 1917, 13BI, and November 20, 24, 26, 1917, 7BI; Breniman to Bielaski, November 14, 1917, 7BI.

115. Jones report, November 28, 1917, 7BI.

116. Jones report, November 21, 1917, 7BI; weekly report, November 24, 1917, 10014-19, MID; *EPMT*, December 13, 1917.

117. Harris report, November 17, 1917, 7BI; Jones reports, November 20, 21, 1917, 7BI; Díaz report, November 30, 1917, 18BI.

118. Díaz reports, December 2, 14, 1917, 7BI.

119. Jones report, November 24, 1917, 7BI; Van Deman to Strauss, November 30, 1917, 8532-347, MID.

120. Jones report, November 26, 1917, 19BI.

121. Jones reports, January 6, March 25, April 18[?], June 6, 1918, 17BI; Burleson report, April 24, 1918, 17BI. Agent Jones also employed a Spaniard, one A. Pigüero, as a confidential informant in Juárez. However, this was one of the Bureau's short-term arrangements: Pigüero received $3 a day for four days' work (Jones reports, November 30, December 3, 18, 21, 1917, 7BI).

122. Jones report, November 27, 1917, 7BI.

123. Díaz reports, December 10, 14, 1917, 7BI; Utley report, December 21, 1917, 7BI.

124. Weekly report, June 23, 1917, 8532-134, MID.

125. Levering report, August 6, 1917, 18BI.

126. Eisenman to Van Deman (misidentified as "Van Dusen"), October 25, 1917, 8532-271, MID.

127. Murguía to Treviño, May 9, 1917, *DHRM*, 17:270–74.

128. MID report, June 30, 1917, 8532-134, MID.

129. Weekly report, December 22, 1917, 10014-24, MID.

130. Weekly report, October 6, 1917, 10014-11, MID.

131. Weekly report, November 24, 1917, 10014-19, MID.

132. Weekly report, December 1, 1917, 10014-21, MID.

133. Weekly report, December 15, 1917, 10014-25, MID.

134. Weekly report, December 22, 1917, 10014-24, MID.

135. *EPMT*, December 30, 1917; "Cresse" [Jones] report, February 11, 1918, 19BI.

Chapter 18

1. *EPMT*, March 15, 17, 19, 20, April 15, 20, 23, 24, June 25, 26, 28, December 11, 1918; *U.S. v. Catherine Schmid*, nos. 394 and 399, U.S. Commissioner, and no. 2360, U.S. District Court, El Paso, Tex., FRC-FW.

2. *EPMT*, November 7, 1918.

3. *EPMT*, August 18, 19, 20, 22, 1918. The customs officers asked to be indicted for murder and tried so there would be no legal loose ends (*EPMT*, November 21, 1918).

4. *EPMT*, November 29, 1918.

5. Northrup report, August 28, 1918; Israel to intelligence officer, September 18[16?], 1918, OMF, roll 21, Investigative Records, 1908–22, RFBI, RG 65, NARA (OMF hereafter cited as BI preceded by roll number).

6. *EPMT*, January 26, 27, 30, 1919.

7. Jones report, April 1, 1918, 18BI; Oliver report, April 3, 1918, 20BI.

8. Barnes to chief, Military Intelligence branch, April 13, 1918, 19BI.

9. Jones reports, January 28, 1918, 19BI, and January 29, 31, February 6, 1918, 18BI.

10. Jones reports, April 1, 1918, 18BI, and April 4[?], 1918, 19BI.

11. *EPMT*, March 8, 1918; Jones report, May 13, 1918, 18BI.

12. See, for example, Whalen report, November 9, 1918, 21BI.

13. Jones report, January 3, 1918, 17BI.

14. Chief to Jones, January 10, 1918, 17BI.

15. Chief to Harrison, January 10, 1918, 17BI.

16. Jones to Breniman, January 14, 1918, 17BI.

17. Howard to Jones, January 16, 1918, 17BI. See also Jones to Bielaski, January 23, 1918, 17BI.

18. Jones report, April 18[?], 1918, 17BI.

19. Burleson report, with the letters attached, April 24, 1918, 17BI; McDonald to Forester, September 22, 1917, 17BI; Jones report, March 3, 1919, 18BI; Jones to Breniman, April 14, 1919, 18BI.

20. Jones report, March 3, 1919, 18BI; Jones to Breniman, April 14, 1919, 18BI. The firm of Miller, Howard, and Gauldin had offices at 719 Caples Building.

21. Albert Neunhoffer report, May 29, 1918, 17BI; Wren report, May 31, 1918, 17BI.

22. Jones report, August 12, 1918, 17BI.

23. Wren report, May 31, 1918, 17BI. See also Wren report, June 1, 1918, 17BI.

24. Jones report, June 7[?], 1918, 17BI.

25. White report, July 1, 1918, 17BI.

26. White report, June 21, 1918, 17BI.

27. White reports, June 21, 27, 1918, 17BI. See also White report, December 20, 1918, 18BI.

28. Villa to American Smelting and Refining Company, Mexico Northwestern Railway, and Potosí Mining Company, October 20, 1918, 18BI. For the Potosí Mining Company's reply to Villa, see White report, December 23, 1918, 18BI. See also Villa to Alvarado Mining Company, October 20, 1918, 17BI.

29. Jones to Bielaski, November 15, 1918, 18BI; Bielaski to Harrison, November 20, 1918, 17BI.

30. Miller to Díaz Lombardo, July 15, 1918, 21BI. See also Miller to Díaz Lombardo, July 25, 1918, 21BI; chief to Pendleton, July 26, 1918, 21BI; Sharp to Pike, July 30, 1918, 19BI; Villa to Miller, September 24, 1918, 17BI.

31. *In re José Sedaño et al.*, June 11, 1918; White report, June 21, 1918, 17BI.

32. White report, June 26, 1918, 18BI.

33. Jones report, November 5, 1918, 18BI.

34. Jones report, June 6[?], 1918, 17BI.

35. Neunhoffer report, June 21, 1918, 17BI.

36. Jones report, January 6, 1918, 17BI.

37. Díaz report, January 15, 1918, 17BI.

38. Bonillas to Lansing, February 16, 1918, DF, file no. 812.00/21763, microcopy 274, RDS, RG 65, NARA.

39. Shaw to inspector general, April 3, 1918, in DF, file no. 812.00/21882; see also acting secretary of war to secretary of state, April 6, 1918, DF, file no. 812.00/1863. The U.S. Army thoroughly investigated the Mexican complaint.

40. Warner to Camp, March 10, 1918, 17BI; district intelligence officer to inspector general, March 15, 1918, 17BI; Jones to Breniman, March 25, 1918, 17BI.

41. District intelligence officer to inspector general, March 15, 1918, 17BI; Jones to Breniman, March 25, 1918, 17BI; Breniman to Camp, March 29, 1918, 17BI.

42. Díaz report, April 2, 1918, 20BI.

43. Sharp to Pike, September 25, 1918, 19BI; Harrison to Bielaski, October 19, 1918, 21BI; Jones report, November 29, 1918, 18BI; White report, December 14, 1918, 18BI. The Bureau also acquired letters that Pancho Villa wrote to John Hawes, his representative in San Antonio. See Wiseman report, April 4, 1918, 20BI.

44. Jones report, August 3, 1918, 17BI.

45. Harrison to Bielaski, August 26, 1918, 17BI.

46. Bielaski to Harrison, September 5, 1918, 17BI.

47. Sharp to Pike, September 25, 1918, 17BI; chief to Jones, September 27, 1918, 17BI; Jones to Bielaski, October 3, 1918, 17BI.

48. *EPH*, October 29, 30, 31, November 1, 1918. The Erupción Mining Company was owned by El Pasoans. It had only resumed operations in July (*EPMT*, July 18, 1918).

49. Jones to Bielaski November 6, 1918, 18BI.

50. *EPMT*, October 29, 30, 31, November 2, 7, 11, 17, 19, December 1, 1918; district intelligence officer to department intelligence officer, November 8, 18, 1918, Central Decimal Files, 1917–25, box 1371, Records of the Adjutant General's Office, RG 407, NARA. In July 1919, Knotts suspended the mine's operation because the Mexican government couldn't provide protection against Villa (*EPMT*, July 27, 1919).

51. Jones report and attachments, November 17, 1918, 18BI.

52. Villa to chief, November 18, 1918, 18BI; Jones to Bielaski, November 27, 1918, 17BI; another copy is in 18BI.

53. John M. Barry, *The Great Influenza: The Epic Story of the Deadliest Plague in History* (New York: Viking, 2004), 4.

54. Bradford Luckingham, *Epidemic in the Southwest, 1918–1919* (El Paso, Tex.: Texas Western Press, 1984), 7, 9, 13; *EPT*, October 13, 1918.

55. Jones report, January 5, 1918, Old German Files, 1909–21, file no. 198744, microfilm publication no. M1085, Investigative Records, 1908–22, RFBI, RG 65, NARA.

56. Kosterlitzky reports, January 5, 6, 1918 (misdated as 1917), January 8, 12, February 18, 24, ca. February 22, 1918, 18BI; Keep reports, January 14, 28, 1918, 18BI; Keep to Bielaski, February 2, 4, 1918, 18BI; Díaz report, February 9, 1918, 18BI; Carusso to "Mario Cartal" [Paz], February 12, 15, 19, 26, 1918, 18BI.

57. See Kosterlitzky report, February 24, 1918, 18BI.

58. Keep report, December 5, 1918, 18BI.

59. Lansing to attorney general and attachments, April 9, 1918, 20BI; chief to Jones, April 20, 1918, 20BI. Along with Krupp, the consulate denounced Juan Lozano and José Tinajero.

60. Jones report and attachments, November 17, 1918, 18BI.

61. *EPMT*, September 12, October 24, December 24, 1916, January 8, 9, 13, April 11, June 23, 24, 25, 1918.

62. *EPMT*, July 4, 5, 1918; White report, July 10, 1918, 21BI; Jones report, August 13, 1918, 18BI. For Adolph Schwartz and his nephew Maurice Schwartz, see Floyd S. Fierman, *The Schwartz Family of El Paso: The Story of a Pioneer Jewish Family in the Southwest* (El Paso, Tex.: Texas Western Press, 1980).

63. Jones report, September 6, 1918, 21BI. As for Mayer, he died in the great influenza pandemic, on October 16, 1918, so the case against him was dropped (Bates report, October 17[?], 1918, 21BI; *EPH*, October 17, 1918).

64. *EPMT*, July 21, 1918; White reports, July 25, 1918, 19BI, and July 25, 1918; Wren report, November 5, 1918, 17BI.

65. *EPMT*, November 30, 1918.

66. Jones reports, February 19, 27, March 13, 1918, 18BI.

67. Jones reports, August 26, 1918, 21BI, and August 26, 27, 1918, 18BI.

68. Jones report, June 6, 1918, 19BI.

69. Jones to Bielaski, June 6, 1918, 20BI.

70. "Cresse" [Jones] report, May 25, 1918, 20BI.

71. *EPMT*, April 19, May 16, 18, June 24, 1918; Jones reports, August 13, 16, 1918, 18BI.

Chapter 19

1. Sharp to Nye, May 14, 1918, OMF, roll 19, Investigative Records, 1908–22, RFBI, RG 65, NARA (OMF hereafter cited as BI preceded by roll number).
2. See, for example, Harrison to Bielaski, January 15, 1918, 18BI; "Cresse" [Jones] report, June 3, 1918, 19BI; Bonillas to Lansing, July 18, 1918, 18BI.
3. Commanding officer to commanding general, Southern Department, May 11, 1918, 20BI.
4. Jones to Bielaski, June 4, 1918, 20BI.
5. Neunhoffer report, June 4, 1918, 17BI.
6. White report, August 2, 1918, 20BI.
7. Jones reports, August 26, September 21, 1918, 17BI. See also Bates report, July 18, 1918, 17BI.
8. Jones report, October 10, 1918, 17BI.
9. Jones reports, November 27, 1918, 17BI, and November 30, 1918, 18BI.
10. Tinklepaugh reports, September 2, 1918, 17BI, and September 3, 1918, 20BI.
11. Tinklepaugh report, September 13, 1918, 17BI.
12. Tinklepaugh report, September 30, 1918, 17BI; *EPMT*, March 12, 1918.
13. Neunhoffer report, October 16, 1918, 17BI; Breniman to Hanson, October 16, 1918, 17BI. Agent Jones vigorously refuted these allegations, stressing that Carroll Bates was cooperating with the Bureau by keeping an eye on Miller and his associates (Jones report, October 21, 1918, 17BI; de Nette report, February 5[?], 1919, 17BI).
14. Tinklepaugh report, October 5, 1918, 21BI.
15. Villa to Miller, October 20, 1918, 17BI; Villa to Miller, September 24, 1918, 17BI.
16. *EPMT*, May 10, 1919.
17. Jones reports, June 20, 24, 1919, 18BI, and July 4, 1919, 23BI. See also consul to García, January 13, 1919, L-E 839, leg. 9, exp. 310, AREM, and García to Bengoechea, L-E 839, leg. 9, exp. 283, AREM.
18. Wren reports, December 13, 17, 20, 1918, 18BI; White report, December 12, 1918, 18BI.
19. Wren report, June 17, 119, 18BI.
20. Jones report, December 26, 1918, 18BI; Jones to Allen, January 15, 1919, 17BI.
21. Jones report, December 26, 1918, 18BI. Alfonso Gómez Morentín was tried for his neutrality violation and acquitted in December 1918.
22. Wren report, December 20, 1918, 18BI; Jones report, December 28, 1918, 18BI.
23. *EPMT*, December 12, 1918.
24. Jones to Bielaski, November 27, 1918, 18BI.
25. Chief to Harrison, November 26, 1918, 17BI; Jones to Bielaski, November 27, 30, 1918, 18BI; *EPMT*, November 21, 29, 30, December 2, 3, 1918.
26. Jones reports, May 13, June 20, October 14, November 30, December 7, 12, 1918, 18BI.
27. *EPMT*, December 6, 11, 13, 16, 25, 26, 31, 1918, January 3, 5, 1919; Jones reports, August 13, October 24, 28, November 5, 12, 1918, 18BI; "Cresse" [Jones] report, November 13, 1918,

18BI. For a biographical sketch of General Castro, see White report, December 16, 1918, 18BI.

28. Jones report, September 19, 1918, 20BI.
29. *EPMT*, December 4, 23, 1918.
30. Jones reports, December 6, 28, 1918, 18BI; White report, December 14, 1918, 18BI.
31. Wren report, December 17, 1918, 18BI.
32. Castro to "Soto," December [?], 1918, 18BI.
33. Castro to "Soto," December [?], 1918, 18BI; Evaristo Pérez to "Soto," December 16, 1918, 18BI.
34. White report, December 17, 1918, 18BI.
35. Ibañez to "Soto," October 31, November 1, 1918, 18BI.
36. Hunt to Montaño, October 21, 1918, 21BI.
37. Jones reports, August 15, September 4, 1918, 18BI; Berliner report, September 14, 1918, 18BI; Sharp to Pike, September 21, 23, 1918, 18BI.
38. Jones report, August 16, 1918, 18BI; Jones to Bielaski, October 1, 18BI.
39. Chief to Jones, September 25, 1918, 18BI.
40. Jones reports, September 26, 28, November 12, 1918, 18BI.
41. Jones report, October 3, 1918, 18BI.
42. Chief to Sharp, October 9, 1918, 18BI.
43. Sharp to Pike, October 10, 1918, 18BI.
44. Jones reports, February 5, 27, 1918, 18BI; Weiskopf report, February 7[?], 1918, 19BI.
45. Harrison to Bielaski, June 12, 1918, 19BI.

Chapter 20

1. Jones reports, January 10, 18, 1919, OMF, roll 18, Investigative Records, 1908–22, RFBI, RG 65, NARA (OMF hereafter cited as BI preceded by roll number).
2. Villa wasn't making idle threats. On February 25, 1918, he had blown up the $1.5 million power plant of the National Mines and Smelter Company at Magistral, Durango, which Carranza troops had been guarding. Villa killed some thirty employees, including several Americans (*EPMT*, March 6, 7, 1918).
3. Jones reports, January 23, 27, 1919, 18BI; Prescott to Raymond, January 25, 1919, 21BI; McQuatters to Alvarado Mining and Milling Company, January 30, 1919, 21BI; *EPMT*, January 24, 1919.
4. District military censor to military intelligence director, January 10, 1919, 21BI.
5. Jones report, January 22, 1919, 18BI; *EPMT*, January 20, February 16, 1919.
6. A translation is in Jones report, February 18, 1919, 18BI.
7. March to United Press, February 24, 1919, 21BI.
8. García to Bonillas, February 15, 1919, 21BI; Jones report, March 5, 1919, 18BI.

9. Jones reports, April 17, 26, 1919, 18BI.

10. Jones report, April 26, 1919, 18BI.

11. *EPMT*, January 10, May 26, July 18, 1919.

12. He did inform the Bureau about his trip to Candelaria, Texas, to confer with a *villista* colonel. He also provided letters that a courier had brought him from General Felipe Angeles (Jones reports, January 2, 27, 1919, 18BI).

13. Jones report, February 26, 1919, 22BI.

14. Wren report, February 19, 1919, 17BI.

15. *Annual Report of the Attorney General of the United States for the Year 1920* (Washington, D.C.: Government Printing Office, 1920), 741.

16. Jones report and attached affidavits, February 9, 1919, 17BI. See also Wren report, February 13, 1919, BI17; Bates report, February 17, 1919, 17BI; Jones report, February 18, 1919, 17BI; *EPMT*, February 6, 7, 8, 14, 1919.

17. Breniman to Allen, February 18, 1919, 17BI; Jones report, February 18, 1919, 17BI.

18. Wren report, February 13, 1919, 17BI.

19. Wren reports, February 20, 22, 1919, 17BI.

20. Wren report, February 19, 1919, 17BI.

21. Jones report, February 25, 1919, 17BI.

22. Wren report, March 8, 1919, 17BI.

23. Jones reports, March 22, 27, 1919, 17BI.

24. Jones report, January 8, 1919, 18BI.

25. Federico Cervantes, *Felipe Angeles en la Revolución: Biografía (1869–1919)*, 3rd ed. (México, D.F.: n. p., 1964), 252–55, 275–76; Kosterlitzky report, January 14, 1919, 18BI.

26. *EPMT*, January 3, 1919.

27. Jones report, January 20, 1919, 18BI. See also Wiseman report, January 2, 1919, 19BI.

28. Cervantes, *Felipe Angeles*, 271–75; Jones report, February 7, 1919, 18BI.

29. Jones report, January 7, 1919, 18BI; *EPMT*, January 2, 6, 7, 1919.

30. A list of the Liberal Alliance's members in El Paso is in Castle report, February 18, 1919, 23BI.

31. Jones reports, January 7, 30, February 5, 1919, 18BI.

32. Jones report, January 23, 1919, 18BI.

33. Jones reports, February 10, 14, 17, 1919, 18BI; *EPMT*, January 29, February 9, July 30, 1919.

34. Jones reports, January 10, 24, 31, 1919, 18BI; Kosterlitzky report, February 4, 1919, 23BI; Wiseman report, September 16, 1919, 19BI; *EPMT*, March 23, 1919.

35. Jones reports, January 18, ca. April 8, 1919, September 26, 1919, 18BI; *EPMT*, January 9, 1919.

36. Luis Liceaga, *Félix Díaz* (México D.F.: Editorial Jus, 1958), 421–26.

37. *EPMT*, April 19, 1919.

38. On April 24, Bureau agents in San Antonio executing a search warrant obtained a mass of García Naranjo's confidential correspondence with other prominent *felicistas*, including Colonel Juan José Rocha, aka Informant AR (Neunhoffer to Allen, April 26, 1919, 18BI; Neunhoffer reports, April 29, 30, May 2, 6, 1919, 18BI; Breniman to Jones, May 5, 1919, 18BI).

39. Jones reports, March 3, 7, 1919, 18BI. See also White report, March 14, 1919, 18BI.

40. See, as three examples out of many, Despit report, February 15[?], 1919, 21BI, and Jones reports, April 10, 15, 1919, 23BI.

41. Ernest Otto Schuster, *Pancho Villa's Shadow: The True Story of Mexico's Robin Hood As Told by His Interpreter* (New York: Exposition Press, [1947]), 171.

42.

Alvarez, Luis	editor, "La Republica"
Angeles, Mrs. Clara K. de	wife of Gen. Felipe, 1800 Montana
Angeles, Eduardo	brother of Gen. Felipe, 1800 Montana
Avila, General Fidel	Las Cruces, N.M.
Ayala, Manuel	member Mexican Liberal Alliance, 1008 S. Santa Fe St
Bonilla, Manuel	brains of Villistas in El Paso, 305 Wyoming
Vega Bonilla, Tomas	member Mexican Union Association
Cesaretti, Pascual	Italian, now with Gen. Angeles
Garcia Conde, Jose	member M. U. A., 306 E. 4th St.
Rocha Chabro, Manuel	member M. U. A.
Chavez, Miguel	messenger between Villa and El Paso junta
Cervantes, Federico, Gen.	now under indictment
Cardenas Garza, Dr.	recent arrival from Silver City, Ashley Hotel
Castelazo, Juan	manager, Los Angeles Mercantile Co., 701 S. El Paso St.
Farias, Andres E.	not active now, 1029 Upson Ave.
Farias, Alfredo	brother to above
Gomez Morentin, Alfonso	"The Admiral"—confidential agent of Villa
Gomez, Filiberto	member M. U. A., grocer, 1001 S. Kansas
Carillo Galindo, Alfonso	member M. U. A., jitneyman, 3805 Frutas St.
Holmes, George M.	now County Jail, indictment violation Neutrality Laws
Howard, Volney G.	Miller & Howard, 719 Caples Bldg.
Jauregui, Carlos	former secretary F. Villa, 3105 E. San Antonio
Jaurrieta, Jose	present secretary F. Villa—now Mexico
Kyriacopulos, Theo.	Greek—Villa's financial agent El Paso (has assumed the mantle of George Holmes) 510 Prospect Ave.
Gonzalez, Manuel G., Sr.	2129 E. San Antonio
Gonzalez, Manuel G., Jr.	former Villa secretary
Flores, Magdaleno	indicted with Cervantes (Villista "colonel")
Landa, Manuel, General	head Mexican Union Association
McManus, Francisco	Irish-Mexican, former Villa consul El Paso bookkeeper, Clint Mercantile Co, Clint, Texas
Medina, Juan	not active, Leckie Hotel
Mier, Pascual C.	director M. U. A., agent Singer Sewing Machine

Lucero, Mrs. M. B.	Villa agent, mistress Juan Medina, 700 Prospect
Miller, Harry C.	firm Miller, Howard & Gauldin, 719 Caples Building
Martinez, Macrino, Gen.	leader M. U. A., Villa's sister married to, 1311 E. Second St.
McClammy, Tod [sic]	associate Geo. M. Holmes, Sheldon Hotel
Medellin, Alberto	recent arrival, intended to leave with Cervantes but "cold feet," Ashley Hotel
Nieto, Carlos A.	secretary M. U. A., floor walker, "White House" [department store], 616 N. Santa Fe
Ramonet, Genaro	director M.U. A., mining engineer, 418 First National Bank Bldg, 220 W. Boulevard
Renteria, Isidoro	director M. U. A., grocer, 1400 E. Boulevard, house 515 Park St.
Reducindo, Mrs. Blanca M.	Villista agent, mother Juan Vargas, trained nurse, rooms 102 Hotel Leckie
Segura, B. R.	member M. U. A.
Sedano, Jose	reported dead, but not confirmed
Terrazas, Sylvestre	editor "La Patria," 830 N. Oregon St.
Torres, Elias L.	civil engineer, member M. U. A. (leader)
Mendez Velarde, Gumesindo	editor "La Vida Nueva," First National Bank Building
Villarreal, Antonio I.	leader M. U. A., 1819 Montana St.
Valenzuela, Jose	director M. U. A., customs broker, 321 Frost[?] Bldg
Velasco, Jose Luis	editor "La Republica" 222 San Jacinto St.

Jones report, May 6, 1919, 18BI; acting chief to Churchill, April 24, 1919, 22BI. The resume is in 23BI.

43. Jones report, April 14, 1919, 18BI.

44. Jones report, April 3, 1919, 18BI.

45. White report, March 27, 1919, 18BI.

46. Jones reports, January 21, February 28, 1919, 18BI.

47. White reports, March 12, 17[?], 1919, 18BI.

48. White report, March 17[?], 1919, 18BI.

49. Díaz report, March 30, 1919, 23BI; Wren report, April 4, 1919, 23BI; Bates report, April 7, 23BI; *EPMT*, March 20, 21, 22, 23, 26, 30, April 10, 11, 1919; Jones report, May 6, 1919, 17BI.

50. Gómez Morentín to Puente, in Kosterlitzky report, April 4, 1919, 19BI. See also Kosterlitzky report, April 7, 1919, 18BI.

51. Bates reports, March 20, 22, 1919, 18BI; Jones report, April 3, 1919, 18BI; White reports, March 24, 1919, 23BI, and March 27, 1919, 18BI; Wren report, March 31, 1919, 23BI.

52. *EPMT*, April 19, July 12, 28, 1918, February 18, 1924.

53. Wren report, March 31, 1919, 23BI; White report, April 17, 1919, 23BI; Bates report, April 6[?], 1919, 23BI; Jones report, April 10, 1919, 23BI; Cervantes, *Felipe Angeles*, 276–77; Bonillas memorandum, March 26, 1919, 23BI; Colvin report, April 26, 1919, 21BI; *EPMT*, April 12, 13, 14, 16, 17, 18, 20, May 18, 1919. The jury split seven to five for conviction, the five perhaps evidencing many locals' distaste for Mexican informants.

54. Kosterlitzky report, May 8, 1919, 23BI; Jones report, May 28, 1919, 23BI; *EPMT*, May 27, 1919.

55. Wren reports, May 2, 10, 1919, 17BI; *EPMT*, April 9, 18, 29, 30, May 5, 1919.

56. Jones reports, April 1, 9, 12, 23, 30, May 2, 1919, 17BI, and April 19, August 6, 1919, 18BI; Bates reports, April 21, 30, 1919, 17BI; Wren report, May 2, 1919, 17BI; *EPMT*, May 1, 1919. The defense attorneys were T. A. Falvey, L. A. Dale, and Charles Owens.

57. *EPMT*, May 4, 14, 18, August 9, 1919.

58. Jones reports, May 5, 1919, 17BI, and June 18, 1919, 18BI.

59. Jones reports, June 16, 17, 1919, 18BI.

60. *EPMT*, June 15, 1919.

61. *EPMT*, June 6, 10, 14, 15, 1919.

62. Jones reports, June 20, July 1, 3, 1919, 18BI; Wren report, June 30, 1919, 18BI; *EPMT*, June 15, 16, 17,18, 21, 24, 1919.

63. *EPMT*, June 18, 23, 1919; Francisco R. Almada, *La Revolución en el estado de Chihuahua*. 2 vols. (México, D.F.: Talleres Gráficos de la Nación, 1967), 2:338–40.

Chapter 21

1. *EPMT*, June 22, 1919.

2. *EPMT*, June 16, 1919.

3. *EPMT*, June 17, 1919.

4. *EPMT*, June 18, 1919.

5. *EPMT*, June 15, 16, 22, July 14, August 13, 23, 1919.

6. *EPMT*, July 11, October 5, November 18, 1919.

7. Jones report, June 20, 1919, OMF, roll 18, Investigative Records, 1908–22, RFBI, RG 65, NARA (OMF hereafter cited as BI preceded by roll number); White report, June 19, 1919, 18BI; Federico Cervantes, *Felipe Angeles en la Revolución: Biografía (1869–1919)*, 3rd ed. (México, D.F.: n. p., 1964), 292–93; *EPMT*, June 21, 1919. Pascual Cesaretti, the Italian *villista* partisan who had accompanied General Felipe Angeles into Mexico, was apprehended by Texas Rangers on June 18 and gave the Bureau a lengthy statement covering his experiences up to the attack on Juárez (Jones report, June 24, 1919, 18BI; *EPMT*, June 21, 1919). Cesaretti later pleaded guilty to entering the United States without a passport and to bringing sixteen quarts of tequila into the country illegally. He was sentenced to two months in the county jail for illegal entry and two years in Leavenworth for receiving and concealing the tequila. "He told the interpreter the sentence was not satisfactory to him" (*EPMT*, October 17, 29, November 11, 1919).

8. Kosterlitzky report, September 27, 1919, 18BI.

9. Berliner memorandum, July 10, 1919, 21BI.

10. For McClammy's smuggling activities in the mid- to late teens, see Jaurrieta to Jaurrieta, June 21, 1917, in Jones report, July 31, 1919, 18BI.

11. Jones report, July 5, 1919, 17BI; Lawrence to Frost, July 12, 1919, 17BI; Wren report, July 12, 1919, 17BI.

12. Jones reports, July 29, October 20[?], 1919, 17BI; White report, August 11, 1919, 21BI; Wren report, August 14, 1919, 21BI; *EPMT*, September 30, October 16, December 10, 11, 1919.

13. Breniman to Burke, July 20, 31, August 16, 1919, 17BI; Wiseman report, August 6, 1919, 17BI; chief to Breniman, August 15, 1919, 17BI; Breniman to Jones, August 15, 1919, 17BI; assistant attorney general to Long, August 23, 1919, 17BI; Miller report, October 17, 1919, 17BI; White report, August 11, 1919, 19BI; Jones reports, August 12, 18, 1919, 18BI; assistant director and chief to Winslow, August 21, 1919, 18BI; *EPMT*, July 3, August 23, 1919.

14. Assistant director and chief to Breniman, September 18, 1919, 23BI. Velasco had written and published in *La República* an inflammatory article on August 30, 1919, the fourth anniversary of Pascual Orozco's death.

15. Jones report, September 16, 1919, 23BI; de Nette to Burke, September 26, 1919, 23BI; Jones to Connell, September 29, 1919, 22BI; Kosterlitzky reports, October 3, 1919, 22BI, and October 13, 1919, 19BI.

16. Assistant director and chief to Connell, September 29, 1919, 23BI.

17. Shelton report, October 3, 1919, 19BI; weekly reports, September 6, 1919, DF, file no. 812.00/23071, microcopy 274, RDS, RG 65, NARA; weekly reports, September 13, 1919, DF, file no. 812.00/23090, weekly reports, September 27, 1919, DF, file no. 812.00/23105, weekly reports, October 4, 1919, DF, file no. 812.00/23146.

18. Jones report, October 8, 1919, 18BI. See also Wren report, March 31, 1919, 18BI.

19. Cervantes, *Felipe Angeles*, 294–365; Jones report, December 1, 1919, 18BI; Stewart to secretary of state, November 19, 1919, DF, file no. 812.00/23210, November 21, 1919, DF, file no. 812.00/23217, November 24, 1919, DF, file nos. 812.00/23225 and 812.00/23226, November 25, 1919, DF, file no. 812.00/23230, November 26, 1919, DF, file nos. 812.00/23234 and 812.00/23235, December 1, 1919, DF, file no. 812.00/23259. Angeles's family and friends appealed to Americans from President Wilson on down to intercede on Angeles's behalf (Angeles to Lansing, November 20, 1919, DF, file no. 812.00/23212; Angeles to Lansing, November 21, 1919, DF, file no. 812.00/23215; Angeles to Wilson, November 21, 1919, DF, file no. 812.00/23220; Angeles to Wilson, November 20, 1919, DF, file no. 812.00/23221; Cobb to secretary of state, November 21, 1919, DF, file no. 812.0/23222; Angeles to Wilson, November 21, 1919, DF, file nos. 812.00/23223 and 812.00/23224; Sheppard to Woodrow Wilson, November 24, 1919, DF, file no. 812.00/23232).

20. Weekly report, January 3, 1920, DF, file no. 812.00/23322.

21. Araiza to Holmes, December 2, 10, 11, 16, 1919, 17BI; Holmes to White, December 3, 1919, 17BI; White to Holmes, December 22, 1919, 17BI; *EPMT*, October 14, November 27, December 9, 10, 11, 21, 1919.

22. *Laredo Weekly Times*, October 24, 1920; John Mason Hart, *Empire and Revolution: The Americans in Mexico Since the Civil War* (Berkeley: University of California Press, 2002), 524; *EPMT*, March 19, 1927; Friedrich Katz, *The Life and Times of Pancho Villa* (Stanford, Calif.: Stanford University Press, 1998), 658.

23. Stewart to secretary of state, August 15, 1919, DF, file no. 812.00/22978, and August 18, 1919, DF, file no. 812.00/22985; weekly report, August 16, 1919, DF, file no. 812.00/22990.

24. *EPMT*, April 15, June 20, 21, July 29, 30, August 19, 3,September 22, 23, 24, 25, 30, October 1, 25, 26, 27, 1919.

25. Miller report, June 11, 1919, 18BI; Jones reports, August 15, 1918, and August 14, 1919, 18BI.

26. *EPH*, June 23, 1916; *EPT*, May 18, 1929, October 10, December 3, 1935, March 16, 1955; *EPHP*, October 9, 1955.

27. *EPH*, May 15, 29, June 1, 1914, May 18, 1915, 21BI; García to Langhorne, February 5, 1919, 21BI.

28. *EPT*, October 4, 1932, June 7, 1937, December 31, 1940, January 2, 1942; *EPHP*, June 5, 1936.

29. Memoranda from the Mexican embassy, September 3, 1919, DF, file no. 812.00/23047, and September 19, 1919, DF, file no. 812.00/23085; weekly reports, December 27, 1919, DF, file no. 812.00/23307, and January 3, 1920, DF, file no. 812.00/23322.

30. Weekly reports, October 4, 1919, DF, file no. 812.00/23146, and November 8, 1919, DF, file no. 812.00/23208; García to Carranza, November 6, 1919, *DHRM*, 18:303–15; Zetina to Ramonet, October 25, 1919, *DHRM*, 18:311–12.

31. *EPMT*, July 20, October 6, November 22, December 9, 1919.

32. *EPMT*, October 10, 1919; Fred Morales, *Smeltertown* (El Paso, Tex.: El Paso/Juárez Historical Museum, 2004), 26–27.

33. Harriet Howze Jones, "Heritage Homes of El Paso: The Krakauer House," *Password* 24, no. 3 (1979): 128–30.

34. *EPMT*, June 2, July 5, 1918, February 11, March 29, May 1, 1919.

35. *EPMT*, September 8, 9, 10, 20, October 2, 1919; Floyd S. Fierman, "Insights and Hindsights of Some El Paso Jewish Families," *El Paso Jewish Historical Review* 1, no. 2 (1983): 163. His brother Julius took over management of the firm.

36. Clifford Wayne Trow, "Senator Albert B. Fall and Mexican Affairs, 1912–1921" (PhD diss., University of Colorado, 1966), 2.

37. U.S. Senate, *Investigation of Mexican Affairs,* 2 vols., Senate doc. no. 285, 66th Cong., 2nd sess. (Washington, D.C.: Government Printing Office, 1920), 3307; Trow, "Senator Albert B. Fall," 271–80; Jane Eppinga, *Henry Ossian Flipper: West Point's First Black Graduate* (Austin: Republic of Texas Press, 1996), 177–203; *EPMT*, April 24, September 6, 7, 17, October 29, November 9, 10, December 10, 1919; Charles H. Harris III and Louis R. Sadler, *The Texas Rangers and the Mexican Revolution* (Albuquerque: University of New Mexico Press, 2004), 481–82; Jones report, February 14, 1919, 18BI.

38. Trow, "Senator Albert B. Fall," 426.

39. Kosterlitzky reports, January 26, February 11, February 18, May 28, 1920, 13BI; Connell report, January 28, 1920, 13BI; Michael M. Smith, "The Mexican Secret Service in the United States, 1910–1920," *The Americas* 59, no. 1 (2002): 80.

40. Kosterlitzky report, April 10, 1920, 13BI; Smith, "Mexican Secret Service," 81.

41. The manifesto is in *DHRM*, 18:265–79; *EPMT*, June 7, 1919.

42. *EPMT*, December 19, 1919.

43. The plan is in *DHRM*, 18:399–404.

44. Michael M. Smith, "Andrés G. García: Venustiano Carranza's Eyes, Ears, and Voice on the Border," *Mexican Studies/Estudios Mexicanos* 23, no. 2 (2007): 385.

45. Agent Jones reported that Villa's surrender had stopped revolutionary activities in El Paso for the present (Jones to Safford, July 31, 1920, ABFP).

46. Douglas V. Meed, *Soldier of Fortune: Adventuring in Latin America and Mexico with Emil Lewis Holmdahl* (Houston: Halcyon Press, 2003), 177–87.

Bibliography

Archives and Manuscript Collections

National Archives and Records Service, Washington, D.C. and College Park, Maryland

RG 38—Office of Naval Intelligence, Confidential General Correspondence, 1913–24

RG 59—Records of the Department of State

Decimal Files, Internal Affairs of Mexico, 1910–1929. Microcopy No. 274

Numerical and Minor Files, 1906–1910, Microcopy M-862

RG 60—Records of the Department of Justice

RG 65—Records of the Federal Bureau of Investigation: Investigative Case Files of the Bureau of Investigation, 1908–1922

Old Mex 232 Files, Microcopy

Old German Files, 1909–21, Microfilm Publication No. M1085

Miscellaneous Files, 1909–21, Microcopy

RG 87—Records of The United States Secret Service

Daily Reports of Agents, 1875 Thru 1936, Microcopy

RG 165—Records of the War Department General and Special Staffs, Military Intelligence Division

RG 204—General Records of the Pardon Attorney's Office, Application for Executive Clemency in behalf of Emil L. Holmdahl, no.31–305,

RG 393—Records of United States Army Continental Commands, 1821–1920

General Correspondence, Department of Texas, 1870–1913

Record Cards, 1909–12, Department of Texas

RG 407—Records of the Adjutant General's Office, 1917–1925

1920 United States Federal Census

National Museum of American History, Kenneth E. Behring Center, Smithsonian Institution, Washington, D.C.

Victor L. Ochoa Papers

Federal Records Center, Fort Worth, Texas

U.S. District Court

El Paso, Laredo, Brownsville, San Antonio

U.S. Commissioner

El Paso, San Antonio

Federal Records Center, Denver, Colorado

U.S. District Court

Santa Fe

U.S. Commissioner

Santa Fe

Federal Records Center, Laguna Niguel, California

U.S. District Court

Phoenix

Archives Division, Texas State Library, Austin, Texas

Texas Rangers, Service Records (microfilm)

Centro de Estudios de Historia de México, Departamento Cultural de Condumex, México, D.F.

President Venustiano Carranza Archive

Archivo Histórico Diplomático Mexicano de la Secretaría de Relaciones Exteriores, México, D.F.

Nettie Lee Benson Latin American Collection, University of Texas at Austin

General Pablo González Archive, microfilm

Lázaro de la Garza Archive

Center for American History, University of Texas at Austin

E. A. "Dogie" Wright Papers

Special Collections, University of Texas at El Paso

Krakauer, Zork & Moye Archive

John H. McNeely Collection

Center for Southwest Research, General Library, University of New Mexico, Albuquerque, New Mexico

Senator Albert Bacon Fall Papers, microfilm

Manuscript Division, New York Public Library

Enrique C. Llorente Papers

Library of Congress

William Howard Taft Papers, microfilm, Series, Executive Office

Correspondence (Presidential Series No. 1)

Texas National Guard Archives, Camp Mabry, Austin, Texas

Texas Ranger Records

Rio Grande Historical Collections, New Mexico State University, Las Cruces, New Mexico

Albert Bacon Fall Family Papers

Government Documents

Annual Report of the Attorney General of the United States for the Year 1906. Washington, D.C.: Government Printing Office, 1906.

Annual Report of the Attorney General of the United States for the Year 1916. Washington, D.C.: Government Printing Office, 1916.

Annual Report of the Attorney General of the United States for the Year 1917. Washington, D.C.: Government Printing Office, 1917.

Annual Report of the Attorney General of the United States for the Year 1920. Washington, D.C.: Government Printing Office, 1920.

Annual Report of the Attorney General of the United States for the Fiscal Year 1923. Washington, D.C.: Government Printing Office, 1923.

U.S. House. *Claims Growing Out of Insurrection in Mexico.* House doc. no. 1168. U.S. Congressional serial set, vol. 6586. 62nd Cong., 3rd sess. Washington, D.C.: Government Printing Office, 1912.

———. *Hearings before the Committee on Expenditures in the Treasury Department: Subject of Hearing—Charges against Collector R. W. Dowe, August 17, 1911.* 62nd Cong., 1st sess. Washington, D.C.: Government Printing Office, 1911.

U.S. Senate. *Brewing and Liquor Interests and German and Bolshevik Propaganda.* Senate doc. no. 62, 66th Cong., 1st sess. Washington, D.C.: Government Printing Office, 1919.

———. *Investigation of Mexican Affairs.* 2 vols. Senate doc. no. 285. 66th Cong., 2nd sess. Washington, D.C.: Government Printing Office, 1920.

———. *Revolutions in Mexico: Hearing before a Subcommittee of the Committee on Foreign Relations.* 62nd Cong., 2nd sess. Washington, D.C.: Government Printing Office, 1913.

Books

Albro, Ward S. *Always a Rebel: Ricardo Flores Magón and the Mexican Revolution.* Fort Worth: Texas Christian University Press, 1992.

Alexander, Bob. *Fearless Dave Allison: A Transitional Lawman on a Transitional Frontier.* Silver City, N.Mex.: High-Lonesome Books, 2003.

———. *Lawmen, Outlaws, and S.O.Bs.: Gunfighters of the Old Southwest.* Silver City, N.Mex.: High-Lonesome Books, 2004.

Almada, Francisco R. *Diccionario de historia, geografía y biografía chihuahuense.* 2nd ed. Chihuahua, Mex.: Universidad de Chihuahua, 1968.

———. *La Revolución en el estado de Chihuahua.* 2 vols. México, D.F.: Talleres Gráficos de la Nación, 1967.

———. *Vida, proceso y muerte de Abraham González*. México, D.F.: Talleres Gráficos de la Nación, 1967.

Atwater, Elton. *American Regulation of Arms Exports*. Washington, D.C.: Carnegie Endowment for International Peace, 1941.

Ball, Larry D. *Elfego Baca in Life and Legend*. El Paso: Texas Western Press, 1992.

Banyai, Richard A. *Money and Finance in Mexico during the Constitutionalist Revolution, 1913–1917*. Taipei: Tai Wan Enterprises, 1976.

Beezley, William H. *Insurgent Governor: Abraham González and the Mexican Revolution in Chihuahua*. Lincoln: University of Nebraska Press, 1973.

Blaisdell, Lowell L. *The Desert Revolution: Baja California, 1911*. Madison: University of Wisconsin Press, 1962.

Blumenson, Martin, ed. *The Patton Papers: 1885–1940*. Boston: Houghton Mifflin, 1972.

Broaddus, J. Morgan. *The Legal Heritage of El Paso*. El Paso: Texas Western Press, 1963.

Burnham, Frederick Russell. *Scouting on Two Continents*. Garden City, N.Y.: Garden City Publishing, 1926.

———. *Taking Chances*. Los Angeles: Haynes Corporation, 1944.

Bush, I. J. *Gringo Doctor*. Caldwell, Idaho: Caxton Printers, 1939.

Butt, Archibald. *Taft and Roosevelt: The Intimate Letters of Archie Butt, Military Aide*. 2 vols. Port Washington, N.Y.: Kennikat Press, 1971.

Carman, Michael Dennis. *United States Customs and the Madero Revolution*. El Paso: Texas Western Press, 1976.

Cervantes, Federico. *Felipe Angeles en la Revolución: Biografía (1869–1919)*. 3rd ed. México, D.F.: n.p., 1964.

Chalkley, John F. *Zach Lamar Cobb: El Paso Collector of Customs and Intelligence During the Mexican Revolution, 1913–1918*. El Paso: Texas Western Press, 1998.

Clendenen, Clarence C. *Blood on the Border: The United States Army and the Mexican Irregulars*. London: Macmillan, 1969.

Downs, Mike. *The Adventurers' Golden Jubilee, 1964: A History of the Adventurers' Club of New York. . . .* New York: The Adventurers' Club Inc. of New York, 1965.

Du Toit, Brian M. *Boer Settlers in the Southwest*. El Paso: Texas Western Press, 1995.

El Paso: A Centennial Portrait. El Paso, Tex.: El Paso County Historical Society, 1972.

El Paso City Directory, 1920. El Paso, Tex.: Hudspeth Directory Co., 1920.

Eppinga, Jane. *Henry Ossian Flipper: West Point's First Black Graduate*. Austin: Republic of Texas Press, 1996.

Fabela, Isidro, et al., eds. *Documentos históricos de la Revolución Mexicana*. 28 vols. México, D.F.: Editorial Jus, 1960–76.

Fierman, Floyd S. "Insights and Hindsights of Some El Paso Jewish Families." *El Paso Jewish Historical Review* 1, no. 2 (1983): Entire issue.

———. *The Schwartz Family of El Paso: The Story of a Pioneer Jewish Family in the Southwest*. El Paso: Texas Western Press, 1980.

Flint, Charles R. *Memories of an Active Life: Men and Ships and Sealing Wax.* New York: Putnam, 1923.

Fuentes Mares, José. . . . *Y México se refugió en el desierto: Luis Terrazas, historia y destino.* México, D.F.: Editorial Jus, 1954.

Furlong, Thomas. *Fifty Years a Detective.* St. Louis: C. E. Barnett, 1912.

Garibaldi, Giuseppe. *A Toast to Rebellion.* Garden City, N.Y.: Garden City Publishing, 1935.

Grieb, Kenneth J. *The United States and Huerta.* Lincoln: University of Nebraska Press, 1969.

Hammond, John Hays. *The Autobiography of John Hays Hammond.* 2 vols. New York: Arno Press, 1974.

Harris, Charles H. III, and Louis R. Sadler. *Bastion on the Border: Fort Bliss, 1854–1943.* Historic and Natural Resources Report no. 6. Fort Bliss, Tex.: Cultural Resources Management Branch, Directorate of Environment, United States Army Air Defense Artillery Center, 1993.

———. *The Border and the Revolution: Clandestine Activities of the Mexican Revolution, 1910–1920.* 2nd ed. Silver City, N.Mex.: High-Lonesome Books, 1990.

———. *The Texas Rangers and the Mexican Revolution.* Albuquerque: University of New Mexico Press, 2004.

Hart, John Mason. *Empire and Revolution: The Americans in Mexico since the Civil War.* Berkeley: University of California Press, 2002.

Henderson, Peter V. N. *In the Absence of Don Porfirio: Francisco León de la Barra and the Mexican Revolution.* Wilmington, Del.: Scholarly Resources, 2000.

———. *Mexican Exiles in the Borderlands, 1910–1913.* El Paso: Texas Western Press, 1979.

Justice, Glenn. *Little Known History of the Texas Big Bend: Documented Chronicles from Cabeza de Vaca to the Era of Pancho Villa.* 2nd ed. Odessa, Tex.: Rimrock Press, 2001.

Katz, Friedrich. *The Life and Times of Pancho Villa.* Stanford, Calif.: Stanford University Press, 1998.

Kerig, Dorothy Pierson. *Luther T. Ellsworth: U.S. Consul on the Border During the Mexican Revolution.* El Paso: Texas Western Press, 1975.

Kruger, Rayne. *Good-Bye Dolly Gray: The Story of the Boer War.* New York: Lippincott, 1960.

Landau, Henry. *The Enemy Within: The Inside Story of German Sabotage in America.* New York: Putnam, 1937.

Leonard, Edward A. *Rails at the Pass of the North.* El Paso: Texas Western Press, 1981.

Liebson, Art. *Sam Dreben: The "Fighting Jew."* Tucson, Ariz.: Westernlore Press, 1996.

Liceaga, Luis. *Félix Díaz.* México, D.F.: Editorial Jus, 1958.

Link, Arthur S., ed. *The Papers of Woodrow Wilson.* 69 vols. Princeton, N.J.: Princeton University Press, 1966–94.

Liss, Sheldon B. *A Century of Disagreement: The Chamizal Conflict, 1864–1964.* Washington, D.C.: University Press of Washington, D.C., 1965.

Lorey, David, ed. *United States-Mexican Border Statistics since 1900.* Los Angeles: UCLA Latin American Center Publications, 1990.

MacLachlan, Colin M. *Anarchism and the Mexican Revolution: The Political Trials of Ricardo Flores Magón in the United States.* Berkeley: University of California Press, 1991.

Mahoney, Harry Thayer, and Marjorie Locke Mahoney. *Espionage in Mexico: The 20th Century.* San Francisco: Austin and Winfield, 1997.

Martínez, Oscar J. *Border Boom Town: Ciudad Juárez since 1848.* Austin: University of Texas Press, 1978.

Martínez Núñez, Eugenio. *Juan Sarabia, apóstol y mártir de la Revolución Mexicana.* México, D.F.: Talleres Gráficos de la Nación, 1965.

Mason, Herbert Molloy, Jr. *The Great Pursuit.* New York: Random House, 1970.

McCreary, Guy Weddington. *From Glory to Oblivion: The Real Truth About the Mexican Revolution.* New York: Vantage Press, 1974.

McNeely, John H. *The Railways of Mexico: A Study in Nationalization.* El Paso: Texas Western College Press, 1964.

Meed, Douglas V. *Soldier of Fortune: Adventuring in Latin America and Mexico with Emil Lewis Holmdahl.* Houston: Halcyon Press, 2003.

Meléndez, A. Gabriel. *Spanish-Language Newspapers in New Mexico, 1834–1958.* Tucson: University of Arizona Press, 2005.

Metz, Leon C. *Dallas Stoudenmire: El Paso Marshal.* Norman: University of Oklahoma Press, 1993.

———. *John Wesley Hardin: Dark Angel of Texas.* Norman: University of Oklahoma Press, 1998.

Meyer, Michael C. *Huerta: A Political Portrait.* Lincoln: University of Nebraska Press, 1972.

———. *Mexican Rebel: Pascual Orozco and the Mexican Revolution, 1910–1915.* Lincoln: University of Nebraska Press, 1967.

Middagh, John. *Frontier Newspaper: The "El Paso Times."* El Paso: Texas Western Press, 1958.

Morales, Fred. *Córdova Island.* El Paso, Tex.: El Paso/Juárez Historical Museum, 2002.

———. *Francisco Villa.* El Paso, Tex.: El Paso/Juárez Historical Museum, 2006.

———. *The Mexican Revolution Trail of El Paso and Juárez.* El Paso, Tex.: El Paso/Juárez Historical Museum, 2003.

———. *Smeltertown.* El Paso, Tex.: El Paso/Juárez Historical Museum, 2004.

Niemeyer, E. V., Jr. *El General Bernardo Reyes.* Trans. Juan Antonio Ayala. Monterrey, Mex.: Universidad de Nuevo León, 1966.

Obregón, Alvaro. *Ocho mil kilómetros en campaña.* 3rd ed. México, D.F.: Fondo de Cultura Económica, 1960.

O'Reilly, Edward S. *Roving and Fighting: Adventure under Four Flags.* New York: Century, 1918.

Ortiz Rubio, Pascual. *La Revolución de 1910: Apuntes históricos.* 2nd ed. México, D.F.: Ediciones Botas, 1937.

Packenham, Thomas. *The Boer War.* New York: Random House, 1979.

Pringle, Henry F. *The Life and Times of William Howard Taft: A Biography.* 2 vols. New York: Farrar and Rinehart, 1939.

Raat, W. Dirk. *Revoltosos: Mexican Rebels in the United States, 1903–1923.* College Station: Texas A&M University Press, 1981.

Richmond, Douglas W. *Venustiano Carranza's Nationalist Struggle, 1893–1920.* Lincoln: University of Nebraska Press, 1983.

Romo, David Dorado. *Ringside Seat to a Revolution: An Underground Cultural History of El Paso and Juárez, 1893–1923.* El Paso, Tex.: Cinco Puntos Press, 2005.

Sánchez Azcona, Juan. *Apuntes para la historia de la Revolución Mexicana.* México, D.F.: Talleres Gráficos de la Nación, 1961.

Sánchez Lamego, Miguel A. *Historia militar de la Revolución Constitucionalista.* 5 vols. México, D.F.: Talleres Gráficos de la Nación, 1956–60.

Sax, Antimaco. *Los mexicanos en el destierro.* San Antonio, Tex.: International Printing, 1916.

Schuster, Ernst Otto. *Pancho Villa's Shadow: The True Story of Mexico's Robin Hood As Told by His Interpreter.* New York: Exposition Press, [1947].

Siller, Pedro, and Miguel Angel Berumen. *1911: La batalla de Ciudad Juárez.* El Paso, Tex.: Berumen y Muñoz Editores, 2003.

Sonnichsen, C. L. *Pass of the North: Four Centuries on the Rio Grande.* El Paso: Texas Western Press, 1968.

Stoker, Donald J., Jr., and Jonathan A. Grant, eds. *Girding for Battle: The Arms Trade in a Global Perspective, 1815–1940.* Westport, Conn.: Praeger, 2003.

Taylor, Lawrence. *La gran aventura en México: El papel de los voluntarios extranjeros en los ejercitos revolucionarios mexicanos, 1910–1915.* 2 vols. México, D.F.: Consejo Nacional Para la Cultura y las Artes, 1993.

Thomas, Lowell. *Born to Raise Hell: The Life Story of Tex O'Reilly, Soldier of Fortune, As Told to Lowell Thomas.* Garden City, N.Y.: Doubleday, Doran, 1936.

Thord-Gray, Ivor. *Gringo Rebel: Mexico, 1913–1914.* Coral Gables, Fla.: University of Miami Press, 1960.

Timmons, W. H. *El Paso: A Borderlands History.* El Paso: Texas Western Press, 1990.

Tinker, Edward Laroque. *New Yorker Unlimited: The Memoirs of Edward Laroque Tinker.* Austin: University of Texas Press and the Encino Press, 1970.

Tompkins, Frank. *Chasing Villa: The Last Campaign of the U.S. Cavalry.* 2nd ed. Silver City, N.Mex.: High-Lonesome Books, 1996.

Trew, Peter. *The Boer War Generals.* N.p.: Wrens Park Publishing, 2001.

Tuchman, Barbara W. *The Zimmermann Telegram.* New York: Viking Press, 1958.

Turner, Timothy. *Bullets, Bottles, and Gardenias.* Dallas, Tex.: South-West Press, 1935.

Ulloa, Berta, comp. *Revolución Mexicana, 1910–1920.* 2nd ed. México, D.F.: Secretaría de Relaciones Exteriores, 1985.

Vanderwood, Paul J. *The Power of God Against the Guns of Government.* Stanford, Calif.: Stanford University Press, 1998.

Vasconcelos, José. *La tormenta.* 7th ed. México, D.F.: Ediciones Botas, 1948.

———. *Ulises criollo: La vida del autor escrita por él mismo.* 9th ed. México, D.F.: Ediciones Botas, 1945.

Vázquez Gómez, Francisco. *Memorias políticas.* México, D.F.: Imprenta Mundial, 1933.

Viljoen, Benjamin J. *An Exiled General.* St. Louis: Noble, 1904.

———. *My Reminiscences of the Anglo-Boer War.* London: Hood, Douglas and Howard, 1903.

Von Rintelen, Franz. *The Dark Invader: Wartime Reminiscences of a German Naval Intelligence Officer*. London: Peter Davies, 1933.

Voska, Emanuel Victor. *Spy and Counterspy*. New York: Doubleday, 1940.

Welsome, Eileen. *The General and the Jaguar: Pershing's Hunt for Pancho Villa*. New York: Little, Brown, 2006.

Wilkie, Don, as told to Mark Lee Luther. *American Secret Service Agent*. New York: Burt, 1934.

Wilson, M. Huntington. *Memoirs of an Ex-Diplomat*. Boston: Humphries, 1945.

Womack, John, Jr. *Zapata and the Mexican Revolution*. New York: Knopf, 1969.

Worley's Directory of El Paso, Texas, 1915. Dallas, Tex.: John F. Worley Directory Co., 1915.

Articles

Almada, Francisco R. "La entrevista Díaz-Taft." *Boletín de la Sociedad Chihuahuense de Estudios Históricos* IX, no. 6 (1955): 862–64.

Barrera Bassols, Jacinto. "El espionaje en la frontera México-Estados Unidos (1905–1911)." *Eslabones: Revista Semestral de Estudios Regionales* 2, no. 2 (1991): 23–28.

Blaisdell, Lowell L. "Harry Chandler and Mexican Border Intrigue, 1914–1917." *Pacific Historical Review* 35, no. 4 (1966): 385–93.

Burks, James. "Colonel James C. Bulger." *The Recount* vol. 5, no. 1 [1960?].

Crawford, Charlotte. "The Border Meeting of Presidents Taft and Diaz." *Password* 3, no. 3 (1958): 86–96.

Crippen, Robert Bruce. "Celebration on the Border: The Taft-Diaz Meeting, 1909." *Password* 29, no. 3 (1984): 114–22.

Cumberland, Charles C. "The Sonora Chinese and the Mexican Revolution." *Hispanic American Historical Review* 40, no. 2 (1960): 191–211.

De Wetter, Mardee Belding. "Revolutionary El Paso: 1910–1917." *Password* 3, no. 2 (1958): 46–59, no. 3 (1958): 107–19, no. 4 (1958): 145–58.

"Elfego Baca vs. The 80 Cowboys." *Albuquerque Journal*, October 8, 2000.

Estrada, Richard. "The Mexican Revolution in the Ciudad Juárez-El Paso Area, 1910–1920." *Password* 24, no. 2 (1979): 55–69.

Gómez-Quiñones, Juan. "Piedras contra la Luna, México en Aztlán y Aztlán en México: Chicano-Mexican Relations and the Mexican Consulates, 1900–1920." In *Contemporary Mexico: Papers of the IV International Congress of Mexican History*, edited by James W. Wilkie, Michael C. Meyer, Edna Monzon de Wilkie. Berkeley: University of California Press and México, D.F.: El Colegio de Mexico, 1976.

Grieb, Kenneth J. "Standard Oil and the Financing of the Mexican Revolution." *California Historical Society Quarterly* 49, no. 1 (1970): 59–71.

Harris, Charles H. III, and Louis R. Sadler. "The 1911 Reyes Conspiracy: The Texas Side." *Southwestern Historical Quarterly* 83, no. 4 (1980): 325–48.

———. "Pancho Villa and the Columbus Raid: The Missing Documents." *New Mexico Historical Review* 50, no. 4 (1975): 335–46.

———. "The 'Underside' of the Mexican Revolution: El Paso, 1912." *The Americas* 39, no. 1 (1982): 69–83.

———. "The Witzke Affair: German Intrigue on the Mexican Border, 1917–18." *Military Review* 59, no. 1 (1979): 36–50.

"Intriguers and Mexico." *The Nation*, July 2, 1914.

Jones, Harriet Howze. "Heritage Homes of El Paso: The A. B. Fall House." *Password* 22, no. 3 (1977): 124–26.

———. "Heritage Homes of El Paso: The Krakauer House." *Password* 24, no. 3 (1979): 128–30.

Katz, Friedrich. "El espionaje mexicano en Estados Unidos durante la Revolución." *Eslabones: Revista Semestral de Estudios Regionales* 2, vol. 2 (1991): 8–15.

Lee, Erika. "Enforcing the Borders: Chinese Exclusion along the U.S. Borders with Canada and Mexico, 1882–1924." *The Journal of American History* 89, no. 1 (2002): 54–86.

Lerner Sigal, Victoria. "Espias mexicanos en tierras norteamericanas (1914–1915)." *New Mexico Historical Review* 69, no. 3 (1994): 230–47.

———. "Espionaje y Revolución Mexicana." *Historia Mexicana* 44, no. 4 (1995): 617–42.

McNeely, John H., Jr. "The Mills Building: El Paso Landmark." *Password* 30, no. 4 (1985): 193–96.

Maluy, Dale C. "Boer Colonization in the Southwest." *New Mexico Historical Review* 52, no. 2 (1977): 93–110.

Meyer, Michael C. "The Mexican-German Conspiracy of 1915." *The Americas* 23, no. 1 (1966): 76–89.

———. "Villa, Sommerfeld, Columbus y los alemanes." *Historia Mexicana* 28, no. 4 (1979): 546–66.

Morales, Fred M. "Chihuahuita: A Neglected Corner of El Paso." *Password* 36, no. 1 (1991): 23–34.

Niemeyer, Vic. "Frustrated Invasion: The Revolutionary Attempt of General Bernardo Reyes from San Antonio in 1911." *Southwestern Historical Quarterly* 67, no. 2 (1963): 213–25.

Persico, Joseph E. "The Great Gun Merchant." *American Heritage* 25, no. 5 (1974): 52–55, 89.

Rausch, George J., Jr. "The Exile and Death of Victoriano Huerta." *Hispanic American Historical Review* 42, no. 2 (1962): 133–51.

Skirius, John. "Railroad, Oil and Other Foreign Interests in the Mexican Revolution, 1911–1914." *Journal of Latin American Studies* 35, no. 1 (2003): 25–51.

Smith, Michael M. "Andrés G. García: Venustiano Carranza's Eyes, Ears, and Voice on the Border." *Mexican Studies/Estudios Mexicanos* 23, no. 2 (2007): 355–86.

———. "*Carrancista* Propaganda and the Print Media in the United States: An Overview of Institutions." *The Americas* 52, no. 2 (1995): 155–74.

———. "The Mexican Secret Service in the United States, 1910–1920." *The Americas* 59, no. 1 (2002): 65–85.

Sotos, John G. "Taft and Pickwick: Sleep Apnea in the White House." *Chest: Journal of the American College of Chest Physicians* 124, no. 3 (2003): 1133–42.

Taylor, Lawrence D. "The Border as a Zone of Conflict: Foreign Volunteers in the Mexican Revolution and the Issue of American Neutrality, 1910–1912." *Journal of Borderlands Studies* 20, no. 1 (2005): 91–113.

Taylor Hansen, Lawrence Douglas. "The Chinese Six Companies of San Francisco and the Smuggling of Chinese Immigrants across the U.S.-Mexico Border, 1882–1930." *Journal of the Southwest* 48, no. 1 (2006): 37–61.

———. "The Great Adventure: Mercenaries in the Mexican Revolution, 1910–1915." *The Americas* 43, no. 1 (1986): 25–45.

Timmons, W. H. "Taft-Díaz Meeting." In vol. 6 of *The New Handbook of Texas*, 193. Austin: Texas State Historical Association, 1996.

Uranga, Rodolfo. "Como vivió Francisco Villa desterrado en Estados Unidos." *La Prensa*, December 28, 1930.

Vigil, Ralph H. "Revolution and Confusion: The Peculiar Case of José Inés Salazar." *New Mexico Historical Review* 53, no. 2 (1978): 145–70.

Voliva, John D. "The Guns of Green River Canyon." *Arms Gazette* 3, no. 14 (1976): 12–15.

Walker, Dale L. "Tracy Richardson . . . Machine Gun for Hire." *El Paso Magazine* 4, no. 3 (1973): 6–7, 15.

Wise, Clyde, Jr. "The Effects of the Railroads Upon El Paso." *Password* 5, no. 3 (1960): 91–99.

Theses and Dissertations

Caleca, John Anthony, "The Vásquez [*sic*] Gómez Brothers and Francisco I. Madero: Conflict Within the Mexican Revolution, 1909–1913." MA thesis, University of Nebraska, 1970.

Estrada, Richard. "Border Revolution: The Mexican Revolution in the Ciudad Juárez/El Paso Area, 1906–1915." MA thesis, University of Texas at El Paso, 1975.

Holcombe, Harold Eugene. "United States Arms Control and the Mexican Revolution, 1910–1924." PhD diss., University of Alabama, 1968.

Johnson, David N. "Exiles and Intrigue: Francisco I. Madero and the Mexican Revolutionary Junta in San Antonio, 1910–1911." MA thesis, Trinity University, 1975.

Rausch, George Jay, "Victoriano Huerta: A Political Biography." PhD diss., University of Illinois, 1960.

Trow, Clifford Wayne, "Senator Albert B. Fall and Mexican Affairs, 1912–1921." PhD diss., University of Colorado, 1966.

Newspapers

Douglas Daily International-American

El Paso Daily Times

El Paso Morning Times

El Paso Times

El Paso Herald

El Paso Herald-Post

New York Herald

New York Times

La Prensa

Laredo Weekly Times

San Antonio Light

Interview

Charles H. Harris III and Louis R. Sadler interview with E. "Bud" Flanagan, February 14, 1970.

Internet Web Sites

Burnham, Frederick Russell: http://en.wikipedia.org/wiki/Frederick_Russell_Burnham

Federal Bureau of Investigation: http://www.fbi.gov/libref/historic/history/historicdates.htm

Flint, Charles: http://www03.ibm.com/ibm/history/exhibits/builders/-flint.html

Holmes, George Milton: http://www.ancestry.com (public member tree)

"Victor Ochoa's Biographical Sketch:" http://www.smithsonianeducation.org/seitech/impacto/graphic/victor/man.html

Index

A page number in italic type indicates a figure on that page.

Acosta, José, 333, 336

Adee, Alvey A., 5, 7–8, 10–11

Adventurers' Club, 185, *236*

Agent X ("Equis"), 300, 302

Aguilar, Cándido, 362, 370

Aguirre, Lauro, 18, 19, 20, 24

Aguirre Benavides, Eugenio, 160

Aiken, Peter S., 77–78

Alanís, Lázaro, 61, 125–26, 129, 372

Alderete, Francisco "Frank", 24, 168, 175, 270, 333; arms, munitions, and supplies and, 196, 292

Alderete, Isaac "Ike", 24; death of, 333

Alderete family, 168–69

Alderson, Leona, 309–10

Allison, William Davis "Dave", 208

Almazán, Juan Andreu, 303

Alvarado Mining and Milling Company, 366–68

American Smelting and Refining Company, 25, 349

ammunition. *See* arms, munitions, and supplies

An Exiled General (Viljoen), 43

Angeles, Felipe, *238*, 244–45, 267, 340, 354–55, 365; attack on Juárez and, 353, 362; declining fortunes and death of, 370–71

Archbold, John D., 35

Argüelles, Alfredo, 289–90

arms, munitions, and supplies, 148–49, 153–54, 155–56, 165, 186–88, 240–41, 249–50, 274–75, 288–90, 336; Alderete family and, 240; Columbus expedition and, 183; Constitutionalists and, 148–49; F. Alderete and, 196; F. Villa and, 161–65; Huerta conspirators and, 194–95; J. M. Arriola and, 298; Ratner brothers and, 193; S. Dreben and, 186–87; S. Guaderrama and, 148–49, 187; submarine and, 163; U.S. arms embargo and, 161–62; *villistas* and, 294–95; V. L. Ochoa and, 186. *See also* smuggling

Arnulfo Chávez, U.S. v., 117–18

Arriola, Jesús María, 34, 48, 278, 310, 374; ammunition smuggling and, 298; Andrés García and, 310–11; Bureau of Investigation and, 291; Carranza government intelligence service and, 268–71; dismissal of, 311; G. Holmes and, 303–4; *villistas* and, 300

Arroyo, Abel, 321

Asociación Unionista Mexicana, 356, 357–58, 368

Atkinson, R. F., 121

Aultman, Otis, *236*

Aultman & Dorman Photographic company, 157

Austin, Carlos B., 297

Avila, Fidel, 259, 276

Azopardi, Louis, 195–96

Baca, Elfego, 90–91, 158–60, 260

Badger, J. B., 145, 146

Banda, Manuel, 248, 252, 300

Bannerman, Francis, 32–33, 136–37

Barbrick, John, 100

Barnes, Robert, 251–52, 255, 264, 267; on border incidents, 319; D. Silva and, 257–58; on J. J. Hawley, 299

Bates, Carroll, 339–40

Beckham, Clifford G.: Huerta conspirators and, 195–96, 199–200; P. Orozco and, 208–9

Belden, Samuel, 286, 301

Bell, George, Jr., 251, 255, 261, 290; E. L. Holmdahl and, 285; G. M. Holmes and, 256

Beltrán, Teódulo R., 76

Bengoechea, Cosme, 347

Bennett, J. J., 35–36

Ben Williams Detective Agency, 251

Bielaski, A. Bruce, 205, 255, 297, 320, 329

Blanco, José de la Luz, 58, 60

Blanford, E. M., 128, 138, 143, 167, 180; arms, munitions, and supplies and, 155–56; C. H. Echegaray and, 174–75; F. Villa and, 171

Blanquet, Aureliano, 250, 259, 345, 346–47, 372; death of, 357

Blatt, Edward M., 38

Bonilla, Manuel, 268, 335, 345, 372; Mexican Peace Committee and, 368–69

Bonillas, Ignacio, 374–75

Booker, Lewis, 25–26

Bordes Mangel, Enrique, 268, 273

Borrego Esparza, Ignacio, 298–99

Boyd, H. H., 205–6

Boynton, Charles, 31, 47

Brahn, Benjamin, 276–77

Breniman, Charles E., 120, 256, 285

Brennan, Milt, 281–82, 291

Brown, Frank Wells, 53, *220*

Brown, Richard, 40

Brown, Volney, 161

Brown and Terry, 161

Buchoz, Numa, 109–10

Bulger, James C., 81–82

Bureau of Investigation: on border conditions 1912–13, 130; Columbus raid and, 255; Constitutionalists and, 143, 172; cooperation with *carrancistas* and, 271; Dictaphones and, 258–59, 379; early 1913 and, 131; E. C. Llorente and, 116–17; F. Villa and, 138; German sympathizers and, 277, 294–98; G. M. Holmes and, 279; H. A. Thompson and, 191; H. J. Phillips and, 108; Huerta conspiracy and, 200–203, 205; H. Villa and, 279; investigative techniques and, 379; J. M. Arriola and, 269–70, 291; *magonista* sympathizers and, 58, 60–61; M. E. Diebold and, 172; Mexican counterparts and, 378; Mexican secret service and, 84–86; Military Intelligence and, 263, 271–72, 280–81, 369; M. Mascarenas, Jr. and, 138–39; munitions sales and smuggling and, 289; neutrality laws and, 57, 242; Orozco rebellion and, 73–74; *orozquista* evacuation of Juárez and, 114; S. Dreben and, 100; State Department and, 348; storage of confiscated ammunition and, 143; United Fruit Company and, 156; V. Huerta and, 193–94, 197–98; *villistas* and, 167, 274–76. *See also specific agents and informers*

Burleson, Albert S., 321, 322

Burnham, Frederick Russell, 15–16, *213*

Burns, Juan T., 163

Burns, Waller T., 177–78

Bush, Ira J., 30, 50

Butt, Archibald Willingham, 3–4, 12, 13

Caballero, Crisóforo, 197, 208, 240

Cabney, T. C. (J. Harris), 104, 108

Cáceres, Felipe, 128, 144

Cal Hirsch and Sons, 165, 194–95

Calles, Plutarco Elías, 271, 292

Camacho, Enrique, 65

Camp, J. L., 181, 285

Campa, Emilio P., 70, 100, 107, 122, *235*, 249, 372

Campbell, Tom, 10, 12

Cano, Chico, 207, 308

Caracristi, C. F. Z., 34

Caraveo, Marcelo, 150, 252, 259–60, 346–47, 372; arms purchases and, 249; Carranza government and, 267

Cárdenas, Julio, 262

Carothers, George, 250, 258, 299, 305, 312

carrancistas: *científicos* and, 192–209; smuggling and, 318–19

Carranza, Venustiano, 48, 135, 137; agents in the U.S. and, 369; *científicos* and, 192–93; F. Murguía and, 344; F. Villa and, 181; Punitive Expedition and, 262–63; racism and, 184; United States and, 242–43, 337

Carranza government intelligence service, 268–71

Carusso, Victor, 165, 240–41, 253, 291–92, 332; *legalistas* and, 268

Casas Grandes, battle of, 40–41

Casillas, Martín, 38

Casso López, Arnaldo, 346, 357

Castillo Brito, Máximo, 154–56

Castro, Jesús Agustín, 344–45, 349–50

Cervantes, Federico, 345, 356, 359–61

Cesaretti, Pascual, 338, 340

Chamizal, 4–5, 7–10

Chao, Manuel, 301

Chapa, Francisco A., 63

Charpentier, Emile L., 40, 49, 55, 59, 60–62, 64, 78; E. C. Llorente and, 115–16

Christmas, Lee, 99

científicos, 55, 62; *carrancistas and*, 192–209; *magonistas* and, 59

Cobb, Zach Lamar, 6, 188, 198–99, 207, 290; D. Silva and, 258; F. Villa and, 241–42; on G. Holmes, 303–4; on M. Medinaveitia, 250. *See also other specific individuals and cases*

Cole, J. Herbert, 47

Collins, James L., 206

Colquitt, Oscar B., 65

Columbus expedition, 179–80, 188–89, 242; *huertistas* and, 183–84; R. H. G. McDonald and, 188

Columbus raid (F. Villa), 250–55

Comadurán, Luis, 278–79

Constitutionalists: arms purchases and, 143–44, 145, 148–49; El Paso junta and, 139; organization of, 135–36

Converse, Lawrence, 38–39, 44; *huertistas* and, 141

Cootes, Harry N., 173

Córdova, José, 124

Corral, Ramón, 27

Corral, Regino, 295

Counts, Carroll M., 341, 351, 370

Crawford, R. E., 309

Crawford, R. H., 323

Creel, Enrique, 12, 13, 22, 259

Creighton, Oscar (James T. Hazzard), 41–42, 46, 52

Cresson, C. C., 175

Crum, Jack R. "Big Dude", 52

Cuéllar, Samuel García, 38, 40–41

Cunningham, Ed B., 35

Cunningham, Thomas Branham, 35, 82, 177

Curry, George, 11–12

Curtis Manning Company, 294

de la Barra, Francisco León, 59–60

de la Vega, José María, 19

De Villiers, Daniel, 53–55, 62–63, 64

Díaz, Félix, 134, 259; *To the Nation*, 250

Díaz, Modesto, 20

Díaz, Porfirio, 1–7, 9–13, 16, *212*, 377; F. Madero and, 28; J. Wilkie and, 14–15; resignation and exile of, 56

Díaz Lombardo, Miguel, 248, 301, 325, 328, 345

Dibrell, John L., 47

Didapp, Juan Pedro, 108, 120, 131

Diebold, Miguel E., 60, 140, 142, 167–70, 172–77; Ysleta expedition and, 168–75

Dorman, Bob, 157, 185, *236*

Douglas Hardware Company, 154

Dowe, R. W., 34

Dreben, Sam, 99–101, 140, 186–87, *222*, *236*, 300; Huerta conspirators and, 195; Punitive Expedition and, 261–62

Dubose, Edwin M., 206

Duncan, General, 22–23

Dunn, Joe, 295

Dunne, William, 53–55

Echegaray, Carlos H., 173–75, 176, 178

Echegaray, Juan N., 280

Edwards, Peyton, 84, 206

Edwards, Thomas D., 6, 56–57

El Eco del Comercio, 109

Elfers, E. D., 287

Elías, Francisco, 148

El Imparcial (Mexico City), 75

El Imparcial de Texas, 63

Elizondo, José, 65–66

El Legalista, 273

Ellis, R. H., 370

Ellsworth, Luther T., 23

El Nacional, 373

El Paso, 377; 1911 events in, 66–67; as "army town", 377; Chihuahuita and, 6, 19, 31; Columbus raid and, 251–52, 254–55; Constitutionalist junta and, 139; Díaz-Taft meeting and, 5–7; economy of, 377; effects of insurrection on, 55; growth and development of, 24–27; influenza pandemic of 1918 and, 332; *maderistas* and, 29–30; *magonistas* and, 17–18, 61, 64; map/drawing of, *210–11*; Mexican government spies in, 75; military presence in, 1916, 283–84; munitions export and, 71; rebel activity in, 18; *reyistas and*, 64; tensions in June, 1916 and, 266–67; *vazquista movement* and, 106; Veracruz, seizure of, and, 176–77. *See also events in Juárez*

El Paso Bank and Trușt Company, 71–72

El Paso del Norte, 251, 254

El Paso Herald, 39–40, 75, 254

El Paso Milling Company, 26–27

El Paso Morning Times, 43, 254, 265

Engelking, S., 30–31

Enos, James, 81

Enrile, Gonzalo C., 83, 98, 250

Erupción Mining Company, 329

Escandón, Governor, 12

Escobar, José Gonzalo, 363, 365, 372

Espinosa, Anastacio, 321–22

Estrada, Agustín, 98

Estrada, Alberto, 108

Estrada, Richard, 19

Everybody's Magazine, 93

Fall, Albert B., 109–10, 251, 300, 373–74; U.S.-Mexican relations and, 354–55

Fargas, César, 325, 342, 370

Farías, Albino, 347

Farías, Rodolfo, 268, 274

Feige, Charles H., 296

felicistas, 179, 345–47, 372; Committee of National Union and, 347; military competence of, 357; *villistas* and, 356

Ferrocarril Noroeste de México (MNW), 26

Fields, Benjamin W., 69

Finley, Ivy, 352–53, 354

Flint, Charles R., 163

Flores, Domingo "El Coyote", 253–54

Flores Magón, Enrique, 17, 23–24

Flores Magón, Jesús, 75

Flores Magón, Ricardo, 17, 20, 22, 44

Folsom, C. S. T., 185, 247, 274

foodstuffs, smuggling of, 318–19

Fornaro, Carlo de, 7

Fort Bliss, 30, 142; ammunition storage and, 169–70. *See also* Military Intelligence

Foster, Thomas, 35

Fountain, Thomas, 78

Fox, Monroe, 253; G. M. Holmes and, 257

Francis Bannerman and Company, 32–33

Fuente, David de la, 70, 110–11, 127, 133, 357, 368; *huertistas* and, 137; Orozco junta and, 126–27

Fuentes, Alberto, 29

Fuller, E. P., 324–25

Funston, Frederick, 263, 276; on ammunition smuggling, 288

Furlong Detective Agency, 35

Gamiochipi, Fernando, 251

García, Andrés, 244, 247, 369; armament purchases and, 240; E. B. Stone and, 276; *El Paso Morning Times* and, 254; J. M. Arriola and, 310–11; *legalistas* and, 274; military intelligence and, 267–68; as refugee, 375; *villistas* and, 245; W. Ibs and, 278

García, Antonio, 49

García, Matías G., 307, 342

García Naranjo, Nemesio, 357–58

Garibaldi, Giuseppe, 42–43, 46, 49, 53, 55, *226*

Garibay, Antonio, 206–7, 209

Garza, Lázaro de la, 163–64, 187–88, 198; *villistas* and, 243–44

Garza Galán, Andrés, 54–55, 137; plot against F. Madero and, 62–63

Gauldin, J. Dean, 321–23

Gavira, Gabriel, 247, 250, 260

George, W. A., 249

Gibbons, Floyd P., 255

Gleaves, William, 296–97

Goldbaum, Louis R., 338

Goldbaum y Padilla, Enrique, 271

Goldstein and Miller, 117

Gómez, Roque, 68, 126, 180, 300

Gómez Morentín, Alfonso, 334–35, 340, 341–42, 360, 365–66

Gómez Robelo, Ricardo, 70, 110, 125, 129, *235*; arrest of, 131; Orozco junta and, 126

González, Abraham, 29–30, 32, 37, 38, 59, 65, 66, 135–36, *226*; Casas Grandes and, 42; L. Converse and, 39; *magonistas* and, 62

González, Francisco, 363; on U.S. troops in Juárez, 365

González, Manuel E., 243

González, Manuel G., 334–35

González, Manuel, Jr., 303, 314, 358–59

González, Pablo, 278–79

González, Santiago, 29, *234*

González Garza, Federico, 47

González Salas, José, 72

Gottwald, Franz, 292–93

Gray, Henry, 166, 249, 271, 306, 369; F. Thayer and, 282; W. Ibs and, 277–78. *See also specific events and cases*

Greer, Wyche, 254

Gresh, Maurice L., 85–86, 118; V. L. Ochoa and, 94–97, 103–5

Grinstead, Robert E., 257, 272, 289–90; Mrs. Lucero and, 261

Guaderrama, Abelino, 91–92; *vazquista movement* and, 112–13

Guaderrama, Jesús, 204

Guaderrama, Sabino, 91–92; arms, munitions, and supplies and, 187; arms smuggling and, 147–48, 160; death of, 249; trial of, 118; *vazquista movement* and, 112–13

Guaderrama brothers, Red Flaggers and, 112

Guerrero, Práxedis G., 18, 23, 24

Gutiérrez de Lara, Lázaro, 24, 61

Gutiérrez-Velarde and Company, 176

Guy, Frederick, 247

Hall, Lee L., 83, 131, 252; Orozco junta and, 125–26; on the *orozquistas*, 128; *vazquista movement* and, 108

Hall, R. L., 167

Hammond, John Hays, 12, 13, 15

Hanson, William M., 34–35, 374

Harrell, Dick N., 351–52, 361

Harrington, R. F., 40

Harris, Hyman, 295

Harrison, Leland, 329

Hart's Mill, battle of, 283–84

Hawes, John J., 298–99, 307

Hayakawa, Lucas G., 264

Haymon Krupp and Company, *231*, 315–16; arms, munitions, and supplies and, 332–33. *See also* Krupp, Haymon

Hazzard, James T. *See* Creighton, Oscar (James T. Hazzard)

Hearst, William Randolph, 299

Heath, Earl, 138

Hebert, C. D., 119–20

Heckelmann, Ben, 353

Hedgson, Lee, 76

Held, Edgar, 80

Henry Mohr Hardware Company, 288–89

Herald, 73

Hernández, Braulio, 39, 67, 107; El Paso junta and, 154

Hernández, J. Evaristo, 109

Hernández, José G., 257

Hernández, Juan, 180

Hernández, Luis H., 35–36

Herrera, Cástulo, 29, 32, 73, 88, 90–91; trial of, 124; V. Ochoa and, 94–96

Herrera, Luis, 289–90

Hill, Benjamín, 183

Hillebrand, H. Richard, 30

Hintze, Paul von, 140

Hitchcock, F. H., 12

Holguín, Epifanio, 329, 331, 372

Holmdahl, Emil Lewis, 127–29, 131, 151, *223*; army enlistment and, 286; Bureau of Investigation and, 247; Constitutionalists and, 141, 144; E. A. Talbot and, 283; F. Villa and, 376; legal action and, 189–90; pardon of, 285–86; Punitive Expedition and, 261–62; trial of, 242; *villistas* and, 167

Holmes, George Milton, 253, 256–57, 327–32; ammunition smuggling and, 274–75, 302–3; Bureau of Investigation and, 279, 343; county jail and, 352–53, 354; death of, 371; E. Jones and, 353; F. Knotts and, 329–31; F. Villa and, 313–14, 327–29; H. Villa and, 274, 275–76; on Miller & Howard, 328; perjury trial and, 371; stolen ammunition and, 351–52; T. F. Jonah and, 272; trial of, 361

Hopkins, Sherburne Gillette, 33, 37, 108, 143; E. L. Holmdahl and, 285; V. Carranza and, 140–41

Hornbrook, James J., 350

Howard, Volney, 307, 320–21, 322–23, 360

Hudspeth, Claude B., 285

Huerta, U.S. v., 286

Huerta, Victoriano, 97–98, 122–23, *233*; arrest of, 203–5; Bureau of Investigation and, 193–94, 197–98; C. G. Beckham and, 199; death of, 247–48; F. Díaz and, 134; Germany and, 193; P. Orozco, Sr. and, 137; P. Orozco and, 192–209; seizure of power and, 135

huertistas: arms purchases and, 146–47; Columbus expedition and, 179–80, 183–84; Juárez and, 136; recruiting and, 179–80; support for, 137, 141–42

Hughes, John R., 6, 15, 66

Hunt, Alice, 300

Hunt, Charles, 300, 346

Huston, Joseph F., 6, 8

Hutchings, Henry, 65

Ibs, William, 277–78

Icaza, Manuel, 358–59

Industrial Workers of the World (IWW), 296

influenza pandemic of 1918, 332

Informant AR, 346, 356, 357, 358, 359, 369. *See also* Rocha, Juan José

insurrectos: Americans and, 39–40; attack on Juárez and, 46–50; El Paso junta and, 29–30; internal divisions and, 51–52; mercenaries and, 40; recruiting and, 44–45; weapons and, 32–33, 37, 45–46

Irwin, James B., 363–64

Iturbide, Rafael, 358–59

Jackson, Dan, 47, 58, 309, 374; *huertistas* and, 196–97

Jahnke, Kurt, 296

Jáuregui, Carlos, 138, 151, 169, 301, 305, 366; bullion smuggling and, 370

Jiménez Castro, Adolfo, 19–20

Jonah, T. F., 272, 274

Jones, Frank C., 324

Jones, Gilford, 79–80

Jones, Gus T. "Buster", *237*, 272, 288–89; on A. García, 327; as agent in charge, 310; on Asociación Unionista Mexicana, 357–58; on *carrancista* smuggling, 319; on C. Fargas, 370; on G. Holmes, 329, 362; G. Holmes and, 315; on H. Miller and C. Fargas, 342; on H. Villa, 368; H. Villa and, 312; intelligence gathering and, 335; on J. M. Arriola, 298; on J. Sedaño, 324, 326; on the Mexican Secret Service, 335–36; on Miller & Howard, 326; on trial of G. Holmes, 361; on V. Howard, 320, 321; on *villistas*, 314. *See also specific events and cases*

Juárez: Carranza government and, 245–46; F. Villa attack on, 362–64; *huertistas* and, 136; *insurrecto* attack on, 46–50; looting in, 52; mutiny in, 67; *orozquista* evacuation of, 114; post-revolutionary unrest in, 59–60; Red Flaggers and, 97

Kelly, C. E., 6, 47, 51, 53, 84

Kerr, Alfred H., 72, 144, 253

Kilpatrick, Dawson D., 308, 315

Kingsberry, Tom, 308–9

Knotts, Frank, 329–31

Knotts, T. H., 331

Knox, Philander C., 4, 5, 9; E. C. Llorente and, 117

Krakauer, Adolph, 6, 87, *220*, 373

Krakauer, Robert, 373; on ammunition smuggling, 288

Krakauer, Zork and Moye, 25, 39, 71–72, 80–81, *229*; Huerta regime and, 136–37; *orozquistas* and, 87–88; Red Flaggers and, 73; trial of, 153–54; *vazquista movement* and, 111

Kramp, Henry C., 37, 58, 60, 131, 190–91, 244; H. Ramos and, 166

Krupp, Haymon, 165, 194–95, 240, 253, 298, 315–16; F. Villa and, 332; H. Villa and, 306

Kyriacopulos, Teodoro, 32, 138, 161, 169, 341, 343; arms traffic and, 240, 291–92; bullion smuggling and, 370; F. Villa and, 254; H. Villa and, 298, 305; J. Sedaño and, 338

La Constitución, 251

Lancaster, Fred H., 47, 51, 53, 269

Langhorne, George, 323, 340; on smuggling, 326

Lansing, Robert, 242

La Opinion Pública, 90

La Patria, 355

La Reforma Social, 18

Larrazolo, Juan B., 106, 252

Laubach, Major, 258–59

Lawrence, David, 55

Lawrence, J. J., 270

Lea, Abraham A. "Kid", 79–80

Lea, Thomas C., Jr., 85, 90–91, 115–16, *224*, 261; arms traffic and, 240; Columbus raid and, 251; E. L. Holmdahl and, 285; *huertistas* and, 196–97; *Morning Times* and, 254; V. Huerta and, 200, 204; *villistas* and, 301

legalistas, 268; Juárez area and, 272–73; *villistas* and, 276

legal profession, 320–23

León de la Barra, Francisco, 56, 259

Lessing, Gunther, 47, 182–83, 186, 190–91

Lewis, A. W., 37, 40, 44, 45–46

Lewis, H. B., 261

Liceaga, Fernando, 358–59

Limantour, José Yves, 259

Limón, Roberto, 103, 105

Limón Molina, Rafael, 65, 66

Linderfelt, K. E., 52

Llewellyn, W. H. H., 47

Llorente, Enrique C., 66, 77–78, 99, 132, 147; 1899 extradition treaty and., 79; arrest of, 148; Carranza government and, 267; Constitutionalists and, 140; *huertistas* and, 196; Mexican Central railroad and, 78–79; neutrality laws and, 115–17, 177–78; V. L. Ochoa and, 186; weapons and ammunition purchases and, 74

Lomelí, Antonio, 6, 32, 34

López, Felipe S., 124–25

López, Francisco, 351–52, 354

López, Martín, 349, 372

Los Angeles Times, 38–39

Loya, Raul, 279

Luján, Abraham, 291; *legalistas* and, 268

Luna, José de, 302–3, 304

Madera Company, 26

maderistas, 30; Bureau of Investigation and, 115; C. F. Z. Caracristi and, 34; H. J. Phillips and, 33; *orozquistas* versus, El Paso press and, 73; recruiting of Americans and, 80; smuggling and, 72–73. *See also insurrectos*

Madero, Alberto, 260–61, 282

Madero, Alfonso, 35

Madero, Francisco I., 40–41, 51, *217*; attack on Juárez and, 48; De Villiers-Dunne plot and, 53–55; discontent and, 58–59; El Paso organization and, 29–30, 33–34; El Paso society and, 53; in Guadalupe, 37; P. Díaz and, 28; on Pineda plot, 54–55; *Plan de San Luis Potosí*, 28; presidential election and, 56; Standard Oil Company and, 36

Madero, Gustavo, 32, 51, 53, 56

Madero, Raul, 53

Madero family dinner party, *220*

Madero government, El Paso and, 74–75

Madison, John M. "Dynamite Slim", 40, 59

Magoffin, Joseph, 6

magonistas, 57–58, 377–78; in Baja California, 57; El Paso and, 17–18, 61. *See also* Partido Liberal Mexicano (PLM)

Mahoney, D. J., 40, 78, 177

Malan, Jack, 44, 55

Mallén, Francisco, 20, 22

Manrique, Francisco, 23–24

Margáin, Alfredo, 172–73

Mariscal, Ignacio, 11

Mármol, F., 175

Martin, Roy, 305

Martínez, Félix, 6

Martínez, José, 83

Martínez, Macrino J., 302, 311, 345

Martínez, Paulino, 70, 109, *235*

Mascarenas, Manuel, Jr., 106–7, 138–39

Mason, Paul, 40, 64, 141

Maurer, Ed, 32–33, 37, 45, 137, 143

Maxey, T. S., 117–18, 127, 132–33

Mayer, Jesse L., 333–34

Maytorena, José María, 140, 245

Maza, Antonio, 21

McClammy, J. Todd, 64, 154–55, 166, *221*, 260–61, 366–68; D. Silva and, 256; F. Villa and, 300; in Valentine, 308; Ysleta expedition and, 168

McCloskey, James Henry, 34

McDonald, R. H. G., 40, 52, 78, 141, 177, 182, 188–89; E. C. Llorente and, 132

McGinnis, John, 90–91

McGinty cannon, 46, 60

McQuatters, A. J., 366–68

Mebus, Ed W., 85–86, 263

Medina, Juan, 261, 301

Medina Barrón, Luis, 193

Medinaveitia, Manuel, 244, 248, 250, 252, 300

Meléndez, Manuel, 126

Mendenhall, Fred, 182, 190, 242

Mercado, Salvador, 157

Mexican Liberal Alliance, 345, 354–56, 360, 368; membership of, 355; *Plan de Rio Florida and,* 355

Mexican Peace Committee, 368

Mexican secret service, 280–81, 310; A. Molina and, 82; Bureau of Investigation and, 84; J. M. Arriola and, 268–70, 280; M. E. Diebold and, 142; W. P. Roberts and, 83. *See also specific agents and informers*

México Libre, 176

Mexico Mine and Investment Company, 96–97

Military Intelligence, 253, 276, 369; Bureau of Investigation and, 263, 271–72, 276, 280–81; munitions sales and smuggling and, 289–90

Miller, Frank, 351–52, 353, 361

Miller, Harry C., 320, 321, 322, 323–24, 325, 339; bullion smuggling and, 370; falling out with the *villistas* and, 341–42; guano and, 339–40; J. D. Gauldin and, 339

Minahan, John H., 351–52, 361

Minck, Charles E., 269–71

Miranda, Fausto, 357

Miranda, Prudencio, 291

Mock, H. B., 276

Mohr, Henry, 91, 270–71; munitions sales and smuggling and, 288–89

Mohr, Henry, Mrs., 291–92

Molina, Abraham, 62, 63–64, 66, 81–82, 83–84; bogus ammunition and, 91; Constitutionalists and, 140; H. Ramos and, 166–67; J. E. Hernández and, 109; as *maderista intelligence chief*, 80–81; *vazquista movement* and, 106, 108; on V. Huerta, 123

Mondragón, Manuel, 259

money, movements of, 298

Montaño, Juan, 345–46, 372

Moore, C. R., 16, *213*

Morales, José, 179

Morales Guevara, Jesús, 73, 116

Moreno Cantón, Delio, *232*

Morine, John A., 208–9

Morning Times, 73

Moya, Cesar, 279

Moye, Max, 39. *See also* Krakauer, Zork and Moye

Murguía, Francisco, 277, 300, 316, 335; F. Villa and, 316–17, 344; in Villa Ahumada, 344

Murguía, José C., 317, 347

Múzquiz, Rafael E., 185

Myer, Albert L., 7, 8

Myles, Homan C., 179

National Alliance (Alianza Nacionalista), 357

Navarro, Juan F., 46, 47, 51–52

Neunhoffer, William, 269

Neville, John, 131

Nieto, Carlos A., 368

Noonan, J. H. "Jack", 78, 131, 141, 177

Obregón, Alvaro, 122, 245–46, 262–63, 375; Comadurán, Luis, 278–79; F. Villa and, 241; *Plan de Agua Prieta* and, 375

Ochoa, Eduardo, 90, 94

Ochoa, Elías, 314–15

Ochoa, Inocente, 19

Ochoa, Manuel, 300, 303

Ochoa, Victor Leaton, 92–97, 103–5, *225*; A. Molina and, 96; arms, munitions, and supplies and, 205–6; arrest of, 182–84; Bureau of Investigation and, 247; *carrancistas and*, 181–82, 185–86, 192; C. H. Echegaray and, 173–74; C. Herrera and, 94–96, 103; Constitutionalist junta and, 139; death of, 287; H. Ramos and, 182; *huertistas* and, 141; imprisonment of, 287; legal action and, 189–90; *legalistas* and, 274; M. E. Diebold and, 169; M. L. Gresh and, 96–97; narcotics and, 287; P. Orozco and, 97; R. Limón and, 103; trial of, 242; *vazquista movement* and, 106

Ojinaga: battle of, 29, 81; C. Cano and, 308; F. Villa and, 155–57, 313; *maderistas* and, 123; P. Orozco and, 122, 197–98

Oliver, George B., 38, 132, 191

O'Reilly, Edward S. "Tex", 40, 81, *222*, *236*

Ornelas, Tomás, 206, 244

Orozco, Jorge, 182, 184, 242

Orozco, José, 170, 182, 242, 249, 286–87

Orozco, Pascual, 30, 37–38, 40, 47, 59, 60, 65, 68, 122, *221*; attack on Chihuahua and, 150; Bureau of Investigation and, 47; C. G. Beckham and, 199–200; Chihuahua rebels and, 70–71; conspiracy against F. Madero and, 54–55; death of, 208–9; defeat at Juárez and, 97–98; escape from captivity and, 202–3; F. Villa's ascendancy and, 157; Huerta conspirators and, 197; *huertistas* and, 137, 179; *insurrecto* attack on Juárez and, 48–50; junta and, 125–27; V. Huerta and, 192–209; Ysleta expedition and, 173–74

Orozco, Pascual, Mrs., 240

Orozco, Pascual, Sr., 123–24, 125, 127, 137, *232*

orozquistas: battle of Rellano and, 72; Juárez evacuation and, 114; United States and, 72

Orpinel, Blas, 168

Orr, O. L., 313

Ortiz, Andrés, 349–50

Osterveen, Adolfo, Jr., 291

Otis, Harrison Gray, 38–39

Padres, Gustavo, 145

Parra, Juan, 128

Partido Liberal Mexicano (PLM), 17, 20; handicaps and, 18–19; organization of, 19, 23–24; P. Díaz's responses to, 19–20; plans of, 19, 23; raids by, 23; U.S. government and, 22–23, 24; U.S. neutrality laws and, 18; village of Palomas and, 24

Paso del Norte Hotel, 73

Patton, George, 262

Payne, D. M., 33, 37

Paz, Octavio, 332

Pearson, Frederick Stark, 26, 27, 66

Pearson Company, 68

Pearson-Farquar syndicate, 26, 66

Peláez, Manuel, 372

pencil pistol, 16, *214*

Pérez, Evaristo, 357

Pérez, Francisco, 108

Perkins, Clifford C., 304–5

Pershing, John J., 187, 192, 206–7; E. L. Holmdahl and, 285; G. M. Holmes and, 256; Punitive Expedition and, 251

Pesqueira, Ignacio, 141

Pesqueira, Roberto V., 298

Peterson/Petersen, Ed, 318

Phillips, Harvey J. (Frank Cody), 33, 37, 108

Phillips, William, 4, 8

Pinckney, Steve, 192–93; D. Silva and, 257; J. Delgado and, 201; P. Orozco and, 201–5. *See also specific events and cases*

Pineda, Rosendo, 54–55, 126

Plan de San Diego, 263

Ponce, Demetrio, 70

Ponce, Lino, 70

Popular Dry Goods Company, 333–34

Portillo, Enrique, 70, 126, 150

Prida, Ramon, 254, 358

Punitive Expedition, 251; Carrizal clash and, 266; U.S.-Mexican relations and, 262–63; withdrawal of, 291

Quevedo, Rodrigo, 126, 170, 179, 180, 300, 372

Quevedo, Silvestre, 179, 180, *235*

Quiroga, Manuel, 63

Raat, Dirk, 19, 28

Ramos, Héctor, 165–66, 178, 180, 204, 244; *carrancistas and*, 182; Ysleta expedition and, 168

Rangel, Israel, 113

Rangel, José M., 60

Ratner, Abraham, 193

Ratner, José B., 193

Ravel, Joe, 147

Red Flaggers, 71, 73; ammunition smuggling and, 88–90; secret agents of, 73

Reeder, J. D., 287, 314

Regeneración, 17, 60

Rellano, 72, 97–98

revolutionary activities, monitoring of, 294

Reyes, Bernardo, 63, 65–66, 134

Reyes, Zeferino, 19–20

Reyes Vázquez, Canuto, 302, 311. *See also* Agent X ("Equis")

reyistas, 63; in El Paso, 64; U.S. government and, 65

Rice, Sedgwick, 112

Richardson, Tracy, 99–100, 101–3, 148, 157, *222*

Richmond, Douglas, 184

Rivera, Librado, 18

Robert, Julius, and Adolph Krakauer, Cástulo Herrera, and Victor Ochoa, United States v., 132

Roberts, John W., 206

Roberts, Powell W., 79, 83, 131, 145; H. Ramos and, 166

Rocha, Juan José, 337, 346–47, 356; Asociación Unionista Mexicana and, 357; G. M. Holmes and, 358–59

Rochín, José, 301

Rogers, John H., 15

Rojas, Antonio, 67–68, 70, 109, 133, *228*; attack on Chihuahua and, 150

Roosevelt, Theodore, 2

Root, Elihu, 2

Ross, Louis E., 37, 57, 62, 63–64, 73–74, 82–86; ammunition smuggling and, 84–86; A. Molina and, 82–83; C. H. Webster and, 120; on cooperation from other agencies, 89–90; E. C. Llorente and, 117, 120–21; F. Sommerfeld and, 79; Guaderrama brothers and, 112–13; J. E. Hernández and, 109; J. Morales Guevara and, 116; *maderista* recruiting and, 79–80; munitions sales and smuggling and, 119–22; Orozco junta and, 127; P. Roberts and, 79, 83–84; S. Dreben and, 101; on Thiel Detective Service, 58; trial of, 121–22; V. L. Ochoa and, 103, 104–5; Western Detective Agency and, 121. *See also specific events and cases*

Rothman, Joseph, 100

Rueda, Policarpo, 108

Ruiz Cortines, Adolfo, 372

Runyon, Damon, 255

Saddler, R. E., 300

Saenz, José S., 106–10, 123, 125, 126

Sage, Russell, Mrs., 256

Salazar, José Inés, 24, 44, 64, 70, 122, 129, 133, 172, *235*, 378; arrest and trials of, 157–60; attack on Chihuahua and, 150; *carrancistas and*, 260; death of, 308–9; in El Paso, 1913, 144; F. Villa and, 275; *huertistas* and, 137; imprisonment of, 273; interrogation of, 207–8; V. L. Ochoa and, 186

Saldaña, F. de J., 172–73, 175, 178

Sánchez, Amador, 137

Sánchez Azcona, Juan, 34

Sandoval, Flavio, 36, 104–5

Santa Isabel massacre, 247–48

Sarabia, Juan, 18, 21–22

Schmid, Catherine, 318

Schuster, Bernard, 109–10

Schwartz, Adolph, 333–34

Schwartz, Maurice, 334

Scott, Hugh L., 263, 272

Sedaño, José, 320–21, 323–25, 326–27; death of, 338–39

Seibel, Bruno, 306

Seibel, John, 295–96

Seijas, Felipe, 173

Shallenberger, Lieutenant, 250

Sheldon Hotel, 31, 71, 73, *218–19*; Orozco and, 47

Shelton, W. H., 33, 145, 154, 341; Bureau of Investigation and, 288; F. Villa and, 162

Shelton-Payne Arms Company, 33, 37, 39, 55, 80–81, *230*; Constitutionalists and, 145–46; Huerta regime and, 136–37; *maderistas* and, 87; trial of, 153–54; *vazquista movement* and, 111–12

Sheppard, Morris, 285

Sierra, E. de la, 167, 175, 178; arrest of, 172–73

Silva, Darío, 255–57, 301–2

Silva, Prisciliano G., 18, 23, 61

Silva, Rubén, 61

Silva de Villa, Mabel, 358

Silver, James, 33

Sitler, Floyd S., 91

Sloan, Richard E., 11

Slocum, Herbert, 256

Smith, J. V., 35–36, 47

Smith, William Alden, 110

Smith, William "Australian Billy", 32, 34, 44, 54, 256

Smith, W. R., 3

smuggling, 31–32, 45–46, 89–90, 339, 373, 379; J. M. Arriola and, 298; L. Ross and, 84–86, 91; railroad employees and, 88; Red Flaggers and, 88–90; S. Guaderrama and, 147–48. *See also* arms, munitions, and supplies

Snowball, Luis J., 131

Snyder, Virgil L., 85–86, 100–101

Solanos, José E., 263

Solomon, T. M., 164

Sommerfeld, Felix, 53, 75–77, 85, 99, 148, *217*, 279; arms purchases and, 143, 156; Constitutionalists and, 139–40; Huerta conspirators and, 195; neutrality laws and, 115–18; S. Dreben and, 101; T. M. Solomon and, 164; *villistas* and, 187

Soriano Bravo, Eduardo, 297–98

Stalder, Ernest B., 351, 361

Standard Oil Company, 35–37, 299

Steever, E. Z., 49–50, 51, 53, 69, 71; on border conditions 1912–13, 130; *orozquista* evacuation of Juárez and, 114

Stevens, Charles, 60, 167

Stewart, C. A., 52

Stone, Edward B., 206, 251, 258; García, Andrés and, 276; imprisonment of, 309–10; L. Terrazas and, 259; Minck, Charles E. and, 271; Mrs. Lucero and, 261; Silva and, 302; W. Ibs and, 277–78. *See also specific events and cases*

Stratton, William P. "Red", 44–45, 64, 182

Summers, C. E., 361

Sweeney, Joseph, 6, 8, 12

Taft, William Howard, 1–5, 7, 9–14, *212*, 377; neutrality laws and, 130

Talbot, E. A., 282–83

Támez, Mariano, 272–73, 300, 315

Tampico News Company, 193

Tatematsu, Gemichi "Gustavo", 264, 307

Taylor, Alonso, 324–25

Terrazas, Luis, 22, 98–99, 171–72, 258–59

Terrazas, Luis, Mrs., 240

Terrazas, Silvestre, 355; Mexican Peace Committee and, 368

Thayer, Frank, 281–82, 304, 307–8, 366; bullion smuggling and, 370

Thiel Detective Service, 37, 58; *orozquistas* and, 82; Red Flaggers and, 73

Thomas, C. R., 138

Thomas, Frank S., 272

Thompson, David, 2, 6, 9–10, 13, 14

Thompson, H. A., 84, 114; Bureau of Investigation and, 191; as Constitutionalist agent, 156; H. Ramos and, 166; on neutrality investigations,

118; on the trial of Orozco, Sr., Herrera, and Hernández, 124

Thord-Gray, Ivor, 151–53; battle of Tierra Blanca and, 152; F. Villa and, 153

Tinker, Edward Laroque, 33

Torres, Manuel, 32

Torres, Tomás, 34, 35

Torres, Zenaido, 258

Torres de Villa, Juana, 258, 261

Treviño, Jacinto, 247, 262, 277; attack on Chihuahua and, 275; *legalistas* and, 273

Troxel, C. R., 35–36

Trujillo, José, 58, 97

Turner, Timothy G., 185, *236*

Turney, W. W., 6

Tuschiya, Hidekichi, 264

Tyler, J. L., 295

Ullman, Robert, 295

Underwood, Oscar W., 285

Union Depot, *215*

United Fruit Company, 156

United States: 24th Infantry regiment, *239*; arms embargo and, 72, 161–62, 176, 262; army presence in El Paso and, 89; Bureau of Investigation and, 31–33, 37, 51–52; C. Aguilar on, 362; E. C. Llorente and, 115; Exclusion Act and, 31–32; *huertistas* and, 146–47; mobilization of the National Guard and, 266; neutrality laws and, 18, 30–31, 378; PLM and, 22–23, 24; policies towards Mexico and, 242; recognition of Carranza government and, 242–43; seizure of Veracruz and, 175–76; Supreme Court, Maxey and, 143; troops in Juárez and, 364; *vazquista movement* and, 131; World War I and, 294. *See also* Bureau of Investigation; Military Intelligence

United States v. Robert, Julius, and Adolph Krakauer, Cástulo Herrera, and Victor Ochoa, 132

U.S. v. Arnulfo Chávez, 117–18

U.S. v. Huerta, 286

Utley, Willard, 299

Valdez, Nicanor, 62–63

Valenzuela, Emilio, 251

Vann, John W., 36, 118

Vargas, Juan, 366–68

Vázquez Gómez, Emilio, 63, 67, 97–98, 109, 137, *232*; indictment of, 131; Juárez and, 70–71; Orozco junta and, 126; *Plan de Tacubaya*, 67; as provisional president, 133–34

Vázquez Gómez, Francisco, 56, 129

vazquistas, 67; ammunition smuggling and, 113; arrests and, 109; El Paso junta and, 106–7, 154–55; mail addresses and, 106; mounting problems and, 110–11; provisional government and, 107; security and, 108–9; Sonora and, 106

Vega, Ramón, 372

Velasco, José Luis, 368, 372

Velázquez de la Rosa, José, 359, 360

Veracruz, seizure of, 175–76; El Paso and, 176–77; Fort Bliss and, 176–77

Vera Estañol, Jorge, 357

Viljoen, Benjamin Johannis, 6, 42–44, 54–55, 57, *226*; Boer War and, 43; *An Exiled General*, 43

Villa, Francisco "Pancho", 30, 51–52, 139, *221*, *227*; Alvarado Mining and Milling Company and, 366–68; amnesty and death of, 375–76; attack on Chihuahua and, 150, 275, 276; attack on Juárez and, 362–64; attack on Villa Ahumada, 343–44; belligerent status and, 300; bullion and, 313, 324, 326–27, 340, 366–68; capture of Juárez and, 150–51; capture of Ojinaga and, 156–57; capture of Parral and, 350; *carrancista* military and, 362; Carranza military and, 316; Columbus raid and, 250; declining fortunes of, 241–43, 371–73; El Paso intelligence network and, 165–67; F. Knotts and, 329–31; Miller & Howard and, 328; Ojinaga capture of 1917, 313; *Plan de Rio Florida and*, 355; racism and, 184–85, 331; Santa Eulalia attacks and, 349; on U.S. intervention in Juárez, 366; V. Carranza and, 181; V. Huerta and, 137–38; Ysleta expedition and, 171

Villa, Hipólito, 187, 191, 204, 245, 274, 304–7, 342; ammunition smuggling and, 298–99; Bureau of Investigation and, 275–76, 279, 312–13; indictment of, 243; Mabel Silva de Villa and, 358; M. Schwartz and, 334–35; U.S. Immigration Service and, 368

Villa, Luz Corral de, 304–5, 307

Villa Ahumada, 343–44

Villalobos, Francisco, 354

Villalva, Ramón, 314

Villarreal, Antonio I., 18, 20–21, 44, 355

villistas: Bureau of Investigation and, 274–76; Columbus raid and, 252; deportation from El Paso and, 248–49; El Paso junta and, 345; expedition to damage railroads and, 327; *felicistas* and, 328–29, 356; funding of, 298–300; network of, 337–38; railroad attacks and, 345; recognition of Carranza government and, 245

Voz de la Mujer, 23

Walthall and Gamble, 172, 175

war kites, 61–62

Warren, Charles, 299

Watts, A. P., 169–70

Weber, Max, 6

Webster, Charles H., 83, 145; J. E. Hernández and, 109

Weiskopf, Victor, 280, 312

Western Cartridge Company, 187

White, T. B., 326

White, Zach, 6

Wilfley, Lebbeus R., 1–2

Wilkie, John, 10, 16; P. Díaz and, 14–15

Williard, H. O., 312

Wilson, Huntington, 4, 9, 14

Wilson, Woodrow, 242, 266

Winter, August, 294–95

Womack, J. D., 35

Worcester, Leonard, 75–76

Wren, John, 155–56, 164–65, 263, 275; F. Cervantes and, 359–60; G. Holmes and, 340; on J. Sedaño, 323. *See also specific events and cases*

Wyatt, John, 7

Ysleta expedition, 168–75

Zapata, Emiliano, 123, 134; P. Orozco, Sr. and, 137

Zea, Leopoldo, 75

Zimmermann telegram, 293

Zozaya, José, 195, 200, 205